Corridors of Migration

Corridors
of Migration

The Odyssey of Mexican Laborers,
1600–1933

Rodolfo F. Acuña

The University of Arizona Press
Tucson

The University of Arizona Press
© 2007 The Arizona Board of Regents
All rights reserved

Library of Congress Cataloging-in-Publication Data
Acuña, Rodolfo.
Corridors of migration : the odyssey of Mexican laborers,
1600–1933 / Rodolfo F. Acuña.
p. cm.
Includes bibliographical references and index.
ISBN 978-0-8165-2636-9 (hbk. : alk. paper)
1. Alien labor, Mexican — United States — History. 2. Mexicans —
United States — History. I. Title.
HD8081.M6A63 2007
331.6'27207940903 — dc22   2007019333

Publication of this book is made possible in part by the proceeds
of a permanent endowment created with the assistance of a
Challenge Grant from the National Endowment for the
Humanities, a federal agency.

12   11   10   09   08   07   6   5   4   3   2   1

Contents

Illustrations

Preface

When I began this project in 1973, I wanted to write the story of the 1933 San Joaquin Valley Cotton Strike. A milestone in Chicana/o history, the strike involved 18,000 cotton pickers and their families, 80 percent of whom were Mexicans. Against all odds, they defied the planter community — which comprised planters, banks, ginning companies, the American Legion, and the Boy Scouts, among others. The enemy were all those who nurtured racism and the willingness to distort truth, to murder, and to deliberately starve men, women, and children, even infants, to maintain total control over their "America." The only missing pieces of the puzzle were, how had Mexicans gotten to the San Joaquin Valley — and how had they endured?

In 1973, the major work on the strike was Paul S. Taylor and Clark Kerr's study,[1] but it had not answered either of these questions. I was going to try. I conducted extensive interviews and read mountains of documents. I made my customary pilgrimage to Berkeley and visited the great Paul S. Taylor in the summer of 1973. I was immediately caught off guard when Taylor launched into a lecture on how Mexicans had fought for "tierra y libertad" in Mexico but, here in the United States, were too apathetic to obtain land. His impressions of the strike were just as disturbing. According to Taylor, Mexicans were leaderless. He described Pat Chambers — the communist organizer of the 1933 strike — as a physically small man, referring me to a photo and saying he would not be surprised to hear Chambers described "as a Brooklyn Jew." The communists, Taylor told me, had taken a leaderless people and brought them down on the law-and-order people. The Mexicans had accepted the communist leadership, which made things all the more difficult because the planters' principal weapon was that the strike leaders were communists. Taylor said that planter after planter would say to him, "Every dime I had in the world was tied up in that crop." Taylor had clearly internalized the collective myths of our society, accepting as absolute truth the illusion that nothing would have happened if the communists had not organized the strike.[2]

The Taylor interview made me think of an article by Ernesto Galarza titled

"La Mula No Nació Arisca"[3] (The Mule Wasn't Born Stubborn) — the old saying ends "la hicieron" (they made it that way). If Mexicans were leaderless and unorganized, what in history had made them that way? This was not a question that could be answered by studying ten days in the lives of workers who were the product of generations of struggle. Hence my quest would require finding how the workers got to the San Joaquin Valley and why they had not organized before the 1933 strike — if that was the case.

Just from common knowledge, I knew that many of the strikers must have been veterans of the Mexican Revolution, with a strong sense of national identity and notions of a just society. The Mexican Revolution had driven millions of refugees to the United States, accelerating movement to the cities in Mexico and the United States. But not all the pickers were immigrants; some were either citizens or longtime residents, while others had served in the United States Army, and a core had experienced strikes in agriculture, mining, and industry. They knew all too well what a just wage was.

The cotton planters responded to the strike by shooting down three strikers in cold blood, starving to death at least nine children — eight of them infants — wounding dozens of others, and orchestrating the arrest of scores of still others. Was this violence the key to why Mexicans had not organized? Did it explain how the growers got away with murder? There had to be more.

I believe it is fair to say that if what happened in the 1933 strike had happened to white workers, it would have been a major page in U.S. labor history. Organizer Caroline Decker told me that it was a good thing that some of the workers were white. If they hadn't been, there would have been a massacre. I agree. The literature of the time formed the popular view of the migrant worker. Look no further than John Steinbeck's portrait of white pickers during the Depression. *The Grapes of Wrath* (1939) tells a gripping story of the "Okies." But Steinbeck chose to ignore the Mexicans' presence. It was almost as if they did not exist. *In Dubious Battle* (1936), he tells the dramatic story of the 1933 Tagus Ranch and the San Joaquin Valley Cotton Strikes, where 80 percent of the strikers were Mexicans. Yet Steinbeck chose to exalt white communist organizers and their efforts to lead white fruit pickers in the Californian apple industry. His choice must have been a conscious one, most likely because he felt he couldn't get his white readers to relate to Mexicans.

As a starting point for my research, I randomly selected Pedro Subia, who had been murdered on a picket line near Arvin, California, on October 10, 1933. I wanted, not to write a historical biography, but to learn more about the experiences of Subia's wave of immigrants. What corridors had they forged on their way to the San Joaquin Valley? I used the metaphor of a corridor because, since time immemorial, living creatures have traveled through natural corridors to survive. These corridors contain and connect natural open spaces; they follow rivers, streams, washes, or other natural courses. Like hallways, they channel human movement back and forth between areas that support life. Historians sometimes call them "cultural and historical routes."

One of the principal corridors leading from Mexico to California passed through Chihuahua. For centuries, Mexican people moved through this central corridor, which I choose to call the Camino Real corridor, on their way to the mines of northern Mexico. They often stayed a generation in places like Zacatecas before moving north. In more contemporary times, some passed through Chihuahua or lived there for a time. The mines were hugely important in pulling people north. In mining camps such as Parral, newcomers formed barrios, where they lived alongside their compatriots. They named these neighborhoods after their former homes, a practice they continued when they moved into the Southwest. The process was constant and persistent. Drawn by a bonanza, large numbers of people would populate mining camps, haciendas, pueblos, presidios, and the like. When the bonanza ended, the population would contract, with thousands migrating to other bonanzas or haciendas and farm settlements.

Over time, Mexicans developed regional differences and identified more with their hometown or region, their *patria chica*, than they did with the Mexican nation. Where a Mexican came from made, and makes, a difference in idiom, food, and music. In the first part of the twentieth century, it often determined where the migrants lived or which corridor they took. Along the way, they named their *colonias* after their homes — Chihuahuitas, Sonora Towns, and the like.

Pedro Subia was born in Camargo, Chihuahua. With thousands of his compatriots, he moved along the Mesilla corridor from El Paso, Texas, to Morenci, Arizona, where he worked for thirty years before migrating to California. The mines of Arizona pulled tens of thousands of Mexicans to the United States from 1870 to 1920. I have attempted to capture the experiences that Subia and his compatriots had before forging corridors to eastern Arizona, and their Chihuahuita in Morenci.

Thousands of Mexicans from Zacatecas, Durango, and other Mexican states also traveled these corridors, even as Sonoran and New Mexican workers and their families forged and followed still others. Major events such as the Mexican Revolution of 1910–20 intruded into their consciousness, as news, rumors, and propaganda flowed back and forth between Mexico and the United States. A huge copper empire was formed in Sonora by copper companies such as Phelps Dodge. During the Revolution, as the mines expanded in the United States and contracted in Mexico, many miners — now politicized by the Revolution — were forced across the line to seek work in the mines of Arizona and in the factory farms of western Arizona and eastern California.

The reclamation project along the Gila River to the Salt River Valley led Subia and other Mexican workers to the final corridor. Tens of thousands like Subia traveled west, often following the crops of the greenbelt that linked the Imperial Valley to Los Angeles, working in factory farms created by the miracle of modern irrigation. Industrialized commercial agriculture, like mining, required huge armies of workers. Many of the Mexican miners drifted into agriculture naturally. Since colonial times, they had worked the land and seasonally gone to the mines to supplement their living. In the late nineteenth and early twentieth centuries, they migrated to larger U.S. municipalities and emerging cities like Phoenix and Los Angeles. The corridors brought them to the San Joaquin Valley in 1933.

From all accounts, Pedro Subia was a decent and hardworking family man. When Subia died in the San Joaquin Valley, he left a son, who also lived and died in the valley, where he made his own Chihuahuita. Like many other Mexican immigrants, Pedro Subia Sr. and his family were looking for somewhere they could enjoy, at least for a time, what so many others did. Throughout their travels, they held on to memories of their homeland.

As with most historical research, few of the documents I accumulated and studied bore directly on my investigation. But some were invaluable: baptismal and death certificates, company records, the papers of the Western Federation of Miners, the U.S. and Mexican censuses and Euro-American, British, and Mexican consular records, for example. I made pilgrimages to university libraries, historical societies, church record repositories, state and national archives — here and in Mexico. Naturally, I went to the Bancroft Library in Berkeley, both to study and to pray. Finally, I conducted extensive oral interviews of Clifton-Morenci miners and residents of Chihuahua, Mexico.

Throughout my investigation, I was struck by how loyal to and enamored with México Lindo Mexican migrants in United States were. Often, when there was a strike, they would turn to the local Mexican consul or they would write a letter to the Mexican president, asking to be repatriated. They expected the Mexican government to defend or rescue them — which it rarely did. It reminded me of the stories told by my students, who idolized their fathers. Time and again, when a student was unjustly accused of misbehavior — often provoked by a racial slur — and the father was called to the principal's office, instead of defending his son or daughter, the father would sit in timid silence while the principal berated him and the student.

I donated more than 200 boxes of research documents and notes to the main library of the California State University at Northridge (CSUN), where scholars can retrace and verify my findings. The documents presented in this volume explode the myth that Mexicans were born apathetic and never attempted to organize.

A final word. One of the problems in accumulating so much information over such a long period of time is keeping the story straight. So I gathered some 2,000 newspaper articles, also available in the Rodolfo F. Acuña Collection, Urban Archives, at CSUN. I have drawn on these article for the central chronology of my narrative. Having gone through a major court case, I realize how important a clear chronology is.

Acknowledgments

Where to start? Given the opportunity to help create a field of study at the age of thirty-five, I will always be grateful to the students whose sacrifices made Chicano Studies departments possible. Because of them, the Chicana/o Studies Department of California State University at Northridge now includes thirty tenured professors and more than forty part-time instructors, more than 60 percent of whom are women. I thank the professors and students for helping build it — and for contributing to my education. The department has become my salvation.

Over the years, friends such as Carlos Vélez-Ibañez have encouraged the writing of this book. The late Mauricio Mazón, Don Ramón Ruiz, and his late wife, Natalia, a gentle human being, are among those who listened. Ignacio Almada Bay of the Colegio de Sonora kindly made information on Sonora available. Apolinar Frías Prieto was one of the first people to appreciate what I was trying to do in drawing the links between Chihuahua and eastern Arizona.

Hundreds of people helped me search for the memories of others. Meeting a half dozen times with the San Joaquin strike organizers, Pat Chambers and Caroline Decker, was inspirational, as was meeting the Subias, despite their reluctance to share their experiences. I am grateful to the miners and their families for the time they spent with me before and during the Clifton-Morenci Strike of 1983, especially Angel Rodríguez and David Velásquez. As with every endeavor, there were those who contributed more than others. I would like to acknowledge the late Joseph F. Park, librarian at the University of Arizona, for expanding my access to knowledge of Mexican workers in Arizona and Sonora. Joe had a deep sensitivity to people and to Mexicans in particular. I thank Armando Miguélez of Alicante, Spain, for placing in my hands more than 300 letters of Carmelite priests, which he rescued from the incinerators. My thanks to Elena Díaz Björkquist for her inspiring oral interviews of Morenci residents. And my special thanks to Armando Durón for keeping me from going under during my grueling battle with the University of California at Santa Barbara, and to Moises Vázquez for his friendship and for winning the case. In many ways, because it is the final chapter in a long struggle, this is their book.

Manuel Servín was my dissertation advisor. We fought, we argued, and we disagreed, but, through it all, he supported me. I will always remember him, as will his many students. I thank Chris Marín of the Arizona State University Library, to whom every Chicano/a doing research on Arizona owes a debt. The late historian Victor Méndoza and Miguel Angel Giner were generous with their time and knowledge, introducing me to scholars and to the people of Chihuahua and scouring local archives for the project. Marty Grajeda, who founded La Familia, which reconstructs Mexican family histories, taught me the importance of census and church records. I am grateful to have Marty, Silvia and Aaron Magdaleno, and Al García, also of La Familia, as my friends.

I want to thank the editors at the University of Arizona Press, without whom the book would not have been published. When my 2,000-page original manuscript had scared most presses off, Patti Hartmann took a chance on it. Thank you, Patti, even for the pain of all those serious cuts. My thanks to Harrison Shaffer, Alan M. Schroder, and Jason S. Ninneman for their advice and guidance; and especially to Harrison for choosing Jeffrey H. Lockridge to be my manuscript editor. Thanks, Jeff, for helping me tame the monster. Cartographer Michael W. Pesses of Bakersfield skillfully navigated a stream of changes and counterchanges. Thanks to Harriet Rochlin — a great scholar and friend.

I also thank the librarians at the University of California at Los Angeles; the Bancroft at the University of California at Berkeley; the University of Southern California Library; the Southern California Library for Social Studies and Research; the Los Angeles Public Library; the Los Angeles Museum of Natural History; the Archivos de Relaciones Esteriores; the Archivos General de la Nación; Condumex; the Museo de Antropologia e Historia; the Universidad Nacional Autónoma de México Newspaper Library Collection; the Universidad de Chihuahua; the University of Texas at El Paso; the University of New Mexico at Albuquerque; the El Paso City Library; the Bakersfield City Library; the Municipal Archives of Camargo, Chihuahua; the Carmelite Archives in Barcelona; the University of Texas at Austin; the University of Arizona; Arizona State University; the Arizona State Library; the Arizona Historical Society; the Sonora State Archives at Hermosillo; the Church of the Latter Day Saints Library in West Los Angeles; the National Archives and Records in Washington, D.C.; and the National Archives and Records Administration at Laguna Miguel.

I thank the interlibrary loan people at CSUN. Those who want to know everyone who helped me are invited to examine the extensive archives of the Rodolfo F. Acuña Collection at CSUN, where the secrets are hidden.

Seeing the value of my work, Associate Vice President of Graduate Studies Mack Johnson allowed me to teach three classes instead of four a semester for five semesters over the course of my research. Mack arranged funding for the initial processing of my archives, hiring a student to inventory them, and sparing me arduous work I could ill afford to do. In 1980, I received an American Council of Learned Societies Award and a Rockefeller Humanities Fellowship, which allowed to take a semester-long sabbatical to Mexico City.

Throughout my career, I have been controversial. This has cost me grants and some recognition. Yet, in the end, it has helped me. Having to do my own research has given me a far surer feel for the history of the events I have explored. I published not because I had to but because I loved it.

I give thanks to life for those around me. For my sons, Frank and Walter, from my first marriage, from whom I stole time, often selfishly absorbing myself in my work. For my grandchildren. For my mother, who always prodded us to do better, to think big. For my father, who was a great artist, a wonderful storyteller, and a decent, gentle man. For my extended family, who made me feel special when I most needed to. For the past twenty-five years, those closest to me have been my wife, Guadalupe Compeán, and my daughter, Angela. Lupita is *mis ojos*. She makes me laugh. She slows me down. And she keeps me going. Angela inspires me, shows me new things. Life would have no meaning without Angela and Lupita, whom I see as one.

Corridors of Migration

◀ 1 ▶

Why Mexicans Moved

Throughout the twentieth century, ever-growing numbers of Mexican workers and their families came to the United States from Chihuahua and Sonora and from south central Mexican states such as Jalisco, Michoacán, and Zacatecas. For centuries, Mexicans had moved through the Camino Real corridor to Zacatecas, often staying there for as long as a generation before moving farther north. Work at the mines of Zacatecas and Chihuahua was an important incentive for the migration from the interior of Mexico. As mining activity expanded and contracted, it pulled and pushed workers along the corridor.

Chihuahuitas

Alongside others from their particular regions, they formed barrios in mining camps such as Parral, naming them after their former homes. Here they were able to re-create their past, at least in part. They continued this practice much later as they moved into the Southwest. Around their campfires, they told stories and shared memories. The tortillas were always better in their home villages.

From the late nineteenth century on, Chihuahuan workers migrating into the United States named their barrios Chihuahuitas (Little Chihuahuas) to remind themselves of where they came from, and where they wanted to return. Chihuahuitas, where they hoped to find work and make a new life — for as short a time as they could — came in all sizes, smaller in mining camps or farming *colonias*, larger in emerging cities. The workers dreamed of having land again and, as soon as their wives arrived, they left their temporary shelters to find houses, however humble, beside which they could plant gardens with familiar herbs and spices. What, after all, was *calabacitas con queso* (squash and cheese) without cilantro? They planted geraniums and other bright flowers in tin cans, ready to take with them to the next Chihuahuita, bringing color to landscapes such as Morenci's, stripped bare by mining and shrouded in smelter smoke. A Chihuahuita was a place of refuge, where they could preserve their identity, where their native Spanish was not drowned out by a foreign tongue. It was like a family that welcomed strangers by putting more water in the frijoles.

As thousands of Chihuahuans passed north, then west, through the Camino Real and Mesilla corridors, thousands of Mexicans from Sonora, Durango, Zacatecas, Jalisco, and other interior states followed them. In the early 1900s, the reclamation projects along the Gila River to the Salt River Valley drew migrating workers west across Arizona to the Cotton corridor, which led through the Imperial Valley and Los Angeles to the San Joaquin Valley. Agriculture, like mining, required huge armies of workers. Many of the Mexican miners drifted into agriculture naturally. Since colonial times, they had worked the land and seasonally gone to the mines to supplement their livelihood. They also migrated to larger towns and to emerging cities like Phoenix and Los Angeles.

This book traces the path of Pedro Subia, murdered at Arvin, California, in the San Joaquin Valley Cotton Strike of 1933, and of those who, like him, traveled the migration corridors from northern Mexico through New Mexico and Arizona to California. Subia was from Chihuahua, but he lived in Morenci, Arizona, until the 1920s before moving to California. Like so many of his fellow *chihuahuenses*, what distinguished him were his memories. Like them, Subia lived in at least three different landscapes before he died. And like his ancestors before him, the nature of his travels helped form his identity.

The Bitter Fruits of Conquest

Christopher Columbus knew that his success depended on making money to pay for his explorations. He also knew that sugar produced by slave labor was a source of huge profits in Europe. When he did not find significant quantities of precious metals, he turned to slavery. Although, in 1493, Pope Alexander VI condemned the taking of Indian slaves, he had left several loopholes. It was permissible to enslave natives if they rejected Christianity, if they reverted to their pagan religions, if they were cannibals, or if they were taken in "just

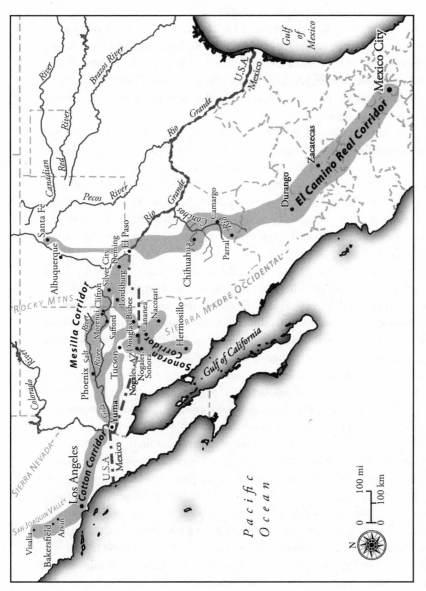

The southwestern United States and northern Mexico, ca. 1933, showing the Camino Real, Mesilla, Sonoran, and Cotton corridors. (Map by Michael W. Pesses)

warfare." Even after these loopholes were closed in 1537, however, hacendados on the frontier continued to use them as justifications for enslaving Indians into the late eighteenth century.[1] In 1494, Columbus sent Spain's Catholic monarchs twenty-six prisoner slaves. The next year, Columbus captured five hundred men, women, and children, ages twelve to thirty-five, and shipped them to Seville as slaves.[2]

In the last decades of the fifteenth century, sugarcane plantations had spread across the Mediterranean from Palestine to Cyprus, Sicily, Calabria, Valencia, and the south of Portugal, then leapfrogged to the Azores, the Canaries, and Cape Verde. As the sugar trade expanded, so did the African slave trade. When cultivation of sugarcane reached the New World, the British, Dutch, French, Portuguese, and Spanish colonizers imported African slaves into the lowlands and offshore islands of South America to replace the natives who had died off.

Slave traders transported at least 10 million Africans to the Americas during the colonial period. They sold more than 5 million to the Guianas and the Caribbean islands (where Spain had established sugarcane plantations by 1516), almost 4 million to Brazil, some 600,000 to Spanish America, and the remaining 900,000 to the British colonies in North America and to Europe in roughly equal shares.[3] Nearly three of every four African slaves shipped to the Americas worked on sugarcane plantations.

The Spanish conquest of the Americas profoundly shaped what it would mean to be a Mexican. The Spanish colonizers disrupted or destroyed the social, political, and economic networks of the indigenous peoples, superimposing a more brutal form of exploitation centered on the control of native labor. One of the first things Hernán Cortés did after conquering Tenochititlán was to seize Aztec records and to resume the collection of tributes. The Spaniards looked upon the natives as savages — "wild Indians" (*indios bárbaros*). Incapable of living a Christian life on their own, they had to have proper direction. To strengthen their control and to make it more difficult to unite against Spanish rule, the colonizers destroyed indigenous networks of regional cooperation, forcing natives to identify with their local communities rather than with their region or people. They concentrated native *rancherías* (encampments) into larger pueblos clustered in townships (*municipios*) around a central pueblo. The townships paid tribute under the *encomienda* and *repartimiento* systems and were governed through local caciques who reported directly to the Spanish authorities.

Both systems furnished forced labor, whether actual or in effect, for agriculture, mining, transport of goods, and public projects. Under the earlier, encomienda system, a form of feudalism used extensively in central Mexico that was much more efficient than slavery, the Crown granted chosen soldiers control over the natives within a geographic region. In return, *encomenderos* were required by law to protect their wards, to instruct them in the Catholic faith, and to defend their right to use the land for their own subsistence. Abolished by the New Laws of 1542 because of widespread abuses, the encomienda nevertheless flourished into the eighteenth century on the frontiers of New Spain, where remoteness from Mexico City made regulation extremely difficult. The New Laws defined natives as free subjects of the Crown yet sanctioned de facto Indian slave labor. They prohibited forced labor without pay yet sanctioned bondage to employers through debt. Under the later, repartimiento system, native workers were forced not only to perform a quota of work, often without pay, but also to buy goods from the Spanish authorities and hacendados.

Three centuries of Spanish colonial rule left a legacy of mixed bloods (*castas*), with privilege assigned according to race measured on a continuum that was affected by variables such as family status. In 1627, responding to pressure from the Catholic Church, the Crown allowed Spaniards in New Spain with wives in Spain to annul their marriages if they did not have children, and to marry native wives. According to Lourdes Martínez-Echazabal, *mestizaje* (interracial mixing) "was designed to maintain the superiority of the whites through . . . 'blanqueamiento' or whitening."[4] Yet being a Mexican was more than being simply mestizo — a mixture of Spanish and Native American cultures and bloodlines. It was a work in progress, and many of the native peoples of Mexico — such as the Maya, Mayo, Yaqui, and Tarahumara — did not, and do not, want to be Mexicans.[5]

In the first century of colonial rule, as New Spain's indigenous population fell by more than 90 percent, some 300,000 Africans were imported into what is today Mexico and Central America — with "roughly 250,000 . . . imported into Mexico during the three centuries of slave trade."[6] In 1560, Africans and mulattoes outnumbered Spaniards in Mexico City, and Africans came to Mexico in greater numbers than whites until the 1700s.[7] Although the Crown abolished indigenous slavery, Spanish hacienda and mine owners used fictions such as "just warfare" to enslave natives well into the late eighteenth century. They sold Indians in the slave markets of Havana, Mexico City, and even Manila. In turn, Manila galleons may have brought as many as 100,000 Filipino slaves as declared cargo to Acapulco or, as contraband, to San Blas, where they were sold to the mines and haciendas of New Spain. The slave traders labeled them African because the law limited slavery to Africans.[8]

Colonization led to the breakdown of the indigenous extended family system. The nuclear family became the center of the new society. Before the arrival of the Spaniards, native couples generally did not marry before the age

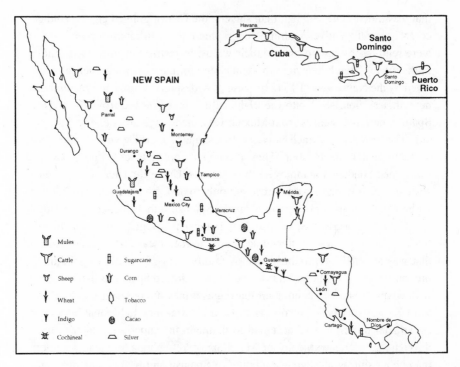

Mining, commerce, and agriculture in New Spain in the seventeenth and eighteenth centuries. (From Socolow, "Introduction to the Rural Past," 12)

of twenty. The Church strongly encouraged native women to marry and thus to have children far younger, at between twelve and fourteen, which resulted in health disorders such as anemia. Early marriage changed gender relations as well, reducing the authority of native women within the clan. The greater age difference between husband and wife favored male dominance. Under colonial rule, men received preferential treatment even in death and were more likely than women to be buried within the church courtyard. By worsening the status of women, colonization increased violence toward them.[9]

After the fall of Tenochititlán in 1521, smallpox and other epidemics swept through the countryside with devastating effect. Over the next century, the indigenous population of Mexico plummeted from 25 million to 4 million — and that of the Americas as a whole, from 100 million to 10 million. Smallpox, measles, and influenza outbreaks struck urban areas the hardest. To deaths from these diseases were added others from typhus, bubonic plague, yellow fever, and malaria.[10]

Too weak to care for their crops or even to make their tortillas, natives became disoriented, depressed, and suicidal. Malnutrition, starvation, and alcoholism claimed still more lives. Before the Spaniards, the natives of Mexico had drunk only one fermented beverage. Made from agave, pulque was rich in vitamins, low in alcohol, highly perishable, and drunk only for religious purposes. Indeed, the use of pulque had been restricted throughout Mesoamerican society, with violators harshly punished. For the first century and a half of colonial rule, however, no restrictions were placed on the consumption of pulque or of the distilled — and nonperishable — alcoholic beverages the Spaniards prepared from agave, tequila and mescal, which provided the Crown substantial tax revenues. It was to these far stronger drinks that natives became increasingly addicted.[11]

Zacatecas: Gateway to the North

Mining drew thousands to the river valleys of northern New Spain. As mining centers developed and urban populations grew, the surrounding river valleys were cultivated and exploited to supply food for the workers and timber for the mines. Using native wars of resistance to their encroachment as the pretext for taking slaves, the colonizers ravaged native rancherías as far to the north and west as Culiacán.

With an army of 30,000 Aztec and Tlaxcalan conscripts, the Spaniards consolidated their control of Nueva Galicia, which comprised all or part of the present-day states of Aguascalientes, Jalisco, and Zacatecas, and its capital, Guadalajara, during the Mixton War of 1540. They pushed farther north, overwhelming the native peoples around Zacatecas, whose mines and lands would be privately developed by Basques as well as by other Iberians. Zacatecas would ultimately produce one-third of Mexico's silver, employ as many as 5,000 workers, and serve as staging area and gateway for workers migrating along corridors in all four cardinal directions.[12]

Spaniards, natives, and African slaves thronged to Zacatecas. Because there were no large river valleys nearby, the mining camps imported huge quantities of food and dry goods from the south, from Guadalajara and from estates in Michoacán and the fertile Bajío. Although most of the workers were Aztecs, Tlaxcalans, Cholultecs, Tarascos, Otomis, or nomadic natives,[13] by the mid-1600s, African and mulatto slaves comprised one-fifth of the workforce. Africans generally worked on the haciendas and above ground, native labor being less expensive and more expendable. By the seventeenth century, Zacatecas was ringed by pueblos, each belonging to a different native people. In later centuries, of those who came to Zacatecas, merchants, administrators, hacendados, and small farmers tended to stay; mine workers tended to move on.

With its link to China, the primary market for world silver, Manila became the Spanish center for transpacific trade soon after its founding in 1571. Lifted by skyrocketing population growth — the number of Chinese increased more than fivefold from 1500 to 1700, when they accounted for more than one in every three persons on earth — Chinese demand for Mexican silver soared. With it so did the fortunes of Zacatecas and, later, of Santa Eulalia–San Felipe. Silver consistently fetched twice as much in China as it did in Europe. Each year throughout the seventeenth century, Spanish galleons carried more than fifty tons of silver bullion from Acapulco to Manila, where it was placed on Chinese junks and carried on to China.

Because labor was scarce, Zacatecan mine owners clamored for and received permission to institute repartimiento in the mid-1600s. The Spanish government tolerated forced labor through the encomienda or repartimiento because it was profitable. The Crown received a fifth of the profits, at least in theory. Though they were supposed to curb abuses, colonial administrators instead took bribes to look the other way. The impact on the natives of the encomienda or repartimiento and of increasing encroachment on their lands by miners and ranchers was disastrous, and their numbers declined drastically.[14]

In the mid-1500s, Zacatecas served as bridge and gateway to Nueva Vizcaya, the first northern province to be explored and colonized and the "heartland" of the northern frontier. Silver or the hope of finding it pulled people north. In the next two hundred years, Spanish colonial rule would spread into almost every river valley of Nueva Vizcaya, which comprised most of the present-day Mexican states of Chihuahua and Durango, with parts of Sinaloa, Sonora, and Coahuila.[15] Zacatecas was the springboard for migration to Chihuahua, where many of the Mexican cotton pickers in the 1933 San Joaquin Valley strike were from.

Chihuahua before the Spaniards

With all but a small western portion of its lower elevations blocked from the rain-bearing Pacific westerlies by the Sierra Madre Occidental, Chihuahua is largely an arid land. Throughout most of the state, apart from the sierra, where it rains much of the year, rainfall is scant. Rising in Colorado's San Juan Mountains and running south through New Mexico to El Paso–Ciudad Juárez, the Río Bravo (Rio Grande) flows for 300 of its 1,200 miles along the northern border of Chihuahua itself, turning southeast to Ojinaga, around the Big Bend, and southeast again to the Gulf of Mexico. At Ojinaga, the Río Bravo is joined by the Río Conchos, which flows three hundred miles east and north from the Sierra Madre Occidental, source of the Ríos Parral, Florido, and San Pedro, and of other, smaller tributaries of the Río Conchos. The valleys of these rivers together form the Conchería, homeland of the Conchos. To the northwest of the Río Conchos and in the heart of the Alta Tarahumara is the Río Papigóchic, the most important source of water for Chihuahua in colonial times.

Frequent droughts severely limited the size of native rancherías, which seldom had more than sixty inhabitants. The scarcity of water precluded the population concentrations needed to build villages and resulted in famines, wars over limited resources, and frequent migration.[16]

Seminomadic hunter-gatherers and subsistence farmers, the natives lived along Chihuahua's narrow desert river valleys. They based their economy on kinship rather than on tributary relations, as was common elsewhere in Meso-america, and their society was largely classless. Availing themselves of the abundant game in both the sierra and the desert, of fish, crayfish, and clams from the rivers, and of more than 250 native plant species, they hunted and gathered away from their rancherías, which comprised several household units clustered together close to water and their farms. In time of war, kin-related rancherías banded together.[17]

The indigenous peoples moved often, to take advantage of seasonal changes such as the rich soil deposited in the valleys by spring floods and to avoid the extreme heat and cold of Chihuahua's climate. The Tarahumara and the Conchos, for example, traveled to the sierra during the summer, where they farmed small fields (*milpas*) on ridges and in mountain valleys. In the winter, they retreated to the river valleys of the desert lowlands or to deep gorges during severe weather.[18]

Santa Bárbara

Located between the Ríos Florido and Conchos in the San Bartolomé Valley, Santa Bárbara was founded in 1567 as the first Spanish settlement in present-day Chihuahua and a logical starting point for Spanish expansion along these two strategic rivers. Its gold and silver deposits and fertile surrounding lands, home to a large encampment of Tepehuan Indians, attracted miners, merchants, and other colonists. Mining created the need for livestock raising and agricultural production. Burros and mules were used to carry ore, pull carts, and mix ore mud. Hides were used to make ore buckets, tallow to make candles, and beef and crops to feed the miners. Because the mineral finds of Zacatecas and of San Juan de Indé in present-day Durango were far richer, however, the mines of Santa Bárbara were shut down and the isolated town abandoned in 1604, not to be repopulated until the founding of Parral, twelve miles to the northeast, in 1631. In 1591, about a thousand Tepehuans worked in the mines of Santa

Bárbara, alongside mostly Tarascans. Decades later, workers included Tarahumaras, Yaquis, Africans, and Spaniards. Relations in the San Bartolomé Valley between those who owned and those who worked the mines and lands were feudal, with the valley's missions acting as labor recruitment centers for both mines and haciendas.[19]

Just before the end of the sixteenth century, Juan de Oñate led a privately financed expedition from Santa Bárbara, sacking the mission lands of the Conchería and conscripting natives from surrounding haciendas. Oñate extended El Camino Real from Santa Bárbara through what would later become Chihuahua to El Paso del Norte and on to Santa Fé. When the Acoma of New Mexico resisted his colonization, he retaliated by destroying their mesa-top pueblo, killing some eight hundred men, women, and children.[20]

Using Santa Bárbara as a springboard for their northern missionizing, Franciscans from the College of Zacatecas began concentrating natives in the valleys of the Río Conchos and its tributaries after 1604. Ultimately, they organized missions the length of El Camino Real, linking the frontier to the center of Mexico. Their key mission was San Francisco de Conchos, founded in 1604 some forty-five miles north of Santa Bárbara and sixty-five miles from what would become Parral. The mission town served as the military and administrative capital of the Conchería. At various times, Conchos, Tarahumaras, Tobosos, Chizos, and other natives would populate its settlements. The area remained unstable because of droughts and frequent native uprisings. By the end of the seventeenth century, the Franciscans operated a dozen missions, most along the well-traveled Camino Real corridor to New Mexico.

Having arrived in Mexico in 1572, the Jesuits were missionizing in the present-day state of Sinaloa by the 1590s. At the Jesuit seminary college in Tepotzotlán, some twenty-five miles south of Mexico City, they trained their missionaries in the native languages and were active in present-day Durango, moving north along the eastern edge of the Sierra Madre Occidental.

By the 1670s, the Jesuits had founded Purísima Concepción de Papigóchic and eight other missions among the Tarahumara of western Chihuahua in the Río Papigóchic's fertile valley, close to the newly founded Villa de Aguilar and to present-day Ciudad Guerrero. The first task of the missionaries was to have the natives break ground and dig irrigation ditches for the missions' cornfields, although some relied on rainfall to water their fields. Missions on central plateaus also raised wheat, and several boasted vineyards and orchards. The Tarahumara resisted this encroachment on their lands by burning the missions and retreating farther into the sierra. Rich mine owners and hacendados purchased or were granted lands in the river valleys where the missions were located. Conflicts over water rights were usually resolved in favor of the large

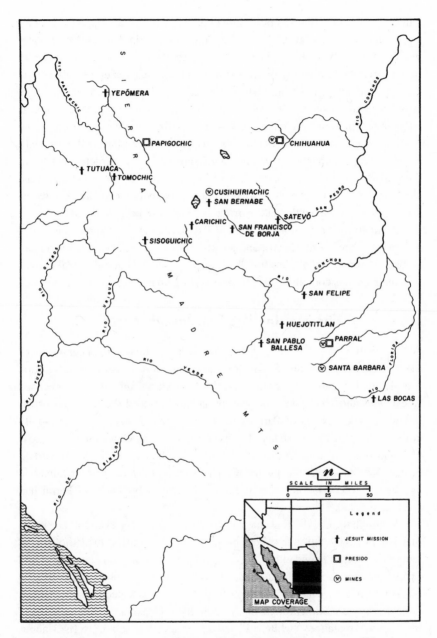

The Tarahumara country, ca. 1700. (From Spicer, Cycles of Conquest, *p. 27)*

landowners. A presidio was built in the upper reaches of the Papigóchic. This was a clear provocation of the Tarahumara, whose principal source of water was threatened. When the natives again resisted, the Spaniards responded with brutal force and the taking of slaves. Insisting that natives embrace Catholic doctrine and adopt the Christian way of life, the Jesuits uncompromisingly strove to eradicate the worship of other gods and "barbarous" practices such as polygamy.[21] In their unrelenting efforts to "civilize" indigenous peoples, the Jesuits concentrated them in pueblos based on nuclear families, with European-style housing. Although they first met with some success in attracting natives to the pueblos, few became permanent residents. As with the Franciscan missions, Spanish encroachment caused friction, especially when hacienda workers diverted water from the native irrigation ditches to hacienda lands.[22]

Occupation of the Río Papigóchic Valley paved the way for mineral exploration of the area in the 1680s, and a rush of Spanish and mestizo miners and colonists from the south. Several Tarahumara missions and individual natives sold their surplus corn and wheat to surrounding Spanish communities.[23]

The Melting Pot: San José de Parral

At an elevation of 6,200 feet (1,890 meters), Parral stood at the headwaters of the Ríos San Gregorio and San Pedro, and of the minor tributaries of the Ríos Florido and Conchos. The foothills northwest of Parral supported an open oak forest. Mesquite, huisache, and various grasses covered the hills and plains below the town. News of Parral's massive silver bonanza in 1631 virtually emptied the present-day states of Durango, Zacatecas, Guadalajara, Michoacán, and much of central Mexico. Yaquis and Opatas from Sonora worked beside Tarahumaras, Tepehuans, Conchos, and Tobosos from Chihuahua as wage or forced laborers. By the mid-1630s, the population of Parral had swelled to 5,000.[24]

Although the Crown discouraged and in some instances even forbade intermarriage or cohabitation between Spaniards and Africans, it made no consistent, serious effort to end either. Mixing of the races continued even after some Spaniards who married Africans were dismissed from their posts and even after others who had African or mulatto mistresses were prosecuted for concubinage — or actually exiled. Through intermarriage with Spaniards, lighter-skinned mestizos and mulattoes "whitened" and rose in social standing. By 1683, about 6,000 mixed-blood colonists lived in the region.[25]

Attempting to segregate Africans from the natives, the Crown forbade them from entering native rancherías or pueblos. Yet the missionaries used Africans as foremen, as did many hacendados. By all accounts, the Africans assimilated more quickly than the natives. Slaves could buy their freedom and receive a document affirming it (*carta de libertad*), and customs limited many abuses. Most Africans in the Parral area were from Angola.

Between 1595 and 1640, New Spain imported more than 132,000 African slaves. Between 1632 and 1676, more than 1,100 African slaves were sold in Parral alone. Many were sold unofficially. Some were even sold by Africans themselves (some of whom would also buy slaves). The slave traders were not limited to a specific race or class. A wide range of Spanish women, merchants, miners, wagon train and team owners, and clergymen engaged in the slave trade. Between 1632 and 1641, the Jesuit College of Durango sold thirty-four slaves in Parral. Although the main suppliers of slaves were the Portuguese, special slave agents (*encomenderos de negros*) were employed to handle the actual transactions. These individuals seldom sold more than three or four slaves, and most sold only one.[26] Between 1632 and 1657, by official record, fifteen Asians were also sold as slaves in Parral. Had dispossessed Indians not been so cheaply available through the encomienda or repartimiento, the number of slaves of whatever race would have been still greater. The clergy were often the only ones who could afford the luxury of African slaves, who, on average, cost five times as much as native slaves.

Although some male African slaves worked as domestic servants, others worked as ore crushers and general laborers, as muleteers and charcoal makers, and occasionally as foremen of labor gangs. A small minority, both as slaves and as freed slaves, were merchants or small shopkeepers. Religion played a huge role in assimilating Africans. An African fraternal society or brotherhood (*cofradía*) observed religious holidays and organized church festivities.

According to Vicente Mayer, between 1634 and 1676, nearly one in every five children baptized was "of African heritage," most being mulatto, and one in every three married couples had at least one African spouse. Between 1649 and 1676, Africans accounted for one-sixth of the deaths.

Parral was a rowdy, mostly male town. All races congregated in La calle de los ladrones, the Street of Thieves, to gamble, drink, and conduct business. African slaves, like their free counterparts, often carried weapons, although authorities levied heavy fines for selling alcohol to Africans, mulattoes, and Indians. Free Africans could acquire property, and some even owned slaves. Everyone enjoyed access to the courts, although justice was far from equally dispensed. Brotherhoods gave the different ethnic groups a stake in the society. A mulatto brotherhood, for example, was the main source of revenue in building Parral's first hospital in 1681.[27]

The number of Apaches sold as slaves in Parral remained small until the 1670s, when the number of natives from New Mexico also increased. We can assume that both worked in the mines, and that many of the natives from New Mexico were also slaves. The governor of New Mexico, Luis de Rosas, was a notorious slave trader, selling Utes and Apaches in Parral.

Mission towns clustered the natives together in *visitas* (native enclaves around the missions themselves), much like pueblos elsewhere, making the natives more accessible for work drafts. Through forced labor or debt peonage, mines, missions, and haciendas alike broke down the native way of life. Every wave of incoming Spaniards demanded native workers, and even the Jesuits accepted the repartimiento of mission natives, viewing it as less oppressive than the encomienda, which flourished elsewhere in Nueva Vizcaya during the seventeenth century, along with African, native, and Asian slavery.[28]

Cycles of Resistance

In the course of the sixteenth century, the natives of Chihuahua suffered the loss of their religion and culture. They were subjected to slavery or forced labor on encomiendas and under the repartimiento. When epidemics and droughts late in the century drastically reduced their numbers or drove them to seek sustenance elsewhere, cattle ranchers encroached on the lands they left behind. The incessant exploitation of timber, salt, saltpeter, and other resources and the more oppressive demands on native labor provoked indigenous uprisings, most notably among the Tepehuan, the Conchos, and the Tarahumara. The Crown responded by constructing military forts called *presidios*.

The demand for labor at the mines, haciendas, and ranchos drew natives away from the missions. Missionaries had continually to import natives from outside to replenish their congregations and to repopulate their native settlements or pueblos. As in the interior, northern mission pueblos were governed through indigenous caciques, who extracted the tribute to which the Spaniards felt entitled.

The first major uprising was the Tepehuan revolt in 1616, which targeted priests and religious symbols. Joining the Tepehuan were the Tarahumara, Toboso, Conchos, and other native peoples who resented the missionaries for not protecting them from work drafts and who blamed the Jesuits for the epidemics that killed close relatives. The revolt forced the evacuation of mines, missions, ranchos, and haciendas between Durango and Santa Bárbara; it cost more than a thousand lives, including three hundred Spaniards and eight Jesuits. The Spaniards brutally suppressed the rebellion and enslaved hundreds of native men, women, and children, whom they sold at auction in Durango.[29]

In the 1640s, in the wake of famines and epidemics, a surge in demand for native labor to exploit new silver finds, the proliferation of haciendas and ranchos along the Río Florido, and the building of a presidio to protect them provoked native unrest in Chihuahua. When the Spaniards responded with slave hunts and increased reliance on the hated encomienda and repartimiento, the Conchos and their allies rebelled.

A band of Conchos burned Christian religious objects and took back their native names. They attacked the church and set fire to the convent at San Francisco de Conchos, killing two Franciscans and the governor of the Conchos. They attacked the haciendas in the San Bartolomé Valley and in Parral, killing workers and confiscating cattle. They destroyed the church at San Pedro de Conchos and attacked a nearby hacienda. Catching up with the rebels some thirty miles from the Río Bravo, an overwhelming force of Spanish cavalry and native allies killed twenty rebels outright, hanged another nineteen, and took ten men and thirty-five women and children prisoner.[30]

Independently, in 1648, Tarahumara rebels attacked the missions north and west of Parral. The Spaniards put down the rebellion the next year, burning three hundred homes and more than 6,000 bushels of corn and demanding the heads of two of the four rebel leaders. This set the stage for a new uprising. In 1650, Tarahumaras destroyed the Jesuit mission Purísima Concepción de Papigóchic and killed its priest. When the Spaniards responded with a show of force, the rebels retreated to an inaccessible rocky mesa. Native resistance was broken by the epidemic of 1651.

In 1652, under the leadership of Gabriel Tepórame, Tarahumaras destroyed the hated Villa de Aguilar, hanging a Jesuit and a militia commander. Captured and himself hanged in 1653, "Tepórame died bravely, chastising his followers for surrendering[, and refusing] the services of the Catholic priest who had come to hear his last confession."[31] He did not want to go to a Spanish heaven.

Native rebellions continued throughout the century as the missionaries founded more missions. Meanwhile, the Jesuits and the Franciscans, who had been quarreling over mission territory, came to an agreement: the Franciscans would work among the Conchos and the Jesuits among the Tarahumara. Spanish colonists repopulated the Río Papigóchic Valley, where friction continued between the Jesuits and the colonists, who charged them with controlling the most fertile land and with monopolizing native labor.[32]

The Great Northern Revolt

Sparked by a general uprising of the Apache in August 1680, the Pueblo revolt swept like a torrent over the province of Nuevo México, destroying towns, haciendas, ranchos, and churches, and killing more than six hundred whites. Natives washed off the "stains" of baptism, annulled Catholic marriages, and destroyed churches. Twenty-two Franciscan missionaries died at the hands of the rebel Pueblo Indians, who drove the Spanish colonists out of present-day New Mexico, not to return until the 1690s. The colonists fled to the area around what is now El Paso–Juárez . Some remained there, while others migrated to the Sierra Madre Occidental in Chihuahua and to Sonora, where they increased the competition for land, food, and natural resources. In Namiquipa and Casas Grandes, Chihuahua, the New Mexicans usurped native lands. In some cases, colonists literally moved natives out of their homes. One in five Pueblo Indians perished in the constant warfare of the 1680s and 1690s. Many Pueblos went to live with the Apache, Navajo, and Hopi.

When the Spaniards reclaimed New Mexico in the 1690s, the rebels were tried in Spanish courts. Some were whipped, dismembered, and hanged. More than four hundred others were condemned to slavery and dispersed among Spanish households. The Spaniards replaced the encomienda with repartimiento, whose excessive use had a devastating effect on the Pueblo communities, depriving them of crops and subjecting them to famines and starvation.

Four years after the Pueblos first rebelled, the Conchos, Tarahumara, Toboso, and other native peoples throughout the northwest, the central valleys, and the northeastern and eastern deserts of Nueva Vizcaya rose up in what came to be called the Great Northern Revolt. Madrid responded by building more presidios. Among them were El Paso del Norte (the Pass of the North) in 1683, San Francisco de Conchos in 1685, Casas Grandes in 1686, and Janos in 1691. As the influence of presidio captains and other officers grew during this period, so did their access to the best lands, which the natives increasingly surrendered. The presidios brought in more colonists, who acquired land and further exploited native labor. The native uprisings continued through the 1690s.[33]

The appearance of a comet, the overflowing of the Río Papigóchic, and an earthquake in April 1696 raised anxiety about the turn of the century to the level of hysteria. The Tarahumara abandoned the missions and fled to the sierra. In 1697, the Franciscans established the mission Nombre de Dios about three miles from present-day Ciudad Chihuahua, laying out the network of missions, presidios, ranchos, haciendas, and mining centers that would become the modern state of Chihuahua.[34]

Consolidating Power

After the Great Northern Revolt of the 1680s and 1690s, with the Conchos all but eliminated and the Tarahumara pushed far back into the sierra, the Apache advanced into present-day Chihuahua, Sonora, Durango, and as far east as

Texas and Coahuila. Their raids depopulated much of Chihuahua and devastated northern Sonora, although Sonora's natives, living in larger and more concentrated settlements along rivers, were better able to resist them.[35]

Central to consolidating colonial rule in Chihuahua was control of the Conchería, the fertile network of river valleys formed by the Río Conchos and its tributaries. Before irrigation, it had been a land of abundance or famine, with native communal land farmers, and later also nonnative ranchers — both hacendados and rancheros — and subsistence farmers, competing with each other for access to water. After Conchos were pressed into digging irrigation ditches, yields increased, as did competition among growing numbers of colonists and declining numbers of natives.

The Apache wars created a siege mentality, reinforcing feudal relations between the rich landowners and poor laborers, both native and nonnative, and popularizing the notion that the colonists were defending civilization and homeland against barbarity and the Apache invader. In the face of ever-mounting Apache raids, the colonists' survival often depended on each presidio's garrison of fifty or so soldiers. With the steady flow of migrants from Durango, Zacatecas, and other parts of the interior along El Camino Real, which linked missions all the way from Mexico City to Santa Fe, native mission settlements on the Río Conchos became enclaves for mulatto and mestizo colonists, who found it easier to encroach on the now largely deserted native lands. Race, which determined who paid and who received tribute, grew even more important as increasing numbers of Spanish-born Spaniards (*peninsulares*) came to Nueva Vizcaya. Spaniards and natives tended to marry their own in frontier regions such as Chihuahua. Social ranking depended on how light-skinned a person was; a mulatto or mestizo could sometimes pass for a Mexican-born Spaniard or criollo.

By the last half of the 1700s, 80 native families and 139 nonnative families lived at the former mission of San Francisco de Conchos and another 1,330 persons of all races lived at the former presidio. Colonists filled the numerous mission towns and settlements on the Río Conchos north of the San Bartolomé Valley and San Francisco de Conchos, an area that would send large numbers of migrants to the United States during the twentieth century. To accommodate the new colonists, authorities encouraged the displacement of natives, in some cases denying that natives returning to their lands had ever lived on them. Both Jesuits and Franciscans neglected the interests of their missions' natives, protecting them neither from labor drafts nor from encroachment, and failing to teach them how to look out for themselves.[36]

Transforming Chihuahua

In 1704, several extensive deposits of silver ore were discovered in central Chihuahua, a third of the way from Parral to El Paso del Norte. They called the mining camp Santa Eulalia de Mérida de Chihuahua. Five years later, the governor designated it as the administrative center of the territory. The mines of Santa Eulalia would produce more than 4,000 tons of silver in their first two decades of operation.

Wanting a level space close to clean water, some miners established a new mining camp fourteen miles northeast of Santa Eulalia, which they called San Francisco de Cuellar, later changing its name to San Felipe del Real de Chihuahua. San Felipe would become La Villa de Chihuahua and eventually Ciudad Chihuahua. By 1709, some two hundred people lived in the Santa Eulalia–San Felipe area, whose population increased more than twelvefold, to an estimated 2,500, over the next ten years.

The discovery of silver and the development of the Santa Eulalia–San Felipe silver-mining complex had far-reaching implications for the eighteenth century. Population growth and the cumulative effect of large and small bonanzas served to accelerate the dispersion of the nonnative population. Demand for food, meat, hides, and staples led to expansion of agriculture in the valleys both of the Río Conchos and tributaries and of the Río San Pedro. China's insatiable appetite for silver kept profits from the mines high, which in turn provided merchants and hacendados with the capital they needed to construct irrigation systems there—and to create trade networks that linked the fertile Río Papigóchic Valley with the rest of the Alta Tarahumara, and Buenaventura, Casas Grandes, Janos, and El Paso del Púlpito with Sonora. The missions were in no position to withstand the new encroachments by Spaniards and mestizos, who usurped land the missions failed to cultivate and moved to monopolize water for agriculture and livestock.[37]

During the mid-eighteenth century, the Crown encouraged settlement of New Spain's northwestern frontier by distributing land to colonists. High-ranking presidio personnel, commingling military, civil, economic, and ecclesiastical roles and powers, got their pick of the best properties, as they did elsewhere on the frontier. San Felipe's elite were the wealthiest landowners in the territory. Spanish-born Spaniards and former military leaders who wanted to command flaunted their wealth, having more servants, slaves, and workers than anyone else.[38] One such leader was Juan Antonio Trasviña y Retes. Arriving from Spain as a youth, Trasviña served in the militia and rose to the rank of sergeant major. He lived first in Parral, then in the mining camps of Cusihuiriáchic in the 1680s. After fighting the Tarahumara, he went to Santa Eulalia, where he claimed the El Rosario and Santa Rosa Mines. With his mining profits, Trasviña purchased large tracts of land, including the San Marcos hacienda, which encompassed more than 250,000 acres and the modern town of Saucillo. Trasviña later moved to Mexico City, donating part of his fortune to the Jesuits to build a college in the Villa de Chihuahua.[39]

From the 1720s to the early 1740s, as the capital of the Chihuahua territory, San Felipe del Real de Chihuahua enjoyed the profits from a mining boom, refining silver ore from the recently discovered mines. Despite depletion of ore and attacks by hostile natives after 1740, San Felipe remained an important government and commercial center for many years to come. Its growth and continued prosperity fueled development of the gateway to New Mexico, what today is the El Paso–Juárez area, and its outlying settlements, San Lorenzo, Senecú, Ysleta, and Socorro, Texas, to the south.

In 1738, as litigation over land and water rights increased, a land judge for the Chihuahua territory ordered the missions to measure their lands in terms of the minimum area of communal land (*ejido*) assigned each Indian pueblo, which amounted to some 4,300 acres (1,755 hectares, or one square league) and was not subject to taxes.[40] Over the years, the Jesuits purchased land beyond the bounds of this minimum, which — to avoid having to pay taxes — they often did not register.

Throughout Mexico, the Society of Jesus owned large haciendas, urban property, slaves, and other assets. In Chihuahua, for example, the Jesuits owned the Mápula, Ciénega de los Padres, Dolores, and San Marcos (present-day Saucillo) haciendas; the Colleges of Hidalgo Parral and Loreto; and mines, refineries, and the Tabaloapa and San Diego haciendas in and around San Felipe. Colonial authorities — many of them mine owners, hacendados, and merchants — believed that the Jesuits' near-monopoly of land and labor in Mexico was stifling the private sector. Seeking royal favor for the expansion of their missions into Alta California, the Jesuits turned over a portion of their mission lands, most in the present-day state of Durango, to secular (lay) priests.

Nueva Vizcaya's Spanish colonists had long demanded privatization. Their demands became more insistent when the province's nonnative population increased fivefold between 1700 and 1750, severely taxing water resources and sharply increasing demand for food. By the 1740s, the missions lost control of communal lands to the regional magistrate (*corregidor*), who, under the pretext of preparing for emergencies, ordered that mission surpluses be placed in storehouses of grain for crises.

The Spanish Bourbons (1700–1807) lacked sufficient resources to defend and expand their empire and to defray the costs of their many wars. To raise revenues and to centralize and strengthen Spain's control over its colonies,

Charles III (reigned 1759–88) undertook a series of reforms in the 1760s. He appointed José Gálvez inspector general (*visitador general*) of New Spain (1765–71) to stabilize the frontier, to overhaul revenue collection, to strengthen Crown monopolies, and to carry out perhaps the most momentous of the king's orders — expulsion of the Jesuits and confiscation of their lands.[41]

The Crown expanded presidios on the northern frontier and garrisoned them with citizen-soldiers, and it imposed heavy taxes and forced loans to pay for its wars. At the same time, siding with mine owners and hacendados and merchants against the missionaries, it loosened trade restrictions and threw its support behind civil officials seeking to privatize mission lands. The Crown's reforms led, in the last decades of the eighteenth century, to a rise in silver production, in traffic along El Camino Real, and in the wealth and power of the merchants who owned strings of haciendas and mines.

In June 1767, the Jesuits abandoned their missions in the Alta Tarahumara and among the Tepehuan. The Franciscans took over, at least at first, establishing their own missions on the abandoned properties. Some administrators were encouraged to sack the missions altogether.

Expulsion of the Jesuits ended all trade between the Tarahumara and the Villa de Chihuahua and isolated the mining town of Cusihuiriáchic, sixty miles to the southwest. Having grown rapidly up to that point, Cusihuiriáchic went into a decline, made worse in the 1760s by a shortage of mercury, needed for silver extraction. It lost almost one-third of its inhabitants in the following decades. To the northwest, however, despite recurring Apache raids, large numbers of mestizos, many of them former presidio soldiers and miners, pushed into the Río Papigóchic Valley, driving the Tarahumara from their fertile river lands and establishing themselves as ranchers and farmers.[42]

The Civil Society of San Felipe

One of the first known workers' strikes occurred in San Felipe. Even though the mines of Chihuahua were isolated, the repartimiento and a steady supply of natives from New Mexico had let mine owners beat down wages. They had adopted the Zacatecan custom of advancing workers ever more credit to bind them in debt, which often grew to fourteen times their monthly earnings and kept them from moving on to other mineral finds. With the *pepena*, however, workers were allowed to keep half the ore they dug in their free time. This let them pay off their debt and encouraged them to migrate to remote mining areas. Time and again throughout the 1720s, the owners attempted to revoke the pepena, only to back down in the face of worker opposition.

Don Manuel San Juan y Santa Cruz, a Basque member of Spain's prestigious Order of Santiago, had served in various presidios and in the Philippines. As presidio captain, he had been given haciendas and mines and natives to work them; as governor, he had crushed a worker rebellion in Parral. In December 1735, San Juan persuaded the mine owners at San Felipe to abolish the pepena. In response, between 300 and 600 miners walked out and armed themselves. Siding with the owners, the government sent fifty armed militiamen, half of them Yaquis with bows and arrows. When San Juan demanded that they fire on the strikers, however, the officer in charge refused. Instead, he ordered his men to surround the mines and to prevent anyone from delivering food or drink to the striking workers. The strike dragged on for four months before the workers were finally starved out. The pepena was retained on a limited basis for a few years, then phased out.

Despite its ever-growing population, Chihuahua officially remained a village (*villa*) until the nineteenth century. Nevertheless, members of its municipal council, though appointed according to class, would on occasion rise above their narrow class interests, such as when they sided with the mine workers over the issue of the pepena in the workers' strike of 1735–36. Moreover, even though the severity of punishment depended on color, the councilmen's commitment to racial orthodoxy did not blind them to outrageous behavior across racial lines. In 1738, for example, the council ruled in favor of a female mulatto slave whose master had broken into her home in search of goods he had falsely accused her of stealing. As part of the final settlement, the slave was granted her freedom.

On the other hand, gender bias thrived in San Felipe's justice system. The municipal council harshly punished women even suspected of threatening "the stability of society." Thus, in 1750, it kept a woman in solitary confinement for seven months while investigating her husband's death at the hand of the woman's Spanish paramour. Women who were raped had the burden of proof, with the benefit of the doubt going to the man. Upholding the centrality of family, the council would jail men for adultery or battery, but it might release an adulterer to support his family.

Having few competitors, Spanish immigrants could freely claim hidalgo status. Some two-thirds were from northern Spain. Although, while in Spain, Basques, Asturians, and Galicians often clashed over cultural and linguistic differences, once in the New World, they were united by the color of their skin. As the elite, they established the social order, working closely with Church and state to strengthen their control of the lower classes. When the elite bought land, they bought those who worked it as well. They required workers to carry papers and forced them to work whether they did or not.

Society, in San Felipe as elsewhere in New Spain, rigidly regulated race until the late 1700s. Available studies show that only one in four mestizos and mulattoes, one in twenty Spaniards, and nearly as few natives married outside their racial groups. Despite the Crown's best efforts, however, toward the end of the century, rates of interracial marriage increased substantially. In 1785, for example, mestizos and mulattoes made up more than one-half of the some 3,700 residents of the Villa de Chihuahua. Yet, even though mixed bloods and Spaniards may have mingled at fiestas and sometimes in the local shops, the social distance between them was wide and would grow wider with time. Because race, or the perception of race, determined social position, there was not much vertical mobility.

Language, especially forms of address and proficiency, conveyed social status. The elite and aspiring elite addressed natives and mixed bloods in the familiar "you" (*tu*), whereas natives and mixed bloods responded in the formal "you" (*usted*). The elite referred to those who spoke Spanish poorly as "Indians" (*indios*) and to workers as "servants" (*sirvientes*).

The mine workers who, together with domestic servants, laborers, and natives generally, lived in the humblest shacks of Santa Eulalia–San Felipe had traveled considerable distances to work in the area's mines and refineries for wages and the pepena. Yaquis, for example, came all the way from Sonora in numbers sufficient to form their own barrio. They were joined by male and female Apaches from New Mexico, both captured slaves and ransomed Indians (*indios de rescate*) — those who bought or ransomed them being entitled to their labor.[43]

The Apache Challenge

By the mid-1700s, relentless Apache attacks had depopulated haciendas, ranchos, and native settlements throughout Chihuahua, although nonnatives could find some safety in urban centers such as Parral and the Villa de Chihuahua, and around presidios. Between 1748 and 1771, Apache raiders killed some 4,000 people and destroyed some 12 million pesos' worth of property in the Chihuahua territory. Between 1771 and 1777, in the area around Parral and the Villa de Chihuahua alone, they killed almost 600 people and took some 215 prisoners. They destroyed or depopulated ninety-four haciendas and ranchos and took or killed more than 55,000 cattle and nearly 1,200 sheep.

The Apache wars unified the territory's disparate classes and races against a common enemy. They molded the cultures of the warring sides, with each side taking prisoners and assimilating them, yet there was also peaceful contact despite the nearly constant hostilities.

In a controversial move, the colonial authorities ordered hacendados to arm their peons and fined them 200 pesos if they did not. When, however, the Apache raids resumed in late 1787 after a short truce, the authorities resorted to the dole, using cash payments, regular shipments of meat, and alcohol to induce the Apaches near the presidios to live in peace. In the 1790s, more than eight hundred Apaches lived at Janos, where they farmed and engaged in crafts. During this time, notes David Weber, "shipping Apache prisoners of war was common, including women and children, from New Spain to Havana" — and very likely to other parts of Latin America, to Asia, and to Europe as well — "so they might never escape and return to their people as earlier deportees to Mexico City had done. [M]ost failed to survive the ordeal of the journey to the Caribbean. Those who did generally spent the remainder of their lives in some form of forced labor."[44] Relative peace between colonists and Apaches lasted until 1831.

Chihuahua before the Storm

Increasingly concerned about social disorder both in Spain and in its colonies, Charles III decreed, in the Royal Pragmatic of 1776, that Spanish subjects under the age of twenty-five could marry only after receiving the consent of their parents. Later legislation extended the scope of the decree to include persons of African ancestry and defined inequality between intended marriage partners as a legitimate basis for parental objection, with race being one measure of this inequality. Rarest between Spaniards and members of other races in southern Nueva Vizcaya (present-day state of Durango), mestizaje in the province as a whole occurred most often between Spanish men and mestizo women, between free mulatto men and native women, and between native men and free mulatto women.

Nevertheless, race mixing increased in the last two decades of the eighteenth century, although the degree to which it did depended on the region. It was more prevalent, for example, in the larger population centers around Durango, Parral, Santa Eulalia–La Villa de Chihuahua, and between Durango and Parral than in the administrative districts (*partidos*) of Cusihuiriáchic, Batolpilas, Conchos, and Cienega de Olivos, most of which had been classified as mission lands until mid-century.

Because the race of a baptized child on a baptismal certificate was based on the race or races of its parents as declared by them or as perceived by the baptizing priest, it is difficult to determine from such certificates the extent of mestizaje for these decades. Workers coming to Chihuahua from as far away as Guatemala were often officially classified as mestizos, even though they may have been natives or mulattoes at home, thus moving up a rung on the social ladder.

At the same time, increasing rates of migration and of intermarriage between citizens from different towns weakened ties to place. In 1777, for example, almost half the heads of household in Parral had migrated there from other places. The Apache raids were a factor in the migration of workers between farms. Moreover, a "floating" population of mine workers migrated from mining camp to mining camp.[45]

At the beginning of the 1800s, only eight missions with their few satellites remained in the territory of Chihuahua. As the native population declined and the nonnative population increased, native rancherías and settlements were replaced by nonnative villages. Chihuahua's population doubled between 1790 and 1823, to 112,000. More people were migrating through the corridors into the territory. La Villa de Chihuahua, which had established the first public elementary school in 1786, officially became Ciudad Chihuahua in 1823. In giving rise to larger, more concentrated markets, urbanization encouraged the expansion of the hacienda system. The Apache raids also encouraged concentration of the population. These developments helped consolidate Spanish colonial institutions, as special interests struggled for access to, and control over, water, pasturage, and farmland.[46]

◄ 2 ►

The Passing of the Saints

Independence opened the way for Mexicans to secularize their culture and education. Influenced by Enlightenment thinking and representative constitutionalism, many of Mexico's new leaders wanted a modern society based on reason rather than theology. The Bourbon reforms had invited scrutiny of the old order, to which religion — the Catholic religion — was fundamental. To build their own nation, Mexicans had to overcome the cumulative effects of three hundred years of Spanish colonialism. To create a new identity for themselves, they had to reject their old, Spanish colonial one, which was inextricably intertwined with the Catholic Church and faith. As a result, Mexico's leaders expelled many Spanish-born Spaniards (*peninsulares*) and came to treat the Church as the foreign agent it sometimes seemed to be. A crucial part of creating a new identity was replacing the old saints with new, secular heroes — heroes who would call on the people to celebrate Mexico and everything it meant to be Mexican.[1]

Independence brought a half century of struggle between conservative and liberal visions for the new nation — a struggle that lasted well beyond the liberal triumph of the mid-1850s. The two factions agreed only that Mexico should be sovereign. The centralist conservative faction, led by wealthy landowners, reactionary clergy, and military men, wanted to retain Church privileges and to preserve the status quo, whereas the federalist liberal faction, led by wealthy, largely reformist merchants and professionals, favored separation of Church and state and a republican form of government.

According to Charles A. Hale, Mexican liberals wanted to "free the new nation from the regime of corporate privilege. [I]ts citizens' allegiance to the civil state must not be shared with the Church or army or with any other corporation, for instance, the university or the Indian community."[2] Because eliminating feudal privileges was foremost on their agenda, liberals aggressively privatized not only Church lands but also Indian communal lands (*ejidos*) and put them up for sale. This had a devastating effect on Mexico's native peoples. Church properties being too expensive, mestizo settlers turned in growing numbers to the relatively inexpensive Indian lands, and the forced sale of communal lands led to repeated rebellions among the dispossessed Indians. Because conservatives, on the other hand, wanted to preserve Mexico's feudal privileges — including those of native peoples — Indians generally supported conservatives over liberals in their civil wars.

Over the colonial period, mining, the Apache wars, and the harsh frontier life had shaped the character of Chihuahuan society. Mining wealth supported an elite of hacendados and merchants and a class system based on race that allowed criollos to dominate the state into the twentieth century. History shaped a military class; the Apache wars strengthened and expanded the hacienda system. The ever-present danger of Apache raids drove many mestizo and native farmers from their lands to work as peons on haciendas, which offered them at least some protection. Mining camps drew on a floating population of resident miners and subsistence farmers who had migrated into the river valleys and who alternated work on their small patches of land with work in the mines. Chihuahuans also traveled to urban population centers to attend fiestas and shop in markets. Truth be told, they traveled longer distances during their lifetimes than most Euro-Americans.

After Independence, many of Chihuahua's ruling elite were the criollo children and grandchildren of Spanish-born Spaniards who had arrived in the previous century. Some helped suppress the first rebellion in the War of Independence (1810–21). At the head of a band of revolutionaries determined to free Mexico from Spain's oppressive colonial rule, Miguel Hidalgo y Costilla had proclaimed Mexico's independence on September 16, 1810. He had called for an end to both slavery and the taxation of Mexico's natives. On September 24, Hidalgo was excommunicated, and on October 13 he was tried in absentia by the Inquisition, which found him guilty of heresy and treason and sentenced him to death.[3] After initial victories, Hidalgo's forces were turned back from Mexico City and finally routed in January of the following year. Taken prisoner in Coahuila on June 26, 1811, Hidalgo was transported to the Villa de Chihuahua. There, along with twenty-two others, he was executed by firing squad on July 30, and his head was displayed in Guanajuato as a warning to would-be revolutionaries. With Independence and the establishment of the Mexican republic in 1824, however, he came to be regarded as the Father of Mexico.[4]

Of all Mexico's institutions, the Catholic Church was the most Spanish. It had a stake in the Spanish Empire. Thus, even though the Spanish Bourbons had privatized and confiscated many mission lands in the previous century, when the revolution reached Chihuahua, nearly all the clergy opposed it. Father José Francisco Alvárez, for example, recruited three hundred Tarahumaras in the Valle de Rosario area to fight for Spain. Also opposed were many members of notable families, whose loyalty to Crown and Church varied greatly, however, depending on which generation they belonged to.[5]

Although the average chihuahuense was culturally Catholic, liberals believed that the power of the Church should be curtailed, whereas conservatives wanted things left the same. Regardless of their opposing political positions, however, liberal and conservative leaders alike were elitists who strove to maintain the cultural and racial dominance of criollos over natives, mestizos, and mixed bloods, whom they regarded as inferior.

Given the leaders' worldview, faced with the hostility of the new mestizo class, who could not accept that most Indians did not want to be Mexican, and used by both liberals and conservatives in their internecine wars, Mexico's Indians fared badly in the first hundred years after Independence. Their share of the nation's population dropped from 60 percent in 1810 to 29 percent in 1920, even as the mestizos' share climbed from 12 to 60 percent (and presumably still higher in Chihuahua).[6] As this happened, however, chihuahuenses came to think of themselves as less Indian, less mestizo, and more white than Mexicans to the south.[7]

"To Populate Is to Govern"

Argentine dictator Juan Manuel de Rosas might just as well have been speaking of Chihuahua when he uttered these words in 1852. Both liberals and conservatives knew that, to govern their state, they had to populate it. But before they could do this, they had to subdue the Apache — and they had to have more people. With the demise of the Chihuahua's natives in the seventeenth and eighteenth centuries, the state's population had been dangerously depleted, encouraging Apaches to occupy Chihuahua's largely deserted lands. The fragile peace with the Apache since Independence fell apart in 1830, when Colonel José Joaquín Calvo, believing in the superiority of the Mexican army, arrogantly suspended the rations and subsidies of peaceful Apaches.[8]

Calvo's folly touched off a fifty-year war with the Apache that almost depopulated Chihuahua's northwestern sierra frontier. The wars furthered the rise of a class of frontiersmen who rode horses and carried guns. Because elites needed the small ranchers and serrano villagers, the appearance of equality between the mestizo majority and the ruling elite developed. Frontier settlements enjoyed considerable autonomy until the last two decades of the century. In the years after Independence, military resources were diverted by frequent coups at the national level, and further resources were needed to respond to the invasion of Texas. The central government's weakness eroded its authority, and Chihuahuans bitterly chastized it for not protecting the lives and property of its citizens. In December 1834, the Chihuahuan newspaper *El Fanal* went so far as to call for the annexation of Chihuahua to the United States to secure just such protection.

After 1830, the state promised settlers small ranchos in the sierra in return for fighting the Apaches. Time after time, however, these ranchos were settled, only to be abandoned, as brief lulls were followed by intense attacks. Sonoran General Francisco García Conde, 36, was appointed governor of Chihuahua to lead the campaign against the Apaches. Son of Alejo García Conde, the last military commander of Nueva Vizcaya, Francisco went back to making pacts and treaties, then offering rations and subsidies to peaceful natives, a policy unpopular with diehards who had developed a "war to the death" mentality. Despite his success, however, he was removed from his post at the end of 1842.

Under constant attack, chihuahuenses abandoned ranchos, small mining camps, and cattle centers. Minerals could not be shipped on the Silver Road (Camino de Plata). Things got so bad by the mid-nineteenth century that Chihuahua entered a joint defense pact with neighboring states. Zacatecas and Nuevo León formed a compact in 1851, and the following year Zacatecas called for another compact between northern Mexican states. Fearing secession, the Mexican government objected to these compacts in December 1852, with the Senate citing the risk of national disintegration posed by parallel military forces.[9]

After the wars of 1836 and 1847, the increased military presence on the U.S. side forced the Apaches south. With the arrival of the southern transcontinental railroad in Texas and New Mexico in the 1880s, the Apache threat gradually came to an end and *serrano* (sierran) ranchos proliferated.[10] This led to the growth of two mostly mestizo townships (*municipios*) — Cusihuiriáchic and Guerrero — that came to symbolize the rancho culture of the region.[11] The serrano ranchers who fought the Apaches, and especially the hacendados who expanded their holdings by acquiring ranchos abandoned in the face of Indian attacks, would play a key role in state politics.

Governing Chihuahua

During the first six decades after Independence, population growth in Chihuahua was much slowed by the Apache wars, but with migration from neighboring states and the rest of Mexico, it greatly accelerated during the next two. Seeking work in Chihuahua's mines and on its haciendas, a steady stream of migrants from Durango, Zacatecas, and the interior passed along the primary corridor to Texas and New Mexico, the Río Conchos, whose river lands had historically supplied labor to Chihuahua's mines. Many would stay there for a time before moving on. By 1900, the state's population had nearly tripled since Independence, to just under 327,800. But where, on average, it had grown by 1 percent per year between 1823 and 1877, it grew by just under 4.6 percent per year — more than four times as fast — between 1877 and 1900.[12]

A liberal-controlled Chihuahuan legislature passed the Land Settlement Law of 1825 to encourage immigration and the settlement of public lands or *terrenos baldíos*, uncultivated and unsurveyed tracts, throughout the state. It also placed a head tax exclusively on indigenous people. Both the state and federal governments, strapped for cash, vied for control of public lands and tobacco taxes as sources of revenue, the first to pay for fighting Apache raiders, and the second to pay for its very existence. The head tax forced some natives to abandon their settlements and allowed nearby haciendas to seize their lands. Of Chihuahua's remaining natives, only the Tarahumara survived in significant numbers, and they responded to the encroachments by escaping into the sierra.[13]

The Heartland

The lands along the Río Conchos are central to our narrative because many of the miners from eastern Arizona would either come from or travel through them. Pedro Subia came from the Camargo (Santa Rosalía) area and many of his relatives were from Delicias, some forty miles farther north on the Río Conchos.[14] Migrant workers were drawn to the region by the bonanzas of Parral, Santa Eulalia, and other mining areas of Chihuahua. Subsistence farmers would work their lands and often seek temporary jobs in the nearest or richer mines. Water was always a problem, either too much or too little. As water rights became further monopolized and campesinos were reduced to dry farming, droughts became more of a factor in their lives.

Throughout much of the colonial period, communal lands, both mission and native, had coexisted with haciendas, ranchos, and small farms along Chihuahua's rivers, although in disputes over water or land the haciendas would almost always prevail. In the last decades of its empire, Spain moved to establish secular pueblos on the Río Conchos and its tributaries, often over objections of hacendados. In 1797, the pueblos of Santa Rosalía and La Cruz were each granted two square leagues (8,600 acres or 3,510 hectares) of lands claimed by the Enramada hacienda, which along with other haciendas had stymied the settling of the pueblos. The pueblos' grants included communal lands, which disappeared in the nineteenth century as the river and its tributaries were dammed and commercial agriculture increased pressure for privatization.

Before the 1800s, there had been little commercial agriculture along the river, whose use had been dominated by the livestock activities of the haciendas. As the productivity of farmland increased with irrigation, however, pueblos such as Santa Rosalía and La Cruz began to attract settlers from within and outside the state. By the mid-1820s, Santa Rosalía had some 2,500 inhabitants. The San Ambrosio canal, dug in 1610, was the oldest acequia in the state. It was joined by the Refugio, Patrocinio, Rosario, and Santa Rosalía canals, most dug during the nineteenth century.[15] Smaller farmers dug and managed acequias by forming farming collectives (*comunidades*) and pooling their labor. Larger farmers pooled their financial resources and sometimes rented out water rights to smaller users. Coexistence with the haciendas was possible because farm production was consumed by the farmers themselves or sold only in local markets.

Who controlled the water and how it was parceled out differed from place to place. For example, water use for San Francisco de Conchos, the oldest settlement in the area, was under the control of one large landowner. In La Cruz, a collective managed most water use, and the larger landowners abided by its decisions. Water for Camargo (Santa Rosalía) and Saucillo was managed by medium property owners.[16]

"Poor Mexico, So Far from God . . . "

The injustice of the United States' annexation of Texas in 1845, its war with Mexico in 1846, and its forcible acquisition of the northern half of Mexican territory in 1848 was not lost on contemporaries. A young lieutenant when the war broke out, President Ulysses S. Grant was and remained "bitterly opposed" to the annexation, which he saw as "a conspiracy to acquire territory out of which slave states might be formed for the American Union." He regarded "the war which resulted as one of the most unjust ever waged by a stronger against a weaker nation." "Texas was originally a state belonging to the republic of Mexico," he wrote. "[Our] colonists . . . introduced slavery into the state almost from the start, though the constitution of Mexico did not, nor does it now, sanction that institution." "Even if the annexation itself could be justified," he concluded, "the manner in which the subsequent war was forced upon Mexico cannot."[17]

Most Mexicans bitterly resented the U.S. invasion of their country and the loss of so much of their patrimony. Soon after Mexico became independent, slaveholders from the southern United States had moved into what was then part of the Mexican state of Coahuila and Texas. The Texans, as they called themselves, would not or could not abide by Mexican laws such as the abolition of slavery, which had been part of Hidalgo's promise. They set out to "re-annex" all Mexican territory up to the Rio Grande, which would have taken in more than half of New Mexico.[18] In 1836, they declared their independence and, owing to Santa Anna's ineptitude, established the Lone Star Republic, which time and again threatened New Mexico and Chihuahua. In 1841, Texas raiders attempting to "re-annex" New Mexico were taken prisoner without a shot being fired and marched through Chihuahua to Mexico City.[19]

When the United States annexed Texas in December 1845, war was inevitable. In March 1846, President James Polk ordered troops into the disputed territory, and in May the U.S. Congress declared war on Mexico over the objections of sixty-seven Whig representatives, most notably Abraham Lincoln. Ohio Senator Tom Corwin accused Polk of involving the United States in a "war of aggression."

In the summer of 1846, Colonel Stephen Watts Kearny left Fort Leavenworth, Kansas, with an army of 3,000 men, following the Santa Fe Trail and using the U.S. merchants in New Mexico as his advance guard. In mid-December, Colonel Alexander W. Doniphan was sent south to conquer Chihuahua with an army of 1,400 men. Chihuahuan troops confronted Doniphan at Temascalitos, not far from El Paso del Norte, on December 25, 1846. Buying arms out of his own pocket, Governor Angel Trías led the resistance.

By late February 1847, Doniphan had captured Ciudad Chihuahua. His troops occupied the state for fifty-nine days, leaving in late April. On September 14, U.S. troops captured Mexico City. Under the Treaty of Guadalupe Hidalgo, signed on February 2, 1848, which ended what Mexicans would call the War of 1847, Mexico ceded some 500,000 square miles — more than 40 percent of its territory — to the United States in return for $15 million, a sum that amounts to less than a nickel an acre for the present-day states of California, New Mexico, Nevada, and for parts of Colorado, Arizona, Utah, and Oklahoma. The U.S. Senate ratified the treaty on March 10, 1848, by a vote of twenty-eight to fourteen. After some difficulty in forming a quorum, the Mexican Senate did so on May 19, by a vote of fifty-two to thirty-five. U.S. Consul

Nicholas Philip Trist, sent to Mexico to negotiate the treaty, said he felt the Mexicans' humiliation: he recognized that the war had been no more than a pretext to seize Mexican land.[20]

The political culture of Chihuahua changed after Guadalupe Hidalgo. The northern portion of the state became more attractive because of its proximity to the United States and its markets. Yet this proximity also put it in harm's way of Apache raiders. A sizable number of New Mexicans expatriated to Chihuahua in accordance with the terms of the treaty. The out-migration concerned New Mexican authorities, who put up barriers to the exodus. In 1848 and 1849 alone, New Mexico lost some 1,200 residents. The following year, a number of wealthy hacendados and their peons left for Chihuahua. The Mexican government actively encouraged a return to the homeland, and according to a Mexican border commissioner, many New Mexicans agreed to return. The Mexican border commissioners complained that New Mexican authorities placed obstacles in the way of the would-be repatriates in violation of the Treaty of Guadalupe Hidalgo.

In December 1850, joint boundary commissioners met at El Paso del Norte to establish the boundary between New Mexico and Mexico, which unsettled Chihuahuans.[21] Reacting to the pronouncements of Euro-American expansionists such as William Carr Lane, General Angel Trías fired back that residents of the Mesilla did not want to be annexed to New Mexico and put the militias of the state of Zacatecas on alert. The Mexican government sent federal troops to Chihuahua. The United States also reinforced its troops, and President Franklin Pierce designated James Gadsden to negotiate a treaty. Gadsden pressured Mexico to sell some 30,000 square miles of its northern territory — about the size of South Carolina. The Gadsden Treaty, known in Mexico as the Mesilla Treaty, was signed on December 30, 1853.[22]

From the beginning, there were problems in establishing the boundaries. In March 1853, even before U.S. commerce had begun to flow through the Mesilla corridor, New Mexico Territorial Governor William Carr Lane claimed that Mesilla belonged to New Mexico and that the United States had therefore given it to Mexico illegally. According to news accounts, the boundary between New Mexico and Chihuahua had been set in 1824 to run about eight miles north of El Paso, Texas, main plaza, but U.S. Boundary Commissioner Bartlett had sold out his country and agreed to a line thirty-four miles north. Bartlett countered that Mesilla had never been part of New Mexico. The controversy continued, with many national politicians supporting Governor Lane.

As could be expected, Mexico responded immediately and gave Chihuahuan Governor Angel Trías authority to go to El Paso del Norte to negotiate with U.S. officials and to defend Mexican territory if need be. Lane did not help matters when he accused Mexico of violating the Treaty of Guadalupe Hidalgo. The Gadsden Purchase effectively ended the controversy in 1853. But the resentment it aroused became part of the historical memory of chihuahuenses.[23]

Although Apache raids emanating from U.S. territory and the territorial ambitions of many Euro-Americans kept relations between the two countries on edge, many Chihuahuan merchants did business in Mesilla, and some even sent their children to parochial schools in Saint Louis.[24] After the war, Mexico gave up requiring that immigrants be exclusively Catholic, although it largely limited immigration to people of European stock. A decade later, Chihuahua would benefit from the U.S. Civil War and the scarcity of cotton. By the late 1860s, the state's nascent cotton textile industry was running some two hundred looms.[25]

Advancing the Liberal Agenda

In February of 1849, Governor Angel Trías painted a dismal portrait of Chihuahua. "Our state," the governor observed, "is a vast desert where there are small spaces of joy and a miserable population that lacks security and welfare for its inhabitants." Having suffered the ravages of the Apaches, Chihuahua was left with an unstable economy and a mining industry in ruins. Mexico's largest state, it covered more than 95,000 square miles — almost twice the size of New York State — yet its entire population could be fit into a third-tier city.[26]

Despite the turmoil to come, Chihuahua and the nation as a whole would eventually take a turn for the better with the rise of the Mexican liberals. Under the leadership of President Benito Juárez and Sebastian Lerdo de Tejada, Mexico adopted the liberal Constitution of 1857, which severely limited Church privileges and nationalized its properties, and the Laws of Reform, which flowed from the constitution. Together with the liberals' almost total victories in the War of Reform and the French Intervention, these events did much to help create a Mexican identity and to confirm the passing of the saints.

The year after the Constitution of 1857 was ratified, conservatives revolted, led by the powerful Zuloaga family. The War of Reform lasted from 1858 to 1860 and served to launch the career of thirty-one-year-old Colonel Luis Terrazas, political jefe of the Ciudad Chihuahua District and cousin to the celebrated military commander and Apache-fighter Joaquín Terrazas. In 1860, Luis was appointed interim governor.[27] The son of a local merchant of modest means, Luis wed the daughter of a wealthy hacendado, Carolina Bustamante Cuilty, and they had fourteen children. Terrazas's sons and sons-in-law would play pivotal roles in building and sustaining his empire. Of his eight sons-in-law, Enrique C. Creel was the most important. An international banker, he was the son of former U.S. consul Reuben Creel and Paz Cuilty, the sister of Terrazas's wife, Carolina. Enrique married Terrazas's daughter Angela. Terrazas was linked, by kinship or business connections, to the major families in Chihuahua. Through his wife, he also had ties with conservative families, such as the Zuloagas, throughout the state. Conservatives were strongly represented among the criollo elite of the state capital. Terrazas used his connections and the state's resources to checkmate opponents, rewarding supporters and, in particular, his cabal — Cuilty, Cordero, Zuloaga, and others — with access to state lands. They profited handsomely from the sale of privatized Church lands, acquiring most of the famous Encinillas hacienda as well as lands in the Galeana District and in the state capital.

In October 1864, during the French Intervention (1862–67), Juárez sought refuge in the Chihuahuan capital. Disagreements arose between Terrazas and Juárez over the sale of terrenos baldíos and of properties confiscated from conservative landowners. Despite these disagreements, however, Terrazas maintained his control of Chihuahua.

U.S. Consul Reuben Creel, father of Terrazas's son-in-law Enrique, reported that Chihuahua was "thinly populated and . . . very poor"; that, having "suffered for four or five years from deficient crops[, t]he people are grumbling very much about taxes";[28] that the state had no more than 3,000 militiamen to defend the republic; and that Juárez was alienating the citizenry by imposing forced loans. The tide began to shift in 1866, when, with the advance of supporters from El Paso del Norte, Terrazas defeated the French in Ciudad Chihuahua. U.S. companies based in El Paso, Texas, were now poised to lay claim to Chihuahua's most prized properties, mines in the western portion of the state.[29]

Although the central importance attached to Catholicism and to notions such as "gente de razón" (civilized people) and "gente decente" (respectable people) meant it was better to be Catholic and not too dark-skinned throughout most of Mexico, the historical struggle between the Church and mining interests in Chihuahua made the relationship between race and social standing more fluid there. U.S. Consul Charles Moye observed in 1867 that, even though nearly all southern chihuahuenses were white or native, the state as a whole boasted a disproportionate number of mixed bloods. Indeed, he described the Chihuahuans as "another race of Mexicans." Consul Moye further observed, however, that many poor Chihuahuans had to work months to afford the marriage fees for a priest (and now also a civil judge), with the unsurprising result that a large number of children were being born out of wedlock; that education was limited; and that the better classes sent their children to the United States to become enlightened and good citizens — much as it had been in colonial times.[30]

By 1868, when Terrazas was only thirty-nine, his cattle ranch holdings had reached 275,000 acres (112,000 hectares). Soon afterward, he acquired the entire Encinillas hacienda, an additional 950,000 acres (386,000 hectares), which had been confiscated from the Martínez del Río family for its support of Maximillian. In 1869, Terrazas was reelected governor.

In the 1870s, Terrazas began to diversify his holdings, setting up a textile factory in 1871 and a flour mill in 1874 and incorporating the Banco Mexicano with members of his cabal in 1879. He remained loyal to the Juárez government during the attempted coups of 1872 and to the Juárez faction of the Reform Party in 1876, when it opposed the Textepecan Rebellion, declared by Porfirio Díaz and supported by the younger Angel Trías (General Trías's son). When an army under the command of Terrazas's cousin Lieutenant Colonel Joaquín Terrazas defeated the *porfiristas* (Díaz supporters), Díaz sent federal troops and installed Trías as governor of Chihuahua. Trías proceeded to raise taxes, impose forced loans, and end the company store (*tienda de raya*), thereby alienating Chihuahua's elites.[31]

In the 1870s, manufactured goods from Europe, and especially from Britain and Germany, sold at lower prices than those from north of the Río Bravo and were therefore favored by chihuahuenses. The arrival of the railroad would generate new trade, however, and give the United States an advantage that Britain, Germany, and even neighboring Mexican states did not have.[32] Although Chihuahua exported chiefly silver and gold, as well as some corn, sheep, and flour, the last to Texas, progress in the export sector was generally stunted by the Apache wars.[33]

Moving On

Pedro Subia, shot to death in Arvin, California, in 1933, Abrán Salcido, leader of the 1903 Morenci, Arizona, strike, who served four years at the dreaded San Juan Ulúa Prison, and the great Mexican muralist David Alfaro Siqueiros all came from the Camargo (Santa Rosalía) area. The first two, both most likely born in 1873, would travel north along the Camino Real and Mesilla corridors, and the third, born just before the turn of the century, would trek south to Mexico City. Their Santa Rosalía was a town in transition, whose population of just under 14,400 would nearly triple, to more than 40,700 between 1877 and 1910.[34]

Subia's and Salcido's people were probably small farmers, but because they were poor, not much is known about them. Irrigation pulled people into the Santa Rosalía area, and droughts pushed them out again. The droughts of 1849–51, the late 1880s, and especially the early 1890s drove many chihuahuenses like Subia and Salcido, who moved to Morenci, Arizona, in the 1890s, to migrate first to mines nearby and then to mines, railroads, farmlands, and pick-and-shovel work north of Mexico.[35]

Luis Aboites Aguilar and Rocío Castañeda González, whose works focus on the monopolization of water in Chihuahua, give us a glimpse of the uprooting of Chihuahuans from the Camargo (Santa Rosalía) area. In most instances, rights to irrigation water were acquired by farmers of some means. Subsistence farmers and sharecroppers depended on rainfall and thus were most affected by droughts and the transformation of agriculture.

Increasingly, throughout the Conchería, the wealthier landholders concentrated control and expanded both their land holdings and the amount of water they were entitled to. The pueblo of La Cruz, not far from Santa Rosalía, was typical. In mid-century, most of the communal landholders had a stake in the 4,300 acres of communal land (*ejido*) originally assigned to the pueblo. Even though the pueblo's water rights were managed by the township council, however, control of much of the its water was concentrated in the hands of one landowner, Merced Valles Baca. Monopolization of the pueblo's land and water intensified in the 1860s. In 1865, for example, as authorized by President Juárez, four *suertes* of the pueblo's communal land — 105 acres (43 hectares) with four days of water per week — were sold to Basilio Muñoz.[36] In 1868, more communal land was sold off when Muñoz was president of the township council. Even though La Cruz's local jurisdiction over water was preserved during the nineteenth century, the sale of township lands opened the way for the hacendados Severino Calderón, Jesús Valenzuela, and Francisco Aguirre to monopolize the pueblo's water in 1875. Along with Valles Baca, they remained in constant conflict with the communal and small landholders over water, or the control of it.[37]

Transforming Chihuahua

The ruling oligarchy in Chihuahua moved to diversify production, establish a market economy, and consolidate their control.[38] Four major developments accelerated the state's economic and political transformation: the defeat of the Apaches, the monopolization of land and water, the arrival of the Mexican Central Railroad, and the massive influx of foreign capital.

Tres Castillos

On October 14, 1880, in the Chihuahuan sierra, Lieutenant Colonel Joaquín Terrazas ambushed Vitorio, fifty-five at the time and by some accounts so arthritic he had to be lifted into the saddle, in the famous Battle of Tres Castillos. Juan Mata Ortiz and his men aided Terrazas, as did the Tarahumara

An Apache camp in Cañon de los Embudos in Sonora in 1886. (Photograph by Noah H. Rose, courtesy of the Denver Public Library, Western History Collection, X-32814)

Captain Mauricio Corredor and his men. The Tarahumaras went from pocket to pocket of resistance, blasting the Apaches out of their rock fortresses with dynamite. The battle lasted through the night and into the morning. The Chihuahuans reportedly massacred seventy-two warriors, Vitorio among them, eighteen women, and some children. They took seventy-eight scalps for bounty and captured and enslaved sixty women and children, including two of Vitorio's sons.

The Chihuahuans held a triumphal march in Ciudad Chihuahua, displaying Apache scalps on lances and marching the prisoners to jail to the sound of bands playing and crowds cheering. They distributed the children among those who wanted them and later sold the adult captives as slaves. Lieutenant Colonel Terrazas was said to have earned more than $27,000 from the scalps and prisoners he personally claimed. The Mexican government promoted him to full colonel and later honored Tarahumara sharpshooter Corredor as Vitorio's killer, giving him a beautiful silver-inlaid rifle.

Apache attacks persisted after the death of Vitorio, and even after the capture of Geronimo in 1886 but at a much lower level. The Apache chief Ju burned Mata Ortiz alive in November of 1882 in revenge for his treachery. Corredor died in a battle with "pacified" Apaches. Eloquent testimony to the assimilation of the small minority of Tarahumaras who fought on the side of the

Chihuahuans, the Battle of Tres Castillos also dashed the small ranchers' hopes for land ownership.[39]

Luis Terrazas: Consolidating Control

By the 1880s, Luis Terrazas had acquired more than 1.5 million acres (624,000 hectares) of land and his close ally, José María Luján, held another 600,000 acres (243,000 hectares) in the Camargo and Hidalgo Districts. Much of this land lay in the area over which Vitorio and his Apache warriors had ranged. Terrazas would acquire still more land through foreclosure and the purchase of terrenos baldíos. In the late 1880s, he and Henrique Muller acquired so much of the communal lands of Cruces (Namiquipa, in the Guerrero District), there was nothing left of the grant made by Teodoro de Croix in 1778. Moreover, they confiscated communal land from the pueblo of Galeana.[40]

In 1884, Díaz sent General Carlos Pacheco to Chihuahua to neutralize Terrazas, who was forever feuding with Díaz appointees. Pacheco allied himself with the Guerrero group, based in the area around the township of Guerrero and led by the Casavantes family — to no avail. Enemies of Terrazas linked to elites in other areas. The Guerrero group had formed the Banco Minero de Chihuahua in 1880, and through partnerships with various surveying companies, it had secured large tracts of terrenos baldíos. Despite its vast land holdings, however, the group lacked the cattle to take to market. When the Mexican economy slid into a depression, the group was forced to sell off the Mining Bank to the Terrazas cabal, which came to hold a monopoly on credit in Chihuahua. Under Terrazas control, the bank generated a million-peso profit between 1883 and 1896, when it absorbed the Banco de Chihuahua, whose assets had been much reduced by the depression.

Terrazas, who would come to own one-tenth of the state's land, reaped huge profits from cattle raising. With these profits and with capital from the Banco Minero, which would become Mexico's fourth largest bank in 1910, he embarked on enterprises in transportation, industry, and mining. Access to government capital helped him weather the depression of 1907. Every step of the way, he used the government to fix the laws in his favor.[41] At the height of his empire in the first decade of the 1900s, Terrazas employed more than 8,500 peons on his haciendas and more than 13,000 workers in his factories — nearly half the industrial workforce of the state. He owned some 400,000 cattle, 100,000 sheep, and 25,000 horses. He controlled almost three-quarters of the state's sales in flour and half its sales in cattle.

During the Díaz years, political power was taken away from local and concentrated in state and then in federal hands. From 1888 on, the state appointed political jefes as district officials; local citizens no longer elected them.

In 1891, the state assumed control over all water not considered federal property under the 1888 law. In 1903 and 1904, the state replaced locally elected mayors with its own appointees, which gave the political jefes control over local councils. The Law for the Organization of the Districts of 1904 replaced locally elected township and district presidents with district jefes appointed by the governor. These officials were almost immediately replaced by Porfirio Díaz with appointees of his own. In 1910, the federal government assumed control of all navigable waters, becoming the sole controller of how those waters were to be used. This consolidation of political control increased tensions between the villagers and state and federal authorities. The townships resented the new officials, many of whom were outsiders. *Serrano* villages and townships resented them even more, having enjoyed considerable autonomy during the Apache wars. Moreover, the rift between Díaz and Terrazas, who had opposed the dictator's coup in 1876, encouraged factions to form.

To put more land and wealth into the economy, the federal government adopted the Settlement Act of 1884. Based on the Reform Acts of the 1850s, the new law granted survey companies generous in-kind franchises (one-third of the land they surveyed, with an option to buy more), transferring thousands of acres of public land into private hands. This infringed on communal land rights in the northwest and led to an all-out assault on the remaining Indian land holdings. It got so bad that in 1884, the Tarahumaras in Norogachi and Andrés del Río rioted in protest. Political jefe Anastacio Porras, a rabid *terrazista*, warned the state government that any further incitement would lead to rebellion and bring ruin to Chihuahua.

Railroads and the Capitalist Invasion

The effective end of the Apache wars and the arrival of the railroad in the 1880s ushered in an era of profiteering and class conflict unprecedented in Chihuahua's history, when peace, stability, new laws and significant changes in old laws, and generous financial incentives attracted huge foreign investment in land and mineral resources.[42]

The Mexican Central Railroad followed the old Camino Real, principal corridor for Mexican miners traveling to eastern Arizona in the late 1880s, and bound Chihuahua with the interior of Mexico and with El Paso del Norte. Terrazas competed with the federal government in building railroad lines: his State Railroad Company (Compañia Ferrocarrilera del Estado) built spurs from Hidalgo to Jiménez and to the Sierra Madre Occidental.[43] The railroad's arrival shifted the balance of trade: it made it easier for Chihuahuans to reach the United States than Mexico City, and it encouraged the massive influx of foreign capital and technology.[44] Far from bringing a higher standard of living to most

Chihuahuans, however, this "capitalist invasion" further concentrated land in the hands of a few large companies in the years between 1870 and 1920, when modernizing forces such as banks and credit institutions began to emerge.[45]

Facilitated by Díaz-controlled political jefes, the relationship between local elites and foreign capitalists was cemented in the 1890s and directed by the national government. Foreigners continued to receive favorable assessments of land and mines throughout the Díaz years. Under this politics of accommodation, foreigner capitalists paid off local political elites, hired lawyers, and received government subsidies if their ventures involved railroad construction. In return for bribes, profits, and perquisites, which financed their conspicuous consumption, these elites presided over the rape of Mexico's natural resources by foreigners. In 1884, U.S. mining interests worked only forty sites in Mexico; by 1892, they worked — and owned — almost 2,400. By 1896, that figure had almost tripled to just under 6,700, and Americans controlled most Mexican mines. The figure would almost double again to just under 13,700 by 1904. By 1902, in Chihuahua alone, foreign capital investment, mostly Euro-American, had reached $30 million; by 1907, it had climbed to $50 million — 70 percent in mining.[46]

"Long Live Tomóchic!"

The last two decades of the nineteenth century were a time of huge prosperity for a few and a time of growing social, political, and religious unrest for the many. The Chihuahuan people awakened from the delusion that Terrazas was their *compadre*, having their best interests at heart.[47] One of the first labor strikes took place in El Paso del Norte in September 26, 1881, when a Mexican Central Railroad foreman cut workers' wages by one-quarter, from two pesos to 1.50 pesos. Like most of the strikes of the period, it was short-lived and uneventful. The first miners' strike, on January 21, 1883, was also short-lived — but far from uneventful. When the British Mining Company of Pinos Altos demanded that its miners spend half their wages at the company store, workers occupied the store. Local authorities intervened on the side of management, deputizing a dozen men to put down the strike. When the manager of the mine attempted to address the workers, however, he was shot and killed, whereupon the township president arrived with twenty-five men and imposed martial law. He arrested the strike leaders and executed five of them, three outright and two later — all three years before the Haymarket Square Riot, when seven policemen and four protestors were killed, and four anarchists later executed.[48]

Supporters of Luis Terrazas and Porfirio Díaz continued competing for power well into the 1890s. Although careful in opposing the leadership of Díaz,

Terrazas shrewdly contested his authority through surrogates. Thus, along with Carlos Zuloaga, he financed Catarino E. Garza's unsuccessful revolt against the Díaz regime in Tamaulipas, on Mexico's northeast coast, in 1891. A former Mexican consul at Saint Louis, Missouri, Garza had helped provide labor leadership for Mexican workers in the lower Rio Grande Valley through *mutualistas* (mutual aid societies) in 1885. Crossing from the United States into Mexico, Garza had attempted on three separate occasions to start a revolution in 1891.[49]

Closer to home, Terrazas supported the Conspiracy of 1889 through Simón Amaya, Celso Anaya, and Santana Pérez, his friends and allies in the Guerrero District, some one hundred miles west of the state capital. Charging that Díaz had violated not only civil liberties but also the spirit of the Constitution of 1857 — having it amended to permit successive presidential terms — Amaya and Jesús María Vásquez, who together led the conspiracy, called for banning the reelection of Mexican presidents altogether. The conspirators also strongly opposed the recently passed Township Revenue Law (Ley de Ingresos Municipales), which limited local autonomy. In a transition zone between ranching country and the sierra, with native settlements near mining and logging camps, the area around Guerrero had been one of constant conflict between mestizos and natives, with Indian revolts in 1879 and 1887. Land surveys and the assault on timberlands had only heightened tensions. Fiercely loyal to Terrazas, Amaya had fought the French in 1860s, the Trías forces in 1879, and the Apache almost all his adult life. He had been a *juarista* in 1872 and a political jefe in 1876 and again in the 1880s.[50] In 1889, he counted on the support of Sonoran dissidents, which did not materialize. Amaya was captured and exiled. Vásquez and Pérez evaded prosecution, the former by betraying his co-conspirators, and the latter by proclaiming his loyaly to the authorities. Celso Anaya escaped to the United States, where he stayed in contact with dissidents. Mexican authorities feared a rebellion would begin from the U.S. side.[51]

Amid the social and political turmoil at century's end, millenarian socio-religious movements, such as the popular devotion to Teresa de Urrea, the Saint of Cabora, mushroomed. Like other such movements, *teresismo* was grounded in religious faith, offering otherwise hopeless peasants the belief that, come the millennium, God would favor them. It had many followers in the pueblo of Tomóchic, near Guerrero, where discontent was growing over encroachment on communal lands and over state-appointed local political jefes.

The caravan that supplied the mine at Pinos Altos, and which retrieved silver and banknotes from it, regularly passed by Tomóchic. In January 1891, the caravan was attacked and robbed some ten miles from Guerrero. Although there was no evidence the Tomochicans were responsible, they were blamed anyway. In November 1891, federal troops were dispatched to the area. Over the following eleven months, tension between the two sides mounted steadily. Finally, on October 20, 1892, a force of 1,200 federal troops surrounded the pueblo. It was met with battle cries of "Long live Teresita!" — "Death to the baldies [*pelones*], sons of Lucifer!" In the ensuing battle, the sixty-eight Tomochican fighters, most of them veterans of the Apache wars, and their wives, sisters, and mothers killed almost five hundred federal troops, wounding hundreds more. They fought under a red cross sewn on a white field, which flew over Cruz Chávez's house. On the orders of President Porfirio Díaz, the parish church was set ablaze, killing most of the women and children, and the defenders were fired upon. Some fifty Tomochicans managed to survive the flames and fusillade, taking refuge in a house nearby. Cruz refused to surrender but, after letting families go, remained in his house without ammunition. The troops soaked the roof with oil, then lit it while firing on the defenders. Although wounded in both legs, Cruz would still not surrender. After ten days, however, the attackers' relentless bombardment and overwhelming firepower broke the Tomochicans' resistance. Finally captured, Cruz and the last defenders were taken away and shot. The troops killed every man and boy over the age of thirteen, and burned the pueblo to the ground. Of the pueblo's 350 inhabitants, only 13 women and 71 children survived. Tomóchic became a symbol of defiance.

The news reached across the border. In his El Paso newspaper *El Independiente*, Lauro Aguirre would charge in 1896 that Díaz had been more cruel, barbarous, and destructive in sixteen years of rule than the Apaches in four centuries of warfare. The Díaz government attempted, without success, to portray the fallen martyrs as fanatics and terrorists. Chihuahuan workers and dissidents took the memory of Tomóchic with them as they traveled "to the North" (*al norte*).[52]

In April 1893, at Santo Tomás, one hundred rebels fought three hundred federal troops. With their two cannons, the troops leveled the pueblo, and only Santana Pérez escaped. Pérez addressed his 1893 manifesto, which outlined the abuses of *caciquismo* (bossism) and the injustice of forced military conscription, to the Mexican soldiers: "We are children of the same mother, our flag is one, our territory one, we speak the same language and want the same things. The tyrants are against democracy and treat us like cattle." The manifesto called Díaz an assassin and his minions imbeciles and bandits. "The rebels adhere to Constitution of 1857. Down with tyrants! Long live the revolution and long live Tomóchic!"[53]

In 1893, Anaya and Amaya met with Victor L. Ochoa, 23, the editor of the *Hispano Americano* in his El Paso, Texas, home. (Born in Ojinaga, Chihuahua, Ochoa was a naturalized U.S. citizen.) The Ochoa cabal was in touch with

Tomóchic and Santo Tomás sympathizers and with the Guerrero and Galeana conspirators. Later, about the time of Garza's 1891 revolt, Ochoa led the Palomas raid from El Paso. His raiders occupied the customshouse, but only three, including Ochoa himself, made it back to the United States.

The official Chihuahua state newspaper characterized the Palomas raid as led by fanatics. The rebels, Ochoa among them, struck again on January 15, 1894, with the intention of concentrating 5,000 men near Ciudad Chihuahua, and then marching against the prefecture of Tomóchic. When the government forces attacked them, Ochoa escaped and made his way to El Paso, where he was arrested for raiding. When arrested, Ochoa had a copy of Santana Pérez's manifesto, with an English translation to be distributed to the U.S. press.

For leading a military expedition against Díaz, Ochoa was convicted and sentenced to two and a half years in the Kings County Penitentiary. In an 1895 interview with the *New York Times*, he attributed his "present trouble" to "the misgovernment of Mexico and the unhappiness of the people." Ochoa cited Tomóchic as an example of Díaz's despotism, calling it a "brutal crime."

Upon his release, Ochoa continued his anti-Díaz activities, selling all his possessions to raise money for "my people's liberation" and joining the Carranza supporters against Pancho Villa. In October 1915, along with José Orozco and E. L. Holmdahl, he was convicted of conspiracy to violate neutrality laws and sentenced to eighteen months in a U.S. federal prison.[54]

Return to the Heartland

Between 1880 and 1910, Camargo was fully integrated into the state's economy: the Mexican Central Railroad made Camargo a stop in the early 1880s, connecting the town to the Villa of Chihuahua and El Paso del Norte, and by 1884 Camargo had telephone service. The shift in control over water from local to federal authorities during the *porfiriato* increased tensions between large and small landholders in the Santa Rosalía area — and, in particular, between wealthy rancheros and hacendados, on the one hand, and subsistence farmers, on the other. The two groups looked at land in distinctly different ways. Large landholders tended to see land, first and foremost, as an economic resource, to be worked for profit by others, whether hired help, renters, or sharecroppers, whereas small landholders tended to see land as a means of survival and as part of their lives, to be worked by themselves and their families. As irrigation spread, the lands along the Río Conchos and its tributaries became more productive and thus more valuable, putting them out of the reach of the smaller farmers. As the wealthier landowners came to monopolize irrigation water, the poorer farmers were increasingly forced off their land.

Construction workers on La Boquilla Dam near Camargo. (Courtesy of Manuel Rosales Villa)

Of the Santa Rosalía area's 26,000 residents in 1910, roughly one in every two lived on a hacienda, estancia, or rancho; one in every ten in a mining camp; and none lived on communal lands.[55] By 1907, the Conchería heartland boasted 41 haciendas and 122 ranchos, with more than 55,100 acres (136,100 hectares) of irrigated land and more than 30,600 acres (12,400 hectares) of dryland in agricultural or livestock production. Among the crops cultivated were peanuts, sweet potatoes, sugarcane, beans, lentils, corn, potatoes, wheat, and tobacco. In addition to mines, the area had four mills, one textile factory, three tanneries, and nineteen public schools — hardly the backward place most Euro-Americans imagined in their stereotypes of Mexico.[56] The completion of La Boquilla Dam, beginning in 1909, would intensify agriculture, pulling in more workers and their families from outside of Chihuahua.

Chihuahua at the Turn of the Century

Chihuahua was not a frontier in the same sense as the Wild West. By 1875, there was free and compulsory education for children from seven to fourteen years of age. The first secondary school for girls opened its doors in the capital in 1896. Shortly afterward, construction began on the government palace costing 390,000 pesos. Railroad lines crisscrossed Chihuahua. The automobile entered the state in 1903.

The state's unprecedented prosperity was reflected in the façades of Ciudad Chihuahua's department stores and other businesses, although the capital maintained its eighteenth-century pretensions, with "respectable people" flaunting their privileged class positions. The new affluence brought with it rapidly growing consumerism, transforming not only Ciudad Chihuahua and other principal cities such Ciudad Juárez but also smaller cities, as well as outlying towns and villages. "By the late nineteenth century," notes Steven B. Bunker, "the residents of Chihuahua lived in an environment [that glorified] personal and family consumption, where definitions of social norms and the ideal image of a modern Mexican centered on the act of consumption."[57] Women became shoppers, and men providers in the consumerist scheme of things.

Businessmen were central figures in the civic and religious life of the capital, much as the Spanish-born Spaniards had been in the eighteenth century. "Gente de razón" ranged from powerful businessmen, government officials, store managers, and shopkeepers, to teachers, journalists, township clerks as well as other white-collar workers, and members of the working classes, particularly artisans.

Between 1871 and 1900, the population of Ciudad Chihuahua more than doubled, to 30,000. Electricity lit its streets and powered its industries, stores, and commercial businesses. Many of its roads were paved, and electric trams took people to work, stores, and entertainment. Telegraph and telephone systems crisscrossed its business districts, and telephones began to be available for home use. These services were extended to places like Santa Rosalía, Parral, and Guerrero during the 1880s, connecting most of the state to the capital and to outlying population centers.

In the 1880s, Chihuahua's northernmost city, El Paso del Norte, clearly benefited from commerce with the United States. Workers converged on this gateway to and from the United States, linked by the Mexican Central Railroad with Mexico City in 1882, and by telegraph with other parts of Mexico in 1884. As testimony to its prosperity and importance, it boasted three newspapers — *La Revista Internacional*, *El Centinela*, and *El Agricultor Mexicano*. El Paso del Norte was officially made a city in 1888 and renamed Ciudad Juárez.

In the last decade of the century, Chihuahua became more and more dependent on U.S. markets. The passage of the McKinley Tariff and the Sherman Silver Purchase Act in 1890 combined with the closing of India's silver mints in 1893 to cause the state's exports of silver to fall by 50 percent. Chihuahua's mining did not revive until the late 1890s.[58]

Growing numbers of chihuahuenses were literate. By 1910, the literacy rate of the state had risen to 25 percent, and that of Ciudad Chihuahua to 28 percent. Newspapers came to play a larger role in the life of the affluent. *El Correo de Chihuahua*, like other urban newspapers, encouraged consumerism through articles, editorials, and especially advertising, which, in Bunker's words, "dangled the possibility of affluence [before] Mexican consumers by linking the cigarette with Porfirian notions of modernity, wealth, and leisure." Entertainment also attracted people to the capital and to the larger cities and towns — bullfights, movies, variety shows, circuses, and free forms of entertainment such as window-shopping and promenading. Instead of pulque, tequila, or mescal, "respectable people" drank beer.

Ciudad Chihuahua was dotted with artisan and small industrial shops. Between 1895 and 1910, the number of professionals grew more than 40 percent, and the number of doctors and teachers by 60 and 100 percent, respectively.

Between 1871 and 1900, the population of the state as a whole almost doubled, to just under 328,000. But though the middle class in Mexico City increased by nearly 70 percent from 1895 to 1910, in Chihuahua, it decreased by 30 percent. One of the very few growth occupations for the middle class in the state was teaching: the number of teachers doubled over the same period. Growing discontent among the middle class and small landowners in Chihuahua in 1910 would lead them to take arms over the theft of land by hacendados and special interests under the land law of 1905. On the labor front, they would be joined by Chihuahua's workers. Conditioned for centuries to survive — and many them now literate wage workers — these were among the most advanced workers in Mexico.

◀ 3 ▶

The Mesilla Corridor

As the railroad forged its way north and south through Chihuahua, the population of the state grew, agriculture became commercialized, and the state's land was privatized and bought up by the larger landowners. The concentration of land ownership and the arrival of migrants from the interior of Mexico transformed Chihuahua's economy and pushed many small farmers, miners, and other workers north along the Camino Real corridor. Their footprints can be found throughout the border region in barrios and *colonias* named Chihuahuita.

The port of entry for most workers from southeastern Chihuahua was El Paso, Texas, although some migrated along the Río Conchos through Ojinaga on the Rio Grande to the Pecos River Valley. Most would work in agriculture, on the railroad, or in mining. Those destined for the mines of central eastern Arizona, such as Pedro Subia, went through the Mesilla Valley, passing to Arizona by way of Santa Ana and Grant Counties in southwestern New Mexico. The first barrio the migrating Mexicans touched after crossing the bridge from Ciudad Juárez to El Paso was Chihuahuita or La Chihuahua, which expanded dramatically in 1881 with the coming of the Santa Fe Railroad, whose tracks isolated it from the rest of the city. Moving west along the Mesilla corridor, they lived in a Chihuahuita in Silver City, New Mexico. In Morenci and Clifton, Arizona, Chihuahuitas were among the first barrios. In Bisbee, Mexicans lived on Chihuahua Hill, near the Zacatecas barrio at the end of Brewery Gulch. Finally, along the Cotton corridor in Southern California, the migrants lived in the Chihuahuitas that sprang up near railroad yards and agricultural fields. Just recently, Pasadena's city fathers corrected the spelling of "Chihuahita," one of the city's oldest barrios near Mission San Gabriel. Truth be told, migrating Mexicans have perpetuated their local identities by living in separate barrios (as in Parral) since colonial times.[1]

Along the Gila

Many migrants were farmers pushed out during droughts or the slow season. They were attracted to the farmlands of the Gila River Valley, where the Pima Indians had long subsisted on fishing and corn and beans, and the valley formed a natural corridor for their travel west. To supplement their farming, they worked in the mines.

In the 1850s and 1860s, Sonoran families from Tucson and northern Sonora moved north into the valleys of central Arizona, where they set up farms and cattle ranches, established a trade network, and founded self-sufficient communities that flourished through much of the territorial period. Overgrazing of the Gila's watershed, however, together with woodcutting and beaver trapping in the upper Gila, severely altered the river's hydrological balance. Flash floods inundated the fields of Pimas and Mexicans alike. In the early 1870s, Euro-American farmers organized the construction of large canals to divert water out of the Salt River above the Pima villages without returning it to the river for others to use. By 1873, after many Pimas had left the Gila River area for good, Euro-Americans began migrating into the territory in large numbers, often moving into Mexican settlements.[2]

The Gila River formed part of the U.S.-Mexican boundary set by the Treaty of Guadalupe Hidalgo, under which Mexico had ceded more than 40 percent of its national territory to the United States in 1848. Many Mexican families from New Mexico, Sonora, and Chihuahua were lured to the upper Gila Valley by the prospect of gold. They first settled in Arizona where the San Francisco River flows into the Gila, at a place they named Pueblo Viejo, Old Town, after the ancient ruins that dotted the valley. In the 1870s, when Mormon settlers started building large-scale irrigation works, many Mexican families sold their land, moved to a new town site, and worked as day laborers for the Euro-American farmers. Others went on to better-paying jobs in the nearby copper mines at Morenci.

Although some of the first Chihuahuans and Sonorans migrating to the United States had been freighters or even indentured servants, many were experienced miners, farmers, or vaqueros. From 1850 to 1880, some 55,000 Mexican workers found jobs in the states or territories closest to Mexico, and a sizable number were attracted to the mines of southern New Mexico and Arizona. When droughts and Apache raids disrupted their lives, they moved on.

Mexico's population grew from about 7 million in 1840 to nearly 10.5 million in 1880. By the end of Porfirio Díaz's three-decade rule (1876–1911), Mexico had 15 million inhabitants (though still fewer than the 25 million it is thought to have had in 1519).[3] Economic pressures attending this rapid population growth uprooted workers, pushing them to migrate to the city nearest their pueblos. In the interior of Mexico, most ended up in Mexico City. The next step was north to the United States. The 5,000 miles of railroad built in Mexico between 1880 and 1910 connected the north-south trunk lines with spurs to mineral deposits and commercial crops. It became easier to travel from Hermosillo, Sonora, to Tucson, Los Angeles, or San Antonio than to Mexico City. As the railroad stretched from Mexico City to Chicago, it played a key role in the dispersal of Mexicans, with Los Angeles, San Antonio, El Paso, and Kansas City becoming reception and distribution centers. During the early 1900s, railroads were the largest employer of Mexicans in the United States.

Along with the economically uprooted came political refugees who brought ideas of a more just society. These ideas proliferated throughout the urban areas and company towns where Mexican lived. Political refugees of every stripe gravitated to San Antonio, El Paso, Tucson, and Los Angeles, settling in or near these communities. Mexican revolutionaries worked the plazas of Los Angeles, Tucson, San Antonio, and countless other localities, condemning injustices in the United States and Mexico. They formed contacts with U.S.-born radicals as well as with European immigrants.[4]

The New Mexican Diaspora

In much the same way as Chihuahua, New Mexico was also undergoing an economic transformation. A sizable number of New Mexicans moved west to Arizona in search of work. These were mostly Spanish speakers who lived in the Chihuahuitas of Clifton, Morenci, and Metcalf. Along with Texas, New Mexico was a large exporter of Mexican labor. The New Mexicans or the *manitos* (from *hermanitos*, little brothers) were related to the Chihuahuans and Sonorans. New Mexican merchants visited California regularly during colonial times and into the Mexican period. New Mexicans such as Julian Chávez, who acquired Chavez Ravine, where the Dodgers play, in 1840. Chávez, his brother, and later his nephew traveled the Old Spanish Trail from New Mexico and settled permanently in Los Angeles. David Weber writes that, by 1845, some thirty New Mexican families had migrated to Los Angeles alone, and another group of Hispanos settled near San Bernardino, California.[5] Although most settled in Southern California, others went to northern California to places such as Vacaville, which they named after Manuel Vaca, in the Sacramento Valley. With the massive influx of Euro-Americans, many chose to return to Mexico to join relatives in Chihuahua and Sonora.

As it did in northern Mexico and Arizona, the desert in New Mexico defined both climate and topography. The Río Bravo — or Rio Grande, as Euro-Americans liked to call it — took on especial importance. New Mexico's early colonizers were descendants of people recruited from Zacatecas and elsewhere in the interior of Mexico. Distance lessened their ties with Mexico. Santa Fe was farther from Ciudad Chihuahua than Tucson was from Sonora's cities. Nevertheless, the history of New Mexico resembled that of Chihuahua during the colonial period. As with Chihuahua, epidemics, Indian wars, and droughts took a heavy toll among the natives, whose pueblos lined the Rio Grande. Although the native population fell, the Spanish and mixed-blood populations grew. As with Chihuahua, the economy of New Mexico was changing even before the arrival of the Euro-Americans. Although New Mexicans traded heavily with Chihuahua well into the territorial period, in colonial times, Chihuahuan merchants had controlled this commerce and derived most of the profit. With Mexican independence, however, New Mexicans organized their own caravans to Chihuahua and garnered more of the economic benefit.

Although New Mexico had no mining bonanzas the size of Parral's, it did have highly productive mines. According to Carey McWilliams, "The Santa Rita is, perhaps, the most famous mine in Western America, for it was here that the techniques of copper mining were first developed in the Southwest." Situated some five miles east of Silver City on flatlands carpeted with creosote bush and dotted with yucca and a wide variety of cacti, the Santa Rita Mine set up operations in 1805. Once smelted in Chihuahua, its copper was carried by relays of up to one hundred pack mules, each loaded with three hundred pounds of ingots, down El Camino Real to the Royal Mint in Mexico City. (Most of the copper coins minted in Spain and Mexico from 1800 to 1840 were made from copper mined in the Santa Rita.) When the Apache renewed their raids in the 1830s, the mine was closed down. After the death of Vitorio and the surrender of Geronimo, however, the Santa Rita was reopened in 1880s, with miners coming not only from New Mexico but also from Chihuahua and even from Texas.[6]

As in Chihuahua, contact with Euro-Americans in New Mexico was limited to the Hispano elite. New Mexican and Euro-American hacendados relied heavily on forced labor and refused to abolish debt peonage or Native American slavery until the U.S. Congress forced New Mexico to do so in 1867. The Civil War attracted a more aggressive and educated breed of Euro-American to the West. Closely paralleling the Chihuahuan experience, Mexican elites formed an alliance with Euro-American adventurers — the Santa Fe Ring. In the 1880s, the ruling cabal used survey companies to privatize communal lands (*ejidos*), making millions of acres available for commercial exploitation. Land values zoomed from $41 million to $231 million, but the takeover of public lands uprooted thousands of villagers, for whom migration became a way of life. The commercialization of agriculture and stock raising made it impossible for the subsistence farmer to eke out a living. Small farming became unprofitable, and many New Mexicans migrated to nearby Colorado.[7]

When men were forced to seek seasonal employment, it placed a heavier burden on their wives and families. As in Chihuahua, women in New Mexico often assumed a greater role in farm production. With the commercialization of farming and ranching, the merchant class became more powerful, the villages overcrowded, the farmland depleted, and the pastureland overgrazed. Thus, in Rio Arriba County, in the far north of New Mexico, sheep men grazed twenty-one sheep per square mile in the 1880s, and by 1900 that number had increased to between 100 and 120.[8] With the coming of the railroad, some subsistence farmers went to work on railroad crews, shifting the agricultural work to their families.

By the end of the century, whole villages worked as farm laborers, shepherds, miners, or railroad workers. These workers and their families had to adjust to the tensions that the changes brought, along with the discrimination, evident in Euro-Americans' earning up to twice the wages of Mexicans for the same work. Meanwhile, access to pastureland was denied to northern New Mexicans who either could not afford or did not have the political connections to obtain grazing permits.

With the development of coal mining in southern Colorado, many New Mexican villagers migrated north. After earning enough money to help their families subsist, they would return home to plant or harvest their crops. Depressions and droughts, such as those which occurred in the early 1890s, forced many others into migration. As Euro-Americans increasingly encroached on public lands, resistance grew among the Mexican ranchers, who began to cut fences. When the courts favored the special interests associated with the Santa Fe Ring, the territory rose up in armed rebellion in the late 1880s. Sixty-six men with rifles and pistols "draped in long black coats and slickers, their faces hidden behind white masks," rode into Las Vegas, New Mexico, in November 1889.[9] The rebellion lasted some ten years before finally being put down by federal troops and company posses. As land resources became ever scarcer, migration from the small villages to the cities accelerated. More than 11,000 New Mexicans moved to southern Colorado in the first decade of the twentieth century. They were followed by thousands more working-class Europeans, making Mexicans a minority.[10]

North and West to Clifton-Morenci-Metcalf

The 1870 U.S. census of Apache Pass in southeastern Arizona gives us a glimpse of where Mexicans came from and what they did before the opening of the mines at Clifton-Morenci-Metcalf. The bulk of the population was male and in its twenties. The white population was mostly in the military. Of the 124 Mexicans counted by the census, which lists most as farmers, laborers, or teamsters, 25 were from New Mexico, 33 from Chihuahua, 64 from Sonora, 1 from Arizona, and 1 from California. The census lists no Subias in Arizona Territory in 1870. The first Subia listed by the census is Luis, age twenty-five, in 1880. He worked in the Clifton Copper Mine in Apache, Arizona.[11]

El Paso had a substantial Mexican population. In the early 1900s, some 2,000 Mexican immigrants were admitted monthly to the United States. By 1907 the number had climbed to nearly 6,000. Towns such as Las Cruces, which had ties with El Paso, Texas, and with Ciudad Juárez, were overwhelmingly Mexican. Las Cruces got its name from La Placita de las Cruces, Little Place of Many Crosses. Migrants would travel up the Camino Real corridor to El Paso, passing through Las Cruces on their way west. Its population grew during the 1880s when the railroad made a stop there. Because the town was treeless, its inhabitants used adobe to build houses.

In 1850, more than sixty families who wanted to remain part of Mexico moved west across the Rio Grande from Las Cruces and founded Mesilla, Little Mesa. Four years later, however, Mesilla was annexed to the United States under the Gadsden Purchase, when a 30,000-square-mile strip of Mexican territory along the U.S.-Mexico border was bought for $10 million. Although a layover for passengers on the Butterfield Overland Stage route from Saint Louis to San Francisco and halfway between San Diego and San Antonio, Mesilla lost out to Las Cruces when the Santa Fe Railroad bypassed it after the Civil War.

Northwest of Las Cruces was Silver City, county seat of Grant County in the 1870s. Nestled in the foothills of the Pinos Altos Mountains at an altitude of 5,900 feet (1,800 meters), Silver City had been founded in 1870 as the Mexican town of San Vicente de la Ciénaga, Saint Vincent of the Marsh. The surrounding area was not only rich in silver, gold, copper, lead, and zinc but also supported ranching, lumbering, and irrigated farming. Silver City's mines and those of nearby Tyrone attracted Mexican migrants, who settled there or who worked for a time on their way west to the mines at Clifton-Morenci-Metcalf.[12]

Some Chihuahuans and New Mexicans settled permanently in the Mesilla corridor. *Arizona Daily Star* reporter Carmen Duarte tells the story of one family that did so — her own. In 1878, after the owners of the copper mines at Morenci had sent recruiters "into Chihuahua, looking for young, strong men to work the veins [and promising] prosperous lives," Duarte's grandfather Florentino, a subsistence farmer, left his wife, Leonarda, and their firstborn, Petra, in Guadalupe Victoria near Casas Grandes for Morenci. There he "broke rock, dug tunnels, lived roughly and saved his wages." After four years, Florentino gave up mining and returned to Chihuahua for his wife and child. Arriving in Mesilla in 1882, Duarte's grandparents had settled along the upper Gila River in San Antonio, New Mexico, a community of Mexican immigrants founded in 1876 near the present town of Virden, eight miles from the Arizona border.[13]

Although Virden's Mexican residents had been outnumbered, discriminated against, and pushed to the margins by the Mormon settlers who came after them, Las Cruces, Silver City, Deming, Lordsburg, and other towns along the Mesilla corridor continued to be overwhelmingly Mexican.[14] But where almost all the earlier migrants traveling the Mesilla corridor had come from Chihuahua and Sonora, those arriving in the 1900s came from the states of Zacatecas, Aguascalientes, Guanajuato, Jalisco, and Michoacán as well.[15]

Gold and Copper: The Early History

Mining was the principal reason why Americans moved to Arizona. As early as 1853, gold was found on the Colorado River. Five years later, Arizona's first major gold rush took place on the Gila River, about nineteen miles east of where it joins the Colorado. By 1861, miners at the find numbered 1,000. In 1863, prospectors working the Colorado River above Yuma discovered gold at La Paz, and the strike attracted 5,000 miners within the year. About twelve miles upstream, Joseph Rutherford Walker led a party of thirty prospectors from California up the Hassayampa River to the Bradshaw Mountains near present-day Prescott. There they found gold along Lynx, Big Bug, and Groom Creeks. White miners gave notice that "no Mexican shall have the right to buy, take up, or pre-empt a claim on this river for a term of six months to date from the first day of June 1863 to December 1, 1863."[16]

After the Civil War, when transportation costs dropped dramatically, interest in copper mining revived. With the development of long-distance transmission of electricity by alternating current and the advent of the Electric Age, demand for copper as a conductor soared. The completion of the transcontinental railroads also played a huge role in making the giant copper camps profitable. Arizona became a global leader in the production of copper: the mining districts of Clifton, Globe, Bisbee, and Jerome, which all opened during this period, would each produce more than five billion pounds of copper.[17]

Apache country had some of the best-watered land in Arizona. Heavy snowfall in the winter months kept its numerous streams running year round and its grasslands lush. After the Civil War, when white men drove large herds through their country to New Mexico for fattening up, relations with the Apache deteriorated. Under Cochise, and later under Vitorio and Geronimo, they resisted this encroachment, raiding ranches near Silver City and in a wide surrounding region. The federal government responded by sending out troops to subdue them, as the need arose, from the late 1860s through the late 1880s. In 1864, when Henry Clifton had traveled to the area near present-day Clifton to look for gold and silver, he had discovered a rich deposit of copper ore, in the limestone cliffs overlooking Chase Creek. In 1870, while serving as scouts for a heavily armed mining expedition, Jim and Robert Metcalfe also found outcroppings of copper ore, near present-day Clifton-Morenci-Metcalf, 150 miles from the Mexican border, and only 65 miles southeast of the San Carlos Apache Reservation.[18] By 1872, the Apache raids had abated. A group headed by Captain Miles Joy established Joy Camp, later known as Morenci, in the foothills of the White Mountains along the Coronado Trail, with alpine forests to the north and desert to the south. Various other groups also staked out their claims, the most important being the Metcalf group (historical sources generally drop the *e* from Metcalfe), which claimed what would become the Metcalf and Longfellow Mines.

Clifton stood seven miles south of Morenci at the mouth of Chase Creek, in a rugged canyon carved out by this tributary of the San Francisco River. Farther up Chase Creek Canyon, three miles north-northeast of Morenci but still in the White Mountains, stood Metcalf. The nearest point of supply for the Clifton-Morenci-Metcalf mines was Silver City, a boomtown with a population of 5,000 some one hundred miles south and east. Las Cruces lay 110 miles still farther east.[19]

The Day of the Merchant Capitalists: The Silver City Connection

Henry Lesinsky had prospected for gold in Australia and for silver in Nevada and had then migrated to Las Cruces, where his uncle, Julius Freudenthal, ran a mercantile house. Operating out of Silver City, Belen, and Las Cruces, Lesinsky and his large extended family set about building a small financial empire, investing in stage and freighting operations. Lesinsky had come to Silver City in 1863 to establish Henry Lesinsky and Company, a large mercantile firm.[20]

When Robert Metcalfe returned there in 1873 to seek financial backing for his mining operations, the ore sample he showed a local merchant found its way to Lesinsky. After traveling to Clifton with Metcalfe and four armed men, Lesinsky immediately bought controlling interest in Metcalfe's Longfellow Mine for $10,000. The next year he bought the remaining interest for another $20,000 and incorporated the Longfellow Copper Mining Company.

In the spring of 1873, Lesinsky went to El Paso del Norte to recruit a small force of Mexicans with experience in copper mining. These men were to construct and operate the first smelter in the district. Known as the Stone House, the smelter was built of stone and adobe, with blacksmith bellows supplying the blast, and located not far from the new mining camp of Clifton, a cluster of adobe houses at the mouth of Chase Creek. At first, all of Clifton's residents were men, who made frequent visits to their native New Mexico and Chihuahua. Needing a more stable workforce, and realizing the importance of the family unit in Mexican culture, Lesinsky commissioned a certain "Don Antonio" to recruit married men with families from El Paso del Norte, which served as the principal labor market for the southeastern Arizona mines. When, instead, Don Antonio returned with twenty-five unmarried Mexican couples, Superintendent Smedberg promptly married them. In 1876, of the 110 voters in the district, 94 were of Mexican-Spanish origin.[21]

By October 1873, some thirty Mexican workers were smelting high-grade ore (70 to 80 percent copper), using Mexican processes. When the price of copper plunged from thirty-five cents a pound in 1872 to twenty-eight cents in 1873, only earnings from the company store kept the company afloat. With transportation costs remaining high, the company struggled to make a profit for a decade. Mexican laborers carried the ore down a steep incline from the mouth of the Longfellow Mine to a wagon road, then hauled it some five miles to the reduction works at Clifton, where other Mexican laborers shouldered the ore baskets and carried them to the smelters.[22]

The lower-grade black ore (15 to 39 percent copper) was sent to Baltimore for smelting. It went by ox-drawn wagons, driven by Mexicans largely from New Mexico, 210 miles to Las Cruces, then 1,100 miles over the Santa Fe Trail to Independence, Missouri, and, by railroad, another 1,200 miles to Baltimore. The wagons then returned with food and supplies. To extract the black ore, horizontal tunnels were drilled into the hillside. In the late 1870s, water-jacketed, charcoal-burning furnaces with water-powered blowers smelted some thirty tons of ore daily. Despite fuel shortages, inadequate transportation, and Apache raids, Lesinsky's miners and work crews maintained a steady flow of ore through the smelters at Clifton.[23]

Meanwhile, investors from Detroit and Silver City formed the Detroit

Copper Mining Company, with a capitalization of $500,000, in 1872. Three years later, Detroit Copper's Eber B. Ward and financial backers purchased the Joy Camp mining claims and changed the camp's name to Morenci, reportedly after a town in Michigan. Morenci was linked to the outside by two stage roads, one forty-five miles long downriver to Solomonville and another to Silver City. Because Clifton and Morenci were Mexican camps, employers ignored the minimum standard of living. The existence of Mexican Camps and American Towns helped ingrain the notion of racial superiority. White workers were placed at the top of the work hierarchy and provided solid houses, whereas Mexican workers were obliged to live in makeshift structures scattered across the hillsides.[24]

Jewish pioneer merchants, most notably members of Lesinsky's extended family, played a key role in financing the early mining ventures and in building the needed infrastructure. J. E. Solomon built charcoal pits in the Gila River Valley when the mines' smelters had depleted the mesquite and timber immediately surrounding the district. Solomon also invested in farming to supply the miners with food and set up a store (the beginning of the town of Solomonville) to supply Mexican laborers.

By spring 1878, Clifton stretched out along the banks of the San Francisco River. At the northern end of the camp stood the Gleason and Sweeny Mine's reduction works, a neat adobe structure encircled by outbuildings and several Mexican huts. The camp's largest buildings were the office and home of Louis Smedberg, superintendent of the Longfellow Copper Mining Company, which employed some two hundred men, mostly Mexican. The largest adobe structure was Lesinsky's store, which, as noted, kept the Longfellow Company afloat when the price of copper, and thus company earnings, fell. A mile below Clifton was a cluster of between thirty and forty Mexican adobes. For their dangerous and mostly underground work, miners were paid an average of two dollars day in checks or in promissory notes printed on stout red cloth and payable entirely at the company's mess hall or store in Clifton, or at the Lesinsky store in Silver City. Strangers were neither welcome nor allowed to eat with the miners. In 1879, Vitorio left the San Carlos Reservation with a band of warriors and raided the Clifton camp, driving off the mules. The continuing Apache threat made it difficult to keep workers.[25]

Ore was brought down long, sharp inclines built almost entirely by Mexican laborers from the district's various mines to Clifton. It was carried there at first also by Mexican laborers and later by mule-drawn cable cars. It was then transported to outside smelters and mills, at first by ox-drawn wagons and later (after 1879) by railroad. The Longfellow incline extended from the mine, located in a triangle between two steep mountains on the west bank of the San

Francisco River, to the bottom of Chase Creek Canyon. The Coronado incline dropped some 1,200 feet from the rugged mountains above the Colorado and Santa Rosa Canyons to the canyon floor. The Coronado Mining Company claims were bought up by the Longfellow Copper Mining Company around 1875. The Shannon incline, owned by the Shannon Copper Company, overlooked the Arizona Copper Company's Metcalf Mine and the town of Metcalf itself.[26]

In mid-November 1878, the Southern Pacific Railroad crossed over to the west bank of the Colorado River. The railroad sent Clifton's fortunes soaring and increased the demand for Mexican workmen. Trying to beat down wages, Henry Lesinsky imported Chinese laborers, who earned $40 per month, $35 less than Euro-Americans and $10 less than Mexicans. When the Mexican and white mine workers reacted violently to the arrival of the Chinese, Lesinsky assured them they would do only work that "neither white men nor Mexicans would accept." Chinese laborers worked in the narrow ravines of the hills, more than thirty-five miles from the copper mines, gathering and burning mesquite for charcoal to fuel the smelters.[27]

Life in Clifton-Morenci

Although the smoke of the smelters shrouded both camps, life was always a bit starker in Morenci than in Clifton. Owned by the Detroit Copper Mining Company, Morenci was connected to Clifton by a tunnel through the Longfellow incline and by a single wagon road that went up the Chase Creek Canyon as far as the Clifton company store. It had no streets, only trails that led to the shanties built on the slopes for the workers. The company boardinghouse, store, library, and other company structures were clustered down in the canyon. The women did their washing at the river and hauled water two miles to their shanties, and the Morenci company store made deliveries by pack mule.

Because children were few and Mexican, the camps had no schools in the 1870s. Not until white children came to the area in considerable numbers was the need for schools recognized. The schools were strictly segregated, like the camps themselves and like mining outposts everywhere in the Southwest. The only public place Mexicans were allowed to go to in Morenci was the post office.[28]

On the other hand, because women were also few and almost all Mexican, cohabitation was tolerated between Euro-American men and Mexican women. During the first years, Jewish men married Mexican women outside the Clifton-Morenci-Metcalf district. In most cases, however, Mexican women were relegated to the role of concubines. Charles Lesinsky, 41, had an affair with Estanislada "Lulu" Bencoma, 15, after whom the Estanislada Mine was named. She is described as coming from New Mexico and having red hair and blue eyes (common among northern Mexicans at the time). Estanislada bore Charles a son out of wedlock, Charles B., who moved away to Los Angeles in 1910. Neither father nor son tried to get in touch with the other. Estanislada moved to Willcox, where she ran a small boardinghouse. Charles moved to Manhattan, where he, his wife Bertha, and their three children lived and died in luxury.[29]

The Day of the Scots

By 1880, both the Longfellow and the Detroit Copper Mining Companies were profitable enterprises, each smelting sixty to eighty tons of 20 percent copper ore per day. Merchant capitalists, however, lacked the capital either to compete with the large copper consortiums, which could readily afford the new technology, or to weather declines in the demand for copper. A crash in copper prices drove many companies out of business.

The mines of the district had produced almost 3.2 million pounds of copper, which they shipped principally to San Francisco and Guaymas, Sonora. Most of the mining was underground in poorly timbered shafts, where the miners were at constant risk, with Chinese laborers put in the most hazardous jobs. Mine workers were paid with chits (*boletas*), redeemable only at the company store, often for less than their face value and for overpriced goods. The store's profits thus offset the expense of workers' wages. That year, the district employed two hundred workers in its mines or at its smelters.[30]

Clifton experienced a major flood in 1880. According to James Colquhoun: "The Mexicans, with their wives and families, were thus left marooned on a island with a raging river in front and rear, threatening to rise and drown them. But those Mexicans were brave, hardy and resourceful. They spent the night in taking their furniture to pieces, making rafts of it, and the next day, after an arduous struggle and great risk, they succeeded in rafting their women and children safely across the raging torrent."[31]

Before completion of the southern transcontinental railroad in 1881, southern Arizona was tied to northern Mexico. After 1881, however, the axis shifted to California and the eastern seaboard, and the heyday of Arizona's early copper era was drawing near. It was also in 1881 that Lesinsky built the Coronado Railroad, the first 20-inch "baby-gauge" railway in Clifton-Morenci, which used a tiny steam engine to haul ore down the Longfellow incline to the smelters in Clifton, and which connected Clifton to Morenci, a distance of about seven miles. The engine also hauled workers up the incline from Clifton and groceries back to the mercantile store in Morenci.[32]

In the spring of 1882, Geronimo's band left the reservation and killed eleven Mexican teamsters at a camp twelve miles south of Clifton. The Apaches also warred on the drivers hauling ore along the track between the mine and the smelters. Sensing a coming crash in the copper market, and lacking the enormous capital needed to stay competitive, the Lesinskys sold the Longfellow and Metcalf Mines in September of that year, to Frank L. Underwood for $1.5 million. Underwood in turn sold the Longfellow Mine to the faltering, Edinburgh-based Arizona Copper Company.[33]

The Scottish company located its Arizona headquarters in Metcalf, north-northeast of Morenci, and its copper works in the boomtown Clifton, as did the other large mining companies. Clifton had no mines of its own, but all roads led to it. The town had a few saloons and restaurants and four stores. Adobe dwellings for the workers dotted the east bank of the San Francisco River. Arizona Copper's offices, made of canvas like those of the other mining companies, its smelter, and adobe outbuildings stood on the west bank.[34]

In 1883, the year nine men were killed when ore cars dashed down the Coronado incline, out of control, Arizona Copper rebuilt the Coronado Railroad, extending it three miles to Metcalf. At a cost of more than $1.5 million for seventy-one miles — a fortune at the time — the company also built a thirty-six-inch narrow-gauge line called the Arizona & New Mexico to connect Clifton with the Southern Pacific Railroad at Lordsburg, New Mexico, in April 1884.[35]

The cost of copper production was high, and the infrastructure of the mines was deteriorating, with frequent cave-ins pushing Arizona Copper toward bankruptcy. Nevertheless, in 1883, the company upgraded its smelter and doubled its workforce in Clifton to a total of four hundred, which included some one hundred Chinese workers despite continued opposition to them.[36]

Meanwhile, also in 1883, a twenty-five-year-old Scottish engineer with grounding in chemistry and metallurgy joined the company. Over the next ten years, James Colquhoun would work his way up from bookkeeper to general manager. Colquhoun explored the region between the Metcalf and Longfellow Mines and found a system of lenses and veins whose sulfide ore deposits ran 5 percent copper. Technology and Colquhoun's management skills allowed Arizona Copper to process the low-grade ore.[37]

Colquhoun made his home in Clifton, which lived up to the reputation of the Wild West. Commenting on the camp's lawlessness, he would later write that, over a three-month period, there was a man killed every day in Clifton. Railroad laborers, miners, drifters, and businessmen converged on its dusty and violent streets. Many were fugitives or wanted simply to strike it rich. They were not interested in building a community. The most notorious were the Texans, who brought prejudices against people of color and, particularly, against Mexicans. Most laborers at the time were Mexicans and Chinese. White and Mexican workers alike felt it was "not a crime to kill a Chinaman . . . since it was an injustice . . . to bring them here in the first place." What little law there was could do nothing about it.[38]

Phelps Dodge Comes to Arizona

The Detroit Copper Mining Company operated out of Morenci. Having acquired options on all the company stock from the Eber B. Ward estate in 1875, William Church desperately needed a smelter but lacked the necessary capital. When he approached Phelps Dodge and Company to sell half interest in Detroit Copper for $30,000, it turned him down but sent out James Douglas on an inspection tour in mid-1880, during which it bought the Copper Queen Mine in Bisbee. Douglas became the intermediary between Church and Phelps Dodge, which, in 1881, finally agreed to buy partial interest in Detroit Copper. Douglas would later write: "Church's entire establishment consisted of a tent and a team of horses with which he had driven originally from his home in Colorado."[39]

With the proceeds of the sale, Church began construction of a copper works. He built a smelter on the San Francisco River, three miles downstream from Clifton. In 1884, Detroit Copper relocated its smelter to Morenci, developed an innovative water delivery system, and improved its blast furnace. That same year, Phelps Dodge acquired the Atlanta claim in Bisbee. Beset by rains, a lack of civil order in the district, and Geronimo's Apaches, Church struggled to survive. Douglas kept a watchful eye over Phelps Dodge's investment, offering Church technical advice, which he often disregarded. After 1887, Church increasingly lived in Denver, and in 1895 he sold his remaining interest in Detroit Copper to Phelps Dodge for $1.8 million.[40]

Mining at Century's End

In by far the worst Apache outbreak near Clifton, Geronimo left the reservation in the spring of 1883 with some two hundred young warriors. For the next three years, until the chief was captured in September 1886, his band raided an area more than five hundred miles in diameter. Soon after the start of this outbreak, five men on their way to Clifton for Gold Gulch, northwest of the town, were attacked by the Apaches. Four of the men were killed; only one survived. On the same day, an ore train from Morenci was attacked, the drivers killed, and the mules taken. The Apaches proceeded down the river to the smelter and attacked it but were driven off when the men at the smelter returned fire. The Apaches continued to raid the mule trains for the next few years. Troops were in and out of the area, contributing to the rowdiness of the camps. Toward the end of the 1880s, however, with as many as 5,000 federal troops pursuing Geronimo and his Apaches, their raids tapered off.

By this time, the Clifton-Morenci mining camps were among the most productive in the world. Even though Mexican families lost most in a 1891 flood that caused $100,000 in damages, Mexicans kept coming to the district, drawn by the prospect of work that paid better than either agriculture or the railroad. Indeed, it was hundreds of Mexican workers who cleared the damage and repaired the railroad tracks, roads, and bridges after the 1891 flood.[41]

A wage cut in August 1886 led to an unsuccessful six-day strike by Mexican smelter workers. In the 1890s, Euro-Americans replaced Mexicans in skilled work, with the percentage of Euro-Americans continuing to increase in the inter-mountain region. Clifton remained a Mexican town, but that did not shield Mexicans or their families from anti-Mexican sentiment.

Until 1906, mining involved shaft sinking, tunneling, and sloping. Ore was, for the most part, mined underground, broken in place, loaded on tramcars, and hoisted through a shaft. The rock was then ground to facilitate reducing, smelting, and refining. Although higher-grade ores were mined out after 1896, Colquhoun's concentrator and the evolution of technology made it possible to produce copper from ever-lower grades of ore.[42]

◀ 4 ▶

The Sonoran Corridor

The largest and earliest wave of migration into eastern Arizona was from Sonora before the Euro-American occupation in 1853. Sonorans populated frontier settlements such as Tucson, where they comprised the bulk of the workforce. In colonial times, Sonora was intimately joined to Alta California on the north and to northern Nueva Vizcaya and southern Nuevo México on the east. During the eighteenth century, natives migrated east from Sonora to the mines of Parral and Santa Eulalia and west from Chihuahua to the mines in Alamos and Cananea. From the middle of the nineteenth century and well into the twentieth, Mexican miners moved north from Sonora, dispersing Sonora Towns in California, Texas, and Arizona. In 1848, they settled what would later be called Sonora Town in the heart of California's Gold Country. By some counts, more than 10,000 took part in the California Gold Rush, and the word "Sonoran" became synonymous with "Mexican." In 1887, they founded Sonora, Texas, sixty-five miles south of San Angelo. And, in 1907, Sonoran workers at the Ray Consolidated Copper Company settled what would become Sonora, Arizona, thirty miles south of Globe. Yet Sonora Towns were far more often barrios, like the one just north of the *placita* church, near Main and César Chávez Streets, in Los Angeles and the one in Gilbert, Arizona.

An old adobe in Sonora Town, Los Angeles. (Courtesy of the Los Angeles Public Library, Security Pacific Collection, 00011134)

The Natives of Sonora

Separated from Chihuahua by the Sierra Madre Occidental, which rises to 11,500 feet (3,500 meters), Sonora is a land of contrasts: it has a vast coastal plain and inland desert, steep mountains, and deep river valleys, with some nine hundred miles of rugged coastline. Sonora's five principal rivers (not counting the Gila and Colorado) are the Ríos Magdalena, Sonora, Metape, Mayo, and Yaqui.[1] These flow generally south into the Gulf of California. Sonora's subtropical desert climate resembles that of Chihuahua: scorching summers and freezing winters, with far more rain falling in the sierra and its foothills than in lower elevations, reflected in vegetation that ranges from pine and oak, to cactus, paloverde, and grasslands, to cactus and mixed scrub, to creosote bush, burr sage, and sparse, if any, grasses. Its climate differs from Chihuahua's in two important respects, however: surface water is available in larger quantities, whether as rainfall or river flow, and droughts are less severe in both frequency and duration. These differences played a crucial role in how the native peoples of the two states developed.

Largely Uto-Aztecan speakers, most of Sonora's natives lived in rancherías averaging between 300 and 400 inhabitants — much larger than those of the Conchos or the Tarahumara in Chihuahua — although some settled in smaller agrarian hamlets (*aldeas*). They led seminomadic lives, raising corn, squash, and beans, and traveling long distances to trade with Chihuahua's natives and the Pueblos of New Mexico. The greater flow of Sonora's rivers and number of fertile alluvial basins gave rise to extensive riverine societies of farmer-gatherers, with greater concentrations of people than in Chihuahua. Most of the natives in Sonora — especially the Yaqui, who were able to field some 7,000 warriors in a 1609 clash with the Spanish army — were clustered in sufficient numbers to effectively resist the Spaniards for a longer period of time than could the natives in Chihuahua.[2]

The Yaqui played a central role in the migration north through the Sonoran corridor to the mines of eastern Arizona and west to the farmlands of the Gila River Valley. Their history was formed by the Río Yaqui, which flows year round from the Sierra Madre Occidental near the junction of the Ríos Bavispe and Papigóchic south and west some 420 miles into the Gulf of California (Sea of Cortés). The Jesuit missionaries estimated that Yaquis numbered 80,000 in 1533, representing approximately one-third of the total indigenous population of the Sonoran Desert at the time. With thirty persons per square mile, the Río Yaqui Valley was the most densely populated area in northwestern New Spain. The Yaqui used cane to build huts and thornbush trees for fence poles. The thick vegetation of the riverbanks supported abundant wildlife.

The Cahita consisted of various tribes speaking similar dialects of Piman, who inhabited the middle and lower portions of the valleys of the Ríos Yaqui, Mayo, and Fuerte in the southwestern part of present-day Sonora and the northwestern part of present-day Sinaloa. Spanish encroachment eliminated many of the Cahitas, the chief survivors being the Yaqui and their cousins the Mayo. During the first decades of the seventeenth century, when the Mayo and Yaqui together are thought to have numbered more than 50,000, the Mayo often allied themselves with the Spaniards against the Yaqui. But Spanish encroachment drove the Mayo to revolt in 1740. Thereafter, they participated in intermittent revolts on the side of the Yaqui until they were vanquished in the 1880s.[3]

Before the advent of farming (ca. 500 BC), the Yaqui and Mayo had lived by gathering some two hundred different species of desert plants and by hunting whitetail and mule deer, rabbits, javelinas, turtles, birds, and wood rats. Even as farmers, they continued to harvest mesquite pods, which they ground into a sweet paste called *pechita*, and to use wild plants for medicine. Like other native peoples of the region, they consumed the tepary bean, a desert legume with high protein content that thrived in the extreme heat, cooked faster than other beans, and did not need salt. Because of Sonora's scant, erratic rainfall, the natives practiced floodwater irrigation. During the rainy season, the rivers overflowed their banks, irrigating their lands and depositing a layer of rich soil. The Río Yaqui, which allowed for two harvests a year, made the Yaqui's lands more productive than those of their neighbors.

Between 1604 and 1623, the Jesuits concentrated the Yaqui's eighty rancherías into seven pueblos: Bahaum, Torim, Vican, Potam, Rahum, Huribas, and Belem. The tribe remained isolated until the late 1660s, when nonnative colonists encroached on the Río Mayo Valley and on the edges of Yaqui country. By 1680, the Yaqui were supplying food and labor for the mines to the north.[4]

Land of Many Nations

The O'odham (the People), as they called themselves, were renamed Pima by the Spaniards. Sedentary dry farmers at the time of the Conquest, through irrigation and intensive farming, the Pima came to live in fairly populous, extended rancherías, loosely linked together in small clusters. Divided into two groups, the Pima spoke a Uto-Aztecan language and were dispersed over a much larger area than the Yaqui, to whom the Lower Pimas were neighbors. The Upper Pimas settled in present-day northern Sonora and southern Arizona. The Lower Pimas were among the first to be evangelized by the Spanish missionaries in the late sixteenth and early seventeenth centuries. Beginning in 1633, they revolted and attempted to kill the missionaries, but their numbers were reduced by epidemics and assimilation.

Though they spoke similar dialects, the Upper Pimas had cultural differences. In the spring of 1687, the Jesuit missionary Eusebio Francisco Kino began concentrating the Upper Pimas, who had already been used as laborers by the Spanish colonists. Noting the fate of the Opata and the Lower Pimas, however, the Upper Pimas resisted mission life. They had heard that the friars required natives to work on mission lands at the expense of the native's own farming, that the Spaniards hanged natives, and that the large number of cattle around the missions drank up all the water. They feared that holy oils might kill them and that the missionaries could not protect them or their lands from the Spanish colonists.

The Opata lived between the Upper and Lower Pimas, most of them in the valleys of the Ríos Sonora, Yaqui, Moctezuma, and Bavispe. Although a single tribal group, they spoke different dialects of the same language. Irrigation supported extensive, larger settlements with substantial houses close to the fields.[5]

Inhabiting the Sonoran coast and offshore islands in the Gulf of California, principally Tiburón, were the Seri, who spoke different dialects of Yuma. They fished and lived off the land or on what they could take from travelers passing by. The Seri derived a sense of tribal identity from their frequent wars, first with the Pima and then with the Spaniards. Although concentrated for a time in missions around present-day Hermosillo, they later revolted, attacking Spanish settlements in 1725 and 1726, and again in 1731. The Spaniards mounted punitive expeditions against them and enslaved many. Seri resistance began to crumble around 1770.[6]

The Tohono O'odham (the Desert People), whom the Spaniards renamed the Papago, inhabited the deserts of southern Arizona and northern Sonora, to the south of the Upper Pimas. Descendants of the prehistoric Hohokam (AD 200–1450) of south-central Arizona, who constructed large-scale irrigation canals and earthen reservoirs for domestic water storage away from perennial streams, the Tohono O'odham were culturally similar to the Pima and spoke a dialectal variant of their language. Because they lived in a far drier and harsher habitat, however, they had to rely more on wild foods, gathered chiefly by their women, and to practice floodwater farming. They planted seeds after the first rains in the alluvium at the mouths of washes, and they used reservoirs, ditches, and dikes to capture the runoff waters along the flood channels. The lack of water forced the Tohono O'odham to move with the seasons, and their rancherías were substantially smaller than those of the Pimas to the north and south of them. Having much less contact with whites than the Pima, the Tohono O'odham were able to retain elements of their aboriginal culture.[7]

Mining: Engine of Expansion and Conflict

Founded in 1686, by the 1700s, Alamos was a boomtown and one of New Spain's principal mining centers, with its own mint and more than 30,000 residents. The wealthiest miners and merchants financed the town's infrastructure, as they had in Parral and Santa Eulalia. Over the next two hundred years, more than $500 million worth of silver would be extracted from nearby mines. In 1781, a colonizing expedition would set out from Alamos for Alta California to settle Los Angeles.

Mining began in northern Sonora in the last third of the seventeenth century with silver finds at Promonotorios and La Aduana, but the region's potential was not fully exploited until the nineteenth century for lack of water. In addition to silver, Sonora's mines produced copper, lead, iron, and later gold. Again as in Parral and Santa Eulalia, each bonanza brought a rush of investors and miners, the further development of haciendas and ranchos, and ever growing numbers of merchants. A few became fabulously wealthy and many more aspired to be.

In 1759, the discovery of gold by placers at San Antonio de la Huerta drew thousands to the Río Yaqui Valley. Between 1770 and 1773, gold was also discovered at Bacanuchi, Bacoachi, and Cieneguilla. Within two years, a sizable number of Yaquis and other Sonoran natives were working in Cieneguilla, whose outlying settlements were prospering, and wealthy stockholders from Mexico City were investing in the valley's mines. Lack of water, however, caused placers to abandon the area for another gold find in the Sierra de San Marcial, east of Guaymas. From 1768 until about 1790, Apache warriors ranged over much of Sonora, but as in Chihuahua, the Spaniards brought the Apache under control between 1790 and 1810 by bribing them to live in peace close to the presidios.[8]

The Jesuits and Native Resistance

When the conquistadores and the Franciscans failed to pacify northwestern New Spain, the Crown turned to the Jesuits, who were given exclusive right to missionize the natives of Sonora and Sinaloa. The Jesuits concentrated Indians living in scattered rancherías of disparate sizes into Spanish pueblos. Each Indian was given a plot of land and, by royal decree, compelled to work the mission lands three days each week. The monopoly of the Jesuits was challenged after 1650, when mining bonanzas attracted greater numbers of colonists. A rivalry arose for the Indians' land and labor, one that would help lay the groundwork for the expulsion of the Jesuits from New Spain in 1767.[9]

Hacendados, miners, and would-be farmers expected the Jesuits to move on and open up the new frontier. They saw the Jesuits as an obstacle to their prosperity, but the Jesuits saw things differently. They had trained the Indians at many of their missions to become skilled workers. Moving on would mean letting their charges revert to barbarism. Among those opposing the Jesuits were merchants who resented the missionaries for purchasing goods through their own cooperative based in Mexico City.[10]

The Jesuits moved into the Pimería Alta in 1687. At first, they had it to themselves, but, by the 1730s, mining camps were encroaching as far north as the Río Altar Valley. The bonanzas brought small but significant numbers of colonists to what is today northern Sonora and southern Arizona. These numbers would swell between 1740 and 1780, as presidios, with their garrisons and surrounding settlements, came to Terrenate, Altar, Tubac, and Tucson. With the Jesuits' departure in 1767, the nonnative communities that had sprung up outside the Indian villages soon penetrated them, and ranchos multiplied in river valleys throughout northern Sonora. The 1772 reform plan stipulated that colonists were to be relocated from presidio sites to house plots and arable land.

To withstand the Apache attacks, officials were to sell them arms at cost — and to give arms to the Opatas, who were used extensively against the Apache, free of charge. As elsewhere in New Spain, the colonists brought deadly diseases in their wake. Smallpox alone killed 10 to 15 percent of Indian children annually in the province of Sonora.[11]

Despite their overbearing, often dictatorial, and paternalistic nature, the Jesuits were good managers. They transformed the Indian societies under their authority, especially the Yaqui, whom they organized into a federation. Their early entrance into the province (1620) gave them time to proselytize the Indians before coming into conflict with the troublesome mestizo colonists, who harassed and abused the natives. On the other hand, the Jesuits' doctrinaire approach to religion, their own exploitation of their Indian charges, their inability to protect them from encroachment or to respond to complaints about overwork or mistreatment at the hands of outsiders, and their intensifying rivalry with civil authorities and colonists led to widespread discontent and repeated rebellions.[12]

Having been subjected to droughts, floods, epidemics, slave raids, the dreaded encomienda and repartimiento, inept colonial rulers, and heavy-handed missionaries, when silver bonanzas drew new waves of encroaching colonists to northern Sonora in the 1680s and 1690s, the Opata and other Sonoran natives rebelled. The Spaniards put down these revolts with characteristic cruelty, hanging their leaders and enslaving many of the rebels. By 1730, civil and ecclesiastical authorities became locked in a bitter struggle over control of native lands and labor, and throughout the province there were small, sporadic uprisings.

In 1740, floods and famine drove Yaquis and Mayos to raid surrounding ranchos for food. When the friars whipped a Yaqui for allegedly stealing the keys to a mission, the Yaqui and Mayo went into open revolt, which lasted until 1741. They were joined by virtually every native people across Sonora, with the exception of the Upper Pimas; even some Apaches took part.

The fighting became so widespread that the Spaniards were able to control only the areas around Alamos, El Fuerte, and Tecoripa. When the native foot soldiers clashed with the heavily armed Spanish cavalry, hundreds of Yaquis and Mayos died at the Battle of the Cerro de Otanahui, and hundreds more perished at Torin. The Yaqui and Mayo leaders, along with forty-three followers, were arrested, and their heads cut off and displayed in the various Yaqui villages. The rebellions were brutally put down, and even though civilian officials were blamed, this was the beginning of the end for the Jesuits in Sonora.[13]

By 1750, Jesuit control over the Pimería Alta had been usurped by civil authorities. The repartimiento was overseen by soldiers, who often abused the

Upper Pimas. Increasingly, the Pimas of the Río Altar and Río Magdalena Valleys complained about encroachments on their lands. Only nine Jesuit missionaries served among them. Pressed into harvesting crops on the encroachers' farms, the Upper Pimas found themselves being slowly killed off or crowded out. Moreover, lacking the political organization of the Yaqui, and having been largely detribalized (assimilated), they found it harder to mount effective resistance. In the Pima Revolt of 1751, however, their visionary leader Luis Oacpicagigua, the Indian governor of Sáric, rallied his people by sending agitators to the various Yaqui villages and among the Tohono O'odham. The rebels killed eighteen colonists before being put down. Oacpicagigua died while in prison in 1755. The Indian revolts of 1740–41 and the 1750s eroded the moral authority and control of the Jesuits among both the natives and colonial officials, who perceived or wanted to believe that the Jesuits were losing control.

The Yaqui were the most changed of the Sonoran native peoples under the Jesuit colonial regime, incorporating many of the farm techniques and trades the Jesuits taught them, and modernizing the structure of their society. They also became more mobile than the other peoples, traveling as far as Parral and the Villa de Chihuahua to work for wages in the mines and on the haciendas. The Yaqui wars heightened their sense of nationalism and attachment to the land. With the departure of the Jesuits, the Yaqui reverted to subsistence farming and adopted a hybrid form of Catholicism. In their blending of traditional and Christian beliefs, Yaqui country became the Promised Land of the Old Testament.[14]

Living next to white settlements, the Mayo never mounted the resistance their Cahita cousins did. Over the colonial period, they were either assimilated or died off. The Seri, perpetually at war, also became nearly extinct. That Pimas and Opatas were often recruited to fight the Apache took a heavy toll on the two peoples, who rebelled and were brutally suppressed. By the 1800s, the Opata had only a third as many people as the Yaqui, numbering fewer than 10,000. Fifty years later, they were all but extinct.

Securing Sonora

To stabilize the Sonoran frontier, the Spaniards built presidios at Terrenate and Horcasitas in 1741, Tubac in 1752, Altar in 1753, and Buenavista in 1765. Like those in Chihuahua, Sonora's presidio commanders had extraordinary powers: they granted prime land to their favorites and grabbed the best land for themselves. It was from military pursuits, mostly against Indian rebels, that many nineteenth-century criollo notables achieved their reputations, and the families of these notables their social and political prominence.

After 1780, a small but significant number of white immigrants arrived directly from northern and eastern Spain. These *peninsulares* got their choice of prosperous farms and haciendas, and they established commercial houses and mines. The Bourbon reforms benefited the landed oligarchy and merchant class, with the lion's share of privatized mission lands going to peninsulares and criollos. The accumulation of property in the hands of a few accentuated class and racial differences. By the 1780s, Alamos had nearly 5,000 residents, with another 5,000 in and around the mining camps of Promontorios and Aduana. As the leading urban center in the northwest, Alamos generated commercial activity throughout Sonora and the interior of New Spain.[15]

The Apache raided Sonora into the final decade of the eighteenth century. Indeed, if it were not for Sonora's native peoples, especially the Opata and the Pima, who were used heavily as fighters, the Apache might very well have driven nonnative colonists out of the province. As it was, many sought refuge in native villages. After the War of Independence, the newly created Mexican government did not extend the Crown's dole, which had kept most Apaches off the warpath. Many Mexican military commanders believed they could defeat the Apache, who, as soon as they learned the gifts of food and dry goods would not continue, resumed their attacks.

Sonora ended up with a highly mixed population. In a 1921 census, nearly 42 percent of Sonorans identified themselves as white, consistent with the myth that Sonora had been a criollo province, where Spanish notables did not mix with other races. Criollos perpetuated the racial prejudices of the colonial period: a Spaniard fell in social standing when marrying a person of another race or mixed blood, although how far he fell depended on his family's prestige or tolerance. In point of fact, of the 40,249 Sonorans counted by a 1793 census, fewer than 0.3 percent were listed as white (with one woman for every sixty men), 42 percent as mestizo or mixed-blood, and nearly 58 percent as Indian.[16] Peter Stern and Robert Jackson suggest a more diverse portrait of race in Sonora than is generally accepted by norteños who view themselves as descendants of criollos. They found that in 1801 in the four northern villages of Santa Ana, San Lorenzo, Ymuris, and Terrenate (on the Río Magadalena in northern Sonora) the 53 whites made up just over 16 percent of the total population of 328. The population categorized by the census as mulattoes (Indo-mestizos and Afro-mestizos combined) composed 79 percent, and the indigenous population made up the remaining 5 percent.[17]

According to Stern and Jackson, because Spanish colonial control was weak, vagabondism (*vagabundaje*) was a major problem on the frontier throughout the eighteenth century, when as many as 200,000 vagrants — or *vagos*, as the priests, peninsulares, criollos, and pretentious mestizos would call them — may have roamed New Spain. Although relatively few in Sonora in the 1780s, these vagos were nevertheless a disruptive element. When they moved onto the land, they used Indian labor to work the fields. After each bonanza, they would crowd into the mining camps — and hang around, living off what they could scrounge or steal.[18] The lingering stigma attached to "other races" was reflected in disparaging words like "vago" and "guacho," which Sonorans used to refer not only to a vagrant or an outsider but also to a mulatto or a mixed blood.[19] Racial prejudice would divide many of the workers migrating north during the next century.

Independence and the Rise of the Criollos

Due to the dominance of first- and second-generation Spaniards, there was little support in Sonora for the War of Independence. This dominance would increase, however, after Independence. When the Mexican government dismantled the remnants of the mission system, wealthy criollo landowners acquired most of the newly privatized Church lands. Because Mexico was too poor to support large contingents of soldiers on the frontier, it relied on local militias instead. Under the feudal leadership of Sonora's criollo notables, the militias served to reinforce the primacy of race and family background.

The opening of Guaymas, one of Mexico's best natural harbors (though blocked by Baja California from direct access to the Pacific), stimulated the growth of Pitic, site of a former presidio at a strategic point on the Ríos San Miguel and Sonora in the geographic center of the province. Considered the gateway to the northern districts, it would be renamed Hermosillo in 1828 and become the capital of the separate state of Sonora. As the area became more secure, it became the province's commercial center Sonora's most important merchants and hacendados, most of them criollo notables, kept business offices and homes there. With the substantial profits they made from exporting silver and wheat, they built mansions and lived lives of conspicuous opulence, the wealthiest and most influential becoming involved in politics.

In the last decades of the colonial period, continual Apache attacks in the north and revolts by the Yaqui, Mayo, and other native peoples in the south combined to drive many small farmers from their land. Criollo hacendados and rancheros took advantage of the disorder to seize the abandoned properties. Criollo military officers made money from bounties on slain or captured Apaches and trafficked in Apache slaves, with women and children parceled out as servants. The new Sonoran state protected these arrangements. Under the state constitution, servants did not enjoy full citizenship rights. The Servants' Law (Ley de Sirvientes), passed by the Sonoran legislature in 1843, permitted voluntary labor contracts between the master and servant.[20]

The Revolt of the Yaqui

Soon after Independence, state legislatures passed laws denying natives communal land rights. Jalisco and Zacatecas went so far as to break up communal lands. Chihuahua and Sonora permitted colonies to be established on unused land or even communal lands, and many criollos and mestizos took the opportunity to grab these lands. The law declared the natives equal, making the native land more accessible. By the mid-1820s, the tax assessors appeared in the Río Yaqui and Río Mayo Valleys. The 1824 constitution of the state of Occidente, which included present-day Sonora and Sinaloa, established the mechanism to alienate native land. Encroachments by settlers stiffened Yaqui and Mayo resistance to the hated Yori — the Yaqui term for anyone who was not a Yaqui.[21] In 1825, the Yaqui mounted their most significant revolt under the leadership of Juan Banderas (Juan Ignacio Jusacamea).

He was called Banderas because he fought under the banners of Our Lady of Guadalupe (Virgén de Guadalupe), Montezuma, and Father Hidalgo. Banderas had visions of a pan-Indian nation and enlisted the Mayo in the Yaqui revolt. According to some accounts, he fielded an army of 2,000 men, joined by the Mayo, Opata, and Pima. The revolt caught the notables and mestizos by surprise, and in 1828, the Sonoran legislature passed a reform act that returned the seized property to the Yaqui and Banderas was made captain-general of the Río Yaqui Valley. This began a pattern of temporary appeasement.

In 1829, the state of Occidente split into the separate states of Sonora and Sinaloa, ending a half decade of wrangling. Alamos, whose first town council had convened in 1814 and which had officially been named a city in 1827, became part of Sonora. It was home to some of the state's richest notables — many of whom had a stake in the Río Yaqui Valley.

In 1830, the federal government abolished Banderas's office of captain general, ending Yaqui self-rule. For two years, he prepared for another revolt, sending envoys to other tribes and making raids on Yori settlements. Expected support from the Opata was not forthcoming and Banderas was captured, tried, and executed in Arizpe. At his trial, Banderas admitted that his purpose had been to exterminate all whites. The Yaqui-Mayo revolt encouraged the Apache to challenge the Sonorans in 1833. This further divided the state, as the northern ranches centered at Arizpe and the southern hacendados competed for funds and whether to concentrate efforts against the Yaqui or against the Apache as the major threat to the state. Meanwhile, the policy of privatizing and encroaching on Yaqui lands continued.[22]

The Criollo Elites Fight over the Spoils

In 1836, a civil war broke out, with *sonorenses* lining up behind General Manuel Gándara, on the right, and José de Urrea Elías, on the left. Gándara headed the conservative hacendados and rancheros living around Ures, who opposed wars of "dubious benefit" against the natives and the incessant raising of taxes to fund such wars. Manuel's father, Juan Gándara, had immigrated to Sonora in the late 1700s, settling near Ures. Gándara, a criollo, shared a feeling of entitlement with his conservative allies and liberal opponents and often switched parties to suit his purposes.

Urrea was a third-generation Sonoran. His paternal grandfather had been born in Altar in 1765. His father, Mariano, had been commander of the presidio of Tucson (1793–1804), where José himself had been born. Mariano served the Crown but joined Antonio López de Santa Anna against the so-called Mexican Emperor Agustín Iturbide. José's mother, María Gertrudis Elías Gonzáles, was the granddaughter of Francisco Elías González de Zayas, who had arrived from La Rioja, Spain, in 1729. José rose to the rank of general and participated in the Texas War (1836), commanding the troops at Goliad.

Appointed commandant general of the departments of Sinaloa and Sonora in 1837, Urrea led the liberal rancheros around Arizpe, who felt that federal and state officials hundreds of miles away were incompetent. They wanted the state's capital moved to Arizpe, so that their legislators might more aggressively pursue the Apache wars. They also wanted to concentrate state business around the Yaqui pueblos, so that Yaquis might more easily be recruited as hacienda and mine workers. When the Yaqui resisted, Urrea brutally suppressed them. The Servants' Law of 1843 served to strengthen debt peonage. Although it gave servants the right to buy themselves out, the law empowered hacendados, rancheros, and mine owners to preserve order by expelling outside agitators. Urrea planned to repopulate the Río Yaqui Valley with non-Yaqui settlers.

The absence of strong state government gave the notables greater access to leadership positions. Merchants, both Sonoran and foreign, became more prominent as the state became dependent on them for revenue. Merchants — including U.S. Consul Juan A. Robinson — often bought favors from the state government.

Meanwhile, the Apache wars ground on, draining the state's treasury. But the central government had neither the resources nor the capacity to end the Apache threat. Sonora's centralists and liberals looked to Mexico City to provide continuity, stability, and the money to put down the Indians. The centralist stronghold was a region of prosperous farms and haciendas worked by Pimas and Opatas–the towns and villages along the Río Horcasitas, the lower Río Sonora around Ures, and the lower Río Moctezuma. Liberals were the ranchero class around Arizpe, the merchants of Guaymas and Hermosillo–in short the emerging capitalist class.

By the mid-1830s, Sonoran elites felt increasingly isolated. They resented sending taxes to the central government while the Apache problem remained unresolved. The frequent coups in Mexico City gave Gándara the opportunity to seize power. In 1842, Antonio López de Santa Anna became president and he appointed Urrea governor and commander general of Sonora and Sinaloa. Urrea immediately led campaigns against the Apache and the Seri, campaigns that provoked armed opposition from the Gándara faction. In 1844, the federal government temporarily ended hostilities between the factions when it sent a neutral outsider to supervise the state.[23]

The Yanqui Wars

In the War of 1847, Sonora was not in harm's way. Governor Luis Redondo prepared to fend off a Yanqui invasion, placing Colonel José María Elías González in charge of defending the homeland. Although three U.S. vessels blockaded Guaymas in 1848, there was no major fighting. Cholera broke out in 1850, just as Yanqui raiders crossed into the state. Conditions worsened in 1853, when James Gadsden bullied an unwilling Mexico to sell a strip of its territory along the border that included the Mesilla Valley of New Mexico and the southern quarter of Arizona, nearly 30,000 square miles all told, of which some 23,000 square miles were in northern Sonora, for $10 million. More than 10,000 sonorenses joined the Yanqui adventurers who were passing through the territory — the Mesilla corridor — on their way to the newly developing goldfields of California.

The loss of the Gila and Colorado Rivers along with the area's known rich mineral deposits is well documented. "On the consummation of the Gadsden purchase in 1854," wrote Hubert Howe Bancroft, "Americans like [Charles] Poston and [Sylvester] Mowry began to open the mines. Eastern capital was enlisted."[24] Sonorans expressed the loss and the aftermath in more anguished terms. In his letter of January 25, 1856, to the Sonoran governor, Joaquín Corella, head of Arizpe's city council, wrote: "The Gadsden Treaty . . . has deprived the state of its most valuable land, and resulted in protecting the Apache who launch their raids from these lands and the North Americans who live among them, because in less than twenty-four hours they can cross the boundary; there the robbers and assassins remain beyond punishment; in our opinion, it is vital, indeed, indispensable to garrison the border with sufficient troops that are always on the alert, since only in this way can they defend the integrity of a state threatened by raiders."[25]

Article eleven of the Treaty of Guadalupe Hidalgo of 1848 obligated the United States to control the Indians (among them the Apache) along the border. Through manipulations and coercion, however, U.S. delegates forced Mexico to to accept a release from this treaty obligation in the Gadsden Treaty of 1853. Adding to Sonoran fears were the separate deals U.S. miners and merchants made with the Apache, which, in effect, encouraged them to attack Mexico, and the rash of U.S.-based raids into Mexico in the early 1850s, most with the intention of annexing both Sonora and Chihuahua. A failed attempt by the French to establish a company to exploit the mines of northern Sonora raised an outcry as far away as New York for intruding into the U.S. sphere of interest. The feeling among the Yanquis was that, if Sonorans could not protect themselves, then it was up to the United States to give them the blessings of democracy and the Monroe Doctrine.[26]

In 1857, Henry Crabb led yet another raid across the border. At the head of some one hundred Californians, Crabb marched into Sonora and refused to leave. The Sonorans ambushed the Californians, executed Crabb, cut off his head, and preserved it in alcohol. The Yanquis in Arizona retaliated against the Mexicans there, and a small-scale war broke out within the territory. President James Buchanan labeled the Mexicans brutal and attempted to use the incident as a pretext to invade Mexico. Many Mexicans fled across the border, abandoning Arizona, and paralyzing the mines and Arizona's economy.

In 1859, as Charles Poston tells it, Buchanan planned to use Governor Ignacio Pesqueira's refusal to allow Charles P. Stone to survey the public lands of Sonora as another pretext for invasion, instructing his consul at Guaymas to prepare to hoist the U.S. flag there. Put off by Stone's arrogance, Pesqueira ordered Stone out of the state. Captain William Porter of the U.S. gunboat *St. Mary's*, anchored just offshore, demanded that Pesqueira allow Stone to continue his survey or he would bombard Guaymas. When, however, Pesqueira replied that he would not be responsible for U.S. property or lives in Sonora if a single shell fell on Guaymas, the *St. Mary's* put to sea. In December 1859, Buchanan asked the U.S. Congress to approve the occupation of Sonora as well as Chihuahua. It declined.[27]

Meanwhile, sonorenses in the United States strengthened their ties to Mexico by forming *juntas patrióticas* in Tucson and throughout California. During the Wars of Reform and the French Invention, most Mexicans had been nationalists who supported President Benito Juárez. In 1863, General Plácido Vega, who fought alongside Pesqueira in the War of Reform, went to San Francisco as a special agent to organize Mexican exile support and to recruit volunteers for the Mexican army. Operating through juntas patrióticas and the Mexican consul, in just over two years, he distributed more than $600,000, a sizable sum for the time. He became active in local politics and throughout the state. Most sonorenses, many Californios, and even J. M. Ainsa, a relative of Henry Crabb, supported his cause. Vega purchased arms and led volunteers back to the homeland.[28]

Sonoran Strongman: Ignacio Pesqueira

Born on December 16, 1820, in Arizpe, Ignacio Pesqueira was a fourth-genera-tion Sonoran. His great-grandfather, Julian Pesqueira, arrived in the 1750s. A century later, the liberal great-grandson challenged the conservative Gándara, himself a second-generation Sonoran. Pesqueira gained the support of many younger state militia officers, as well as that of merchants from Hermosillo and Guaymas. In the tradition of Urrea, he sought to control the strategic Río Yaqui and Río Mayo Valleys, which had the richest lands in Sonora.

After Pesqueira became governor of Sonora in 1857, the Wars of Reform and French Intervention, the Yaqui and Mayo revolts, and the Apache wars would drain the state's coffers. Pesqueira was ruthless in punishing both civil insurgents and Indian rebels. After a battle in May 1868, for example, on the governor's orders, Colonel Salazar Bustamante herded hundreds of captured Yaquis into a church at Bacum and demanded that they surrender their arms. When they refused, the soldiers shot their chiefs and fired upon the other Yaquis. By 2:00 a.m. some 120 Yaquis lay dead, and only 59 remained alive. The Sonoran militia lost only four soldiers in this massacre. Through constant, heavy taxes to fund the continuing wars, Pesqueira alienated the townspeople of Alamos and then used the wars as a pretext for confiscating the property of rich *alameños*.

Early in 1868, the governors of the northern states asked the federal gov-ernment to help finance their campaigns against the Apache and the Yaqui. To no avail. In 1869, the U.S. consul in Sonora observed that stepped-up military operations in Arizona had simply caused the Apache to shift their attacks to Sonora. Pesqueira's failure to control the Apache eroded his power. Between 1860 and 1870, Sonora's population fell by almost 20 percent, to 108,000, with nearly 20,000 Sonorans leaving for Arizona and California, more than the number killed during the French Intervention and the Apache wars combined. By 1874, Mexico City became convinced that state efforts to control the native uprisings had failed and Mexico City and moved to take a more active role, placing General Jesús García Morales in charge of operations. Pesqueira tem-porarily retired to his hacienda at Las Delicias.[29]

The Yaqui Wars

Rebellions by the Yaqui and Mayo continued under the Yaqui leader Cajeme (José María Leyva), who had spent much of his childhood among the Mexican people, spoke Spanish, and knew Mexican ways. In 1849, Cajeme went to California with his father to prospect for gold and then returned to Sonora and lived in Guaymas during the 1850s. During the War of Reform, Cajeme joined the liberal cause. A partisan of Pesqueira in the 1850s and 1860s, fighting against his own people, Cajeme was promoted to captain for his role in putting down the Yaqui Revolt of 1867. He helped Pesqueira suppress the Conant revolt in 1873 and was rewarded by being made chief alcalde of the Yaqui and Mayo and captain general of the Yaqui.

In 1875, Cajeme changed sides, however, joining Francisco Serna, the customs chief of La Libertad and a member of the Sonoran elite, to fight against Pesqueira. As a result of the Constitution of 1873, which institutionalized the reforms of the Constitution of 1857, such as the privatization of Church and Indian lands and the ending of Church privileges, encroachments on Yaqui lands had increased. The Yaqui prepared for war by building forts and tending to their lands. When the Sonoran militia attacked, killing more than sixty natives and wounding twenty more, the Yaqui and Mayo responded by burning the ranchos and pueblos of Cocorit, in the Río Yaqui Valley, and the seaport of Santa Cruz, at the mouth of the Río Mayo.[30]

With the overthrow of Pesqueira and the coming to power of a more vigorous generation of liberals, encroachments on Indian lands intensified. By the 1880s, only the Yaqui lands remained in native hands. In the early 1880s, Governor Carlos R. Ortiz led 1,200 federal troops into the Río Yaqui Valley to club the Yaquis into submission. After Cajeme was captured and executed in 1887, the federal presence in Sonora grew and foreign capital poured into the Río Yaqui and Río Mayo Valleys. Regrouping under their new leader, Tetabiate (Juan Maldonado), the rebels were determined to fight to the end. During the brief peace in 1897 — the Peace of Ortiz — each Yaqui male was to receive some ten acres (4.5 hectares) to farm. But Tetabiate insisted that no Mexican settlers or troops be allowed in the valley. When the Sonorans did not abide by this condition, the Yaqui again rebelled and fought on, even after Tetabiate was killed in 1901.

Sonorans attempted to control not only the flow of arms and food to the Yaquis but also where they lived and worked. Nearly half of Sonora's Yaquis lived outside Yaqui country and worked throughout the state. By 1907, the mines and railroads had been cleared of Yaquis. *Rurales* searched the haciendas looking for others, which many hacendados resented because the Yaquis were trusted laborers. Between 1902 and 1908, as many as 15,000 Yaquis were deported from Sonora, half of them to Yucatán. Revolutionaries would recruit heavily from among their ranks. Several hundred Yaqui men, women, and children were rounded up and jailed. Authorities farmed out the children to be "civilized," left some of the men to die in prison, and returned the women to their bosses. They sentenced other Yaqui men to work for merchants or other businessmen in Hermosillo and Guaymas, while still others were given the choice of informing on the rebels (*broncos*) or being deported — or they were simply hanged.[31] By 1908, the rebellion was completely crushed. The brutality of the Yaqui wars — and the ruthless punishments meted out to rebels and non-rebels alike — left a lasting imprint on the consciousness of Sonorans and tested their good conscience.

Transforming Sonora

Between 1880 and 1900, Sonora was politically and economically transformed into one of the wealthiest and most prosperous states in Mexico. Although its central and northern districts still had fewer than three persons per square mile in 1890, Sonora's population doubled over the last two decades of the nineteenth century, with many of its new residents drawn from other states.

The political fragmentation within Sonora led to the rise of a liberal triumvirate — Luis Emeterio Torres (1844–1935), Ramón Corral (1854–1912), and Rafael Izabal (1854–1910). Torres, a native of Chihuahua, had been an early supporter of Díaz. A veteran of the French Intervention, he migrated to Sonora after the war, where he supported the Alamos group against Pesqueira. Torres was best man at the weddings of both Corral and Izabal. Corral, though a native of Alamos, was raised in Chinipas, Chihuahua, and was not from Sonora's elite families. Corral's father died when he was fourteen, so, lacking formal schooling, Corral became a printer, rising through government service to became part of the Alamos group. The intellectual leader of the three, he served as secretary of state under Díaz and as governor of Sonora, Corral supported the Serna revolt in the late 1870s and General Lorenzo Torres against Governor Carlos R. Ortiz in 1883. He collaborated with Torres and Izabal until 1911, acting as the link between the Alamos group and Mexico City.

Izabal was born in Culiacán, Sinaloa. His mother, Dolores Salido, was from the prominent Salido family of Alamos. A hacendado, he served in state and federal governments and as governor in the 1890s. Izabal had close ties to foreign investors, was very active against the Yaqui, and led military campaigns against the Seri. He was the political front man in Sonora.

The rise of the triumvirate coincided with the rise of foreign influence —

and capital — in the state. Mexico City had been reluctant to allow construction of the north-south railroad for fear of Yanqui encroachment. And indeed, with the coming of the railroad in 1882, trade, which had been mostly south to north, would soon reverse direction. The city of Tucson would take on added importance as Arizona and Sonora merchants integrated their operations. By 1883, of the railroad's nearly 2,000 employees, though more than 40 percent were Yaquis, almost 25 percent were Euro-Americans.

The absence of the Apache threat, together with liberal taxes and liberal land concessions, attracted foreign capital, allowing Sonora's industrial development and its integration into U.S. markets. In 1879, the first telegraph linked the Sonora to Arizona. In 1880, a short line linked Guaymas and Hermosillo, and by the middle of the decade, telegraph lines crisscrossed the state. By 1884, the railroad linked the Sonoran interior with the railroad lines of Arizona. At least for a time, the seaport of Guaymas remained a vital link to the outside, with lumber arriving from Oregon and rails, cars, and locomotives, from the U.S. East Coast. This influx of raw materials and manufactured goods from abroad hastened the flight of Mexican capital and solidified the control of the state by the merchant oligarchy.

The aggressiveness and economic advantages of Euro-Americans caused inevitable tensions. Euro-American employees built separate facilities for Euro-Americans and Mexicans. Empalme, the Yanqui colony in Guaymas, had separate housing and a country club reserved for whites only. Tennis, golf, boating, swimming, dancing, playing cards, and other recreation became a symbol of Yanqui affluence and dominance. When Mexican workers objected, employers threatened to import Chinese workers from California.

As demand for miners climbed, Sonoran haciendas and ranchos experienced a shortage of labor: increasingly, farmworkers ran away for higher wages. Between 1897 and 1907, the number of mine, mill, and smelter workers in Sonora nearly tripled, to just under 17,400 — which did not include the thousands of Sonorans working across the border in those jobs in Arizona. The Yaquis were an integral part of this labor force.

Meanwhile, miners bought appliances and furniture through the company store, where automatic payroll deductions were made. Then, as now, the credit system acted as a form of social control. As Clifton-Morenci, Douglas, and Pirtleville grew, so did Cananea and Nacozari. One company — Phelps Dodge — eventually owned all. By the end of the 1870s, Arizona had become the supplier rather than the consumer of goods, and Sonora had a well-formed merchant class and trade relationships with San Francisco.

Soaring growth in commercial agriculture brought great wealth not only to Sonora's larger landowners but also to its merchants, who, with the new order,

Freight at the railroad station in Nogales, Arizona, ca. 1890. (Photograph by Ira Knee-land, courtesy of Special Collections Library, California State University, Fresno, To-polobampo Collection)

could ship produce to buyers in San Francisco and Los Angeles via Nogales, breaking Guaymas's import-export monopoly. Merchants monopolized the production and export of flour, causing shortages at home — and a near riot in Guaymas in April 1878. Their newfound wealth also came at the expense of subsistence farmers, especially the Yaqui and Mayo, who had been awarded small plots after 1886. As in Chihuahua, commercial agriculture and liberal legislation set off a wave of land speculation in the 1880s, with speculators buying up millions of acres of terrenos baldíos.

By 1912, Sonora was raising 7.6 percent of Mexico's cattle — only Chihuahua and Jalisco had more. With an initial investment of $50,000, ranchers could earn $25,000 annually. Mining also prospered, with Arizpe and Moctezuma becoming bastions of copper production. Railroads and proximity to the border served to drive this prosperity. In the 1890s, trade between Sonora and Los Angeles grew as Sonora's demand rose for farm machinery, mine equipment, and other products sold in Los Angeles. The *Los Angeles Times* called Sonorans Mexico's "most progressive" citizens. As the dominance of trade shifted from other foreign merchants to U.S. merchants, more goods were received and shipped through Nogales. By 1910, Sonora had become dependent on the United States; the Sonoran merchant class had lost its grip on the state's economy. Mexicans were becoming increasingly resentful of Euro-American arrogance and control.

Hermosillo's merchants, for their part, grew rich from the sales of imported goods: its bankers prospered, and it became the financial capital of the state. Towns along the railroad, like Magdalena, became trade centers, whereas those the railroad bypassed, like Ures, moved to the periphery.

Although the railroad made it easier to travel to Los Angeles than to Mexico City, with Mexican musical groups touring both sides of the border, it was still too costly for the poor, who continued to travel hundreds of miles in search of work or a good fiesta. The discovery of new deposits of copper, silver, and gold pulled ever more settlers into Arizona, whose numbers doubled during the 1880s.[32]

By the 1870s, English was in common use in Sonora. Sonorenses living in Tucson celebrated Thanksgiving, and those from Guaymas, Hermosillo, and other Sonoran towns played baseball (*béisbol*). English words crept into the Sonoran vocabulary. Indeed, in the last two decades of the century there emerged a new Sonoran elite of merchants, hacendados, government functionaries, and ambitious members of the middle class who spoke English as well as they did Spanish, went to school in the United States, and bought U.S. products.

Although only the more affluent could afford to send their children to Mexico City, Sonora spent more per capita on education than any other state. Between 1887 and 1891, the number of schools increased by more than 25 percent, to 175, and the number of students by more than 70 percent, to 9,500.

By the 1890s, Ramón Corral and Luis Torres looked upon the mining complex at La Colorada–Minas Prietas, connected to the outside world by a narrow-gauge rail line, as a model for attracting foreign capital. A hundred adobe houses were being built every month, and miners were being paid higher wages (1.50 to 5.00 pesos a day) than in other parts of Mexico.

By 1895, Yaquis and nonnative sonorenses made up close to 90 percent of La Colorada's population of just over 3,000. Out-of-state migrants accounted for less than 5 percent, with the largest numbers coming from Sinaloa, Baja California, Chihuahua, Durango, and Jalisco in that order. A 1895 census of La Colorada–Minas Prietas lists 30 percent as unmarried men or women, 30 percent as married, and 40 percent as children, some 2,000 out of a total population of nearly 5,000.

Besides the Yaquis, Sonorans, and other Mexicans, there was a growing number of foreigners at the mining complex. Indeed, between 1890 and 1895, foreigners at Minas Prietas increased fivefold, to just under three hundred. Many were veterans of other mining camps, and like the Yaquis and Sonorans, brought their own particular life experiences with them. For example, the British managers had previously operated mines in South Africa, and the Euro-Americans had run mines in Chihuahua. Many of the Yaquis, Sonorans, and other Mexican miners had also worked in Chihuahua and Arizona.

Euro-American and British managers also worked as engineers, book-keepers, mechanics, machine operators, blacksmiths, and carpenters. According to Manuel Tinker Salas, European and U.S. foremen looked different from their Mexican and Sonoran counterparts, no matter the hue of their skin: they wore blue overalls and usually sported a tie. Most often, they had assistants (*ayudantes*) when they supervised Mexican work gangs and oversaw operations in the mine shafts. With few exceptions, the rank and file were Yaquis and nonnative Mexicans, who worked as miners and as field hands (*peones de campo*) on the ranchos and haciendas that supplied the mining complex.

Mine wages as high as five pesos a day attracted Mexicans from Chihuahua, Sinaloa, and the interior of Mexico in ever greater numbers. Of the nearly 7,000 out-of-state Mexicans at La Colorada–Minas Prietas in 1895, more than half came from Sinaloa, Chihuahua, and Jalisco, in that order. The presence of federal troops in the Río Yaqui and Río Mayo Valleys also brought non-Sonorans into the state, giving rise to the demeaning epithet "guacho," cultivated by the Sonoran elites, who extended it to mean all Mexican outsiders they deemed socially undesirable. The epithet, along with the stereotype of *sureños*, southern Mexicans, as working for less and being less industrious than the sonorenses, only added to Sonora's growing social resentments during the *porfiriato*. Sonorans resented not only the non-Sonorans Díaz sent to occupy their state but also those all-too-often non-Sonoran favorites to whom Díaz apportioned Sonoran state lands.[33]

Cananea

Twenty-five miles south of the international border, at an altitude of 5,200 to 5,400 feet (1,600 to 1,650 meters), in the northeastern part of the state lay the Cananea mining district, part of a copper belt extending from Globe, Clifton, Morenci, and Bisbee into Sonora. Cananea was legendary, as were nearby Nacozari and the Moctezuma and Arizpe districts, which had gigantic deposits of copper ore. Though not eclipsing Minas Prietas, Cananea was more symbolic of the intimate economic relationship between the United States and Mexico, in which boom, bust, and recovery cycles produced the depressions of 1893, 1901, and 1907 — crises that became part of the historical memories of the participants.

Lack of capital, peace, and water had blocked development of Cananea.

Enter William C. Greene, active in ranching and farming on the San Pedro River near Fairbank, Arizona, who acquired the holdings of the Empress Mexican Mining Company (Empresa Minera Mexicana) and other properties in the 1890s. After shipping the slag he found there to a smelter he established in Fairbank, Greene organized the Cananea Copper Company in 1896 and, three years later, the Cananea Consolidated Copper Company, better known as 4C. Green then built a railroad connecting Cananea and Naco in 1901.

Cananea's population swelled to 20,000 in 1906. About a fifth of these were Yanquis living in the separate and unequal facilities of La Mesa, which had its own exclusive club and saloons. To the west of the Yanqui colony lay the shantytown world of the Mexican miner. Makeshift houses of wood, mud, or discarded materials, lacking sanitation and disease-ridden, stood in stark contrast with the stone houses of the Yanquis. The main Mexican barrio, El Ronquillo, bordered those of Cananea Vieja and Mesa Sur. This pattern was repeated in Nacozari, where some 5,000 Mexicans lived apart in mining camps such as Minas Prietas and La Colorada.

One of the first recorded labor actions in Sonora occurred in 1889 in La Trinidad, a community of 4,000 in the isolated mining district of Sahuaripa in the sierra of eastern Sonora. The Trinidad mine belonged to a British group. Its workers were paid 1.50 pesos a day, but in paper chits (*boletas*) rather than money, redeemable only at the company store. Local stores refused to take the chits. The workers demanded to be paid in silver. When management refused, they struck. Town Councilman Manuel Pablo Encinas agreed to represent them. After first promising reforms, English Superintendent Edmund Harvey appealed to local officials to break the strike. Prefect Loreto Trujillo posted guards around the mine property. Ordered by Díaz to protect the interests of the British company, which generated nine-tenths of the revenue of the Sahuaripa district, Governor Corral proceeded to drive off most of the strike leaders. Town officials sought a compromise, but nothing came of their meeting with the company, which promised only that local merchants would now accept the company chits. Corral ordered that all strikers return to work or be jailed as vagos. After some delay, the mayor jailed six ringleaders, and the strike was over.[34]

The China Chapter

Well aware of the benefits of Chinese immigration, especially with the building of infrastructure during the Díaz years, Mexico signed the Treaty of Amity and Commerce with China in 1883, over the protests of the British and the Euro-Americans. After the U.S. Congress passed the 1882 Chinese Exclusion Act and its later amendments, many Chinese workers used Mexico as a backdoor to the United States. By 1904, nearly half of those who stayed to work in Mexico lived in Sonora, and many sonorenses soon acquired an antipathy toward them. Meanwhile, U.S. authorities pressured Mexico to exclude the Chinese altogether. At first, even at the risk of economic ties with the United States, the Díaz government resisted these pressures and the entry of armed U.S. border patrolmen into Mexico in pursuit of Chinese. Gradually, however, it yielded, as Mexican newspapers, particularly those in Sonora, caught up in the virulently anti-Chinese sentiments of the public and labor on the U.S. side, followed the example of their Yanqui counterparts in creating a climate of hysteria. Whatever the source or motivation, coming after the brutality and cruelty of its wars against the Indians, the racist treatment of Chinese workers was a blot on the historical record of the state.[35]

◄ 5 ►

Corridors, Convergence, and Community

After speaking with dozens of people who took part in the Mexican Revolution, Apolinar Frías Prieto, former curator of the Pancho Villa Museum in Ciudad Chihuahua, came to realize the importance of spreading ideas through conversation. Mexicans love stories, now as much as then, he explained. Even before the twentieth century, thousands traveled back and forth between Chihuahua and Arizona, bringing stories about their experiences with them. Many were peons, who had no patrimony and were therefore footloose. Others were small ranchers with a hundred acres to divide among their sons. Migration was natural to both these groups.

Because chihuahuenses had a history of warring with the Apache, and many had even received military training, they were natural rebels. When tensions between the haves and the have-nots passed the snapping point, the mine owners and hacendados blacklisted workers who left for the mines of Arizona and New Mexico. Shrinking resources pushed them north to Lordsburg, New Mexico, and to Morenci, Arizona, where Apolinar's father and two brothers would work in 1908. Dry farmers, idled between November and May, when there was no work to be done, would go to the mines out of habit. Though they often did not know how to read or write, they would listen to radical organizers who told them about just wages and treatment and about racism, which took on different meanings in the United States.

From the beginning of the Conquest, workers in Sonora and Chihuahua had alternated between mission fields, their own small plots, and the mines. Centuries later, border towns would mark La Linea, which Mexicans would cross and recross on their frequent trips away from, and back to, their homeland. Since the seventeenth century, small prospectors (*gambusinos*) had been trickling into Arizona. Over time, this would change, as the missions and large landowners came to dominate the labor of the indigenous peoples.

Hired by mine owners, farmers, the railroad, and other industries in the United States, Apolinar's father and brothers and thousands of other Mexicans would migrate north. The mines of Sonora and Chihuahua became staging areas for migrant workers, drawing them from outside the area in times of expansion, and sending them elsewhere when the economy contracted. Early on, the economics of the mines in Arizona became intimately tied to that of the mines in northern Mexico: labor flowed north and south in response to the cycles of boom and bust. At the turn of the cetury, the Mexican mines began to ship in bulk to U.S. refineries. As Mexican workers moved to Arizona's mining camps, middle-class Mexicans and small merchants followed them. For the more pretentious Mexicans, however, the mecca was Tucson.[1]

Tucson

Seventy miles north of present-day Nogales, Tucson developed as the commercial center of the region that would be home to many current and former members of Sonora's elites. In 1775, the Spanish army moved its garrison from Tubac to the Presidio of San Agustín de Tucson. With Mexican independence and the secularization of the missions, Sonora's elites turned to southeast Arizona, dispossessing the Indians of their lands along the Santa Cruz River. The Apache depopulated the area north and south of Tucson, whose population in 1831 was just over 950, with "pacified" Apaches (486) slightly outnumbering Mexicans (465). Renewed Apache attacks, a divided Sonoran government, and the exodus of Sonora settlers for the gold fields of California in 1848 left the pueblo of Tucson as the only populated settlement on Sonora's northern frontier. By 1860, its Mexican population had increased by almost 40 percent, to just under 650, nearly all U.S.-born, a phenomenon that would largely reverse itself within a decade.

According to the census of 1864, Arizona had a white population of nearly 4,600, including Mexicans who identified themselves as white. During the Civil War, President Abraham Lincoln asked the U.S. Congress to grant Arizona territorial status and to name Prescott the capital. Despite its reputation for lawlessness, Tucson garnered enough political clout by 1867 to have it voted territorial capital instead. As the the most populous and important trading center in Arizona, the Old Pueblo remained the capital for ten years, until northern mining interests moved to restore Prescott to that position.

Not all of Tucson's Mexicans were poor miners or farmers. Among their number were wealthy members of northern Mexico's elites, who brought considerable financial and human resources to the town. Some started small mercantile businesses; others freighted ores and dry goods.

Thus Esteban Ochoa moved to Tucson in 1860 and partnered with Pinckney Randolph Tully to freight cargo. Originally from Chihuahua but educated in Independence, Missouri, Ochoa had first settled in Las Cruces, where he had traded goods along the Chihuahua Trail. In 1876, Ochoa and Tully purchased a copper mine, the Margarita, in the Papago district, and they later had an interest in the Santa Rita Mine near Tubac. Ochoa built a smelter in Tucson and joined Indian Agent Tom Jeffords in a Sonora gold-mining venture.

Mariano G. Samaniego had successful businesses in Mesilla before arriving in Tucson in the 1860s. Born in Sonora, raised in Chihuahua, and a graduate of Saint Louis University, Samaniego was a conservative who sympathized with the Confederates during the U.S. Civil War. He became a member of the Society of Arizona Pioneers in 1884 — one of the few Mexican "Pioneers." Although membership was limited to those who arrived in Arizona before 1870, fewer than 10 percent of the members were Mexican Americans. Samaniego also speculated in mines, owning substantial mining properties at his death in 1907.

The Eliases, Leóns, Ochoas, Redondos, and Samaniegos engaged in commercial agriculture and livestock ranching, and moved to monopolize the waters of the region's river valleys. In 1874, Ochoa experimented with cotton. In 1877, he erected a windmill to irrigate his fruits and vegetables, and created an artificial lake near Tullyville, which he planned to stock with fish. In the 1880s, when new markets emerged for farmers and ranchers, only the wealthiest Mexicans could afford to mechanize, experiment with new farming techniques, or upgrade their livestock. Employing hundreds of men on his ranchlands, José Redondo purchased cattle in Sonora and Chihuahua to supply the Indian reservations at Mohave and San Carlos in Arizona.

Much of the early success of the Mexican elites depended on political connections. But, despite their supposed *palanca*, pull, with the territorial governor, no Mexican was ever appointed to a position of influence, much less power. The few Mexican Americans who were elected to the Territorial Legislature came from heavily Mexican districts, and even then, were limited to Samaniego, Ochoa, Redondo, León, and the Elías brothers.[2]

In the 1870s, Texans who had migrated to nearby Tombstone began to hound and rob Mexicans on both sides of the border. As Tucson's Euro-American population grew, cultural tensions also increased. In 1872 and 1873, vigilantes lynched several Mexicans, and Mexican consul Manuel Escalante feared they might soon attack all Mexicans. In July 1877, *Las Dos Repúblicas* entreated Mexicans not to abandon either their culture or their dreams of recapturing lands lost to the United States. The newspaper predicted that Mexicans would eventually overwhelm the Yanquis because of the superiority of their morals, customs, and language. Toward that end, *La Sonora* promoted, indirectly at least, the teaching of Spanish in town's public schools, complaining in 1879 that "the policy of . . . excluding the study of the Spanish language from their curriculum is somewhat to be wondered about, especially in those places where a large percentage of the population is Spanish and the necessity for a knowledge of that tongue is so apparent."[3]

Racism also polarized the Mexican community. Some labeled those who had assimilated with the belittling epithets "americanizados" and "agringados." Although Tucson's Mexican elite were concerned about racism, they looked upon *la plebe*, the people, in barrios such as Tucson's Barrio Libre, the Free Zone, with disapproval and sometimes contempt. Their indifference to the interests of working-class Mexicans made it easier for U.S. ranchers, farmers, merchants, mine owners, and railroads to exploit them.

Even after the railroad linked Arizona to the U.S. market system, Arizona's Mexicans continued to trade with Mexico. They celebrated *fiestas patrias* (Mexican national holidays), and San Juan's (Saint John the Baptist's) Day on June 24 with dancing, picnicking, and swimming in the Santa Cruz River. Many traveled to Magdalena, Sonora, for the feast of San Francisco in early October. Traveling Sonoran musical and theatrical troupes regularly entertained the Tucson Mexican community. Spanish-language newspapers accentuated the literary and social life of Mexicans. As the twentieth century approached, Arizona's Mexicans and Euro-Americans grew further apart.[4]

The Second Wave: The Ties That Bind

By the 1880s, fewer Spanish surnames were appearing in the social columns of Tucson's English-language newspapers. On November 30, 1881, the *Daily Arizona Journal* listed guests arriving at Tucson's Porter, Grand, Palace, Russian House, and Cosmopolitan Hotels — and not a single one was Mexican. Of the town's 4,400 Mexicans, fewer than 30 percent had been born in the United States. Much of the Tucson's prime real estate changed hands during the decade, driving most local farmers, particularly Mexican farmers, out of business. In addition, the lack of an industrial base slowed Mexican immigration. Tucson's Spanish-language newspapers — *Las Dos Repúblicas*, *El Fronterizo*, and later *El Tucsonense*—regularly complained about negative stereotypes of Mexicans, and associations such as the Club Unión and the town's many *mutualistas* served as a refuge from growing anti-Mexican sentiment. Through it all, ties between Tucson's Mexicans and Mexico remained strong.

Like other Sonorans, Federico José María Ronstadt was drawn to Tucson by the new opportunities that came with the railroad. When he arrived in 1882, at the age of 14, from Magdalena, where he had spent his early years, the Santa Fe Railroad Company was building a line from Guaymas, Sonora, to Benson, Arizona. The route the tracks would take was of great interest to Mexicans on both sides of the border. Nogales had not yet emerged, and La Linea was more an abstraction than a reality. In Tucson, Ronstadt lived with his aunt, worked as an apprentice to his mother's brother-in-law, and attended night school. Ronstadt felt strong cultural ties with his homeland. Like Tucson's other Mexicans, he celebrated the fiestas patrias and Mexican religious holidays and enjoyed performances of the traveling theatrical troupes and musical groups that came to Tucson from Sonora.

The recognized leaders of the Tucson's business and professional elites were Antonio Amado and Alejandro and Perfecto Elías. "Despite their political activism and their protests against discrimination, these business and professional men were unable to forge lasting ties with miners, migrant workers, or other members of the Mexican working class."[5] Their class pursued its economic and social interests and an idealized vision of Mexican society and culture.

Fernando Laos arrived in Tucson from Hermosillo in 1888, at the age of 19. He worked first as a butcher, then a barber, then for the Southern Pacific. He set up a fashion barbershop, as well as tobacco shops and pool halls. Other Mexican immigrants established clothing stores, restaurants, and cigar stores; still others were lawyers, doctors, journalists, and politicians. Most were active in planning the fiestas patrias.

Some immigrants, such as Ignacio Bonillas, would return to Mexico after pursuing successful careers in the United States. Born in San Ignacio, Sonora, in 1858, Bonillas was educated in Tucson, became a schoolteacher, then worked for Governor Anson Safford, husband to Bonillas's sister Soledad. In the early 1880s, Bonillas studied mining, engineering, and surveying at the Massachusetts Institute of Technology and taught a class in engineering at the University of Arizona. He never surrendered his Mexican citizenship, and he returned to Mexico, where he was elected mayor of Magdalena. He later became Mexico's Ambassador to the United States. He was a supporter of Venustiano Carranza, who chose Bonillas to succeed him as president of Mexico in 1920.[6]

The arrival of the Southern Pacific drew mining and cattle consortiums, whose vast capital investments and powerful monopolies unleashed an "irresistible torrent of civilization and prosperity," with devastating consequences for Tucson's Mexican elite. Although Mexicans made up nearly two-thirds of the town's more than 7,000 residents in 1880, they were in the political minority. Only a fifth of them worked in white-collar occupations.[7]

In Defense of Lo Mexicano

In 1878, Tucson's first Mexican newspaper, *Las Dos Repúblicas*, condemned workers' societies as consisting of "idle and depraved people who wanted a repetition of the [1789] Revolution in France." By the early 1880s, Tucson's Barrio Libre was notorious among the Mexican elite for its vice and destitution, even though nearly all its residents were neither criminals nor vagrants but poor Mexican workers. The elite championed their Mexican culture, yet they seldom, if ever, questioned capitalism, not even its systematic exploitation of working-class Mexicans.

A May 29, 1880, article in the Tucson newspaper *La Sonora* complained that "Americans try to humiliate Mexicans." The author found it "extremely disgusting to hear Americans make the remarks 'the white and the Mexican population,' 'a white woman and a Mexican woman.' " Such remarks implied that Mexicans were of African descent, he went on to say, yet there were, not just thousands but millions of Mexican men and women, who could "boast of as clear and fair complexion as may be found" in the United States.

Tucson's newspapers contained frequent correspondence from and news of Sonora. Thus, in a June 5, 1880, article praising Díaz as the greatest Mexican president since Juárez, *La Sonora* described the abortive revolt of General Manuel Márquez in Magadalena, who marched on Altar with 130 men. *El Fronterizo* also reported on the revolt, which allegedly had partisans in Jalisco, Durango, Sierra de Puebla, and Baja California.

Meanwhile, the politics of Porfirio Díaz had produced a large, restless labor pool in northern Mexico. Massive industrialization had pushed and pulled Mexicans not only into the United States but also into northern Mexico, contributing to a vigorous racial mixing of the Mexican population. Much of this migration had gone to developing trade centers such as Tucson, even before the porfiriato.

Before the 1880s, the most common currency was the peso, the "adobe dollar," which was worth as much as an actual dollar. After 1880, Tucson merchants continued to accept pesos but at a 10 percent discount. This affected Sonorans and other working-class people along the U.S.-Mexico border who received their wages in pesos. *Las Dos Repúblicas* urged workers to demand payment in dollars rather than pesos.

A series of incidents throughout the decade strained relations between Mexicans and Euro-Americans. In 1883, a fight broke out between drunken Euro-Americans and a Mexican in Mesilla during the fiesta of San Agustín, and police were barely able to control the two sides. In 1885, a Mexican youth was lynched in the Huachuca Mountains. In 1888, after a white man made advances to a married Mexican woman in a railroad car at the Pantano Station in Tucson, the husband attacked him, and other Mexicans and Euro-Americans jumped in. When Mexicans entered the car with rocks in hand, the armed Euro-Americans fired on them. Such incidents became ever more numerous and widespread.[8]

Between 1882 and 1889, a disproportionate majority of criminal defendants listed in Pima County court records were Mexican: twelve of the seventeen charged with murder, ten of the fourteen charged with larceny, and all five of the five charged with robbery. Convicted Mexicans were more severely punished, being sentenced, on average, to more than 3.5 years in prison, versus only one year for Euro-Americans. In 1889, Arizona passed a law denying hospital care to anyone who was not a citizen. Matters got so bad that *El Fronterizo* called for the creation of a Centro Radical Mexicano for legal aid.

In 1893, a drought devastated the U.S. cattle industry. Euro-American nativists succeeded in having a tariff put on Mexican beef, arguing that Mexican cattle were inferior to and smaller than U.S. beef, much like the Mexicans themselves, whom they characterized as dumb. Naturally, Mexicans retaliated by putting a tariff on U.S. goods. This exclusion of Mexican cattle echoed calls for the exclusion of Mexican labor. The Society of American Workers, for example, lobbied to limit work on railroads to "legitimate Americans."[9]

Tucson's Mexican elite belonged to a host of patriotic and civic societies. In 1875, Estebán Ochoa, Jesús Pacheco, and Juan Elías formed the Mexican Society for Mutual Benefit to help the destitute. It had 120 members, who paid monthly dues of twenty-five to fifty cents. It was followed by the founding of other such societies: the Sociedad Hispano-Americana Beneficencia in Florence, Arizona, in 1886; the Sociedad de Beneficia Mutua de la Raza Latina in Phoenix in 1888; the Sociedad Hidalgo in Solomonville in 1889; and the Sociedad de Beneficencia Mutua in Clifton in 1893. The most important and long-lasting society, however, would be the Alianza Hispano Americana, formed to protect Mexicans from the nativist American Protective Association.[10]

Many of the Alianza's leaders brought the political biases of their class with them. Carlos I. Velasco, whose father, José Francisco, had been mayor of Hermosillo and a deputy in the Mexican Congress, published *El Fronterizo*, supported Republican candidates, and believed that Catholicism was the moral foundation of Latin culture. Carlos was to become a friend of Ramón Corral, Luis E. Torres, and Rafael Izabal, and a staunch supporter of Porfirio Díaz.

Velasco traveled to Sonora during the French Intervention (1861–67) and followed Governor Ignacio Pesqueira back to Tucson in 1866. Velasco did not return to Sonora until the 1870s, serving as a state legislator and a pro-Pesqueira journalist. When Pesqueira's star fell in 1877, he returned to Tucson.

Velasco's *El Fronterizo* campaigned enthusiastically for the repatriation of U.S. Mexicans, waxing eloquent about the opportunities that awaited them in the Río Yaqui and Río Mayo Valleys. According to the paper, not only did many Mexican families in California, Arizona, and New Mexico want to return home, but their homeland — and President Díaz in particular — wanted them to as well. The paper urged its readers to write to Asunción Sánchez and Samuel Brannan, agents for the Sociedad de Colonización de Sonora.

When a Matamoros newspaper labeled *El Fronterizo* an "American journal," nationalist Velasco replied on June 16, 1882: "We were born Mexicans, we live Mexicans, and we will die with pride in being Mexicans. Let them know." Though it vigorously championed equality for U.S. Mexicans and attacked derogatory stereotypes of Mexicans, *El Fronterizo* just as vigorously opposed socialism and labor unions.

The economic changes of the 1880s collapsed the dreams of Tucson's Mexican elite. In 1890, they formed the Club Democratico Mexicano, which succeeded in having laws translated into Spanish. But poorer Mexicans continued to live in a barrio on the south side of town, which *El Fronterizo* described as a place of drunken brawls, gambling, and prostitution. Toward the end of the century, Tucson was fast becoming a health resort. The mines outside Tucson, owned by Michigan capitalists, were nonunion and relied heavily on Mexican labor.

When the depression of 1893 fanned U.S. nativism, some Arizona Mexicans chose to repatriate. The Alianza Hispano Americana, whose motto was "Protection, Morality, and Instruction," pledged to lift the dignity of "those of our race." Lodges spread to Clifton, Bisbee, and Globe and, in the early 1900s, to Tempe, Nogales, Yuma, Metcalf, and Brawley. The Alianza was essentially a fraternal insurance society. There is little evidence that it involved itself in labor movements. It did not take sides, for example, in the Clifton-Morenci Strike of 1903, or in the Cananea Strike of 1906, although reportedly some of its officers did. Velasco was, in effect, a social Darwinist as were, we can safely assume, Ochoa, Samaniego, and Jesús María Elías — all held important offices, all were wealthy, and all numbered themselves among the "fittest." The Alianza continued to focus attention on Tucson, however, with its substantial number of Mexican Americans and influential businessmen. By contrast, nearly all the Mexicans in Arizona's mining towns were immigrants and influential businessmen were few.[11]

King Copper

From 1880 until World War I, mining was the main pull of Mexican labor to Arizona. Although poor Euro-Americans also worked the mines before 1880, most pick-and-shovel workers were Mexican. The systematic gap between the lowest pay for Euro-Americans and the standard rate paid Mexicans, no matter their skill or experience, became institutionalized as "Mexican wages." Mexican mine workers labored twelve hours a day, six days a week. The mine operators actually paid even lower wages if profits from company stores, which sometimes reached 300 percent, are factored in. Preferential treatment for Euro-Americans drove the wedge of ethnic division into what might have become a unified working class. Throughout the period, the gap between Mexican and Euro-American widened.[12]

Mining stimulated cattle and farming enterprises and attracted large numbers of Texas cowboys, who imposed "on the region their English language and dislike of Mexicans."[13] The influx of Euro-Americans into Arizona intensified discrimination and segregation. Mexican newcomers moved into barrios, neighborhoods, and *colonias*, isolated from Tucson's Yanqui residents. Commercialized cattle and sheep operations overgrazed the rangelands in the 1880s, causing substantial ecological damage. The raising of livestock for export left Arizona increasingly at the mercy of national and international markets, suffering greatly during times of drought and economic depression.

The rise of copper is critical both to the rise of modern Arizona and to the history of Mexicans. Between 1880 and 1920, Arizona's share of the national copper market grew ninefold, to nearly 50 percent, while the U.S. share of the world copper market more than tripled, to nearly 60 percent. In time, Arizona's four mining districts would each produce more than 5 billion pounds of copper.

Copper became the mainstay of Arizona's economy. Demand for the metal grew as its uses increased. Changes in technology and engineering led to changes in production methods. Mexican labor had been used during the exploration phase, but, once transportation made it possible to ship greater quantities of copper, skilled hardrock miners, many of them Cornishmen, worked the rich veins. As the higher grades of copper played out, improvements in concentration and refining methods made it profitable to mine lower-grade ores, for which less-skilled labor could be used. Larger corporations bought out the smaller companies, which lacked the resources for such capital- and labor-intensive production. Pick-and-shovel Mexican workers took the place the of hardrock miners, who blamed the Mexicans instead of the mine owners for displacing them. Tucson was no longer the principal destination of Mexican migrant workers.

The exploration of most of Arizona's major copper deposits took place in the period from the mid-1860s to the mid-1880s, with the mining camps of Globe, Bisbee, and Jerome joining Clifton-Morenci. Although several smelters were built in 1865 and mining laws were adopted in the 1880s that made it easier to stake mining claims, it was completion of the transcontinental railroads that made the giant copper camps profitable and, even more important, the Electric Age that made copper a valuable commodity.[14]

In 1880, Arizona had 40,000 residents, more than 60 percent of whom were born there. Euro-Americans became a majority in 1884. Between 1900 and 1910, the Mexican population alone more than doubled, to just under 29,500. In Tucson, the number of Mexican immigrants nearly doubled as well, to just under 4,300.[15] The mining boom contributed to this population growth, as did the attendant demand for food and services. The new mining facilities received increased federal protection, which meant more army forts, which in turn meant more government contracts. Supplying Indian reservations was also a source of profit. The demand for large quantities of lumber for mine shafts spread the boom to northern Arizona.

In 1897, at Mammoth Tank, California, forty miles southwest of Yuma, Arizona, 260 Mexican railroad workers went on strike. Summoned by the railroad to the scene to arrest the leaders, Yuma County Undersheriff Mel Greenleaf arrived just after his two deputies, George Wilder and James Jones, who supposedly were pursuing a murderer having nothing to do with the strike. As the three lawmen approached, one of the strikers let out "a peculiar cry." Wilder drew his pistol and fired two shots in the air. Feeling threatened, the workers responded by throwing rocks and knocked Wilder unconscious, whereupon Jones got a shotgun from the stationmaster and dispersed the crowd. A posse of twenty-five men arrived the next day. Eighteen workers were arrested and taken to San Diego, California, where they were brought before a judge, who dismissed all charges and released them. Most strikes during this early period were spontaneous. The more militant union organization would take place later, when mine workers were grouped together year-round in intense industrial environments.[16]

Few made the connection between racism and the exploitation of Mexican and other workers, however crucial racism was in building Mexicans' identity as Mexicans.

Other Morencis

Around 1874, Ben Regan staked a rich silver outcrop in central Arizona and named it Globe. As the silver ore ran out, a rich copper carbonate ore was discovered along the Old Dominion vein. The Globe Mining Company bought the claims and began copper production. The isolation of the camp made profitability problematic, and the Globe mines struggled until 1895, when the Lewisohn brothers of New York bought control of the Old Dominion. A new smelter was built, and the mine owners ran a railroad line to the Southern Pacific.

In the next twenty years, Globe and the Old Dominion Mine would rank among the greatest copper camps in the world, with mine shafts reaching a depth of 1,500 feet, where a "river of water" kept huge pumps working around the clock. Not having the capital to carry production to the next phase, the Lewisohns sold to Phelps Dodge, which modernized the operation. A few miles west of Globe, a prospector named "Black Jack" Newman located a rich copper prospect. Nearby, another group of prospectors staked a claim they named Miami in honor of their hometown in Ohio. Newman eventually sold to the Lewisohns, who formed the Miami Copper Company, and the Ohio group sold to the Inspiration Mining Company. Miami Copper and Inspiration Mining became two of the biggest copper producers in Arizona.

Situated in central Arizona overlooking the Verde Valley, Jerome would become the "billion-dollar copper camp." In 1875, army scouts discovered mineral outcrops on Mingus Mountain. This discovery attracted both prospectors and investors, chief among whom were James Macdonald and Eugene Jerome, to the area. With others, MacDonald and Jerome formed the United Verde Copper Company and began to exploit the surface copper oxide ores. When these were exhausted, they sold to William A. Clark, of Butte, Montana, who controlled the New Jersey refinery that processed the United Verde's matte. Clark discovered a bonanza ore body that ran 20 percent copper.

The last great copper camp was Bisbee. Members of an army scouting party to the Mule Mountains registered the first claim in 1877. They contacted George Warren, who enlisted several other prospectors and, after six months of exploration, filed dozens of claims. Although Warren and four friends had discovered what would become the Copper Queen Mine, Warren lost his share gambling on a horse race, and his friends sold their interest to San Francisco investors, who struck 20 percent copper ore. In 1885, the San Francisco company merged with Phelps Dodge, which had bought an adjoining claim. Bisbee developed into one of the premier copper camps in the country.

Before mining, the hills around Bisbee were covered with oak, piñon pine, and juniper. The trees were soon cut down for fuel. Tents and cabins were piled on one another on hills and hillside ledges. By 1900, the canyon bottom and most of hillsides were crowded with buildings. Chinese were not allowed to own property in or even to spend the night in Bisbee. They lived on farms near

San Pedro River, where they grew vegetables. Mexican women cleaned and mended clothing for more than eight hours a day. Mexicans were not allowed to enter public places, and, for lack of water and space, they could not grow gardens, as they could in other mining camps. Euro-American males joined the Ancient Order of United Woodmen, the Masons, Elks, Moose, Eagles, Odd Fellows, and the Royal Order of Redmen. They were Bisbee's most politically powerful and business-connected residents. Mexicans joined the Alianza Hispano Americana, and African Americans joined the Silver Leaf Club. Neither was listed in the town directory.[17]

Technology and Mexicans

The richer veins of copper ore were played out at Clifton in the first two decades of operations. Forced to produce copper from ever lower grades of ore, the Arizona Copper Company would not have survived without Mexican labor. The company store, by recovering most of the workers' wages, kept profits high. The company also charged workers for housing, water, and hospital care. By 1904, Arizona Copper's annual output of more than 29 million pounds of copper exceeded that for the entire territory in 1882. Electric cars hauled ore through the shafts to the elevators and then to the surface, to be processed through modern concentrators, smelters, and leaching plants.

As in Mexico, even the unskilled Euro-American workers felt entitled to higher wages than the Mexicans. In 1890, there were nearly 3,700 Mexicans employed as common laborers in Arizona, of whom almost 60 percent were Mexican immigrants. Immigration increased nativism, especially during the depression of 1893, when many Euro-Americans feared the "Mexicanization" of Arizona.[18]

During the 1890s, the Detroit Copper Mining Company at nearby Morenci was forced to shut down for a time, and the Clifton mines often had barely enough money to pay wages, and none to meet payments on a million-dollar mortgage. The low-grade oxidized porphyry ore could not be efficiently processed using the old mechanical methods, and much of its copper content wound up in the dumps. Colquhoun developed a leaching process that recycled the tailings, increased production by 40 percent, and reduced the cost of producing copper by two cents a pound. The increased efficiency compensated for declines in copper content. To sustain high levels of production, Clifton's Arizona Copper Company doubled, then tripled the number of surface and underground workers.[19]

Mexican Space

From at least the sixteenth century, Mexican women brought seeds, cuttings, and other treasures of the past as they followed their migrating husbands and fathers. The first wave of migration to the mines of Arizona was mostly male, but many of the Mexican miners soon brought their families to the mining camps.

Mexicans used space differently than Euro-Americans. They planted peppermint, corn, pomegranates, squash, chilis, fig trees, nopalitos, verdolaga (purslane), rosemary, abaca, and cilantro, and tried to re-create traditional Mexican food unavailable in their new homes. They socialized in their *corrales*, yards. This worked out better in Clifton than in Morenci, where the company controlled space, and water was at a premium.[20]

Within this space, women were much more than the keepers of gardens. Like their husbands, they were the keepers of memories, having to endure the layoffs, the strikes, and the racism of their larger communities. Often, they were the agitators inside and outside the home. They were always the minority among men but the majority among women of all colors. By the turn of the century, there were even more of them, and, with them, came other concerns, such as housing, education, and health. They stressed the need for *mutualistas* with insurance benefits for families. They were essential in forming communities.

Clifton-Morenci-Metcalf at the Turn of the Century

By the 1890s, Clifton had three general stores, seven saloons, two doctors, and several Chinese restaurants and laundries. Euro-Americans from the U.S. East and Midwest found adobe repulsive in appearance. They disliked its Mexican origins and replaced it with wood and brick as soon as possible. On the outskirts of town stood a large machine shop and a roundhouse for the Arizona and New Mexico Railway. The railroads, reduction works, and mines all belonged to the Arizona Copper Company, which employed hundreds of men. Most were Mexican, but there were also many Chinese, along with some Italians and several Jewish itinerant merchants. The Chinese worked as house servants, gardeners, laundrymen, and restaurant cooks.[21]

In 1890, Clifton was a busy little Mexican camp owned by absentee capitalists, mostly Scots. Four hundred men worked in the mines and another 2,000 depended on the miners' labor. Clifton served as the administration and smelting center for a cluster of camps, connected by a 36-inch narrow-gauge railroad to the Southern Pacific at Lordsburg, New Mexico, seventy-one miles away.

But lawlessness was a real problem. It was almost impossible for a stranger to visit Clifton without being held up. The road from Duncan to Clifton was alive with rustlers. Outlaws like Big Dan, Curley Bill and Doc Baker operated freely. Kid Lewis shot a girl and Clifton Constable Olguin killed him.[22]

Clifton was beset by frequent floods, which seemed to recur in ten-year cycles. After a bad flood in 1891, no fewer than five bad floods swept the town between 1903 and 1906. The flood of 1891 covered the whole town, from mountain to mountain, with water, washing away buildings and twisting the rails so that the no trains could run for several days. It washed away the Wells Fargo safe, in which many people had left valuables and cash for safekeeping. It was never found. The greatest flood, according to some sources, was that of December 4, 1906, when it rained for thirty hours and killed eighteen people.

Henry Hill laid out Clifton's first subdivision, Hill's Addition, a large, flat area in the south part of Clifton, a mile from town's center, where he built his brick residence. It soon became the town's most desirable neighborhood. The Arizona Copper Company built elegant, wood-and-brick homes for its manager and officials.

Morenci surpassed Clifton in population in the 1890s. Its saloons, brothels, and other enterprises stood out in the central district. Most other buildings — a boardinghouse, a store, a hospital, and the workers' shacks — clung to sides of the Longfellow incline. There were no real roads, just paths leading to the workers' huts. The Detroit Copper Company owned everything, even the air. Metcalf resembled Clifton and Morenci. The fertile valleys to the south supplied Mexican labor.[23]

Having bought out William Church for $1.5 million in early 1897, Phelps Dodge immediately built a concentrator near the West Yankie underground mine between the towns of Old Morenci and Longfellow.[24] That same year on Christmas night, Arizona Copper's oxide concentrator at Clifton burned down. The company demolished a large part of its buildings and rebuilt them with steel and concrete. These improvements did nothing to improve Clifton's foul air, however. Colquhoun even tried to convince residents that the sulfur was good for their health. In 1901, the Clifton smelter was entirely rebuilt.

The Shannon Copper Company, organized in November 1899 in nearby Metcalf, was the third major producer in the district. It paid its worker higher wages than the Arizona Company. Clifton's first school was built in 1895. Realizing it needed a better-educated workforce to run the more complex smelters, Arizona Copper built a new school in 1898, with some thirty students, mostly Mexican, who were the children of the better-skilled smelter workers. The company also built its hospital in Clifton in 1908. Meanwhile, the economy improved. By 1907, the market value of Arizona Copper stock had climbed with the company's mounting production, to eighty dollars a share from its 1892 price of seventy-five cents a share. Most of the mines remained around Morenci and Metcalf. By this time, the district had gone electric.[25]

Capital, Workers, and the Times

As the grade of copper ore decreased, demand for larger mills increased. Driven by the de-skilling of the mining industry that accompanied modernization, the miners desperately sought to protect their jobs and status through collective bargaining. Labor agitation began in the railroads in the 1880s and in the mines by the 1890s, a process that accelerated the development of the institution of the U.S. marshal, which "represented the propertied class." The hardrock miners formed the first unions. Mass production led to the importation of large numbers of Mexicans, whom hardrock miners blamed for their replacement. Banning Mexicans from their camps and restricting Mexican immigration were often the first priorities of the new unions. Instead of educating the rank and file, union leaders often pandered to prejudice as a means of gaining worker solidarity. They branded Mexican workers "cheap labor." This lack of working-class unity allowed employers to continue paying Mexicans less than Euro-Americans. Mexicans, in turn, resented not only getting paid less for the same work but also what went with it — segregated housing and facilities.

Since most mines were located in remote, isolated, rugged, mountainous terrain, the mining camps were harsh and inhospitable. They were owned by eastern or foreign corporations whose prinipcal concerns were moving rock, earning the greatest profit, and providing sufficiently high dividends for their stockholders. They made little effort to improve the poor living conditions, viewing wages as controllable expenses, and workers as expendable pieces of equipment, to be used until they could no longer produce, then discarded. A dual wage system, with different wages for Euro-Americans and Mexicans performing the same work, was standard in most camps.[26]

On June 8, 1898, the *Arizona Republican* ran an article saying that trouble was expected between Mexicans and Americans at Clifton-Morenci-Metcalf. The cause of the trouble, according to the author, was that many Mexicans sympathized with Spain in the Spanish-American War, a farfetched notion, considering the Mexicans' antipathy toward Spain. The author went on to say that Mexicans were mostly recruited from Chihuahua and had come to the Arizona mining camps to save their own skins.[27]

Both the Longfellow Mine and the Detroit Copper Company were highly profitable enterprises by the 1890s, each smelting sixty to eighty tons of 20 percent copper ore per day. To Arizona's advantage, the construction of the Southern Pacific Railroad in southern Arizona allowed many of the fledgling Arizona copper camps to become profitable. But the profit often came out of the hides of the Mexican workers. Thus, in 1900, shifts were increased from eight to ten hours at Ray, thirty miles south of Globe. When Mexicans demanded added compensation, the response was to replace Mexican workers with Euro-Americans. Discouraged Mexicans left the area, a prelude to the 1900s.[28]

◀ 6 ▶

Becoming Mexican

In 1900, Arizona had almost 123,000 people. A decade later it had more than 204,000 — an increase of 66 percent. Right across the border, Sonora's population grew by less than 20 percent, to just under 265,400. The number of U.S.-born Mexicans in Arizona increased by about the same rate, 21 percent, whereas the number of Mexican immigrants in the territory increased seven times as fast — by more than 153 percent — for a combined total of almost 71,100 in 1910.[1]

In 1900, the Old Pueblo had more than 7,500 residents, and slightly more than half were of Mexican extraction. Settled in the 1870s, Phoenix was mostly Mexican, although, by the turn of the century, Euro-Americans were becoming the majority. Phoenix had a huge agricultural base in Salt River Valley, which attracted huge numbers of agricultural workers, who soon became largely Mexican workers. Reclamation projects of the first decade of the century swelled the Mexican population to tens of thousands during the harvest seasons.

Monopolization during the porfiriato brought a decline in Mexico's rural population, as subsistence farming was no longer an option for many. It also brought Mexican families to the rapidly industrializing United States from the border states of Chihuahua, Sonora, Coahuila, and Baja California, as well as from Zacatecas, Guanajuato, Michoacán, Jalisco, and the interior. At the same time, Mexican workers were ever more vulnerable to the capitalist cycle of boom and bust, being pulled toward jobs when the economy expanded and pushed away when it contracted, as it did during the 1907 world depression.

The Arizona-Sonora and New Mexico–Chihuahua borders became a revolving doors, with miners and pickers moving back and forth through the Sonora, Camino Real, and Mesilla corridors.

The Octopus, the Workplace, and the Worker Ants

Colonialism shaped the Euro-American and Mexican identities in Clifton-Morenci-Metcalf. Besides those of Arizona Copper, Phelps-Dodge, and Shannon Copper, smaller copper mines operated in Clifton-Morenci-Metcalf area. Many originally mined for gold or silver, but copper eventually carried the day, attracting huge investments and proportionally huge numbers of workers. Phelps Dodge was both aggressive and ubiquitous, mining copper not only in Morenci but throughout the area, burrowing into the hills above Metcalf on the east bank of Chase Creek.

In Clifton-Morenci-Metcalf, the inferiority of Mexicans was a fact in the minds of white people. "The Mexicans, naturally indifferent to sanitation," wrote Remington Barr, "conducted and aided in the spread of all the filth disease by their habits and carelessness. The doctors and the schools crusading for health, were immeasurably aided by nature in torrential summer rains that flushed out the accumulated filth."[2] It was these same rains and the filth they washed downstream that made summer the season of epidemics among the Mexican workers and their families.

The *Engineering and Mining Journal* wrote that, on the one hand, "common sense" said the Mexican peon was in large part superior to Indians. The peon enjoyed fiestas, mescal, and cockfights, and "all the lower-class Mexicans are of a contented disposition." On the other hand, the journal pointed out, Mexicans treated their wives like "Indian squaws." And even though they loved children, large families, and supported aged parents, they had low morals and spread a variety of diseases. Moreover, as underground miners, their fearlessness led them to be reckless.[3]

A road joined Metcalf to Clifton in 1903, in 1908, Arizona Copper built its hospital there, and by 1910 Clifton had a population of around 3,000. Most of the adobe huts that made up the town's three barrios — Chase Creek, Shannon Hill, and North Clifton — stood on flat ground next to the creek, directly in the path of Clifton's frequent floods. Others were scattered across the mountain slopes. Almost none had windows. In Clifton as in other mining camps, the mines shaped Mexican women's work: they continuously made tortillas and fetched and heated water for their mine worker men, and more water still, when their families had their weekly baths. Laundry consumed much of the women's time:

the miners' clothes had to be constantly washed, mended, and maintained. Water carriers (*aguaderos*) delivered water, furnished by the Clifton Water Company and loaded in leather or canvas bags onto burros, selling it for twenty-five cents a bag or four dollars a month, In sharp contrast, whites mostly inhabited houses with indoor plumbing, first installed by Pete Gámes, a plumber and blacksmith from Sonora.

The poorest Mexican families sent their children to work. The ten-year-old son of Leonida López and the two youngest sons of José María and Refugia Vargas worked as ore sorters. Daughters worked as domestic servants or seamstresses. Their social life revolved around baptisms and communions.

Morenci's one street was Burro Alley, named so because only a burro train could pass through it. The area where the whites congregated, between the Morenci Hotel and Detroit Copper's company store, was paved with cement, and a flight of cement steps connected it with the town's plaza. The town's focal point was the stuccoed wood-and-brick Morenci Hotel, owned by Detroit Copper, whose basement boasted a two-lane bowling alley, a billiard room, and a gym. Detroit Copper also owned a whites-only social club, which charged its members $1.25 a month in dues. Colonists and colonized were clearly distinguished by the quality of their houses and neighborhoods.[4]

Mexican workers learned about Morenci by word of mouth. Pedro Gómez's grandmother and uncle migrated there in 1910 by way of El Paso, where they stayed for a time. The Gómezes lived in the scorpion-infested El Seis in structures made from cheesecloth with no bathrooms. The whole family bathed on Saturday, and the children attended segregated schools.[5]

Mexicans lived close to the Italians and the Spaniards, most of whom were unmarried males, as were most Euro-Americans in Morenci. In time of crisis, Mexicans were vulnerable because many had their families with them. Euro-Americans, Spaniards, and Italians, having no families, were more mobile and could devote more of their earnings to accumulating capital.

After a fire in the late 1890s, Morenci was rebuilt — that is, all but the Mexican section, where Mexicans continued to live in adobe huts. In the beginning, Mexicans paid rent for the land where they built their huts.

Superintendent Charles E. Mills made sure that "Americans" had access to better housing. Detroit Copper supplied housing for white families and deliberately segregated both housing and workplaces. Even the showers were segregated into the 1950s. In 1900, a Morenci masquerade ball was an all-white affair, at which Miss Ella Parker dressed as a Mexican peasant. E. L. Griswold came as a Mexican gentleman, C. E. Vanling as a black man with a razor, and A. Schwarg as a "Chinaman."[6]

The social lines were blurred between Christians and Jews, on the one hand, and between Catholics and Protestants, on the other — that is, unless you happened to be Mexican or a person of color. The white elite recognized Jewish merchants as leaders. Louis Ferber, a prominent Jewish merchant, opened a brokerage house in Clifton. Sam Abrahams's hotel was the headquarters for many of the elites. His wife, Laura Abrahams, was not Jewish. Intermarriage between Jews and non-Jews was common, the white and Mexican communities accepting Jews as white. Because of their money and because they identified with the norms of the white community, the Abrahams were also accepted into white society. Louisa Gatti was identified as Italian and listed in the census as "Luchia" even though born in Arizona, supposedly of German parents. Her husband, Jonn Gatti, was an Italian immigrant with pretensions to French ancestry. Although working-class, the Gattis had money, hence were considered white.[7]

The Mexican men who labored in the mines also built the company houses, where their women worked for twenty-five to fifty cents a day. Mexicans owned fewer businesses in Morenci than in Clifton. To keep its Mexicans happy, Detroit Copper paid for a Christmas celebration in the central plaza below the club, hotel, and the company store. The celebration usually featured a Mexican band and spotlighted Mexican leaders close to the company. But Mexican food was not served at these events since it was considered vulgar.[8]

The more Mexicans in a mining camp, the less was spent on education. Clifton allocated nearly ten dollars per student, whereas Morenci, whose students were predominantly Mexican, allocated just over five dollars. Clifton had four elementary schools: the North Clifton school had a mixture of races, segregated in separate classrooms; South Clifton had an all-white school; and Chase Creek had one Mexican and one white school. Yet, in 1905, even Mexicans voted not to consolidate the schools.

As the towns modernized, segregation became more rigidly observed. Few Mexicans attended white schools, and then only for the first three grades. The area had no high schools. Whites formed segregated clubs, fraternal organizations, and saloons on the eastside and in South Clifton. There were also formal public balls for whites that upper-class Mexicans attended. Mexicans held dances, more often in the open, which were internally segregated by class. The Mexican elite less frequently mixed with the white elite at their own large formal events. The social life of many of the Mexican elite revolved around Tucson.[9]

Mexican wages lagged well behind those of their Euro-American counterparts. In 1909, most Mexican-born workers earned $1.50 a day; fewer than 2 percent earned $3.00 a day. Most white workers earned at least $2.50 and many earned more than $4.00. The wage differential prevailed into the 1940s. The changing rooms were separate and unequal with Mexican miners crowded two to three to a locker. Even U.S.-born Mexicans were simply listed as "Mex." It was common to secure work through labor brokers, who always took their cut of the workers' pay. The Mexican worker had to go to the labor brokers for special requests such as a day off to attend to a sick child. These brokers lent workers money at high interest, and pressed them to buy chances in lotteries that never paid off.[10]

Although most male Mexican immigrants worked as miners, some got jobs as clerks. Mexican women worked as maids and cooks. Throughout the latter part of the nineteenth century, the Mexican middle class failed to support working-class struggles, generally accepting a racially stratified society as normal, showing little desire to challenge or even question white hegemony, and considering themselves superior to the socially inferior Mexican workers. In fact, many openly opposed the workers' rebellions. Only discrimination against them as Mexicans mattered.[11]

Mexican miners and their families from neighboring New Mexico, Chihuahua, and Sonora frequently left for home after three months' work. They would visit their families for a time before returning to the mines. Quitting was a form of protest. Miners were a source of pride for their families back home, and they would frequently send photos of themselves dressed in suits. Most miners who could afford to brought their families to the camps.

Although Mexican mine workers generally could not vote, or did not even if they could, 45 percent of registered voters in Clifton, Morenci, and Metcalf in 1894 had Spanish surnames. In the early 1900s, Mexican workers read the Spanish-language newspaper *El Obrero*, while white Republicans read the *Copper Era*. During this period, the courts generally favored the interests of larger white farmers and ranchers at the expense of smaller Mexican ones.[12]

Ranchers and farmers joined together to limit the dumping of slag and tailings from the mines into the streams. When the townspeople sought to incorporate Clifton, however, Arizona Copper opposed them. It was not until 1909 that the townspeople prevailed. At issue was whether the company would pay its share of taxes.[13]

Mexicans patronized their own bars on Chase Creek. Even Italians learned the value of being white, distancing themselves from Mexicans. Alcoholism became a major problem, not just in Clifton, Morenci, and Metcalf but in all the mining camps. In a letter to the *Miners' Magazine*, the secretary of the Ray miners' union, W. S. Crowe, complained that saloons, where unions were forced to meet for lack of halls, were getting to be too numerous and too rowdy at night — indeed, that "the saloon is the worst enemy the working man has."[14]

By the turn of the century, the Arizona's Chinese population had thinned out. Where, in 1883, the Chinese comprised a quarter of workforce, by 1900, fewer than seventy Chinese remained, mostly serving the mining communities in menial occupations, such as produce farmers, cooks, and laundry workers, where they were subject to constant abuse.

Light-skinned Mexicans sometimes joined Spaniards and darker-skinned Europeans as Euro-Latinos. Although most Euro-Latinos were Catholics, few went to church. They considered the Catholic Church a Mexican church. Some Italian and a few other non-Mexican surnames appeared in the Sacred Heart parish records. Euro-Latinos were the last to be included as white, which was not an option for Mexicans in white men's camps. Italian miners in Morenci more often lived in Mexican than in white neighborhoods. Intermarriage between Mexicans, Spaniards, and Italians was common.

In Clifton, there was some intermarriage between working-class whites and Mexicans. It was seen as a chance for Mexican women to move up the social and economic ladder. In 1900, two-thirds of Mexican women who intermarried in Clifton and Morenci married white males who earned better pay than Mexicans did. Of every six Mexican women who intermarried, three lived in the Mexican barrios, two in mixed neighborhoods, and only one in distinctly white areas. Color mattered less to men not climbing the social ladder. Mexican women often assimilated white standards of beauty, and wanted their children to be light-skinned. They gained a reputation for being both extraordinary housekeepers and more submissive than white women.[15]

Before the turn of the century, Mexicans ran most, if not all, of the businesses that supplied mining camps with vegetables, meat, flour, dairy, wood, water, liquor, tools, and so on. By 1904, Euro-Americans had taken over these enterprises. Mexicans had to turn to less lucrative pursuits, working as barbers, shoemakers, grocers, peddlers, and sellers of water and firewood.

There were exceptions, of course. Primitivo Medina prospered as a rancher and dairyman on the spread he bought from the brother of Sheriff Jim Parks. A group of Mexican landowners in the Gila River Valley built a toll road from Solomonville, charged travelers ten cents per horse or wagon, and sold them food and water. Arturo Elías, half brother of Plutarco Elías Calles and a naturalized U.S. citizen, became a merchant and later a porfirista consul and government spy. With the triumph of the Revolution of 1910, he landed on his feet and worked for the constitutionalists. Several Mexicans who worked as foremen or labor contractors were regarded as "better-class Mexicans" or "Spaniards" because "Mexican" by itself meant "poor, ignorant, and degraded."[16]

The Irish Union

Arizona's first mining strike took place in Tombstone in April 1884, when miners, told their wages would be cut from four dollars a day to three, refused to accept the cut. In May, the companies closed the mines, called for troops from Fort Huachuca, and planted a spy in the union. At first popular and receiving outside support, the strike was eventually broken when the townspeople withdrew their support, forcing the workers to accept the three-dollar daily wage.[17]

Born at Coeur d'Alene, Idaho, in 1892, the Western Federation of Miners (WFM) earned its reputation for militancy at Cripple Creek and Leadville, Colorado, in 1894 and in 1896, the year the WFM formed its first local in Arizona — at Globe. Managers responded by dismissing anyone who joined. Globe was a white men's camp. When workers struck against wage cuts in 1896, management brought in Mexicans to replace the strikers. The union promptly blamed the Mexicans for depressing wages. And when the strikers got a small raise, the Mexican miners were discharged. The Globe Miners' Union hall, built in 1900, became the center of union activity and bigotry for the town.

Located in the middle of the San Carlos Reservation, Jerome employed a thousand miners. In 1900, a 518-member union was formed at the Verde Mining Company around the campaign for the 8-hour workday. By 1903, skilled or crafts workers in Globe-Miami, Bisbee, and Jerome had joined unions affiliated with the American Federation of Labor (AFL), whereas unskilled white workers belonged to the Western Federation of Miners, which had withdrawn from the AFL in 1897, after only a year.[18]

It would have seemed a natural for the WFM to recruit Mexican workers. Like them, the Irish immigrants who dominated the union had a history of oppression, and they were also Roman Catholics. But the Irish leadership neither supported nor attempted to recruit Mexicans. Instead, the WFM spread the myth that, being a rural people newly arrived from a nation of peons, Mexicans could not become good union members because understanding trade unionism was simply beyond them.

Formed in Butte, Montana, in 1878, the Butte Miners' Union was, by 1900, the largest local labor union in the world. Conditions in Butte were so stark that an Irish priest wrote to his mother "there is not a tree nor a shrub nor a blade of grass up here but all the wealth is underground." But miners there were paid more than those in Arizona, earning $3.50 for a nine-hour shift, double what most industrial workers earned and more than double the Mexican rate in Arizona. By 1905, Butte had a red light district second only to New Orleans.

Irish immigrants entered the United States in three main waves: 106,000 between 1845 and 1849, another 1.1 million between 1848 and 1854, and 3.1 million more between 1856 and 1921. Each succeeding wave was more Catholic and more politicized than the previous one. Believing they had been driven from their homeland by English treachery, the new immigrants formed Irish fraternal organizations, which expressed their rage, found them jobs, and facilitated their social mobility. While these organizations helped, in the end most Irish mine workers were muckers — men with shovels.

In the early 1880s, Irish miners had drifted into Butte, drawn to the Anaconda properties, developed by Marcus Daly, an Irishman who converted Anaconda from silver to copper. Daly was the first president of Anaconda Copper Mining Company. He joined Irish associations and paid for churches and purposely blurred class lines by contributing to workers' funds. In 1892, Daly paid $10,000 to bail out Peter Breen, an Irish attorney and Butte Miners' Union officer, accused of murder and conspiracy in Coeur d'Alene. In 1894, he sided with workers in the Great Northern Railroad Strike. Daly guaranteed Irish workers jobs; they could not be persuaded he was an evil man.

The Roman Catholic clergy who missionized the Mexicans of Arizona were foreigners. John Brondel Bishop of Montana went to Ireland for priests. Bishop Brondel regularly ordered parish priests to take up collections for Ireland. The Sisters of Charity trained Irish minds. However, there were divisions among the Irish by 1910. The younger generation was more radicalized by revolutionary events in Ireland. A division occurred within the Irish fraternities that were dominated by nationalist and better-off Irishmen. These organizations, like the Mexican mutualistas, were conservative and cooperated and collaborated in controlling the community's radicalism.

WFM militants knew that Daly controlled the Butte Miners' Union and, in 1902, moved the WFM headquarters to Denver. Four years later, the Butte leadership accused the WFM of radicalism and bolted the convention.

The Catholic Church actively resisted the radicalization of the union, which had close ties to Irish nationalist organizations. Irish American Bishop of Montana John Carroll regularly denounced socialism and labor radicalism. Carroll branded the Industrial Workers of the World (an offshoot of the WFM, founded in 1906) as socialist and anti-God. For its part, the WFM regularly took the Catholic hierarchy to task in the pages of the *Miners' Magazine*. During this period, there is no evidence the prelates sought to bring social justice to the Mexicans they missionized.[19]

Teresa de Urrea and the Revoltosos

Even before the 1903 strike, Clifton, Morenci, and Metcalf were centers of labor militancy. Mexican political exiles would regularly recruit followers there. This came as no surprise: Phelps Dodge owned properties in northern Sonora as well. Personages such as Teresa de Urrea, popularly known as "la Santa de Cabora" or "la Niña de Cabora," sought the protection of friends in Clifton-Morenci-Metcalf's large Mexican community. Although Teresa did not engage in revolutionary activity while at Clifton, her father and his father's common-law wife and confidante, Gabriela Cantúa, lived there. It was also headquarters for the Partido Liberal Mexicano (PLM) activists and revolutionaries such as Práxedis Guerrero and Manuel Sarabia, who lived in Morenci, and they organized in Clifton-Morenci-Metcalf camps.

Teresa, the natural child of Cayetna Chávez, a mestiza, and Tomás de Urrea, was born on October 15, 1873, in Ocoreni, Sinaloa. Tomás was a member of a prominent Sinaloan and Sonoran family. When Teresa's mother disappeared, she went to live with her father. Political problems with the governor of Sinaloa led the two to move to Tomás's hacienda in Cabora, Sonora, in the mid-1880s. Teresa suffered her first seizure at the age of 16, and appeared to be dead for fourteen days. Thereafter, she was reputed to have healing powers. Thousands of adherents visited Cabora. She is reported to have cured many, winning a huge following among the indigenous and poor people.[20]

Millenarian movements among the natives of Sinaloa and Sonora flourished at the time. Many believed that the end of the century would mark the return of Christ to bring justice, annihilate hostile powers, and take them to his kingdom on earth. Due to the horrendous state of affairs caused by the Yaqui wars, millenarianism was especially attractive to the tribe. Government officials became suspicious and sent spies to Cabora. Dozens of other saints roamed among the Yaqui and Mayo. One such saint was Damián Quijando, a youth of 16. Natives abandoned their haciendas and pueblos to listen to Quijando, who, like John the Baptist, spoke in the name of God and the Santa de Cabora.

On May 15, 1892, shouting "¡Viva la Santa de Cabora!" the Yaqui attacked San Ignacio and Navojoa. Teresa was arrested on May 19, 1892, when an army of five hundred federal troops arrived in Cabora, expecting to engage an army of insurgents. Instead of seditious literature, they found prayers and other orations. Teresa was taken to Guaymas under arrest.[21]

Upon her release from jail in Guaymas, Teresa and Tomás fled to Nogales, where Tomás asked for the protection of the U.S. authorities. Also in Nogales was Lauro Aguirre, who had fled to Sonora as well. A spiritualist and friend of

Tomás, having worked for him as a construction engineer, Aguirre was fascinated with Teresa's mystical powers and considered her a medium. Aguirre wielded considerable influence over both the Urreas. Meanwhile, news of Teresa's presence in Nogales spread. Pilgrims traveled hundreds of miles on foot to see her, alarming the Díaz government, which realized that the mob could be dangerous. The Mexican consul at Nogales, Arizona, asked Mexico City to intervene. Meanwhile, within five months of the Yaqui revolt, 1,500 federal troops laid siege to Tomóchic in the Sierra Tarahumara of Chihuahua, wiping out the village of 350. Although there is no direct link between the Tomóchic revolt and Teresa, she had become increasingly critical of the clergy for charging parishioners fees. The clergy, in turn, had preached against her. In April 1893, a second rebellion occurred, this time at Temósachic, and again the battle cry was "¡Viva la Santa de Cabora!"[22]

Meanwhile, Lauro Aguirre, 33, who himself was a member of the Methodist Church was in touch with other insurgents. Many Protestants joined the insurgent ranks when Díaz resurrected many of the Catholic Church's privileges. On April 6, 1895, Teresa was reported to be living in El Bosque, Arizona, ten miles from Nogales.

The Urreas moved to San José, near Solomonville, around 1896. Rumors surfaced that Teresa de Urrea was leading an assault on Mexico. In March 1896, the *Los Angeles Times* traced the rumors to Lauro Aguirre's *El Independiente*. Aguirre had published the paper for a short time but left for El Paso, after a fight with the printer, Pedro de la Gama. Hounded by the police and the Mexican government, the Urreas followed Aguirre. El Paso was a den of political intrigue, and Aguirre fell in with the Victor Ochoa cabal. Ochoa had been sent to prison the year before and, like Aguirre, become obsessed with the brutality of Tomóchic. U.S. officials described Teresa as a "young Mexican without education and ignorant."[23]

Meanwhile, on July 12, 1896, a band of forty U.S.-based Mexicans unsuccessfully attacked the customshouse at Palomas. Upon returning to the United States, they were arrested. U.S. officials investigated Tomás and Teresa on suspicion of violating U.S. neutrality laws. The Mexican government pressed for extradition. Copies of *El Independiente* were found on the bodies of rebels at Ojinaga and Palomas with orations to Teresa. Even after the U.S. crackdown, the conspirators continued to meet in the home of Tomás.[24]

Another invasion took place in Nogales, Sonora, on August 12, as rebels attacked the customshouse there. Mexican authorities rushed sixty members of the rural constabulary under Colonel Emilio Kosterlitsky from Magdalena by train to Nogales. Fourteen were killed in the raid and the rebels retreated to the U.S. side, where a posse chased them. A news account read: "The Yaquis seem to be crazy on account of the fanatical worship of Santa Teresa de Cabora. On the body of one leader were found a picture of the saint, tied in ribbon, and a half dozen copies of *El Independiente*, published at El Paso by Lauro Aguirre."[25]

Although the Urreas denied any involvement, they must have known about Aguirre's political use of Tomóchic and Teresa. On August 21, Teresa wrote that, since her exile, every revolution had been attributed to her. She was blamed for revolts in Oaxaca, Guerrero, Durango, Veracruz, Guanajuato, Jalisco, Michoacán, and Coahuila.[26]

U.S. marshals cooperated with Mexican Consul Francisco Mallén and kept the Urrea home in El Paso under surveillance. On October 30, Pomposo Ramos Rojo living under the name of Antonio Altamirano was arrested, along with Francisco Ledesma, at Las Cruces. Without much prodding, Ramos Rojo became an informer and confessed to everything. (Also present was the notorious Patrick F. Garrett, Sheriff of Dona Ana County). The informer implicated the Urreas and Lauro Aguirre. According to Ramos Rojo, a Señor Izaguirre was the revoltosos' (insurgents') agent in Ciudad Guerrero and was sent money by Aguirre and the Urreas. The plan was to attack Nogales, Palomas, Ciudad Juárez, and Nogales.

The Mexican government hired the Thomas Furlong and Pinkerton Detective Agencies to spy on dissidents. In all, 180 political refugees were returned to Mexico. Ansel T. Samuels, who sold advertising for *Regenerción*, spied on the group. After hounding Aguirre, Consul Mallén bribed U.S. Marshal George Scarborough to deliver him to Mexico.[27]

Ramos Rojo boasted that he could infiltrate the Urrea home in El Paso at will. The Mexican consul already had the Urrea home under surveillance. On November 1, 1896, Ramos Rojo met with William L. Rynerson, and planned how to get proof on the so-called conspirators. The plan was for him to infiltrate Aguirre's cabal. Ramos Rojo left Marfa on November 19 for Shafter, Texas, arriving on the 30th, where he learned of another conspiracy. According to Ramos Rojo, he was in touch with an informer, who told him the group was planning a raid on Ojinaga. The informer later named members of the crew and tied them to Teresita. The Díaz government continued to press for the Urreas' extradition, which probably would have succeeded, had it not been for favorable press coverage.[28]

By 1897, the Urreas, accompanied by heavily armed bodyguards, moved to Clifton, where the father established profitable dairy and firewood businesses. A news account reported that Tomás and Teresa's brother would go to work in the mines of Morenci. It was rumored that Aguirre would soon join them. In Clifton, Teresa gained notoriety as a healer, and became the darling of whites, who invited her to dinner.

In 1900, Teresa married Guadalupe Rodrigues but divorced him when he turned out to be a Díaz agent assigned to lure her back to Mexico. Rodrigues took Teresa away from her family to Metcalf, where he shot her and threatened to kill her family. Rodrigues was arrested and returned to Clifton. Don Tomás died in 1902, leaving a wife in Sinaloa and a partner in Clifton. The Rodrigues affair had alienated father and daughter. Teresa went on tour and held rival meetings in other parts of the country, not returning too Clifton until the autumn of 1904, shortly after the "great Arizona orphan abduction," in which white vigilantes forcibly abducted white babies adopted by Mexican families from their homes. Teresa used her money to build a two-story hospital, but her curative powers had diminished. She died in 1906.[29]

Tomás's common-law wife, Gabriela Cantúa, is listed as his actual wife in the 1900 U.S. census, and he was evidently devoted to her. This longtime union produced many children, whose descendants live in the Southwest. Gabriela was the daughter of Ramón Cantúa, a Sonoran vaquero. She lived with Tomás at Cabora. In all probability, she was close to Lauro Aguirre, who spent time at Cabora building Urrea an irrigation system. Urrea brought Gabriela and their children to the United States soon after he arrived there. He remained married to his wife in Sonora, although his marriage does not seem to have been a meaningful relationship. One biographer speculates that Tomás never made a complete break with his family, and this prevented him from declaring for a revolution, because he feared that Díaz would confiscate his Sonoran properties, leaving his family without support.

It should not be assumed, however, that Urrea or anyone else opposing Díaz was necessarily a radical. Many across the political specturm opposed Díaz's policies, which were becoming ever more oppressive. Thus many old, conservative families in Sonora opposed Díaz for tolerating, if not actually supporting, the excesses of Corral, Izabal, and Torres. There is evidence that Gabriela was close to Teresa and that Gabriela's children considered Teresa an aunt or first cousin. Be that as it may, it seems clear that Gabriela prepared the way for the Mexican Revolution.[30]

The 1903 Strike

The Clifton-Morenci Strike of 1903 was a defining moment in the history of Mexicans not just in Arizona but in Mexico itself. It was linked to the Cananea Strike of 1906, a precursor to the 1910 Mexican Revolution. This strike was Mexican made and was not — as reported in many history books — supported by the Western Federation of Miners. True, there were a few inclusionists who urged the WFM to organize the Cananea camp — but nothing more. For the next decade, the union leadership would debate whether they were advanced enough to organize there. A prime example was Bill Moyer, who later became president of the WFM. Moyer purposely dragged his feet even though he knew it was in the best interest of the union to organize Mexicans. Indeed, a close reading of the *Miners' Magazine* and the proceedings of the WFM during the decade shows a deep antipathy toward Mexican miners within the union's rank and file and even its leadership. Its involvement in Clifton, Morenci, and Metcalf was minimal. On the other hand, the union's racism and history of isolating the Mexicans only contributed to Mexican solidarity.[31]

In 1903, the Arizona legislature passed a labor-sponsored law establishing an eight-hour workday, a practice already in place in white mining camps. Mexicans worked ten hours a day for $2.50. The mine owners argued that, if they reduced the Mexicans' workday by two hours and paid them the same daily wages, it would amount to a 25 percent pay hike. So the mine owners cut the Mexican workers' wages by 10 percent.

On the morning of June 3, three days after the law went into effect and management announced its pay cut, one source reported that 3,500 workers went on strike.[32] The number was probably closer to 1,500 strikers, 80 to 90 percent of whom were Mexican, mostly U.S.-born. Jeanne Parks Ringgold, granddaughter of then-Sheriff Jim Parks of Clifton, would call the strike the "bloodiest battle in the history of mining in Arizona." The mining companies stonewalled the strikers.[33]

The *Bisbee Daily Review* of June 3, 1903, reported: "The Mexicans belong to numerous societies and through these they can exert some sort of organization and stand together." Initially, there was cooperation among the Mexican, Italian, and Spanish workers. The strike leaders were Abrán (sometimes called Abraham) Salcido, from Camargo, Chihuahua, who was president of a Mexican society;[34] Frank Colombo, an Italian; and Weneslado H. Laustannau and A. C. Cruz, both of whom were Mexican, although Jeanne Parks Ringgold called "Jack Laustenneau" a "half-breed Spaniard." The Yuma Territorial Prison cemetery records list him as "Laustannau," also known as "Three-Fingered Jack." Fellow miners called Laustannau "el Negro," "Three-Fingered Jack," and "El Mocho."[35]

On June 5, the *Bisbee Daily Review* observed, "the strike is now composed almost entirely of Mexicans. Quite a number of Americans have left." During the strike, tempers and racial animosities flared. Parks Ringgold admitted that "existing conditions were deplorable," and that the company did not furnish the Mexican workers locker rooms. "After the men came off shift in the mines, they had to walk over the hills to their homes in their wet working clothes, even during the cold winter weather."[36]

The managers notified Sheriff Jim Parks, who lived in Solomonville.

Strike leader Abrán F. Salcido, who was sentenced to two years in prison and fined $1,000. (Courtesy of the Yuma Territorial Prison State Historic Park)

Strike leader Weneslado Laustannau, sentenced to two years in prison and fined $2,000. (Courtesy of the Yuma Territorial Prison State Historic Park)

Parks's family was from Kentucky. W. John Parks, the youngest of the clan, and father of James Parks, moved first to Missouri, then to Texas, where he married. Traveling along the Rio Grande, W. John's family moved to New Mexico and settled in Silver City in 1879 because of a drought. They stayed in Lordsburg for two months, where James started a meat packing business but moved to the Duncan area soon afterward.

In the 1880s, James became a deputy in Solomonville. The ranchers with large land and cattle holdings like Jim Parks and his brothers George and Deputy Sheriff John Parks possessed the only economic interest that could challenge the mining interests. Cowboys and shopkeepers resented the mine owners' arrogance and felt that they did not pay their fair share of taxes. Jim himself distrusted men behind desks, and the mine owners distrusted Parks.[37]

When Parks's posse arrived in Clifton and then Morenci, it found that the mine owners had drawn the proverbial line in the sand. Parks and his thirty-two deputies tried to mediate. He reportedly told Phelps Dodge Superintendent Mills that many of the workers' demands were reasonable. The Mexican miners were underpaid and their living and working conditions deplorable. Meanwhile, Thiel Detective Agency spies infiltrated the strikers.

Mills and Colquhoun pressured the governor to call in the Arizona Rangers. Arizona legislators were aware of the new militancy among miners of all colors, and passed a special law in 1901 that created the Arizona Rangers, who closely resembled the Texas Rangers. By 1903, the rangers had grown to a squad of twenty-four, headed by Captain Thomas H. Rynning. This was their first strike-breaking assignment. They arrived by special train early on the morning of June 8.[38]

Rynning had been a second Lieutenant in the Rough Riders and had served with Roosevelt in Cuba. Born in Norway in 1866, he immigrated to the United States when he was two years old. Rynning had fought the Apache and helped chase Sitting Bull. He was full of himself and would later become involved in other strike-breaking activities.

What happened depends on who is telling the story. According to J. H. Bassett, one of the fifteen or sixteen rangers at Clifton, Sheriff Jim Parks of Graham County and the rangers stayed in Morenci for four or five days and shared the space with National Guard and U.S. troopers. As Rynning tells it, the strike leaders were a "wild bunch of killers and cattle thieves," who threatened the sheriff and his men. They were led by el Mocho, "which is Mexican for 'crippled hand,'" Rynning explains. "He'd been an Austrian army officer." Rynning claims to have hit el Mocho, stepped on his revolver, and hollered out orders to Parks.[39]

Afraid for his life, ex–Rough Rider Mills left Morenci at 2:00 a.m. on June 7, for El Paso. The strikers interpreted Mills's departure as a signal that he would not negotiate, which only increased their resolve to prevent scab labor from crossing their lines.

On the morning of June 9, the deputies on the Longfellow incline could see hundreds of strikers gathering at a lime quarry and the Mexicans from the Metcalf mine coming by the hundreds down Metcalf Canyon on their way to quarry. When 2,000 miners assembled, speaker after speaker mounted a boulder to address the crowd, which yelled and cheered, waving red flags. After the demonstration, strikers began gathering in front of the Longfellow company store. According to Ringgold, "The strikers were well armed, more or less drunk, and in a dangerous mood." John Parks and Dave Arzate, an Italian who could talk "good Mexican," went to meet the strikers. When they reached the ridge, they saw that the miners had white men in custody.

Reportedly, the Deputy Sheriff Parks had pushed into the crowd, when he noticed Dave was not following him. The miners had issues with the Italian. Paul Nicholas, superintendent of the Longfellow Mine, came to the store early, and "knowing that they [the Mexicans] were drunk and desperate, he locked the store, went into the tunnel at the rear of the store, and closed the tunnel door." Laustannau agreed to let Nicholas go to Clifton to talk to Morenci officials, promising to use his influence with the supervisors. Arzate, who had been taken prisoner, was released on Laustannau's orders.[40]

About 10:30 a.m., the strikers scattered and went home. They waited for deputies to go eat before suddenly coming out of every quarter of Morenci and Longfellow. Meanwhile, the sheriff and his deputies, backed by the National Guard and the Arizona Rangers, readied themselves. According to Jeanne Ringgold, Rynning panicked and turned tail. John Parks wanted to move on to Morenci, but Rynning insisted that they would be massacred.[41]

Tensions remained high as 2,000 workers staged a one-hour demonstration in direct defiance of the Rangers and in the midst of a torrential rainfall that had suddenly started. The workers marched down the streets of Clifton in the driving rain but were forced to disperse when water rushed down the mountain-sides, ripping through Clifton and flooding many of the strikers' homes. The water rose to a height of ten feet, causing $100,000 worth of damage. The rains killed thirty-nine people, mostly women, children, and the elderly and mostly Mexicans. However, this did not totally destroy the strike, and as a result, Sheriff Parks wired the governor requesting more help. The governor rushed federal troops to the strike-bound district, followed by six companies of the national guard.[42]

Thus the flood, and not the overwhelming show of force, ended the strike. A confrontation would have in all probability occurred, had not the rains been so devastating. The Clifton strike had all of the makings of the Ludlow Massacre, which would occur less than a dozen years later.

The damage was compounded by the negligence of the mining companies. The Arizona Copper Company mill was on the Longfellow side. Beyond it, down in Chase Creek Canyon, were a tailings dump and a tailings dam. When Arizona Copper's tailings dam could not hold the floodwaters, $100,000 in damages resulted. John Gatti chaired the citizens' committee, and no Mexicans were on the negotiating committee. Some leaders and workers continued their resistance, meeting at a lime pit, only to be dispersed by the army. By July 1, the cavalry was still in Morenci, and the good white citizens tried to establish their own cavalry under A. M. Tuthill, a Detroit Copper physician. Phelps Dodge and Arizona Copper made some concessions, giving the Mexican workers changing rooms and a small raise. They also established a blacklist and permit-ted their foremen and managers to charge workers 5 to 15 percent for housing, obtaining jobs, and other services. Many Mexicans quit in disgust and left the area.[43]

Abraham Salcido, Frank Colombo, Weneslado H. Laustannau, and others were convicted of inciting a riot. Laustannau died in the Yuma Territorial Prison under suspicious circumstances. Out of 112 deaths, Laustannau's was the only death from heat prostration.[44] Phillip Mellinger points out that many strikers were longtime residents of Clifton, Morenci, or Metcalf. Half of those living in Clifton were homeowners. Morenci was a company town and consequently all the property belonged to the company. The Detroit Copper payroll for May 1903 showed that 384 Mexicans, 54 Italians, and 79 Euro-Americans and Irish worked at the mine. Nearly two-thirds of the Mexicans earned less than thirty cents an hour, whereas only 20 percent of the Italians and 1 percent of the whites fell into this category. Laustannau, a Sonoran, and Salcido, a Chihuahuan, belonged to mutualistas. Salcido was the president of a mutualista. Other leaders were, for the most part, literate. However many states the rank and file were from, most of the leadership came from northern border states, preponderantly from Chihuahua.

During the strike, the managers called Arturo M. Elías, a merchant in Solomonville, to Clifton to mediate. Elías met with Charles Mills. Some Mexican workers believed the Mexican government would intervene on their behalf, which was highly unlikely given that the United States cooperated with Díaz in keeping an eye on Mexican exiles. Elías was a key player in the surveillance and harassment of Mexican exiles.

A. L. Solis wrote to Díaz complaining about the injustice suffered by Mexican and Italian workers. Solis wrote that Abraham Salcido was the leader of the miners. According to him, Wensesloa Laustannau spoke good English and knew the law. The miners were peaceful and Laustannau told them not to fire unless fired upon. Mills became very aggressive when the Arizona Rangers and the National Guard soldiers arrived. Laustannau went Clifton to see Colquhoun but was detained by police. The strikers had high expectations when Elías arrived. After secreting himself with the mine owners for an entire day, however, Elías went to the home of the elder Canuto Vargas and told the strikers there that the company had expenses. Elías advised them to return to work. Solis speculated that Mills had paid Elías off. The strike leaders were taken to Solomonville, where Elías spoke to them. Solis wanted protection for them and was also writing to the governor of Sonora.

Elías denied that Mills had bought him off. He said that the Mexican strikers were violent and had taken unarmed deputy sheriff David Arzate prisoner. For this reason, the government sent the militia to Clifton-Morenci-Metcalf. Laustannau was a U.S. citizen and thus no concern of the Mexican government. Elías claimed that Salcido, A. Caballero, and Rafael Váldez were not Mexican citizens. Mills told him he could not pay the same daily wages for only eight hours' work. According to Elías, none of the strikers were Mexican citizens. The Mexican minister of foreign relations dismissed the charges against Elías because of an alleged lack of evidence.[45]

Salcido had been in the Clifton-Morenci-Metcalf area since he was twenty-two. He was president of the Alianza chapter there, and Laustannau was vice president of the same chapter, which listed Italian-surnamed members. The strikers were dependent on the mutualistas for meeting places. Among the Mexican males, 22 percent were registered voters in Clifton-Morenci. Many Clifton voters voted socialist in 1904. When the army occupied the area, the authorities banned workers' meetings, which the strikers protested as a denial of their rights as American citizens. The strike raised fears among the mine owners. James Douglas had called a meeting of owners, and they colluded to hold the line on wages for workers. The mine owners knew that the Mexican strikers would not receive outside assistance. Even though the strike transformed the image of Mexicans among the workers, the WFM was stll not ready to accept them as brothers. A *Miners' Magazine* review of the situation in Arizona from November 12 to December 31, 1903, says not one single word about Mexican workers.[46]

Salcido is listed on the 1900, or twelfth, U.S. census of Morenci as "Abrán Salcido."[47] He was born in 1874, was single, and shared a home with two other men. He and his parents were born in Mexico. Arriving in Morenci in 1896, Salcido worked at the smelter. Pedro Subia, the Mexican striker murdered in the 1933 San Joaquin Valley Cotton Strike, who we know from other data was from Camargo, Chihuahua, is listed on the 1900 census as being about the same age as Salcido.[48]

Subia lived in the same precinct as Salcido, listed as born in 1873. His wife, Francisca, was born in 1879 in Arizona. Her father was from Texas and her mother from New Mexico. However, her death certificate lists her as born in Mexico. In 1900, Francisca and Pedro had a son, Ramón, born in 1899 in Arizona. According to the census, Pedro arrived in the United States in 1894 (his son said he arrived in 1891). Francisca died of influenza at the age of forty on March 16, 1919, during pregnancy. The probability that Salcido and Subia knew each other is very high. Morenci was no New York.[49]

◀ 7 ▶

Mexican Miners

By the twentieth century, the corridors to and from eastern Arizona had lit up like a pinball machine. A logical source of institutional support at the end of the corridor was the Catholic Church. But, like the unions, it was headed by Europeans, who were culturally, racially, and linguistically different from Mexicans, the majority of Catholics in the region. The entire territory of Arizona, divided by the Church into three regions, was served by twenty-eight missionaries. Most of the priests were non-Mexicans, who felt that the Mexican "half-breeds" and the Indians in their parishes had to be protected from the heathens, that is, the Protestants. Most were put off by the isolation of the mining camps. They found life in Clifton-Morenci-Metcalf to be Third World, if not the end of the world.

In February 1904, Father Constant Mandin replaced Father Peter Timmermans, who had returned to Belgium for a time because of ill health. Speaking little English and limited Spanish, the twenty-five-year-old priest relied on a handful of devoted Mexican women for assistance in carrying out his duties. Shortly after his arrival, Father Mandin read a circular to his mostly Mexican parishioners. It was from the Catholic-run New York Foundling Hospital (NYFH), asking good Catholics to adopt Irish orphans. The parishioners said, yes, they would, and agreed to adopt forty of the orphans.

On October 1, 1904, some sixteen months after the Clifton-Morenci Strike of 1903, three nuns and four nurses got off the train from New York at Clifton with forty Irish orphan children in tow. The children were part of a group of

THE PRETTY AMERICAN CHILDREN WHO WERE
RECOVERED FROM MEXICAN HOVELS IN
MORENCI, ARIZ., WHERE THEY HAD BEEN
PLACED FOR ADOPTION.

The New York foundlings. (From Leslie's Weekly, *Oct. 27, 1904, as reproduced in*
Brophy, Foundlings on the Frontier, *52)*

fifty-seven orphans brought to the Southwest by train to Clifton and by stage to
Morenci. Their arrival touched off a violent reaction from the white citizens of
the mining camps.[1]

According to the Arizona Supreme Court case, which would make its way
to the U.S. Supreme Court in 1906, "good American citizens, moral [who] had
no children of their own" were infuriated when they learned these white children were going to "half-breeds."[2] An angry white mob in Morenci threatened
to lynch the priest. Armed with buckets of tar and feathers, rope, gasoline, and
Winchester rifles, and egged on by the women, the white men of Clifton
marched on the Mexican barrio of North Clifton to "rescue" the blond orphans.

Phelps Dodge enforced a strict policy of racial separation. Superintendent
Charles E. Mills stood behind the "good American citizens." A bachelor pa-
triarch, whom the miners called *patrón* or *mayordomo*, Mills was still smarting
from the humiliation of the previous year. In 1898, he had resigned his job to ride

with the Rough Riders in Cuba. Investments in mining and banking had brought Mills considerable wealth and he prided himself in knowing his Mexicans.

Mills told George Whitney Swayne, the Foundling Hospital's agent, that Mexicans "were indigent, had no trade, no means, and did not draw sufficient salary to support families or educate them either; that they didn't educate their own . . . that five or six of them would stop in the same room. . . didn't even have a bed to sleep in."[3] He pressured Swayne to reassign the children. Refusing to cooperate at first, Swayne eventually struck a compromise, parceling out some of the children to white families but allowing none to remain with Mexicans. Numbed with fright, Sister Michaella bowed to Mills's bluster and gave an orphan to Dr. W. F. Davis, a longtime Morenci physician and friend of Mills.

One of the nuns told the *Tucson Citizen* that the Morenci women "called us vile names, and some of them put pistols to our heads. They said there was no law in that town; that they made their own laws. We were told to get the children from the Spaniards and leave by Tuesday morning. If we did not, we would be killed."[4]

The Graham County Probate Court granted guardianship of the orphans to the vigilantes. The state Supreme Court later accepted John Gatti's allegation that the New York Foundling Hospital had "abandoned [a particular orphan] to the keeping of a Mexican Indian." The hospital "conceded that a great blunder was committed in the . . . delivery of the children to these degraded half-breed Indians."[5] Its only concern was that the orphans would be raised Catholic.

For his part, however, Tucson Bishop Henri Granjon saw the vigilante activity as an affront to the Catholic faith. He fumed that the Foundling Hospital had made Father Mandin the fall guy and had chosen a young and inexperienced lawyer to defend the Church's interests. He feared that the New York Chancery was advising the sisters to drop the case, sacrificing the interests of Arizona Catholics, most of whom were Mexican. "How hollow are the claims of superiority of the so-called Americans who objected to the children being placed in Mexican families," the bishop went on. "A girl was given to a divorced Jew, another to a saloon keeper and gambler; a man and wife, both Mormons, obtained a little girl."[6]

On October 16, 1904, in an editorial titled "Foundlings in Arizona," the *New York Times* that said the nuns should have known better. They were naive in not anticipating the reaction of the white Euro-Americans. "The point is that to hand an American child over to a 'greaser' to be reared was to assure that the child should become a foreigner of a particularly undesirable type."[7] The *Times* hoped the nuns had learned their lesson.

On October 22, 1904, Mariano Martínez of Benson, Arizona, responded to the editorial: "I believe that you, being a true American, love truth and justice

NEW YORK ORPHAN CHILD IN A FULL-BLOOD MEXICAN FAMILY IN ARIZONA. HALF-BREED NEGRO CHILD (AT RIGHT) ONE OF THE WOMAN'S FAMILY.

Mexican family, racist headline. (From Leslie's Weekly, *Oct. 27, 1904, as reproduced in* Brophy, Foundlings on the Frontier, *70)*

above everything [and would want] to know the truth." The Mexican families were carefully selected, he explained. "The priest did his duty without race prejudice." He read the circular sent by the Foundling Hospital in both English and Spanish. Martínez took issue with calling the mob "American" because most so-called Americans in Arizona could not vote. "Probably the only claim you have to call them 'Americans' is that they have blue eyes, red hair, a face full of freckles, and long feet." In contrast, the " 'low down' Mexicans whom you refer to are nearly all native-born American citizens and voters, as the great register of Graham County will prove." Martínez concluded that his parents were born in the territory and that he was born and raised in Tucson but that the editorial made him rethink whether he was an "American citizen" after all.[8]

At trial, the white witnesses called the Mexican women whores. The court allowed hearsay tales of liquor given to the children. Louisa Gatti, a crude and uneducated woman, when asked to describe the Mexican women, replied that they had "dirty faces, and wore black shawls over them and they had ragged dresses on." When asked if she knew the Mexican women personally, she answered "No, sir. There are so many Mexican women around there, I don't know one from the other . . . they are Indians; they are not real Mexicans."[9]

One the nuns told the *Tucson Citizen*: "Some of the children were taken to refined, dependable, prosperous Spanish people, whose homes were neat and clean."[10] Virginia and Silvestre Galván, for example, had been married for twenty-four years. Silvestre had arrived in Arizona in 1869 and worked as a stage driver and saloon keeper. The couple had three teenagers. Five of their ten children had died. Roja Guerra, a fifty-year-old widow, ran a seventeen-room boardinghouse. She had five grown children. Abigail, 47, and Andrés de Villescas, 51, were a stable couple. He worked at the smelter. They had two grown children, who were not living with them. Lee and Refugia Windham were one of few mixed couples. Lee was a registered voter, 36, and worked for a smelter. Although they had once simply lived together, they were married when they applied for adoption. Yet the white community insisted on calling Lee's wife "his Mexican woman." Father Timmermans described Refugia as a good woman "living a good life."[11] Angela Flores had recently married her longtime partner, Juan Esquivel, who now called himself John Maxwell. Son of a Euro-American and a Mexican woman, John worked at Shannon Copper concentrator and made three dollars a day. He was from New Mexico and she from Texas. Baleria and Ramón Balles, married nine years, were childless, as Baleria was infertile. Ramón finished school in Clifton. They lived in a frame home.

Francisco Alvídrez, a smelter worker was married to Trancita. His son Frank became a businessman and political big wheel. Francisco was the first Mexican to join the Elks in the 1950s. His sixty-year-old father, a registered voter, lived with them. Josefa Holguín, a dressmaker, was married to Rafael Holguín, a skilled worker. Josefa was born in Mexico, and he in Texas. Married for two years, they were childless. Rafael had attended elementary school in Clifton and was a registered voter. He was on a select list of Mexicans whom James Colquhoun invited to his functions.[12]

Interpreter Margarita Chacón, 24, was born of German and Mexican parents, and Her maiden name was Margaret Miller. Raised in an El Paso Catholic orphanage, she was Father Mandin's assistant. Her husband, Cornelio Chacón, 42, whom she had married in El Paso six years before the abduction, had fled Mexican debt peonage for the United States. Mrs. Chacón gave religious and basic writing classes in Spanish and English in her home. Highly religious, she arranged for the placement of the orphans, met them at the train station, and stayed with them at the church. Despite overhelming evidence of their status in the community, all the women were presumed to be whores.[13]

Indeed, the Mexican parents never had a chance to refute charges against them. Not one was allowed to testify. On November 16, 1904, Judge P. C. Little denied the Foundling Hospital's petition and gave the Clifton white parents guardianship. In the end, the U.S. Supreme Court dismissed the Foundling Hospital's appeal, noting that, of the forty children, nineteen had been taken out of the Foundling Hospital's jurisdiction.[14]

The white women felt it was their duty to save the kids. One of the orphans reportedly begged her adoptive parent, "Won't you watch me so the Mexicans can't get me?" However, it is not the Mexicans that she had to fear. One of the "good people" raped a twelve-year-old adoptee.[15]

The Revoltosos

Meanwhile, resistance to Porfirio Díaz was growing in Mexico. Political exiles who crossed into the United States were attracted to the large Mexican populations of places such as Clifton-Morenci-Metcalf.[16] These exiles were seeking not only safe havens but also money, arms, and recruits. The militancy of Clifton's Mexican miners in 1903 did not go unnoticed. By this time, forerunners to the Mexican Revolution could be found in U.S. cities and towns reading their newspapers in the plazas of most of the larger Mexican barrios. They gathered together to form revolutionary groups, chief among which was the Partido Liberal Mexicano (PLM), headed by Ricardo Flores Magón (1873–1922).[17]

Arrested in Mexico for political activities, upon their release in 1904, Ricardo and his brother Enrique migrated to San Antonio, where they resumed printing *Regeneración*. Harassed by Díaz's and U.S. federal agents, they moved again, to Saint Louis, Missouri, where they again published their newspaper and issued a manifesto calling for revolution. By 1905, they had followers in Douglas, Arizona, as well as in Cananea. They also had supporters in Morenci among disaffected miners. Indeed, in 1905, Consul Arturo M. Elías recommended that the Mexican consular office be moved from Solomonville to Clifton due to the large "seditious" population there. Among the Magones' sympathizers was Práxedis Guerrero, who had read the PLM's 1905 manifesto

Ricardo Flores Magón. (Courtesy of the Yuma Territorial Prison State Park)

and contacted the party's Junta Organizadora. A worker at the Detroit Copper Company, Guerrero, in collaboration with Manuel Sarabia, who also operated out of Morenci, established Obreros Libres in Morenci in June 1906.

A year before the Cananea Strike of 1906, *magonistas* organized the Club Liberal "Libertad." Lázaro Puente operated out of Douglas and founded branches of the club in Tucson, Metcalf, and Clifton. Key to the exile strategy was the Arizona-Sonora mining triangle. Douglas had railroad links to Cananea and Nacozari, where there were also large caches of arms and money, on the Mexican side. Bisbee had links to Morenci and Tucson on the U.S. side — as well as to the growing Mexican population in the Salt River Valley and Phoenix.

The Mexican workers moving up the Sonora corridor to Arizona joined with those moving up the Camino Real corridor to Chihuahua and then west through New Mexico to Arizona. A Chihuahua employer complained that, of 8,000 workers arriving from Zacatecas and central Mexico, within a year, 80 percent had moved to United States.

Plácido Ríos regularly traveled to Douglas to confer with members of the Club Clandestino and Club Liberal "Libertad" there. The Douglas revoltosos coordinated events in the triangle. Ríos fled to Douglas after the Cananea strike and became secretary of the Revolutionary Junta that planned the September 1906 invasion of Sonora.[18]

Released from the Yuma Territorial Prison in early 1906, Abrán Salcido became a member of the Partido Liberal Mexicano. On May 5, 1906, he gave a fiery speech before 2,000 mine workers at Metcalf, calling Porfirio Díaz a traitor, a tyrant, and a thief. The crowd went wild, but the mine owners and the

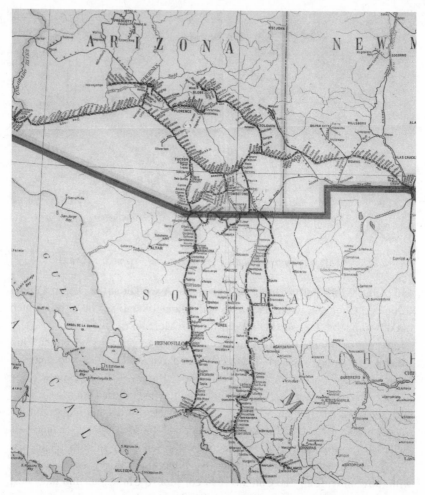

Railroad networks that knit together Arizona and Sonora. (Detail of Union Pacific and Southwestern Pacific Systems *map, Union Pacific Railroad Company, 1911; reproduced by permission of The Huntington Library, San Marino, California)*

Mexican consul forced him to leave the mining district. Salcido then went to Douglas, although some say he returned to Cananea.[19]

The Douglas revoltosos, who had links to the El Paso cabal of Lauro Aguirre, worked throughout the mining districts of Arizona and Sonora. The group also had contacts with Práxedis Guerrero and Francisco Manríque, who had established the Club Liberal "Libertad" in Morenci. The home of Modesto Díaz in Morenci's Chihuahuita was a gathering place for the rebels, who ran arms into Mexico through contacts in Ciudad Juárez. The spy Quirino Maese turned the plans of the El Paso cabal over to Juárez police. Captain Adolfo Jiménez Castro and Lieutenant Zeferino Reyes set a trap for the rebels, gaining their confidence by promising to surrender a garrison to them.

The Club Liberal "Libertad" circulated propaganda throughout Arizona and Sonora in 1905. Clubs also operated in Hermosillo, Cananea, Nogales, and Sahuaripa. In the spring of 1905, the Douglas club sent Antonio P. Araujo, Enrique Bermúdez, and José López to Cananea. Plácido Ríos made frequent trips to Douglas to buy arms and spread propaganda. Bermúdez published *El Democrata* in Douglas, and Fernando Palomares, a Mayo and member of the PLM, worked in Cananea. After the 1906 strike, he went to Arizona, where he continued organizing. The group initially planned a general uprising for June 30. Palomares had connections with the Yaqui and Mayo.[20]

Araujo also distributed *Regeneración* in Cananea. Araujo, along with Lázaro Puente and Tomás Espinosa, organized the Club Liberal of Douglas. Journalist José Bermúdez, Enrique's brother, also operated in Douglas. By May 1906 Enrique was in Cananea, publishing the radical newspaper *El Centenario*, which reprinted material from *Regeneración*. Luis G. Monzón, a teacher from San Luis Potosí, had been a member of the Club Verde in Sonora and later worked with the Cananea-Douglas cabal.[21]

By early 1906, Estebán B. Calderón and Manuel M. Diéguez were in contact with the magonistas' Saint Louis junta. Calderón later recalled that he arrived in Cananea in March of 1905 without the proper clothing and was helped by a "humanitarian Chinese gentleman," who gave him a warm coat and lodging. He contracted pleurisy and had to go to Buenavista, a mining camp halfway up the sierra, to rest. While there, Calderón began reading *Regeneración*, which, along with conditions at the camp, politicized him.

In October 1905, Francisco Ibarra introduced Calderón to Diéguez. Together with Francisco M. Ibarra and thirty miners, they formed the Unión Liberal Humanidad in January 1906, a secret cell with ties to the Saint Louis junta. The members later formed the Liga Minera de los Estados Unidos Mexicanos. In March, Diéguez received a letter from Ricardo Magón, telling him that he had heard about tensions in Cananea and requesting more information to publicize the cause in *Regeneración*. Three days later, Diéguez and Calderón received a letter of apology from the Revolutionary Junta, who were afraid the article they had published would increase Mexican government harassment.[22]

By the end of April, the Unión Liberal Humanidad had organized the *junta patriótica* for the Cinco de Mayo celebration at the Buenavista camp. *El Centenario* covered the event. Diéguez was president of the Patriotic Society and Calderón, the secretary. The May issue of *Regeneración* wished the organizers well. The committee invited Lázaro Gutiérrez de Lara as a speaker and Professor Amado Cota Robles recited the poem "¡A las Armas!" Calderón delivered a lengthy and explosive speech, which began on a solemn note and ended passionately. Calderón told the group that it was a disgrace that in their own land the capitalists used them as beasts of burden. Invoking the issue of racism, he made a veiled call to arms.[23]

Soon afterward, Gutiérrez de Lara formed the Club Liberal "Libertad" of Cananea in the colonias of Mesa Grande and El Ronquillio. On May 12, 1906, *El Centenario* published Calderón's speech. On May 20, the president of the Municipio de Cananea informed Governor Rafael Izabal about the existence of the two liberal clubs and ordered an investigation. At El Capote mine on May 26, members of the PLM unsuccessfully tried to persuade Diéguez and Calderón to postpone the strike until June 15, to coordinate strikes with miners at other mining camps, most notably, Rosa Morada and Nueva Rosita in Coahuila, Avalos in Chihuahua, and Santa Rosalía in Baja California.[24]

The Cananea Strike of 1906

Consolidated Copper's Bill Greene owned the hospital, the schools, the Café de Cananea, the hotel, the bank, the company store, and most of the property surrounding Cananea. Campesinos, hacienda peons, small property owners, day laborers, displaced farmers from all parts of Mexico mingled together in Cananea. Anti-American feelings were high and in January, the U.S. consul reported a hesitancy on the part of Nogales merchants to sell to U.S. citizens. Tensions between the races were not new. In 1899, a fight had broken out after a baseball game in which four were killed and one was wounded. According to news reports, cowboys were poised on the border to invade Naco, Sonora. Things got so bad that the U.S. consul called for state troops.[25]

Cananea was about twenty-five miles south of the border. Part of a network of towns running through the north-south corridor, it was linked to Arizona copper as much as it was to the center of the state. The Río Sonora rose south of Cananea, near the Mexican-U.S. border, and flowed southward. Below Hermosillo, the river crossed the coastal lowlands and emptied into the Gulf of California opposite Tiburón Island.

Bill Greene's Consolidated Copper Company, which received generous grants, owned 37,000 acres (15,000 hectares) of mineral lands, 350,000 acres (142,000 hectares) of timberland, and thirty miles of railroad connecting Cananea and Naco. Everything within ten square miles of Cananea, which had a population of some 25,000, belonged to Greene. The Cananea Mine employed 5,360 Mexicans as miners and 2,300 foreigners, mostly Euro-Americans, as managers and administrators.

On the evening of May 31, two foremen at the Oversight Mine told the workers that, as of June 1, they would be working by piecework contract, rather than on salary. The next morning, the Mexican miners walked off the job, demanding five pesos for an eight-hour workday. They carried signs saying, "¡Cinco pesos y ocho horas de trabajo! (Five peso for eight hours of work!) ¡Viva México!" "El pueblo obrero" (The Worker Community). They wanted equal pay and the opportunity for promotion. William Green armed his Euro-American workers and asked the Mexican state for help. In the early afternoon, workers marched through the streets of the town.[26]

Strikers marched to the Cananea Copper lumberyard, where they invited workers to join them. The Metcalfs, uncle and nephew, fired on the workers, who responded by burning the lumberyard and killing the Metcalfs and another Euro-American. Governor Rafael Izabal panicked and allowed some 275 Euro-Americans, Rynning's Rangers, under Captain Thomas Rynning to enter Sonora. General Luis Torres gave an ultimatum to miners — go back to work or get drafted into the army. The general arrested a hundred men and sent dozens to prison. Colonel Emilio Kosterlitsky entered Cananea and came into immediate conflict with Rynning's Rangers, who shot at and wounded one of his troopers. Hysteria gripped the U.S. side.[27]

Governor Izabal blamed the Magones. Greene blamed the Western Federation of Miners. The *Los Angeles Times* on June 2 announced: "Americans Killed in Mexican Race War." According to the *Times*, refugees were pouring into Naco, Arizona, and "liberated" Euro-Americans were telling graphic stories of rioting. "Forty-five Americans Killed," the *Times* headline ran. Mexicans, it would seem, had wiped out the entire Cananea police force.

A frantic consular agent at Nogales, W. J. Galbraith, sent a telegram to Washington, "Send assistance to Cananea. American citizens being murdered" and Mexicans were dynamiting Euro-American property. On the next day, Galbraith praised the "brave American boys of the camp." On June 3, Vice Consul Albert W. Brickwood Jr. sent yet another telegram, claiming the strikers had killed four Americans and martial law had restored order. Brickwood kept asking permission to go to the battlefront. He maintained that Americans and law-abiding Mexicans welcomed the American volunteers. He went to Cananea and praised the Euro-American volunteers for their restrained behavior.[28]

What Caused the Rebellion?

According to W. Dirk Raat, the Western Federation of Miners organized a local in Bisbee in the spring of 1906. Joe Carter, the union's organizer, distributed literature and money to agitators in Cananea and Nacozari. Although Norman

A gathering of smelter strikers in front of the Cananea Copper general office on June 1, 1906. (Courtesy of the Arizona Historical Society/Tucson, no. 97311)

Caulfield contends that WFM organizers in 1906 were cooperating with the PLM at Cananea, there is no hard evidence of this, and it is unlikely the WFM played any role in the organization of Mexican workers. Since the mid-1890s, Aguirre and others had led raids on Mexican soil. Opposition to the Díaz regime was mounting. Labor dissidents, some of them veterans of the Clifton-Morenci Strike of 1903, joined forces with the revoltosos — they were not waiting for the WFM or the Saint Louis junta to organize them. Rising nationalism, industrialization, the obvious disparity in treatment of Mexicans and Euro-Americans at the mines made choices clearer to Mexican workers.[29]

Another instance of the disparity was that Euro-American miners were paid in dollars, but Mexican miners were paid in pesos. In 1905, Mexico had devalued the peso by 50 percent, while wages remained the same. A rise in the cost of living and a drop in price of silver worsened conditions. Mexicans working side by side with Euro-American miners received only one-third as much in wages, on top of which they had to pay inflated prices for food staples imported from the United States.[30]

The Douglas Connection

By 1903, Phelps Dodge had linked by rail Douglas, Nacozari, Bisbee, and El Paso, which helped connect their Liberal Clubs with one another and with others in the lower Rio Grande Valley, from Del Rio, Eagle Pass, and Laredo to Brownsville.[31] Douglas served as a staging area for activities in Cananea and Nacozari, and was tied by railroad lines to El Paso and Del Rio on the U.S. side and to Agua Prieta, Cananea, and Nogales on the Mexican. It was in Douglas, shortly before the 1906 strike, that Mexican authorities shut down Enrique Bermúdez's newspaper *El Azote* (The Whip) for libeling the Mexican vice consul there. Tried and convicted in Hermosillo, Bermúdez was briefly jailed. Upon his release in the spring of 1906, he began editing *El Centenario* in Cananea. Meanwhile, Lázaro Puente formed the Club Lerdo de Tejada in Douglas, which had three hundred members and links to Clifton and other mining camps. On July 3, 1906, revoltosos formed the Mutualista Obreros Libres in Morenci, with Práxedis G. Guerrero as president and Agustín Pacheco (a government spy) as treasurer. Mexican secret agents kept the groups under strict surveillance.[32]

By June 1906, groups had been organized in Solomonville, Clifton, Mowry, Morenci, and Metcalf. The Douglas group, consisting of some three hundred partisans, with Tomás R. Espinosa as president and Luis García and Abrán Salcido as officers, appointed Javier Guitemea delegate to the Yaqui and Mayo nations. Born on a hacienda, Guitemea had worked on the railroad, traveling to the Nacozari and Cananea mines and to El Paso. In 1900, he worked in the smelters of Douglas, not returning to Sonora until 1908, as a member of the PLM.[33]

By late August 1906, the revoltosos prepared to invade Sonora. Clifton-Morenci-Metcalf was one of the bases of operation for the September 1906 events. Manuel Sarabia and Práxedis Guerrero were both active in Clifton-Morenci-Metcalf, and received their mail there. A secret junta in Morenci sent operatives to Metcalf to inform the partisans there.

With Cananea authorities close on his heels, Plácido Ríos fled to Douglas and hid out among partisans. Ríos was no stranger to the town, having runs arms between Douglas and Cananea before the 1906 strike. During the Revolution of 1910, Juan G. Cabral and Salvador Alvarado would also recruit miners for their army in Ray and Tucson. The Saint Louis junta kept in close touch with Douglas and with groups along the border network. Making visits to Cananea, Salcido operated openly in Douglas, where he associated with Bruno Treviño and Plácido Ríos.

The Douglas group held meetings at a halfway house called Oro Plata. Government spies reported the presence of José Treviño and Abrán Salcido, whom they characterized as having bad reputations. Clifton and Morenci were under constant surveillance. Spies reported on armed groups of Mexican miners leaving the district. Although the *Morenci Leader* expected problems on Mexican Independence Day, 6,000 attended the celebrations without incident.[34]

The insurgents planned the invasion for September 1 but postponed it to October 5. However, in mid-September, fifty agents surrounded the home of Luis García and arrested eighteen rebels. Rynning played a role in the raid, as did Douglas Sheriff Sam J. Hayhurst and U.S. federal agents. They made twelve arrests and issued fifty warrants. Among those arrested were Tomás Espinosa, Rubio Gabriel, Luis Garcia, Ildefonso Martínez, and Lázaro Puente. Identifying Tomás Espinosa as the chief conspirator, the *Los Angeles Times* described him as "a repulsive little fellow with ape-like features, blear eyes, negro lips, unwholesome skin and hands like claws."[35]

Defendants Gabriel Rubio, Tomás D. Espínosa, Miguel Godínez, Refugio Mascarenas, Elephonso Martínez, Guadalupe López, and Eugenio Soto were charged with violating U.S. neutrality laws. E. C. Becher testified he saw Abrán Salcido and Eugenio Soto at the meetings. The court sentenced Espínosa to two years in the Yuma Territorial Prison, and Luis García and Gabriel A. Rubio were handed over to Mexican authorities.

When arrested, Salcido confessed his revolutionary activities and was turned over to Mexican authorities. He was fined 1,000 pesos and sentenced to eight years and eighty days in the dreaded San Juan de Ulúa Prison. He had already spent two years in the Yuma Territorial Prison.[36]

By the end of September, Manuel M. Diéguez, Estebán B. Calderón, and Plácido Ríos had been arrested in Sonora and sentenced to fifteen years in San Juan de Ulúa. Luis G. Monzón, director of the School for Boys in Moctezuma, who would play an important role in the Constitutional Convention of 1917 at Querétaro, was arrested in Douglas. A member of the Club Lerdo de Tejada and one of the few communists among the Mexican revolutionaries, Monzón escaped and returned to Moctezuma, where he continued to work in education and prepared for the revolution.[37]

Greene continued to be obsessed with the PLM. Through the Furlong Detective Agency, he hounded Ricardo Magón and forced him to flee with Modesto Díaz to El Paso, where Ricardo Flores Magón, Juan Sarabia, Antonio I. Villarreal, and Librado Rivera secretly met at the home of Lauro Aguirre. On September 1, 1906, Magón, Villarreal, and Rivera were arrested and charged with conspiracy to violate U.S. neutrality laws.[38] Villarreal escaped and made his way to Sacramento, California.

Hired by Greene to shadow the Revolutionary Junta in Los Angeles, the Furlong Detective Agency worked closely with two Mexican American Los Angeles police officers, who, on August 23, 1907, arrested Magón, Rivera, and Villarreal in their house on Pico Street. The officers discovered a cache of mail from anarchists all over the world, including Emma Goldman.

The PLM defendants stood trial in Tombstone, Arizona, for the 1906 con-

Tomás D. Espinosa, 39.
(Courtesy of the Yuma Territorial
Prison State Park)

spiracy to violate U.S. neutrality laws. Some 1,800 supporters attended a Los Angeles rally for "los tres." Representing Mexico, Consul Arturo Elías used private detective Manuel Peña del Pino and, through him, Miguel López Torres in Clifton to gather evidence. Elías pressured U.S. Attorney J. L. B. Alexander and the sheriff of Graham County to hound other PLM members. The U.S. government actively participated in this violation of civil liberties, allowing the private detectives access to postal records. In August 1910, after the defendants had spent two years in jail, it took the jury eleven hours to find Ricardo Flores Magón, Antonio I. Villarreal, and Librado Rivera guilty.[39]

A Return to Clifton-Morenci-Metcalf

The years 1905–07 saw a transformation in the consciousness of Mexican workers and a number of white union organizers. The formation of the IWW initially pushed the WFM to the left, bringing IWW organizers such as Fernando Velarde into the field in April 1906. Velarde was prepared to organize Mexicans in Arizona, New Mexico, and Mexico and was preparing a manifesto. But less than two years later the WFM split into syndicalist, moderate, and socialist wings and thus began a fight that ten years later would force the WFM to grudgingly accept Mexicans into its ranks. The greatest change, however, was among the Mexican miners. The 1903 Morenci Strike had forced them to accept more direct forms of action to achieve parity. White-Mexican tensions in Cananea and the 1906 strike politicized them, as did the response of Arizona/Sonora copper barons as they moved aggressively to control the labor process through classifications, technology, and a homogenizing of skills. The activity of the PLM and the revoltosos cannot be discounted in this dialectic, and a majority of white organizers saw the broader picture.[40]

WFM organizer Marian W. Moor was aware of the transformation. In 1905 he said, "I would suggest that the W.F.M. as soon as possible secure a man to act as organizer who can talk Mexican and Italian and keep him busy in Arizona and Southern California," where Mexican and Italian workers would join by the hundreds and make good members. The next year, Moor went to Clifton to investigate labor conditions. In a letter to WFM president Charles Moyer, he wrote that the mining camps were in the absolute control of the companies that owned everything, including the government and the militia. He noted that Fernando Velarde was a tireless organizer. Despite this and individual efforts, the WFM leadership remained ambivalent about organizing Mexicans. In contrast, the companies actively recruited supervisors who could handle *their* Mexicans.[41]

The Clifton-Morenci-Metcalf complex was second in economic importance only to Bisbee. The mining corporations' control permeated local businesses, churches, schools, and law enforcement: they built YMCA buildings, supplemented the preachers' salaries, paid the salaries of schoolteachers and principals, appointed the sheriffs and justices of the peace and paid their salaries. They owned the streets, roads, halls, and parks. They had the power to permit or deny free speech.[42]

In July 1907, the Arizona Copper Company smelting plant was shut down by a strike of 140 mostly Mexican employees. Wage increases at Globe had motivated the workers. According to the *Los Angeles Times*, the men refused to affiliate with the WFM and even ousted Frank Little from a strikers' meeting. The failed strike, which lasted a few weeks, did not affect Arizona Copper's 4,000 miners. Then Southern Pacific workers in Tucson struck, which caused an exodus to the mines of Sonora. By this time, the telegraph connected the principal towns of Arizona, increasing the flow of information and ideas.[43]

By November, the bottom fell out of the economy, and the copper mines closed down, beginning a period of consolidation of capital and the beating down of wages. Only a few months before, it had been difficult to find miners. The shutdown affected 30,000 people. In Sonora, the *Los Angeles Times* reported, "American miners are coming across the border by the trainload and many Mexicans will be drafted into the interior for work upon railroad construction." A retrenchment took place in Bisbee, but no further reductions at the Copper Queen were predicted. At Clifton, the price of producing copper even from low-grade ore was low because of the low wages paid Mexican workers.[44]

High unemployment made the Mexican miners likely recruits for the rebels. Even those who were still employed were still underpaid, as the mining companies rode out the depression on the backs of their mostly Mexican workers. The depression underscored the injustices reported in rebel newspapers. In Clifton, an era ended with the resignation of Arizona Copper's James Colquhoun on December 6, 1907. Few could foretell that, within a dozen years, Phelps Dodge would gobble up Henry Lesinsky's old company.

Vice Consul Isidro Romero, the Revoltosos, and the Spies

On June 5, 1907, Agua Prieta's commandant of police, Libero Vásquez, wrote the secretary of the State of Sonora in Hermosillo that a band of Mexicans had left from Clifton for the frontier. The Mexican minister of foreign relations told the chief of the customshouse at Fronteriza to set up surveillance. Often spies worked for government and mine owners alike. For example, Agustín Pacheco, 45, from Zacatecas migrated to Chihuahua in 1883, and then to Morenci in 1892, where he spied for the Detroit Copper Company. Pacheco was outed and expelled from the Clifton Mill & Smeltermen's Union Local 158. A founding member of the Mutualista Obreros Libres of Morenci in 1906, Pacheco would later testify for the government against the revoltosos.[45]

Mexico's consuls generally ignored U.S. abuses of its citizens. Vice Consul Isidro Romero was an exception. Graham County Sheriff A. A. Anderson complained to Consul Arturo M. Elías about Romero. In February 1907, Romero had wired the governor, charging that Anderson was giving Charles Wright, who had killed a Mexican by the name of Luján, special treatment. Romero demanded that Justice of Peace Smith keep Wright in solitary confinement, and that Officer John Patty be discharged because he had taken Wright from the jail to his saloon on Chase Creek without shackles. Anderson's lack supervision gave Wright the opportunity to escape.[46]

Romero complained that Euro-Americans who committed violent crimes against Mexicans were allowed to wander about unrestrained. Deputy Sheriff Len Scott allowed a man who raped a Mexican woman on September 16, 1907, to go free altogether. Then, on December 26, Scott assaulted Abraham Rico of Morenci publicly without provocation. (Rico was probably the Abraham Rico involved in the 1903 strike and active in the PLM.) In January 1908, Romero demanded that Scott be dismissed, and threatened that, if he did not get justice, Mexicans would take matters into their own hands. Anderson accused Romero of being a meddler and of taking graft. On February 8, 1908, Justice of the Peace Smith also complained about Romero, who "believes we do not know anything regarding the United States Laws"[47]

Mexican spy Salvador Martínez del Toro and Mexican Consul Arturo M. Elías actively shadowed the magonistas. In July 1908, Elías wrote El Paso Consul Antonio V. Lomelí that Clifton, Morenci, and Metcalf were centers of revolutionary activity — and particularly the Metcalf home of Ramón Treviño, brother of Leocadio Treviño, one of the main revoltoso leaders. There was great interest in Ramón because he was married to the sister of Teresita (Teresa de Urrea). Elías alleged that Treviño had assaulted the customshouse at Nogales with Lauro Aguirre and been involved in the Tomóchic revolt. Elías speculated that Treviño, released from jail on July 7, might have been in communication with Lauro Aguirre. Elías also mentioned that other key revoltosos were in the Clifton-Morenci district. Elías urged Consul Lomelí to send him evidence of wrongdoing by any of the men mentioned in the report, so that he could have them prosecuted. Inés Salazar and Angel Salazar also lived in Metcalf. Mexican authorities were preparing charges against Lauro Aguirre, whom they had linked with the Morenci cabal.[48]

In August, Graham County Sheriff Munguia asked a Señor Lugo to spy on the house of Treviño. The authorities were interested in Ramón and his brother Leocadio, who allegedly had participated in the PLM's June 28 attack on the town and customshouse of Las Vacas on the Texas-Mexico border. Some fifty magonistas, including Práxedis Guerrero, José Salazar, and many other residents of the area, took part in this bloody but unsuccessful encounter. Del Toro wrote that it was common knowledge that all Mexicans in Morenci and Metcalf had guns in their homes. Del Toro was making sweeps of South Clifton with Sheriff Munguia. Munguia then sent Señora Micaela Delgado to the home of Señora de Urrea in Clifton. Señora Delgado was well received. She reported who was there and that the magonistas were directing operations from Morenci and Metcalf, leaving instructions with Señora de Urrea. An attack was planned for September 15. Del Toro wrote that "The house of Señora de Urrea is in a neighborhood called 'La Barranca' or 'Chihuahua,' not very far from a house that Vice Consul Romero frequents almost every evening."

According to del Toro, Nepomuceno Ríos had given Reynaldo Ornelas money for the Revolutionary Junta in California. He also mentioned that Inés Salazar had written his wife to sell their home in Metcalf and go to Zacatecas. Meanwhile, a group of revoltosos left for Agua Prieta. The Sonoran secretary of state was told that Teléforo Ortega Salazar was returning to Mexico, where Douglas Consul Luis E. Torres wanted him arrested. Torres emphasized the urgent need to keep watch on Clifton and Morenci. Reports continuously repeated that Práxidis Guerrero, a delegate of the Los Angeles junta, was a resident of Morenci. Correspondence said that Guerrero had been involved in the 1906 conspiracy at Douglas.[49]

The huge role that Teresa de Urrea's stepmother, Gabriela Cantúa, played in preparing the way for the 1910 Revolution has been almost entirely overlooked by historians. In 1908, Gabriela was living in Clifton with her eleven children and grandchildren.[50] Del Toro notes in his August 26 report that she had for a long time had "seditious sympathies." Revoltosos met at Gabriela's house, and many of them received their orders through her.

By 1909, Vice Consul Romero had become a liability to the Díaz administration, which was seeking greater cooperation with the United States. By mid-March, Romero was reassigned to Amapola. As soon as he left, he was accused of having ties with the revoltosos. Carlos Palafox of Clifton wrote the secretary of foreign relations that, when Romero failed to pass information on to authorities concerning the rebels, Palafox had concluded he was their friend.

Originally, the consular service had sent Romero to Morenci-Metcalf in 1906 to investigate the activities of the Douglas conspirators. When Abrán Salcido, Juan B. Treviño, Fernando Muñoz, and Juan Muñoz left Metcalf, Romero identified them as members of the PLM. Felix Rubalcava, also a member of the PLM, migrated from Morenci to Aguacalientes. Romero noted that Práxedis Guerrero was president of the Mutualista Obreros Libres in Morenci. Given the quality of his 1906 report, we must conclude that Romero was loyal to the Díaz government at the time. Once appointed vice consul, however, a change in his behavior becomes apparent. We can also speculate that Romero's financial problems may have played a role in this change.[51]

The Surveillance of Morenci Continues

As mentioned, Morenci was a center for revolutionary activity. Different organizers met, developed relations, and collaborated there. Manuel Sarabia, who recruited Práxedis Guerrero for the PLM, had been in contact with Douglas, Arizona, since 1905. Along with Manuel Vázquez, Sarabia and Guerrero founded Mutualista Obreros Libres in 1906. By the spring of 1907, Guerrero was in Douglas and had become a member of the Supreme Junta. In June he moved to Bisbee, where he met with Sarabia, and lived in the same house. In 1908, Guerrero, as second in command of the junta, would move to El Paso.[52]

Meanwhile, U.S. authorities cooperated with Enrique Creel, who directed the spy activity at the highest levels. Captain Harry Wheeler arrested Manuel Sarabia in Douglas, and abducted him to Sonora. Sarabia's arrest and abduction triggered effective protest campaigns to get him back. Luis Torres and Wheeler arranged his return. At the end of August 1907, Thomas Furlong located Ricardo Magón and had him arrested, along with Rivera and Villarreal. Gutiérrez de Lara was also arrested on trumped-up charges, detained for three months, then freed on $3,000 bail, a fortune at the time. The Mexican government attempted to extradite him, without success. Juan Sarabia was arrested in Chihuahua, convicted of sedition, and sent to San Juan de Úlua Prison.[53]

Heavy surveillance continued throughout 1907, and Mexican officials targeted Práxedis Guerrero. Investigating possible violations of U.S. neutrality laws in Phoenix at the behest of the Mexican Embassy in Washington, D.C., Special Agent John C. Wallis of the Department of Justice found evidence of a conspiracy. Meanwhile, del Toro infiltrated the union at Morenci, disguised as a worker, and sent Detective José Gonzales Carrillo to Clifton to work with Deputy Sheriffs Len Scott and Muñoz.

Agustín Pacheco, acting as a spy for Chihuahuan authorities, reported that revoltosos left Morenci on July 10, 1907, from the home of a "Don Miguel." In Tucson, Arturo M. Elías continued to play a pivotal role in gathering intelligence.[54] Detective José González Carrillo and other government spies reported the movement in and out of the mining camp. Scott and Munguia monitored the mail and newspapers from Mexico and locally. The surveillance paid off.[55]

By September 1908, the surveillance had intensified. The Mexican government prepared Agustín Pacheco to testify against Magón, Rivera, and Villarreal, who were held incommunicado. The authorities also wanted to know the whereabouts of Guerrero and Inés Salazar, who they suspected were in Cananea. At their trial in Tombstone, the three defendants were first charged with plotting to assassinate Díaz. Labor lawyer W. B. Cleary of Tucson handled their defense. The proceedings were a tumultuous trial: at one point, the Villarreal sisters jumped to their feet and called the prosecutor a liar. The jury convicted the three of violating U.S. neutrality laws and sentenced them to eighteen years in the Yuma Territorial Prison.

As expected, in 1908, there were uprisings along the border in Chihuahua, Sonora, Coahuila, Nuevo León, and Tamaulipas. Key to the success of the rebellion was a Yaqui revolt, which never materialized. Ricardo Magón would write: "We are poor Mexicans. We are revolutionaries and our ideas are very advanced but we are Mexicans. This is our fault. Our skins are not white."[56]

In March, Guerrero had instructed Javier Guitemea, 40, a bachelor and laborer from Hermosillo, to return to Sonora and seek an alliance with the Yaquis. When he crossed the border, Guitemea (also spelled with an *H*) came under suspicion when Mexican inspectors found a rifle and ammunition in his luggage. He also had a copy of the revolutionary plans of the PLM, various other letters linking him to Manuel Sarabia and Guerrero, and plans for inciting the Yaquis. The Mexican court sentenced Guitemea to six years and eight months in prison.[57]

The planning was hatched in El Paso's Chihuahuita barrio, and a rendezvous house was designated on the corner of First and Tays Streets. Práxedis Guerrero and José Inés Salazar led the magonistas. When, hoping to enlist their assistance, Consul Antonio Lomelí told U.S. marshals that Villareal and Guerrero were in El Paso, they replied that the two had departed for Los Angeles.[58]

On June 18, in what appears to be coordinated raids, Mexican authorities raided the magonistas in Casas Grandes, Chihuahua. On June 23, Texas Rangers raided the home of Prisciliano G. Silva in El Paso and seized 3,000 rounds of ammunition and important documents, which listed PLM cells within Mexico, and which identified Benjamin Silva, José María G. Ramírez, León Cárdenas, Enrique Bermúdez, Manuel and José Aguilar as members of the cabal. U.S. authorities immediately handed these documents over to the Mexican government. Despite the setback, the revoltosos crossed the border on the night of June 24–25, taking the town of Viesca, Coahuila. Led by Práxedis Guerrero, Benjamín Canales, Encarnación Guerra, and Jesús M. Rangel, they then attacked the town of Las Vacas, Coahuila. Guerrero retreated to El Paso. On July 1, Guerrero, his neighbors Enrique Flores Magón and José Inés Salazar, and his close friend Francisco Manrique attacked Palomas, Chihuahua, and Manrique was killed in the assault.[59]

In Douglas, Práxedis Guerrero contacted Jesús M. Rangel and planned a third uprising. They recruited and raised money from the mining camps. Meanwhile, military authorities alerted U.S. troops at Fort Huachuca, Douglas, Naco, and Nogales. U.S. Consul Luther Ellsworth, who spoke fluent Spanish, had close ties to Mexican officials and did undercover work for the Mexican government. In 1909, the Justice Department appointed him to coordinate enforcement of U.S. neutrality laws. Ellsworth characterized revolutionary activity in Tucson, Clifton, Morenci, Metcalf, Phoenix, and Arizona as critical. He quoted Consul Gustavo Levy, Tucson, and Consul Arturo Elías, Phoenix, as saying that revoltosos had "infested" Arizona.

Mexican superspy Miguel Peña del Pino assigned Francisco Solis to Morenci. There were forty revoltosos in the Clifton area that year, mostly male and less than forty years of age. The average age of Clifton group was less than thirty-five. Solis was very detailed in reporting their age, height, and place of origin. Most were artisans and craftsmen, managers and skilled workers. Ironically, there were no peons or campesinos.[60]

Meanwhile, in 1910, congressional hearings exposed the collusion of the U.S. and Mexican authorities. Among other things, the hearings exposed that

the U.S. collector of customs at El Paso was in the pay of the Mexican government to spy on Mexican refugees. Representative Champ Clark stated, "I say
that the agents of the Mexican government, or any other government, have no
right to come into the United States and violate our laws and do things to
persecute the poor Mexicans."[61] The Thomas Furlong Detective Agency confessed it was in the pay of the Mexican government. That the hearings took
place at all was a tribute to the radical network developed by supporters of the
revolutionary forerunners.[62]

The Myth of the
Western Federation of Miners

The WFM clearly represented the interests of the white miners, but most enlightened organizers knew that the future of the union depended on organizing
Mexican workers. They also knew, however, that a majority of white miners
would not tolerate Mexicans. Two of the WFM's strongest locals, Jerome and
Globe, were white men's camps. In 1907, the Globe local favored withdrawing
from the IWW, and the WFM paid considerable attention to Globe. Moyer
frequently referred to Mexicans as "greasers" and blamed them for organizational failures. Although he knew it was in the best interest of the WFM to
accept Mexicans, he was cautious about upsetting the rank-and-file members
who considered Mexicans genetically prone to being scabs.[63] As one organizer
said, "The race prejudice among Texans is very strong against Mexicans, and
Arizona is filled with Texans."[64] But not everything can be blamed on Texans.

In 1907, H. W. Kane noted that, since the Clifton-Morenci Strike of 1903,
the WFM had not attempted "to organize the men employed in and around the
mines, mills and smelters of this district." He added that the "Clifton-Morenci
district which bears the distinction of being about the worst that has ever
happened in the southwest, and which, like a hog wallowing in a bed of filth,
has heretofore been quite indifferent as to what anybody thought about it."[65]

The WFM was very active in Douglas, which had 1,200 Mexican and
Euro-American smelter workers. When the *Arizona Republican* spoke of
"1,200 vicious and idle Mexicans loose" in Douglas, the *Miners' Magazine*
responded, why would any company want Mexican workers if they were
vicious?[66] The quality of life of Mexicans in Douglas as elsewhere depended on
their class. Some old Mexican families had books and were better off. But there
were few examples of ethnic solidarity between Mexicans and white workers.

For example, in the Mexican colonia of Pirtleville, just north of the smelters, where residents could keep farm animals because it was unincorporated,
houses cost fifty dollars, a quarter of what they cost in Douglas. The low cost of

housing attracted Serbians, Italians, and French smelter workers. Mexicans of all classes found a common identity during the fiestas patrias. As in most of Arizona, Mexicans went to Mexican schools, whites to white schools, and blacks to black schools. Pirtleville was a breeding ground for dissidents, who filled the ranks of the troops in various rebellions.[67]

In his 1907 report, D. Haberbosell noted that 80 percent of the workers in Clifton-Morenci-Metcalf were Mexican and "not one in 500 spoke English," but that there was no direct evidence that the companies had recruiting agents in Mexico. Haberbosell said that, because the mine owners played the races against each other, it was up to the union to educate the Mexican workers and to use their militant spirit intelligently. He contrasted the nearly all-Mexican workforce in Morenci with Bisbee's Copper Queen, which did not hire Mexicans and maintained a blacklist.[68]

Meanwhile, the Mine Owners' Association of Arizona was becoming ever more oppressive. As of July 1910, the WFM did not have a single Mexican organizer. Of 970 Mexicans working in the smelters in Clifton and Douglas, only 25 — less than 3 percent — were foremen, engineers, or mechanics. By 1910, the Detroit Copper Company was overtaking Arizona Copper, with a return of 36 percent in 1909 and 1910.

Clifton-Morenci-Metcalf was home not only to revoltosos but also to followers of the Mexican revolutionist Francisco Ignacio Madero. In 1910, a group of mine workers sent a letter to the minister of foreign relations. It complained that the Mexican colony had for years suffered at the hands of U.S. authorities, who treated them worse than they did Chinese and blacks. Mexicans, according to the letter, suffered like dogs. The hatred of Mexicans was intransigent and unconditional, worsened by weak Mexican consuls, who conspired with the mine managers. They called their consul in Clifton a "decorative figure," who did not seek justice nor protest, much less defend against, the lack of it.[69]

The End of the Decade

As 1910 drew near, the number of Mexican miners living in Arizona reached critical mass. Politicized by revolutionary activities, labor agitation, and racism, some of the leaders of the dissident community resided in, and operated out of, Clifton-Morenci-Metcalf. They were neighbors of Abrán Salcido, Práxedis Guerrero, and dozens of others such as Teresa and Tomás de Urrea. They belonged to the same mutualistas, frequented the same saloons, and played on the same pool tables. Their families knew each other's stories.

◄ 8 ►

The Mexican Revolution

On November 3, 1910, Texans lynched Antonio Rodríguez, 20, at Rock Springs. *Regeneración* thundered: "Mexicans know that there are no guarantees in our country nor abroad."[1] An angry Toribio Ortega and some sixty-five villagers less than a week later clashed with federal troops at Cuchillo Parado in the Río Conchos Valley of northeast Chihuahua. Ortega had worked as a ranch hand in Shafter and Marfa, Texas, knew English, and knew the Texans. At Ciudad Chihuahua, students demonstrated, as they did in Mexico City, Guadalajara, and throughout the country. Mexican Foreign Minister Enrique Creel apologized for violence to Euro-American property.[2]

In June 1911, a mob yanked fourteen-year-old Antonio Gómez from his cell in Thorndale, Texas, beat him, tied him to the back of a buggy, and dragged him around the town. The following month, in Pecos, Texas, Texans lynched León Cárdenas Martínez, 15. "I have not witnessed a people as imbecilic as Americans in general," seethed Ricardo Flores Magón. "They are taught in school that the United States is unique. The Mexican is brutally hated. There is no justice in court for the Mexican, who is considered to be subhuman. Miserable cowboys!"[3] Unfortunately, these were not aberrations: William D. Carrigan estimates that "between 1848 and 1928, mobs lynched at least 597 Mexicans."[4]

Other humiliating occurrences fanned unrest. U.S. health authorities, reinforcing the stereotype of the dirty Mexican, sprayed visitors from the neighbor country with noxious and toxic chemicals such as Zyklon-B (later used by the

Nazis in their death camps). On January 28, 1917, at 7:30 a.m., Carmelita Torres, 17, a maid en route to work in El Paso was stopped on the Santa Fe Bridge and ordered by the customs officials to take a gasoline bath. She refused. Thirty female passengers the *El Paso Times* labeled "the Amazons" joined her. An hour later, more than two hundred Mexican women blocked traffic entering the city by lying down in front of the railroad tracks. Within four hours, "several thousand" were demonstrating. Troops from Fort Bliss were joined by those from the Carranza "death squad." When José María Sánchez shouted "¡Viva Villa!" he was escorted to the Juárez cemetery and shot. The resistance lasted for several days, and shots were fired as the Mexican women were driven back across the bridge. The headlines of the *Los Angeles Times* of January 30 read: "American Troops Attacked by Juarez Rioters Incited by Villa."[5]

The Mexican Revolution

People communicated differently in the 1910s. The telegraph made news more accessible — sensational and brief. The telephone cost too much for most workers, and the radio was not yet in common use. Newspapers and new arrivals were important sources of information. Balladeers expressed their repugnance to race and class oppression through *corridos*.[6]

In cities and towns across the Southwest, in the plazas close to factories and working-class barrios, workers would listen to magonistas and other radicals read the newspapers. As with Cuban and Puerto Rican cigar makers, not everyone could read — but they understood. In Los Angeles in the 1930s, a free speech forum was constructed to avoid conflicts.[7]

Newspapers created a sense of community. In the first two decades of the twentieth century, Mexican newspapers filled the spaces in between. Although concentrated in California, the Upper Rio Grande Valley, and south Texas, these appeared also in communities such as Tucson, which had supported several Mexican newspapers since the 1870s. Indeed, from 1900 to 1920, no fewer than ten Spanish-language newspapers functioned at one time or another in Arizona.[8]

The industrial nature of mining concentrated large numbers of workers at mine sites. As a rule, these workers owned rifles and ammunition. Frequent economic recessions and depressions made them willing recruits for the rebels. Hence, with the outbreak of revolutionary hostilities, border consulates kept an eye on the copper camps.[9]

Chihuahua's population had changed during the porfiriato, as economic expansion and contraction pushed people north. "Part of this population was originally from Durango, Zacatecas, and other places in the interior of the nation," Luis Aboites Aguilar writes. "[They] were attracted by the high sal-

Soldaderas. (Courtesy of The Center for American History, The University of Texas at Austin, Runyon Collection, 00211)

aries that were paid in Chihuahua."[10] As agriculture was commercialized and water projects completed, ranchos and farms multiplied, attracting workers from within and outside the state. Thus, in the areas around Ciudad Guerrero and Cusihuiriáchic alone, the number of ranchos more than tripled, from seventy-nine to 297, between 1893 and 1908.

There were many kinds of Chihuahuans. The serrano Chihuahuans, whose isolated sierran pueblos resembled the Rio Arriba villages of New Mexico, differed from Chihuahuans in the Río Conchos Valley — and both differed from those in Ciudad Chihuahua and Ciudad Juárez. Chihuahua was more industrialized than other states. According to Michael Meyer, it had "a relatively large middle class of merchants, artisans, coachmen, railroad men, and clerks," which socialized migrants and residents alike.[11]

The Magonistas

The Partido Liberal Mexicano (PLM) formed cells along the northern edges of Sonora, Coahuila, and Chihuahua during the first decade of the century. As ardent supporters of their revolutionary leader Ricardo Flores Magón, the magonistas were not fond of Francisco Madero, who lacked a revolutionary plan. Indeed, they refused to recognize Madero's authority. Madero reacted to this insubordination and lack of respect by jailing six magonista leaders. For a short time, during the ill-fated rebellion of January 1911, the PLM controlled Baja California. But its expeditionary force, composed mostly of Mexican and Euro-American volunteers, lacked discipline, and was quickly routed. Stalwarts such as José María Leyva, a veteran of the Cananea Strike of 1906, could not keep the Baja revolt from falling into the hands of opportunists. The Los Angeles–based junta was unprepared for the impossible task of raising funds, supplying arms, and offering leadership all at the same time.[12]

Moreover, Baja was too close to Los Angeles, where *Los Angeles Times* publisher General Harrison Gray Otis, his son-in-law Harry Chandler, and William Randolph Hearst of the *Los Angeles Examiner* held court. Otis and Chandler owned the California-Mexico Land and Cattle Company and had a vast agricultural empire in the Mexicali Valley. Not only did they pressure Washington to intervene, but they also subverted the revolt through financial intrigues of their own. In March, the United States mobilized 20,000 men, moving much of its Atlantic Fleet to the Pacific Coast and putting 2,000 U.S. Marines on alert.

The Baja revolt had a continuous turnover in leadership. Once Madero defeated Díaz's forces in June 1911, support for the venture dropped off. Madero pressured the U.S. Department of Justice to arrest magonista leaders in the United States, even as Mexican federal forces pointed their guns at the PLM in Baja. The end came in the summer of 1911. Former commanders testified against the junta. Federal prosecutors jailed Ricardo and Enrique Flores. Meanwhile, PLM insiders such as Lázaro Gutiérrez de Lara, Juan Sarabia, and Antonio Villarreal and their network of socialist and trade union supporters defected. After the Baja fiasco, the magonistas ceased to be a factor.[13]

Two Villistas, including an Indian sharpshooter. (Courtesy of the El Paso County Historical Society, Stevens-Darbyshire Scrapbook of the Battle of Juárez, 1911, and Family Photos, 1908–1913)

Chihuahua: A House Divided

The election of Francisco Madero on October 1, 1911, temporarily lessened tensions along the border. But differences within the revolutionary ranks widened. The most critical defection was that of Pascual Orozco Jr., 30, a middle-class muleteer from the Guerrero area.

Orozco did not genuflect before Madero, a Coahuilan aristocrat who would rather rule than govern, and even flirted with running against Madero's designate as governor of Chihuahua. This was enough to cast suspicion on his loyalty. *Maderistas* speculated that Orozco was in the thick of the plots of Bernardo Reyes and Emilio Vásquez Gómez. By November 1911, Emiliano

Zapata circulated his Plan of Ayala and named Orozco the head of the Revolution. Although Orozco campaigned against the *vasquistas*, in January 1912, he resigned his command rather than fight against Zapata.

On March 3, 1912, along with the Chihuahuan magonistas, Orozco issued the Plan of the Empacadora, which condemned Madero, expressed strong anti-American sentiments, and hit at the heart of serrano grievances. The plan demanded local autonomy, a one-term limit for presidents of the republic, and redistribution of land. Pursued by General Victoriano Huerta, in August, Orozco retreated to the United States.

In February 1913, the Revolution took another turn. Having arrested first Madero and then Governor Abraham González, General Victoriano Huerta had them both shot. A civil war erupted, with Governor Venustiano Carranza and Pancho Villa leading the assault. At this point, Huerta reached out to Orozco, who agreed to recognize him as president on the condition that he adopt Orozco's plan.

On paper, Huerta agreed to redistribute the land in Chihuahua and to pay both the debts of the *orozquistas* and pensions for widows and orphans. Orozco would name two cabinet members. In return, the leaders of the Orozco revolt agreed to help protect the public safety. Suffice it to say, the distribution of land did not happen, the widows and orphans did not receive their pensions — and Orozco was painted as a traitor.[14]

¡Viva Villa!

After 1913, the Chihuahuan revolt was reduced to two words: Pancho Villa. Villa's exploits formed U.S. attitudes toward Mexicans north of the Río Bravo. In spring 1913, Woodrow Wilson refused to recognize Huerta and placed an embargo on arms shipments to Mexico. Villa took Torreón on October 1, 1913, and his reputation soared. In December, Villa entered Ciudad Chihuahua and named himself governor. Early the next year, President Wilson lifted the embargo, helping the rebels.[15]

As Villa expropriated the money, land, and cattle of the hacendados and paid his army, he put his soldiers to work improving the infrastructure. He formed a bank and protected Euro-American mining interests. Meanwhile, U.S. Navy warships had been sent to Tampico and Veracruz — ostensibly to protect U.S. and other foreign interests in the rich oilfields of the area. When, in April 1914, a group of sailors went ashore to retrieve supplies, Mexican authorities arrested them. Although they were shortly released, the U.S. admiral demanded not only an apology but also a twenty-one-gun salute to the U.S. flag. Huerta agreed — providing the admiral would return the honor.

Pancho and Luz Villa. (Courtesy of the El Paso County Historical Society)

The naval commander angrily notified Washington of the insult to the U.S. flag, and the Republican senator from Idaho, William Borah, bellowed, "If the flag of the United States is ever run up in Mexico, it will never come down. This is the beginning of the march of the United States to the Panama Canal!"[16] President Wilson received a standing ovation in Congress for vowing to defend American honor. The U.S. consul warned that a German ship was expected to deliver arms to Huerta on April 21. Wilson ordered the U.S. Navy's Atlantic Fleet to Mexico's Gulf Coast.

Presidential advisers urged Wilson to call up 400,000 reservists. Instead, he sent a force of 5,200 to occupy Veracruz. When a force of some eight hundred marines and sailors landed, Mexican soldiers fired on them, and a violent street battle broke out. Mexicans killed four Americans and wounded twenty, while sources estimate that between 152 and 172 Mexicans were killed and between 195 and 250 were wounded. By the end of the month, the U.S. Army's Fifth Infantry Brigade arrived at Veracruz. In July, Huerta resigned from office, and the occupiers left Veracruz in late November.

With Huerta eliminated, President Wilson played cat and mouse. Tension between Zapata and Villa, on the one hand, and aristocrat Carranza, on the other, intensified now that source of their common hatred had been removed. In the late summer, an assembly was called in Aguascalientes to nominate a president. When Carranza boycotted the assembly, it chose Fernando Iglesias Calderón, whom Carranza refused to recognize. This set off hostilities with Villa and Zapata. In October 1915, over the objections of the Catholic lobby, Wilson recognized Carranza and enforced an arms embargo against Villa.[17]

After this point, Villa became increasingly anti-American. At Santa Ysabel in January 1916, *villistas* captured seventeen Yanquis off a train and killed all but one. Companies ordered their U.S. employees out of Mexico. Anti-Mexican feeling ran high, as press and politicos alike took cheap shots. The incident touched off a series of raids south and north across the Mexican-U.S. border, which peaked the following March, when Villa raided Columbus, New Mexico.[18]

Why Villa chose Columbus, a small town with one hotel, a few stores, some adobe houses, and 350 Euro-Americans and Mexicans, is open to conjecture. Its Camp Furlong was home to the five hundred troopers of the Thirteenth U.S. Cavalry Regiment. That noted, Villa could hardly be accused of raiding defenseless civilians. Nor was it a surprise attack: spies warned the military commander that a raid was imminent.

Villa invaded Columbus with nearly five hundred men on March 9. According to the War Department, ten U.S. soldiers and eight civilians were killed. Approximately a hundred Mexicans were killed, and seven were wounded and captured. The U.S. public clamored for the army to punish Villa. The commander of the Southern Department telegraphed the War Department the day after the raid and urged that U.S. troops be given authority to pursue Villa. Wilson ordered Secretary of War Newton Baker to organize a "punitive expedition."[19]

From March 16, 1916 to February 14, 1917, Brigadier General John J. "Black Jack" Pershing chased Villa with more than 14,000 soldiers. One Arizona newspaper claimed that 210,000 men had been mobilized for border patrol duty, approaching the entire population of Arizona.[20]

Some U.S. Mexicans applauded Villa's raid; others protested he was ruining Mexico. On May 6, *El Tucsonense* told its readers that Villa had committed acts of vandalism and urged them, as "guests in this country," to refrain from all action. The Tucson elite wrote that, despite rumors, the U.S. government would not interfere with those who minded their own business. Nevertheless, tensions were rising in the Tucson Mexican community.

A year before, at its annual convention in Phoenix, Lodge Number 8 of the Liga Protectora of Tucson had passed a resolution that members not side with any faction in the Revolution, and it had expelled members who did. Although constitutionalist leaders in Sonora condemned the Villa raid, largely because it shut off revenue from the mines, most Mexicans condemned the U.S. violation of Mexican sovereignty that followed on its heels.[21]

Pershing was unable to find Villa, whose forces captured twenty-three enlisted men and one civilian interpreter. The villistas took the prisoners to Ciudad Chihuahua, where they were released. Even so, the U.S. press was furious. The "punitive expedition" officially ended on the afternoon of February 5, 1917, and the individual soldiers returned home as "veterans." Twice in four years, the United States had invaded Mexico, on the pretext of extending "American" democracy.[22]

Sonora Querida

Whether originally from Sonora or from elsewhere in Mexico, Sonoran workers and their families constantly moved to and from the mines and the agricultural fields of Arizona. They also crossed La Linea to visit or shop in cities like Tucson. The 1910 census put the Mexican-born population of Arizona at 29,542 out of a total of 294,353 — a dramatic undercount. Using the 1900 census as a basis, there were at least twice as many U.S.-born residents as Mexican-born.[23]

As in Chihuahua, opposition to Díaz existed prior to 1910. In 1901, young student activists published the newspaper *El Combate* and named their group El Club Verde, after a popular waltz by Sonoran composer Rodolfo Campodónico. When the youths mounted a protest over the lack of fair elections, the prefect of Hermosillo, Francisco C. Aguilar, a member of the Ramón Corral cabal, called out his troops. A deadly confrontation was averted when Carmén Serna, the mother of two of the protest leaders, interposed herself between the students and the troops. Tales of her heroism were circulated throughout the region.[24]

The Club Verde molded its share of activists. Plácido Ríos participated in the great Cananea Strike of 1906. Eduardo Ruiz and his family supported Madero. Outside this circle, Adolfo de la Huerta was reportedly a PLM fellow traveler and ardent opponent of Díaz. De la Huerta was from Guaymas, like José María Maytorena, whose family defied the Díaz regime by opposing the genocide of the Yaqui.

Maytorena emerged as the leader of the Sonoran revolutionaries largely because of his links with Madero and his own family fortune. Prominent in the influential Guaymas group, composed of middle- and upper-class adherents, Maytorena could readily raise money for the cause. But even before the fighting broke out, militant supporters of Madero challenged Mayortena's leadership. The opposition came from Cananea, where, in December 1909, Juan Cabral, Salvador Alvarado, Rafael Romero, and Pedro Bracamonte had begun planning a revolution. When their plot was discovered, they fled to Arizona. Alvarado and Cabral went to Tucson and then to the Del Rey mining camp, where they set up a small business, recruited men, and collected money and arms.

In September — two months before the 1910 Revolution — maderistas met and parceled out leadership posts. José Antonio García was named head of the Sonoran operations. Later, the Sonoran rebels met at Nogales, where García, Alvarado, and Cabral demanded proof that Madero had anointed Maytorena the leader. Aside from age differences, class and regional tensions divided the revolutionaries. Maytorena, a rich hacendado, was from Guaymas; the others were from more rustic venues in northeastern Sonora. But the *guaymenses* had the upper hand: Mayortena funded the rebels at Nogales and elsewhere in the state. Cabral, Alvarado, and Rafael Romero independently formed the Junta Revolucionaria Sonorense and distributed propaganda to the various mining camps. Maytorena was not asked to join. On November 20, they crossed south into Sonora with seventeen armed men.[25] Initially, the magonistas had a number of supporters but they were diverted to Baja California, hence were unable to challenge Madero for leadership.

Because of their large investments in the state, Walter Douglas and L. D. Ricketts kept a close eye on Sonora. They knew that both sides had a stake in keeping the mines operating and revenues flowing. The border was of strategic importance because it controlled access to customshouses, arms, and recruits. However, there was the danger that heavy fighting on the border would provoke the United States to intervene. Sonora was strongly maderista, and Yaqui reinforcements helped the revolutionaries overwhelm the federal army. Even so, the intensity of the fighting in Sonora could not be compared to that in Chihuahua. As late as the end of December, George Young, the secretary of the Cananea Consolidated Copper Company, wrote that the political situation in Cananea was quiet and never looked better.[26]

The resignation of Porfirio Díaz in late May 1911 raised the expectations of the miners and railroad workers. When Juan Cabral entered Cananea early in May, miners received him with open arms. About that time, Ricketts gave Cabral 15,000 pesos. By the fall, after serving less than five years at San Juan de Ulúa, many 1906 strike leaders returned to the camp.

Although the state was calm throughout the year, there were threats of revolution. The maderistas broke into small bands, whose reputations rose with the number of their recruits. Meanwhile, the state legislature quarreled with Maytorena, whose critics multiplied. By the summer, many of the Sonoran revolutionaries left the state for Chihuahua and elsewhere. But, as they left, the orozquistas began to penetrate the state. In September 1912, magonista Inés Salazar (who lived in Metcalf; see chapter 7) attacked El Tigre Mine, demanding $100,000 and threatening to destroy the $2 million plant there, while hauling away $20,000 in gold and silver bullion, a hundred horses, and four cannons. By the end of September, the orozquista revolt was almost dead.[27]

Meanwhile, the state was plagued with other problems. Many of the rebels were becoming disenchanted with Madero. In October 1911, workers had formed the Unión de Obreros of Cananea. When the Cananea Consolidated Copper Company dismissed six workers in December, the union went on strike. On the one hand, George Young, the secretary of Cananea Consolidated, minimized the problem posed by the strike, saying the union represented only 10 percent of the company's workforce, or 500 workers. On the other, Young insisted that the dispute be brought before Governor Maytorena: the union "agitators" had escalated the firing of a few miners into demands for a 20 percent increase in wages, a reduction of one hour of work a day, and official recognition of the union. Moreover, according to him, union workers planned to use their Sunday demonstration calling for a general strike as a pretext to raid company stores for food and clothing. He had reliable information that the Western Federation of Miners wanted revenge—the culprit was Charles Moyer, "who has a very bad record," and is "very dangerous man." The Chamber of Commerce was considering measures because "Mexican working men are easily excited."[28] Local officials sided with the miners, but interim Governor Ismael Padillo sided with the company. Although the strike failed, Arizona and Sonora union activists were now clearly communicating with each other.

The Sonoran political situation had just begun to stabilize when Huerta assassinated Madero in February 1913. Governor Maytorena hesitated in confronting Huerta. But, led by veterans of the Cananea Strike of 1906—Manuel Diéguez, Esteban Baca Calderón, Juan José Ríos, and Salvador Alvarado—the Sonoran workers pushed him to revolt. In 1913, Maytorena was 46, wealthy, and anointed by fellow aristocrats Madero and Carranza. The pretenders, Juan Cabral, 30, Salvador Alvarado, 33, Plutarco Elías Calles, 36, Benjamín Hill, 39, Adolfo de la Huerta, 32, and Alvaro Obregón, 33, did not have Mayotena's prestige, nor had they yet broken free of the pack. Although unified in their hatred of him, they nonetheless began to feud.

In what was to become an all-too-familiar pattern, once the fighting began, Mayortena took his leave. Ignacio Bonillas, 54, became the interim governor but deferred to Ignacio L. Pesqueira, 46. Much to the chagrin of veterans such as Alvarado—who resented Obregón for failing at first to support Madero and for being a *científico* with ties to Ramón Corral—Alvaro Obregón was named

El Pasoans watching the Battle of Juárez in May 1911, in which Francisco Madero captured Ciudad Juárez. (Courtesy of the El Paso County Historical Society, Dr. H. E. Stevenson Scrapbook of the Mexican Revolution)

head of the state forces.[29] This appointment served as platform to launch Obregón into national prominence. Meanwhile, the *Los Angeles Times* and other U.S. newspapers formed a Greek chorus warning Euro-Americans that U.S. property in Mexico was in danger.[30]

There was a constant stream of revolutionary volunteers from the U.S. side. In March 1913, 120 maderistas met at Café Jesús Quiros in the Old Plaza area of Los Angeles. Because of the U.S. neutrality laws, the meetings were clandestine. The only person identified at the March meeting, for example, was Emanuel García, probably an alias. A call went out to small towns in eastern California for volunteers and money.[31]

Héctor Camín Aguilar describes the activities of the "brokers *fronterizos*" — largely relatives of the leadership — profiteers who smuggled cattle across the border and purchased arms. Among them was Roberto Pesqueira, an attorney for the Cananea Consolidated and a cousin of the governor. Foremost was Francisco Elías, 31, a ranchero cousin of Plutarco Elías Calles, as well as many of the other pretenders. Smuggling and taxes imposed on the copper companies allowed them to buy munitions — it also made the brokers even richer.[32]

Both sides ignored promises not to fight at La Linea. Bullets flew across the border, and the U.S. commander warned *huertistas* and *constitutionalistas*

Mexican revolutionaries in Pancho Villa's army. (Courtesy of the Los Angeles Public Library, Shades of L.A. Archives, 00002615)

alike to cease fire or else. After an all-day battle, Emilio Kosterlitzky crossed over and surrendered to the Fifth United States Cavalry.[33] Meanwhile, Pesqueira challenged Maytorena, who had returned from self-imposed exile, expecting once more to assume the governorship. Most rebel leaders opposed Maytorena's return, fearing that the fattest jobs would go to the friends and relatives of the guaymenses. Maytorena clung to power through the grace of Carranza and his own personal wealth.[34]

Keeping Afloat

Nineteen thirteen was an eventful year. Benjamín Hill and Ignacio Pesqueira challenged Maytorena, whose frequent absences eventually gave Hill, Pesqueira, and Calles a foothold. Only their common opposition to Huerta kept the fragments from falling apart. At the beginning of the year, leaders such as Diéguez were key to keeping workers and revolutionaries on the same page. However, a middle leadership vacuum developed as militant labor leaders joined the revolutionary ranks — Diéguez and Calderón and others became colonels, then generals, during 1913. Maytorena was becoming a liability. On his return that spring, he demanded back pay for himself and his staff, emptying the state treasury.

In the summer of 1913, George Young claimed that Lázaro Gutiérrez de Lara had called to tell him he planned to sue Cananea Consolidated for defamation, false imprisonment, and malicious prosecution. Young admitted that they had exaggerated the value of de Lara's alleged theft so they could extradite him. De Lara had received permission from the prefect of Cananea to lecture in the area. "De Lara's hobby is the division of lands among the poor people. And it will naturally be the theme of his lectures." The antagonism of the land barons would take on more significance five years later.[35]

The problems of obtaining money and arms and controlling the border persisted. Meanwhile, the anti-Maytorena faction was gaining wider support. Rumors of the rift in the ranks of Sonora's revolutionaries unsettled the people. When Carranza visited Cananea toward the end of the year, he found widespread dissatisfaction with Maytorena.

On April 23, 1914, as U.S. forces seized Veracruz, Wilson used the pretext that he was preventing a shipment of arms bound for Huerta's army. Later in 1914, Carranza's forces occupied Mexico City, and Huerta left the country. About this time, 2,500 miners struck at Cananea. The *Copper Era* wrote that Mexican officials sided with the owners and rounded up radicals. In late April, "rioting" broke out in Cananea, renewing the Greek chorus's calls to evacuate Euro-Americans from the camp and invade the country. The strike lost steam as famine brought 40,000 to 50,000 Mexicans to the brink of starvation. Fields had not been cultivated because of the fighting. The *Los Angeles Times* reported: "A few scattered ranches, producing small amounts of frijoles, corn and wheat, offer at this time the only relief to the famine-threatened State."[36]

The national disaster did not totally dampen the fervor of the Unión de Obreros, now under the control of anarcho-syndicalists. The union demanded that Phelps Dodge assign and manage fair piecework contracts with workers. It was clearly gaining strength: 2,500 workers walked out, whereas the year before it had been only 1,400. The mobilization involved entire families, as women took to the streets. Cananea Consolidated resumed operations on May 8, 1914, after assurances from Military Commander Plutarco Elías Calles that he would protect the company. At Nacozari, Euro-Americans abandoned the camp on the advice of "conservative Mexicans." They returned a few days later expecting to resume operations with the help of "trusted Mexican foremen." Apparently the copper barons received the support of the various revolutionary factions.[37]

Workers demanded more control over the workplace, a goal the new revolutionary bureaucrats did not always support. Although the prefect of Arizpe,

Federico Platt, called the rhetoric of the Cananea strike "propagandistic," the township president sided with the strikers and forced George Kingdon, the superintendent of Greene Cananea, to accept the union's demands. The workers wanted a 25 percent rise in wages and a 20 percent reduction in the prices at the company store. George Kingdon claimed he did not have the authority to approve the demands, and would have to confer with his superiors. Kingdon and three associates arrived in Naco on the night of July 2. At this point, the constitutionalists had a mere two hundred troops in the Cananea area and were strapped for cash. So they made every effort to force the strikers to withdraw their ultimatum.[38]

In June, the owners shut down the mines, leaving 3,800 workers unemployed. At Nacozari, a quarter of the workforce was laid off due to a weak market. This was a blow to Calles, who had committed six hundred troops to guarantee the mines' protection and was banking on increased revenues.

Meanwhile, Maytorena barely survived as governor, saved by the timely arrival of Yaqui troops. A rift between Carranza and Villa gave him precious time. Maytorena formed an alliance with Villa. By early August, fighting broke out, as both factions vied for control of Nogales. Villa and Carranza supported Maytorena, while Benjamín Hill replaced Calles as the commander of the army.[39]

In September 1914, the forces of Maytorena and Benjamín Hill–Plutarco Elías Calles clashed at Naco. The fighting between Maytorena and Hill, who had once been close, can be characterized as anything but fierce. In November, Hill played cat and mouse around Cananea, burning some bridges in the process. Things were so quiet that the twenty or so Euro-Americans were thinking of reopening the Cananea Club. Walter Douglas wanted the bridges along the Nacozari Railroad line repaired, but Maytorena, who wanted to keep Hill bottled up in Nacozari and Naco, would not allow this. Hill was losing 100,000 to 125,000 pesos for every month he could not move his troops. For fear of bullets across the border, Maytorena would attack neither Naco nor any of the other border towns. Toward the end of the year, everyone was suffering from cold weather and heavy rains. Hill barricaded his army in circular trenches around Naco. Begun in October, the siege of Naco was lifted in late November.[40]

Although speculation was rife that Villa would invade Sonora, Villa was bogged down by uncertainties as to when hostilities against Carranza would break out, and sent fewer than 1,500 men to the state. At this point, it was expected that the augmented troops of Maytorena would defeat Hill, securing the border and the copper camps.

Because of the heavy fighting there, Woodrow Wilson ordered General Hugh Scott to the border with a large army in December. When Maytorena hesitated to abide by the cease-fire, Scott asked Villa to intervene. Villa had broken with Carranza and Obregón. Hopeful of U.S. support, he cooperated. President Wilson then warned Carranza that the United States would intervene if hostilities continued near the border.

Meanwhile, torrential rains wiped out wheat crops, killed cattle, and destroyed railroad properties in Sonora. (In 1916, floods would sweep away roads and telegraphic lines.) Food was scarce. Nor could the government help: the Revolution made it impossible to collect taxes of any type.

Encouraged by the division between the two sides in November 1914, Burdet Aden Packard defied an order by Hill not to move his cattle; they were needed by the army. Packard, a former partner of Greene and president of the First National Bank of Douglas, had received 100,000 acres and 10,000 head of cattle as his share of his investment in Greene's holdings. Packard moved 6,000 head into Arizona — duty-free — with the cooperation of Arizona authorities. He had thirty-five gunslingers, many of whom were former Arizona Rangers. Mexicans and Euro-Americans fired at each other across the border as Packard drove *his* cattle home.[41]

In January 1915, Villa replaced Maytorena with Juan Cabral, who had switched sides after the Aguas Calientes Convention of July 1914. This ended the crisis. Villa appears to have earned points with U.S. military officials. Being a realist, however, he knew he had to keep the border open to ensure the flow of arms. Meanwhile, General Scott returned to Washington.

A flood destroyed towns in the Río Sonora Valley, slowing operations. It was unrealistic for either side to pull back. Unless it could control the border, the war was lost. By March 1915, the Revolution had bankrupted the nation and destroyed its infrastructure. In Sinaloa and Sonora alone, nearly three hundred bridges were destroyed. Claiming that Yaqui raids threatened the property of sixty-five Americans in the Río Yaqui Valley, the U.S. Navy sent the cruisers *Raleigh* and *New Orleans* to patrol the waters off Guaymas.[42]

By October 1915, Wilson's recognizing Carranza had dealt a deathblow to Villa, who crossed over the Sierra Madre Occidental into Sonora in hopes of reviving his movement. Sonora was isolated and had not experienced the heavy fighting of Chihuahua and Durango. When Villa left Chihuahua, Maytorena was winning the war: he had 3,000 *carrancistas* bottled up in Agua Prieta. But true to form, he made off once again to the United States, where, this time, he threw in the towel: "I will not rejoin the Villa army, Carranza has won." Incredibly, believing he might land a post, Mayortena offered his services to the new government. Meanwhile, Wilson gave Carranza free passage to send troops across U.S. soil to Agua Prieta, whose defenders had dug trenches and put up barbed wire barriers similar to those used in Europe. But Villa had not expected the searchlights. His once powerful Division del Norte was smashed on November 1, 1915.[43]

Bowed but not yet defeated, Villa operated in the area for several weeks. He recaptured Naco and Cananea, where he took hostages and demanded taxes from Cananea Consolidated. Still in a foul mood over Wilson's recognition of Carranza, Villa was quoted as saying he would devote the rest of his life to killing gringos and destroying their property. Cananea Consolidated was caught in the middle, paying both Villa and Maytorena's Governor Carlos Randall taxes, while knowing that the constitutionalists would not recognize these payments.[44]

When the new regime assumed power, some of the mines began operating again, chiefly at Nacozari. Cananea Consolidated, which bore the brunt of Villa's occupation, did not resume production for some time. The constitutionalists executed large numbers of villistas but spared Governor Randall at President Wilson's request. Others surrendered as Calles prepared to send troops to western Chihuahua.[45]

The Big Picture

In 1916, upon the resignation of his father as president and chairman of the board, Walter Douglas took charge of Phelps Dodge. His brother, James S. Douglas, was shifted to the United Verde extension in Jerome. The Douglas family tightened control of operations in Arizona and Sonora. Walter Douglas was angry because of the 1915 strike (see chap. 10), in which Mexican miners at Morenci had won major concessions and defied his authority. In Sonora, Douglas ruled through bribes and control of communication. Expecting to get their way, he and other mine managers lavished praise on Calles as savior of Sonora's economy. Calles, in his dual capacities of governor and military commander of the state, assured U.S. investors that no law-abiding person need fear harm and promised to protect U.S. property. Like the hidalgo in the sixteenth century Spanish novella *The Life of Lazarillo de Tormes and His Fortunes and Adversities*, even though the state treasury was all but empty, Calles, with a gold toothpick in his mouth, allocated monies for education, veterans' benefits, reconstruction, and agrarian reform.[46]

Although Frederick Simpich, the U.S. consul at Nogales, accused Calles of sanctioning "numerous depredations" against U.S. citizens and property, in general, the railroad and mine owners welcomed the defeat of Villa and the emergence of a "strongman", and they planned to resume operations. Meanwhile, Calles's labor policies were mixed. In 1916, he set the minimum wage at

1.50 pesos day. But miners already made twice that, and for an eight-hour workday. The bottom line was that Calles needed money and only the mining companies could provide it.

As the economy seemed to right itself, the demand for labor increased. Because merchants needed a reliable currency, Calles moved to stabilize it and to curb counterfeiting: he ordered that state and federal workers be paid in silver. Carranza countermanded his order for federal workers, while insisting on new paper currency as a uniform medium of exchange.[47]

This led to protests of federal workers in Hermosillo. Under Carranza's national policy, all the states collected taxes in gold or silver and sent it to the national treasury — Guanajuato, Hidalgo, and Zacatecas had already sent $66 million in gold — where it was exchanged for new paper money. Widespread counterfeiting made the new money almost worthless, however. Indeed, large U.S. corporations profited from illegally trafficking in counterfeit money. Southern Pacific, for example, purchased 150,000 counterfeit pesos per month for several months before U.S. agents made arrests. Calles wanted to build new schools and had allocated millions to that end. He had twenty engineers surveying and subdividing lands to be distributed to the poor and tooks steps to prevent them from falling into the hands of speculators. To carry out his ambitious plans, he needed to revive Sonora's economy and to generate revenues. Thwarted by Carranza, Calles submitted his resignation in February, only to have it refused. During his term as governor, Calles succeeded in enacting reforms such as prohibition, the expansion of education, and the reorganization of state government.[48]

Meanwhile, Carranza caused another crisis when he appointed a favorite and former cabinet member as governor, Adolfo de la Huerta. Although de la Huerta had helped Calles become police commissioner of Agua Prieta early in the Revolution, the appointment did not sit well with Calles. Suffering from a huge hangover, prohibitionist Calles bluntly told de la Huerta, to his face, that he would not take orders from him. But though there continued to be disputes between the two, in May, Calles turned over the government to de la Huerta and proceeded to step up Sonora's military operations against the Yaqui. Calles ordered that every captured Yaqui child be sent to Hermosillo to attend an Indian school.

The copper barons disliked de la Huerta, who sought to strengthen labor in October 1916 through creation of the Chamber of Workers, which assigned each section of labor a representative for every 1,000 workers. The chamber arbitrated disputes and drafted labor legislation. De la Huerta's labor reforms were temporary and in line with what was happening nationally, namely, the Constitution of 1917.

Adolfo de la Huerta teaching singing in Los Angeles in 1929. (Courtesy of the Los Angeles Public Library, Herald-Examiner Collection, 00054785)

Walter Douglas wrote to the U.S. Army commander at Douglas, Arizona, that he believed that Calles would do everything possible to protect U.S. lives and property, so long as "the integrity of the state is not seriously menaced." Louis D. Ricketts, in a note to General Hugh Scott, described Calles as a good organizer and disciplinarian but added that he was not a particularly good commander. Ricketts dismissed Hill and Obregón as untrustworthy.[49]

In desperate need of money for his social programs, Calles confiscated the property of the Porfirian elite and levied high taxes on the mining companies.

Although the copper barons complained, they paid the taxes because demand for copper was up. Calles naively believed that he could persuade Euro-American supervisors to remain in Mexico, but even without them, the Cananea plant was producing a little better than fifty tons of copper per day. "The Mexicans are doing surprisingly well in handling the plant."[50]

Calles's reputation as a radical was in large part due to his anticlericalism. He deported six "científico" priests who were "spreading the gospel of strife and intervention instead of the Gospel of God," in spring 1916, adding that the expulsion was not directed against the Catholic Church, which had plenty of good priests. On the secular side, state authorities expelled Kosterlitsky's son-in-law, Carlos Terán, for sedition. Meanwhile, 2,000 women joined the Sonora Women's Rifle Association and offered their services to defend the state should the United States invade.

Border towns bulged with refugees. Calles formally protested to Douglas authorities about the ill treatment of Mexican refugees by immigration authorities. The main complaint was that they were crowded into detention camps and put on limited rations. Immigration officers refused to let many of the detainees return to Mexico, claiming they were rebels. In the meantime, Calles asked U.S. mining men to return to their mines. Calles assured them that he would guarantee their safety, that peace had returned to the state, and that there would be no war between the United States and Mexico.[51]

Calles Country

When Obregón's brother, José, ran against Calles for governor, Pershing reported in April 1917 that the political situation in Sonora had worsened and that tensions were high between Calles and Obregón.[52] In the end, Obregón's supporters, except for those among Tucson's Sonoran elite, reconciled themselves to Calles's overwhelming victory in the election.[53]

From 1916 to 1920, Calles and de la Huerta shared the governorship. Adolfo de la Huerta was provisional governor of Sonora from May 16, 1916, until August 31, 1917. He increased labor's role in the civic life of the state through the Chamber of Workers, extending the eight-hour workday and minimum wage to the poorest sectors of society. He initiated a workmen's compensation law and took the lead in forming the Unión Sonorense, composed of farmworkers.

Carranza's attempts to recall Calles were blocked by de la Huerta and Obregón, who got him reprieves. Meanwhile, a shift in the political wind favored Calles. Since 1915, Walter Douglas had declared an all-out war on miner organizations. After his defeat at Clifton-Morenci-Metcalf in 1915,

Douglas vowed to shut down operations rather than concede one iota of control to the unions. At the same time, the Industrial Workers of the World challenged the Western Federation of Miners for the hearts and minds of the workers. Dissatisfied with the WFM's leaders and at odds with the IWW's anarchist policies, many progressive miners spit off to join the Arizona State Federation. Mexican miners benefited from the split as they became more militant traveling between the Arizona and Sonora mines. The IWW took control of the Cananea mines, which were twenty-five miles from Naco. Through a small army of spies, Walter Douglas closely followed the events. He was not about to make concessions to Mexican miners on the Mexican side that he had refused to white and Mexican miners on the U.S. side.

At Nacozari, irritated by negotiations with the Chamber of Workers and de la Huerta, the owners temporarily closed the mine down in April 1917. When the workers attempted to run the mine, Phelps Dodge cut off their electric power. The workers had banked heavily on the skyrocketing price of copper, but the barons were looking at the "big picture." And when de la Huerta approached Cananea Consolidated and naively suggested the government take over its management, the owners refused point blank. Moreover, the monthly cost of operating the company was approximately 500,000 pesos, 200,000 pesos in salaries and 300,000 in fuel and power. In June, El Tigre workers struck when the mining companies would not allow their union to determine a fair day's work. The Chamber of Workers also protested, insisting employers could not fire Mexican workers without its consent.

Mexican miners continued to rail at the company's contract system. Their grievances were identical to those of miners in Arizona. Workers complained that Cananea Consolidated hired supervisory personnel who did not speak Spanish and who preferred foreigners. They demanded to be paid biweekly and for overtime.

Calles seemed to believe he could placate the owners by making concessions. He ordered local authorities at Nacozari and El Tigre to expel all labor agitators, he ordered workers at El Tigre back to work, and he forbade the removal of food from Cananea. Calles became increasingly frustrated when Douglas closed down operations at Cananea, which was unjustified in his view. This coincided with the Bisbee deportations. Calles put a train at the disposal of any worker who wanted to leave Cananea, and transported thousands to agricultural lands in Sinaloa and elsewhere.[54]

Calles thought if he could only meet with the executives of the mining companies, they could resolve any problems. But when, with Carranza's blessing, he traveled to New York to lobby the copper magnates, they gave him smiles and empty assurances.[55]

Between June 1 and June 21, 1917, nearly 16,000 persons crossed La Linea into Arizona. Because the mines had been idled, most sought work in agriculture. When a strike broke out at El Tigre Mine, Calles sent trains to resettle people in other parts of the state. Food was scarce and only a few mining companies, such as Moctezuma Copper, were still operating. Because of the crisis, many expected Calles to give in to all the mine owners' demands.

Cananea Consolidated alone had set a standard of how many feet would be drilled in an eight-hour workday and the rate of pay. The company insisted there be no hearing before they assessed a fine. In face of resistance, the company shut down its mine. Yet Brigadier General J. Parker of Fort Sam Houston reported that there was no bitter anti-American feeling in Sonora.[56] Strike conditions became even more critical for the Sonoran government, which received 90 percent of its revenues from duties levied on Cananea Consolidated. Incredibly, *El tucsonense* blamed the strikers.[57]

When Calles returned to Sonora from Mexico City on July 28, 1917, Sonorans feared hostilities with the United States — according to a quote attributed to Calles in secret session with the legislature.[58] In August, there was no improvement in the economic situation, and the Yaqui threat in western and southwestern Sonora triggered U.S. saber rattling.[59] Meanwhile, even though Cananea was deserted and its stores were closed, Brigadier General Parker attributed anti-American sentiment there to German propaganda. "Criticism of Americans and the American government," he explained, "has disappeared from press articles in Sonora since General P. Elías Calles took his office as Governor."[60]

Calles almost immediately began to roll back de la Huerta's labor reforms in order to make Sonora more business friendly. In conjunction with the federal authorities, the state abolished the graduated Employer's Liability Act, as well as the Chamber of Workers. Even as they extracted more promises from Calles, Walter Douglas and Phelps Dodge attempted to discipline the workforce by shutting down production at will. It had an effect. In September, the U.S. consul at Nogales reported desertions from Calles's army to agricultural companies in California, where growers contracted some 1,300 Mexican workers, half of them miners.[61]

A freezing winter damaged corn and bean crops, which yielded 50 percent less than expected. According to Colonel Malvern-Hill-Barum, "Shortage of corn and other staples in Mexico is no doubt responsible for the effort now being made to effect a more liberal arrangement of the Mexican mining laws and regulations, which have been the source of much hardship to foreign mine operators."[62]

Natural disasters also hit Chihuahua: cloudbursts and floods in central

Chihuahua caused widespread property damage, destroying irrigation projects on both sides of the Río Conchos, from La Boquilla near Camargo to Ojinaga, and depositing six to eight feet of gravel. The dry weather that followed slashed crop yields, severely affecting areas such as La Laguna in Coahuila, which employed thousands of migrant workers. "Southern and Eastern Sonora," U.S. officials announced, "is permeated with refugees from Chihuahua, looking for work, . . . with arms in their possession, or hidden for possible future use."[63]

In February 1918, news sources reported that the mine owners were not able to make a deal with Calles. *El Tucsonense* called Cananea Consolidated's shutdown lamentable but placed the blame squarely on Calles, who it insisted had bankrupted the state. This was an incredible claim, especially in light of the ruthless treatment of the Tucson Mexicans in the Arizona mines.[64]

The next year, 2,000 miners were discharged from Cananea and 600 from Nacorzari. Finally acknowledging that the mines would not reopen anytime soon, Calles shipped some of the workers from Nacozari to Culiacán and others to Chihuahua. More important than the recession that followed the European Armistice was the unfolding larger plan to purge the workforce of union members and to restructure taxes.[65]

On the other hand, efforts emanating out of El Paso were already under way to unify the labor refugees against Carranza in California, Arizona, New Mexico, and Texas. Tension still existed between Calles and Obregón with the tucsonenses remaining pro-Obregón. The activity of the Yaqui forced the moving of the state capital to Nogales. The tucsonenses reported on the continued exodus of miners from Cananea to pick cotton in Arizona.

Meanwhile, there was a clampdown on the Wobblies, as the IWW organizers were called, on both sides of the border, diverting attention away from the copper barons.[66] As late as 1919, the companies believed that its agents were influencing Calles by giving him sizable loans. He owed Cananea Consolidated $18,000 and he requested another $30,000. Sonora's military commander needed money for the state's army and for his power struggle with Carranza. Meanwhile, de la Huerta attempted to prevent worker confrontations at the mines but to no avail — the die had been cast.[67]

The Death of an Icon: Lázaro Gutiérrez de Lara

Hated by the copper barons, especially by Walter Douglas, Gutiérrez de Lara had a high profile during the Arizona mining strikes of 1915. In a telegram to President Carranza, General Plutarco Elías Calles boasted that he participated in the capture of the "famous agitator" Lázaro Gutiérrez de Lara when he attempted to enter Sonora through the Altar District. He ordered de Lara's immediate execution, along with that of a Russian agitator, in Hermosillo on January 18, 1918.

The *Los Angeles Times*, no fan of de Lara, announced on February 17, 1918: "Say de Lara Was Put to Death by Enemies." De Lara had gone to Sonora as a self-appointed trade emissary. While he strongly empathized with the miners' union, he was a socialist. The difference between his ideology and the IWW was as significant as the differences between Shiites and Sunnis. Calles probably feared more agitation at the mines, principally those at Cananea, which he had pledged to safeguard. Calles was still under the illusion that they would resume operations.[68]

The Río Yaqui Valley

Yaquis worked in the mines and farms of Sonora and Arizona. The Yaqui wars drove them across La Linea, where they formed enclaves in and around Tucson and Phoenix. According to James Robert Kluger, they sought out the mines of Arizona rather than taking their chances with either of the warring revolutionary factions in Mexico.[69] Yaquis were often indistinguishable from nonnative Mexicans in the eyes of the Yanquis.

Esteban B. Calderón was politicized by the horrible plight of the Yaqui: "I arrived in Sonora about the middle of 1904. I was disillusioned to learn the real motives behind the never ending war against the Yaqui that had caused so many victims between the Yaquis and the Yoris."[70]

As early as 1895, the U.S. consul reported that the Yaqui did not molest Euro-Americans. As they began to interfere with U.S. interests, however, they became bloodthirsty savages, according to the U.S. press, torturing and clubbing Mexican children to death. A consul complained that millions of dollars in U.S. capital were at the mercy of the Yaqui. In 1905, Consul Albert R. Morawitz wrote that nearly all Americans and many Mexicans believed that the government did not really want to put down the Yaqui rebellion. Izabal, Torres, and Corral had made millions in the previous thirty years out of the war in the purchase of rations, horse feed, and other supplies.[71]

The rebel factions recruited Yaquis to their ranks, promising them a better life, even as they coveted their land. Once in power, revolutionary leaders acted like científicos. The privatization of the Río Yaqui Valley was the key to the state's progress. The Díaz government had given U.S. investors large grants in the Río Yaqui Valley. Under siege, the Yaqui once more rose up between 1913 and 1916. U.S. interlopers pressured Washington to intervene. Woodrow Wilson sent the Marines to Guaymas, forcing a Mexican mobilization against the Yaqui.[72]

A group of more than thirty Yaqui women and children prisoners under guard in Guaymas, Sonora, ca. 1910. (Courtesy of the University of Southern California, on behalf of the USC Specialized Libraries and Archival Collections)

Newspapers such as the *Los Angeles Times* exaggerated tales of refugees fleeing the "savage" Yaqui, painting portraits of "Americans" being victimized by Yaqui warriors near Hermosillo, gouging out their blue eyes and cutting off their ears. The only solution for the United States was to save the Mexican people and give them democracy by taking the Río Yaqui Valley off their hands. In the meantime, the transformed Sonoran elite concluded, as many other elites had before them, that the Yaqui were bad for business. Because neither mining nor meaningful agrarian reform was possible without resolving the Yaqui question, Plutarco Elías Calles waged an all-out war against them, one that would lead to their total surrender. Many revolutionaries urged Calles to live up to the promises made to the Yaqui by the Revolution.

The Río Yaqui Valley's importance was dramatized by the widespread famine of 1916 and 1917, during which the Yaqui tenaciously fought for their lands. In July 1916, they raided Euro-American property in their valley.[73]

The Richardson Construction Company had begun operations in the valley in the 1890s, when the Southern Pacific had built a trunk line there. The company widely distributed a pamphlet, printed in English and Spanish, claiming that it had opened the economic potential to the valley, and added that "unless the Yaqui Indian question is definitely and permanently settled, these benefits cannot be realized." Davis Richardson obtained water flow rights to 45 percent of the Río Yaqui from the Mexican government, equaling 1,750 cubic feet per second (50,000 liters per second).[74]

The Richardson Construction Company lost favor during the Revolution, when it failed to pay taxes, and when Mexicans themselves wanted the valley's land. The federal government promised to allocate 10,000 pesos per month to rehabilitate the Richardson canal system, money that it did not have. The United States placed tremendous pressure on the federal and state governments to protect Euro-Americans living in the Río Yaqui Valley. The Yaqui uprisings gave the United States an excuse to intervene. In 1916, the *Los Angeles Times* reported that Carranza had seized the Los Angeles–based company, which had made great investments in their valley colony. Shortly afterward, it was reported that the land had been restored to its "rightful owners" — the Richardsons. In 1918, Calles saw this monopoly as scandalous. Furthermore, the land companies were not paying their way. By the time they resumed operations in 1923, the Campañia de Terrenos de Sonora owed $173,000 in back taxes, the Wheeler Land Company $162,000, and the Richardson Construction Company $352,000.[75]

To his credit, de la Huerta remained sensitive to the Yaqui plight. As governor of Sonora, he wrote a letter to President Carranza on April 10, 1920, saying that he had read that Carranza planned to send an army up the coast under General Manuel M. Diéguez. De la Huerta emphasized that the state government was there to solve problems but that the presence of large numbers of troops would only hurt his efforts among the Yaqui, indeed, would provoke them, for they still harbored ill feelings toward Diéguez. De la Huerta was a personal friend of Diéguez, who later supported him in the 1923 revolt against Obregón.[76]

"Los Hombres del Norte": The Sonoran Triumvirate

The controversy over the shutdown of the mines continued throughout 1919. George Young said the company found it necessary to shut down operations because of a lack of a market. De la Huerta believed that it was part of a ploy of the owners and accused them of using the dispute to undermine his candidacy for governor. Although Young said he would investigate de la Huerta's complaint, in reality, the copper industry was going through a restructuring and was using the economy (as we will see in chapter 10) to clean radicals out of the mines. The excuse was the IWW, which had moved from Clifton-Morenci into Sonora.[77]

Nationally, a crisis occurred when Carranza did not support Obregón as his successor, instead backing the Sonoran Ignacio Bonillas. This led to a revolt, which ended with the defeat and assassination of Carranza. De la Huerta, 39, was named interim president pending the election of Obregón. As president, de la Huerta made peace with Villa. Alvaro Obregón, the president-elect, took office in December 1920.

In 1924, Obregón supported Calles, and de la Huerta mounted an unsuccessful revolt. Although a substantial portion of workers and revolutionary generals supported de la Huerta, nonetheless he lost and went into exile in Los Angeles. In retrospect, Sonorans never developed a popular leader such as Pancho Villa. The members of the vaunted Sonora Triumvirate were from old families; they had little in common with the emerging working class.

The Exiles

The de la Huerta revolt unsettled the large Sonoran colony in the United States. Since the 1850s, Los Angeles had been a refuge for sonorenses, as had Tucson. In the early twentieth century, waves of revolutionary exiles joined their ranks. The villistas, for example, who included personages such as José María Maytorena, migrated north in significant numbers between 1915 and 1920. The treatment of the exiles varied, depending on the politics — theirs and the Euro-Americans' — and the year they came.

The exiles for the most part lacked funds, and their quality of life diminished. Those in the first wave were conservative and former supporters of Díaz. Then came the opponents of Huerta between 1913 and 1915. Many exiles continued to cross back into Mexico. Depending on the whim of the U.S. authorities, they were arrested or let go. Some spent time in Leavenworth Penitentiary.

Circumstances make strange bedfellows. To protect U.S. mining and petroleum interests, some Republicans, such as Edward L. Doheny, who owned the Mexican Petroleum Company, wanted Villa to set up a government in northern Mexico and to break away from the rest of the republic. Wealthy Republicans sponsored several reunions of exiled villistas and donated money to their cause. Their efforts did not bear fruit because Villa himself completely opposed the idea of secession.

As a group, exiles did not return to Mexico until the mid-1930s, when Lázaro Cárdenas and his cabinet invited political refugees to come back with assurances of pardons. By this time, there were a hundred political exiles in Los Angeles. They met to consider the offer. Adolfo de la Huerta, 54, was ready to return.[78]

◀ 9 ▶

To the Other Side of La Linea

According to a 1912 *Mining and Scientific Press* report, 30 percent of the smelter workers in Arizona were Americans, 60 percent were Mexicans, and 10 percent were British or northern Europeans. Significantly, the report distinguishes U.S.-born whites from northern Europeans. It excludes Spaniards or Italians (southern Europeans), who were heavily represented in other racial breakdowns of workers at the turn of the century. The central thesis of the report was that Mexicans were not assimilating. It underscored this point by noting that nearly half the Mexican workers had lived in Arizona for less than five years, and three-quarters for less than ten years, whereas most English, Irish, German, Scots, and Swedish workers had lived in Arizona for ten years or more; that only 8 percent of the Mexicans spoke English and fewer than 5 percent read and wrote English, whereas all the Germans and Swedes spoke and read English; and that only 5 percent of the 210 Mexicans working in the smelters had become citizens.

The report's comparisons make little sense when you consider that the Europeans had to sail across an ocean and travel more than halfway across a continent, whereas the Mexicans had only to cross an imaginary line. Its comparisons make even less sense when you consider that Mexican immigrants, no matter how recent, are lumped in with U.S.-born Mexicans who had been in Arizona, often for several generations, and most of whom spoke, read, and wrote English. The report completely overlooks the role played by racism—

that almost all Mexican workers, immigrant and U.S.-born alike, worked under segregated conditions imposed by the companies hiring them and that they lived in segregated barrios built and maintained by these same companies.

It is important to remember that most Mexican mining workers worked in the mines. Of those who worked in the smelters, which represented the elite sector of mining, three-fifths were general laborers: only a few worked on the smelter crews. And those few who, despite institutional racism, were able to break the "adobe ceiling" to become foremen or skilled workers were almost all U.S.-born. For, no matter where they worked in mining operations, almost all immigrant Mexicans and U.S.-born blacks worked as unskilled laborers.

As a result of occupational segregation, Mexicans worked harder and were paid less. The workday at the smelters was eight to twelve hours. Skilled workers toiled for eight to nine hours, and unskilled for as many as twelve hours. Whereas most white general laborers were paid $3.50 per day, 87 percent of the Mexican workers earned less than $2.50 for the same work. And whereas 85 percent of non-Mexican immigrant workers earned more than $2.50 per day, fewer that 15 percent of Mexican immigrant workers did.[1]

Censuses, as a matter of course, overlook both the racial biases of their compilers and the historical context of the populations they enumerate. In 1910, Graham County encompassed the largely Mexican camps of Clifton, Morenci, Metcalf, and Solomonville and their environs. According to the 1910 census, only 46 percent of the county's 3,550 Mexican-born persons were classified as "white" — and 54 percent as "other." Examination of the census forms, however, reveals clear evidence that the census compiler, a Doctor B. Jones, reviewed and changed the racial classification of most of the Mexicans, crossing out "white" and replacing it with a mark, which later appears to have signified "other," and noting "Mexican" on the left margin of the census form beside each Mexican person, whether born in Mexico or the United States.[2]

Mexicans, Go West

Large waves of Mexican workers continued to arrive through Nogales, even though the railroad would not link Sonora to Sinaloa until 1919. Between 1910 and 1921, as the overall population of Mexico fell by more than 5 percent, to just under 14,335,000, that of Sonora rose by nearly 4 percent, to just over 275,000, indicating heavy migration into and out of the state.

The direction of the migration changed when completion of the Roosevelt Dam and others like it permitted an incredible expansion of agriculture in the valleys of Arizona, attracting thousands of farmworkers. With the contraction of mining activity, Mexican miners migrated west from the camps along the

Mesilla corridor to the cotton fields of Arizona, as the state became the nation's leading producer of cotton, a crop that required armies of pickers. They were joined by other Mexicans traveling north along the Sonoran corridor. Headlines such as "Big Crops of Cantaloupe" and "Sugar Beet Seeds," competed for space in the *Graham Guardian*. The "Big Harvest" had come to Arizona, and cantaloupes were a $1.2 million crop, involving 2,300 acres. As with mining companies, most agribusinesses had absentee owners and hired managers. They were not so much farms as what Carey McWilliams would later call "factories in the field."[3]

Among the migrants was José Galván Amaro, born in Durango, Mexico, on May 28, 1902, the son of gold and silver miners. His family had for five generations worked in the mines just south of Parral. He joined Pancho Villa's army but deserted after his commanding officer was killed. He went north to El Paso, where he worked laying tracks for the railroad, and then west to Arizona, where he picked cotton near Phoenix. In 1923, he ended up in Los Angeles, where he worked in construction, attended night school, and studied English. During the Depression, Galván Amaro moved northward in search of work, to the Santa Maria area, where he became a leader in the 1931–35 strikes.[4]

The Revolution Rolls On

In February 1911, some fifty revoltosos recruited by "Hernández" — twelve from Metcalf, sixteen from Morenci, and the rest from Clifton — left Metcalf for the Sonora. Brigadier General W. S. Schengler of Fort Huachuca reported in March 1911 that the "mining district of Morenci and Clifton, Arizona, which has been persistently represented to us as a fertile recruiting ground, from which men and arms were being sent to the revolutionists in Chihuahua. I met there several gentlemen who are in a position to know what is going on, and also the Mexican consul recently arrived."[5]

There were reports of 5,000 rifles being stockpiled in San Antonio, 1,600 in Laredo, and another 5,000 in Bisbee. Throughout the decade, Clifton, Douglas, and El Paso bustled as revolutionary centers. Porfiristas expected an invasion of Sonora through Nogales and Douglas. La Liga Protectora de Refugiados Politicos organized chapters in Ray, Arizona, and in Santa Rita and Hurley, New Mexico, to protect the rights of Mexicans. They sponsored a dance for General Emilio Campa, a partisan of the Mexican revolutionist Emilio Vásquez Gómez, at Saint Patrick Saloon. The event was considered highly inflammatory: Campa was rumored to have told workers at the San Geronimo Mine that all gringos remaining in Mexico after September 15, 1912, would be slaughtered.

Spies reported that Julio T. Mancillas, Ramón Martínez, and Isabel Rangel were leaving Morenci for Nogales and then Cananea to organize a strike.[6] The *Graham Guardian* reacted with headlines like "Americans Are Leaving Mexico" and "Mexico Needs Spanking."[7] Cananea continued to be a center of revolutionary dissension. Mexican government sources whispered that a cannon was hidden near Cananea and would soon bombard the city.[8]

Miguel Aguilar, a Díaz operative, reported that Luis L. Hernández, who was organizing revolutionary clubs throughout the Southwest, had come to El Paso, offering $20 and a rifle to anyone joining the rebels. Though not every Mexican was a revolutionary, Aguilar conceded that, at this point, many of the deputy sheriffs were in sympathy with Hernández and the Revolution. Aguilar was also in touch with Brigadier W. S. Schuylar, as small parties left Clifton-Morenci-Metcalf to return to Mexico.[9]

U.S. detectives cooperated with the Mexican foreign office, which kept regular tabs on the *Copper Era* and other newspapers. Mexican consul S. M. del Toro at Clifton reported on revolutionary activity in Agua Prieta and elsewhere in Arizona and Sonora. Although Clifton-Morenci-Metcalf miners were not enthusiastic either for Vásquez Gómez or for Orozco, political friction among the workers caused the *junta cívica* to suspend patriotic activities. Spies identified Nepomuceno Ríos, who had been with Inés Salazar, as well as Ursulo Martínez, and Guillermo Espinosa as revoltosos.[10]

With the overthrow of Díaz, the forerunners to the Mexican Revolution were released from prisons. In a simple but compelling letter to Chihuahua Governor Abraham González, Abrán Salcido wrote that, having taken part in the revolutionary movement of 1906, he had been sent to San Juan de Ulúa Prison, along with three hundred compañeros, where conditions had been difficult. He served four years and eight months and was among the seventy-nine survivors. After congratulating González on becoming governor, he stated he was in bad health and asked for a job. If the revolutionary government was distributing land, he wanted some for himself and his five brothers. Salcido would also appreciate a recommendation to President Madero.[11]

Echoes of the Revolution

In the first decade of the twentieth century, Arizona became the world's leader in the production of copper. The Western Federation of Miners remained a Montana affair, and Butte Local 1 its linchpin. By 1910, however, the Industrial Workers of the World had opened the door for nonwhite workers. The WFM could no longer ignore the Mexican workers, and fights broke out between the

IWW and WFM partisans. WFM's Charles Moyer was shouted down at one meeting, where a shooting occurred. The *Miners' Magazine* correspondent blamed the Wobblies, calling them liars and thugs.[12]

The IWW was the WFM's Frankenstein monster. Almost immediately after the federation organized the IWW in 1905, factionalism developed. The radical leadership wanted locals to advance revolutionary goals. Moyer sought recognition and written agreements with employers, but IWW radicals called the arrangements reactionary. Although the WFM was willing to pour resources into the IWW, it was not willing to surrender its hard-won gains to the radicals. Accordingly, the WFM was the model of organization, whereas the IWW was just the opposite. The WFM claimed jurisdiction over all "workers in and around mines," a political claim the radicals refused to recognize.[13]

Before 1910, IWW radicals and the WFM had been united in their hatred of the American Federation of Labor. Afterward, the WFM gravitated toward the AFL, rejoining it in 1911. As the largest union within the IWW federation, the WFM had an alleged membership of 20,000. The radicals of the IWW abolished the presidency as reactionary and insisted that the WFM organize workers politically in an industrial union. The WFM, for its part, wanted to maintain its status as a trade union and to organize workers across the entire industry.

Readmitted to the American Federation of Labor through the offices of the United Mine Workers in 1911, the WFM veered farther to the right. Because of the challenge of the IWW, and the realities of the workforce, however, it had no choice but to organize Mexicans, whom the IWW had heavily recruited. This new direction clashed with the race prejudice of both its members and leadership, which, at the level of locals, was overwhelmingly white. In Jerome, an organizer claimed that only a fifth of the 1,300 miners belonged to the union. Workers spoke twenty foreign languages, and it was difficult to communicate with them, let alone interest them in the union.

Although union organizers complained about the difficulty of organizing Mexican workers, in reality, Mexicans readily participated in job actions when allowed to. For example, when a United Verde foreman, Martin Griffin, forced workers in the fire department to kick back wages, they demanded the company fire him. The men gave the superintendent forty-eight hours to discharge Griffith. When the superintendent replied that he had to investigate the matter, other Mexican miners then stepped up and filed affidavits against Griffith.[14]

Se Habla Español

When, as late as 1912, the WFM stated at its convention in Arizona that "Mexican miners are slowly but surely driving out the organized men in this state,"[15] the statement went unchallenged. According to many white miners, being peasants, Mexicans were incapable of understanding class consciousness.[16] As troops were deployed in ever greater numbers on the U.S. side, the likelihood of yet another U.S. invasion unsettled the increasingly nationalistic Mexicans. At the same time, there were Euro-Americans who sympathized with, or at least took note of, the revolutionary character of the revoltosos.

In 1910, the U.S. consul in Mexico, Luther T. Ellsworth, wrote: "I have the honor to report increasing activity of the very intelligent class of Mexican exiles in the Cities and Towns along the Mexican-American Border line, between the Gulf and the Pacific Ocean. [They] are busily engaged [in] writing and publishing inflammatory articles intended to educate up to date, in new revolutionary ideas, the thousands of Mexicans now on the American side of the Border line, and as many as possible of those on the Mexican side."[17] The number of Mexican workers was also growing in the mills and smelters of El Paso, gateway to New Mexico and the rest of the Southwest, staging area for the mines of eastern Arizona, and a center for labor militancy. Born in California of a Mexican mother and a Mexican American father, Fernando Velarde had worked for the IWW in Phoenix since 1906, organizing the separate Local 272 there in 1908. The following year, he published the first revolutionary industrial unionist paper, *La Unión Industrial.*

Soon afterward, Velarde moved to Southern California and participated in the PLM-IWW invasion of Baja California. On his return to Los Angeles, he published *La Huelga General* from 1913 until September 1914, and later, a third, unofficial newspaper, *El Rebelde,* which carried IWW news. These publications rarely reached beyond California. For a short time, Velarde had worked with Frank Little as a labor organizer in Clifton-Morenci-Metcalf.

Velarde questioned the commitment of the IWW's national leadership to addressing the ethnic issue, pointing to its failure to promote the education of the U.S. Mexican community. Velarde and his followers received little support from the IWW's Spokane offices. Manuel Rey, the IWW's only Latino national organizer, did not travel west during this period, and there were no Spanish-speaking members on the IWW executive committee. As Philip Mellinger points out, the IWW had an ethnic separation policy that "ran counter to its own acceptance of ethnic diversity." It had "language federations" and ethnic "branch" locals. "Most often, IWW national leadership either ignored or deliberately avoided organizing among Greeks, South Slavs, Spaniards, Mexicans, and Spanish Americans in western mining areas."[18]

The flow of IWW members from Arizona along the cotton corridor to Los Angeles, and back again, is noticeable in these years. IWW organizers were permanent fixtures in and around the Old Plaza of Los Angeles. On August 11,

1912, Leonidez Gutiérrez, a Mexican anarchist, was killed, and a riot ensued. Another riot broke out about a year later, when a hundred Wobblies and sympathizers marched behind a red flag "carried by two Mexican women of Amazonian proportions . . . at Third and Los Angeles Streets."[19] Throughout the decade, police kept close watch over the Old Plaza, which remained a center for radical agitation.

At the eastern end of the Mesilla corridor in El Paso, the mounting number of Mexican workers made organizing possible. The highly industrialized Gateway City was an early battleground for the IWW and the WFM adherents. In 1912, the IWW's Fernando Palomares, Rosendo A. Dorame, and S. Lomas were sent from Phoenix to El Paso, and were promptly arrested for organizing. A news account called Palomares a Mexican agitator who was in trouble in Los Angeles, and Dorame — a "California Mexican Indian."

The IWW was ordered out of town in 1913, during a strike called by the El Paso Mine & Smelter Workers Union, when a riot broke out and a Texas Ranger shot a striker. At this point, the WFM took control of the strike, sending Charles H. Tanner to El Paso. Although an experienced organizer, Tanner was also a blatant racist, constantly calling blacks "niggers." He acknowledged the Mexican workers' militancy but said they lacked class conscious and knew little of unionism. Due to the length and intensity of the strike, the union arranged to ship many strikers and their families to New Mexico, where they worked at jobs such as construction work on the Elephant Butte Dam, which paid $1.50 for eight hours' work, or for the railroad, which paid $1.50 for nine hours' work. Others worked in agriculture or the mines. Many sent money to feed the strikers who stayed behind. By Labor Day 1913, the back of organized labor seemed broken in the Gateway City.

Phillip Mellinger makes the logical assumption that many politicized El Paso strikers ended up in Arizona mining camps. The American Smelting and Refining Company, which had smelters in Ciudad Chihuahua, Aguascalientes, Mathuala, and Valardiania, closed down operations in December 1913, citing the growing turmoil in Mexico. Many of the company's 7,000 Mexican workers made their way north. Ciudad Juárez was at the center of the storm, as Euro-American workers also exited Chihuahua.[20] This only added to tensions brought by unemployment, labor strife, and the Revolution. The prospect of martial law on the U.S. side of the border drew nearer.[21]

Production in the Globe and Miami mines, which peaked in late May 1913, was linked to El Paso. Much of the ore secured by foreign, Los Angeles, and other out-of-state capitalists based around Phoenix ended up in the El Paso smelters. Low-cost electricity, the gift of the Reclamation Service via the Roosevelt Dam, made unparallel expansion possible. Electric plants networked the

Calumet and Arizona Copper mines in Globe, Miami, Superior, and Ray and the rest of the state.

The WFM-IWW war intensified. The various labor enclaves appeared split and at war with each other. Even the normally united Southern Pacific shops had become nonunion amid the squabbling. The Southwestern Railroad would not allow a union man to work for it. After the El Paso smelter management defeated the union there, management at the Pearson mills and other cement factories followed suit.

By 1914, even the Butte Miners' Union, a stronghold of the old WFM, was under the control of the Wobblies. A desperate Moyer demanded that the governor call out the troops to get rid of the IWW. The WPM's only hope was to ally itself with the AFL, whose membership had grown to just over 2 million by early 1914. Reflecting the WFM's decline in membership, the *Miners' Magazine* switched to a magazine format in mid-decade.[22]

Sonora, Arizona

Ray, Arizona, was located in the mountains near the colonias of Sonora and Barcelona, about eighty miles southeast of Phoenix and two hundred miles, by circuitous trails, west of Morenci. Ray was thirty-six miles southwest of Globe, the union stronghold of Arizona. In 1912, underground mining was still used to extract low-grade copper ore. The Ray Consolidated Copper Company owned everything, including the law in the towns of Ray, Sonora, and Barcelona.

In the early 1900s, Mexican and Mexican American workers and their families arrived in larger numbers, and by 1907 they had founded the community of Sonora, Arizona, which emerged from Sonora Camp a mile south of Ray and had its own post office. Workers were segregated not only physically but also by a dual wage system. Spanish Carmelite priest Pascasio Hériz described Ray as the "poorest of the poor."[23] In another letter, he said he was "shocked by lamentable state of Mexicans, without faith and without morals."[24] Many of the miners in Ray were from Hermosillo. In 1914–15, Sonora had a population of about 5,000, and Barcelona, the Spanish colonia next to it, had about 1,000, as did Ray itself, most of whose residents were Euro-American and Irish.

In March 1914, in response to growing labor militancy, forty copper barons met in Tucson to form a new association. Unable to attend because of problems in Mexico, J. S. Douglas was represented by a proxy. Ray Consolidated employed 1,400 men, most of whom were Mexican nationals. The rest of the workforce were Spaniards and white Euro-Americans, the latter of whom held skilled craft positions. The Guggenheims owned Ray, while Moyer wanted to consolidate the Globe, Miami, and Ray Districts and the Guggenheim mines and smelters throughout the West.[25]

The Western Federation of Miners reinforced Ray Consolidated's racial policies. According to Andrea Yvette Huginnie, "Anti-Mexicanism remained an important issue for the W.F.M. throughout the World War I period. Union leaders repeatedly fell back on excluding Mexicans from the mining workforce as a means of protecting and bettering Anglo workers' position — at least in the short run."[26] Tempers flared when the WFM supported the Arizona Alien Labor Law — the "80 percent Law" — which severely limited the number of Mexicans who could work in the mines by requiring companies to employ at least 80 percent "American" labor. Governor George Hunt favored the law.[27] Mexican miners resented it.

Violence broke out in the summer of 1914, when Euro-Americans chased Peter Smith, a "half-breed Mexican," as the press called him, after he allegedly stole a horse in Ray and took to the hills. Angry because they had not been paid after being laid off, Smith and two or more companions ambushed the posse. When several shootings followed the stabbing of the Mexican boss of an all-Mexican mine crew while he slept, the situation exploded. On August 20, 1914, the *Los Angeles Times* announced: "Race War in Arizona; Death List Is Sixteen." Four Euro-Americans and twelve Mexicans were killed in the bloody riot. As the *Times* reported:

> Infuriated at the news of the death of posse members, white residents of Ray invaded the Mexican section of town, driving the terror-stricken men, women and children of the section from their homes. One American and seven Mexicans were killed when a number of the Mexican residents resisted the attack upon their homes. The others fled to the hills. Reports said that many Americans were searching the hills near Ray tonight, bent upon killing every Mexican they meet. Officers and citizens have been sworn in as deputies, were sent to patrol the entire section to prevent a spread of the race rioting, if possible.[28]

According to the PLM newspaper, white scabs attacked nineteen Mexican workers in Ray, Arizona. Sheriff Brown died along with two Mexicans in Devil's Canyon near Ray. That night, in another confrontation, another Mexican was killed. White mobs descended on the Mexican barrio, forced their way into its homes, and committed atrocities. They scoured the hills looking for Mexicans. "The American working class is the most mentally retarded class," wrote *Regeneración*, not knowing its interests as workers.[29]

The reign of terror was encouraged by the management of Ray Consolidated. Desperate Mexicans wired Lázaro Gutiérrez de Lara in Los Angeles, who telegraphed Governor Hunt, asking him to intervene. Hunt, originally from nearby Globe, investigated the killings in August 1914. The governor called labor relations there feudal, stating that Mexicans were justifiably angry. Matters remained unresolved into 1915.

Ray Consolidated played on ethnic hatreds to consolidate its control. Anyone Consolidated believed was a troublemaker — read union activist or labor organizer — was beaten, jailed, and kicked out of town, as were WFM organizers E. J. Moreno and Julio Mancillas, sent to Ray in 1914. Moreno berated the Mexican workers for accepting lower wages than whites, and challenged them to organize. Mellinger has credited the mutualistas for organizing Mexican workers. In reality, the mostly conservative, middle-class membership of these groups wanted, more than anything else, to fit in, and they realized they could do this only by staying quiet.[30]

Revolt in the Mexican Camps

A dramatic rise in the price of both copper and food while wages remained low stirred discontent among the miners. In Miami, skilled workers voted to strike. The Mexican workers' union, Comité por Trabajadores en General (General Workers' Committee), walked out in solidarity. Owners settled the strike in two weeks, when workers reluctantly accepted a company offer that tied wages to the New York wholesale price of copper.

With fighting just over 150 miles to the south, Spanish and Mexican miners at the nearby Ray Consolidated Copper Company grew nervous. Would the United States intervene? Would Villa invade Sonora? When a devastating flood destroyed many homes in Sonora in mid-January, they worried about the safety of their relatives. Toward the end of March, heavy fighting broke out once more in Sonora. Throughout the year, different Mexican factions visited the Mexican mining camps seeking volunteers and money.[31]

As the Yaqui wars heated up, the U.S. press once again called for intervention. In mid-May, the U.S. Navy sent a cruiser to just off the coast of Guaymas to protect "Americans" from the Yaqui. U.S. news accounts recalled the "American pioneer spirit" as their countrymen confronted the "murderous" Yaqui. Coverage of the Yaqui rebellion resembled the tales of the "marauding Apache." Another crisis arose when Governor Maytorena sent 850 troops to the Río Yaqui Valley, raising the possibility that villistas intended to repel the Marines if they invaded Sonora.[32]

Believing that Mexico and the United States were going to war, the Mexican miners of Ray called a meeting in the spring of 1915. Mellinger speculates that it "may have begun as a Plan of San Diego meeting. Rumors were rife, especially in areas which were in close proximity to the international border."[33]

Yaqui Indians at Agua Prieta, Sonora, Mexico, in November 1915. (From Finley, "The Yaqui Fight in Bear Valley"; courtesy of the Fort Huachuca Museum)

The plan had called for a general uprising of Mexicans and other minorities on February 20, 1915, in which the rebels would execute all white males over age 16 — but spare African Americans, Asians, and Native Americans. The Southwest would become a Mexican nation, with blacks and Native Americans forming other independent nations. Although we can assume some of the plan's supporters may have resided in Arizona, there is no evidence it had significant support among the Mexican miners of Ray.[34]

Writing in *Regeneración*, Ricardo Flores Magón never supported the plan, stating that authorities wanted "to make it appear as if the Mexican uprising in that section of the United States is part of the Plan of San Diego."[35] Indeed, Euro-Americans used the plan as a pretext for widespread terror against Mexicans. In 1917, George Marvin reported in *World's Work* magazine:

> The killing of Mexicans . . . along the border in these last four years is almost incredible. . . . Some Rangers have degenerated into common mankillers. There is no penalty for killing, no jury along the border would ever convict a white man for shooting a Mexican. . . . A great deal was made of the intention of Mexicans to kill Euro-Americans and minimize their own atrocities, although reading over Secret Service records gives one the feeling . . . it was an open gun season on Mexicans along the border.[36]

U.S. historian Walter Prescott Webb excused the reign of terror — blaming the Mexican Revolution, the Plan of San Diego, and even the "nature" of Mexicans. "Without disparagement it may be said that there is a cruel streak in the Mexican nature, or so the history of Texas would lead one to believe. This cruelty may be a heritage from the Spanish or the Inquisition. it may, and doubtless should, be attributed partly to the Indian blood."[37] Webb alleged that

Germany had agents scattered throughout Mexico, training Mexican soldiers, and that Germany had a powerful wireless station in Mexico City. Webb even dragged in the IWW, saying that it was passing out incendiary literature. Americans could not simply stand by; "their anger was lashed into fury." On the other hand, Webb noted: "In the orgy of bloodshed that followed, the Texas Rangers played a prominent part, and one of which many members of the force have been heartily ashamed."[38]

What is amazing is that a force of fifty Mexicans caused the Texans to panic. On June 18, 1915, President Wilson put the National Guards of Texas, New Mexico, and Arizona, a force of 100,000 men, under federal command to patrol the border. Arizona copper barons had pressured Wilson to take this action to quell labor agitation, which was also supposedly German-inspired. In any case, between July 1915 and July 1916, Rebels made a total of thirty raids into *Texas*. Officially, U.S. authorities claimed that 300 "suspected" Mexicans were shot, hanged, or beaten and that twenty-one Americans were killed by the rebels.[39]

Back in Ray, Mexican miners decided to strike Ray Consolidated on June 27, 1915, when there was considerable turmoil 150 miles to the south. Mexican mine workers were well organized, and they wanted justice and equality with white workers in the workplace. The Comité por Trabajadores General pushed the issues of fairness and an end to Ray Consolidated's absolute control. Organizers E. J. Moreno and Julio Mancillas were jailed, beaten, and thrown out of Ray. The company allowed white union members to work at its facilities but would not let Comité members on its premises.[40] When white miners struck at Miami, Mexican and Spanish workers, whom the union had excluded, walked out in solidarity.

The Comité, which represented between 1,000 and 1,500 workers, demanded the Miami wage scale and equality with white workers. C. L. Salcido and José Miranda solicited Governor Hunt's support when he visited Miami. Ray Consolidated went on the offensive and beat several strikers, including Refugio M. de J. Muñiz and A. N. Tribolt. The managers threatened to arrest strikers.

The Mexican and Spanish workers tasted power: although they did not get the Miami scale, they won a 60-cent increase in their daily wages.[41] Of the statewide network of mutualistas, only the Liga Protectora Latina came out in support of the strike, and only toward the end. And even though WFM organizers Henry S. McClusky and Guy Miller, an executive board member, were in Ray during the strike, the WFM did not rally its AFL base, as it had during the Utah and Nevada strikes of 1912.

At Miami, there was a power struggle between the WFM and the IWW.

Dissatisfied with Moyer's leadership, the Globe Miners' Union was largely in the camp of the Arizona State Federation of Labor, formed in 1911 and chartered in 1914 as an international. Many of the federation's officers were Globe Miners' Union members.[42]

Governor George W. Hunt had strong ties to labor. The business community and mayor of Globe were all pro-union. However, the Globe Miners' Union was torn by internal power struggles. Whereas Guy Miller was enthusiastic about organizing Mexicans, Moyer was paranoid about the new mass movement and WFM's Miami Local 70, which he believed was under IWW influence. According to Mellinger, "The Miami men were opening the way to large-scale and long-lasting ethnic unionism."[43] Meanwhile, Phelps Dodge posted a 23 percent yield on a capitalization of $45 million, and Detroit Copper a 146 percent yield on a capitalization of $1 million. The copper market was heating again up as the war in Europe expanded.

The 80 percent Law and the Loyalty League spearheaded efforts to make mining camps "all-American." Nativism gained steam during the depression of 1914. The state election was noteworthy because of conflicts between the copper barons and labor. As the mine owners began the Great Spring Drive with a wave of discharges, the WFM decided to fight back.[44]

The race question loomed. Veterans like Miami local's George Powell feared race violence and "uncontrollable Mexicans" who were agitating the Mexican rank and file. Company operatives used the division — warning the Mexicans about the Anglo-Irish, and the Anglo-Irish about the Mexicans. Although Powell feared Mexican radicalism, he and Charles Tanner opposed the exclusionists. They were pragmatic — the IWW set about actively organizing unorganized Mexicans.

Even after Mexicans on both sides of the border flocked to unions, Moyer still appeared to be afraid of alienating white miners by admitting Mexicans into the WFM. The IWW was challenging Moyer, however, and more practical organizers such as Guy Miller called "unorganized" workers a menace. Racist nativism extended back to 1896, when the Globe miners excluded Mexicans from the camp. Labor lined up against the immigrants in the 1903 fight over the Eight Hour Law, the 1909 Arizona Literacy Law, proposals in the 1910 state constitution that targeted Mexicans, and the Kinney Bill of 1914. The American Federation of Labor and the WFM passed anti-immigrant resolutions and failed to temper the ranting of Hunt's attorney general Wiley Jones, and Arizona Senator Henry Ashurst talked incessantly about dangerous aliens who were driving "Americans" (white people) out of Arizona. The Mexican middle class, although against organized labor, resented this racist nativism.[45]

The price of copper was badly depressed in 1914, falling to sixteen cents a pound. Hard times and a surplus of labor made it difficult to organize. In September 1915, Ray miners told Governor Hunt they did not want anything to do with the WFM. Why should they when it had excluded them? They told Hunt that they did not care how much they earned so long as it was equal to what "American" miners earned. They did not care if that meant reducing "American" wages. Why should they?[46]

A Return to Clifton

Between 1911 and 1912, copper production increased by more than $58 million. In 1913, the Arizona Copper Company built a $2.5 million smelter on Smelter Hill south of Clifton, replacing the old smelter in the heart of town. The next year, Arizona Copper built a mansion for its president, Norman Carmichael, on the east side. Chase Creek Street, the business section of Clifton, was lined with pool halls and saloons, player pianos played day and night. The Empire and Royal Theaters were also on Chase Creek. On Clifton's east side stood two banks, two hotels, two restaurants, and a Chinese laundry. From 1911 to 1913, there was major building boom in Clifton. When a fire burned down the commercial district in April 1913, they rebuilt it on a grand scale: "arches, balconies, and Victorian and Neoclassical detailing, combined with the narrow street, dense one-and two-story façades and natural setting, give Chase Creek an ambiance unequaled anywhere in the state."[47]

The London-Arizona Consolidated Copper Company brought together well-known capitalists from the United States and London with a capitalization of $12 million to monopolize Arizona's mining claims. In November 1913, F. S. Stephens, representing Scottish capital, purchased seven copper claims near Jerome. Doctor L. O. Davenport of Humboldt Copper headed another syndicate purchasing placer claims. That year, the Copper Queen smelter produced almost 11.5 million pounds of copper, and the Greene-Cananea smelter 7 million pounds.[48]

Racial incidents were common. According to *Regeneración*, lawmen threw Julian Ramos into jail on trumped-up charges, and Jesús Urrea was beaten up in the streets of Clifton.[49] On August 13, 1913, an accident killed nine men on the Coronado incline, among them a twelve-year-old Mexican boy.[50] That year, both Arizona Copper and Shannon Copper contributed money to Morenci and Clifton fiestas patrias.[51] On September 18, 1914, the *Copper Era* reported: "Shannon Company Shuts Down Mines and Smelter." Shannon had not sold copper since July 20, and approximately six hundred Mexican miners were idled in Metcalf and Clifton. Morenci remained a gloomy place and in 1914.

Three Mexicans were wounded at Chihuahua Hill, and there were also four attempted suicides. Fights frequently erupted in these communities, where there were few recreational facilities for workers of their families. The companies fought against taxes, even for improvements to safety.[52]

Enter the Carmelites

The logical institution to protect the Mexican immigrant was the Catholic Church. But its hierarchy was rabidly anti–trade union and against radicalism of any sort, although an occasional priest of Irish descent would champion the rights of Irish workers. Cardinal James Gibbons questioned the use of strikes: "They paralyze industry, foment passion and lead to the destruction of property." They were an "unwarranted invasion of commercial privileges guaranteed by government to every business firm."[53]

In Arizona, Bishop Henry Regis Granjon called labor organizing a "barbaric invasion led by Protestants." During the 1910s, Granjon saw the Mexican population mushroom and, with it, the demand for Spanish-speaking priests. Enter the Spanish Carmelites.

After being expelled from Mexico in the nineteenth century, the Spanish Carmelites had drifted back in the late 1899 — bringing with them memories of a century of Church and state tensions. Most were from Barcelona, the scene of bitter street fighting.[54] They had expected to be received as saviors. But when, in 1903, the order's growing internal rift surfaced, Mexican-born and Spanish-born Carmelites divided the province of Mexico between them. By 1905, the Spanish Carmelites were actively looking to expand to the United States. Father Pedro de Santo Elías (Hériz) was sent to the United States to seek refuge in case they were expelled by the Mexican revolutionaries. After negotiations with Bishop Granjon, the order was given to a small parish at Winkelman, on the Gila River.[55]

Father Alejo Coll Coll (de la Virgen del Carmen) joined Pedro, José María de la Concepción Inmaculada, and Brother Pedro Tomás del Infante Jesús. The Carmelites expanded into the mining camp of Ray, where they developed good relations with General Manager Louis Cates, who donated two candlesticks and a crucifix to their church. The Carmelites placed great emphasis on learning English in order to cross over. There is no indication they stood up for their Mexican parishioners or were concerned about their material welfare. They seemed oblivious of the camp's segregation, with Father Pedro Hériz noting that, in Tucson, there was one cathedral for the Mexicans and another for the *americanos*.[56]

Father Alejo arrived in Morenci in May 1913.[57] He was born José Alejo Coll

Coll on August 26, 1884, in Leridana de Aramunt in the Pyrenees of Catalan. His parents, Buenaventura Coll and Antonia Coll, had six children, three of whom died while still quite young. One sister became a nun, the other a servant mother in Barcelona. His mother died when Alejo was ten, and he entered the noviate in 1900. In April 1912, the Carmelites ordered Alejo to the United States during what one biographer called "years of great social agitation."

Everything seemed to be going smoothly in Morenci until a bomb exploded in the parish house on July 11 — and another on July 31. The bombings had a profound impact on Alejo, who wrote Bishop Granjon: "I was very unhappy because at one o'clock in the morning of the 11th day of this month, I was the object of a savage and criminal attempt; some tubes of dynamite were placed in the room where I slept. The fire cracker made a horrible explosion, destroying the walls made of lumber and part of the roof, but, I, thanks to God, came out unhurt, although the explosion took place at a distance of about four feet from my bed." He wrote on August 2 that "a bomb which was placed under the church and some dynamite cartridges right under the sacristy and at the place over which I slept, all exploded at the same time.[58] Bishop Granjon asked whether there been any signs of discontent? He cautioned Alejo to exercise moderation, as non-Catholics did not like the ringing of bells on weekdays.

Father Pedro's brother, Pascasio — or Paschasius, as he was also known — arrived in Arizona in early 1913. Assigned to Ray, he wrote, "Don't think that I am discouraged. My initial reaction was one of shock at the lamentable state of these Mexicans, without faith and without morals, damaged terribly by immorality. Little by little, I am converting some of them and awakening them to the slumber in which they find themselves."[59] Pascasio later wrote from Hayden that, unlike the people, "the Hayden company is very warm to me, it has given me cement at sixty cents a sack" and sold him zinc sheeting much cheaper than the market price.[60] Pascasio was generally negative about Mexicans. On the spiritual remissness of Mexicans, Granjon wrote Pascasio: "It is a matter we all deplore. They came from the border states of Mexico with vices deeply rooted in their nature, and of course, their association with the infidel and Protestant elements of this country does not tend to improve them. Far from it. God will bless us for our efforts, at any rate. — I shall consider the suggestion of giving you a strong letter on the subject."[61] Father Paschasius would later be sent to Morenci, where he would be a key player in the 1915 strike.

The bishop assigned José María de la Concepción Inmaculada to Clifton. Granjon said that Clifton would help finance the poorer parishes, such as Ray.[62] Meanwhile, Pedro met with displaced white priests and learned of their displeasure with the bishop. Granjon had not consulted with the priests of the diocese before assigning the Carmelites to Clifton-Morenci-Metcalf. Three priests were sending a protest to Rome. Morenci and Clifton were considered plums. Granjon continued to press Pedro to remain in Clifton-Morenci-Metcalf, where detectives were investigating the bombings and would guarantee the priest's life.[63]

Rumors abounded that the bombers were terrorists. According to one source, they were Spanish anarchists who had migrated from Barcelona to Arizona. On temporary assignment to Morenci, Pedro wrote the vicar general in Cataluña that it was rumored that a friend of the displaced priest, unhappy about his removal, had placed the bombs. "Things around me are tranquil and I do not believe I am in danger, but I am nevertheless cautious."[64] Meanwhile, three Mexicans were arrested as suspects but were released for lack of evidence. The investigation reached a dead end. By the fall, it was still believed that radicals were to blame. In November, Granjon said he would not spend more money on detectives and, because the state authorities were not cooperating, he was bringing the matter to the attention of the U.S. Attorney in Arizona.[65]

During the Mexican Revolution, Carmelite priests were arrested and the order's property nationalized.[66] Father Simon de Jesús wrote about the sacking of Durango, calling the rebels barbarous. On the other hand, the Carmelites received money from exiled families. Father Pascasio Hériz moved to Morenci, and his correspondence suggests divisions between the younger priests and between them and Father Pedro.[67]

Alejo had a difficult time raising money from the community, prompting him "to reexamine the commitment of Mexicans in Sonora, Arizona."[68] Pedro was disillusioned with Alejo. He complained that Granjon did not answer his letters, which also suggest that the Carmelites spent an excessive amount of money on the religious art and statues they imported from the Tomás Márques Taller in Barcelona.[69]

According to Pascasio, during the great Clifton-Morenci-Metcalf Strike of 1915, the union passed a resolution giving him twenty-four hours to leave Morenci, a claim supported by the Tombstone *Epitaph*. Pascasio did so after consulting with the supervisors of the mining companies. The union felt that both Pascasio and José María of Clifton were undermining the strike and were out to destroy the union. After speaking to the president of the Clifton local, Juan Guerra, José María decided to stay. The priests did not make extended comments about the strike. On October 2, 1915, Vicar General Father Lucas, who had come to Morenci, barely mentions the strike. Meanwhile, Pascasio kept in communication with some parishioners and reported that the company had evacuated foremen Varela and others, who, according to Pascasio, were peaceful and only escaped to Clifton with their lives. Pascasio sympathized with the scabs.[70]

Alejo believed that Pascasio had left prematurely and was at least partially responsible for what happened. Alejo was disturbed by the abrupt departure of Pascasio. He wrote Lucas that Pascasio had left Morenci and did not intend to return because of calamities and rumors. Alejo felt compelled to go to Morenci and offer his services out of respect for the parishioners. Alejo charged that Pascasio could have avoided the problem — adding that neither he nor José María were in danger. The priests seemed angry with Pascasio because they were now overworked.[71]

After leaving Morenci, Pascasio spent several days in Tucson and Hayden, before proceeding to Sonora to minister to some "americanos mal casados" (Americans living in sin). He wanted to return to Morenci but the strike was not resolved and that he knew the strikers did not like him.[72]

Alejo remembered being bombed and predicted that the strike would end in two or three months. Alejo was much more sympathetic to the suffering of the strikers and said that the union people were hungry and exclaimed, "Poor people!"[73] In May 1916, Pascasio wrote to Alejo, "In all of the mining camps of Arizona, religion is suffering great perdition, and loss of religion and liberality are assuming an alarming strength." In the face of this wave of godlessness, the priests must pray and be patient and preach so the Devil will not win out.[74]

The Carmelites' letters suggest panic over a possible war between Mexico and the United States. Pascasio requested that, since the Yanquis were going to war with Mexico, Alejo send him the bullets for his gun. He did not say which way he would point the gun. In October, Pascasio and other Carmelites traveled to Washington, D.C., and went to Catholic University, where they were greeted by Cardinal Gibbons and treated "like angels."[75]

Alejo was active in cultivating vocations among the Mexicans. Bishop Granjon cautioned: "My experience has been to the effect that not one Mexican woman in a dozen remains in the convent. There are few who, *sooner or later*, do not leave it. Be prudent."[76] No mention is made of the strikes that consumed Arizona in 1917. In May 1918, Father Alejo bought property for a parochial school, which shut down in August 1921. He left for Spain that October.[77]

By 1927, the Carmelite priests assigned to the mining camps wanted to live in urban communities, preferably in Los Angeles. Pedro agreed with them. Father Lucas in Rome wrote Pedro that he personally did not believe that the priests were so dissatisfied they would abandon the souls of their parishioners. He reminded Pedro that Arizona's large Mexican population was the reason they had been given sanctuary there. Simply put, the other bishops did not want them in California, which was a popular site.[78]

The Arizona Carmelites insisted they be allowed two priests per parish, like the Jesuits. In the 1920s, the Carmelites would pull out of the mining camps that were not prosperous. The move was made possible by the growth of the Mexican population, who needed Spanish-speaking priests. The lessening of the persecution of Catholic priests in Mexico led exiled priests to return to Mexico. In the Diocese of Los Angeles alone, there were forty parishes that had been ministered by "Mexican priests who returned to Mexico."[79]

Throughout his exchanges with his fellow Carmelites, Father Lucas showed his displeasure: "I want to deal with reality, and I do not have the luxury of dreaming." The Arizona Carmelites had been able to accumulate a substantial amount of property. But Lucas attacked them on other grounds. He scolded Pedro for mistreating the Spanish Carmelite nuns and requesting that the bishop replace them with American nuns.

> I do not know definitely what has happened with the nuns! [What] I have heard is second- and third-hand rumors. . . . I have always believed that excessive familiarity with our good Religious Sisters would in the end bring disagreeable consequences. I never thought that things would reach the point they have. Without a doubt, we are all at fault. At least three times, I ordered the door closed, and personally nailed that interior door of the garden, and others again opened them. I assumed that, after the Visitor General's visit, that it has been permanently closed.

The bishop and R. P. Timmermans, as vicar general, rejected the request. "If this is true, we have lost considerable moral ground in the eyes of the esteemed Bishop. I beg that you to tell me the truth."[80]

◄ 10 ►

The Great Copper Wars

In November 1914, Arizona voters passed an initiative requiring that at least 80 percent of the workers be naturalized citizens or native-born Americans. The growing presence of Mexicans not only in mining but also in agriculture, added to the Euro-American angst over the 1913 recession. Mine owners opposed the initiative process as mobocracy because it bypassed their lackeys in the state legislature, and they opposed this particular initiative as a reflection of the growing power of organized labor.[1]

The copper barons lined up with Walter Douglas and planned an all-out assault on labor as Europe in 1914 plunged into war. By the end of the year, Europe was buying copper once more. In Miami, after a brief strike on January 23, 1915, workers won a sliding scale that tied wages to the price of copper. Shortly afterward, workers received small raises at Bisbee. Miners were unsettled by the prospect of war between Mexico and the United States. A short, successful strike occurred at Ray in July, when Mexican workers won concessions, aided by the Globe-Miami WFM. The cluster of mines at Ray, Globe, and Miami was owned by the Guggenheims and the Lewisohns, whom Douglas viewed as permissive.

Douglas had made concessions at Bisbee, but these were to white miners. He was determined to hold the line at Morenci, where the workforce was overwhelmingly Mexican, had less popular and union support, and was more isolated—and where the pretext for resisting workers' demands was the need to maintain efficiency in processing the low grade of copper.

The 1915 Miami strike was hugely important. When Mexican strikers at Ray sought equality with white workers, it was the Miami scale they demanded. After two weeks, workers reluctantly accepted a company offer that tied wages to the New York wholesale price of copper, though at rates slightly below the Miami scale. This victory energized workers in other camps. Guy E. Miller and a "half-breed Mexican" A. N. Tribolet slipped into Morenci and held meetings in nearby Newton.

Miller and Tribolet used Mexican workers' societies to contact miners throughout the cluster. Their initiative was significant because it had not been approved by the WFM's executive board, which probably would not have authorized a strike anyway—it had other priorities.

The conditions were ripe at Morenci and the surrounding camps. Abuse was systemic. Petty foremen and minor officials forced workers to buy chances on worthless prizes. Shift bosses collected from five to fifteen dollars a month for mythical services. Foremen rented shacks to the workers for ten dollars a month. And the mining companies charged inflated hospital and water fees. In mid-July 1915, the Mexican miners had formed the Club Cosmopolita, which functioned as a union rather than a mutualista or WFM chapter, in Metcalf.[2] By September, Guy Miller, an executive board member of the WFM, telegraphed the union headquarters: "Advise you wire L. Gutierrez de Lara 420 West Fourth Street, Los Angeles . . . and instruct him to come here."[3]

Many old timers, the *Copper Era* reported, opposed striking on principle. Company loyalists flooded the area with pro-management circulars. Over the years, the more militant miners had been cleaned out through blacklisting. One vocal critic of the labor organizers was mine metal foreman Refugio G. Murillo, 45, of Metcalf. Although born in Mexico and married to a Mexican woman who spoke mostly Spanish, Murillo listed his primary language as English. Murillo's two eldest children had been born in Texas; the other five, two of them adopted, had been born in Arizona. He Anglicized the names of all seven.[4]

The Industrial Workers of the World were not a factor in Morenci. WFM loyalists Canuto Vargas Jr., secretary of the Morenci District Miners Union, and Pascual Vargas y Soto, president of the local, had cleaned them out. Canuto Vargas Sr. had been a leader of the Clifton-Morenci Strike of 1903. He had emigrated from Mexico in 1892 with his wife, Estanislada, and his infant son, Canuto. The younger two siblings were born in Arizona. Pascual Vargas—no relation—was from Texas.[5]

The walkout began on September 12. Within a few days, some 5,000 mine, mill, and smelter workers were on strike. The Morenci workforce went out

Officials of the Morenci District Miners Union, including Henry S. McCluskey (third from left, top row) and Canuto Vargas and Pascual Vargas y Soto (second and third from left, bottom row). (Courtesy of the Arizona Collection, Arizona State University Libraries, Henry S. McCluskey Photographs, CP MCC-82)

nearly to the man, demanding the Miami scale. "In Metcalf," the *Miners' Magazine* wrote, "the walkout was 100 per cent; at 1:00 close, the men came out of their holes; they came down the hills in order." At 2:00 in the afternoon, there were parades, as Mexican families prepared to march into Clifton.[6]

Meanwhile, the organizers were gathering. E. J. Moreno, driven out of Ray and elected the "Spanish conductor" of the Miami union, came to Morenci, as did Guy Miller, George Powell, Henry McCluskey, Ed Crough, Charles Tanner, A. N. Tribolet, W. F. Burleson, and E. A. Redwanz. Lázaro Gutiérrez de Lara came from Los Angeles, and Juan Rico from South Texas.[7]

On September 27, strikers accused company loyalist Pedro Michelena, 57, of being a spy, and ordered him out of Clifton-Morenci-Metcalf. Originally from Sonora, Michelena lived with his wife, Luisa, and their seven children, who were all born in Arizona. He was a longtime resident of Solomonville and employed by the Arizona Copper Company as an interpreter.[8]

Telegraphed by Sheriff James G. Cash, Governor George Wiley Hunt arrived in Clifton on Tuesday, September 18, and checked into the Reardon Hotel. Hunt, fifty-five and an ex-miner, met with the mine managers and suggested an arbitration committee. The managers balked. They invited him to supper, but he declined, saying he had come to settle the strike, not to eat.[9] For two days, he toured the camps, sitting down with the workers and listening to their grievances. Hunt was mindful of the Colorado Ludlow Massacre of April 20, 1914, where twenty men, women, and children had been killed by National Guard troops and company goons. In calling out the Arizona National Guard, he was determined to have it prevent bloodshed — not cause it.

Two days later, a mass meeting was held at the Clifton Library Plaza. Workers from Morenci and Metcalf began to arrive at noon with large female contingents. More than 3,000 wives, children, miners, businessmen, clerks, deputy sheriffs, and others poured into the plaza. A Mexican orchestra serenaded the governor. Lázaro Gutiérrez de Lara fired up the crowd and interpreted for Hunt, who told the audience they should pursue their demands, "but in an orderly and law-abiding manner." Everyone would be treated equally from the owners to "the poorest Mexican they control." The response was enthusiastic. After the speech, Hunt drove to Lordsburg, where he took a train to Phoenix.[10]

Meanwhile, the managers, who refused to deal with the WFM and who declined the governor's offer to arbitrate, turned the mines over to Sheriff Cash. Miller was conciliatory and did not insist on WFM recognition. Loyalists defended the companies, saying that, if a man was willing, he could always find work in Morenci, and blaming the 1915 walkout on agitators.[11]

Worker support of the strike followed racial and class lines. For Mexicans, the Miami scale meant equality with white miners. Initially, the merchants' association, whose members were tired of the mining companies' monopoly, supported them. Dick Frantz of Becker-Franz Mercantile Company, who owned a chain of mercantile stores, gave the strikers $10,000 in credit, and reportedly distributed $26,000 in goods. Other camps sent money; the Globe-Miami miners donated $15,000. The rail workers helped, as did the Arizona State Federation.[12]

"We Will Fight before We Starve!"

During a speech on September 14, Juan Guerra, president of the Clifton local, pointed at Celidonia Trujillo, 43, a foreman of the Arizona Copper Company, and said: "Here you have one of the men who had been sold to the company. He was the one who lowered the wages to $1.40 and he is one of the men who has done the most wrong to the people and he has done nothing good for the people."

Trujillo worked at the smelter, and he was married with six children. On September 17, he left Clifton — and his wife Francisca and family — behind.[13]

On October 2, a drum corps followed by miners, women, and children marched along Chase Creek to the center of Clifton with signs saying "Mine Managers Too Proud to Confer." Two days later, their ranks swelled to two bands and 3,000 marchers. Rumors circulated that the main between Morenci and Newton would be dynamited to cut off the workers' water supply.[14] Also on October 2, managers Norman Carmichael, J. W. Binnie, and Milton McLean fled to Lordsburg and then to El Paso. Sheriff Cash and a deputy chased their train by car to New Mexico, in an effort to prevent them from leaving.[15] Hunt characterized their departure as unjustified, especially in light of the WFM's accommodating attitude. The governor requested that Secretary of Labor William B. Wilson conduct a federal investigation, and Wilson sent Joseph S. Myer (later joined by Hywell Davies) to Arizona as a conciliator.[16]

As mentioned in chapter 9, Father Pascasio, who had close ties with Arizona's Mexican elite and the mine owners, opposed the strike and was, according to him, ordered by militant workers to leave Morenci.[17] One of the elite, J. Y. Ainsa, a language instructor at the Arizona Copper Company and a member of the Alianza Hispano Americana and the Liga Protectora Latina, sided with the owners and passed out a circular highly critical of the strike. The union labeled Ainsa, Murrillo, and two loyalist Spaniards traitors.

As the strike entered its second month, the mood of the strikers darkened and they grew more militant. Scab Gregorio Ramírez, 50, for example, was jailed for six hours after an altercation with strikers on October 2. Between October 8 and October 16, by relief committee reports, the number of families and single men in need of food jumped tenfold overall, to 2,300 and 130, respectively. On October 10, the Morenci strikers, among whom were Abraham Rico and Carlos Casalay, had ordered L. J. Owens, manager of the Phelps Dodge Store, to leave town, along with the company scabs. Rico had been active in the 1903 Clifton-Morenci strike and was reputed to have had ties to the Partido Liberal Mexicano. Casalay, forty-seven, had immigrated when he was ten and was a neighbor of Pedro Subia.[18]

On October 19, the *Prescott Journal-Miner* featured testimony "by men who suffered attacks" from the WFM strikers. J. I. Watson, for example, who described himself as "a pump repairer . . . employed for five years here," married with one child, "an American citizen, a property owner and taxpayer," claimed the strikers had broken his nose.[19] On October 21, the *Prescott Journal-Miner* called Governor Hunt's assertion that there had been no violence at Clifton-Morenci-Metcalf a lie. It reported that between 700 and 800 men had been driven from Clifton-Morenci-Metcalf by threats and harassment.[20]

Judge Ernest W. Lewis, the managers' spokesperson, said that the managers objected not to employing union men as such but to employing those of the WFM because it was violent. The managers were ready to keep mines closed until 1920 if need be. The *Los Angeles Times* labeled the job actions "strike-riots." It blamed them on Arizona's progressive state constitution, which favored labor, and accused the WFM of misleading "ignorant Mexican miners" and of wanting to take control of Arizona.[21]

The Arizona Federation of Labor endorsed the strike, largely muting the WFM issue. The newspapers reminded Clifton merchants and anyone who would listen that the miners' payroll amounted to $450,000 a month. A pay hike, the *Copper Era* contended, "would cause a substitution of white miners for the Mexicans."[22]

Negotiations for a meeting in El Paso dragged on. Time favored the owners because their plates were full, whereas the strikers were starving. They also counted on the division between Mexican and white workers — unskilled versus skilled tradesmen. The copper barons launched a recall of Hunt on October 22, citing the high cost of keeping soldiers in the district. More troops arrived in late October, much to the chagrin of Phoenix businessmen, who accused Hunt of malfeasance. When Hunt called on people to donate food and clothing for the strikers, the attitude of managers, company loyalists, and the white community in general was to let the strikers — and their families — starve.[23]

Juan Guerra and Ricardo Rodríguez resigned on October 23 as president and secretary, charged with breaches of confidence. Guerra had bragged that he had absolute control of the workers and could send them back to work any time he wanted. The mood of the strikers grew angrier and Guerra and Rodríguez had to leave town.[24] According to the *Copper Era*, Juan Guerra was found wandering the hills half-starved. And although the organizers continued to work through the mutualistas, these became divided when the Tucson Mexican elite failed to support the strikers.[25]

Well-Fed Loyalists

Some thirty miles to the south of Clifton, the town of Duncan was thriving.[26] It had two large bunkhouses with 120 men each. On occasion, loyalists who had left for Duncan during the strike would wander back into Clifton-Morenci-Metcalf. For instance, in late November, Casimiro Martínez, 25, returned to Morenci and was accused of being a scab. He refused to go to union headquarters and went instead to his home in Burro Alley. When Lucano Ramírez tried to drag him from his home, Martínez shot him. After pinning a sign saying "Esquirol" (scab) on Andrés Télles Gándara, a clerk at the Phelps Dodge

Mercantile store, twenty strikers escorted him back out of town. The store manager complained that no deputy had come to the aid of Télles.[27]

On December 10, a group of a hundred businessmen formed the Clifton Citizen's League for mutual protection and for safeguarding life and property. Two weeks later, the miners celebrated Christmas with the Mexican orchestra and grumbling stomachs. On New Year's Day 1916, the managers offered a compromise that was rejected by a majority of the strikers. Again the vote was along racial lines with the Mexicans voting no and the Euro-Americans yes. The strikers formally returned their charters to the WFM and were rechartered by the Arizona Federation of Labor, whose vice president, John L. Donnelly, told the strikers that the union was proud of their struggle.

There were still bitter feelings, as 250 more men returned from Duncan on January 7. The workers agreed to go back to work on January 17 for fifteen days provided talks continued. They wanted no discrimination against union men, but the managers refused. The union insisted that Duncan people should not be allowed to return. But the union finally agreed to a gradual reincorporation of the company loyalists under the direction of Sheriff Cash and deputies. On January 24, the settlement was approved. When, however, management hired a new man over an old employee on February 1, the workers of Morenci walked out once more. Abraham Rico, Manuel Rico, J. R. Cabrajal, and Manuel Lucero were among the leaders who were not heard of after the strike.[28]

The Illusion

The Mexican miners were no longer afraid. They demanded equality with white miners. Throughout the next three years, spontaneous strikes rocked Miami, Globe, Ray, Ajo, Jerome, and Warren, as well as Clifton-Morenci-Metcalf. Like good oligarchs, however, the copper barons were not about to give up power. Led by Phelps Dodge's Walter Douglas, they bought control of local newspapers and actively separated labor from its small-business and farmer allies.[29]

The mine owners had their reasons for keeping the WFM out of Clifton-Morenci-Metcalf. It was the most moderate of the three unions. Douglas wanted a total victory; he wanted a showdown with labor activists. During 1916 and 1917, the companies tightened control. The Arizona Copper Company management gave Euro-American timbermen supervisory duties, claiming that the shift bosses could not be everywhere. A timberman would take over when the shift boss was absent. This put more white men over Mexican miners, who rose up in protest. In the next months, Morenci and Mexican underground workers participated in nineteen wildcat strikes (*strikitos*) over the issue of the timbermen. In one incident, mine owners claimed that Jim Maggi, a timberman, had been murdered and thrown down a ladder way. When the owners refused to yield on the timberman issue or any other issue, the miners and aboveground workers went out on strike.[30]

Charles Moyer's failure to support the 1915 strike discredited the WFM. But Moyer still had his partisans. Canuto Vargas Jr. led a purge of radicals and IWW supporters. The alliance with the Arizona Federation of Labor leaders such as John L. Donnelly, George D. Smith, and Thomas Croaff remained a marriage of convenience. Because of their inclusion into union ranks, Mexican workers would not become strikebreakers during the 1917 strikes and would be among the most united camps.[31]

They were often provoked by a grievance process set up to favor management, and one that provided no mechanism for prompt resolution. The reality was that the copper barons wanted to frustrate labor. They wanted to paint unionists as irrational — and they wanted another fight. At Metcalf, a walkout lasted for two months. At Metcalf in early February, two union men, a Mexican and a Spaniard, were discharged because they allegedly threatened an Italian from Tyrone, whom they accused of being a scab. The men walked off the job. When Donnelly arrived in Metcalf, there was already a backlog of thirty grievances. At Arizona Copper's Colorado Mine, led by Enrique Barquín, muckers struck in June 1916. In November, Elizando Ordoñez led another strike at Arizona Copper's Humboldt Mine.[32]

Splits within the union movement divided Mexican miners. Mexicans were members of the WFM, the Arizona Federation of Labor, and, no doubt, the IWW as well. Anti-Mexican feelings increased with Pancho Villa's raid on Columbus, New Mexico, in March 1916. Adding to the drama was the expected town hall meeting of Euro-American patriots, who now talked of preemptive action because of the fighting in Mexico. Friction spilled over into the streets, as Euro-Americans attacked Mexicans, who constituted 75 percent of Clifton-Morenci-Metcalf's population and workforce. The president of Morenci's Mine, Mill & Smelter Workers' Union protested the invasion of Mexico, which, he said, had been instigated by the copper barons.[33]

By September, the Wobblies acquired a presence in the district. Authorities jailed Aurelio V. Azuara of Los Angeles, editor of *El Rebelde*, a Spanish-language labor paper, and Benigno Medina. They took them to Clifton, where they were released on $5,000 bail.[34] Along with Deputy Sheriff O'Neal, Donnelly rescued the IWW members who had been surrounded by a hundred or more members of the Arizona State Federation of Labor. Later in the week, Donnelly was himself accused of threatening a Wobbly.[35]

During this same period, rancher Austin Morris, 44, reportedly knocked down three Mexicans in a fight over politics near Chase Creek. In the ensuing melee, fearing for his life, barber W. H. Lantz shot and killed a Mexican anarchist named Martínez. In another incident, E. J. Moreno, now an organizer for the state federation, shot and killed Federico Básquez. Moreno had made a speech against the IWW. An argument broke out in front of a pool hall, and Moreno drew his .45 and shot Básquez, who was not from Morenci. Moreno surrendered his gun to Constable Johnny Hoffman.

"The Mexican employees of the copper companies are the despair of even their American union associates," the *Los Angeles Times* declared, "for they stop work when they will, on any pretext." The wages they were paid were the highest they had ever known, the *Times* maintained, and there was prosperity in every hut.[36] Be that as it may, Mexicans continued to stop work over dismissals of their coworkers. In November 1916, first 200 and then 1,500 left work. In 1915 and 1916, no fewer than seventeen strikes occurred within the span of a year. Throughout this period, Pedro Subia and the Mexican miners who would eventually migrate west lived in the area of conflict.[37]

Before the Storm: The Long, Thin Line

In 1915, the WFM claimed 17,000 dues-paying members, but the actual number was closer to 9,000. The next year, the World Federation of Miners changed its name to the International Union of Mine, Mill & Smelter Workers (IUMM&SW). Increasingly paranoid, Moyer refused to charter new locals in Arizona on the assumption that they would favor his rivals. On their own, Ray strikers won a flat 65-cent increase in their daily wages the year before, although they still earned less than workers at Globe, Miami, and Bisbee. Exercising their newfound power, Mexican miners challenged racial discrimination, intimidation, and petty despotism in, for example, leasing and contract arrangements. They challenged the compulsory nature of contracts and their arbitrary management, as well as the white monopoly on the positions of resident manager and shift boss. And they challenged the company store's raising prices even as the company cut their pay.[38]

In 1917, John L. Donnelly, George D. Smith, and Thomas Croaff of the Arizona Federation continued their efforts to topple Moyer. Donnelly had even flirted with the IWW. But he was ideologically incompatible with the Wobblies. His principal goals were union recognition, a dues checkoff system, and a closed shop. What kept Moyer in power was the support of the Samuel Gompers, the Woodrow Wilson administration, and the upcoming war.[39] The companies' trump card in turn was Bernard Baruch, chairman of War Industries Board, with whom the barons entered into a price-control arrangement at the expense of workers' earnings.

When Germany resumed submarine warfare in February 1917, the United States broke off relations. On April 6 it entered the war. As tensions built up in mining camps throughout Arizona in the spring of 1917, Moyer curried favor with the Wilson administration by directing his Clifton local to keep down trouble.[40] When labor relations rapidly deteriorated, Secretary of War Newton D. Baker ordered commanding officers to repress acts of sedition within their forces and to comply with any local request for federal troops. The troopers regularly intimidated strikers and escorted scabs to work.[41] In June, Walter Douglas demanded troops be sent to Bisbee because the sheriff had "lost his nerve."[42]

The Imperious Scot

Walter Douglas was not a man to be trifled with. It was his company, his company towns — his empire. When the *New Republic* criticized Phelps Dodge's suppressive tactics during the 1915–16 strike, Douglas lashed back saying his facts "leave no room for legitimate dispute." He bristled at the comparison between Clifton-Morenci and Ludlow, which he once claimed had never even occurred. He denied that workers' demands had been presented to the companies or that strikebreakers had been imported. He blamed the strike on the WFM, which, according to Douglas, had offered no material help to the strikers. He called the strike peaceful and benevolent. In short, he reinvented reality.[43]

Named vice president and member of the board of directors of Phelps Dodge in early 1916, Douglas was soon afterward elected president of the American Mining Congress in Chicago. He looked with horror on the growing political strength of labor. A popular coalition of trade unionists, small business owners, and farmers controlled state politics — people who resented the copper companies not paying their share of taxes. Starting in 1914, through a campaign of intimidation, subversion, libel, and slander, the copper barons succeeded in breaking up the reform coalition. For Douglas, Clifton-Morenci was a defeat, and the Mexican Revolution an annoyance. His enemies were tax laws, corporation laws, labor laws, workmen's compensation, and the unions, which were all un-American.

Through the publications he owned or controlled, such as the *Engineering and Mining Journal*, which he bought for more than a million dollars, Walter Douglas regularly misquoted the price of copper, directing that it be reported at lower than actual levels, thus driving down miners' salaries. His newspapers manipulated the news. Douglas punished non-mining communities for their support of labor. He also punished newspapers and businesses dependent on copper advertising when they failed to support his policies.[44]

On April 14, 1916, the manager of the Arizona News Service pled guilty to federal charges of falsely publishing an advertisement as news and was fined $500. Douglas regularly sent material to newspapers for publication — already fully prepared as typeset plates. By September 28, 1915, Walter Douglas owned the Tucson *Daily Star*, the Phoenix *Arizona Gazette*, the *Bisbee Daily Review*, the *Douglas International Gazette*, the Clifton *Copper Era* and other newspapers. Through them, Douglas sent the message that unions were wasting taxpayers' money and that anyone who did not agree with him was a dangerous radical and un-American.[45]

The growth of large agribusinesses supported the copper barons' agenda. Under Douglas's reign, school appropriations were cut by 80 percent, from $500,000 to $100,000, taxes on the rich were repealed, and assessment on mine property lowered. Greenlee County, established in 1909, became his kingdom. Heavily invested in banking, Douglas used his economic power to influence universities, state colleges, public schools, and churches. And he used an army of spies to root out the troublemakers.[46]

The July Offensive

Former Rough Rider James H. McClintoch, a member of the state militia and a would-be historian, wrote after the strikes that the IWW was radical — it demanded six dollars a day![47] Clearly, the copper barons based their moral authority on the assumption they were fighting an evil force that was un-American and a threat to American democracy. On the other hand, a mine owner told Robert Bruere of the *New York Evening Post* that Bruere could not fairly represent the interests of the mine owners because "you believe in democracy and we don't run our mines in a democratic basis." To apply democratic principles to the mining industry was absurd: managing mines was a problem of mechanical engineering, not politics. "Democracy implied intelligence, initiative," wrote Bruere, "and these were precisely the most undesirable qualities in a mucker, the man who shovels the ore deep down in the stopes and drifts, the man who feeds the machines." The mine owners preferred IWW to conservative mainstream union workers — they were easier to purge. And this was precisely the strategy carried out against labor in the month of July 1917. The owners raised the specter of the IWW while making an all-out assault on organized labor under the guise of patriotism. They would not deal with "alien enemies, pro-German conspirators, traitors to their country at war."[48]

As in other mining camps, the miners in Clifton-Morenci-Metcalf made their demands for higher wages and better work conditions. When the owners would not budge — even though they knew there was no IWW involvement in their mining camps — John Donnelly called a strike on July 1, 1917. As usual, the mine managers took off to El Paso. When federal investigator Joseph Meyers asked them to return, the managers blamed the workers, who they said already had everything they had asked for. Sheriff Arthur Slaughter, 36, native of Texas, swore in townspeople as deputies to protect Detroit Copper property.[49] A Mexican named Acosta gathered the names of union men who wanted to work and anyone who refused was expelled.[50] The strike lingered on into August, when Meyers again asked the managers to return to negotiate. Meanwhile, the nion was conciliatory, willing to sacrifice the discrimination issue for the good of country. Manager Carmichael said he could not make a commitment without a letter from the company's Scottish directors. In a secret ballot was taken on July 27, workers voted 1,363 to 230 to stay out until a settlement was reached.[51]

On May 20, 1917, at Jerome, after the union voted to strike, vigilantes put a gun to McCluskey's head, and marched him across the state line to California. The mine owners' position was they did not want to deal with "alien enemies, pro-German conspirators, traitors to their country at war." Bruere, however, found the Mexicans to be "the most docile people imaginable." All they wanted was an American standard of living. The irony was that the IWW had been trying to block the strike.[52]

The mine workers returned to work on July 4, but the IWW continued to agitate. It called a strike for July 6. There were fist fights between IWW and Jerome Miners Union partisans. On the July 10 — two days before the Bisbee deportations — more than two hundred armed men rounded up more than 2,500 miners. Despite his treatment at the hands of the vigilantes, Henry McCluskey volunteered to break the IWW strike at Jerome and clean out the camp. The town leaders met at Jerome High School and made preparations for deporting strikers. McCluskey cooperated, checking off deportees from a membership list of Jerome Miners' Union.[53] Vigilantes raided every "cheap boardinghouse" and the IWW headquarters at the local pool hall. They deported 250 miners. "The mine managers and the I.W.W. have two things most strikingly in common," Bruere wrote, "love for direct action and contempt for the slow processes of organized democracy for which the 'legitimate' unions stand."[54]

Although there was labor strife throughout Arizona, the most flagrant affront to constitutional rights — and one that was applauded by conservatives — occurred at Bisbee. When, on July 12, 1917, Phelps Dodge deported strikers from the Bisbee mines, Superior Court Judge G. Walter Shute of Globe upped the ante, saying he "would like to go up there and mow those sons of bitches down with a machine gun."[55] Judge Shute's attitude was not uncommon in states, such as Arizona, that were run by absentee owners. According to Alice

Hamilton, "Lawlessness in labor disputes, even on the part of officers of the law, is an old American tradition and usually an outbreak does not attract much attention, but this was too highhanded and dramatically ruthless to be passed over."[56] The price of copper had skyrocketed, and World War I boosted demand. But, for the copper barons, it went beyond wages and came down to control. Branding all unions radical, extremist, and terrorist, and equating them with the IWW, they dared the workers to strike. By seeking higher wages (however justified their demands), the workers were hurting the troops, which was un-American. The owners infiltrated the unions, employed labor spies, and goaded miners to commit acts of violence.[57]

Agents of the Burns International Detective Service swarmed over Jerome's United Verde Copper, while those of the Thiel Detective Agency were everywhere in Globe, Bisbee, and Jerome. They paid provocateurs and created dissension. Even where the IWW had few operatives, as in Clifton, Morenci, and Metcalf, Douglas and the Greek chorus blamed the Wobblies. The chief of Bureau of Investigation of the Department of Justice cooperated in this campaign. The strategy was that, if enough violence were used, organized labor would fold its tents and go away. If all else failed, several hundred gunmen could be mustered into the militia or deputized, as they had been at Ludlow.[58]

The IWW represented the downtrodden. They offered hope. Waving red flags and marching under the banner "There Is Power in a Union," the IWW demonstrators included Mexicans, although by no means were all or even most Mexicans Wobblies. But their participation in IWW demonstrations allowed pseudo patriots to paint Mexican workers as terrorists and traitors. It allowed Douglas to perpetuate the myth that they posed an imminent danger and that preemptive action was necessary. The *New Republic* made the point that the IWW was a creature of the copper barons, whose "combination of autocracy and exploitation gave the I.W.W. their chance."[59]

Sheriff Harry Wheeler, a former Rough Rider, directed the Bisbee deportations. Born in Florida in 1887, Wheeler took his stepfather's name. He served in the cavalry and later in the Arizona Rangers under Rynning, whom he replaced as captain. When the rangers disbanded in 1912, he became a lawman — and one of the fastest guns around, hitting bull's-eyes 197 times out of 200. The stereotypical small man at five feet four inches, he was obsessed with Villa. For Wheeler, who spent his vacations chasing bandits, the IWW were the bad guys.[60]

Watching 4,500 Mexicans march up and down the street every day, Wheeler believed the country was being invaded by aliens. "I knew that they hated us, and I heard through Mexican sources that some of the villistas had rifles all cached in the Ajo Mountains . . . and that when the opportunity presented itself they would secure these rifles." When Secretary Wilson of the president's commission investigating Clifton asked Wheeler whether there was any attempt to separate villistas from the rest of the Mexicans, he replied: "How could you separate one Mexican from another?" Yes, he had tried to separate leaders, but he said, "No Mexican, hardly, will testify against another. Even if one is dying, stabbed by another, when you get there and ask him who hurt him he will tell you he does not know." Wheeler said he was acting in defense of the community, and, turning tables on the secretary, asked, "Are you an American, or are you not?"[61] The sheriff had orders from Walter Douglas to break the strike. So he arrested every nonworking miner.

Douglas ran a segregated camp and thought it "desirable that American employees should own their own homes," although he thought that "where the Mexican is concerned, it will be difficult to induce him to obligate himself to pay for the house in which he is living." Instead, Douglas preferred to rent "tenements or cheaply constructed houses" — read "made of scrap wood" — to his Mexican workers at Clifton-Morenci-Metcalf (Phelps Dodge hired few Mexicans in Bisbee).[62]

Just prior to the deportations, Governor Thomas E. Campbell sent Lieutenant Colonel James J. Hornbrook to investigate conditions in Bisbee. Hardly pro-labor, Hornbrook reported that everything was peaceful. What he did not see was that Bisbee was awash with patriotism. The Phelps Dodge people bought and strongly promoted the purchase of Liberty Bonds, and patriots reviewed what their fellow citizens were doing for America. The atmosphere became so intense that, by July 2, at least three hundred strikers had left Warren for Globe and Clifton. The Loyalty League claimed it had recruited 1,600 men in forty days. Yet the IWW workers did little to provoke these avowed patriots, other than refuse to participate in the Fourth of July festivities.

Having decided preemptive action was necessary to prevent bloodshed in the streets of Bisbee, Wheeler called a meeting on July 11. "We will not compromise with rattlesnakes," Walter Douglas had said, "this goes for the International — the A. F. of L. organization — as well as the I.W.W."[63] The Loyalty League had known about the deportations a week beforehand. So had the 75 to 80 members of the Bisbee Rifle Club, "all loyal and Patriotic Americans," as Bykrit described them.[64] For his part, however, Lemeul Shattuck, owner of Bisbee's third copper company, found the whole affair "obnoxious" and did not cooperate.[65]

The Loyalty Leaguers were out early on the July 12. About 2,000 deputized vigilantes took to the street, wearing white armbands, seizing the Western Union telegraph office, and cutting outside communication to the town. At 6:30 a.m., Sheriff Wheeler began the roundup.

Ramón Valenzuela, who was described as a deaf and dumb agitator and deported from Bisbee. (Arizona State Library, Archives and Public Records, Archives Division, Phoenix, George W. P. Hunt Collection, no. 96-1757, Ph D009)

The patriots marched the strikers two miles to a makeshift bullpen in the Warren Ballpark. Miners loyal to the company rushed home and got their rifles, put on white armbands, and joined the vigilantes in an enormous parade. Any worker willing to put on a white armband and denounce the strike was let go. According to James Ward Byrkit, "Women sympathizers outside the park, using strong, explicit language, [urged] the men not to weaken."[66] Notices were posted reading, "ALL WOMEN AND CHILDREN KEEP OFF THE STREET TODAY."[67] Amado Villalovas was in a neighborhood store when "about ten gunmen all armed came in and told me to get out. I asked them to let me take my groceries home to my family. They dragged me out of the store, hit me, and knocked me down."[68]

At 11:00 a.m., a train pulled up, and 1,186 men were herded into cattle cars, whose floors were thickly covered in manure. The train set off, with a contingent of 186 armed guards and a machine gun on top of the cars. Frank H. Moore, a Los Angeles attorney, was among those deported. His crime was that he represented the IWW. There were twice as many Mexican deportees as their proportion overall: "Bisbee's mining labor force was about 13 percent Mexican, but at least 27 percent of all deportees were Mexican — and probably more." Having had no water for twelve hours, the deportees were dumped in Hermanas, New Mexico, near Columbus, on one of the hottest days of the year. The military detained many of the men for months.[69]

The *New Republic* condemned the lawlessness of the operation: "During the deportation, officers of a great mining corporation with headquarters in New York City forcibly seize[d] the local telegraph office and impose[d] a censorship upon Associated Press dispatches so that the deportation [might] not be interfered with by the authorities of neighboring towns or states."[70] For months the Citizen's Protective League required passports before entering Bisbee. The 3,000 members of the Loyalty League and Protective Association patrolled the streets. The Bisbee patriots forbade the deportees to return. Wheeler continued playing Buffalo Bill along the roads in and out of Bisbee. That same day, 170 deported Mexicans decided to walk to Naco. Mexican Consul Ives G. Lelevier promised to transport them to the Río Yaqui Valley. None of the men were connected with the IWW or any other labor organization.[71]

El Tucsonense wrote, "We must remember that the U.S. is at war, sending its sons to the front, and those who remain at home cannot tolerate strikes nor the paralyzing of industry because this is what our enemies want and this leads to the sacrifice of our sons in the war." *El Tucsonense* blamed the IWW, and claimed that owners had good relations with Mexican workers.[72] Meanwhile, the Bisbee deportations heightened anti-Americanism in Mexico.

Truth be told, organized labor cooperated with the copper barons. It was a matter of "winning." Writing in the *Miners' Magazine*, Joseph D. Cannon accepted without comment the companies' requirement that miners pledge loyalty to the flag if they wanted to work and their desire to exclude foreigners, specifically Mexicans. On the other hand, Cannon was impressed with the Mexican workers' "loyalty to unionism and their understanding of economic conditions[, which] have completely surprised the employers, who brought them here in the first place to make a strike of the mines either impossible or ineffective."[73]

Although the leaders of the deportations were taken to court, as with the 1904 foundling case, the verdict was predictable. The all-white male jury accepted the defense argument that the kidnapping and deporting of nearly 1,500 presumed Wobblies "was legal under the 'Law of Necessity.' " A "nationwide conspiracy" made it essential because "a lot of disloyal, un-American anarchists" were sabotaging the war effort. "Necessity knows no laws"; a person is entitled to protect himself.[74]

President Woodrow Wilson responded by appointing a presidential mediation commission to study the problem. After two years, the courts punished no one, although evidence proved that the copper barons, specifically Walter Douglas, had planned the deportations at Bisbee. Historians speculate that President Wilson did not take any action because of his intimate friendship with Cleveland Dodge, who was a member of his cabinet, and who had been on the board of trustees of Princeton University when Wilson was appointed president of Princeton. The Wilsons and the Dodges vacationed together.[75]

Although Clifton had been a model of ethnic solidarity in 1916, the white tradesmen became impatient with their Mexican coworkers over the frequent strikitos, and fights broke out. Because the craft workers comprised less than 15 percent of the workforce at Clifton-Morenci-Metcalf, however, the Mexican workers outvoted them on August 27. By September, the mine operators were winning the war of attrition. Thousands of Mexican miners had fled the state in search of other employment. Many went to the Salt River, Imperial, and San Joaquin Valleys to pick cotton.

Felix Frankfurter served as counsel to the President's Mediation Commission. Frankfurter realized that the mine owners had acted criminally and that the Wobblies were a small, powerless faction. However, Gompers was the commissioners' guy and they moved to protect the WFM. Despite mediation, bayonets, and deportations, the companies had not been able to start up again. Meanwhile, tempers flared when Mexican women assaulted a group of scabs on their way to work. Sara and Josefina Medina, mother and daughter, were arrested. The owners offered to resume operations and to pay wages in conformance with government recommendations so long as the men returned to work immediately, before any further negotiations.[76]

On September 24, the *Copper Era* listed the names of draftees, inducted into the cavalry and sent to Fort Riley.[77] That same day, Canuto Vargas called a meeting. The mine managers had announced they would resume production only if the workers would submit grievances to the managers themselves. The union members voted almost unanimously against returning under that condition. On October 1, the government settled the wage dispute, but the companies would not negotiate any other issue. The union responded by putting a picket line around the mines and smelter. Later that day, Sheriff Slaughter and four deputies disarmed 250 Mexicans and Spaniards who reportedly had set out from Morenci to "clean up the Americans." Six shots were fired, and eighty strikers were charged with inciting a riot.[78]

Mexican Consul Enrique Gutiérrez said the Mexicans were marching to Clifton to find work and had no intention of disturbing the peace. Later, when angry Morenci strikers attempted to stop five hundred scabs from entering the area, sixty-four were arrested. Deputy Sheriff Brooks Brown had killed Gregorio Zorillo on October 3. Zorillo had lived in the district for fifteen years and had a good reputation. A coroner's jury cleared the deputy. The presiding judge said there were no witnesses. When the consul objected that there were witnesses, but they were afraid to testify, the sheriff accused him of agitating the strikers. Gutiérrez warned his superiors that the situation was dangerous. Despite the severe crackdown, the workers continued marching. Seeing the strikers as dangerous, the local justice of the peace ordered their arrest but said, "If they want to go to work, I'll turn 'em loose now." Bail was set at from $500 to $1,000.[79]

The workers wanted seniority, a checkoff system, and the Miami scale. "We reserve the constitutional right to protect ourselves," they declared in their formal statement, "and will certainly do it. If we are quiet and submissive in the face of manifest injustice, it is not fear that prompts us; it's a desire to keep order and show forbearance to those whom would defame the honor of our state and nation, and making Arizona another Colorado. Just men do not fight without a great and just cause, and then only after much provocation."[80]

On October 15, the union telegraphed President Woodrow Wilson that the 4,000 Mexican miners of Clifton, Morenci, and Metcalf had unanimously asked President Carranza of Mexico to repatriate them. Desperate, many miners left for Phoenix, which had become a clearinghouse for employment referrals to railroad and construction crews and increasingly to cotton plantations.[81]

The record clearly shows that Douglas waged a guerilla war against labor and got away with it. When he began his campaign, the Arizona constitution and labor laws and tax laws were among the most progressive in the nation. In the end, he succeeded in getting the employers' liability, workmen's compensation, and mine inspection laws repealed, and in rolling back other labor standards. Laws mandating a dry room for miners, abolition of the chit system, and pay twice a month, railroad safety laws, women and child labor laws — all were sacrificed on the altar of copper.[82]

Absolution: The Hearings

According to testimony by P. M. Vargas y Soto before the President's Mediation Commission, a Justice Department agent by the name of Harris had told the union at Clifton-Morenci-Metcalf in 1917 that the United States was at war and wanted no strikes. When union members told Harris of a worker's complaints about the contract system, Harris asked: "Is he a citizen?" Told he was not, Harris responded, "If he likes it, he can stay here; if not, he can go away." Harris said he had the names of all the union officers — if there was any trouble, they would be taken to prison.

Workers told the commission how the foremen manipulated assays of ore and refused to pay for ore mined, how one foreman held a lighted lamp to a worker's back. In 1911, a boy lost a leg in a mining accident. He sued but did not get one cent in damages, and had to wait five years to hear that decision. Then, because he *had* sued, he could not get job in the company store. He was blacklisted.[83]

Manager Carmichael testified, "We know our Mexicans and the Mexican character and the Mexican regard for truth, and the Mexican imagination, and we are not surprised that you should receive plenty of affidavits," and that they would not amount to anything serious. He distinguished between contracts and leases, and said the company could not operate without them. Many Mexicans lived there for many years and did not want to work all day and would rather go back into the hills and work independently. The company treated them fairly but believed in systematic development. According to Carmichael, the best workers left in 1915 because they were driven out by the WFM.[84]

According to J. F. Nichols, who had worked with Mexicans for thirty-five years, "You work Mexicans six days and let them lay off one, and you get five days work a week. You never get a day's work on Monday when they come back." Nichols to Commissioner R. T. Walker: "The Mexican is the easiest man to control that is if you control him right." On race relations, Nicols said you could not get Texans to love Mexicans or vice versa. "In dealing with Mexicans, when you state you will do a thing, that you will punish him in a certain way if they do certain things, you have to punish one or two of them before they will believe what you say."[85]

J. Y. Ainsa, who had opposed the 1915 strike, voluntarily testified. He said that people would say things about him and that he wanted to tell his side. He said that he was born in Fresno, California, in 1876, and that his father was a U.S. citizen, who in 1882 went to northern Sonora to establish a gold mining business. He said that his father was wealthy and led a privileged life, that he was raised in Mexico but loved democracy.

Ainsa migrated to Morenci in 1910 and helped start a private school. He taught English and citizenship and in 1913 was put on the payroll of the Arizona Copper Company. He criticized Vargas and other leaders for not Americanizing the workers. All they wanted was an office and to draw five dollars a day. He knew Tribolet, as well as his father, in Nacozari and called him an outlaw and highwayman. Ainsa admitted making speeches against the union during the 1915 strike. Ainsa handed the commission a list of 300 to 400 names of those of the good element who belong to associations opposing the strike. He made it clear that he opposed the 80 percent law because it was anti-Mexican.

Ainsa belonged to the Alianza and was a friend of Canuto Vargas's father. Ainsa did not approve of what happened in Bisbee: "Do you think I approve of the way the Mexican people live there, the way they are treated there? No, I don't approve of it, but that hasn't anything to do with me."

Ainsa was a member of various Mexican organizations, along with Emilio Váldez, Jesús Estrada, and Francisco Bénites in Clifton, and along with Amado Cota Robles in Tucson. Ainsa headed the Legislative Committee, whose members believed they were men of influence and reason and that the governor would listen to their petitions. They resented the unions, which they saw were dominated by non-Mexicans.[86]

Gracious to the end, the Mexican community serenaded the head of the commission. "In all three camps," Henry S. McCluskey reported, "meetings have been an almost daily and nightly occurrence, for a Mexican miner's union hall is his school, library, court of social justice and place of recreation." In Metcalf, the company owned everything, so they met on hillside and had their debates in the open. "The Mexican miners know that here, on the border, international fraternity is being put to the test." There were 10,000 Mexican workers in Arizona mines.[87]

The commission published its report, and the workers were forced to settle. The agreement had an anti-IWW proviso that was used against socialist, pacifist, and anti-Moyer leaders. "These Mexicans are supposed to be all that is bad," said Frankfurter, "when the truth is that they are merely different," adding that the managers were "blind to what's going on in the world." Frankfurter called the copper barons pathetic and cruel.[88] No fewer than three hundred men drifted from Morenci in the months to come. The union lost its best men. Arizona Copper at Clifton posted the names of those who allowed to return. When the union protested, the company said it was just testing whether they were there. U.S. citizenship became the litmus test for new employment. Mexican strikers were blacklisted. The Mexican consul registered eighty complaints with the Mexican ambassador and with the Department of Labor.[89]

The Death of the Unions

By 1918, the agreement brokered by the President's Mediation Commission the year before had disintegrated, and the copper barons began to restructure and phase out the unions.[90] Using the low grade of ore and inefficiency as pretexts, they idled the mines at Clifton-Morenci-Metcalf. A major supporter of the agreement, Canuto Vargas complained that unions would have been better off if they had agreed to discriminate against the more militant miners. The mediation commission and immigration service solved the unemployment problem by shipping the miner-strikers to Salt River Valley farms. The Bureau of Investigation reported that Clifton-Morenci-Metcalf was a hotbed of agitation.[91]

Following the November 11, 1918, armistice, the copper market collapsed once more, and Douglas went to Europe looking for buyers. In Jerome, miners walked out when management cut their daily wages by seventy-five cents. The 1918 influenza pandemic killed many miners and their family members, among them Francisca Subia, wife of Pedro, who fourteen years later was murdered in Arvin California.[92] With their large percentage of Mexican members, the miners' unions found themselves vulnerable. The owners effectively played the race card, preferring "Americans," as before.

Time worked in Phelps Dodge's favor, allowing to gobble up other mining companies, not pay taxes, and concentrate on developing its capital plant. The copper companies maintained it was their right to lower wages — after all, they had a surplus of copper. Meanwhile, they diverted attention from their role in shutting down the mines, by blaming the IWW and the Bolsheviks. The unions were rapidly dying.[93]

Even as labor conditions in Arizona worsened, Moyer wrote to McCluskey that he was concerned about anarchists and syndicalists within union ranks. Gloating that union leaders had cleaned the IWW element out of Arizona Federation of Labor, Moyer now spoke as though the salvation of the unions was to be found in recruiting large numbers of Mexican workers.[94]

The Class Line

Arizona's Mexican elites rose to the defense of Mexican-born Mexicans, as they recognized nativism as racist. They were sensitive to the treatment of Mexicans in United States but did not want to be viewed as revoltosos or un-American. They castigated a Mexican consul whose negative remarks about the United States were used in a German newspaper. During the Jerome and Bisbee deportations, the elite sided with vigilantes. When the mine owners were not able to make a deal with Governor Calles, they sided with the owners. Less than two weeks before the deportations at Bisbee, the Mexican elite's principal newspaper, *El Tucsonense*, ran a column claiming that 65 percent of the Mexican workers had been duped by agitators.

El Tucsonense condemned the anarchists at Bisbee, Globe, and Jerome, arguing, "The methods employed by Arizona authorities are undoubtedly radical but we are in the throes of a war; this makes it necessary to deal with infectious diseases, which must be segregated from the social body . . . to avoid infecting the whole organism and, as such, the great masses of workers." On November 7, 1917 it announced that negotiations had collapsed and blamed the workers. It was not that they did not know better. In Tucson, there was a great shortage of labor because so many were returning to Mexico to avoid the draft.[95]

The Alianza Hispano Americana continued to be the premier civic society for Mexicans in the United States, spreading throughout the Southwest and into Mexico. For the most part, Tucson's Mexican elites stayed aloof from the labor wars. In Phoenix, leaders of the Mexican middle class formed the Liga Protectora Latina in 1914 to oppose Claypool-Kinney. Led by Ignacio Espinosa, Pedro G. de la Lama, and Jesús Meléndez, the Liga supported striking miners at Ray in July 1915. By 1917, it had thirty lodges, which focused on political and legal action to protect the rights of Mexicans, increased mutual aid for Liga members, and greater emphasis on education.

Many members of the Mexican elite immigrated after 1911 and were supporters of Porfirio Díaz. Judging from its editorials and articles during the 1910s, *El Tucsonense* clearly supported Republican candidates and U.S. policy toward Mexico, as did many of its elite readership. The paper's editors as well as Mexican civic, patriotic, and social organization maintained good relations with leading coroporations such as the Southern Pacific and Phelps Dodge. For the most part, the members of the elite were nationalistic. Immigration policy was the litmus test, which Democrats failed.[96] Meanwhile, the societies to which they belonged were by no means radical. Most Mexicans appeared to have been interested in their own economic survival.

Tucson's Mexican elite based their distinction more on family affiliation than on money. At the Liga's 1914 convention in Phoenix, Ignacio Espínosa, Pedro G. de la Lama, Jesús Mélendez, and others pledged to protect and educate Mexican Americans and pay funeral expenses. Educated at a Jesuit College in Spain, de la Lama had gone to a Mexican naval college and later become an officer in the Mexican army. In 1896, he had come to Arizona, where he worked as a teacher in Solomonville, later moving to Phoenix.

Arizona's Mexican middle class continuously integrated members of the Sonoran elites. According to Carlos Vélez-Ibañez, "proving and gaining class legitimacy was a major effort" among this class. The Mexican middle-class, though remaining centered in Tucson, spread throughout Arizona, linked together by mutualistas and fraternal organizations, whose active social calendar further reinforced the class network. Amado Cota Robles, for example, was a member of the Alianza Hispano-Americana, the Sociedad Mutualista Porfirio Díaz, the Leñadores del Mundo, the Sociedad Mexicana-Americana, and the Liga Protectora Latina — the Alianza being the most prominent of these organizations.

"As early as 1904, Bernabé Brichta spoke out against the Locomotive Stokers Union, the Locomotive Engineers Union, and the Machinist Union because they refused to admit Mexicans, Blacks, or Chinese as members." At the same time, Bernabé argued that Mexicans should not be lumped in with African Americans and Chinese. He demanded an end to the unions' war against Mexicans. The most important industry in Tucson was the railroad, where the Euro-Americans dominated the skilled trades. Even there, *El Tucsonense* failed to support strikes.

The Liga developed strong ties to the Republican Party, holding a series of meetings with Republican Governor Tom Campbell, for example. Like *El Tucsonense*, it reflected the goals and aspirations of the Mexican elites, although it sided with the miners at Ray in 1914–15 and the Arizona cotton workers in 1919–20.[97]

At its third annual convention, the Liga established a commission headed by Amado Cota Robles to lobby the state legislature for bilingual education at the primary level. Under Cota Robles's leadership, the Liga began night classes in Spanish, arithmetic, geometry, geography, and Mexican history. Its leaders spoke of the need to establish night school classes to teach English, especially in the mining districts, of the sacrifices of Mexicans in Arizona during the war, and of their right to the same privileges as others.

By 1919, the Liga had lodges in Arizona, California, New Mexico, and Philadelphia, with nearly 3,800 members and its own journal, *La Justicia*. Membership fell the following year, when the initiation fee was raised to $3.00 and monthly dues to $1.25. Poorer members protested, and the league divided along class lines, going into a decline, before finally disappearing in the 1930s. For all the criticism of the Liga, however, it was a middle-class nationalist organization that worked to protect the rights of Mexicans. It dealt with Republicans because the Democrats and union leaders wanted to exclude Mexicans.[98]

Lessons of History

Just before its 1918 convention, Antonio I. Villarreal of the newly formed Pan-American Federation of Labor (PAFL) raised the issue of racism.[99] According to Villareal, millions of Mexican workers toiled in the United States for starvation wages, suffering humiliation. Most were general laborers, but some were skilled workers, and many were farmers. As a rule, the skilled workers, who were among Mexico's best, knew how to read and write, and some were highly educated. Villareal criticized organized labor for neither protecting these workers nor tapping their initiative and motivation in crossing the border. These workers were progressive, with "over a half million of them" belonging to trade unions. Villareal considered the Pan-American Federation of Labor a positive sign that the AFL would recruit Mexicans. But, he cautioned, Mexicans were unwilling to give up their citizenship and that Euro-Americans should not make it a condition for membership. The movement should be for international worker solidarity.

At the PAFL convention itself, the issues of discrimination and the treatment of immigrants were again raised. Henry S. McCluskey of the International Union of Mine, Mill & Smelter Workers blamed the Mexican immigrant workers for their failure to organize or support AFL unions. He claimed that the union spent money and time trying to organize Mexican workers in recent years, with almost no success, except in Clifton-Morenci-Metcalf. Because they were willing to work for lower wage, Mexican workers made unionization next to impossible. "This went on until no American miners were left in Arizona." According to McCluskey, the copper companies used Mexicans to break down the standard of living for Euro-Americans.[100]

In their response to these remarks, Mexican delegates were almost apologetic, when they should have been outraged. Pascual M. Vargas, the first vice president of the Arizona State Federation of Labor, talked about his union's efforts to eliminate abuses and promote harmony of races. Another Mexican delegate noted that the organization of Mexican workers in the United States had been studied in Mexico for some time. Researchers had concluded that discrimination existed because Euro-Americans lacked information about Mexicans. White delegates responded that labor had spent money in the Gallup, New Mexico, strike, for both American and Mexican workers. After intensive debate,

The citizens of Sonora, Arizona, celebrate Mexican Independence Day on September 16, 1919, with floats decorated with both Mexican and American flags. (Courtesy Club Sonorense Records, Chicano Research Collection, Arizona State University Libraries)

a compromise was reached. They commissioned an AFL-CROM[101] committee to investigate the situation at the border.

Shortly before the convention ended, the question of exchange of union cards came to floor. Guillermo Quiroz from IUMM&SW Local 86 asked three important questions. Would Euro-American unions agree to admit Mexican workers into their ranks? Would Mexican union members have the same rights and privileges as white members? Would the antagonism of races continue within the labor organizations? The official reply was that each union had its own rules and was autonomous. The exchange of union cards had been one of main reasons Mexicans accepted concept of the PAFL in the first place.[102]

The decade ended much as it had started. Euro-American labor remained ambivalent about Mexican workers, whose numbers had increased dramatically, both in the mines and in agribusinesses. Mexicans in general had been politicized by events in Mexico and the United States. World War I had changed those who served in the armed forces and the growing number of second- and third-generation Mexican Americans. Through violence, the closing of the mines after World War I, and the intentional "cleaning out" of the Clifton-Morenci-Metcalf mines, the copper barons had destroyed the Mexican unions, at least for the time.

◀ 11 ▶

The Cotton Corridor

The post–World War I depression forced most Mexican workers and their families from the mining camps of eastern Arizona. Many migrated west, to the farmlands of the Salt River Valley and, along the Cotton corridor, to the Imperial and San Joaquin Valleys. Even before the advent of land reclamation and massive agribusinesses, since colonial times, workers had traveled similar routes in search of work. But starting in the mid-1920s, they would come by the thousands from the mines to pick cotton and produce in California.

The 1918 influenza pandemic hit every section of Arizona so severely the state fair had to be postponed. By the end of October 1918, seven hundred cases had been reported in the state. In March 1919, Francisca Subia, like hundreds of others, died of the "Spanish flu." A devastated Pedro and his young son soon left for Los Angeles, where a daughter lived.[1]

Under the guise of patriotism, Walter Douglas's henchmen flushed Mexican radicals and known union activists out of the Clifton-Morenci-Metcalf mines. Phelps Dodge then broke the unions' backs by shutting down operations in 1919. As the mines slowly resumed production, the loyalty leagues added a new wrinkle to blacklisting: citizenship was made a precondition for employment.[2] From January 1919 on, the copper companies repatriated thousands of Mexican workers and their families, retaining mostly white and trusted Mexican American miners to do development work and mine, and letting the others go.

Mexican Consul Miguel Limón wrote that Clifton, Morenci, Metcalf, and

Duncan had a combined population of 20,000 in 1919. Of these, 5,000 were Mexicans, 2,000 Spaniards (the majority of whom had been born in Mexico or New Mexico), 2,000 Italians, and an unspecified number Arabs, "Mongolians," and of course whites. The consul noted that the growth of U.S. nationalism had forced a great many Mexicans to apply for U.S. citizenship. The copper barons, who had once welcomed Mexicans from Mexico with open arms, now required them to become naturalized citizens to get a job. During this period, the Club Mexicano Benito Juárez of Morenci and the Gran Círculo Cooperativo de Emancipación Mexicana helped many Mexican families make the transition to U.S. citizenship.[3]

Born in Jalisco, Pedro Gómez, twenty in 1921, worked in a Phelps Dodge machine shop. Speaking of his fellow Mexicans during the 1921 depression, Gómez said, "Many took passage to California. Others went to New Mexico and Colorado. And others, who preferred, went to Mexico. Free because the company gave them [passage] to wherever they wanted to go.... Many of them went to Mexico and a year later when Morenci started again, many came back to Morenci." His family stayed during the Depression. According to Gómez, there was work in Los Angeles, which was rapidly industrializing and was also one of the leading agricultural counties in the United States. "Some would go to work in Los Angeles and leave their families in Morenci. They would send [them] money." Many decided to remain because there was no employment in Mexico.[4]

As Josephine Martínez Granado of Morenci remembered, "We were real close, all the people there. We were mountain climbers [in our neighborhood of El Espinazo]. There was El Seis, La Arizona, Longfellow"[5] — with most of the barrios perched on steep hillsides. They would be uprooted again, only more cold-bloodedly this time, in 1921. Early one morning in April, between 1,600 and 1,800 Mexican men, women, and children assembled at the Morenci Southern Railroad station. There the copper companies loaded them onto a special train bound for Mexico via El Paso. When company representative José Y. Ainsa proposed that some of the men be placed in cattle cars, Mexican Consul Váldez angrily refused. The deportees were destined for Aguascalientes, Chihuahua, Durango, Jalisco, and Zacatecas, carrying their household goods, utensils, and pets with them.[6]

In 1919, the Arizona Copper Company had bought the Shannon Copper Company mines, based in Metcalf, which would be gobbled by an open pit. By May, General Manager Norman Carmichael announced that Arizona Copper would close permanently. Phelps Dodge purchased Arizona Copper and its transportation system. By early 1921, the bottom fell out of the economy. Walter Douglas used the occasion to close down the mines in order to reduce

The deportation of Mexican nationals from Morenci in 1921. (Courtesy of Arizona State University Libraries, Southwestern Photograph Collection)

taxes and to clean the last of the union men out of the camps. The next year, the industry began to rebound, although there is little evidence that many of the miners displaced during the recession made their way back to the mines.[7]

A Hole in the Safety Net

Mexicans had worked in and around the Salt River Valley since the 1880s. Their dominance in the cotton fields, however, did not take place until after World War I. The flow of miners back and forth between mining and farming dated back to the seventeenth century, when Mexican miners alternated between the mines and their small farm fields. This was part of the life Mexicans in Arizona, who turned to agriculture when times were slow, or harsher than usual, in the mines. The *Copper Era* regularly carried stories of the expansion of agriculture.[8] Most Mexicans heading for Los Angeles worked their way across the green belts linking western Arizona to California. Even if they were lucky enough to have a car, they had to earn money for gasoline and repairs. The family farm was disappearing in Arizona, where farmland was even more concentrated than in California. The demand for cotton grew as its use in tires, textiles, and other products increased. In 1916, the year Goodyear became the world's largest tire manufacturer, it acquired its first cotton ranch in Arizona.

The Salt River Valley was the first large beneficiary of the Federal Reclamation Act of 1902. Completion of the Roosevelt Dam in 1911 launched huge cotton plantations. When irrigation put 200,000 acres into production, Phoenix blossomed, although few of the its Mexicans, whose families had been in the town since its founding, benefited.

When José María Ruiz, who had lived in Clifton, could not adapt to work in the mines, he became a cowboy and a carpenter. For a time, he worked for the railroad before drifting to the Phoenix area, where he joined thousands of refugees from the mining camps.[9]

Phoenix's development depended on railroads, which linked the fields to the city. Southern Pacific acquired land nearby. Pacific Gas and Electric, a Phoenix–Los Angeles corporation, monopolized Arizona's hydroelectric power. Angelinos speculated in Arizona real estate and reaped tourist dollars from their investments. With its extra-long fibers, Arizona's new Pima cotton soon became a premium variety. Agricultural expansion meant more pick-and-shovel jobs.[10]

Tire manufacturing contributed to the boom, supplying Los Angeles's mushrooming auto market. Goodyear Tire and Rubber Company decided to build a $20 million factory there, and bought cotton ranches in Arizona to supply it. Between 1918 and 1921, the Arizona Cotton Growers Association (ACGA) imported more than 30,000 Mexican farmworkers at a cost of $300,000. Plantations produced cotton on 210,000 acres, of which 186,000 were in the Salt River Valley.

As the Mexican population increased, however, so did incidents of racist nativism. In 1919, the Liga Protectora Latina of Arizona charged Rafael Estrada, a labor contractor for cotton growers in Arizona, with bullying and abusing Mexican workers. The Arizona Federation of Labor moved to organize the state's underpaid cotton pickers. Planters responded by having the authorities arrest six Mexican workers near Glendale, among them Apolino Cruz, who was taken away and his eight-year-old son left alone by a ditch. When friends took the boy to Tempe for safekeeping, the ACGA arranged to have him shipped back to Mexico unescorted. To end the flow of migrants to the United States, union organizers met with Mexican President Adolfo de la Huerta. Even though nothing came of the meeting, cotton growers were outraged.[11]

During the 1921 depression, demand for agricultural workers fell off dramatically, leaving thousands of Mexicans who had come to the green belts stranded and destitute. Growers had deducted their transportation to Arizona from their wages, but now they refused to pay the workers' way back. On March 5, Mexico City's *El Universal* reported, "When they arrived at Phoenix, a party of Mexican workers were taken to Tempe and introduced to a concentration camp that looks like a dung heap." It said Mexicans were forced to work on chain gangs.[12]

In 1920–21, a joint Arizona-Sonora commission investigated working conditions in the Salt River Valley. It found that ACGA job bosses had subjected 12,000 to 15,000 Mexican workers to substandard housing — tents where temperatures often reached well above 100 degrees — abusive treatment, and illegal deportation. Siding with the ACGA, the U.S. Justice Department directed its agents to raid the Arizona Federation of Labor Hall. The union struggled on. By 1921, it had formed fourteen locals, averaging 300 to 400 workers per local, mostly in Maricopa County. Then disaster hit. The 1921 depression dried up jobs and, within a year, the union locals as well.[13]

On February 25, 1921, the *Los Angeles Times* reported that Arizona's congressional delegation was attempting to exclude Mexicans from the mines, even as it requested $25,000 for destitute Mexicans. As of June 21, 1921, out of an estimated total of 73,000 farmworkers imported into California and Arizona, some 35,000 had returned to Mexico, some 15,600 were still employed in the United States, 414 had died, 494 had been permitted to remain as legal permanent immigrants, and some 21,400 had simply disappeared. Many of the disappeared workers made their way to Los Angeles.[14]

Mexicans, Go West

In 1920, when California devoted nearly 130,000 acres to cotton, more than twice what it had before, "talk of importing Mexicans became more noticeable than ever," according to Paul S. Taylor. Ira Aten, a Texan and one of California's early cotton planters, announced: "We mean to get Mexicans for the work and we can get all we need. Mexicans are the best pickers we know of. They come from Mexico City for the work and make good pay at it in Texas."[15] From this point on, Mexicans would dominate California's farm workforce, their particular numbers depending on the crop.

As cotton production increased in the El Centro–Calexico area, its cotton gins served the Arizona-California–Baja California triangle. By the late 1920s, after picking cotton in Baja, Mexican farmworkers would travel to the San Joaquin Valley, which was becoming the major producer of cotton in California. Arguing that there was a labor shortage, representatives of both Baja and California lobbied to keep Mexicans off the immigration quota.

By 1929, some 20,000 Mexicans worked in the Imperial Valley. Half lived in urban areas, and more than half of their children enrolled in schools were born in the United States. Many migrated to Los Angeles to the San Joaquin Valley and other parts of California, with a large number returning home.[16]

Mecca: Los Angeles

The opening of the Panama Canal in 1914, the expansion of the city's harbor facilities, and World War I all contributed to the rapid urbanization and industrialization of Los Angeles, as did its new warehouses, rail lines, and highways. Like Parral and El Paso del Norte in colonial times, Los Angeles was both magnet and transfer point for those seeking work. Its interests extended south, east, and north. In 1911, the Chandler family, owners of the *Los Angeles Times*, had formed a syndicate, and purchased 300,000 acres of sprawling ranch land in Los Angeles and Kern counties, known as Rancho Tejon. The syndicate lobbied for a road linking Bakersfield with Los Angeles and running through its Tejon holdings.

By 1917, the Port of Los Angeles had surpassed those of San Francisco and Seattle in export tonnage. In the first three decades of the twentieth century, the city's population grew more than tenfold, to 1.2 million. Just over 40 percent of its Mexican population worked and lived near the Old Plaza and close to the railroad yards. Almost 70 percent were manual laborers, working in the city's new industries or on its agricultural and construction projects.[17]

Between 1920 and 1930, the number of Mexican children attending Los Angeles public schools more than doubled, to 55,000, or one-seventh of the total student population. Infant mortality in Los Angeles among Mexicans ran two and a half times that among whites. Mexicans, who represented between 12 and 14 percent of the city's population, accounted for one-fourth of the tuberculosis cases at city clinics in the 1920s. In 1924–25, after pneumonic plague claimed thirty lives in Sonora Town, the city's exterminators killed some 140,000 rats.[18]

By the late 1920s, five Little Mexicos formed in Belvedere Park, Maravilla Park, Boyle Heights, Palo Verde, and Lincoln Heights. Taking note, Protestant churches there vied with one another in saving Mexican souls. Some 30,000 Mexicans lived in the Belvedere-Maravilla barrio by the end of the 1920s. Mexicans also filled the crevices of Boyle Heights. Some lived in the arroyos and under the bridges that connected the Heights, while the better-off were beginning to nudge residents of the Heights. Other Mexicans lived along the Pacific Electric routes, working in the maintenance crews. Still others lived on the outskirts of Los Angeles in small colonias near farms, brickyards, and mills.[19]

In May 1920, immigration officials announced that hundreds of refugees were headed for Los Angeles. Middle-class Mexicans had come in the stormy days of the Revolution and lived on the outskirts of the barrios or among white Euro-Americans. Now, new immigrants came in larger numbers from all classes, with workers moving into the barrios. Members of Los Angeles Mexi-

Mexican American women factory workers in 1922. (Courtesy of the Los Angeles Public Library, Shades of L.A. Archives, 00002826)

can elite gathered at the Centro Hispano Americano on West Adams Street, where they held weekly formal balls. The *Times* observed that the Mexican señorita was fast becoming a "modern girl" who spoke perfect English and benefited from the "independent qualities borrowed from the American girl." Mexican social life thrived along Main and North Spring Streets. Aristocratic Mexicans gathered at Café Cuba on Main. Immigrants, day laborers, track drivers, and trackwalkers frequented the Old Plaza, where the Mexican consul held court, and where fiestas patrias attracted Mexicans from all classes.[20]

World War I had heightened Euro-American nationalism. By the 1930s, Mexicans were typically listed as members of the "red" race, or just "Mexicans," on census forms and on birth and death certificates. White racism made Mexicans more conscious of their identity. Americanization programs often had the opposite effect.

A native of Nuevo León and the founder of *La Prensa* in San Antonio in 1913, Ignacio Lozano moved to Los Angeles, where he founded *La Opinión* in 1926. Lozano's new paper defended the interests of Mexican homeowners in the incorporation controversy of Maravilla-Belvedere — opposing city annexation of the area. It also protested racial slurs by whites and police harassment of

Members of Los Angeles' Mexican elite gathered for the Círculo Cosmopolitano's Black and White Ball in 1931. (Courtesy of the Los Angeles Public Library, Shades of L.A. Archives, 00002821)

Mexicans. Yet, like *El Tucsonense* of the century before, *La Opinión* remained an instrument of the better-off Mexicans.[21]

In the late 1920s, six of the city's ten public schools having more than 90 percent Mexican students were in Belvedere, which had the largest concentration of Mexicans in the Los Angeles neighborhoods. By the end of the 1930s, and in sharp contrast to the extreme poverty of Maravilla Park, Belevedere boasted one Presbyterian, two Pentecostal, one Spiritualist, one Baptist, and one Catholic church, in addition to a settlement house, as well as the Santa Maria Community Center and hospital. Boyle Heights also had its share of middle-class Mexicans. In the 1930s, it seemed almost as if every other social commentator clamored to stereotype "the Mexican." Reverend Samuel M. Ortegón observed: "That the Mexican is emotional is very obvious. This susceptibility is derived from the Spanish and the Indian stock. Latin blood has always been emotional."[22]

As a trade center that mixed industry with farming, Los Angeles was the perfect warehouse for temporary labor between harvests. Displaced miners and

Mexican American women at a pottery company, ca. 1928. (Courtesy of the Los Angeles Public Library, Shades of L.A. Archives, 00002885)

farmworkers filled its barrios. This influx increased after the completion of the Guadalajara–Nogales–Los Angeles rail line in 1927.[23]

Bonding

Discrimination played a big part in forging a common identity among Mexicans. In 1921, police arrested Manuel Hondon, a Mexican dancer, in an alley behind a bathhouse and took him to the Venice Police Station, where they severely beat him, broke his jaw, and left him in a cell without medical attention. According to police, Hondon had been intoxicated. Although two witnesses corroborated Hondon's story that officers had assaulted him, the police were not charged. As early as 1925, the press carried accounts of Mexican gangs.[24]

The Mexican community reacted with outrage to what they saw as a miscarriage of justice. Aurelio Pompa, 21, killed his foreman, William D. McCue, after an argument in 1922. McCue struck Pompa, who went home, got a revolver, and shot McCue. Mexican witnesses swore that this happened only after Pompa and McCue had argued for a second time. Euro-American witnesses said Pompa shot McCue without warning. When, after two mistrials, Pompa was convicted and sentenced to death, the Mexican spectators were so angry that District Attorney J. B. Costello asked deputies to escort him from the court.

The Sociedad Melchor Ocampo supported Pompa. Along with other mutualistas, it pressured the Mexican consul to intervene, as Mexican organizations collected nearly 13,000 signatures on a clemency petition. To no avail. In May 1924, the People of California executed Pompa. For two nights, Pompa's body lay in state in Los Angeles before being shipped back to Caborca. Like so many Mexicans in Los Angeles, Aurelio Pompa had migrated to California from his native Sonora simply to survive. "Tell my race not to come here," a *corrido* has him say, "For here they will suffer; there is no pity here." Asked if he were Spanish, he responded, "I am a Mexican and proud of being so."[25]

Identifying with heroes from their ranks, such as prize fighters, also helped Mexicans to bond. Boxing, writes Gregory S. Rodriguez, "has served as a mechanism of solidarity, promoting a sense of identity, unity, status, and esteem; as an instrument of confrontation between national and ethnic groups." It has also served to relieve racial tensions and to undermine the myth of white supremacy. Boxing reinforced Mexican nationalism and, for the successful few, provided a way out of poverty. Through the first great Chicano boxer, Aurelio Herrera, Mexicans experienced what it meant to win as a Mexican. Born in San Jose, California, on June 17, 1876, Herrera grew up in Bakersfield but fought in Los Angeles from 1898 to 1909. For Mexicans, he was the symbol of Mexican greatness. After being badly mismanaged, however, he was forced to retire from the ring. Now penniless, he became a drunk and roamed the streets. Herrera was arrested for vagrancy in 1926.[26]

Throughout the 1920s, Bert Colima, "el Mexicano de Whittier," was constantly in the news. As the Mexican middleweight boxing champion, Colima symbolized the fame and fortune coveted by so many Mexican Californians of modest means. Pride in Colima came in a decade of intense Americanization. World War I had ushered in a wave of anti-immigrant hysteria that, during the 1920s, took the form of nativist immigration laws, the creation of "Mexican schools," which segregated Mexican children, and Americanization programs designed to transform Mexicans into brown gringos.[27]

Even sympathetic Euro-Americans wanted to transform Mexicans, differing from conservatives only in their not wanting to eradicate Mexican culture altogether. Thus the Friends of the Mexicans, under the auspices of Pomona College and the State Board of Public Instruction, hosted educators, social workers, agriculturalists, and others at its annual meetings in the 1920s. Although the group promoted teacher exchanges and improvement of relations with Mexico, its primary focus was on the Americanization of Mexican women and children.[28]

Back and Forth

"The Roaring Twenties," wrote Frank Medina in his autobiographical novel of the wanderings of Juan López in search of a community, "were like an engine running out of gas." The Arizona mines resumed operations but were subject to frequent layoffs. Medina described a program called Renganche, in which farmers got together with the state and mine owners to ship unemployed miners to the fields by rail to alleviate labor shortages. This displacement of Mexicans accelerated in 1931, when the Phelps Dodge cut back operations in Morenci to 400 miners three days a week. More than half the population of the towns of Morenci and Clifton was shipped back to Mexico or migrated west.[29]

Writing in 1928, Paul S. Taylor characterized agriculture in the Imperial Valley as "tenant farming, absentee ownership, and a general condition of instability and impermanence."[30] Planters used Mexicans for picking melons and lettuce, with labor contractors delivering them at agreed times. Upon the demise of a few short-lived independent unions, the Federation of Mexican Societies, mostly mutualistas, met in Los Angeles in March 1928 to form the Confederación de Uniones Obreros. The Confederación, which included nationalists, communists, and IWW fellow travelers, established twenty-one locals with a total membership of 2,000 to 3,000.[31]

At about the same time, a year-round Mexican population of field hands, merchants, and general laborers, assisted by the Mexican consul, formed the Union de Trabajadores del Valle Imperial. In May 1928, the union sent letters to cantaloupe growers and the chambers of commerce at Brawley and El Centro demanding that workers receive pay raises, free picking sacks, and ice, and that their wages be deposited in a bank instead of with contractors. When the growers refused, the workers walked out at the Sears Brothers Ranch. Claiming that the Wobblies had instigated the walkout, Sheriff Charles L. Gillett brutally crushed the strike. If the Mexican did not like the working conditions, the sheriff was heard to observe, they could always go back to Mexico.[32]

On the Eve

In January 1930, 5,000 Mexican workers in the Imperial Valley, led by the Asociación Mutúa Mexicana and together with Filipino workers, struck lettuce growers. Workers later changed the name to La Asociación Mutúa del Valle Imperial. This time, the Communist Party became a player. When the Sixth

World Congress of the Communist International declared that the American Federation of Labor was no longer a viable instrument to pursue working-class and revolutionary goals, the Agricultural Workers Industrial League (AWIL) had been formed in 1928. The militant tactics of the Trade Union Unity League, AWIL's organizational vehicle, attracted many disaffected workers in the Imperial Valley.[33]

The growers exploited the factionalism between the AWIL and the Asociación Mutúa Mexicana. Much as Consul Arturo Elías had with the copper barons, the Mexican consul conspired with the Western Growers Protective Association and immigration authorities to get rid of the AWIL. The nationalism of the Mexican association led to the defection of the Filipino pickers, who were highly politicized and united. The presence of the Communist Party was both positive and negative. On the positive side, it gave the plight of the workers national and international exposure. On the negative, it made the strikers ready targets for conservatives and "patriots."

During March and April, cantaloupe growers monitored the Communist Party and planted three spies. Local authorities cooperated with the Los Angeles Police's "red squad" and infiltrated the party. The Workers International Relief and the International Labor Defense Committee branded the Mexican union reactionary. In April, while himself under indictment for corruption and police brutality, Sheriff Charles L. Gillett arrested 103 strikers. Bail was set at $40,000, later reduced to $15,000, and union leaders were charged with criminal syndicalism. A lower court convicted and sentenced the defendants to from two to twenty-eight years.[34]

In July 1931, the AWIL changed its name to the Cannery and Agricultural Workers Industrial Union (C&AWIU). In November 1932, the C&AWIU entered the bloody Vacaville strike, where growers severely beat scores of strikers, and angry vigilantes kidnapped six leaders, shaved their heads, and doused them with red paint. The governor refused to intervene, claiming he had no power to interfere with local authorities. According to Pat Chambers, the violence at Vacaville went well above the norm for such a strike, with 75 to 100 severe beatings. Chambers called Vacaville a milestone. Communist Party organizers were charged with criminal syndicalism.[35]

In 1933, California growers were hit with thirty-seven strikes, involving nearly 48,000 farmworkers. The C&AWIU participated in twenty-five of these, involving just under 33,000 workers. The Santa Clara Valley pea strike, the El Monte berry strike, and the summer strikes in sugar beets, apricots, pears, peaches, lettuce, and grapes all contributed to politicizing farmworkers, when police, armed guards, and secret agents attacked them as they held mass meetings. Most of the strikes resulted in partial victories. They created a cadre for the San Joaquin Valley Cotton Strike of 1933.[36]

The Control Center

Southern California's vast agricultural industry operated out of downtown Los Angeles, where the chamber of commerce was in constant contact with California agribusinesses. There was a constant flow through the city of seasonal pickers, many from the Imperial Valley, Mexico, and the Dust Bowl, on their way to the San Joaquin Valley and points north. Those who stayed in Los Angeles worked in the city's canneries, packinghouses, and the clothing industry, or as maids or pick-and-shovel workers.

California growers wanted Mexican farmworkers available at harvesttime and expected Los Angeles to warehouse them until then. To do this a welfare system was needed that could feed those unable to accumulate or earn sufficient funds to tide them over the off-season. The growing number of Mexicans on relief drew the attention of relief bureaucrats, charity workers, politicians, and nativists, who uncritically assumed Mexicans had come to Los Angeles for welfare.

To put everything into perspective, by the 1930s, Los Angeles was the fifth largest city in the United States, surpassing Cleveland, Saint Louis, Boston, Baltimore, and Pittsburgh in size. It had evolved from an agricultural market center to one of the country's top producers of foods. During this transformation, Angelinos constantly tore up and replaced the old. They leveled farms for factories and homes, and they bulldozed homes to make way for office buildings. By 1930, the city's movie industry had fifty-two studios employing 15,000 people. The Los Angeles region accounted for 9 percent of U.S. and 5 percent of world oil production.[37]

In the 1920s, the city's population grew by 115 percent; its Mexican population, by 226 percent. With the increased visibility of Mexicans and the ravages of the Depression came an upsurge of racist nativism. The California legislature in 1931 passed the Alien Labor Law, excluding Mexicans and other "aliens" from the construction of public school and government office buildings, as well as of highways.

Newspapers played an enormous role in manufacturing and promoting the politics of fear during the Depression. The major newspapers ranged from the *Hollywood Citizen-News* to metropolitan newspapers such as William Randolph Hearst's *Los Angeles Examiner* (morning) and *Los Angeles Evening Herald and Express* (evening). Hearst had a $220-million press empire that included the *Readers Digest*, nineteen big-city newspapers, and one of the nation's largest news agencies. Starting out as an ardent advocate of organized labor, Hearst degenerated into a rabid right-wing Republican and anti-Bolshevik crusader. Hearst's newspapers competed with the *Evening Express*, the *Daily News*, the *Los Angeles Post-Record* (1933–34), and the *Los Angeles Times*. Of these, Hearst's were by far the most right-wing in their political agendas.[38]

According to Walter J. Stein, "During the 1920s, Los Angeles Mexicans were studied, analyzed, and 'Americanized' by social workers as few other groups in the state's history, and agriculturalists favorable to Mexican labor became concerned over the 'habit' of relief and what some noted as an un-familiar 'surliness' developing among them." Even social workers and teach-ers who owed their jobs to them justified the repatriation and exploitation of Mexican workers. Mexicans were called criminals — and depicted as carriers of disease. The 1930 C. C. *Young Report* greatly exaggerated the financial burden in caring for tubercular and impoverished Mexicans.[39]

The Greek Chorus

An angst-ridden United States turned on the "foreigner" during the Great Depression. On January 6, 1931, Secretary of Labor William N. Doak re-quested that Congress appropriate funds for the deportation of illegal Mexican immigrants, alleging that 400,000 aliens had evaded immigration laws. The California senate proposed a bill prohibiting immigrants without papers from engaging in business or seeking employment, and making it a misdemeanor to have an alien as a business partner.[40]

On January 19, 1931, Assemblyman George R. Bliss of Carpinteria intro-duced a bill that, had it passed, would would have legalized the segregation of Mexican and Mexican American students in separate schools. As a Carpinteria school board member, Bliss had successfully established one such school by calling it an Indian School. Under the California school code, school districts had the power to establish separate schools for Indian children and children of Chinese, Japanese, and Mongolian ancestry. Mexico City's *Excelsior* blasted the bill: "The measure intended to put into effect with respect to Mexican children is degrading, ignoble, and devoid of justice, and it has raised waves of indignation."[41]

Meanwhile, C. P. Visel, the Los Angeles local coordinator for unemploy-ment relief, telegraphed Washington that conditions in Los Angeles were des-perate and that local citizens needed the jobs that undocumented Mexicans were taking from them. Visel circulated leaflets in the Mexican community stating that deportations would include both legal and illegal Mexican resi-

Mexican repatriation from Los Angeles, 1932. (Courtesy of the Los Angeles Public Library, Herald-Examiner Collection, 00052947)

dents. He claimed that "20,000 deportable aliens were in the Los Angeles area." Los Angeles officials took the position that, by deporting the Mexicans, they were doing them a favor. They likened the planned exodus of immigrants to that of the "children of Israel" out of Egypt. The Mexicans who had lived in the United States would take civilization to their less civilized relatives south of the border. Others argued that repatriation was simply a "weeding out."[42]

To assist in this effort, Los Angeles Mexican leaders formed the Cooperativa de Repatriación, composed of more than fifty groups. Alejandro Wallace, head of the Comité Mexicano de Beneficencia, estimated that between 60,000 and 75,000 Mexicans had departed by mid-summer 1931. In the early 1930s, the Comité and Asociación Mutúa joined forces to help the city's destitute Mexicans. Consul Rafael de la Colina raised funds for the unemployed. The Sonora Town Businessmen's Association and the Sociedad de Damas Católicas set up a charity kitchen, lodging was furnished at little or no charge in Sonora Town hotels, and milk and medicine were dispensed. The Comité purchased return tickets for some 1,500 repatriates, furnishing lawyers for those caught up in immigration dragnets.[43]

In 1932, the repatriates formed the Unión de Repartiados Mexicanos to pressure the Mexican government to live up to its promises of assistance. When the government failed to do so, the Unión sent word back to the United States. The much-advertised plight of these repatriates dampened the enthusiasm of many Mexicans for returning home. By 1935, the deportation and repatriation campaigns had both slowed considerably.[44]

Fighting Back

Mexican women left their homes to work in sweatshops and packinghouses. A lucky few got clerical jobs and some even worked as secretaries. A quarter of Mexican and Mexican American women had industrial jobs. Los Angeles alone had an estimated 150 dress factories, employing about 2,000 workers, three-quarters of whom were Mexican females (the remaining quarter being Italians, Russians, Jews, and Euro-Americans). In the summer of 1933, the garment industry began to restart production and workers demanded pay increases. Employers violated the National Recovery Act (NRA) code requiring a pay rate of fifteen dollars a week and hired replacements at less than five dollars a week.[45]

Up to this point, the International Ladies Garment Workers Union (ILGWU), which considered Mexican women unorganizable, had isolated them. That was to change with organizer Rosa Pesotta, an anarchist Jewish immigrant, sent from New York. She had another viewpoint.

Many of the women had been poorly paid and hard-driven farmworkers, who, seeking to leave their thankless labors, naturally gravitated to California's principal cities, where their compatriots had preceded them. On their way into the Los Angeles garment industry, they were joined by hundreds of Mexican women and girls, traditionally skillful with needle and eager to get away from family domination.[46]

According to Pesotta, the Mexican women lived on the outskirts of town "at the end of the car-lines, in rickety old shacks, unpainted, unheated, usually without baths and with outside toilets." "We get them," Pesotta explained, "because we are the only americanos who take them in as equals. They may well become the backbone of our union on the West Coast." The reaction to the first ILGWU strike was fierce: Captain William Hynes and his Red Squad attacked and arrested the Mexican women strikers. This and other strikes in the garment industry, although not always successful, expanded the leadership corps and the political awareness of the participants and their families and friends.[47]

Meanwhile, Los Angeles still operated nearly 14,000 farms in the county,

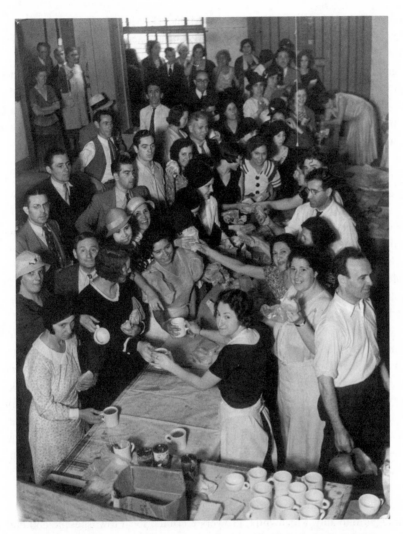

Striking Los Angeles garment workers being served lunch at the strike headquarters, 1933. (Courtesy of the Los Angeles Public Library, Herald-Examiner Collection, 00050657)

representing an annual income of $76 million, more than triple that of the Imperial Valley. Hard times accelerated the seesawing of farmworkers between city and farm. More Mexicans joined urban unions and were often caught up in urban protests sponsored by groups such as the Unemployed Councils.

Among the early farmworkers' strikes was the El Monte Berry Strike of 1933, which touched off a string of other strikes engulfing the onion and celery fields of Venice, Culver City, and Santa Monica. El Monte, a town of 4,000, was in the eastern half of Los Angeles County. Located across from a dry gulch next to El Monte was Hicks Camp, a Mexican shantytown. In May 1933, the Mexican Farm Labor Union (MFLU), associated with the Confederación de Uniones Obreros Mexicanos (CUOM), demanded twenty-five cents an hour and the abolition of child labor. The employers were Japanese tenant farmers who operated 80 percent of the 600 to 700 acres of berries. The strike commenced on June 1. Shortly afterward, the C&AWIU joined the strike and a power struggle arose between the Mexican Farm Labor Union's Armando Flores and Vice Consul Ricardo Hill, on the one hand, and the C&AIWU communist leadership, on the other.[48]

Hill and Consul Alejandro Martínez cooperated with the Los Angeles Police's Red Squad, even as Los Angeles Phelps Dodge harassed workers and broke up communist protests. They labeled the C&AWIU organizers as reds, who in turn distributed leaflets branding the consuls as sellouts. Because the Mexican Foreign Service and CUOM advised local consuls on strike strategy, many Mexican workers expected the Mexican government to intervene on their behalf.[49]

Contributing to the division was the Stalinist tactic of setting up dual unions. "In 1920," as Todd Chretien explains it, "Lenin personally intervened in American Communist trade union policy with his book *Left-Wing Communism: An Infantile Disorder*." He criticized the strategy of forming dual unions as playing into the hands of the bourgeoisie. Lenin saw the need to work within reactionary trade unions and not abandon the space or workers to reactionary leaders. But directly contradicting this, in 1929, Stalin ordered U.S. communists to desert the American Federation of Labor and to set up dual unions. According to Pat Chambers, many C&AWIU organizers accepted partial responsibility for the division.[50]

Local authorities backed the Mexican Farm Labor Union and the strike dragged into July. Meanwhile, growers recruited local townspeople and children to harvest the highly perishable berries. The Japanese consul worked privately with the Mexican consul to arrange a settlement effective on July 6. Because the peak of the harvest season had passed, growers offered a rate lower than that previously rejected by the union, so the union turned it down, calling for $1.50 for a nine-hour workday and demanding that growers recognize the union, whose members would receive preferential hiring. In the middle of July, the Mexican Farm Labor Union became part of the new Confederación de Uniones de Campesinos y Obreros del Estado de California, whose leaders had been prominent in the CUOM. The Confederación was affiliated with CUOM, and Flores became its first general secretary.[51]

In Dubious Battle

Farm wages plummeted from 35–50 cents an hour in 1931 to 15–16 cents an hour by mid-1933, culminating in what Stuart Jamieson called "a series of strikes of unprecedented scope and intensity throughout the country." The C&AWIU led sixty-one strikes involving 57,000 farmworkers in 1933, four-fifths of them in California. Not only did these strikes politicize workers, but they also trained organizers through trial and error, taking many beyond ideo-logical rhetoric, and introducing them to new strategies. The organizers prof-ited from the mistakes of El Monte and embarked on a series of more ambitious and successful strikes such as the one at Tagus Ranch in August 1933.[52]

The first wave of large walkouts in the San Joaquin Valley under C&AWIU leadership took place in Fresno in early August. Prior to this, a few small strikes succeeded in raising wages from fifteen to seventeen cents an hour, building the expectations of workers. When the National Recovery Administration fixed wages at between twenty and thirty cents an hour, farmworkers naturally be-lieved that this included them. The Sierra Vista Ranch in Delano, part of the DiGiorgio Corporation, announced it would comply with the NRA and that, to employ more workers, it would shorten their hours. The expected minimum rate was twenty-seven cents an hour, and peach workers demanded a raise to meet that rate.[53]

When their expectations were not met, "all hell broke loose" at Tagus Ranch, near Tulare, one of the largest fruit ranches in California. In Merced County, a hundred miles to the north, 2,000 workers of the California Packing Corporation also struck. The going rate was fifteen cents an hour. The union demanded the abolition of piecework contracts, equal pay for women, the abolition of child labor, and good sanitation.

Tagus Ranch had orchards, grape vineyards, cotton fields, and a cotton gin on the property. Its manager, H. C. Merritt Jr., had expanded the ranch to 7,500 acres. With the largest acreage in peaches and apricots in the world, the ranch used 87 million gallons of water daily — two-thirds more than the entire city of San Francisco. On August 11, some seven hundred pickers walked off Tagus Ranch. "The growers' initial reaction verged on panic." Pleas went up for the National Guard. Merritt seized the car keys of roving picketers and harassed them. The strike paralyzed local packinghouses when 2,000 women at Tulare canneries were thrown out of work.[54]

Although Tagus Ranch was at the center of the storm, the strike spread north, to the California Packing Corporation's ranches in the Merced area. When Merritt imported two hundred scabs to Tagus from the Fresno area, Chambers faced off with him. Sheriff R. L. Hill seized ten guns found in the possession of Tagus Ranch guards. Ray Edwards, a former Tulare police officer, was found carrying submachine gun during eviction of the workers. Alleging he was armed, authorities arrested Luis Mancello, a strike leader, for disturbing the peace. The California Highway Patrol asked county supervisors to hire more special officers. Chambers and dozens of other strikers were arrested for disturbing the peace. When Merritt claimed he had broken the back of the strike, Chambers responded by threatening a statewide walkout of 10,000 agricultural workers.[55]

Sheriff R. L. Hill and dozens of deputies, backed by American Legion volunteers, guarded the ranch. Superior Court Judge J. A. Allen issued a temporary restraining order to the strikers, forbidding them to hinder the transaction of business on the ranch. Under Chief E. Raymond Cato, thirty-six officers of the California Highway Patrol reinforced Fresno and Kern county deputies. Merritt ejected four hundred fruit pickers from the Tagus Ranch. Authorities dumped the workers' family possessions on the Golden State Highway, which ran through the gigantic ranch. The welfare of women and children was of little concern. "It is not our duty to provide for them when they refuse to work," said county welfare agent Emily Tubbs of Tulare. "That has always been our policy."[56] As the strike spread, the court issued sixty warrants for violating Judge Allen's injunction.

In Fresno, the State Division of Labor Statistics and Law Enforcement moved to arbitrate the strike, with Governor Rolph appointing a mediator. NRA regional director George Creel attempted to bring farmworkers under NRA code, which would give power to the federal government to prohibit strikes. The state mediator recommended raising the wage level. The deadlock was broken when the California Packing Corporation announced a wage hike. Merritt also raised wages to twenty-five cents an hour (up from 17½ cents) and acceded to most of the strikers' demands, although he refused to recognize the union. On August 19, some five hundred Mexican workers in Fresno celebrated the Tulare victory. "The news of any gain in wages was infectious among the workers. The workers seemed to feel: 'If they can do it, why can't we?' "[57] Like the peach and pear pickers, grape pickers walked off the fields, demanding twenty-five cents an hour.

Farmworkers throughout the San Joaquin Valley demanded twenty-five cents. Amid escalating strike activity and tensions, a rancher's son ran over two workers who tried to stop his truck. Meanwhile, Chief Cato, who said it was his duty to keep roads open, regulate traffic, and not take part on strike activities, did little to control the farmers. Evidently, he considered the strikers' car caravans an obstruction to traffic. "When hot-headed agitators publicly advocate violence," Cato declared, "it is time for law-abiding citizens to uphold their officials in protecting individuals and property, and the Board of Supervisors and the American Legion are to be commended for their attitude on the matter."[58]

When, on September 4, another strike broke out on at Lodi, thirty miles south of Sacramento, farmers under the leadership of Colonel Walter Garrison, fifty-seven, the "Führer of California," attacked the strikers. Garrison was born in California but apparently liked to play at being a Southern gentleman. He was the first president of the Associated Farmers in 1934, which, under his leadership, expanded and formed alliances with organizations such as the American Liberty League. Grape growers tried to form a Mexican Workers' Alliance, a company union to counteract the C&AWIU. The grape harvest was the largest in years. Walkouts began in Fresno and Modesto. On September 7, the owners met and agreed to pay 1½ cents a crate. The pickers insisted on two to four cents a crate. On September 13, several hundred workers met and demanded fifty cents per hour. Two weeks later, two hundred hundred pickers struck 150 ranches.[59]

Law enforcement recruited special deputies to combat the guerilla picketing. They arrested any car carrying picketers for disturbing the peace. Ranchers held mass meetings of more than 1,000 local people. At one meeting in Lodi, Garrison told businessmen and legionnaires, "All they have got is mob rule. Let's beat them to it." Growers broke up gatherings of strikers with fire hoses and tear gas. A striker was shot and a ranch foreman killed. When a striker demanded a jury trial, the Municipal Court Justice replied: "Juries be damned. . . . Juries are reminiscent of medieval times. They are a means of escape for guilty men. If I were innocent, I would rather go before a judge. They usually got twelve boneheads to sit on the jury."[60]

The Tagus Ranch strike leaders led the grape strike that raged for most of September. C&AWIU organizers were arrested and charged with violating the criminal syndicalism laws. Newspapers listed M. Esparzo, Y. López, and John García as ringleaders. G. S. Herrera, José Cota, and Willie de la Hoya were charged with criminal syndicalism. From Fresno, the strike spread to the Reedley-Dinuba area and Tulare. During this period, one of the most respected communist organizers, Pat Callahan, arrived from San Jose with Caroline Decker. Finding that it had overextended itself and that the preponderance of small growers made it difficult to organize the pickers, the C&AWIU abandoned the grape strike. By mid-September, it was over.[61]

The Tagus Ranch and subsequent strikes set the stage for the San Joaquin cotton strike of October 1933. Growers, workers, and union organizers knew the landscape. The August 1933 strikes infused the "workers with a tremendous unifying spirit."[62] Meanwhile, the C&AWIU held its first convention in August 1933. It was open to all field, cannery, and picking shed workers. Dues were twenty-five cents a month for the employed and five cents for the unemployed. The goal was seventy-five cents an hour for skilled workers for an eight-hour workday, and time and half for overtime.

In September, Chambers paid visits to every cotton camp to enlist members, and the union's strike committee arrived at the figure of $1 per hundredweight. At the same time, the San Joaquin Valley Peace Officers Association met in Fresno to find "ways and means of coping with agitators."[63] During the August walkouts, union organizers noticed the vulnerability of strikers who resided on company property and consequently devised new strategies such as setting up private camps and roving pickets. Although union organizers increasingly focused on the large orchards, they also attempted to win over the smaller farmers. After a prolonged strike, the grape pickers had won a significant pay hike — to twenty-five cents an hour. This victory fueled worker militancy, but growers were bitter, and more determined than ever to break the worker movement.[64]

◀ 12 ▶

The San Joaquin Valley
Cotton Strike of 1933

> The consciousness of a worker is not a curve that rises and falls with wages
> and prices; it is the accumulation of a lifetime of experience and socialization,
> inherited traditions, struggles successful and defeated. . . . It is this weighty
> baggage that goes into the making of a worker's consciousness and provides
> the basis for his behavior when conditions ripen . . . and the moment comes.
>
> — E. P. Thompson[1]

The summer spilled over into October, giving off a "dry and hazy . . . breeze" that heightened the edginess of San Joaquin Valley planters. Thousands of workers and their families had arrived in the valley to pick cotton and earn enough for food and gas to carry them to the next bonanza. When planters refused to offer survival wages, what followed was the largest farmworkers' strike in California to that point, involving 18,000 workers and their families — 80 percent of whom were Mexican.[2]

Farms along the cotton corridor produced more cotton per acre than the Old South.[3] Although the cultivation of cotton was recent in the San Joaquin Valley, in less than a decade it was the leading producer of the staple. San Joaquin cotton was whiter and had longer fibers, and it yielded and paid more per acre. In Texas, the cost of production was as high as twenty-two cents a pound, whereas, in the San Joaquin Valley, it was eleven to fifteen cents a pound. Even so, planters had to take out large loans for the electricity to pump up water. In turn, the large output attracted armies of pickers.[4] In 1929, the Depression lessened demand for cotton, and many marginal planters lost their land to the Bank of America and the ginners, who held the notes. By 1933, the federal government came to the rescue and offered planters subsidies.[5] The pickers hoped that farmers would share their bounty with them. When this did not happen, the cry went up for *huelga* (strike). This was a familiar word for Pedro

Subia, who had participated in the 1903, 1915, and 1917 Morenci strikes — as well as strikitos.

The Indian summer gave the planters more time to harvest the cotton and starve the pickers and their families. The summer of 1933 had registered highs of 116 degrees on July 26 and August 13. Even in October the temperature was in the low 80s.[6] And it was even hotter in fields. The planters worked themselves into a frenzy, shooting down two Mexican strikers at Pixley, some fifteen miles south of Tulare, and another near Arvin, some fifteen miles southeast of Bakersfield, on October 10, 1933. Although only a few pulled the triggers, the community of bankers, merchants, ministers, and even the Boy Scouts had egged them on.

The Bank of America, the San Joaquin Ginning Company, and the Anderson Clayton Company owned the contracts the planters signed in the spring, setting costs and picking rates. They held the mortgages and leased land to smaller operators. The planters could buy and sell only through them. Without capital, the planters could not turn on electric water pumps to water the crops. The community, the chambers of commerce, the farm bureaus, the American Legion, the Boy Scouts, local and state authorities, newspapers, supported their own.[7]

"Rolling Labor"

The planters derisively described the caravan of pickers as "rolling labor."[8] The automobile had given workers more independence as they migrated over wider areas. They drove, sometimes with radiators boiling over, or walked the Ridge Road, which connected the San Joaquin Valley with Los Angeles. Many had worked in mines or on railroads, on farms or in urban industries. Some had homes in Southern California and Arizona, and others lived year-round in the valley. A minority had picked cotton in La Laguna of southwestern Coahuila, traveling to the Rio Grande River Valley of Texas, the Salt River Valley of Arizona, and the Imperial Valley of California. They had fought in the Mexican Revolution, and they were veterans of other labor struggles. Most lived from day to day and spoke limited English. Almost all were victims of racism.[9]

From April and December 1933, some 50,000 farmworkers staged thirty-seven strikes in California. In August, the Cannery & Agricultural Workers Industrial Union, a communist union, won important concessions for farmworkers harvesting fruits and vegetables in the San Joaquin Valley. They did so against insurmountable odds[10] — and against one of the best organized groups of growers in the nation. San Joaquin planters organized and funded the San Joaquin Valley Labor Bureau in 1926 and hired Frank J. Palomares, 62, who had worked for both the Spreckels Sugar Company of California and the Arizona

A cotton strike picket caravan, October 1933. (Courtesy of the Library of Congress, Prints & Photographs Division, LC-USF344-007487-ZB)

Cotton Growers Association. Palomares called himself Spanish. Born in California, he lived in a white neighborhood in Fresno with his wife and thirty-three-year-old son, who was a director of labor for the chamber of commerce.[11]

Planters preferred Mexican pickers, who they thought could be "easily handled." In less than twenty years, cotton became a Mexican crop in western Arizona, eastern California, and then the San Joaquin Valley. Paid low wages, these farmworkers were, in effect, left to their own devices. As Paul Scharrenberg, an American Federation of Labor official, would later say: "Only fanatics are willing to live in shacks or tents and get their heads broken in the interest of migratory labor."[12]

On September 18, seventy-eight men and women met in Tulare to plan the cotton strike. They concluded that it took the average picker 10 hours to harvest 300 pounds. Planters offered forty cents a hundredweight — that was not enough to buy enough food and gas to get to the next job. The workers demanded a dollar per hundredweight. W. D. Hamett of Tulare, an Oklahoman, was chosen chairman of an executive strike committee that included regional representatives. The day before, the Associated Farmers of Tulare had met at McFarland, some forty miles to the south, and Kern County growers had formed a group to "assist" farmers.[13]

Picker expectations were high. The New Deal had brought a partial recovery, which the planters closely followed and organizers reported. On June 30,

1933, the *Pixley Enterprise* had informed that the U.S. Department of Agriculture was paying growers six to twelve dollars an acre to retire land. On September 23, the *Bakersfield Californian* informed readers that the price of cotton had been pegged at ten cents per pound (ten dollars per hundredweight). Subsidies and guarantees would be paid under the Agricultural Adjustment Act crop reduction program. This would guaranteed profits with less cotton to pick. Thus the workers believed farmers could afford to pay them more.[14]

Responding to public pressure, the ginners, bankers, and large growers reluctantly agreed to raise the offer to sixty cents per hundredweight. This was still not enough, so the strike unofficially began on October 2. Reminiscent of Walter Douglas in Arizona, planters mobilized for an all-out war against the "Reds" — a charge that became ever shriller in the course of the strike. "When people are paralyzed with fear," C&AWIU organizer Caroline Decker said, "they seldom think or believe rationally. The farmer lived with fear. He breathed fear, he talked fear, he grew fear, and he spread fear." Business leaders, newspapers, chambers of commerce, farm bureaus, elected officials, and city and county police lined up on the side of the growers.[15]

No Rights for the Landless

When they received word of the strike, seventy-five Kings County planters gave pickers and their families five minutes to load all their belongings on trucks and then dumped them on the highway. "The sheriff and I told the growers not to worry about the pickers' rights anyway," said Kings County District Attorney Clarence Wilson.[16] Fortunately, the C&AWIU had rented camp spaces close to the cotton-picking centers. The most important was Corcoran. J. E. Morgan, 50, who owned a gas station across from the Santa Fe Railroad tracks leased the union four acres. Pickers erected a water tank, five hundred feet of water pipe, fourteen toilets, and garbage pits. Morgan was from West Virginia, and his wife Felicia, from Arkansas. The Morgans had five daughters and one son, ages one through thirteen. They would not be told what to do by the big guys. The Corcoran camp, governed by Mexicans, was in the middle of the "Little South."[17]

Alejandro Rodríguez, about thirty-five at the time of the strike, worked for J. G. Boswell on October 1. His father-in-law, Mateo Castro, was a foreman. Rodríguez went to the camp because Boswell had kicked all the Mexicans off his land. He went on picketing caravans and stood guard to protect the camp from the planters.[18]

Lilly Cuellar, 17, from Brawley, arrived at the Corcoran camp with her husband, Arnulfo Cardena, after their employer evicted them. Cuellar remem-

A campsite of striking Mexican workers in Corcoran, California, October 1933. (Courtesy of the Library of Congress, Prints & Photographs Division, LC-USF344-007487-ZB)

bers security guards patrolling the camp. According to Cuellar, families could barely survive on wages they earned in grapes. Cuellar's husband had previously participated in Imperial Valley strikes.[19]

As a straw boss and contractor, Mateo Castro was loyal to Boswell. He had left a foreman's job at a ranch in Tlazazalca, Michoacán — and his first wife — to come to the United States in 1909. His son Roberto followed but did not see his father again until 1922. Roberto's mother would never see her husband again. Whereas Mateo bitterly opposed the strike, Roberto sided with the pickers, formed a strike committee, and remained loyal to the workers throughout his life.

Why Mateo never returned to Mexico is not known. In 1930, he was living in Corcoran with his second wife, Mary Castro. The 1930 census (which spelled his name "Matteo") listed Mateo's birth date as 1876, making him fifty-seven at the time of the strike.[20] Mary was about forty-nine and their son, Rudolph, eleven at the time of the strike. Rudy was friendly with Boswell's son, Jim (J. G. Boswell Jr.).

At the Boswell camp, the pickers' families were housed in some forty tents and huts, each twelve feet by fourteen feet in size, whose stench rivaled the Boswell hog pens, although Rudy Castro claimed his family lived in three deluxe cabins. Young Rudy was impressed by all the out-of-state license plates, from Texas, Arizona, Colorado, and New Mexico, as pickers drove in from Los

Angeles, Corona, Riverside, and Oxnard. Some, like Fidel Medina, had traveled across four or more states before settling into the Corcoran camp. Medina left the Santa Fe Railroad when he and his six sons went to work for Boswell.[21]

Rudy Castro remembered how "in the eyes of the growers we were just about equal to . . . mules." On Saturday nights, thousands of workers would shop at Corcoran's grocery stores, drugstores, and dress shops, and would frequent its main street theaters. The townspeople barely tolerated them. Adding to their troubles, Mexicans had a hard time getting medical care. When Rudy took his pregnant sister-in-law, who was suffering from complications, to a hospital and pled with the maternity nurse to take care of her, the nurse responded, "No, we have to give her a bath first. You Mexicans are all dirty." When Harry Glenn's car struck Eliador Hernández while walking down Whitley Avenue, Glenn, who owned the local telephone exchange, did not even stop to check to see if Hernández was alive. The day the strike began, Rudy saw the California Highway Patrol roar through town and, two blocks from the railroad crossing, mount a machine gun pointed in direction of the strike camp. "They were ready to mow down these strikers," he said, "all because they had the audacity to ask for more money."[22] Because Mateo's son Roberto was a union man, Bill Boswell questioned Mateo's proven loyalty and evicted the Castro family.

The nearly 3,800 strikers at the Corcoran camp outnumbered the town's residents almost two to one. A tent school was set up for some seventy children. In an area of the camp specially set aside, Lino Sánchez, fifty-one, held court over the nightly mass meetings, which growers called the Aztec Circus. Lino had been a resident of Corcoran since at least 1920, arriving in California from Mexico about 1910. He died in Corcoran in 1969.[23]

"If You Don't Like It, Go Back to Mexico"

J. W. Guiberson, one of the first men to plant cotton in a dry lake bottom, saw Mexicans as "one big parade of nomads." They were the kind of workers "we want . . . the kind we can send home when we get through with them." In an interview with Paul S. Taylor, Kings County District Attorney Clarence H. Wilson said, "The conditions for the Mexicans were far from ideal but they aren't used to living in palaces. They are better off in the camps and at sixty cents [per hundredweight] than they were in Mexico."

Although Los Angeles was not in the San Joaquin Valley, it controlled it. Aside from warehousing many pickers in between picking seasons, the city was headquarters for the cotton, fruit, and various other crop exchanges. Cotton in Kern County alone generated 5,000 jobs and 450,000 man-days of work each year. According to the valley newspapers, the cotton growers were being extremely fair: they had increased wages by 50 percent at a time when cotton prices had increased by only 30 percent.[24]

At first, the growers believed the Indian summer would delay picking some ten days without damage. This would make it easier for them starve strikers out. To fortify the planters, Kern County Sheriff (John) Cass Walser, sixty-three, had sworn in five hundred special deputies. Walser was born in California, but, like most of the valley's establishment, he had Southern roots — his parents were from Missouri. Walser was a growers' man: he issued hundreds of firearm permits to planters and indiscriminately arrested strikers as he directed the evictions.[25]

Meanwhile, to the north, in Tulare County, Constable Delos O. Howard, 49, of Pixley arrested three men considered to be strikers Jesús Chavirin of Earlimart, Paul Sánchez, and Primes Harrell.[26] Howard and his wife were born in California, his father was born in Missouri, and his wife's father was born in Kentucky. Hiram C. May, 42, of Earlimart filed the complaint against Chavirin. May and his wife, Lola, were born in Texas. They shared deep Southern roots and an abiding antipathy toward Mexicans.[27]

The *Visalia Times Delta* was rabidly pro-grower. When union leaders warned that a Tulare judge and the district attorney would be held accountable for any calamity, the *Times Delta* editorialized on October 7: "The orders issued by strike leaders in Stockton to Sheriff (Bob) Hill and District Attorney [Walter C.] Haight to keep their hands off the cotton strike in Tulare County, under the penalty of being held directly responsible for any resulting violence, remind us of the threats which George (Machine Gun) Kelly made to federal marshals and attorneys." Sheriff Hill, 61, admitted that there had been no union violence but added that "ranchers were losing patience with the strikers and a continuance of the [strikers'] present tactics might result in violence." Hill was born in California, but his father was from Kentucky and mother from Texas.[28]

The Vigilantes

On Saturday, October 7, a truck full of growers wielding pistol and rifle butts pulled up to the strikers at Woodville, southwest of Tulare. "I will shoot to kill the first striker I see in the road," one of the growers told Caroline Decker, all of four feet eight inches tall, "and it won't be the first . . . I've killed."[29] According to news accounts, the strikers overwhelmed seventy growers. Among the vigilantes, Woodville District Attorney John Nelson suffered a fracture of his arm. Sheriff Hill came to the rescue of the vigilantes but made no arrests. Hill announced that the Farmer's Protective Association had been formed to combat

A picket line in Tulare, California, October 1933. (Courtesy of the Library of Congress, Prints & Photographs Division, LC-USF344-007484-ZB)

agitators and escort them to the county line. Meanwhile, the American Legion was put on full alert.[30]

Rabbi Irving Reichert, a newly appointed director of Mediation and Adjustment for the NRA in California, complained of the "lawlessness" and "high-handed and outrageous methods of the so-called vigilantes." The rabbi continued, "Gangsterism has been substituted for law and order in the cotton areas." Reichert demanded the curbing of vigilantism and implored that peace officers be instructed to "exercise intelligence and self-control."[31] Rolph half-heartedly admonished local authorities.

In the meantime, vigilantes ousted two hundred more families from their hovels in Kern County. Strikers responded by parading through the streets of Bakersfield with placards reading: "Hold the Line!" "Negro and White Unite and Fight!" They demanded an end to evictions, hot lunches for their children, removal of the camp guards, recognition of their right to picket, respect for their right to peacably assemble in public places, sanitary conditions in all camps, and the release of leaders arrested the previous week.[32]

The *Bakersfield Californian* praised members of newly formed growers' association, calling them Minutemen whose mission was to "protect pickers" from the strikers. A 5-mile-long convoy of 1,000 automobiles carrying 4,000 businessmen, civic leaders, and growers arrived at Hoover Ranch in northern Kern County at noon on October 8. A spokesperson said the growers were demonstrating show of force. Word arrived from Los Angeles that the U.S. Immigration Service had sent agents to the fields to investigate the worker leadership.[33]

The night of October 9, workers held meetings throughout the strike area. State Labor Commissioner Frank McDonald said that the strikers were "sitting on dynamite," that the growers were "ready to go outside the law." According to Sam Darcy, that same evening, a delegation of three hundred small farmers met with the strikers and offered to work out favorable changes with the finance companies. The offer boosted the strikers' morale. A delegation of large farmers offered strikers at the Corcoran camp seventy cents per hundredweight, but the strikers rejected the offer.[34]

Many of the strikers were from Los Angeles or had spent time there. Joe Ambris, Albert Ambris, Silverio Mena, and Gavino López, all of Corcoran, were arrested for disturbing the peace when they attempted to persuade pickers on the John Held Ranch to join the strike. Like many of the strikers, the Ambris family was once from Los Angeles, where the senior Ambris worked in cement construction in 1930. Joe Ambris, 38, was a single father, whose sons Albert, 20, Raymond, 18, and Tony, 14, lived with him. Born in Mexico, Joe came to the United States in 1909.[35]

The Minutemen

On October 10, the Tulare Farmer's Protective Association published a manifesto in the *Visalia Times Delta*, branding the strike Communist and promising ranchers "armed aid." The Tulare Board of Supervisors authorized Sheriff Hill to hire as many deputies as he needed and to arm them with shotguns loaded with tear gas. California Highway Patrol Captains W. E. Riley of Tulare and B. W. Olivas of Madera County reported that ranchers told their patrolmen that, starting October 10, they would "blow to hell every striker who so much as laid a hand on the fences of their property."[36] In Kern County, local sheriffs handed out six hundred citizen's permits to carry concealed weapons. That same day, two strikers were killed at Pixley and another at Arvin.

In the morning of the October 10, strikers set up a picket line of nearly two hundred at Alpaugh, near Pixley. According to news reports, when thirty strikers urged pickers to join the strike, Alpaugh Constable Ira Knox, forty-one, arrested seventeen and took them to the Justice Court in Pixley. Knox was inexperienced and, as recently as 1930, had been a laborer for the Irrigation

District.[37] According to Constable Delos Howard, who had deputized farmers in the event of "trouble," a worker delegation went to the Justice Court to demand the release of the picketers. Fearing trouble, Howard telephoned the Tulare County Sheriff's Office for backup.

Meanwhile, the farmers worked themselves into a frenzy, claiming that strikers were going to free the prisoners. So they made a preemptive strike. Thirty cars full of growers pulled up next to a worker rally and took cover behind their cars and began shooting. Seeing the growers, the strikers retreated to the union hall. Growers alleged that a speaker spoke disparagingly of the American flag, so a grower aimed his shotgun at the crowd and fired. The next day, the *Visalia Times Delta* quoted striker Billy Thomas as saying: "The farmers opened fire on us from behind automobiles without warning last night."

Big Bill Hamett told a reporter, "I told [a planter] not to shoot into the hall, into the women and children in there." The planters killed Dolores Hernández, 53, and Delfino Dávila, 50. They severely wounded seven others: Isabella Ward, 47, Felipe Estrada, 48, Joe Rymer, 43, Gonzales Carnejo, 32, Cruz Alvárez, 47, John Clemment, 19, and Felipe Mascora, 41 — all residents of the valley. Meanwhile, growers were mobilizing in Porterville and Corcoran to invade worker camps.[38]

One of the few major California newspapers to condemn the violence was the *San Francisco Chronicle*: it wrote that there must be no compromise with lawlessness and violence. More typical of newspaper coverage was a letter to the editor in the *Los Angeles Times*: "From the south San Joaquin Valley come accounts of cotton pickers on the ranches being threatened by mobs of ruffians who motor from place to place urging terrified pickers to strike for a 66 percent raise in wages." The contrast between the two papers' positions was nowhere more evident than in the columns of the *Chronicle*'s Clifford Fox and the *Times*'s Chapin Hall.[39]

By all reliable accounts, the strikers were unarmed. Constable Howard, a six foot four inch Gary Cooper look-alike, admitted this, yet apparently did nothing to stop the violence. According to O. W. Bryan, a local merchant, Howard was a conciliator who never drew a gun because he saw no need for one man to draw on another.[40]

On the day of the shooting, Howard saw the planters drive up. He knew them by name, and he knew they intended to make trouble. Yet he made no attempt to intervene, even though he saw that women and children were among the picketers. *Fresno Bee* reporter Ronald B. Taylor, who interviewed Howard, and who did extensive research on the strike in the 1970s, called what happened at Arvin and Pixley massacres. He concluded that the planters had planned both confrontations, and that focusing on the role played by the ginners and bankers distracted attention from the virulent redneck prejudice of the growers. The San Joaquin Valley was California's Confederate South, with all its trappings, according to Taylor.

Staying inside because he was afraid the strikers were going to release the prisoners, Howard watched as the planters' convoy drove up, rocks were thrown, and strikers shot. He told a horrified Taylor he found it funny when a "fat black lady with a big butt" was shot through both sides and ran around with blood squirting out. Although Howard openly sympathized with growers, he conceded that they were wrong for shooting the strikers.[41]

The California Highway Patrol (CHP) played a suspect role. Ira Cross was struck by stories told the Governor's Fact Finding Committee of the patrol "interfering with the strikers and their movements." Later he wrote: "When the Pixley shootings occurred, the strikers rushed into their hall and attempted to get out . . . into the alley in order to escape the bullets of the growers. They were met by a patrolman with drawn gun, who shouted at them to get back into the hall." Although Cross was careful not to accuse the patrol of collusion, he raised a serious question. Why did CHP officers, who were clearly on the scene, make no attempt to restore order? Less than two months later, a mob in the Imperial Valley, reportedly led by a CHP officer, abducted ACLU attorney A. L. Wirin.[42]

According to the *Bakersfield Californian*, Pedro Subia, 57, a resident of Kern County for eight years, was killed by a bullet from a fellow striker's weapon at Arvin "at E. O. Mitchell Ranch two miles Northwest of Arvin High." Subia worked on several cotton plantations in the area. According to growers, 150 strikers stood at the edge of field "harassing" a dozen pickers and yelling for them to come out. A fight ensued and the strikers reportedly clubbed grower Hugh S. Jewett, 51, knocking him unconscious during the melee. Jewett was one of the firebrands and president of the Agricultural Labor Bureau of the San Joaquin Valley and a leader in the newly formed Farmer's Protective Association. He headed the Kern County Water Development Commission. Strikers allegedly also beat another planter, Lloyd W. Frick, 42, who was from Iowa.[43]

Deputy Sheriff Thomas J. Carter, 35, originally from Texas, said he stepped aside when someone shot Subia in the chest. The *Californian*, in an attempt to divert attention from the killings, repeated the misinformation that a fellow striker killed Subia.[44] "Three men lie in morgues, twenty-two persons are nursing injuries that range from crushed skulls and broken arms to bullet wounds, and eight alleged strike leaders are in Kern County Jail on 'suspicion of inciting a riot.' " CHP commander Roy Gallion and Deputy Sheriff William Young arrested Alonzo Andrews, 27, a strike leader from Arvin, for Subia's murder. *Chronicle* reporter Fox summed it up: "At Arvin, Kern County, one man was shot to death and five wounded when a posse of officers, armed with drawn guns and tear gas bombs, charged a picket line drawn around the largest cotton plantation in the district."[45]

The coroner's report suggested a cover-up. Pedro M. Subia, 20, who was in Arvin when his father was killed, identified the body.[46] There had been fighting at the Mitchell Ranch for thirty minutes before ranchers fired two shots. E. O. Mitchell, the owner of the ranch, was present. James M. Stewart, a farmer living on Bear Mountain Road testified that the sheriffs fired more than five tear gas bombs. William E. Stewart, a laborer who lived on the neighboring Bonfield Ranch, testified he had not seen any guns among the strikers. Eliza N. Margraves testified to the all-white jury that she had heard a man with "stipped [sic] overalls and . . . glasses" admit to shooting Subia.

According to H. E. Clark, "the one they call Mitchell, got mad and slapped someone in the face. That's what started the rumpus." Several shots came from the other side of the fence, where the farmers were. Clark got eight stitches for a wound to his head as a result of the melee.[47]

The Subia murder gave the planters an excuse to clamp down on the strikers. They issued an ultimatum. Demonstrations or meetings would be met with prompt action. To drive home their point, farmers from throughout the county, armed with baseball bats, pistols, shotguns, and rifles, attended an emergency meeting. In the end, they decided to let Sheriff Cass Walser clean up the mess. Planters said they had the duty to arm and protect themselves so they took action to preserve the peace — in other words, to take preemptive action. Kern County Under Sheriff Tom Carter told Paul S. Taylor on November seventeen that growers had two machine guns and had bought $1,000 of tear gas.[48] In response to pressure by the Committee in Defense of Political Prisoners headed by Lincoln Steffens, Governor James Rolph ordered Clarence Morrill, director of the State Bureau of Criminal Identification, to look into events surrounding the strike. Before initiating his "impartial" investigation, Morrill blamed the "Communists."[49]

According to Sam Darcy, on the night of the shootings, "we moved from camp to camp in an effort to discipline the outraged anger of the workers." Meanwhile, Hugh S. Allen, 49, from Kentucky, sent a memo to his fellow vigilantes: "Gentlemen: the cotton strike is still very serious. The fight in Arvin County yesterday and the demonstration staged last night convinced the Sheriff of Kern County and the District Attorney that they must do something so that now they are prepared to move the crowds off the roads and arrest the leaders. We have been trying for a week to get the Sheriff to do this but it took yesterday's melee to bring this about." Allen had been in the area at least since 1900 and listed himself on the 1930 census as a mining engineer for the Kern County Land Company, a powerhouse in the San Joaquin Valley.[50]

The Death of a Strike

Although the sheriff had arrested Alonso Andrews, 27, on suspicion of shooting Subia, he had six other suspects: H. E. Clark, 23, Jessie McHenry, 33, Viola Andrews, 34, the wife of the prime suspect, William Johnson, 47, A. C. Summers, 43, and Henry Mitchell, 27. Apparently, Merced Véloz, 25, who had his left arm amputated, was not charged.[51]

Clad in pair of trousers and an undershirt, Pat Chambers was also arrested. Chambers was in good spirits, telling a reporter that the communists were the only ones fighting for workers. The news account made it clear that the State Bureau of Criminal Identification listed Chambers as an organizer for the Communist Party, who had been arrested twice before on criminal syndicalism charges and seven times for vagrancy. Attorney A. L. Wirin sought a writ of habeas corpus for Chambers's release. The growers attempted to drive a wedge between the organizers and the rank and file by asking why Chambers was being bailed out and not the Mexican workers. Kings County District Attorney Clarence Wilson blamed Chambers for the strike: "He is just a radical and an agitator. But I guess there is a place for such people after all. These ignorant Mexicans aren't able to get any degree of justice for themselves."[52] As Wilson later bragged: "We were in control of the strike because [the Mexicans] didn't amount to anything and couldn't even vote, but the growers were well known and had lots of influence and we were much more afraid we wouldn't control them." He made his double standard clear in his assessment: "I guess the growers said things just as likely to incite to violence as Pat Chambers did but they couldn't be guilty of criminal syndicalism because they weren't trying to overthrow the government."[53]

Just before the shootings, the following ad appeared in the local newspapers:

> We, the farmers of your community, whom you depend upon for support, feel you have nursed too long the Viper that is at our door. The communist agitators MUST be driven from towns by you, and your harboring them further will prove to us your non-cooperation with us, and make it necessary for us to give our support and trade to another town that will support and cooperate with us. Farmer's Protective Association.[54]

Because the bulk of the strikers were Mexican, Enrique Bravo, the Mexican consul in San Francisco, found the notice inflammatory. Barely thirty when the strike began, Consul Bravo and his German wife, Ada, had lived in a white neighborhood in Los Angeles in 1930, when he was vice consul there. Bravo had been in the San Joaquin Valley for at least two years and had experienced other strikes both in the valley and, before, in Los Angeles. Although he was clearly distressed when planters murdered Dávila, who had worked as a volunteer in the consular office, Bravo was careful not to offend the growers. Nevertheless, the consul said that the Mexican government would protect its nationals and he called on Governor Rolph to disarm the ranchers. Authorities knew that Kern County had issued six hundred gun permits to growers and that Tulare County had followed suit with "hunting licenses."[55]

Days after the killings, Bravo softened his tone. He said he was satisfied with the conditions at the Corcoran camp, echoing Sheriff Buckner's evaluation that it was "quieter than it has ever been since the strike developed,"[56] and that the strike had promoted unrest. The growers quoted Bravo as saying that Mexican farmworkers were satisfied with sixty cents and would return to work if it were not for the communists who were sowing radicalism.

Bravo's close associate, Leoncio Acosta, 53, president of the Fresno Comisión Honorífica, earned highest praise from the growers. Acosta lived in Fresno and was an interpreter. Acosta said he was from Chihuahua and a veteran of the Mexican Revolution. Arriving in 1913, he become active with the consular office and curried the friendship of the growers. When Bravo arrived as vice consul in Fresno in 1931, more than a thousand compatriots welcomed him greeted him. Acosta was the toastmaster for Bravo's welcome. Bravo found Fresno, whose Mexican colonia numbered 6,000, too stressful; he relied on Acosta and other brokers.

Bravo attended elite Mexico City schools and went to Columbia University for a year, where he received unimpressive grades but was fluent in English. He joined the consular corps in 1925. Bravo had developed *comisiones honoríficas* in Hanford, Pinedale, Tulare, and Fresno, and self-help organizations in Madera, Fresno, and Selma, as well as the Escuela Mexicana Benito Juárez in Fresno.[57]

Anticommunist Bravo had pretensions to being upper-class. He wanted peace with the growers and for the Mexican workers to negotiate without the union and accept the old rate. He went to the Corcoran camp and tried to persuade the workers to reach a separate settlement, apart from the union. He also helped repatriate Mexicans who wanted to return home. Meanwhile, *San Francisco Chronicle* columnist Clifford Fox reported that there were 4,300 hungry women and children in the tent cities.[58]

The shootings temporarily steeled the strikers' resolve. Scabs deserted the fields, and on October 11, close to 1,000 strikers converged on Visalia. In Fresno, 1,000 to 4,000 workers took the streets. Sympathy strikes took place near San Francisco, when tomato pickers walked off the job. On the steps of the Visalia Courthouse, pickers demanded that the growers be charged with murder.

Bravo warned strikers of the consequences if they continued and pleaded with the pickers to return to work. Bravo told anyone who would listen that the strikers had four hundred rifles and were ready to defend themselves. Bravo again accused the union of fomenting revolution while cheating workers by collecting unnecessary dues.[59]

Despite the murders, the state bureaucracy sided with the growers. "I have operatives down there in jail as agitators," Chief Morrill of the California Bureau of Criminal Investigation opined. "They have been preparing for this for some time." He claimed that the communists had committed thefts from armories. Morrill told Sheriff Robert Hill from Visalia that Robert White, 43, a mulatto, in jail at the time, was a red, and that there were communists in high places. George Aydelotte, Kings County NRA director, told Paul S. Taylor, "Chambers is a coyote. You can see that by looking at him." Aydelotte also claimed that a man could pick thirty-six pounds in an hour — six pounds more per hour than strike organizers had determined.[60]

The insinuation that Pat Chambers — probably of British or Irish extraction — was a Jew kept crept into reports. The press referred to "red agitators from New York," a euphemism for communist Jews. W. L. Walker, manager of the State Employment office in Bakersfield and vice president of the California State Employee Association told Paul S. Taylor, "It was a fight between Communist Jews and [the San Joaquin Valley Agricultural Labor Bureau,] which is a racket."[61]

California Highway Patrol Captain Raymond Cato named Chambers and E. H. Ernest as the principal agitators in Kern County, in effect, declaring an open season on them. The governor appointed Morrill and Cato to bring about a fair solution in the valley. Although there was no evidence that Chambers had been armed, he and indeed all the strike organizers were treated as violent. Timothy A. Reardon, the state director of industrial relations, said, "California cannot tolerate civil warfare such as marked the strike during the last two days." Reardon called upon strikers and growers to disarm at once — even though there was no credible evidence that the strikers had fired a shot.[62]

Enraged by the arrest of Chambers, the union redoubled its efforts. It prepared to strike more than 3,000 ranches, using women extensively on its picket lines. Strikers demanded an audience with Governor Rolph but were put off. The killings embarrassed state officials. Governor Rolph lashed out at "smart alecs who want to be clothed with authority and are running around taking the law into their own hands. I'm not going to turn a lot of men loose to run around and help out the regular police forces when the police haven't asked for it. I am cooperating with the rightful authorities in every county of this state and holding them responsible for preserving the peace. They need have no fear whatever because when they really need help I will give it."[63]

On October 12, the C&AWIU passed out a leaflet: "Comrade strikers. The weather is threatening. The growers are becoming desperate. We must mobilize. All of Our Forces to Keep the fields clean. Do not let stool pigeons or anyone else call off the picket lines. There must not be a Scab in the Fields. Mobilize more picket lines to cover."[64]

◀ 13 ▶

Bitter Warfare

Author Ella Winter described a tour of the Corcoran camp in the dark of night:

> We stumbled along in almost pitch-darkness among tents, people, burning oil stoves, refuse, wretched and smell as in the shack towns, smells of greasy cooking, stake fish, damp clothes, and sewerage. [T]here were small muffled sounds that gave the feeling of a crowded city. Though we could not see the crowds. A sick baby wailed — and I had a sense, in the darkness, of people waiting, waiting. . . . A frowsy woman came out with a bundle, a tiny wizened baby whose face was almost black — black as I had seen them in Vienna; his tiny eyes gazed unseeing. . . . "The baby's dead!" Mexicans stood around unmoving, wondering, I supposed, who these strange people were, commiserating all of a sudden with a wretchedness they had always lived inside.[1]

On October 10, the day of the killings, three-month-old Jennie Roque, daughter of Mr. and Mrs. Philip Roque, was taken to a Kings County hospital with another sibling. Both were critically ill from starvation. Jennie died. Three more babies died at Corcoran on October 14.[2] The doctors reported the cause of death — malnutrition and exposure. Local hospitals treated more than a dozen other children for starvation and exposure. "Thousands of strikers and their families in the squalid tent cities dotting the countryside," the *San Francisco Chronicle* reported, "were facing hunger and disease as County and State officials enlarged their relief agencies."[3] The planter community showed no remorse. Yet they were infuriated when, the next day, the *Chronicle* exposed their strategy for what it was — "a plan to 'starve out' the cotton field strikers," undertaken with the complicity of "County Supervisors, a District Attorney and Sheriff, a chief of police and 'other officials.' " "We realize," the paper concluded, "how necessary it is for the State to step in with impartial authority to stop this conflict."[4] Meanwhile, a hospital at Corcoran refused admission to expectant striker wives ready to give birth. A doctor from the San Francisco Bay Area tended to patients in the Corcoran camp under an assumed name, fearing grower pressure would get his license lifted.[5]

On October 18, the *Visalia Times Delta* headline read: "Infant, Victim of Strike, Dies of Malnutrition." Two-month-old Henry Sparca died of pneumonia, malnutrition, and bowel disorder at Corcoran.[6] The Corcoran City Council, the Corcoran Chamber of Commerce, the American Legion, and the PTA adopted resolutions to close the camp. Refused treatment at a local Kings County hospital, Mrs. Sabas Aguila died of pneumonia. On October 18, Sam Darcy wrote, "5th baby dies at Hanford camp," thirty-five miles north of Corcoran. On that same day, the mothers assembled at the Corcoran camp refused to accept state relief milk because they were required to sign cards pledging they would return to work at the old rate.[7] On October 19, a 4-month-old girl succumbed to malnutrition at Corcoran. On October 22, the *Chronicle* and the *Hanford Morning Journal* reported that 5-month-old Francisco "Komocho" (probably "Camacho") son of José "Komocho" died of malnutrition at Hanford. Four days later, Rudolph Urteaga, four years old, died of pneumonia, the second child of the Urteaga family to succumb — and the ninth to die during the strike.[8]

"Let's Appoint a Commission"

As with most Euro-American disasters, the governor appointed a fact-finding commission to find out what everyone already knew. After some dithering, San Francisco Archbishop E. J. Hanna, University of California Professor Ira B. Cross, and President Tully C. Knoles of the College of Pacific were appointed to the commission.[9] The growers adamantly opposed any state or federal interference and expressed their outrage that state and federal authorities would even listen to the other side. The National Recovery Administration (NRA) said it was powerless to give workers relief until they submitted to arbitration.[10]

Governor Rolph met with a delegation of strikers who asked for relief and the right to arm themselves. Although, in April 1933, Congress had formed the Federal Emergency Relief Administration to provide workers with immediate relief, it had excluded migrant workers from that relief. Yet there was a loophole. The feds were empowered, through the State Emergency Relief Administration, to funnel money to state and county offices in an emergency, provided the emergency was nationwide and that relief was a national and not a local problem. Harry Hopkins made it clear that relief should be dispensed according to need and not whether a controversy such as a strike existed. This was not acceptable to the planter community, which demanded local control.[11]

The supervisors of Kern and Tulare Counties refused to assist the strikers. Faced with mass starvation and pressured by the federal authorities, Governor James Rolph ordered the California Emergency Relief Administration to give the strikers and their families' assistance. "The California Governor overrode federal regulations withholding relief from strikers under arbitration," reported the *San Francisco Examiner*, "and, over the protestations of local boards of supervisors, sent in trucks of milk and food to the embattled camp." This was the first time workers in any industry had received food from a federal agency during a strike.[12]

Relief did not start until October 14 and ran into an immediate roadblock. R. C. Branion, state and federal director of relief, complained that, asked to reveal their history and sign affidavits in return for their children receiving food, the strikers had refused. Many were mindful of the repatriations taking place — some 1 million Mexicans were sent back to Mexico during these years. Most of the strikers refused out of fear that the state would deport them as charity cases. Others accepted the food only after receiving repeated assurances they would not be deported for doing so.

Behind the scenes, state and federal officials pressured both sides to settle. With their full plates and political influence in the state legislature and Congress, the growers had clear leverage over the starving strikers. NRA Administrator George Creel feared another outbreak of violence and gave the governor an ultimatum to resolve the dispute or the federal government would step in. He also told the planters that failure to cooperate could cost them their Agricultural Adjustment Administration subsidies.[13]

In a telegram to Governor Rolph, State Director of Industrial Relations Timothy Reardon proposed that the federal government settle the strike by subsidizing the pickers' salaries. "I have found that the growers cannot pay more than sixty cents per one hundred pounds, but I have also determined that the pickers should receive no less than eighty cents." Reardon suggested that government pick up difference, claiming that, as things stood, relief to strikers would attract the unemployed from other areas and drive up federal outlays without returning workers to productive employment.[14]

Mexican strikers held a mass meeting in which anyone could speak on the subject of accepting relief. In the end, many strikers gave in to the pleas of their starving women and children. When the relief authorities arrived with milk, news reporters said Mexican mothers begged for it. According to relief workers, "Children clung to their mother's skirts crying for a bottle of milk." Although the Corcoran camp was the largest and most militant, other camps were as determined to resist. At Mexican Camp and at Hoover City in Bakersfield on October 25, strikers were also on the verge of starvation. Relief workers were shocked, "We saw a little baby dying from lack of milk."[15]

Private and public relief was vital to keep a strike alive. The Workers International Relief Fund brought donations of food and clothing and, for a brief time, the State Emergency Relief Administration furnished limited relief. Small farmers and city people also donated truckloads of meat and vegetables, although these were often seized by the sheriffs. Relief, no matter how temporary or how little, only angered the growers, as did the presence of civil rights groups from Los Angeles pressuring government institutions to protect the strikers.

After touring the strike area, Edward O'Neal, president of the American Farm Bureau, blamed the communists and the Mexicans: "The Mexican population . . . has no roots in California soil. Hence the Mexican laborer is very susceptible to the whispers of agitators." "The California planter," he explained, "receives forty cents an acre return on his crop. The fixed costs are twenty cents an acre. He pays the pickers half of what is left and keeps the other half for himself." His conclusion? "I can only say, in surveying this situation, that I'd rather pick the cotton than own the land."[16]

The Communists Made Them Do It

According to Joe Gladney, twenty-one at the time, the growers were armed and the strikers were not. Gladney was born in Texas, and his parents were from Oklahoma. In 1920, the Gladneys lived in Heard, Arizona, where his father farmed. Many of his neighbors were Mexican at the time. According to Gladney, the growers did not hate the Mexicans, they hated Pat Chambers. They resented his passing out leaflets, and believed Chambers wanted to convert the workers to communism in return for gas money. The years 1932 and 1933 were difficult, but he blamed outside agitators for the strike. He questioned where the strikers got the money for gas to drive around in their caravans. They would pull up to the fields and call out to the field hands, who left the fields because they were afraid. Although Gladney was pro-grower, he conceded that the Mexicans were not getting paid enough.

Gladney dwelled on hard times. The only source of financing was the ginning companies. The growers and ginners had set a price in the spring, so the planters simply could not pay more money than the ginning companies had budgeted for them. According to Gladney, most of the Mexicans during the early 1930s came to Tipton from Watts, California.[17]

Small farmers, caught in the middle, understood the plight of the near-starving Mexicans and their families and tried to help. In the Arvin area, a group of Bakersfield women led by Genevieve Hunt helped cotton strikers' wives who were expecting babies. Emma Cutler of the International Labor Defense argued that, although the small farmers also had it hard, "the farmers' wives at least have a roof over their heads, and a chance to grow their own food, but the pickers work through the season for wages which will not permit them to live decently even while they are working." Moreover, "the strikers have no weapons so far as I know and are pledged to conduct themselves lawfully. They realize the farmers are helpless, but feel the finance companies will be forced to act if the strike continues."[18]

A Tipton dairy farmer interviewed in 1973 testified that most of the cotton production was centered in the Earlimart-Pixley district. Like other interviewees, he repeated that planters were at the mercy of the ginners. The planters had to pay ginners' charges, inspection fees, and so on. Most cotton planters were not as big as they are today.

But even though he returned, over and over, to the theme of planters caught in a squeeze between pickers and ginners, the dairy farmer sympathized with the Mexicans. He said there would not have been any problem if the planters had compromised and paid eighty cents the hundredweight. But he noted that many planters were Southerners, who did not like Mexicans and even regarded them as slaves.

The dairy farmer knew some of the indicted planters, and did not like the elder Stark, who he said had been a U.S. marshal in Texas before coming to Tipton. The farmer recalled that Stark had held a gun on Mitchell's boy while one of Stark's boys beat him. The Mitchell boy had beaten Stark's boy in a fair fight. Stark bragged about the incident.[19]

J. Boyd, a farmer, told Paul S. Taylor, "Matt Stark always goes around with a gun. He didn't do the shooting at Pixley but he would have if he'd been there. There are a lot more like him." After the trial, Boyd heard that the planters intended to celebrate their victory. A government man told the planters to stay calm. The verdict was a foregone conclusion. The planters would have gotten away with no trial at all if the California Highway Patrol had not been present.[20]

Justice Denied

Even though their sense of justice was badly shaken — Subia's killer or killers had gotten away with murder — the strikers still did not submit. On October 12, they marched to Visalia demanding that the state prosecute growers for the murders of Delfino Dávila and Dolores Hernández.[21]

"Although 'eye witnesses' of the fatal melee [in Arvin] were almost unanimous in blaming the farmers for not only starting the riot but also doing the only shooting in the mix up," the *Bakersfield Californian* wrote four days after the killings, "a coroner's jury returned an open verdict that angered the strikers. The witnesses blamed the [pickers] now under arrest."[22] The coroner's jury found that "Pedro Subia, Mexican victim of last Thursday's strike riot at Arvin, was killed 'by a person or persons unknown; [and that his death was] accidental.' " Witnesses testified that a "large white man in striped overalls" did the shooting. Meanwhile, a hundred strikers demanded the release of Viola Andrews, Herschel Real, Jess McHenry, H. E. Clark, Arthur Summers, and William Johnson, jailed for rioting and resisting arrest. A first-degree murder indictment was issued against Alonzo Andrews. Conspiracy charges were eventually dropped against defendants Viola Andrews, Alonzo Andrews, Herschel Real, Jesse McHery, H. E. Clark, and William Johnson.[23]

Ralph Kreiser, a *Los Angeles Times* reporter at the time, covered the inquest, each day phoning in his story in time to make that day's edition. Kreiser blamed the banks, especially the Bank of America, and called the Pedro Subia coroner inquest a farce. A female reporter from the *San Francisco Chronicle* became so outraged Kreiser had to restrain her. Although Kreiser had been at Arvin, he did not see the shooting. He said that the Mexicans were caught in middle, and that the communist leadership was responsible for the violence. Over the years, Kreiser became part of the Bakersfield establishment, working for the *Bakersfield Californian* and developing close ties with many planters. Kreiser said he knew who killed Subia but would not name the killer because "it would serve no purpose."[24]

Burying the Dead

The National Guard at Hanford and Visalia was put on alert, as mourners marched to a small Catholic church in Tulare to bury Hernández. "When the casket of Dolores Hernández emerged from the church," the *Chronicle*'s Clifford Fox wrote, "a sudden hush fell on the group. It was succeeded by the shuffle of feet that came like the rustle of wind through the trees. As the casket started for the cemetery with the armed motorcycle police in close attendance, the marchers fell in behind, the shuffle of the myriad feet becoming a steady thump like distant drums. And so they buried Dolores Hernández." After the funeral, the strikers announced their intent to reinforce Corcoran.[25]

The funeral of Pedro Subia took place in an old warehouse building in

Bakersfield on October 16. Father A. C. Stillman celebrated Mass. The headlines referred to Subia as "Comrade," suggesting that he and his mourners were communists, although there is no evidence that they were. Workers came from all the camps around Bakersfield to gather in his honor in front of the Bakersfield City Hall. They included "Whites, Mexicans and Negroes, some of them once farmers in their own right, tall fair men from the mountains of the South and their wives leading little towheaded children, some desperate, many hopeless." The marchers' only weapons were no larger than hairpins: "Any weapons they may have had were pawned long ago to buy food." [26]

Tulare Sheriff Kerr swore in more deputies. The California Highway Patrol pulled back, which further irritated the planters. Kings County Sheriff Buckner alleged that the person in charge of food distribution at the Corcoran camp was bribing the strikers with food to continue the strike. Buckner protested federal relief, saying it worsened the situation. Meanwhile, newspapers reported that the Kern strikers had returned to the fields for seventy-five cents per hundredweight. [27]

The Eviction

Although the shootings broke the larger strike, a small core of strikers voted on October 15 to fight on. The strike committee recommended putting more women on the picket lines. Tulare Sheriff Robert L. Kerr, 61, warned that "the Federal Government is very liable to throw some of these people into a bull pen and ship them out of the area if they remain recalcitrant." Rumors circulated that the union was sending armed agitators. Although the coverage of the *Chronicle* was generally good, it occasionally lapsed into stereotypes: "Gifts of food, tobacco and other articles were brought by dark-eyed señoritas to the Mexican prisoners [at Visalia] and passed through the bars under the watchful eyes of armed guards." [28]

Consul Bravo urged Mexican workers to be orderly and law-abiding, even as growers continued to harass and menace them. He dissipated any moral authority the Mexican government might have had by putting more blame on the strike leaders and thus minimizing the role of the planter community. "Show me a single leader or agitator who has led you into this strike," he dared the workers on October 18, "who has ever picked a stalk of cotton." For his part, Governor Rolph announced: "We're not going to force these strikers into arbitration by starving them into it. Not in my state! These people are hungry. Get down there — fly down there by plane and feed them as soon as you can." That said, Rolph took care not to alienate the growers further. [29]

Back in Corcoran, Sheriff W. V. Buckner, 74, laid down the law at Corcoran, ordering the speakers to "talk only in American." Local authorities criticized NRA Administrator Creel for telling the workers that peaceful picketing was legal in the United States. Initial public sympathy for the striking pickers soon faded before the growers' propaganda drumbeat that the "riots" were the fault of communist agitators. By October 17, some 2,000 scabs had come to the fields of Kern County to pick cotton, and the strikers were going down for the count. It was left only for L. W. Frick and the San Joaquin Valley Growers' Association to declare victory.[30]

Planters now claimed that Corcoran strikers were threatening, intimidating, beating, and even kidnapping the new pickers who refused to go on strike. Lieutenant Gordon Marmaduke, commander of the Hanford National Guard, and Sheriff Buckner agreed that the situation was out of control. They requested that the state send in a hundred California Highway Patrol officers. News accounts had the growers arming themselves.[31]

When strikers announced they would visit all the plantations in Kern, Kings, and Tulare Counties to urge scabs to leave the fields, the planters accused them of adopting "semi-military tactics." Sheriff Buckner told the strikers he would not permit anyone to leave the Corcoran camp. Caroline Decker replied, "No man will stop us."

Planters suddenly gave Federal Conciliator Edward Fitzgerald a vote of confidence, a bad sign for the union. As the Indian summer drew to an end, they were starting to panic. They suggested school holidays on Monday and Tuesday for the children to pick cotton, pouring 12,000 schoolchildren into the fields.[32] The Farm Bureau and the valley grocers demanded that immigration authorities round up "illegals" and ship them back to Mexico.

Erasing Memory: Absolution

The fact-finding commission established by the governor and California NRA Administrator George Creel got under way on October 21. The governor and everyone connected with the strike knew the attitude of both planters and strikers. Even so, it was hoped that reasonable people could somehow bring the two sides together.[33]

Because Pat Chambers was in jail, Caroline Decker headed up the union delegation. On the second day of the commission's hearings, however, Decker and attorney H. L. Wirin refused to participate unless Chambers was present. Authorities conceded to their demands. Chambers entered the room to applause.[34] As Sam Darcy later wrote, "One worker after another, unused to speech, to whom action came unhurried yet nevertheless sure, rose and in simple halting words urged that the union not retreat one inch. One had to be humble before such courage."[35] Robert Lee submitted a signed affidavit:

On October 7, about 1:30 p.m., I was called to a camp in Tulare County to see a lady who was sick. I [went] to this lady's tent, [found] her [sick], took her temperature which was 104, pulse, 120, respiration, 30, I returned to Corcoran, called union headquarters to have a doctor from Tulare County go and visit this patient. Before he came, I called [the] County Welfare Office [in Visalia] and asked them to admit this lady into the hospital. Telling them my findings. They asked me if this was a striker's wife. I told them, yes. He answered me. 'We have no beds.' Doctor Van Vorkis, from the Kings County volunteered the following day to visit this woman, finding her in serious condition, too serious to remove to the hospital, the [woman] died this date, October 19, at six a.m.[36]

W. B. Kearney, a small grower, said, "I listened to attorneys picking to pieces the testimony of working mothers, with babies in their arms, dressed in rags, some of them with bleeding fingers, telling how much cotton they could pick and how they had to leave their babies lying in the field, while they picked cotton for a mere existence." Charging that the violence used against the strikers was organized at a growers' meeting four days before the Pixley shooting, Kearny added: "I do not think that either the large or small farmer, the way things are being manipulated, could pay [more than sixty cents a hundredweight]. If the finance companies and the San Joaquin Light and Power Company . . . put in their right [share,] we could pay enough so that [the pickers] could eat."[37]

Kearney testified that the growers had met in the Corcoran stadium, where Kings County cotton ginner Louis D. Ellett, 62, urged them to "arm and drive the strikers out" to make room for new pickers. "The time has come when we have to take the law into our own hands. We will have to use force to get rid of these workers and get new ones."[38]

The press described Decker as the brains of the union. Reporters watched with fascination as she questioned woman after woman, establishing that they could pick two hundred pounds in eleven hours. Several Mexican women testified they had children from six to eleven years of age. They would start work at 6:00 a.m. and were so tired that they slept in the fields. Decker asked Mrs. Pauline Domínguez how many children died at the camp? She responded, "Two that I know of." Of what? "Undernourishment." Decker also established that the women were afraid to sign the paper they were presented and that Sheriff Hill told them they would be put in bull pens if they did not return to work.[39]

The commission recommended raising the rate to seventy-five cents per hundredweight. "Without question," it found, "the civil rights of strikers have

A Mexican cotton picker in the southern San Joaquin Valley. Photo by Dorothea Lange. (Photograph by Dorothea Lange, courtesy of the Library of Congress, Prints & Photographs Division, LC-USF34-009950-C)

been violated. We appeal to constituted authorities to see strikers are protected in rights conferred upon when by laws of the state and by federal and state constitutions."[40]

The growers took exception to the report. Growers hated the fact-finding commission and member Ira Cross in particular. Years later, a planter testified: "You tell [Cross] it won't be healthy for him if he comes down into the valley — the respectable citizens will take care of him."[41] H. V. Eastman, chairman of the Regional Farm Bureau, accused the commission of being biased against the growers and said its report had "no binding force either legal or moral." Nevertheless, "in the interests of good American citizenship, law and order, and to forestall the spread of communism and radicalism and to protect the harvesting of other crops," the growers finally accepted the commission's recommendations.[42]

The System

Meeting with Administrator Creel and Governor Rolph, the growers flatly told them that they would adopt the 75-cent rate only on condition that more federal aid was forthcoming. The press made their case: the *Los Angeles Times*'s Chapin Hall labeled the militant strikers un-American for refusing to accept the 75-cent rate and the growers patriots for agreeing to it — but failed to mention that the patriots had asked for a bribe.[43]

Rolph ordered one hundred California Highway Patrol officers into the valley to guard the plantations, and arranged for a million-dollar loan to seal the planters' cooperation. Chief Cato moved to break up the Corcoran camp, calling it a "danger spot." Secretary of Agriculture Henry Wallace ordered authorities to shut off relief funds to "able-bodied idlers." Kern County would dispense aid only on condition that the workers returned to work. R. C. Branion assured farmers that the state would not distribute food to strikers who refused to work at the new rate. State Commissioner Frank MacDonald warned the union to go back to work or else.[44]

Prohibition ended in early December, which was a boon to Tulare County, second in the nation in the production of grapes. The repeal of the 18th Amendment would be a windfall of more than $6 million annually. For all intents and purposes, grape production had resumed. Chapin Hall of the *Los Angeles Times* on December 5 predicted: "Horizon Bright in Kern County." The newspapers of the time give a sense of the planters overweening power and influence — in the meetings of chambers of commerce, of women's clubs, of farm bureaus, of boards of supervisors, of the American Legion.[45]

The cotton planters received a federal subsidy of 3½ cents per pound or $1,015,000, for a total income twice what it had been in 1932. The Agricultural Adjustment Administration announced the success of its program. The Bank of America also had a good year, with the common shares of TransAmerica's first stock issue since 1931 gaining almost $3 million in value. The Bank of America was a major player in the valley.[46] The only thing spoiling the party was the trial of planters complicit in the October 10 massacres.

The San Joaquin Valley Peace Officers' Association deplored the cotton strike violence, blaming the strikers. Caroline Decker was arrested in Porterville for allegedly telling workers not to wait for wages but to take what they wanted. CHP chief Raymond Cato bragged that the troublemakers scattered as soon as the California Highway Patrol showed up and insisted that the union leaders had no interest in the workers: the C&AWIU had moved on to the citrus harvest. Growers beat the anti-union drums, saying that industrious workers in the citrus fields asked only to be left alone. Chambers's trial on criminal syndicalism ended in a deadlocked jury (6–6), and the judge declared a mistrial. Upon his release, Chambers went on a speaking tour. Meanwhile, the trial of the planters was postponed.[47]

The Death of Chihuahuita

On October 25, the *Los Angeles Times* headline read, "Troops Gather for Crisis of San Joaquin Strike." "The strike situation in the San Joaquin Valley," chanted Chapin Hall, leader of the Greek chorus, "is rapidly approaching a crisis. National Guard units at Hanford and Visalia are mobilized. The Kern County motorcycle traffic squad and seven Bakersfield patrolmen have left for the front. The Tulare County fairgrounds have been turned into a stockade and the police are rounding up strikers and rioters and putting them incommunicado." Hall accused the federal government of prolonging the strike by feeding the strikers and families. "Strikers, with their stomachs full, and confident that the government is back of them," he continued, "insolently rampage from ranch to ranch." He added, "I entered the war zone today with an open mind," ending, "so while heads are broken, gins are idling and a $10,000,000 crop is at the mercy of elements, an issue is joined . . . which may be settled by early and determined action on the part of established authority or which may very easily slip over the border line to a condition wherein machine guns hold the trump card."

Back at ground zero on October 26, Doctor Giles Porter of the State Department of Health went to Corcoran and declared the camp a dangerous health hazard. When the sheriff tried to enter the camp at 10:00 a.m., "the Mexicans were ready for him. They got some 30-30 rifles and some ammunition." "There were some young rebels over in the camp," wrote Commissioner MacDonald, "young dare devils that had been in the Mexican army and they was ready for a scrap." Fearing international repercussions, authorities restrained themselves throughout the strike.[48]

According to the *Chronicle*, Sheriff William V. Buckner, 74, and 460 deputy sheriffs stood outside the Corcoran camp, carrying sidearms, "while the unmistakable bulge of tear gas 'pineapples' in their blouses gave indication of the grim intention of the State of California to carry out its ejection mandate."[49] Rabidly pro-grower, Buckner told Paul S. Taylor that Ira Cross was a communist, that the communists were the source of the trouble, and that the Mexicans did not want to strike. Buckner had advised the owner of the camp to tell the pickers to pick or get out. Buckner was seen as a "good guy" because he had restrained a grower from killing a Mexican — although he did not arrest the man.[50]

When the sheriff informed the pickers that growers would take them back to the fields, they booed and jeered him. L. D. Ellett and J. W. Guiberson then told the strikers that commissaries would be opened and credit extended as soon as they picked one bag of cotton. The Mexican families refused to listen, and began hammering on buckets, pots, and other metal objects.

At eleven a.m. on October 26, Buckner ordered camp residents to evacuate by three p.m. — even though Commissioner MacDonald told him that the ultimatum was not necessary, that the central strike committee had accepted seventy-five cents per hundredweight. Angry pickers yelled, "We won't leave!" MacDonald and others went to Tulare and persuaded strike leaders to go to Corcoran to talk the Mexicans into leaving. But even though Decker went to the camp and called off the strike, the Mexican workers refused to pick in Corcoran. As they told L. J. Acosta, a consular representative, they would not pick because "strikers had been illegally beaten, shot and murdered by growers and their sympathizers in that district."[51]

Now desperate, however, the strikers posted a huge red sign at the entrance of the camp: "We Want No Overthrowing. We Are Waiting for Orders from Our Government to Be Repatriated. Keep Out." They sent a telegram, signed by the camp mayor, Lino Sánchez, to the Mexican minister of war: "We are 5,000 compatriots in the Corcoran strike district and we are disposed to migrate to our own country because of pressure by local authorities and business interests. Can you arrange transportation home for us?"[52]

Yet still the strike continued: a hundred pickers walked off their job at Merced. California Highway Patrol Chief Cato blamed "well-fed un-American agitators who lived in hotels with preventing a more general resumption of picking." Some workers, defying the authorities, refused to accept the new rate, although others did. Kings County District Attorney Clarence H. Wilson later told Paul S. Taylor that he was not sure that evictions were legal, and that sanitation at Corcoran was not that bad, even though the planters were complaining about it although six miles away.[53] Meanwhile, another 14-month-old boy died at the Porterville camp, of dysentery.[54]

Undersheriff Tom Carter of Kern County mirrored Buckner. He was unrepentant: "We protect our farmers here in Kern County. They are our best people. They are always with us. They keep the county going. They put us in here and they can put us out again, so we serve them. But the Mexicans are trash. They have no standard of living. We herd them like pigs." Carter said that the planters "knew strike was coming — we were prepared — had two machine guns — bought 7,000 of tear gas [bombs] — swore in forty-five deputies during the strike." He claimed he tried to prevent trouble at Arvin. The situation was tense: "Two growers were just hoping one [of the strikers] would put his foot across the line and he would have been plugged him full of holes." "In McFarland we were ready to clean them out," Carter added. "We built bull pens, one for the women and the one for the men."

Even after the evictions, some Mexican families fought on without the union. On November 2, Margarita Váldez, Ofelia Estrada, Dolores Ramírez, Pedro Váldez, Francisco Silva, and Fred Rivera were charged with rioting, although charges of vagrancy and disturbing the peace were dropped against five others at Corcoran.[55] Meanwhile, a central strike committee, composed of thirty representatives of various locals, turned thumbs down on the settlement. Promising to intensify picketing, they demanded eighty cents. The committee argued that the government was guaranteeing cotton at ten cents a pound. But the leaders knew it was a lost cause. According to Sam Darcy, "gentle" Caroline Decker, "quiet-spoken" Pat Chambers, and rugged Bill Hamett urged workers to return for seventy-five cents the hundredweight. But, for a core of workers, it went beyond wages; it was a matter of human dignity.[56]

On November 3, 1933, the *Bakersfield Californian* headline read: "Select 4,000 L.A. Families to Harvest Cotton in Valley." Pickers were chosen from lists of unemployed on relief and shipped by train, cotton trucks, and automobiles to the cotton fields. "Everyone" was happy — Los Angeles saved $250,000 and workers could probably earn $2 to $2.50 a day, according to the article.[57]

Herding Mexicans

Ella Winter's delegation met with District Attorney Walter Haight, who was prosecuting Chambers, the trespassers, and the eight planters who had been indicted for the Pixley murders. Haight and Alfred J. Elliot, chairman of Tulare Board of Supervisors and James R. Fauver, foreman of the grand jury, had asked the immigration authorities to deport the Mexican strikers. Haight had also waived the provision that a trial take place within thirty days. "We've come to see you about the strikers in jail," Emily Joseph of the delegation said. "We consider their bail excessive and you've just raised Pat Chamber's from two thousand to ten thousand." Haight responded, "Criminal syndicalism is a very serious charge." Noel Sullivan asked about the planters carrying guns. "I would have no right [to take the guns.] [I]t is for the sheriff to see the peace is kept." When the sheriff was asked about the guns, he responded, "Folks, I can't take the guns from the farmers, they go hunting and they have hunting licenses." Asked if the strikers could have guns: "They couldn't have a gun a minute in their hands without shootin'. They means harm and violence." When pressed, the sheriff said, "I don't care about the Constitutiootion [sic] of the United States, I am the law of Tulare and [what] I say in Tulare County while I am sheriff — ." He never finished the sentence.[58]

Again, the courts legitimatized the killings and the violence against the strikers. The Pixley planter defendants were acquitted of murder and the Taylor Ranch worker defendants found guilty of rioting. International Labor Defense Counsel A. L. Wirin said, "What the South does to its exploited Negroes, California has done to its exploited Mexican cotton pickers. There is only one explanation for this outrageous verdict. Workers may expect one kind of justice and ranchers another." All the Taylor Ranch defendants were Mexicans except one. The maximum sentence was two years for rioting and five for resisting an officer.[59]

Getting Away with Murder

On Friday, October 27, the KKK lit fiery crosses to warn the valley strikers of terror and raids. The *Visalia Times Delta*, October 29, 1933, encouraged the notion that the KKK should take active part in suppressing strike. Meanwhile, the report and the actions of state authorities left the impression that planters and strikers were equally to blame. Even the liberal press urged Mexicans to be reasonable.[60] The strike lasted twenty-three days, with 3 strikers killed, 42 hurt, and 113 jailed, most in Tulare, Kings, Kern, and Fresno Counties, although some also in Merced and Madera Counties. Nine children died of malnutrition or disease.

The district attorney, who had earlier indicted Chambers on criminal syndicalism charges, indicted the P. T. Taylor Ranch defendants for two counts of rioting and resisting arrest. Meanwhile, the Tulare County Grand Jury returned eight indictments for two counts of murder. Robert Culpepper, 61, Roy McAvee, 40, and J. N. Stark, 53, considered ringleaders, were not indicted.[61]

In the Bakersfield area, Judge Allan Campbell presided. District Attorney Tom Scott prosecuted Viola Andrews, Alonso Andrews, H. L. Real, Jesse McHenry, and Homer Cullingsworth for rioting in the Arvin shooting. The jury was composed of all-white residents of Visalia and Porterville. Real testified that he saw Marvin Hayes, a farm hand, born in Tennessee, take dead aim at Subia and fire the bullet that killed him. Alonzo Andrews also testified to seeing Hayes, Bogue Vastbinder, and Henry Wallace fire at the strikers. After a three-week trial, Homer Collingworth and the others were acquitted of murder but convicted of lesser charges.[62]

At their trial in Visalia, the Pixley defendants pled self-defense. Witnesses testified that the growers pulled up but left their guns in their cars. J. N. Stark, who was identified as one of the armed farmers, was not present in the courtroom; Stark had been questioned and released. J. J. Heflin, a state witness, stated that he heard ranchers assembled in front of the strike headquarters shout for someone "to get" individual strikers. Helfin saw E. G. Kruger, 39, of Earlimart, who wore a special deputy badge issued by Kern County, as well as a holster and gun, wave his hand, and heard him shout, "Let's get the leader!" as Chambers led the strikers to the hall. The ginning companies in Pixley had paid Kruger's bail.[63]

Witnesses testified that Henry Santens, 40, of Earlimart, told a Mexican, "I'll get you." The Mexican then fell to the ground, apparently wounded, but did not know who had shot him. A. W. Keen of Porterville saw Roy Nichols, 28, a gas station operator, shooting from the highway. Keen also identified Leland Thompson as being among those who opened fire on the strikers.[64]

Theodore R. Smith, a reporter from San Francisco, testified that the vigilante committee fired at the strikers but that the firing stopped with arrival of the California Highway Patrol. Smith contradicted the testimony of a defense witness who testified that, from the sound of the bullets, the shots must have come from inside strike headquarters.[65]

Cruz Alvárez was shot attempting to help a woman and child escape. Alvárez gave direct testimony that the man who shot Delfino Dávila wore a badge. Many of the strikers blamed Kruger for the shootings and, on October 25, the *Bakersfield Californian* reported: "Two Bombs Hurled to Intimidate Farm Crew." An unidentified shooter shot five shots into Kruger's home in Pixley at about the same time that the bombs exploded at the E. O. Mitchell Ranch.

It took the all-white, mostly male jury only one and a half hours to reach its verdict, although the trial itself had taken three weeks. When the verdict was announced on February 2, the courtroom burst into applause, many wept. The law said the planters were not guilty: they had gotten away with murder. The townspeople had treated the killers as heroes. The planned victory celebration was called off, however, because of possible negative public opinion. On February 3, the *Tulare Advance Register* ran an editorial of the *Porterville Recorder* speculating whether it was not time for vigilantes to take care of gangsters.[66]

Disciplining the Public

Los Angeles Times columnist Chapin Hall opined that "red propagandists" were using the schools and churches to preach the gospel of social destruction and to trample on the American flag. Hall singled out "social evangelist" E. P. Ryland at the Southern California Annual Convention of the Methodist Episcopal Church. Local leaders in the San Joaquin Valley also railed against communist influence in the schools, especially in the universities. Planters looked with angry suspicion on the students from Berkeley, Stanford, and the San Francisco Bay Area who visited the valley throughout the strike.[67] No one noted the Catholic Church's failure to use its considerable influence to feed the hungry and to end the violence against them, even though nearly all the Mexican strikers were Catholic.

Communist organizers recruited crucial outside support, to include actors such as James Cagney, who regularly contributed to humanitarian causes. When, however, it was revealed that Ella Winter, wife of Lincoln Steffens, had named Cagney as a supporter, in her letters to Caroline Decker, on trial for criminal conspiracy in 1934, Cagney responded by declaring himself a 100 percent American — and later by filming *Yankee Doodle Dandy*. Film stars Ramón Navarro, Lupe Vélez, and Dolores Del Río, whose names appeared on a slip of paper seized from Decker, were singled out as unpatriotic for allegedly contributing to communist causes.[68]

Truth be told, the half dozen or so communist organizers at the cotton strike did serve as its organizers. Although reporters considered Caroline Decker to be the brains of the strike, most contemporaries concede that Pat Chambers, a five-foot, six-inch Irishman and thirty-two at the time of the strike, was the leader. In interviews forty years later, however, Chambers gave credit to the Mexican families for keeping the strike alive. Yet neither he nor Decker could remember the name of a single Mexican leader during that strike. Labor reporter Ronald B. Taylor wrote that Pat Chambers spoke Spanish fluently, but he did not. Nevertheless, Chambers was able to communicate with the strikers and to earn their trust. Chambers was not a good speaker, according to Decker, but an excellent man.[69]

Caroline Decker was four-feet, eight inches tall, of medium build, weighing 107 pounds, and with blonde hair and blue eyes. *Times* columnist Hall traced Decker back to Pittsburgh, Pennsylvania, where she had been arrested for the first of numerous times. Decker joined the Communist Party because she felt that it was the only organization doing anything about poverty. Decker had been a communist since she was 16.[70]

Chambers was well liked by the workers. Decker, constantly called the "blonde secretary" of the C&AWIU, was eye candy for the press. Years later, several Mexican strikers including Pedro Subia Jr. asked me about her. Her fiery speeches and courage had attracted them, as well as students, a cause of concern among the planter community. Decker recruited literary figures such as Lincoln Steffens and his wife, Ella Winter. Winter in turn brought in a network of intellectuals such as millionaire Noel Sullivan and the black poet Langston Hughes.[71]

The leadership of the C&AWIU had helped organize the Tagus Ranch strike. They included men such as W. D. "Big Bill" Hamett, 46, a former preacher and ex-justice of the peace in Oklahoma, and Alan A. Clark, a former Visalia Chamber of Commerce member. Big Bill Hammett was likened to abolitionist John Brown: he had battled growers at Woodville and at Pixley. The organizers made him the public leader. No Mexican or African American leader was allowed to have anything like his visibility.[72]

As heroic as Decker and Chambers were, there was room for criticism. Both remembered Big Bill, the great Oklahoman leader of the strike, but not a single Mexican, which, considering that 80 to 95 percent of the strikers were Mexican, was telling, although also a reflection of the labor movement and progressives at that time. Decker said that if it had not been for the Okies, she did not believe that the Mexicans and Filipinos would have had the courage to step forward. The strike could not have happened without the "indigenous Americans."

Were Mexicans involved as strike leaders? They certainly appeared to have been active in the strike's principal union, the C&AWIU, and in the Communist Party. The U.S. Military Intelligence Division released a report entitled "Active Communists in California Compiled by Advisory Associates" in January 1934. After listing Sam Darcy as District 13 organizer for the Communist Party, A. L. Wirin, of Los Angeles, as an International Labor Defense attorney, and Pat Chambers as the initial C&AWIU organizer in the Imperial Valley, the report went on to list Frank Samora as secretary of the C&AWIU, Fred Martínez as an organizer for the Young Communist League in Imperial Valley, and Angelo Fernando, Tony Poso, John Nava, and Ralph Rodríguez as Communist Party activists in Sunnyvale. The research of Devra Weber and others has established the Mexicans' presence in both the party and the union. According to Weber, Francisco Medina, 68, was a member of the Communist Party and a founder of the C&AWIU, who worked closely with Pat Chambers and John Díaz, a C&AWIU organizer.[73]

A Confederate Heritage

The "Little South" was held together and protected by a common history. The leader was Colonel J. G. Boswell, from Greene County, Georgia. The colonel owned land in California, Arizona, Oregon, Colorado, and Australia. His California empire was founded on lake bottomland. The colonel ran Corcoran: "Mexicans, they were the workforce" there. Blacks lived in nearby Allensworth and worked on its plantations, although minstrel shows were performed in Corcoran.[74]

Corcoran was the heart of the Boswell empire, which extended to Tipton, Porterville, McFarland, Mendota, Guernsey, and Tulare. The colonel ran his empire from Los Angeles, with offices among the fifteen cotton dealers in the downtown Los Angeles Cotton Exchange Building on West Third Street. He frequented the California Club and the Midwick Country Club. Although an archconservative who ranted against FDR for steering the country toward "socialism, communism or some other type of ism," he made his fortune from government subsidies, which provided him the capital in 1933 to buy thousands more acres of land. The land in turn allowed him to buy water rights from Portuguese farmers along the Kings River.

The colonel worked behind the scenes, letting L. D. Ellett do most of the public speaking. At one point, he told J. W. Guiberson, a leading grower and banker himself, "You ought to have the guts to go in and clear them out. The cotton industry in the San Joaquin Valley will never be worth anything unless you do."[75]

The colonel was above getting his own hands dirty. But the Virginia hillbilly Clarence "Cockeye" Salyer, 38, was not. His son Fred told *Los Angeles Times* reporters that his father was present at Pixley. When he came home after the shooting with his hands covered with blood, Clarence said he could not be 100 percent sure his bullet had killed Dolores Hernández, so he damn sure wasn't going to take a chance it hadn't.

Although just nine at the time, Fred Salyer was still angry with the communists. Pat Chambers was nothing but a communist agitator, and "it was a war, and people died in war." The only question here is why, if Clarence was at Pixley, why did Constable Delos Howard not see him? Surely he would have recognized him, and if he did, was it a cover-up? Or was this the memory of a nine-year-old, growing old, and caught up in the culture of the time and place?[76]

In Kern County, cotton planter, banker, and government bureaucrat Wofford B. Camp was a lifelong Democrat, a Baptist, and a legend. Born on a farm in Cherokee County, South Carolina, the fifth of eight children, he graduated from Clemson College in 1916 with a degree in agronomy. Camp was not as rich as Boswell, but his power was indisputable. Camp worked for the Bank of

America as head agricultural appraiser. He joined the Roosevelt administration, where he drafted and operated the Cotton Program. Throughout his lifetime, Camp exercised considerable influence on the Department of Agriculture. President Lyndon B. Johnson praised him and made him a member of the Federal Bureau of Water Resources.

In an interview at the Bancroft Library, University of California at Berkeley, Camp said he was proud of the fact that his father was a member of the Ku Klux Klan. "I look upon his activities in that just the same as I do my own activity in Associated Farmers in California." Camp saw the KKK of the 1920s performing the same function it had in the 1870s and 1880s. "All it was protecting their homes and women folk and the children, and any man who is a man is certainly going to try to protect his home." Camp equated this to his own activity with the Associated Farmers. "Our purpose all of the time was just one thing: fighting Communism." According to Camp, the original KKK stood for a fine and honorable purpose. The communists were carpetbaggers, agitators. Men not ready to defend their homes against them were not men. "All we were organized for and all we tried to do and did was fight Communists."

Camp hated *The Grapes of Wrath*, finding none of its accusations true: "Caroline Becker [*sic*] was a fat communist. [W]e knew that folks trying to organize the agricultural workers were definitely communists or dominated by communists, and therefore the organization was to fight communism. . . . We didn't care about them being organized, but those things with the closed shop, we just can't operate that way." Camp accused the La Follette Committee of being communists and the WPA of being riddled with agitators and "controlled by, directed by, people who don't love America like I do."[77]

Historical Amnesia

Forty years later, Ormond W. Bryan, 75, a smaller version of Burl Ives, white goatee and all, declined to return to "the bitter memories" of the strike. In a 1973 letter, he told me he had arrived in the area not long before 1933. He had been a grocery store owner and bachelor at the time and had lived with a brother and sister. Accordingly, he had wanted to remain neutral in the especially heavy encounters between farmworkers and planters. He had done well since the strike; he was a justice of the peace for fifteen and a half years. Bryan was from Iowa, the southern part of which had sympathized with the South in the Civil War.[78]

Art González said that forgetting the Pixley killings was "convenient for men like Bryan," but that he chose not to. González remembered Hank Santens and Sam White or Miller — still alive in 1973 — as men with violent tempers.

A Mexican migrant family with tire trouble, February 1936. (Courtesy of The Bancroft Library, University of California, Berkeley, 1942.008 PIC no. 8:5)

On September 29, 1935, after Chambers (in a new trial) and Decker had been convicted of criminal syndicalism, the *Los Angeles Times* reported: "With the leaders of former farm strikes in California safely behind prison bars, State officials today found it a matter of comment that the harvest season in the State has passed thus far without a serious labor disturbance. In contrast with the bloody riots of former years in the Imperial and San Joaquin Valleys and elsewhere, Timothy A. Reardon, State Director of Industrial Relations, pointed to the practically unruffled manner in which [growers] moved California's vast agricultural crops to markets and canners."[79] California was safe with the white communist agitators now in jail. Mexicans didn't count.

◀ 14 ▶

La Mula No Nació Arisca

Ernesto Galarza took the first part of an old Mexican saying for the title to an article he wrote in 1966: "The mule wasn't born stubborn" — the second part goes: "they made it that way." Galarza related the saying to the larger society's treatment of Mexican Americans and African Americans, to its attributing certain behavior to these subcultures rather than looking to itself as the source of antisocial behavior or poverty.[1] Soon after Galarza's article appeared, someone asked him why Mexicans had never successfully organized. He answered that was why he wrote books. Truth be told, Mexicans have always organized, but they have seldom done so formally — in part because non-Mexicans assumed it was not in their "nature," and in part because non-Mexicans have violently resisted their efforts to do so.

Mexicans from Chihuahua, Sonora, and other Mexican states traveled hundreds, sometimes thousands of miles in search of work. Beginning as far back as the seventeenth century, many planted their crops and traveled to nearby or faraway mines for money or goods. By the time they came to the United States, their experiences with capitalism had shaped their identity. Some of the strikers in the San Joaquin Valley Cotton Strike of 1933 had taken part in the Mexican Revolution, and many were veterans of World War I. Yet the myth persisted that Mexicans were peasants, that they lacked the sophistication or intelligence to appreciate trade unionism and to want a decent standard of living.

What happened in the 1933 cotton strike was well and widely known

Misael Lopez, a Mexican American soldier, 1921. (Courtesy of the Los Angeles Public Library, Shades of L.A. Archives, 00002870)

among Mexicans, and is remembered to this day. As *New York Times* reporter Frederick F. Forbes wrote on October 22, 1933: "Although the actual bloodshed has not been great — four persons and perhaps a score wounded — the psychology of war has prevailed over the troubled area of the southern San Joaquin Valley." Despite clear evidence that growers had gunned down three strikers and been responsible for at least nine children starving to death, Forbes blamed the "Reds." Yes, the planters had colluded with local authorities to prevent food from reaching the worker camps. But that didn't matter. Nor did it matter that the workers were demanding less than a decent living wage. The communists had taken advantage of the Mexican pickers and made them go on strike. They, not the planters, were to blame for the violence that ensued.[2]

The simple fact is that the killings and the poverty at Pixley and Arvin, like those at Ray and Clifton-Morenci-Metcalf and Bisbee, were not aberrations but part of the "American culture." Planters, copper barons, and respectable townspeople worked themselves into a frenzy, using communism as a pretext to make preemptive strikes against Mexican workers as the Other. They had to stop the Reds from keeping *their* Mexican workers from working. They had to keep the Reds from taking over *their* fields or *their* mines. And each time gross constitutional and human rights violations occurred, they pushed these out of their minds.

The Facts and Nothing But the Facts

Again, years after the 1933 cotton strike, Fred Salyer, son of Clarence, told *Los Angeles Times* reporters how he had helped his father clean up the blood and melt down his father's Colt .38 special. Clarence Salyer believed that his bullet killed Dolores Hernández. If true, Sheriff Delos Howard was complicit, for he had witnessed the shootings. Salyer was hardly an invisible man. Governor Edmund G. Brown later named him to the state agricultural board.[3] So why didn't Howard mention Salyer in his accounts of the killings?

Within hours of the Pixley murders, planters murdered Pedro Subia. Coincidence? Ronald Taylor and scores of others did not think so. Wofford B. Camp was the leader of the Kern County growers. Camp was an ideologue. He was proud of the way they treated the communists and glorified the Klux Klux Klan. The Associated Farmers in California were patriots — "all we tried to do and did was fight Communists [who were] people who don't love America like I do."[4]

The tragic truth was that the justice system absolved the killers, just as those who paid taxes wanted it to. Everyone knew who killed Subia, and they knew who killed the strikers at Pixley. Robert Powers, a captain in the Bakersfield Police Department's Traffic Division at the time, said that the police were there to see that things did not get out of hand and to control the angry strikers. Indeed, the National Guard was readied. Yet columnists like the *Los Angeles Times*'s Chapin Hall said nothing about gross violations of the U.S. Constitution — calling instead for military action against the strikers.

The killing forced Powers to think about the Constitution. Subia's murder angered the strikers, and they were about to march on the Bakersfield City Hall with his body. The police chief panicked. His first impulse was to block the entrance to the city. The mayor and the city manager discussed using tear gas. Powers volunteered to take over the operation.[5]

Ralph Kreiser remembers Powers sitting by a window staring out. Kreiser asked him what he was going to do. Powers responded, "Let them march." At the time, he presumed the marchers were communists. He asked the organizers what they were going to do. They told him that they were marching on City Hall. Were they contemplating violence? No, not unless someone "bothered" them. Powers told them that he would see that no one did. They got into a column of fours and marched to City Hall. Afterward, they marched back without incident.[6]

The event left a deep impression on Powers. His views of civil rights conflicted with the accepted notion that people were without rights if they could not vote. A gut sense forced him to react against the mob mentality of the planter community: "I am opposed to people who push others around." The strikers' peaceable march helped transform this self-described grammar school dropout into a liberal.

In contrast, Kreiser, a graduate of Franklin High in Los Angeles, a major in history at Pomona College, and a graduate of the University of California at Los Angeles, rationalized both the planters' violence and their violation of the Constitution. According to him, when people's property was threatened, they were justified in killing to defend it.[7]

The Face of Pedro Subia

Pedro Subia was born about 1873, according to the 1930 census. A Chihuahuan baptismal certificate establishes that a "Pedro Zubia" ("Subia" is often spelled with a "Z") was baptized on February 16, 1873 at the Church of Santa Rosalía de Camargo. It further establishes that Father José de la Luz Márquez baptized a boy of one and a half months named "Pedro de Jesús," son of Juan Zubia and Manuela Gutiérrez, and that Juan Zubia was in turn the son of Manuel Zubia and Josefa Martínez.[8] This *may* have been the first document at any location listing Subia.

The earliest available U.S. document to list Subia is the 1900 census, on which Subia's wife, Francisca, born in 1879 in Arizona, also appears. Francisca's father was from Texas and her mother from New Mexico. They had a son, Ramón, born in 1899 in Arizona. Subia arrived in Arizona in 1894. We also know that one of the leaders of Clifton-Morenci-Metcalf Strike of 1915 was a neighbor and that Subia joined the strike. A Pedro Subia fitting this Subia's description did not appear in either the 1910 or the 1920 census.[9]

My search for Subia began forty years after his murder. In the beginning, he was faceless. I interviewed several of Pedro Subia's relatives in the San Joaquín Valley. Pedro Subia had lived in eastern Arizona, and the family had roots in the Clifton-Morenci mining district. Some believed that Pedro was from the Delicias area. Pedro's son, twenty or twenty-one at the time of his father's murder, was living in Mendota, California. Pedro Jr. (Pete) had built a good life for himself there. As manager of a large mercantile store, he was a respected member of the community.[10]

Pete Subia was less than enthusiastic about resurrecting the past. His own consciousness had changed over the years, and he had internalized his initial anger. He no longer blamed only the growers but included also the organizers. He did not leave the area after the shooting because, as he said, he had to survive. Shortly after the strike, he attended a few meetings of the Communist Party in Los Angeles, where organizers tried to recruit him. He remembered being about fourteen during the shooting. As mentioned, he was actually closer to twenty-one.

Pete described his father as an innocent bystander who simply wanted a better life for himself and his family. His father was about five foot, ten inches, of stocky build, weighing about 190 pounds. He was a nondrinker, nonsmoker, and had many friends. His family was from Camargo, Chihuahua, and had arrived in Morenci about 1891, when he had become a miner. He had married in 1898. The death of his wife of the "Spanish flu" in 1918 had shaken the family.

When the strike began, the planters kicked the Subias off the plantation, and they had no choice but to join. Pete verified that his father had participated in many strikes in Morenci—though not a leader, he was also not the kind of man to be duped. Pete spoke of a brother Ramón and a sister in Burbank, who were not there when the killing occurred. He asked that I not contact his sister, a request I was careful to honor.[11]

From other sources, I verified that Pedro Subia migrated to Bakersfield by way of eastern Arizona, Clifton-Morenci-Metcalf, and Los Angeles. Pedro was in the Bakersfield area three years before the strike. He lived just outside Bakersfield, close to but not in the town of Arvin. According to the 1930 census, Pedro Subia, age 55, lived with his son, Pedro Jr., age 18, and two boarders: Paul Jaramillo, age 16, and Alejo Delgado, age 50. (The census spells Delgado's first name "Alego.") The elder Subia and Delgado were born in Mexico, and Pedro Jr. and Jaramillo were born in the United States — Subia in Arizona and Jaramillo in Texas. The neighbors were of mixed nationalities: Mexicans, Italians, Germans, and whites from states other than California, mostly from Arkansas and Oklahoma.[12]

By 2000, the Arizona Subias I contacted were for the most part guarded, and reluctant to talk about their family histories. Some said that the family was originally Spanish but did not offer any proof. A search of the archives of Camargo and surrounding towns suggests that the Subias had been in Chihua-hua for at least a hundred years before arriving in Morenci. Many still live in the Clifton area, and, most referred me to a relative employed by Phelps Dodge. Like Pedro Jr., they had carved out lives for themselves and had hidden memo-ries of Mexican-white conflict.[13]

The Linkages

As with most workers, there were few direct linkages between Pedro Subia and strikes. One of the few was through another Pedro Subia, born into a family of farmers on June 29, 1887, in San Pablo, Chihuahua.[14] While he was still an infant, the family rode burros from San Pablo to Morenci, following the grand-mother, and being followed in turn by Pedro's two uncles. At the time, many people came from Chihuahua, and many returned.

When he was old enough, the other Pedro hauled lumber but seldom worked in the mine, having promised his mother he would not. He was in Clifton in 1907, and he knew our Pedro Subia, who lived in Morenci in a barrio called Las Carpas and whom he remembered as a dark, stocky, peaceful man, thirteen years older. Because they had the same last name, they speculated whether they were related but treated each other like family anyway. The other Pedro left for California in the 1920s after his wife, Francisca Márquez, died of influenza (spelled "Marcus" on Pedro Jr.'s birth certificate). He remembered that the union came to Morenci in 1915, that the governor was on the side of the union, and that the strike was over low wages. He was working as a woodcutter at the time. He remembered that our Pedro Subia joined the union and sup-ported the strike. The other Pedro migrated to California near Hanford, where he met Pedro Jr. (Pete) at a funeral and Pete drove him to Fresno. The other Pedro remembered that Subia had a brother, Ramón, who died in Los Angeles and two sisters, Josefa and Lara.[15]

Thus our Pedro Subia appears to have experienced strikes and the turmoil of life in Morenci from the 1890s to 1921. He was a neighbor to Práxedis

Guerrero and Ramón Treviño, who operated there. Abrán Salcido was from Camargo, had arrived in Morenci in 1896, about two years after our Pedro Subia, and lived not far from him, according to the 1900 census. Abrán and Pedro were about the same age In all probability, both traveled to and from Camargo, which was no Chicago at the time. If our Pedro Subia identified with his namesake, what is the probability that he would also know and talk to Salcido?

The Scapegoats

Speaking again of the 1933 cotton strike, Robert B. Powers said, "Whether the leaders were Communists or not seems to me unimportant. The two I met appeared to me to be Communists — at least they sure as hell were skillful and knew how to organize and handle the affairs of the strike. Their motives may have been to turn this country 'Red,' but their activities in attempting to get a living wage for the workers were certainly justified. As to the growers being 'wanton killers' — no, no. Some, no doubt were willing to go to any lengths in oppressing the workers, but the only killing I recall was done by a deputy sheriff."[16]

What this monograph clearly shows is that significant social change does not come about without opposition to the established order, and that raising the issue of radicalism in one form or another is a pretext to destroy all opposition, whether radical or reformist. The Mexicans were outsiders, the Western Federation of Miners was socialist, the Industrial Workers of the World were anti-American, and the Communist Party was out to destroy the country — these are themes that ran throughout the anti-Mexican campaign. Each time capitalists made preemptive strikes on labor, they first sounded the alarm that American civilization was in imminent danger.

This pattern is discernible in the Clifton-Morenci Strike of 1903, the Cananea Strike of 1906, the Clifton Strike of 1915, and the tumultuous year of 1917, as well as in the Ludlow and Wheatland strikes. The owners spoke in ideological terms but the word "Mexican" could easily be substituted for "Communist" or "Red." The similarities between the San Joaquin Valley Cotton Strike of 1933 and other California agricultural strikes are striking, and go a long way in answering the question why Mexicans were not formally organized.

Accusing workers of being Wobblies and Communists was used to drown their legitimate demands. Yet the IWW and the Communist Party played a crucial role in forcing established labor to accept Mexicans as members and in clarifying the issues. For, when all is said and done, the American Federation of

Labor was hostile to Mexicans and indeed all immigrants. Its craft unions often collaborated with management against the interests of industrial workers. The Mexican middle class and the Catholic Church, with few exceptions, did not fight injustice. They did not seek to improve the material conditions of Mexicans, and they allowed gross racism to go essentially unchallenged and unchecked.

Magnates such as Walter Douglas, J. G. Boswell, and Wofford B. Camp bare a striking resemblance to one another. Through flag waving and fear mongering, they exploited and manipulated economic and political conditions. They were supported by a gaggle of patriotic and civic groups. Together, as the establishment, they controlled the press, elected officials, and law enforcement. They created the "common sense" that sanctioned violation of constitutional rights and murder. Each would say that he loved America, insinuating that any who opposed him did not. In each case, the Mexican workers paid the price. After 1917, substantial evidence exists that Douglas and other mine owners deliberately reduced the number of Mexican workers under the guise of hiring only Americans. After 1933, the California Chamber of Commerce came to favor workers from Oklahoma and west Texas over Mexican workers. By 1934, the agricultural workforce had turned half white. Indeed, even the literature of the time concentrates on the plight of the Oklahomans, lapsing into historical amnesia over the murder of Mexican workers at Pixley and Arvin, the starvation of nine Mexican children, almost all of them infants, and the injuring of scores of others.

The Associated Farmers

Planters officially formed the Associated Farmers in 1934 out of vigilante groups they had formed during the 1933 agricultural strikes. The Associated Farmers was the creature of the California Chamber of Commerce, the Farm Bureau, the Boy Scouts, and Americana. The association hired the Pinkerton Detective Agency to "get the goods on communists." The Associated Farmers sent photos of labor agitators to Frank J. Palomares of the San Joaquin Valley Labor Bureau, an organization funded by growers, sugar companies, oil companies, railroads, and utilities. Many small farmers refused to join the Associated Farmers because they were tired of the "bunch of big fellows who ran things." The Associated Farmers controlled local police, "influenced" the state legislature to pass laws that barred picketing, and, finally, secured the arrest, and later the conviction, of labor leaders.[17]

George P. Clements, in a letter to Guernsey Fraze, Executive Secretary of the Associated Farmers of California on January 23, 1935, wrote: "Unfortunately, Los Angeles has no Mussolini. I believe that we must now turn to the agricultural interests in an endeavor to provide finances to carry on work we have begun as well as prepare for the inevitable, the mutterings of which are already to be heard." Clements offered to solicit funds for the Associated Farmers, and Harry Chandler, publisher of the *Los Angeles Times*, helped him.[18]

"The Associated Farmers," wrote Clark Chambers, "opposed the closed shop, the hiring hall, and picketing — union practices that it was willing to concede might be necessary in industry but regarded as impractical to agriculture."[19] The Associated Farmers created a special strategy committee, which compiled lists of trusted members who would be available for law enforcement in case of a strike, as well as lists of likely suspects. Philip Bancroft stated before Commonwealth Club: "We are not willing to give any group of labor agitators the power to destroy us at will and we are not going to do it . . . Gentlemen, the farm workers of California are going to be protected and the farmers of California are going to harvest their crops!"[20]

The Mexican strikers fought to the bitter end. But the aftermath of the 1933 cotton strike resembled that of the 1917 Bisbee miners' strike. The union was broken — the C&AWIU was crushed and its leaders jailed — and Mexican workers were replaced. The news media played a huge role in spawning and feeding anti-Mexican and anticommunist hysteria. For example, the *Los Angeles Times* cheered the planters' vigilantism with headlines like "Growers Push Fight on Reds." Even Simon L. Lubin shied away from condemning the growers' gangsterism, telling the San Francisco Commonwealth Club that "the employers, victims of a totally inadequate economic system, are hardly in position, or in the mood, to work upon their problems calmly and with due consideration . . . having little or no control over the market."[21] Yet the fact remains that the growers received government handouts and that the workers went on to another location hoping for change.

The Last Nail in the Coffin

Farmworker organizations were no match for the Associated Farmers, which allied urban commercial and industrial interests. Its membership reached 100,000, and Standard Oil, Southern California Edison, San Joaquin Light & Power, Holly Sugar, Spreckels Sugar, the Fresno Chamber of Commerce, the Kern Farm Bureau, Libby, McNeil & Libby, the California Packing Corporation, Mortgage Guarantee, and San Joaquin Cotton & Oil were among its benefactors. Thanks to the association's relentless campaign, communist organizers were rounded up throughout the state. Pat Chambers and Caroline Decker were among those who stood trial for criminal syndicalism in 1935.[22]

Although California newspapers called for the heads of the defendants, the *New York Times* was more balanced. George P. West wrote that, although Chambers and Decker had been found guilty of "attempting to overthrow the government of the United States by force and violence," as a result of their work in the 1933 agricultural strikes, "wages were raised and working and living conditions improved for thousands of vagabond itinerants on whom California growers depend for the harvesting of their crops." West expressed an admiration for the Communist Party organizers, describing them as idealists.[23]

In the course of the trial, Melville Harris, a disaffected member of the Young Communist League, testified against Pat Chambers, Caroline Decker, Jack Crane, Albert Hougardy, and Martin Wilson. Nora Conklin had recruited him. Frank M. Peterson, an Earlimart rancher who participated in the Pixley killings, testified against Chambers and Decker. On February 27, the *Los Angeles Times*'s Chapin Hall wrote: "Russia loomed large in today's proceeding. The red banner of the commune persistently intervenes across the mental vision until the flag of freedom . . . is all but obscured."[24]

The press hyped the trial, and rumors spread of gathering violence. Pat Chambers, Caroline Decker, Nora Conklin, Mark Wilson, Albert Hougardy, Lorene Norman, Norman Mini, and Jack Crane were found guilty. Like with the Wobblies the actions of the growers were justified because the country was in imminent danger.[25]

Caroline Decker, Nora Conklin, and Lorine Norman were sent to Tehachapi. According to Chambers, it was a horrific experience for Decker. The convictions were reversed two years later. The appellate court found that "clearing the defendants on the charges of resorting to the spoken and written word or personal conduct to advocate criminal syndicalism logically meant that they could not have been convicted of organizing, managing and joining associations for the purpose of teaching criminal syndicalism." The court reaffirmed the constitutionality of the state's criminal syndicalism laws.[26]

The C&AWIU, though in existence for only four years, succeeded in forcing employers to raise wages and government agencies to improve some of the worst conditions. On the other hand, it galvanized the fight against unions whose motto became "Drive out the Reds." Its strength and effectiveness was based on its support among rank and file, low initiation fees and dues, and "democratic participation in union affairs." The growers based their power on fear and a "rule or ruin" mentality.[27] The union and the Communist Party alike had made mistakes, yet they had achieved substantial results. For their parts, neither the Catholic Church, the Roosevelt administration, the Mexican American middle-class organizations, nor white radicals maintained any presence within the Mexican farmworker community or acted on its behalf.

Postscript: Why Mexicans Did Not Organize

From June 1983 to December 1984, the Clifton-Morenci area was the scene of a bitter strike, provoked by Phelps Dodge, in which the company exploited ethnic and religious differences among workers. The National Labor Relations Board teamed up with state authorities to defeat unionized workers. Even though Kennecott, Asarco, Magma Copper, and Inspiration Consolidated all quickly accepted the workers' demands, Phelps Dodge pushed to destroy the United Steelworkers. President Richard T. Moolick's strategy was to deny the cost-of-living adjustment, the only nonnegotiable provision. In breaking the union, Moolick followed a road map developed by the University of Pennsylvania's Wharton School and funded by Phelps Dodge.[28]

The strike encompassed Clifton, Morenci, Bisbee, Douglas, and Ajo, although the center was Morenci, which, despite Phelps Dodge's protestations that it was unprofitable, was the brightest star in its constellation of mines. During the strike, Arizona's Department of Public Safety (DPS) harassed and terrorized strikers. The Arizona Criminal Intelligence Agency joined the department in taking videotapes and photographs of the strikers, spying on union meetings, tapping their phones, and maintaining files on union activists at Clifton, Morenci, and Ajo. Liberal Arizona governor Bruce Babbitt deployed state troopers — to protect the replacement workers. Or, as Babbitt put it, to make sure there was no violence. Much as Walter Douglas did in the 1910s, and agribusinesses did in the 1930s, corporate America has discredited the very idea of unions in the public's mind, giving corporations mastery over workers' lives. Corporations have achieved what Douglas, J. G. Boswell, Walter Camp, and others strove for — unquestioned control of the workplace.

Women played a major role in the 1983–84 miners' strike. Many were themselves miners. The role of wives and female partisans went beyond that of a women's auxiliary. Defying the authorities, female leaders served on the picket lines. Much as in the Salt of the Earth Strike, they also had to fight the sexism of their husbands. The president of the women's group confronted the president of the local and wrote, "We object to being called a 'Ladies' auxiliary.' We are the Morenci Miners *Women*'s Auxiliary. We fight for our homes, our livelihood, our children's futures and dignity as productive human beings." Alongside other strikers, they endured teargassing and the armed occupation of their community. Law enforcement officers stormed the home of Diana Vega and handcuffed her in front of her four-year-old son. Afterward, the courts found evidence of a company conspiracy to break the strike, as the commissions had of constitutional violations after the Bisbee deportations and the 1933 killings. And just like the commissions, they did nothing.[29]

Many of the 1983–84 strikers had parents and grandparents who had participated in the 1903, 1915, and 1917 strikes. Many were originally from Chihuahua. David Velásquez, a founder of Mine Mill in 1946, was a veteran, whose parents had lived on Chihuahua Hill in Morenci. The strike divided the Torrez family, whose grandfather had arrived from Chihuahua at the turn of the century, with brother fighting brother.

After the strike, the other companies followed Phelps Dodge's lead. Some of the blame has to go to the United Steelworkers national leadership. Like the Western Federation of Miners in 1903, 1915, and 1917, it did not properly support Mexican locals. The leadership at Phoenix under Frank McKee, the international treasurer, stood in the way of innovative strategies and did not rally the union's base. The American Federation of Labor also failed to mobilize what forces it had. It was a time for labor to stand up and fight — and it did not. Meanwhile, the price of copper rose steadily and, with it, Phelps Dodge's profits, from $29.5 million in 1985 to $504 million in 1989.

For the Mexican American miners, the union was more than a bargaining agent. It was part of their community. After World War II, meeting in graveyards around Morenci, they built the largely Mexican Mine Mill local. Through it, they did away with the dual-wage system, segregated facilities, and the indignity of "No Mexicans Allowed." Alex López, a negotiator during the 1983–84 strike, accused Phelps Dodge of trying to break the union, and faulted the international for not raising the race issue.[30] There were 640 strikebreakers at Morenci, 500 Euro-American and 140 Spanish-surnamed scabs. Before the strike, half of the workforce had Spanish surnames. The strike changed the balance from Democrat to Republican, from Mexican American to white.[31]

Abbreviations

The following abbreviations are used in the notes and Sources Cited.

AAM	Archivo de Armando Miguelez
ACDC	Arxiu de los Carmelites Descalcos de Catolunya
AGN	Archivo General de la Nación
AHS	Arizona Historical Society
AMGR	Archivo de Manuel González Ramírez
ARE	Archivos de Relaciones Exteriores
ASA	Arizona State Library, Archives and Public Records, Archives Division
ASU	Arizona State University
C&AWIU	Cannery and Agricultural Workers Industrial Union
CSUN	California State University at Northridge
GCP	George Clements Papers
F&HRC	Fred and Harriet Rochlin Collection
HSMC	Henry S. McCluskey Collection
IWW	Industrial Workers of the World
JMC	John Murray Collection
NARA	National Archives and Records Admininstration
NARS	National Archives and Records Service
NSDC	Nicholas Schenck Davis Collection
PAFL	Pan-American Federation of Labor
PBS	Public Broadcasting System
PSTC	Paul S. Taylor Collection
RFAC	Rodolfo F. Acuña Collection

RFAFN	Rodolfo F. Acuña Field Notes
RRC	Ridgeway Ryder Collection
SC	Special Collections
SJFBF	Sam J. Freudenthal Biographical Files
UA	University of Arizona
UCB	University of California at Berkeley
UCLA	University of California at Los Angeles
USMID	U.S. Military Intelligence Division
WFM	Western Federaton of Miners

Notes

Preface

1. P. Taylor and Kerr, "Documentary History of the Strike of the Cotton Pickers in California: San Joaquin Valley Cotton Strike, 1933."
2. Paul S. Taylor interview.
3. Galarza, "Mula No Nació Arisca," 199–200. See chapter 14.

Chapter 1. Why Mexicans Moved

1. In 1537, Pope Paul III prohibited the enslavement of Indians, with no exceptions, "under penalty of automatic excommunication."
2. Ferdinand and Isabella rationalized that these slaves were "prisoners of war."
3. Sued-Badillo, "Christopher Columbus," 71–102. Sale, "What Columbus Discovered," 444–446. Cruz, "African Americans in Caribbean."
4. Martínez-Echazabal, "Mestizaje," 21.
5. Menchaca, *Recovering History*, 55–59.
6. Wolf, *Sons of Shaking Earth*, 29.
7. Richmond, "Legacy of African Slavery." Villa-Flores, " 'To Lose One's Soul,' " 439.
8. Vincent, *Legacy of Guerrero*, 78–81. Estimates of Filipino slaves brought to Mexico vary widely. Though high, Vincent's estimate of 100,000 is altogether possible, based on my reading of the literature. Even at half that figure, however, Filipinos would be a significant addition to Mexico's racial mix.
9. Carmack, Gasco, and Gossen, *Legacy of Mesoamerica*, 181.
10. N. Cook, *Born to Die*, 206.
11. Brooks, "Revising Conquest of Mexico," 1–29. Kellogg, "Hegemony Out of Conquest," 29. Crosby, *Columbian Exchange*, 48–58. N. Cook, *Born to Die*, 132, 139, 140, 168, 170, 193.
12. Aboites Aguilar, *Breve historia de Chihuahua*, 13. Bakewell, *Silver Mining and Society*, 12–13, 124, 134–135. Engerman and Sokoloff, "Factor Endowments, Inequality," 44, 48.
13. Throughout this volume, whether in Mexico or in the United States, by preference of the University of Arizona Press, native peoples will be called by their English rather than Spanish names. Thus "Aztecs," "Tlaxcalans," "Otomis," and so on, rather than "Aztecas," "Tlaxcalanes," "Otomís," and so on.

14. Bakewell, *Silver Mining and Society*, 129, 115, 125. Sheridan, "Limits of Power," 160, 167. Radding, *Wandering Peoples*.

15. Bakewell, *Silver Mining and Society*, 1, 19. Flynn and Giráldez, "Cycles of Silver," 393, 398, 400, 413.

16. Roca, *Spanish Jesuit Churches*, 1–7. Phillips, "Prehistory of Chihuahua," 373–376. Swann, "Population and Settlement," 50. Holbert, "Rural/Urban Conflict over Water," 2–5, 19–22.

17. Weigand and García de Weigand, "Huichol Society before Arrival." Deeds, "Rural Work in Nueva Vizcaya," 429–430. Spicer, *Cycles of Conquest*, 86, 231. Roca, *Spanish Jesuits*, 7.

18. Sheridan, "Limits of Power," 157. Radding, *Wandering Peoples*, 47. Deeds, "Rural Work in Nueva Vizcaya," 429–430.

19. Cramaussel, *Santa Bárbara*, 22–23, 33, 50. Algier, "Feudalism on New Spain's Northern Frontier," 8, 15–16, 25.

20. Cramaussel, *Santa Bárbara*, 49, 50. Lister and Lister, *Chihuahua*, 24. Rocha Chávez, *Tres siglos de historia*, 9–24.

21. The Jesuits arrived in Mexico in 1572. They purchased haciendas — and slaves — throughout Latin America, often using African slaves as foremen. On the Jesuits' contemptuous attitude toward indigenous peoples, see Pérez de Ribas, *History of the Triumphs*, an account of Jesuit missions from 1591 to 1643 in present-day Sinaloa and Sonora.

22. Swann, "Population and Settlement," 53–54, 70. Deeds, *Defiance and Deference*, 54. Griffen, *Indian Assimilation*, 4, 99, 100. Rocha Chávez, *Tres siglos de historia*, 43, 70–71.

23. Deeds, "Mission Villages," 348–350. Meyer, *Water in Hispanic Southwest*, 47–49. Deeds, *Defiance and Deference*, 17, 21, 81. Gerhard, *North Frontier of New Spain*, 185, 187. Lister and Lister, *Chihuahua*, 40–44. Aboites Aguilar, *Norte precario*, 63–65.

24. Gerhard, *North Frontier of New Spain*, 218. Roca, *Spanish Jesuit Churches*, 21. Almada, *Resumén de historia*, 58. Griffen, *Indian Assimilation*, 99. Mayer, "Black Slave," 20, 23–24. Castañeda González, *Irrigación y reforma agraria*, 21. Rocha Chávez, *Tres siglos de historia*, 24–25.

25. Mayer, "Black Slave," 78. Swann, "Population and Settlement," 124, 128.

26. Mayer, "Black Slave," 16–18.

27. Mayer, "Black Slave," 27–29, 77, 90. Weckmann, *Medieval Heritage of Mexico*, 400–402. Aboites Aguilar, *Breve historia de Chihuahua*, 29–32.

28. Griffen, *Indian Assimilation*, 109. Deeds, *Defiance and Deference*, 63. Deeds, "Mission Villages," 346.

29. Cramaussel, *Santa Bárbara*, 51. Swann, "Population and Settlement," 70. Deeds, *Defiance and Deference*, 30–38.

30. Griffen, *Indian Assimilation*, 5–7. Deeds, "Mission Villages," 349. Almada, *Resumén de historia*, 62, 66. Deeds, *Defiance and Deference*, 66–66. Rocha Chávez, *Tres siglos de historia*, 115. Aboites Aguilar, *Breve historia de Chihuahua*, 34–36.

31. Deeds, *Defiance and Deference*, 68–70. Almada, *Diccionario . . . chihua-huenses*, 521–522. Almada, *Resumén de historia*, 68.

32. Aboites Aguilar, *Norte precario*, 63–64. Deeds, *Defiance and Deference*, 70–72. Aboites Aguilar, *Breve historia de Chihuahua*, 36–38, 76. Swann, "Population and Settlement," 71–72. Voss, "Societal Competition in Northwest," 192. Deeds, "Land Tenure Patterns," 455, 458.

33. Forbes, *Apache, Navaho and Spaniard*, 200–224. Almada, *Resumén de historia*, 78. Martin, *Governance and Society*, 20. Aboites Aguilar, *Norte precario*, 34, 59–61, 65. Aboites Aguilar, *Breve historia de Chihuahua*, 40–41. Deeds, *Defiance and Deference*, 82, 86. Rocha Chávez, *Tres siglos de historia*, 23. Griffen, *Indian Assimilation*, 11–12.

34. Deeds, *Defiance and Deference*, 87. Aboites Aguilar, *Breve historia de Chihuahua*, 42–44. Martin, *Governance and Society*, 20. Altamirano and Villa, *Chihuahua: Una historia*, 13–14, 17. Méndoza Magallanes, *Pueblo viejo*, 87.

35. Griffen, *Apaches at War*, viii–ix, 11. Hadley, *Minería y sociedad*, 168–170. C. Martin, *Governance and Society*, 42–44, 49–55, 62–63, 65, 56–60.

36. C. Martin, *Governance and Society*, 21, 23. Griffen, *Indian Assimilation*, 110. Deeds, *Defiance and Deference*, 104–106, 107–108, 114, 141, 162–163. Gerhard, *North Frontier of New Spain*, 184–185. Deeds, "Mission Villages," 355–356. Hadley, *Minería y sociedad*, 111. In an unsuccessful effort to correct some of these lapses, missionaries and natives filed a flood of complaints against nonnative encroachers in the 1720s.

37. Griffen, *Indian Assimilation*, 101. C. Martin, *Governance and Society*, 21, 23. Almada, *Resumén de historia*, 69, 89. Hadley, *Minería y sociedad*, 31. Deeds, *Defiance and Deference*, 183.

38. Hadley, *Minería y sociedad*, 99–100.

39. Hadley, *Minería y sociedad*, 52, 127, 223. C. Martin, *Governance and Society*, 78, 98. 164.

40. The assignment of at least one square league of communal land (4,300 acres) to each Indian pueblo for farming and ranching was first made in 1573 and reaffirmed in 1713.

41. To counter the rising economic and political power of the Church and of the Society of Jesus in-particular, Charles III ordered that the Jesuits be expelled from Spain and all its colonies in 1767.

42. Aboites Aguilar, *Norte precario*, 79–80. Swann, "Population and Settlement," 112. Almada, *Resumén de historia*, 115–120. Valerio-Jiménez, "Neglected Citizens and Willing Traders."

43. Swann, "Population and Settlement," 103–106. Deeds, *Defiance and Defer-ence*, 120. Hadley, *Minería y sociedad*, 60, 62–65, 168. C. Martin, *Governance and Society*, 29–46.

44. D. J. Weber, *Spanish Frontier*, 212. Aboites Aguilar, *Norte precario*, 37, 38–39. Forbes, *Apache, Navaho and Spaniard*, 7. Valerio-Jiménez, "Neglected Citizens and Willing Traders."

45. Swann, "Population and Settlement," 350, 363.

46. Almada, *Resumén de historia*, 130–131. C. Martin, *Governance and Society*, 188, 199–200. Aboites Aguilar, *Breve historia de Chihuahua*, 69, 71–72, 73–78. Deeds, *Defiance and Deference*, 184–185.

Chapter 2. The Passing of the Saints

1. See García Ayluardo, "World of Images," 77–78.

2. Hale, "José María Luis Mora," 197. See also Knowlton, "Expropriation of Church Property," 389, 400–401, and "Some Practical Effects," 256.

3. Archbishop's Confirmation of Excommunication of Miguel Hildalgo, Sept. 24, 1810, and Inquisition's Denunciation of Miguel Hidalgo, Oct. 13, 1810, in "Bando contra la Esclavitud," Oct. 19, 1810, Valladolid. Electronic copies found in Archives of Father Miguel Hidalgo, DeWitt Colony, http://www.tamu.edu/ccbn/dewitt/hidalgoar chive.htm#excom.

4. Almada, *Diccionario . . . chihuahuenses*, 253. Aboites Aguilar, *Breve historia de Chihuahua*, 76–78. Fuentes Mares, *México se refugió*, 171. Altamirano and Villa, *Chihuahua: Textos*, 59. Lister and Lister, *Chihuahua*, 83–85. Almada, "Imprenta y periodismo en Chihuahua," 247. The state of Hidalgo is named after Miguel Hidalgo; towns and cities throughout Mexico were renamed in his honor; September 16, when Hidalgo proclaimed his revolt in 1810, is celebrated as Independence Day, rather than August 24, when Spain formally granted independence to Mexico in 1821.

5. Aboites Aguilar, *Breve historia de Chihuahua*, 76.

6. Cue Cánovas, *Historia social y económica*, 134. Redfield, "Indian in Mexico," 132.

7. John P. Schmal, in "Indigenous Chihuahua," quotes the 1921 Mexican census, where residents of each state were asked to classify themselves by race. In Chihuahua, 12.8 percent claimed to be of pure indigenous stock, versus 29.2 percent nationally; 50.1 percent, to be mestizo, versus 59.3 percent nationally; and 36.3 percent, to be white, versus 9.8 percent nationally. Quite a difference. For an excellent discourse on race in Chihuahua, see Aboites Aguilar, "José Fuentes Mares," 479, 481–484. See also Chance, "On Mexican Mestizo," 162–163. Powell, "Mexican Intellectuals and Indian Question," 19–20. González Navarro, "Mestizaje mexicano," 36, 40.

8. Aboites Aguilar, *Breve historia de Chihuahua*, 87–88.

9. Orozco, *Guerras indias*, 23. Aboites Aguilar, *Breve historia de Chihuahua*, 89, 91, 94–95. Sandels, "Silvestre Terrazas," 19–20. Wasserman, *Capitalists, Caciques, and Revolution*, 13–14. Almada, *Diccionario . . . chihuahuenses*, 216–218. Lister and Lister, *Chihuahua*, 111, 136. Almada, *Resumén de historia*, 235.

10. Lister and Lister, *Chihuahua*, 83–85. Almada, *Diccionario . . . chihuahuenses*, 253, 527. Altamirano and Villa, *Chihuahua: Textos*, 59, 61–62. Almada, "Imprenta y periodismo en Chihuahua," 247. Aboites Aguilar, *Norte precario*, 90. "La opinión de Chihuahua ante el Congreso," in Altamirano and Villa, *Chihuahua: Textos*, 234. D. J. Weber, *Mexican Frontier*, 22, 25, 33, 37. Wasserman, *Capitalists, Caciques, and Revolution*, 13–14. Aboites Aguilar, *Breve historia de Chihuahua*, 76–78.

Serrano villages and ranchos had also operated during the eighteenth century, often alongside the Jesuit and Franciscan missions and the presidios and military colonies established by Spanish authorities to combat the Apaches, as was the case with Santa Rosalía on the Río Conchos. Here small ranchers and farmers had used their family members to herd or to work the land. Their extended families and neighbors had banded together in small rural enclaves to defend themselves against the Apaches. See Aboites Aguilar, *Breve historia de Chihuahua*, 102.

11. For in-depth discussions of the *serrano* rancho culture, see Nugent, *Spent Cartridges*, and Alonso, *Thread of Blood*. Once the Apache threat was largely removed, the hacienda owners expanded their holdings still further, at the expense of the small ranchers. Benedict, "Hacienda Management," 395. Wasserman, *Capitalists, Caciques, and Revolution*, 13.

12. Aboites, *Breve historia de Chihuahua*, 113–114, 121–122. Aboites Aguilar, *Norte precario*, 99. State authorities renamed Parral as La Villa de San José de Parral in 1825 and Ciudad Hidalgo in honor of the revolutionary priest Miguel Hidalgo y Costilla in 1833. Wanting to preserve their town's identity, however, Parralans changed its name once again, to Hidalgo del Parral, which it is called to this day. Chihuahua, Secretaría del Gobierno, Sección Estadistica, *Anuarios, 1905–1909*, in Wasserman, *Capitalists, Caciques, and Revolution*, 110.

13. Altamirano and Villa, *Chihuahua: Textos*, 61–62.

14. Arturo Armendariz, July 10, 1982. Most Subia surnames are spelled "Zubia." Camargo Registro Civil de Nacimientos, Roll 1, Book 8, ARCCC, lists a "Zubia," born on Nov. 10, 1883, and Book 14 lists several "Zubias," but nowhere could I find a "Pedro." See also Lambert, "Zona minera de Naica," 156–158, 168, 173. Altamirano and Villa, *Chihuahua: Textos*, 60, 63.

15. Aboites Aguilar and Morales Cosme, *Breve compilación sobre tierras*, 12. Castañeda González, *Irrigación y reforma agraria*, 51–53, 59. Documentación Relativa a la Revalidación de una Concesión de Agua de la Hacienda San Diego del Tecuán, 1865, in Aboites Aguilar, *Agua y tierra*, 43–58.

16. Rosales Villa, *Mis puntes*, 8–15, 16, 17. Founded in 1740, Santa Rosalía had been abandoned because of Indian rebellions and land disputes with surrounding haciendas. It was repopulated in 1797 under the same name by twenty-eight residents from San Francisco de Conchos. Castañeda González, *Irrigación y reforma agraria*, 18, 22, 67–68, 74, 83.

17. Grant, *Personal Memoirs*, 22–24.

18. Stephen Austin to Edward Lovelace [Josiah Bell?], Mexico City, Nov. 22, 1822, http://www.tamu.edu/ccbn/dewitt/slaveryletters.htm. This Web site has most of the documents and letters of the Euro-American Texas colonists and their Mexican counterparts relating to the takeover of Texas. In the Mexico City letter, Austin favors Emperor Agustín Iturbide for his favorable attitude toward the slave interests of the Texas colonists.

19. Zavala, *Journey to United States*, 2–3, 50, 79, 90, 107. In this 1830 account, leading Mexican liberal Lorenzo de Zavala reveals his admiration for Euro-Americans

and his disdain for the castes in his own country. He was later elected vice president of the Lone Star Republic. Letter from President M. B. Lamar to the People of Santa Fe, Apr. 14, 1840, http://www.tamu.edu/ccbn/dewitt/santafeexped.htm.

20. For an in-depth look at Nicholas Trist's reaction to the terms imposed on Mexico, see A. Sobarzo, *Deber y consciencia*, 283–285.

21. Bartlett, *Personal Narrative of Explorations*, 1st div., 4, 187, 189.

22. Aboites Aguilar, *Breve historia de Chihuahua*, 98–99. Altamirano and Villa, *Chihuahua: Textos*, 107. Almada, *Resumén de historia*, 240–242. "Late from El Paso," *New York Daily Times*, Oct. 30, 1851. "Chihuahua," *New York Daily Times*, Aug. 27, 1852.

23. During 1853 and 1854, the *New York Daily Times* carried numerous articles on the boundary survey and the controversy surrounding it. See esp. James Bartlett, "Mexican Boundary Commission," Dec. 20, 1852. "Governor Lane's Movements in New Mexico," Apr. 30, 1853. "The Mexican Boundary Question," May 3, 1853. John R. Bartlett, "New Mexico," May 4, 1853. "The Mesilla Valley: Lane's Manifesto," June 20, 1853. "The Gadsden Treaty," Mar. 17, 1854. A full listing of these articles can be found in RFAC, Urban Archives, CSUN, where earlier drafts of this monograph are housed. See also H. Bancroft, *History of North Mexican States*, 2:693.

24. One such child was Mariano G. Samaniego, a graduate of Saint Louis University, born in Sonora and raised in Chihuahua, who had successful businesses in northern Chihuahua as well in Mesilla and Tucson. See Sheridan, *Los Tucsonenses*, 2, 41–54, 108. M. G. Gonzales, "Mariano G. Samaniego," 141–160. Almada, *Diccionario . . . chihuahuenses*, 479–480. Another Mariano Samaniego, assumed to be related to the first, was also born in Sonora, and moved to Chihuahua, where he served as governor. He was closely allied with Luis Terrazas.

25. *Periodico Oficial del Gobierno del Estado* (Chihuahua), Oct. 8, 1878. Among Chihuahuan farming communities that cultivated cotton for local factories or export to the interior were Meoqui, Camargo, and Jiménez. Foley, "Estado Chihuahua," 130–139. Ruiz y Sándoval, *Algodón en México*, 14, 173. Cotton had been grown in Mexico since pre-Columbian times, and the varieties grown in Louisiana and Texas were essentially Mexican. In the 1880s, cotton was grown in Chihuahua around El Paso del Norte and around Santa Rosalía and San Pablo on the Río Conchos. Schoonover, "Mexican Cotton," 429, 434. Aboites Aguilar, *Breve historia de Chihuahua*, 96–97, 107, 109. Zamora, *World of Mexican Worker*, 16. As early as the 1890s, many Mexican workers would migrate from La Laguna (near Torreón, Durango) up the Camino Real corridor to Ojinaga and to the Rio Grande River Valley in Texas to pick cotton.

26. Aboites Aguilar, *Breve historia de Chihuahua*, 100.

27. In 1859, U.S. Consul George L. MacManus reported that Chihuahua was in a state of revolution and that it impossible to earn a livelihood. Apparently, Euro-American merchants favored the liberals. Zuloaga was defeated and escaped to the United States. George L. MacManus to Secretary of State, Lewis Cass, July 12, 1859, Despatches from United States Consuls in Ciudad Chihuahua, 1830–1906, Micro Copy 283, Roll 1, NARA, 1964.

28. Reuben Creel to Secretary of State, July 14, 1865, Despatches from United States Consuls in Ciudad Chihuahua, 1830–1906, Micro Copy 283, Roll 1, NARA, 1964.

29. Reuben Creel to William H. Seward, Aug. 18, 1866, Despatches from United States Consuls in Ciudad Chihuahua, 1830–1906, Micro Copy 283, Roll 1, NARA, 1964. Terrazas established ties with conservatives in 1852 and with foreign interests in 1860s. Wasserman, "Social Origins of 1910 Revolution," 16.

30. Charles Moye to William H. Seward, June 3, 1867, Despatches from United States Consuls in Ciudad Chihuahua, 1830–1906, Micro Copy 283, Roll 1, NARA, 1964.

31. Wasserman, *Capitalists, Caciques, and Revolution*, 35–36. F. MacManus and Sons to John W. Foster, Minister of the United States, Mar. 5, 1877, Despatches from United States Consuls in Ciudad Chihuahua, 1830–1906, Micro Copy 283, Roll 1, NARA, 1964. The occupation of Chihuahua by Díaz's forces, even though it paralyzed business, made Chihuahuans feel secure, according to the consul. The younger Trías was aligned with Díaz. Almada, *Resumén de historia*, 314.

32. Charles Moye to Hamilton Fish, Sept. 16, 1870, Despatches from United States Consuls in Ciudad Chihuahua, 1830–1906, Micro Copy 283, Roll 1, NARA, 1964.

33. William H. Brown, Acting Consul, to Second Secretary of State, Oct. 1, 1871, Despatches from United States Consuls in Ciudad Chihuahua, 1830–1906, Micro Copy 283, Roll 1, NARA, 1964.

34. Aboites Aguilar, *Breve historia de Chihuahua*, 114, 122.

35. "Starvation in Mexico," *Los Angeles Times*, Oct. 11, 1891, 4. "Garza's Ally, the Drought," *New York Times*, July 19, 1892, 8. Liverman, "Drought Impacts in Mexico," 50. Endfield and O'Hara, "Degradation, Drought, and Dissent," 402–419.

36. Located between a pueblo's acequia and the river that fed it, a *suerte* of land was 26.3 acres with the right to twenty-four hours of water weekly. One of the first to receive water rights in the La Cruz area was José Claudio Muñoz, who surveyed his land to establish a farm, a house, and a soap factory, in 1807. Twenty other individuals also petitioned for land. Castañeda González, *Irrigación y reforma agraria*, 71–72.

37. Castañeda González, *Irrigación y reforma agraria*, 57.

38. Lloyd, *Proceso de modernización capitalista*, 11–12, 18–30.

39. Terrazas, *Memorias*, 77–89. "Chihuahua," *El Fronterizo*, Sept. 26 and Nov. 28, 1880. Louis H. Scott to Assistant Secretary of State, Oct. 23, 1880, Despatches from United States Consuls in Ciudad Chihuahua, 1830–1906, Micro Copy 283, Roll 2, no. 57, NARA, 1964. Fuentes Mares, *México se refugió*, 138.

40. Almada, *Resumén de historia*, 334.

41. Wasserman, "Enrique C. Creel," 648. Founded in 1882 with a modest 100,000-peso investment, under Enrique Creel's supervision, the Mining Bank of Chihuahua accumulated assets of 23.2 million pesos and paid out more than 6 million pesos in shareholder dividends by 1910.

42. In 1883, the Mining Code was radically revised to permit private exploitation of the subsoil. Until then, Mexican law had followed Spanish law, with the subsoil belonging to the nation, as it had to the Crown. *Herald* (Washington, D.C.), July 29, 1883, ARE, 11-2-34.

43. "Proyecto para la construcción de dos lineas de ferrocarril en el estado," *Periodico Oficial del Gobierno del Estado* (Chihuahua), Sept. 24, 1884. "Desprendimiento," *Periodico Oficial del Gobierno del Estado* (Chihuahua), Jan. 24, 1885.

44. Brand, "Historical Geography of Northwestern Chihuahua," 114–116, 124–125, 140–144. Bauer, "Modernizing Landlords."

45. Wasserman, "Foreign Investment in Mexico," 3–5. Wasserman, "Enrique C. Creel," 647, 648, 650. R. Holden, "Priorities of State," 579, 581.

46. With the radical revision of the Mining Code in 1883, revenues from Mexico's silver production doubled, from nearly 40 million pesos annually in the 1880s to more than 80 million pesos by 1905. Hart, *Empire and Revolution*, 152, 153. See also Wasserman, "Foreign Investment in Mexico," 3–4, 6–7.

47. One of Terrazas's favorite ploys had been to present himself as godfather (*compadre*) to the people.

48. Almada, *Resumén de historia*, 330. "Apuntes Historicos del Distrito Rayon por Francisco R. Almada" (Obra Inedita), chap. 16, pp. 129–136. "Huelga de Pinos Altos, 1883," pp. 1–11, AMGR, vol. 4, AGN. R. Anderson, *Outcasts in Own Land*, 87–88. Almada, *Diccionario . . . chihuahuenses*, 257.

49. Garza was extensively covered in the *New York Times*; see RFAC, Urban Archives, CSUN. See also Notes to Foreign Legations in the United States, 1834–1906, Mexico: May 2, 1884–Nov. 20, 1893, NARA, no. 99, Roll 72. For Garza's biography, see Garza Guajardo, *En busca de Catarino Garza*.

50. Osorio, *Tomochic en llamas*, 50. Almada, *Diccionario . . . chihuahuenses*, 32, 257. Almada, *Rebelión de Tomochi*, 15–16. "Conspiración de C. Guerrero," Documento del Jusgado de Primera Infancia de C. Guerrero, Jefatura Política de D. Guerrero, Estado de Chihuahua, Paquete 20. "Conspiración de C. Guerrero, Guerrero Chihuahua," Aug. 24, 1889, pp. 1–3, AMGR, AGN.

51. The best single source on Tomóchic is Almada, *Rebelión de Tomochi*, 27–30. See also folder entitled "Conspiración de Ciudad Guerrero," in AACG, AMGR, AGN, which contains copies made by Almada. These can also be found in RFAC, Urban Archives, CSUN. See also Almada, *Revolución en Chihuahua*, 97.

52. The most comprehensive English-language monograph on the Tomóchic revolt is Vanderwood, *Power of God*. See also Almada, *Rebelión de Tomochi*. Frías, *Tomochic*. W. Holden, *Teresita*. Chávez Calderón, *Defensa de Tomochic*, 5–9. Valadés, *Porfirio Díaz*, 28, 62. See also AACG, AMGR, AGN. *Periodico Oficial del Gobierno del Estado* (Chihuahua) 15, no. 28 (Nov. 26, 1892). "A Probable Revolution" Aug. 21, 1892, ARE, 7-3-670, vol. 1, 00368. "Indios Bárbaros: Años 1882–1887" and "Los Sucesos de Tomochi, 1891–1892," AMGR, vol. 7, AGN. Documentos Tomados del Archivo de la Secretaría General del Gobierno del Estado de Chihuahua, Ramo Gobernación, Paquete 590, Rxpte. 134, pp. 1–3.

Ochoa was a protégé of Lauro Aguirre—confidant of Teresa de Urrea and her father, Tomás. Through them, the Ochoa cabal had links with Mexican revolutionaries in Clifton-Morenci, whose activities are discussed in chapter 6.

53. "Rebels Defeat Federals at Santo Tomás," *El Paso Times*, Apr. 20, 1893. "Los

Pronunciados de Temosachi," *El Norte*, Apr. 27, 1893. Almada, *Rebelión de Tomochi*, 130. Almada, 357–359. Gonzales Ramírez, *Manifestos politicos*, 93–95. See folder entitled "Rebelión de Santo Tomás, 1893," in AACG, AMGR, AGN.

54. Almada, *Resumén de historia*, 357–358. "Mexican Revolt," *El Paso Evening Tribune*, Apr. 18, 1893. "More Fighting," *El Paso Evening Tribune*, Apr. 19, 1893. "All Quiet on Potomac," *El Paso Evening Tribune*, Apr. 20, 1893. "The Chihuahuan Troubles," *El Paso Evening Tribune*, Apr. 24, 1893. "Perez Issues Manifesto," *El Paso Times*, Dec. 3, 1893. "Rebels Hang Federal General," *El Paso Times*, Dec. 13, 1893. "Alarma Infundada," *El Norte* 3, no. 130 (Nov. 13, 1893). "Charged with Aiding Rebels," *New York Times*, Dec. 1, 1893. "To Mexico for Revenge," *New York Times*, Aug. 17, 1895. "Sentence Carranza Agents," *New York Times*, Oct. 21, 1915. "Rebelión de Palomas y El Manzano, Años de 1893 y 1894," and "El Robo a la Aduana de Palomas," *El Norte* 3, no. 129 (Nov. 19, 1893). "Rebelión de Palomas y El Manzo: Años de 1893 y 1894," AMGR, vol. 8, AGN.

55. Castañeda González, *Irrigación y reforma agraria*, 14–18, 22–26, 42–43, 57–63, 67–70, 88–89, 147. La Cruz Registro Civiles, Books 1872–1877. Hart, *Empire and Revolution*, 105, 121–122, 134–135, 167. O'Horo, *American Foreign Investments*, 154, 174. Almada, *Resumén de historia*, 314.

56. Ponce de León, *Datos geográficos y estadísticos*, 65–69.

57. Bunker, " 'Consumers of Good Taste."

58. Wasserman, *Capitalists, Caciques, and Revolution*, 76. Schell, "Money as Commodity," 70, 71, 73. Mexico accounted for 34 percent of the world's silver supply in 1900. Like Mexico's other silver-producing states, Chihuahua relied heavily on export. With the object of making huge profits, the United States led an attack on the Mexican peso. J. G. Woodman, Superintendent, to John Robinson, General Agent, Cusihuiriáchic Mining Company, Chihuahua, Feb. 14, 1882, Despatches from United States Consuls in Ciudad Chihuahua, 1830–1906, Micro Copy 289, Roll 2, NARA, 1964.

Chapter 3. The Mesilla Corridor

1. Uhl and Meglorin, "Chihuahuita in the 1930s." Duarte, "Mama Santos's Story," chap. 2. García-Acevedo, "Forgotten Diaspora," 218. Prewitt, " 'We Didn't Ask,' " 1. Chihuahuitas dotted the Southwest. In Texas, barrios called Chihuahuita can be found in Del Rio, San Antonio, and Corpus Christi. There was a Chihuahuita in Gallup, New Mexico, and the Chihuahuita in Roswell was probably the town's oldest settlement.

2. Ridgway, "Sanchez Name Spices," Owens, "Growth and Development of Safford," 4, 8–9. Corle, *Gila*, 9.

3. McCaa, "Peopling of Mexico," 604–608. Borah and Cook, *Aboriginal Population of Central Mexico*, 88.

4. Corle, *Gila*, 249–271. "Sonoran Pioneers." Willeford, "Mexican Settlers." Cardoso, *Mexican Emigration*, 23. R. Anderson, *Outcasts in Their Own Land*, 18, 38, 43.

5. D. J. Weber, *Mexican Frontier*, 195.

6. McWilliams, *North from Mexico*, 142. D. J. Weber, *Mexican Frontier*, 142–143. Perrigo, *Our Spanish Southwest*, 113, 117, 153.

7. Marez, "Signifying Spain," 267–307. Sheridan, "Limits of Power," 167. Havstad, "Improving Sustainability." R. Gutiérrez, *When Jesus Came*, 300, 304. Sinclair, "Town That Vanished." Deutsch, *No Separate Refuge*, 13–14.

8. Deutsch, *No Separate Refuge*, 21.

9. Schlesinger, "Las Gorras Blancas," 97.

10. Deutsch, *No Separate Refuge*, 15–17. Weigle, *Hispanic Villages*, 151. W. Taylor and West, "Patron Leadership," 79.

11. The 1870 census, Series M593, Roll 46, Page 10, Image 19, Apache Press, Pima Territory, lists the state in Mexico that Mexican workers came from. Found at http://www.Ancestry.com (accessed Oct. 23, 2004). The first two Mexican workers listed are Joaquin Salazar, 27, laborer, Sonora, and Tomas Quiros, 26, laborer, Sonora. The 1880 census, Series T9, Roll 36, Family History Film 1254036, Page 9B, Enumeration District 35, Image 0025, lists the following Subias: Luis Subia, 25, Clifton Copper Mine, Apache, Arizona, single; Delfina Subia, 38, Faustina Subia, 38, and Francisco Subia, 35 — all single and all from El Paso, thus U.S.-born. Found at http://www.Ancestry.com (accessed Mar. 1, 2003).

12. Martínez, *Border Boom Town*, 9–11, 35, 42. Gonzales-Berry and Maciel, *Contested Homeland*, 20. De La Vara, "Return to Mexico," 43–57. "New Railroad Towns; Railroad Building," *Los Angeles Times*, Mar. 25, 1883.

13. Duarte, "Mama Santos's Story," chap. 1.

14. "Life in Lordsburg," *Los Angeles Times*, June 14, 1883. "New Mexico; Santa Fe Lot Owners Sorely Troubled," *Los Angeles Times*, Mar. 11, 1897. Duarte, "Mama Santos's Story," chaps. 2 and 3. Gonzales-Berry and Maciel, *Contested Homeland*, 3.

15. Mellinger, *Race and Labor*, 34.

16. Spude, "Walker-Weaver Digging," 64–74.

17. Bideaux and Wallace, "Arizona Copper," 10–27. Sargent, "Copper Star," 30–31.

18. *Arizona Gazette*, Dec. 6, 1880. Cogut and Conger, *History of Arizona's Clifton-Morenci*, 10.

19. Vinson, "Vanished Clifton-Morenci," 184. Fenn, *Clifton Editor*, 2, 4. Watt, "History of Morenci," 10, 183–187. Mellinger, *Race and Labor*, 2. Carmichael and Kiddie, "Development of Mine Transportation," 1, 4–5. Emersley, "Clifton Copper Mines," 133. "Clifton, New Mexico," 121–122. Watt, "History of Morenci," 17. Bideaux and Wallace "Arizona Copper," 10–27.

20. Freudenthal, "Narrative," 4. Freudenthal provides an excellent narrative of his family history and experiences in Clifton and Grant Counties, New Mexico. Watt, "History of Morenci," 11–13. Colquhoun, *Early History of Clifton-Morenci* (pamphlet), 8; (1924), 21.

21. Patton, *History of Clifton*, 11, 17, 69. Lamb, "Jewish Pioneers in Arizona," 137, 146. See also SJFBF, AHS. Henry Lesinsky's estimated birth year was 1834. See 1910 census, Series T624, Roll 1043, Part 1, Page 73B. Freudenthal, "Narrative," 4, 9. Watt, "History of Morenci," 11, 13. Colquhoun, *Early History of Clifton-Morenci* (pamphlet), 8; (1924), 21. "Letter from Rover," *Arizona Star*, Apr. 25, 1873. Bachelder, "Reminiscences," AHS. Arrieta, "Mexican Community of Clifton-Morenci," 128.

22. Gamble, "Clifton and Old Graham," 1, 8–9. Colquhoun, *Early History of Clifton-Morenci* (1924), 35–37. Patton, *History of Clifton*, 11. Lesinsky, 1874, F&HRC, SC, UCLA.

23. Patton, *History of Clifton*, 13. Cleland, *History of Phelps Dodge*, 83.

24. Hyde, *Copper for America*, 113–132. Cogut and Conger, *History of Arizona's Clifton-Morenci*, 10. Myrick, *Railroads of Arizona*, 16. Vinson, "Vanished Clifton-Morenci," 187.

25. Vinson, "Vanished Clifton-Morenci," 184. Patton, *History of Clifton*, 12, 72. Huginnie, " 'Strikitos,' " 59–62. Byrkit, *Forging Copper Collar*, 21. Park, "History of Mexican Labor," 252–254. Gleicher, "Spielbergs of New Mexico." Solomon, "Solomonville." Hopkins, *Financing the Frontier*, 3–5.

26. Cogut and Conger, *History of Arizona's Clifton-Morenci*, 79. Myrick, *Railroads of Arizona*, 24–25.

27. Fong, "Sojourners and Settlers," 1–30. "La Cuestión China," *El Fronterizo*, Mar. 7, 1880.

28. Ringgold, *Frontier Days*, 164. Patton, *History of Clifton*, 127. Kingsolver, *Holding the Line*, 66–67.

29. *Clifton Clarion*, July 29, 1885. These events were verified by Harriet Rochlin and the census data. See F&HRC, SC, UCLA. On Estanislada Bencoma and Charles B. (Bencoma) Lensinsky, see 1910 census, Series T624, Roll 38, Part 2, Page 229B. On Charles Lensinsky, see 1880 census, Series T9, Roll 36, Family History Film 1254036, Page 6C, Enumeration District 35, Image 0016; 1900 census, Manhattan, New York, Series T623, Roll 1116, Page 15B, Enumeration District 792; and 1910 census, Manhattan, New York, Seires T624, Roll 1020, Part 1, Page 142A. Charles Lesinsky, at age 30, also lived with Angelita Garcia, 20, an unmarried Mexican seamstress, while in Fort Davis, Texas. See 1870 census, Series M593, Roll 1601, Page 530, Image 604.

30. Myrick, *Railroads of Arizona*, 31. Byrkit, *Forging Copper Collar*, 27.

31. Colquhoun, *Early History of Clifton-Morenci* (pamphlet), 22. Arhelger, A.695, AHS. Edward Arhelger arrived in Arizona in 1882.

32. "Lesinsky Mines," *Southwest Sentinel*, June 14, 1884, in F&HRC, SC, UCLA. Sheridan, *Arizona*, 167. Vinson, "Vanished Clifton-Morenci," 183–206.

33. Patton, *History of Clifton*, 17, 35. "Arizona," *Engineering and Mining Journal*, Dec. 30, 1882, 349–350. Arhelger, A.695, AHS. "Arizona Mines and Mining," *Los Angeles Times*, Mar. 10, 1882. Freudenthal, "Narrative," 7. Colquhoun, *Early History of the Clifton-Morenci* (pamphlet), 22. "Lesinsky Mines," *Southwest Sentinel*, June 14, 1884, in F&HRC, SC, UCLA. Sheridan, *Arizona*, 167. Vinson, "Vanished Clifton-Morenci," 183–206. Cogut and Conger, *History of Arizona's Clifton-Morenci*, 39, 132. "Clifton Memories," *Arizona Republican*, Apr. 18, 1925. Barr, "Integrated Results," 8–9.

34. Patton, *History of Clifton*, 21–22. Carmichael and Kiddie, "Development of Mine Transportation," 7. Hildebrand and Mangum, *Capital and Labor*, 86–87. Cleland, *History of Phelps Dodge*, 99–101. Allen, *Company Town*, 35, 45–46. Huginnie, " 'Strikitos,' " 48–49. Gamble, "Clifton and Old Graham," 1, 8–9.

35. Gamble, "Clifton and Old Graham," 1, 8–9. Hildebrand and Mangum, *Capital and Labor*, 86–87. Sheridan, *Arizona*, 167. Patton, *History of Clifton*, 18, 72–73.

36. Patton, *History of Clifton*, 52, 91. Carmichael and Kiddie, "Development of Mine Transportation," 6, 7. Hildebrand and Mangum, *Capital and Labor*, 86–87. Cleland, *History of Phelps Dodge*, 99–101.

37. Hildebrand and Mangum, *Capital and Labor*, 43, 50. Barr, "Integrated Results," 79, 81–82.

38. Allen, *Company Town*, 35, 45–46. Cogut and Conger, *History of Arizona's Clifton-Morenci*, 18, 61–62, 72–73. Patton, *History of Clifton*, 18, 21–22, 35, 52, 72–73, 91, 102–104, 108. Carmichael and Kiddie, "Development of Mine Transportation," 7. Hildebrand and Mangum, *Capital and Labor*, 86–87. Cleland, *History of Phelps Dodge*, 99–101.

39. James Douglas, as quoted in in Cogut and Conger, *History of Arizona's Clifton-Morenci*, 47.

40. Watt, "History of Morenci," iii, 5–7. Cleland, *History of Phelps Dodge*, 83. Cox, "History of Bisbee," 37–38. Graeme, "Bisbee, Arizona's Dowager Queen," 58.

41. "Flood Sufferers," *Los Angeles Times*, Mar. 6, 1891. Patton, *History of Clifton*, 79.

42. Arrieta, "Mexican Community of Clifton-Morenci," 130. Cogut and Conger, *History of Arizona's Clifton-Morenci*, 63. Barr, "Integrated Results," 79, 81–82. Patton, *History of Clifton*, 21. *Arizona Bulletin*, Jan. 12, 1900. *Clifton Clarion*, Feb. 18, 1885. Hildebrand and Mangum, *Capital and Labor*, 43, 50, 86–87. Schwantes, *Bisbee*, 21.

Chapter 4. The Sonoran Corridor

1. Otero, "New Agrarian Movement," 31. Eduardo Villa, in *Historia de Sonora*, 27, includes the Gila River, which most Euro-American scholars do not.

2. Radding, *Wandering Peoples*, 3, 12, 21–23. Dabdoub, *Historia del Valle de Yaqui*, 6–7. Hu-DeHart, in *Missionaries, Miners, and Indians*, 1, estimates the population as 30,000 at the time of the Spanish *entrada* (entry). Sheridan, "Limits of Power," 167.

3. O'Connor, "Among Mayo Indians," 260–268.

4. Villa, *Historia de Sonora*, 28–32. Yetman, *Sonora*, 7. Dunbier, in *Sonoran Desert*, 45, says the Río Yaqui was 680 kilometers (about 420 miles) long; Hu-DeHart, in *Missionaries, Miners and Indians*, 8, 10, lists the river's length as 400 miles, whereas the *Encyclopaedia Britannica* says 380 kilometers (about 240 miles). Almada, in *Diccionario . . . sonorenses*, 842–843, does not give a length. I went with 680 kilometers (approximately 420 miles) because Dabdoub, in *Historia del Valle de Yaqui*, 6, also gives this figure. Spicer, *Yaquis*, 9, 12. Bowden, *Killing the Hidden Waters*, 51.

5. Evans, "Yaquis vs. Yanquis." Radding, *Wandering Peoples*, 10. Spicer, *Cycles of Conquest*, 91–100. Gerhard, *North Frontier*, 279–281. Officer, *Hispanic Arizona*, 32–44. Meyer, *Water in Hispanic Southwest*, 79. Velasco, *Sonora*, 51, 91–104. Hu-DeHart, *Missionaries, Miners and Indians*, 9–10. Officer, *Hispanic Arizona*, 28–31. Villa, *Historia de Sonora*, 40–42.

Notes to Pages 66–71

6. Spicer, *Cycles of Conquest*, 112. Nabhan, "Cultural Dispersal of Plants."
7. Radding, *Wandering Peoples*, 48–49, 51–55. Spicer, *Cycles of Conquest*, 121–123, 131–133. Meyer, *Water in Hispanic Southwest*, 11. Vigil, "Spanish Bluecoats." Bayman, Palacios-Fest, and Huckell, "Botanical Signatures." Gaillard, "Papago of Arizona and Sonora," 293–296. Villa, *Historia de Sonora*, 47–51, 51–55.
8. Pradeau, *Sonora y sus casas de moneda*, 11. Mosk, "Economic Problems in Sonora," 343. Chilcott, "Yaqui World View and School." Officer, *Hispanic Arizona*, 31–32. Hansen, "Fiebre del oro," 110. R. Jackson, "Demographic Change in Northwestern New Spain," 83. Del Río, "Auge y decadencia de los placeres," 83–86, 90–91, 96. Stevens, "Mexico's Forgotten Frontier," 36–37.
9. Voss, "Societal Competition in Northwest," 185, 187–188, 190, 192, 195. Treutlein, "Economic Regime of Jesuit Missions," 289.
10. Voss, "Societal Competition in Northwest," 192.
11. R. Jackson, "Demographic Change in Northwestern New Spain," 464, 466. Stern and Jackson, "*Vagabundaje* . . . in Colonial Northern Sonora," 464.
12. Mosk, "Economic Problems in Sonora," 341. Treutlein, "Economic Regime of Jesuit Missions," 289.
13. Dabdoub, *Historia del Valle de Yaqui*, 82, 88–97. Meredith, "Yaqui Rebellion of 1740," 222, 226, 229. Voss, *Periphery of Nineteenth-Century Mexico*, 15–16. The Meredith article has translated documents investigating causes of the Yaqui revolt. Hu-DeHart, *Missionaries, Miners and Indians*, 70. Radding, *Wandering Peoples*, 283–284.
14. Hu-DeHart, *Missionaries, Miners and Indians*, 3–5, 37, 44–46, 52. Hu-DeHart, *Yaqui Resistance and Survival*, 4, 7, 14–17. Acosta, *Apuntes historicos sonorenses*, 85–86, 90–92; Spicer, *Perspectives in American Indian Culture*, 40. Radding, "From Counting House," 83, 84. Caywood, "Spanish Missions of Northwestern New Spain," 8. Evans, "Yaquis vs. Yanquis." Radding, "Insurgencia y autonomia." Calvo Berber, *Historia de Sonora*, 31. Kroeber, *Uto-Aztecan Languages of Mexico*, 10–12.
15. Vigil, "Spanish Bluecoats." Polzer, "Evolution of Jesuit Mission System," 170–172. Voss, *Periphery of Nineteenth-Century Mexico*, 17, 29–32. Gerhard, *North Frontier of New Spain*, 284–285. Meyer, *Water in Hispanic Southwest*, 77. Radding, "From Counting House," 86.
16. Schmal, "Indigenous Identity in Mexican Census." Robert H. Jackson, in *Indian Population Decline*, 195n48, writes that it is difficult to establish with precision the racial-ethnic origins of the Sonoran population. As in Chihuahua, parish priests exercised wide discretion. Despite this, from selected northern Sonora parish rolls in 1796–1814, he shows it was quite common to see the listing of "coyote," "mulato," "pardo," and "mestizo." Aguirre Beltrán, *Población negra de México*, 234–237. M. Gutiérrez, *Álbum de mujer*, 44.
17. Stern and Jackson, "*Vagabundaje* . . . in Colonial Northern Sonora," 472.
18. Stern and Jackson, "*Vagabundaje* . . . in Colonial Northern Sonora," 462.
19. H. Sobarzo, *Vocabulario sonorense*, 153. Tinker Salas, *In Shadow of Eagles*, 3, 26–27.
20. Lempriere, *Notes in Mexico*, 148–149. Tinker Salas, *In Shadow of Eagles*, 54.

Villa, *Historia de Sonora*, 163–175. Voss, *Periphery of Nineteenth-Century Mexico*, 33, 37, 44–45. R. Ruiz, *People of Sonora*, 119, 122. Stevens, "Mexico's Forgotten Frontier," 51–53, 63–66.

21. With ever mounting encroachment, first by Spanish colonists and then by Mexican settlers, "Yori" more and more came to refer to *non*native outsiders.

22. Voss, *Periphery of Nineteenth-Century Mexico*, 50–54, 66–67. H. Bancroft, *History of North Mexican States*, 2:639, 645. Troncoso. *Guerras con tribus yaqui*, 20, 112. Hu-DeHart, *Yaqui Resistance and Survival*, 7, 20–25, 48.

23. Officer, *Hispanic Arizona*, 92, 98–99, 199. Acuña, *Sonoran Strongman*, 16–19, 60–62, 66, 85–94, 101–104. Almada, *Diccionario . . . sonorenses*, 528–529. H. Bancroft, *History of North Mexican States*, 2:656. Tinker Salas, *In Shadow of Eagles*, 65–67. Officer, *Hispanic Arizona*, 43, 53, 117.

24. H. Bancroft, *History of North Mexican States*, 2:579.

25. Pesqueira, "Documentos para la historia de Sonora."

26. Wyllys, *French in Sonora*, 52–55, 162–164. Soulie, *Wolf Cub*. Voss, *Periphery of Nineteenth-Century Mexico*, 117–120. The *New York Daily Times* carried daily articles on Sonora and the Monroe Doctrine such as H. du Pasquier de Dommartin, "What the French Are Doing in Sonora," Dec. 22 and 24, 1852. See RFAC, Urban Archives, CSUN.

27. *La Voz de Sonora*, Nov. 16, 1885. Reid, *Reid's Tramp*, 209–215. *La Voz de Sonora*, May 9, July 4 and 12, 1856, Sept. 12 and 19, 1856, Mar. 6, 1857. *San Francisco Bulletin*, May 27, 1857, reported the Crabb saga. "Arizona Territory," *New York Times*, May 10, 1858. *Arizona Weekly Star*, quoted in Park, "History of Mexican Labor," 29, 64. Stone to Lewis Cass, Guaymas, Dec. 23, 1858; Alden to Cass, Guaymas, Nov. 18 and 21, 1859; Thomas Robinson to Alden, Guaymas, Nov. 20, 1859, Despatches from United States Consuls in Guaymas, 1832–1896, RG 59, NARA, 1964. Edward Conner to Cass, Mazatlán, Mexico, May 26, 1859, Despatches from United States Consuls in Mazatlán, 1826–1906, NARA, 1949. *La Estrella de Occidente* (Sonora), Nov. 18, 1859. Acuña, "Ignacio Pesqueira," 152–154.

28. Miller, "Plácido Vega," 137, 143, 144.

29. *La Estrella de Occidente*, Feb, 28, 1868, Mar. 28, 1868. *El Eco de Sonora*, Apr. 17, 1871. *La Estrella de Occidente*, Oct. 30, 1874, Nov. 6, 1874. Stevens, "Mexico's Forgotten Frontier," 27, 48, 165–166. A. Willard to State Department, Guaymas, Sept. 30, 1871, Despatches from United States Consuls in Guaymas, 1832–1896, RG 59, NARA, 1964. Corral, *Obras historicas*, 25, 26, 76–78, 85. Garza, "¿Don Ignacio Pesqueira?" 19–22. Almada, *Diccionario . . . sonorenses*, 574. Manson, "Indian Uprisings in Sonora, Mexico," 65.

30. Corral, *Obras historicas*, 118. R. Ruiz, *People of Sonora*, 170, 175–176. Dabdoub, *Historia del Valle de Yaqui*, 115–120. Hernández, *Razas indigenas de Sonora*, 123–124. Villa, *Galeria de sonorenses ilustres*, 97. Troncoso, *Guerras con tribus yaqui*, 60.

31. Hernández, *Razas indigenas*, 120. Dabdoub, *Historia del Valle de Yaqui*, 150–155.

32. Almada, *Diccionario . . . sonorenses*, 406–408, 792–794. R. Ruiz, *People of Sonora*, 1–3, 7–9, 11–13, 16–20, 55, 123–125, 126–128, 135–143, 200–201. Tinker Salas, *In Shadow of Eagles*, 14–16, 36–43, 112–113, 128–129, 133, 136–137. Calvo Berber, *Historia de Sonora*, 254–255. Heyman, *Life and Labor on Border*, 53–55, 58, 64. Schell, "American Investment in Mexico."

33. Tinker Salas, *In Shadow of Eagles*, 176–182, 184–185, 189, 201–222, 230–238. R. Ruiz, *People of Sonora*, 8, 212–227. Goldstein, "Americanization and Mexicanization," 24. H. Sobarzo, *Vocabulario sonorense*, 153.

34. Almada, *Diccionario . . . sonorenses*, 139–141. R. Ruiz, *People of Sonora*, 14, 33, 38, 56–58, 85–88, 90–98, 100–116, 205. Morehouse, Carter, and Spouse, "Implications of Sustained Drought," 783–811. Corral, *Obras historicas*, 167–172.

35. Dennis, "Anti-Chinese Campaigns in Sonora," 65. See the Dennis article for examples of yellow journalism in the Mexican press. Cott, *Mexican Diplomacy and Chinese*, 64, 67, 72, 74, 77, 78.

Chapter 5. Corridors, Convergence, and Community

1. Professor Apolinar Frías Prieto interviews, July 10 and 15, 1982.

2. Sheridan, *Tucsonenses*, 42, 85, 267. *Arizona Miner*, Dec. 7, 1867. Vélez-Ibañez, *Border Visions*, 95. Getty, "Interethnic Relationships," 208–209. M. G. Gonzales, "Mariano G. Samaniego," 141–160. Goldstein, "Americanization and Mexicanization," 245–246, 268, 273. M. G. Gonzales, *Hispanic Elite*, 16–25, 152. Tinker Salas, *In Shadow of Eagles*, 103.

3. "Spanish in Our Public Schools," *La Sonora*, Nov. 30, 1879.

4. Sheridan, *Tucsonenses*, 42, 85, 267. *Arizona Miner*, Dec. 7, 1867. Vélez-Ibañez, *Border Visions*, 95. Getty, "Interethnic Relationships," 208–209. M. G. Gonzales, "Mariano G. Samaniego," 141–160. Goldstein, "Americanization and Mexicanization," 245–246, 268, 273. M. G. Gonzales, *Hispanic Elite*, 16–25, 152. Tinker Salas, *In Shadow of Eagles*, 103.

5. Sheridan, *Tucsonenses*, 93–95. The Mexico/Arizona Project, http://www.mexico arizona.com/fp1.htm (accessed Dec. 22, 2004), lists the genealogy of many elite families having roots on both sides of the border. *El Fronterizo*, Feb. 22, 1880. Ronstadt, "Memoirs." Coverage of the social life of the elite is in every issue of *El Fronterizo*; see Aug. 1 and 21, 1880, and Apr. 3, 1881. See also *La Sonora*, May 29, 1880. "Sonora," *El Fronterizo*, May 16, 1880. "Spanish in Our Public Schools," *La Sonora*, Nov. 30, 1879, is an early example of the demand for bilingual education. Briegel, "Alianza Hispano Americana," 22.

6. Bonillas was defeated by Álvaro Obregón in the 1920 presidential election.

7. Sheridan, *Tucsonenses*, 55, 87.

8. Sheridan, *Tucsonenses*, 81–82, 88–89. From Department of State to Mexican Legation, Washington, D.C., Jan. 9, 1885. Notes to Foreign Legations in the United States, 1834–1906, Mexico: May 2, 1884–Nov. 20, 1893, File Microcopies in RG 99, Roll 72, NARA.

9. Sheridan, *Tucsonenses*, 89–91. *Arizona Champion*, Sept. 28, 1889, Arizona, Reel 1, 1867–1893, Bancroft Library, UCB.

10. Sheridan, *Tucsonenses*, 109.

11. Officer, "Barriers to Mexican Integration," 7–16. Briegel, "Alianza Hispano Americana," 39–40, 47–48. M. G. Gonzales, "Mariano G. Samaniego," 145–152. *El Fronterizo*, Sept. 29, 1878. *El Fronterizo*, Sept. 29, 1878. The fiestas in 1878 were sponsored by the Club Unión. *La Sonora*, May 29, 1880. "Mexico," *El Fronterizo*, Dec. 9, 1881. "Imigrantes Mexicanos," *El Fronterizo*, Jany 20, 1882. "La colonización del Yaqui," *El Fronterizo*, June 10, 1891. "The Mexican Lodge Will Build a Hall in Mexican Quarter of Jerome," *Jerome Mining News*, Nov. 20, 1899, 16. *Miners' Magazine*, Feb. 1900, 42. *Miners' Magazine*, Apr. 1900, 4, 12–13.

12. Bideaux and Wallace, "Arizona Copper." Sargent, "Copper Star of Arizona," 30–31.

13. Goldsmith, "Hispanics in Arizona," 14.

14. Tuck, "Fifty Years of Mining." Hyde, *Copper for American*, 81–82. *Los Angeles Mining Review*, Mar. 21, 1901, AHS. Hugginie, " 'Strikitos,' " 86–95. Caulfield, "Mexican Labor and State," 13–22.

15. Goldstein, "Americanization and Mexicanization," 16–18. Sheridan, *Tucsonenses*, 169.

16. "A Labor Riot," *Los Angeles Times*, Oct. 26, 1897. "At Mammoth Tank," *Los Angeles Times*, Oct. 27, 1897; "Sixty-seven Cuts," *Los Angeles Times*, Oct. 28, 1897. "San Diego County," *Los Angeles Times*, Nov. 14, 1897. "San Diego County," *Los Angeles Times*, Nov. 20, 1897. Love, *Mining Camps*, 141–143.

17. Vaughan, "Everyday Life in Copper Camp," 57, 61, 72, 78. Briegel, "Alianza Hispano Americana," 48, 77. Servín, *Awakened Minority*, 34. Bideaux and Wallace, "Arizona Copper."

18. Huginnie, " 'Strikitos,' " 55, 57, 103–104. Patton, *History of Clifton*, 79. "A Look at Clifton," *Arizona Republican*, July 20, 22, and 24, 1890. "Clifton," *Arizona Citizen*, Dec. 27, 1890. "Morenci," *Arizona Citizen*, Aug. 8, 1891. "Clifton," *Arizona Citizen*, Aug. 8, 1891 "Lively Times," *Arizona Citizen*, Aug. 15, 1891. "Three Days in Clifton," *Arizona Enterprise*, Sept. 12, 1891.

19. Goldstein, "Americanization and Mexicanization," 207–208. Huginnie, " 'Strikitos,' " 70–72. Colquhoun, *Early History of Clifton-Morenci* (1924), 21–22. W. Jackson, *Enterprising Scot*, 179. Patton, *History of Clifton*, 91.

20. Goldsmith, "Seasons, Seeds, and Souls," 141–153.

21. Patton, *History of Clifton*, 108.

22. "A Look at Clifton," *Arizona Republican*, July 20, 1890. "Three Days in Clifton," *Arizona Enterprise*, Sept. 12, 1891. "Lively Times," *Arizona Citizen*, Aug. 15, 1891. "Morenci," *Arizona Citizen*, Aug. 8, 1891, "Clifton," *Arizona Citizen*, Aug. 8, 1891. W. Jackson, *Enterprising Scot*, 179.

23. Ross, *History of Arizona Federation*, 15, 19–20, 46, 101–102. Vinson, "Vanquished Clifton-Morenci," 187–190. "Morenci," *Arizona Enterprise*, Aug. 15, 1891. Owens, "Growth and Development of Safford," 4, 8.

24. Caulfield, "Mexican Labor," 13–22. Arrieta, "Mexican Community of Clifton-Morenci," 130. Huginnie, " 'Strikitos,' " 120. Cogut and Conger, *History of Arizona's Clifton-Morenci*, 13.

25. Patton, *History of Clifton*, 24, 129–130. Cogut and Conger, *History of Arizona's Clifton-Morenci*, 99–100, 131–132. McBride, "Labor Unions in Arizona Mining," 60. Carmichael and Kiddie, "Development of Mine Transportation," 7. *Los Angeles Mining Review*, Mar. 21, 1901, AHS. Huginnie, " 'Strikitos,' " 140.

26. Hugginie, " 'Strikitos,' " 53.

27. Meinig, *Southwest*, 41. Ball, "Office of United States Marshal," 7–8, 289–290. *Arizona Bulletin*, Jan. 12, 1900, supplement. Carmichael and Kiddie, "Development of Mine Transportation," 7.

28. "Arizona Copper Mines," *Copper Era*, Nov. 16, 1899. Patton, *History of Clifton*, 55. Hildebrand and Mangum, *Capital and Labor*, 86–87. Huginnie, " 'Strikitos,' " 35, 37–38. Cleland, *History of Phelps Dodge*, 117. *Arizona Gazette*, Dec. 6, 1880. Arrieta, "Mexican Community of the Clifton-Morenci," 130.

Chapter 6. Becoming Mexican

1. Gordon, *Great Arizona Orphan Abduction*, 48. Meier and Rivera, *Dictionary of Mexican American History*, 287. Gutmann et al., "Demographic Impact of Mexican Revolution." *Población total nacional y estatal*, 4.

2. Barr, "Integrated Results," 77.

3. Rogers, "Character . . . of Mexican Miner," 700–701.

4. Gordon, *Great Arizona Orphan Abduction* 125, 130–137. Barr, "Integrated Results," 21. Patton, *History of Clifton*, 69.

5. Cogut and Conger, *History of Arizona's Clifton-Morenci*, 163–164. Congut and Conger's interview of Pedro Gómez was biased in favor of Phelps Dodge's people. Elena Díaz Björkquist's interview of Gómez is much more balanced. See "Valentine Subia Herrera," in Björkquist, "Mexican Americans in Morenci." Patton, *History of Clifton*, 35. Segregated schools were common in mining camps at this time. Watts, *Morenci*, 104.

6. "Masquerade Ball,' *Copper Era*, Mar. 1, 1900. "Morenci Ball," *Copper Era*, Dec. 14, 1899. All in attendance were white, except for a Miss G. Salcido of Metcalf. Fenn, *Clifton Editor*, 17.

7. Gordon, *Great Arizona Orphan Abduction* 174–175.

8. Gordon, *Great Arizona Orphan Abduction*, 177–179. Patton, *History of Clifton*, 35. Watts, "Morenci," 104. Barr, "Integrated Results," 3, 21.

9. Rogers, "Character and Habits," 700–701. Gordon, *Great Arizona Orphan Abduction*, 194, 198. *Graham Guardian*, Mar. 15, 1901. *Copper Era*, Dec. 13, 1900. *Valley Bulletin* (Solomonville), Dec. 20, 1889. John Hay to Manuel de Azpiroz, Mar. 15, 1905, Notes to Foreign Legations in the United States from Department of State, Mexico, Feb. 2, 1903–Aug. 14, 1906, M-95, Roll 74, NARA.

10. *Valley Bulletin* (Solomonville), Dec. 20, 1889, lists an honor roll, with three Spanish-surnamed students.

11. Heyman, "Oral History," 189–192.

12. Gordon, *Great Arizona Orphan Abduction*, 100, 170.

13. Cogut and Conger, *History of Arizona's Clifton-Morenci*, 14. Gordon, *Great Arizona Orphan Abduction*, 171–172.

14. W. S. Crowe, as quoted in *Miners' Magazine*, May 1902, 42. Heyman, "Oral History," 189–190. 191–192. Sheridan, *Tucsonenses*, 85. Gordon, *Great Arizona Orphan Abduction*, 122–125. Ringgold, *Frontier Days*, 126–127. Cogut and Conger, *History of Arizona's Clifton-Morenci*, 14, 100–105. Fenn, *Clifton Editor*, 41–42. Kluger, *Clifton-Morenci Strike*, 10.

15. Gordon, *Great Arizona Orphan Abduction,*, 100–105.

16. Fenn, *Clifton Editor*, 41–42. Gordon, *Great Arizona Orphan Abduction*, 121–122. The 1900 census, Precincts 3, 11, 19, and 15, Graham County, Arizona Territory, Series T623, tracks Jesús Martínez, Arturo Elías, and Primitivo Medina.

17. McBride, "Development of Labor Unions in Arizona," 43–44. "Tombstone," *Prescott Weekly Courier*, Aug. 8, 1884.

18. Hugginie, " 'Strikitos,' " 201–202. Casillas, "Mexicans, Labor, and Strife," 6. J. Torres, "Globe Strike of 1896," 1–14. *Miners' Magazine*, Dec. 1901, 8, 15, 17–18. "In Arizona," *Miners' Magazine*, Sept. 1900, 10. Casillas, "Mexicans, Labor, and Strife in Arizona," 6, 40. "Arizona Federation," *Los Angeles Times*, Aug. 5, 1903. Casillas, "Mexican Labor Militancy," 35, 45. Harrison, "Development of Arizona Labor," 6–7.

19. Emmons, *Butte Irish*, 20–27. This is the best source on the Butte miners; this section draws heavily from it. Freeman, "Catholics, Community, and Republicans," 257, 259. Glasscock, *War of Copper Kings*, 70, 91. *Miners' Magazine*, Sept. 3, 1903, 9. *Miners' Magazine*, Apr. 14, 1904, 6. A Letter from M. J. Hoban, Bishop of Scranton, Dec. 15, 1907," *Miners' Magazine*, Jan. 2, 1908, 4. John M, O'Neil, "My Answer to the Bishop of Scranton," *Miners' Magazine*, Jan. 2, 1908, 5. "The Millionaire Robber," *Miners' Magazine*, July 1, 1909, 8.

20. Domecq, "Teresa de Urrea," 144–146. "Miss Teresa Urrea: The Mexican Jeanne d'Arc," ARE, 11-19-11. W. Holden, *Teresita*, 8–13. Vanderwood, "Using Present," 102–103.

21. "Miss Teresa Urrea: The Mexican Jeanne d'Arc," ARE, 11-19-11. Vanderwood, *Power of God*. W. Holdem, *Teresita*, 8–13. Montoya, "Empowered or Subordinated?" "Informes sobre indios," pp. 50–59, Sept. 6, 1890, Primera Rama Militar — Linea del Mayo, AMGR, vol. 7, AGN. On millenarian movements, see also Macklin and Crumrine, "Mexican Folk Saint Movements," 89–105.

22. Madrid, "Corrido de Tomochic." Domecq, "Teresa de Urrea," 151, 165. "María Teresa Urrea: 'La Santa de Cabora,' " Félipe A. Zabadie, Consul, Nogales, to Secretario de Relaciones Exteriores, Nogales, Arizona, July 5, 1892, III/5.3, "890"/2, ARE, 11-19-11. Mariscal to Consul Nogales, July 16, 1892, III/513; "890"/2. ARE, 11-19-11. Vanderwood, "Using Present," 104. Vanderwood, *Power of God*, 182, 221.

23. Aguirre can be traced through the 1920 census, Series T625, Roll 1799, Page 5B, Enumeration District 91, Image 0847; Draft Record 1953281, Draft Board 1, El Paso. Prior to *El Independiente*, Aguirre published *El Progresista*. Mallen to Secretario

de Relaciones Exteriores, El Paso, June 19, 1901, ARE, 15-9-11. Lauro Aguirre Expediente. ARE, 15-8-11. "Arizona News," *Los Angeles Times*, Apr. 3, 1896. "Santa Teresa," *Los Angeles Times*, Apr. 6, 1895. Consul at El Paso, Texas, to District Judge, Ciudad Juárez, Jan. 6, 1896. "Called a Fake," *Los Angeles Times*, Mar. 11, 1896. Rodríguez and Rodríguez, "Teresa Urrea." 57–58, 63. Domecq, "Teresa de Urrea," 146–147, 156.

24. Roberto U. Culberson, Promotor Fiscal, West Texas District, El Paso, Texas, to Attorney General of United States, Washington, D.C., Oct. 9, 1896, ARE, 11-19-11. Domecq, "Teresa de Urrea," 147–149, 160–162. Almada, *Revolución en Chihuahua*, 105.

25. "Not Revolutionists," *Los Angeles Times*, Aug. 23, 1896. W. Holdem, *Teresita*, 170–171. Valadés, *Porfirismo*, 105. Almada, *Revolución en Chihuahua*, 105. Lauro Aguirre to Enríque Acevedo, Aug. 12, 1896, ARE, 1-3-670, vol. 2, Exped. III, 252, AMGR, vol. 8, AGN. See Correspondencia Particular de Coronel Emilio Kosterlitsky, Nogales, Sept. 5, 1896, Tomo 2650-1910, Ex. 1, AMGR, vol 8, AGN. See also "Rebelión de Pomposo Ramos Rojo y Demetrio Cortés," Estado de Sonora, 1896, ARE, 9-3-670, vol. 7, in Sonora, AMGR, AGN.

26. W. Holden, *Teresita*, 117. Teresa de Urrea, "Mis Ideas sobre las Revoluciones," *El Independiente*, Aug. 21, 1896. "El Asalto de Nogales," *El Fronterizo*, Aug. 15, 1896, Correspondence on and from Aguirre found in ARE, 7-3-670 and 7-3-673, vol. 1, AMGR, vol. 8, AGN. For full citations, see earlier drafts in RFAC, Urban Archives, CSUN.

27. Peña Del Pino to Corral, Gobernación, Feb. 19, 1901, L.E. 942, ARE. Documentos Tomados de "Relación de la Rebelión de Pomposo Ramos Rojo y Demetrio Cortés," 1938, by Francisco Almada, in *Rebelión de Pomposo Ramos Rojo y Demetrio Cortés*, 1896, AMGR, vol. 8, AGN. Huberman, *Labor Spy Racket*, 156. Langham, *Border Trails*, 33. Furlong, *Fifty Years*, 137–139. *Hearings on S. Res. 106*, 2:36.

28. Transcript of hearing before Magistrate William E. Baker, Mar. 5, 1897, ARE, 11-19-11. W. L. Rynerson, Las Cruces, New Mexico, to R. C. Ware, U.S. Marshall, San Antonio, Dec. 26, 1896, ARE, 11-19-11. "Arizona News," *Los Angeles Times*," Sept. 7, 1896. "She Is Not a Saint," *Los Angeles Times*, Sept. 20, 1896.

29. W. Holden, *Teresita*, 172–177, 196. Maximino Gairto, to Secretario de Relaciones Exteriores, Bisbee, July 10, 1897, ARE, 11-19-11. "Santa Teresa Blamed," *Los Angeles Times*, Aug. 7, 1899. W. Holden, *Teresita*, 188. "Hubby 'Shot' Saint," *Los Angeles Times*, July 1, 1900. "The Troubles of Santa Teresa," *Copper Era*, June 28, 1900. *Copper Era*, Feb. 26, 1900. Domecq, "Teresa de Urrea," 166. "Wealthy Exile Dead," *Los Angeles Times*, Oct. 10, 1902. Tomás de Urrea had a wife in Sinaloa, reportedly worth $100,000. He left a friend in Clifton $2,000.

30. The 1900 census, Clifton, Precinct 3, Graham County, Arizona Territory, Series T623, Roll 45, Page 44B, Enumeration District 19, Image 89, lists Tomás Urrea, 40, and his partner, Gabriela, 35. They had seven children at the time. Letter from S. M. del Toro to Consul in Tucson, Clifton, Aug. 26, 1908, states that Ramón Treviño was in Morenci and that Teresa de Urrea's son-in-law was under surveillance. He refers to Teresa's

house: "The house of Señora de Urrea is in a neighborhood called 'la Barranca' or 'Chihuahua,' not far from the place frequented every night by Vice Consul Romero," ARE, 939, vol. 22, AMGR, vol. 40, AGN. According to the report, Treviño was involved in planning the Sept. 1908 attacks on Mexico and, by implication, on Teresa de Urrea.

31. Mellinger, *Race and Labor*, 17–32. *Miners' Magazine*, Dec. 1902, 11. *Miners' Magazine*, Jan. 9, 1905, 13. *Miners' Magazine*, Jan. 12, 1905, 1. Híjar, "Notas sobre cultura obrera mexicana," 12–14. Casillas, "Mexican Labor Militancy," 35. Harner, "Copper Mining . . . in Sonora," 6. Mellinger, " 'Men Have Become Organizers,' " 332–333. J. T. Lewis, Member of the Executive Board, *Moyer Report*, Denver, May 27, 1903, WFM, *Official Proceedings of the 11th Annual*, Denver, Colorado, May 25–June 10, 1905.

32. Mellinger," 'Men Have Become Organizers,' " 329.

33. Jeanne Parks Ringgold, as quoted in Park, "History of Mexican Labor," 257. Gordon, *Great Arizona Orphan Abduction*, 241. Brophy, *Foundlings on Frontiers*, 18. Mellinger, *Race and Labor*, 34. Fenn, *Clifton Editor*, 60, 111. R. Anderson, *Outcasts in Their Own Land*, 85–86. Mellinger, " 'Men Have Become Organizers,' " 328–334.

34. Francisco Avila to Juez de Distrito del Estado de Sonora, Sept. 24, 1906, p. 3, and to Rafael Huacuja y Avila, Dec. 20, 1906, L.E. 922, ARE. Salcido described as 33, a bachelor, and a miner living in Morenci, from Camargo, Chihuahua. Later in Douglas, Salcido worked in the lumber department of the Southwest Railroad, knew Gabriel Rubio, and lived with Romo Mascareñas and others.

35. Wagoner, *Arizona Territory*, 386. Ringgold, *Frontier Days*, 165. Laustannau was also spelled "Loustaunau" in the Tucson area and in Sonora. "Convictions in Arizona," *Miners' Magazine*, Nov. 2, 1903, 7, identifies "Laustennan" as leader of the Morenci strike. He was sentenced to two years and fined $2,000. Abrán F. Salcido, Manuel L. Flores, and Francisco Figueroa, all from Chihuahua, were given two years, one year, and one year, respectively. Most of the inmates of the Yuma Territorial Prison were Mexican. "Miners Forced to Declare a Strike," *Miners' Magazine*, July 1903, 35. Harrison, "Development of Arizona Labor," 6. Casillas, "Mexicans, Labor, and Strife," 67–69. Arrieta, "Mexican Community of Clifton-Morenci," 130. One of leaders of 1903 strike, Abraham Rico, was president of the Morenci union and was also involved in Partido Liberal Mexicano activities. Watts, "Morenci," 61. The *Morenci Leader*, July 8, 1905, reported that an Italian was a member of the Mafia.

36. Ringgold, *Frontier Days*, 165–166.

37. *Arizona Silver Belt* (Globe), Jan. 24, 1879, NSDC, AHS. Ringgold, *Frontier Days*, 56–57. 78. Gordon, *Great Arizona Orphan Abduction*, 234–237.

38. Ringgold, *Frontier Days*, 167–168. Mellinger, *Race and Labor*, 47, 51. *Arizona Silver Belt* (Globe), Jan. 24, 1879, NSDC, AHS. Hopkins, *Financing Frontier*, 57. Born in Illinois in 1867, Charles Mills was the silent czar of Morenci. The Mexicans called him "El Indio" because was said to be Indian-like: he had a powerful physique, a grim reticence — speaking mostly in monosyllables — and a gloomy intensity of mind and mood.

39. Rynning, *Gun Notches*, 231. J. H. Bassett Folder, ASA.

40. Ringgold, *Frontier Days*, 170. Watt, in "Morenci," 57–58, recounts the strike, claiming that Parks was friends with Laustaunnau.

41. Ringgold, *Frontier Days*, 172, 174. Full of bravado, Rynning contradicts Ringgold, in *Gun Notches*, 231, 232–253.

42. McClintock, *Arizona*, 424. Hugginie, " 'Strikitos,' " 213. "Historical Annual National Guard of Arizona." Jackson, *Enterprising Scot*, 182. Fred L. Waterman Collection, ASA. Frank E. Frazer was a Major General in the Arizona National Guard. Adjutant General to Fred L. Waterman, Sept. 19, 1956. The *Los Angeles Times* reported extensively on the 1903 strike, as it did on most such strikes.

43. Park, "History of Mexican Labor," 258. Byrkit, *Forging Copper Collar*, 51. "Copper Mines Out," *El Paso Herald*, June 6, 1903. "Guards Disarmed by Strikers at Clifton," *El Paso Herald*, June 9, 1903. Ringgold, *Frontier Days*, 173.

44. William H. Laustannau, no. 2029, also known as "Three-Fingered Jack," died Aug. 20, 1906, of heat prostration brought on by prolonged solitary confinement. "Yuma Territorial Prison Cemetery." Jeffrey, *Story of Arizona Territorial Prison*, 7, 23, 78–79. According to Jeffrey, who described him as a burly Romanian labor agitator, Laustannau "was probably one of the most violent and vicious of the prison's incorrigibles." "Another Mine Disaster Here" and "Morenci Rioters Free," *Morenci Leader*, July 8, 1905. "Union Miners' Strike Was Almost a War," *Los Angeles Times*, June 26, 1903. Identifies Laustannau as a Mexican.

45. Arturo M. Elías, ARE, 2-17-14, vol. 4, pp. 16–18. En el Corte Distrito del Segundo Distrito del Territorio de Arizona, en y por el Condado de Graham, [signed] Frank Dysark, clerk, June 13, 1903, Solomonville, Arizona. Detroit Mining Co. of Arizona v. Abrán Salcido y Otros, Arturo M. Elías, Expediente, and Arturo M. Elías sobre Su Expediente Personal, Año 1947, ARE, 2-17-13, vol. 7. Elías was still in service in 1953. Arturo M. Elías, ARE, 2-17-14, vol. 4, pp. 16–18. A. L. Juan Solis to Díaz, Lordsburg, New Mexico, July 6, 1903, Arturo M. Elías, ARE, 2-17-14, vol. 4, p. 19. Arturo M. Elías to Juan Solis, July 31, 1903, ARE, 2-17-13, vol. 4, and 2-17-14, vol. 4. Mariscal to Elías, Aug. 7 1903, ARE, 2-17-13 and 2-17-14, vol. 4. Gordon, *Great Arizona Orphan Abduction*, 221–224.

46. Gordon, *Great Arizona Orphan Abduction*, 224–228, 231–233. Arrieta, "Alianza Hispano Americana," 55–57, 60–71. Arturo M. Elías, Vice Consul Record, Prt. VII; Solomonville, Arizona, Vice Consul, 1904, regarding 1903 Strike, "Elías Helped Round Up Magonistas," 1906, IV. Elías to Secretario de Relaciones Exteriores Mariscal, July 20, 1903, regarding letter from Juan Solis in Lordsburg, ARE, 2-17-13. Gordon, *Great Arizona Orphan Abduction*, 229. John Hay to Manuel de Azpiroz, June 22, 1903, Notes to Foreign Legations in the United States from the Department of State, Mexico, Feb. 2, 1903–Aug. 14, 1906, M99, Roll 74, NARA. The U.S. State Department reported that a conspiracy to raid Cananea was being hatched in Phoenix. "The Arizona Cactus Heard From," *Miners' Magazine*, Nov. 12, 1903, 9.

47. Salcido is important because, aside from anticipating the Revolution of 1910, he was originally from Camargo, Chihuahua. In Morenci, he lived close to Pedro Subia. Abrán Salcido, 1900 census, Precincts 3, 11, 19, and 15, Graham County, Arizona

Territory, Series T623, Roll 45, Page 25B, Enumeration District 19, Morenci Township, Image 51.

48. See 1900 census, Precincts 3, 11, 19, and 15, Graham County, Arizona Territory, Series T623, Roll 45, Page 5B, Enumeration District 19, Morenci Township. That year, Pedro Subia also registered under the name of "Pedro Suvia," same wife and child. 1900, Precincts 1, 5, 6, 7, 10, 12, and 13, Graham County, Arizona Territory, Series T623, Roll 45, Page 18A, Enumeration District 21.

49. Francisca Subia (listed as "Francisca Marcus" on Pedro Jr.'s birth certificate), Place of Death: Morenci, Greenlee County, Arizona, Arizona State Board of Health State Index no. 160, Local Registrar 47, Mar. 16, 1919. Pedro Jr. was born six years before his mother's death. Arizona State Board of Health State Index no. 189, Census Register no. 123, Local Registrar 46, Morenci, Greenlee County, Arizona, Mar. 31, 1913, lists both mother and father, a miner, as born in Mexico.

Chapter 7. Mexican Miners

1. Gordon, *Great Arizona Orphan Abduction*, 80–81, 87–89, 90–96, 105–106. Patton, *History of Clifton*, 139–140, 143–144. Byrkit, *Forging Copper Collar*, 2. Brophy, *Foundlings on Frontier*, 13. Hugginie, " 'Strikitos,' " 203–206. Mulligan, "Foundlings at Clifton-Morenci," 56.

2. *NY Foundling Hosp. v. Gatti*, 203 U.S. 429 (1906). Argued Apr. 26, 1906; decided Dec. 3, 1906.

3. Gordon, *Great Arizona Orphan Abduction*, 110.

4. *Tucson Citizen*, Oct. 19, 1904.

5. *NY Foundling Hosp. v. Gatti*, 203 U.S. 429 (1906). The lawsuit made specific reference to only one orphan, although it was brought on behalf of all the white familes seeking to adopt the Irish orphans.

6. Gordon, *Great Arizona Orphan Abduction*, 300.

7. "Foundlings in Arizona," *New York Times*, Oct. 16, 1904. The coverage in the *New York Times* and *Los Angeles Times* was anti-Mexican.

8. Mariano Martínez, "Arizona Americans," *New York Times*, Oct. 31, 1904.

9. Louisa Gatti, as quoted in Gordon, *Great Arizona Orphan Abduction*, 72. Brophy, *Foundlings on Frontier*, 101. "The Innocents," *Weekly Arizona Republican*, Jan. 19, 1905.

10. *Tucson Citizen*, Oct. 19, 1904.

11. Gordon, *Great Arizona Orphan Abduction*, 153. S. Johnson, "Sharing Bed and Board," 37. Because there were so few white women in Arizona in the 1860s, cohabitation and intermarriage were common between Mexican women and Euro-American men. Briegel, "Alianza Hispano-Americana," 27. Such intermarriage declined when the population of white women increased after the arrival of the railroad.

12. Gordon, *Great Arizona Orphan Abduction*, 154.

13. Gordon, *Great Arizona Orphan Abduction*, 37–43, 118, 119–120. Many of the Mexican parents were involved in *mutualistas*. By 1902, the Alianza Hispano Americano had established lodges in Clifton, Morenci, and Metcalf. By 1907, it had 1,171

members in twenty-two lodges. Both the *Morenci Leader* and the *Copper Era* carried items on this club's activity.

14. *NY Foundling Hosp. v. Gatti*, 203 U.S. 429 (1906). Brophy, *Foundlings on Frontier*, 61, 101. Mulligan, "Foundlings at Clifton-Morenci," 62. *Report of Cases Argued*, 105. Criminal no. 209, filed Jan. 21, 1905, 79 Pac 231, 106–111. The 1920 census, Clifton, Greenlee County, Arizona, Series T625, Roll 48, Page 8B, Enumeration District 69, Image 304, listed Margarita and Cornelio Chacón.

15. "Prefer Statutory Charge," *Los Angeles Times*, Apr. 14, 1914. George F. Sattler, a well-to-do grocer, was accused of molesting and impregnating Gladys Freeman, 12, one of the foundlings adopted by Olive Freeman, and several other younger girls. "Denies Charge of Young Girl," *Los Angeles Times*, July 9, 1914. Sattler was an ex-convict, who had served thirteen years in San Quentin Penitentiary. Upon his release in 1906, he had become a church deacon.

16. Elías to Secretario de Relaciones Exteriores, Feb. 24, 1906, and Isidro C. Romero, El Expediente Personal, Relaciones Exteriores, Phoenix, Jan. 31, 1905, ARE, 5-5-59, document this importance. Mexican officials had close relations with the white establishment. "A. M. Elías, Mexican Consul Tucson," *Copper Era*, Sept. 14, 1905: "Arturo is always a welcome visitor to this section and his many friends in Graham County are glad to see him getting along so well."

17. Albro, *Always Rebel*, 3–22. Henderson, "Mexican Rebels in Borderlands," 207–219. By 1906, *Regeneración* had a circulation of 20,000.

18. "Cannot Cross Border with Guns," *Copper Era*, Sept. 6, 1906. Martínez Nuñez, *Vida heroica*, 40–41, 77–80. Raat, *Revoltosos*, 29, 43. Rivera, *Revolución en Sonora*, 139, 169. Medina Hoyos, *Cananea*, 34–38. Almada, *Diccionario . . . sonorenses*, 56, 218–219, 337–338, has numerous biographical sketches. Gordon, *Great Arizona Orphan Abduction*, 51.

19. "Morenci Rioters Free," *Copper Era*, July 6, 1905. Mellinger, *Race and Labor*, 55. When he was booked on Oct. 25, 1903, Abrán Salcido listed a brother, Joaquín, in Chihuahua.

20. The U.S. Department of Justice, Feb. 24, 1911, wrote that Fernando Palomares, Tucson, claimed his mother was Mayo, and that he had gone to an American school in the United States in 1904, U.S. Department of Justice, RG 60 90755, no. 2, Justice 90755, Reel 1, Film 1413.

21. Rivera, *Revolución en Sonora*, 164. Jenkins, "Ricardo Flores Magón," 78–82. Lloyd and Azoala, *Formación . . . del Partido Liberal Mexicano*, 67, 71–77. Aguilar Camín, *Frontera nomada*, 123.

22. Albro, *Always Rebel*, 35. Hernández Padilla, *Magonismo*, 30–46. Calderón, *Guerra del yaqui*, 24–28, 28–31. Barta, *Regeneración*, 18. Medina Hoyos, *Cananea*, 42. Calderón, *Guerra del yaqui*, 33–39, 81. R. Anderson, *Outcasts in Their Own Land*, 113. "Dirección de *Regeneración*," Profesor Librado Rivera and Antonio Y. Villarreal, Saint Louis, Missouri, to José María Valenzuela, Cananea, Nov. 1, 1905. Ricardo Flores Magón, Saint Louis, to Manuel M. Diéguez, Mar. 1, 1906, Junta Organizadora del Partido Liberal Mexicano, Saint Louis, to Estebán B. Calderón and Manuel M. Diéguez,

Cananea, Mar. 3, 1906, Junta Organizadora del Partido Liberal Mexicano, Saint Louis, Manuel M. Diéguez, Cananea, Mar. 29, 1906, Ricardo Flores Magón, Mar. 30, 1906, in Hoyos Medina, *Cananea*, 30, 34–38.

23. *"El Centenario*: Seminario independiente y liberal," Director responsable y administrador, Enrique Bermúdez, Cananea, May 12, 1906, no. 6. Quoted in Medina Hoyos, *Cananea*, 44–46. Trueba Urbina, *Evolución de la huelga*, 77. Medina Hoyos, in *Cananea*, 69, 80, writes that Cota-Robles was commissioned by the township president to help the police recover the bodies of the dead and wounded.

24. *El Centenario*, May 12, 1906, as quoted in Medina Hoyos, *Cananea*, 47–49. Calderón, *Guerra del yaqui*, 44–49, 51. Dr. F. Barroso, Cananea, June 1, 1906 to Sr. Juez 2do de Primera Instancia en Cananea. "Huelga de Cananea," AMGR, vol. 23, Archivo General del Estado de Sonora, AGN, vol. 2184 (1906), exp. 11. Calderón, *Guerra del yaqui*, 50, 79.

25. James Walsh, Deputy Collector of Taxes, Custom House, Port of Bisbee, to J. F. Darnal, Consul, Nogales, Oct. 27, 1899; "Cowboys Threaten Naco Sonora," Despatches from United States Consuls in Nogales, 1889–1906, Micro Copy 283, Rolls 3 and 4, NARA, 1964. *El Paso Herald*, Oct. 10, 1899. Albert R. Morawetz to Robert Bacon, Assistant Secretary of State, Jan. 17, 1906; Sariego Rodríguez, *Enclaves y minerales*, 88–90, 109–111. M. Bernstein, "Colonel William C. Greene," 187, 190–192.

26. Harner, "Copper Mining . . . in Sonora," 3–4. W. J. Galbraith, Cananea, Sonora, to Albert R. Morawetz, June 9, 1905, Despatches from United States Consuls in Nogales, 1889–1906, Micro Copy 283, Roll 4, NARA, 1964. Rivera, *Revolución en Sonora*, 150. Sonnichsen, *Colonel Greene*, 166, 191–200. Medina Hoyos, *Cananea*, 69. Calderón, *Guerra del yaqui*, 61–62, 88–90. Rénique, "Frontier Capitalism and Revolution," 450.

27. Calderón, *Guerra del yaqui*, 98–99. Rivera, *Revolución en Sonora*, 155–156. Raat, *Revoltosos*, 81–85, 89. R. Anderson, *Outcasts in Their Own Land*, 110, 116. Frank M. Crocker, Guaymas, to A. Morawitz, June 19, 1903. "George A. Metcalf, Death Certificate," June 13, 1906, Consul at Nogales, Despatches from United States Consuls in Nogales, 1889–1906, Micro Copy 283, Roll 4, NARA, 1964.

28. Izabal to Corral, June 5, 1906, in Medina Hoyos, *Cananea*, 40. Trueba Urbina, *Evolución de la huelga*, 74. "Americans Killed in Mexican Race War," *Los Angeles Times*, June 2, 1906. "Serious Trouble at Cananea," *Copper Era*, June 7, 1906. Telegram, Naco, June 13, 1906, to Bacon; "Report of Visits to Cananea, Sonora, Mexico, during Outbreak: Confirmation of Telegrams," June 22, 1906. "Report on the Disaffection among Mexican Laborers at Cananea, Sonora, Mexico," June 22, 1906. "Report of Americans Injured June 1st and 2nd during Outbreak on Part of Mexican Laborers at Cananea, Sonora, Mexico," Nogales, June 22, 1906. "Reports of Deaths of American Citizens"; Albert W. Brickwood Jr. to Hon. Elihu Root, Secretary of State, Nogales, June 30, 1906, no. 283, Roll 4, vol. 4, Nogales, NARA.

29. Raat, *Revoltosos*, 44, 78, 90. Caulfield, "Mexican Labor and State," 47. Greene, "Huelga de Cananea," 1906 a el Comité de Huelgistas," June 1, 1906, v. 22, AGS, vol. 2184 (1906), exp. 11, AMGR, AGN.

30. Sariego, *Enclaves y minerales*, 129–131. David Cole, General Manager, to Greene, July 20, 1906, Denver, Albert Fall Collection, Huntington Library. John Hay to Manuel de Azpiroz, Washington, D.C., June 22, 1903, Notes to Foreign Legations in the United States from Department of State, Mexico, Feb. 2, 1903–August 14, 1906, M-95, Roll 74, NARA, 1950. Louis Hostetter to Robert Bacon, Assistant Secretary of State, Nov. 20, 1906, Despatches from United States Consuls in Hermosillo, 1889–1906, Micro Copy 293, Roll 1, NARA, 1964. Caulfield, "Mexican Labor and State," 47.

31. M. J. Gonzales, "Copper Companies . . . and Mexican Revolution," 656.

32. Casillas, "Partido Liberal Mexicano," 8–14. Raat, *Revoltosos*, 27, 29. Sariego, *Enclaves y minerales*, 133–138.

33. Ricardo Flores Magón has copies of correspondence between the junta and its operatives during the summer of 1906. For instance, in letter dated Aug. 31, 1906, the Saint Louis junta commissioned Javier Guitemea of Douglas to confer with the Yaqui and enlist them in uprising, promising restitution of properties and giving them "the advantages of the working classes." Ricardo Flores Magón, Saint Louis, to Tomás D. Espinosa, Douglas, Sept. 2, 1906, warned of a traitor and called for secrecy; Junta Organizadora of the PLM to Ildefonso R. Martínez; Ricardo Flores Magón, Saint Louis, to Gabriel Rubio, Douglas, July 27, 1906, U.S. Department of Justice, RG 60 90755, no. 2, Justice 90755, Reel 1, Film 1413. Albro, *Always Rebel*, 58. Rénique, "Frontier Capitalism and Revolution," 420. Rivera, *Revolución en Sonora*, 165. Calvo Berber, *Historia de Sonora*, 279. Hernández Padilla, *Magonismo*, 85, 92.

34. Manuel Sarabia to Henry Max Morton (Tomás Sarabia), June 10, 1907, refers to Luis Mata, Práxedis Guerrero, and Reynaldo Ornelas; Manuel Sarabia to Samuel F. Jiménez of Jerome, Arizona, June 10, 1906. L.E. 925, ARE. "Cannot Cross Border with Guns," *Morenci Leader*, Sept. 8, 1906. There is considerable correspondence between the junta and the *revoltosos* at Douglas and between Mexican and U.S. authorities. Antonio Maza, consul, to James Kibbey, Governor of Territory, Aug. 18, 1906; Ricardo Flores Magón junta, Toronto, to Bruno Treviño, Moury, Arizona, Aug. 18, 1906. Librado Rivera, to Gabriel Rubios, Sept. 1, 1906; Ricardo Flores Magón to Ildefonzo R. Martínez, Sept. 2, 1906. G. Cosio to Relaciones Exteriores, Sept. 24, 1906; Corral to Secretario de Relaciones Exteriores, Sept. 25, 1906, L.E. 1241, ARE. Rivera, *Revolución en Sonora*, 166, 171. *Morenci Leader*, Sept. 8, 1906. Ricardo Flores Magón to Tomás D. Espinosa, Aug. 2, 1906; Ricardo Flores Magón to Tomás D. Espinosa, Sept. 2, 1906; A. Salcido to José B. Treviño, Aug. 28, 1906, U.S. Department of Justice, RG 60 90755, no. 2, Justice 90755, Reel 1, Film 1413.

35. "Conspirators in Arizona," *Los Angeles Times*, Sept. 19, 1906. Gabriel Rubio was alleged to have urged the crowd to "kill the gringos." He, like Salcido, had contact with Cananea.

36. Mariscal to Vice Consul, Solomonville, Sept. 12, 1906, AMGR Gobernación, AGN, Section 1a 3517, 1906–07, Mexico City, Asuntos Federales, Revoltosos Magonistas, Relaciones Exteriores, Mex.–E.U., Información e Algunos Clubs, C-12, Bls. Exp. 1, F 25, Mexico City, Sept. 17, 1906, Asuntos Federales, Revoltosos Magonistas, Jan.–Aug. 1908, C-7, Exp. 5, 19086, has extensive correspondence from and about

Morenci. *United States v. Rubio, Espinosa, et al.* was heard before U.S. Commissioner Albert M. Sames at Douglas on Sept. 17, 18, and 19, 1906, L.E. 1242, ARE. Elías to Secretario de Relaciones Exteriores, Tucson, Sept. 12, 1906; Guillermo Macalpin, Nogales, Sept. 17, 1906; Mariscal to Canciller, Consul, Nogales, Sept. 18, 1906, L.E. 124, ARE. "Mexican Case," *Miners' Magazine*, Sept. 10, 1908, 7. "Salcido Not Shot," *Morenci Leader*, Oct. 20, 1906. "Salcido Deported," *Copper Era*, Sept. 20, 1906. "Cananea Quiet," *Morenci Leader*, Sept. 20, 1906.

37. Aguilar Camín, *Frontera nomada*, 123. Rivera, *Revolución en Sonora*, 168. Guillermo Malalpina to Secretario de Relaciones Exteriores, Sept. 11, 1906; Telegram from L. Hobbs, Deputy Sheriff, Clifton: "Armed groups of ten leaving with rifles and revolvers to Nogales and Sonora," L.E. 1240, ARE. Translation of Babino Davalos, Oct. 29, 1906, no. 227, Embassy of Mexico, U.S. Department of Justice, RG 60 90755, no. 2, Justice 90755, Reel 1, Film 1413.

38. "Col. Greene Ridicules That Mexican 'Junta,' " *New York Times*, Sept. 9, 1906.

39. Morgan, *Domestic Intelligence Monitoring*, 18. Furlong, *Fifty Years*, 142–145. Elías, Phoenix, to Sheriff of Graham County, Solomonville, Sept. 19, 1908; J.L.B. Alexander, U.S. Attorney, to Elías; A. A. Anderson to Elías, Oct. 25, 1908; Elías to Secretario de Relaciones Exteriores, Tombstone, May 7, 1909, AMGR, vol. 40, AGN, L.E. 944 XXVIII, ARE. Asuntos Federales, Revoltosos Magonistas, Relaciones Exteriores, Manifesto de los Magonistas al Pueblo Americano, Arizona, Feb.–Mar. 1908, E. 7, no. 10, 19055, Mexico City, E.E. AMGR Gobernación, AGN. Antonio Lozano, Los Angeles, to Secretario de Relaciones Exteriores, Dec. 3, 1907, L.E. 1242, ARE. *Magon et al. v. United States*, 212 U.S. 589 (1909).

40. For the sense of the argument, see the *Miners' Magazine*, 1902–1907, and WFM, *Official Proceedings of the . . . Annual Convention of the Western Federation of Miners of America*, 1902–1907.

41. Marion W. Moor, WFM, *Official Proceedings*, June 9, 1905, 76, 252, 253–54; ibid., May 28–June 13, 1906, 148. Moor to Charles H. Moyer, *Official Proceedings*, May 28–June 13, 1906, 218. Marion W. Moor, "Stenographic Report," in WFM, *Official Proceedings*, May 23–June 7, 1907, 146–148, 252–254. *Morenci Leader*, June 19, 1907.

42. McCluskey, "Absentee Capitalists," 2–5.

43. "The Situation in Bisbee, Ariz.," *Miners' Magazine*, July 4, 1907, 4. "Strike Continues," *Miners' Magazine*, July 11, 1907, 3. "The Fight in Arizona," *Miners' Magazine*, July 25, 1907, 5, 7. D. Haberbossell to James Kirwan, Acting Secretary of WFM; "Conditions in Clifton, Metcalfe and Morenci Arizona," Sept. 23, 1907, in *Miners' Magazine*, Oct. 10, 1907, 14–15. "Unions Court Disaster," *Los Angeles Times*, July 28, 1907. "Strikers Fail to Affiliate," *Los Angeles Times*, July 31, 1907. "Strikers Many, Regrets More," *Los Angeles Times*, Aug. 19, 1907.

44. "Copper Mines Closed Down," *Los Angeles Times*, Nov. 3, 1907. "Cananea Runs Small Force," *Los Angeles Times*, Dec. 29, 1907.

45. Libero Vásquez, Comandante de Policía, Agua Prieta, to Secretario del Estado, Hermosillo, June 5, 1907, A.G. de Sonora, v. 43, vol. 2524, 1908, AMGR, AGN. Lomelí to Lic. D. Miguel Lira y Lira, Sept. 1, 1908, says Mexican authorities feared an uprising,

asks whether Pacheco would testify against the Ricardo Flores Magón junta, Villareal, and Sarabia. Lomelí to Antonio Maza, Douglas, Consul, Sept. 1, 1908, L.E. 821, ARE. Pacheco cooperated with the U.S. government in the trials against Ricardo Flores Magón and his cohorts. See "Another Labor Spy," *Miners' Magazine*, Feb. 6, 1908, 11.

46. A. A. Anderson to Elías, Feb. 19, 1908, ARE, 5-5-59. *Morenci Leader*, Feb. 9, 1907.

47. Thomas Smith, to Arturo M. Elías, Feb. 8, 1908, ARE, 5-5-59. "Dave Arzate Dep. Sheriff," *Copper Era*, Nov. 10, 1905.

48. Arturo M. Elías, Clifton, July 12, 1908 to Consul El Paso, L.E. 821, ARE, in Fabela, *Documentos históricos de la Revolución*, 70–72. Arturo M. Elías, Clifton, July 13, 1908. Elías to Lomelí, July 16, 1908, Elías to Consul Lomelí, El Paso, July 19, 1908 (Lomelí is listed as sender — probably an error), L.E. 821, ARE, in Fabela, *Documentos históricos de la Revolución*, 72–73, 96–97. Del Toro to Elías, Aug. 3, 1908, Clifton, L.E. 821, ARE.

49. Del Toro to Elías, Aug. 3, 1908, Clifton, L.E. 821, ARE. S. M. del Toro, Clifton, to Consul in Tucson, Aug. 26, 1908. AMGR, vol. 40, AGN, 939 XXII, ARE. Corral, May 20, 1909, to Governor of Sonora, no. 1948 (in 1908 file) AMGR, vol. 43, AGN; From A.G. de Gobierno del Estado de Sonora, vol. 2524, 1908, exp. Rebelión Sonora y Chihuahua; Ramón Corral to Secretario de Relaciones Exteriores, July 11, 1908, L.E. 936, no. 378, ARE. Elías to Lomelí, July 12, 1908, L.E. 937, ARE.

50. See 1910 census, Clifton, Graham County, Arizona Territory, Series T624, Roll 39, Page 39A, Enumeration District 41, Part 3, Line 7.

51. Romero to Ignacio Mariscal, Secretario de Relaciones Exteriores, Feb. 22 1909; Romero to Secretario de Relaciones Exteriores, Mar. 15, 1909. Carlos Palafox, Clifton, Nov. 23, 1909, to Secretario de Relaciones Exteriores, ARE, 5-5-59. Isidro Romero, Vice Consul, Solomonville, Clifton, to Secretario de Relaciones Exteriores, Sept. 12, 1906, L.E. 1241, ARE. Lomelí to Elías, Aug. 3, 1908, L.E. 821, ARE. Charles A. Boynton, U.S. Attorney, Waco, Sept. 9, 1909, RG 60 1–1413 DOJ 90755. "Carceles y Presidios. Informe de la Prision Formal de Salcido y Socios," Mexico City, Veracruz, 1908, AMGR Gobernación, AGN. "Asuntos Federales, Revoltosos Magonistas." Jan.–Aug. 1908, C-7, E.5, 19086, AGN.

52. Lloyd and Azoala, *Formación . . . del Partido Liberal Mexicano*, 78, 80–81. Araiza, *Ricardo Flores Magón*, 74–75. Luther T. Ellsworth, Ciudad Porfirio Díaz, to Secretary of State, Washington, D.C., Mar. 22, 1911, in Hanrahan, *Documents on Mexican Revolution*, 255–260.

53. "Kidnaping in Arizona," *Miners' Magazine*, July 18, 1907, 6–7. Charles A. Boynton, U.S. Attorney, Waco, June 28, 1909 to Attorney General, Washington, D.C., U.S. Department of Justice, RG 60 90755, no. 2, Justice 90755, Reel 1, Film 1413. Ethel Dolsen, "Mexican Revolutionists in the United States," *Miners' Magazine*, June 11, 1908, 6–10. There is extensive documentation on Gutiérrez de Lara, in Lázaro Gutiérrez de Lara Su Expediente Personal, L.E. 1883, ARE, and in AMGR Gobernación, AGN. Cited extensively in earlier drafts, RFAC, Urban Archives, CSUN.

54. Luther T, Ellsworth, San Antonio, to Secretary of State, Mar. 3, 1911, in Hanrahan, *Documents on Mexican Revolution*, 273. Albro, *Always Rebel*, 148. Dale Lloyd

and Azoala, *Formación . . . del Partido Liberal Mexicano*, 78. Phoenix Consul to Elías, Sept. 1909, AMGR, vol. 43, AGN, L.E. 948 XXXI, ARE. T. Furlong to E. Creel, Ministro de Secretario de Relaciones Exteriores, Mar. 2, 1911, L.E. 638, ARE.

55. A. V. Lomelí to Secretario de Relaciones Exteriores, El Paso, Aug. 22, 1908; J.L.B. Alexander, U.S. Attorney, Memo to Elías: Elías to Secretario de Relaciones Exteriores, Tucson, Sept. 15, 1908; J.L.B. Alexander to Elías, Sept. 11, 1908; Elías to Secretario de Relaciones Exteriores, Tucson, Sept. 17, 1908, AMGR, vol. 40, AGN, L.E. 941-XXIII, ARE. Caro to Governor Alberto Cubillas, Sept. 17, 1908; José González Carrillo to Elías, Morenci, Sept. 28, 1908; José G. Carrillo to Elías, Morenci, Sept. 30, 1908; Elías to Secretario de Relaciones Exteriores, Tucson, Oct. 5, 1908, Arturo M. Elías File, 1953, ARE, 2-17-13, vol. 1. File on Salvador Martínez del Toro, born Ciudad Guzmán, Jalisco, Apr. 14, 1879, Archivo General del Gobierno del Estado de Sonora, vol. 2524, 1908, L.E. 943 XXVI, ARE, AMGR, vol. 40, AGN. Luther T. Ellsworth, American Consular Service, Ciudad Porfirio Díaz, to Assistant Secretary of State, Feb. 12, 1910, RG 60 1-1413, U.S. Department of Justice, RG 60 90755, no. 2, Justice 90755, Reel 1, Film 1413.

56. Ricardo Flores Magón, as quoted in Albro, *Always Rebel*, 101. Antonio Maza, Douglas, to Lomelí, Sept. 4, 1908; Lomelí to Lic. D. Miguel Lira y Lira, Sept. 1, 1908; Lomelí to Antonio Maza, Sept. 1, 1908; Josefa G. Madrid to Sra Micaela Delguilo from Las Cruces, July 31, 1908, L.E. 821, ARE. *Magon et al. v. United States*, 212 U.S. 589 (1909). J. Turner, *Barbarous Mexico*, 239.

57. Agustín Farrara, District Judge of State of Sonora, Nogales, Oct. 15, 1908, AGS, vol. 2524 (1908), AMGR, vol. 40, AGN.

58. Almada, *Revolución en Chihuahua* 114–118, 179–180. Martínez Nuñez, *Historia de la Revolución*, 131. E. Turner, *Ricardo Flores Magón*, 185. J. Herbert Cole, special agent, El Paso, to Bureau of Investigation, Washington D.C., Jan. 5, 1911, 120-13; U.S. Marshal to Antonio V. Lomelí, Dec. 31, 1910, in Hanrahan, *Documents on Mexican Revolution*, 110.

59. Almada, *Revolución en Chihuahua*, 114–116. Martínez Nuñez, *Historia de la Revolución*, 159–170.

60. Luther T. Ellsworth, American Consular Service, District of Ciudad Porfirio Díaz, Mexico, Phoenix and Tucson to the Honorable Assistant Secretary of State, Aug. 1, 1909; O. F. Miller, to Ellsworth, Aug. 3, 1909, U.S. Department of Justice, RG 60 90755, no. 2, Justice 90755, Reel 1, Film 1413. Miguel López Torres, Vice–consul, Clifton, Feb. 8, 1909, to Secretario de Relaciones Exteriores, L.E. 942, ARE. Miguel López Torres, Clifton, Feb. 12, 1909, to Secretario de Relaciones Exteriores, L.E. 942, ARE. Kerig, "Luther T. Ellsworth," 7, 21, 24, 60, 70. Carman, *Customs and Madero Revolution*, 13. Smith, "Mexican Secret Service," 66–76. Raat, *Revoltosos*, 30–31, 191–192. Private detective Manuel Peña del Pino was in the pay of Miguel López Torres, Vice Consul of Clifton, Arizona. From 1909–1911, the FBI worked with the Treasury Department's Secret Service in the surveillance of the rebels.

61. U.S. House, *Alleged Persecution of Mexican Citizens*, 3, 5, 9, 14.

62. Mexican Consul, Phoenix, to Secretario de Relaciones Exteriores, Sept. 12,

1909, AMGR, vol. 43, AGN, ARE, L.E. 948 XXXI. *Revolución* 1, no. 29 (Los Angeles; Mar. 1, 1908). U.S. House, *Alleged Persecution of Mexican Citizens*, 4, 21, 60, 70.

63. Report by Charles Moyer, *Official Proceedings*, May 26–June 7, 1902, 140–46. "Reason and Fanaticism," *Miners Magazine*, July 25, 1907, 5. RAAT, *Revoltosos*, 44.

64. Marion W. Moor, "Report"; Marion W. Moor to Charles H. Moyer, Apr. 10, 1906, in WFM, *Official Proceedings of the 14th Annual Convention*, May 28–June 13, 1906, pp. 148, 218. Harrison, "Development of Arizona Labor," 18. *Copper Era*, Jan. 23, 1908.

65. H. W. Kane, "Arizona Labor Conditions," *Miners' Magazine*, Feb. 14, 1907, 8. WFM, *Strike for Liberty!* 120–122.

66. *Miners' Magazine*, July 25, 1907, 7.

67. Heyman, "Oral History," 194–195. Harner, "Copper Mining . . . in Sonora," 93, 102. "The Sixteenth Celebration," *Copper Era*, Sept. 20, 1906. "The Celebration at Morenci," *Copper Era*, Sept. 27, 1910.

68. D. Haberbosell, "Conditions in Clifton, Metcalf, and Morenci, Arizona, Sept. 23, 1907, Western Federation of Miners," *Miners' Magazine*, Oct. 10, 1907, 14–15. Patton, *History of Clifton*, 53. "Phelps-Dodge Co. Said to Be after Market Control," *Copper Era*, June 3, 1910.

69. J. Alvárez, Concepción Ríos, Nepomuceno Ríos, Joaquín Urrea, and others, to Ministro de Relaciones Exteriores, Aug. 4, 1910, L.E. 1327, ARE. Pedro E. Ortiz, Secretary of Club Anti-revolucionista Mexicano, to Enrique Creel, Ministro de Relaciones Exteriores, Clifton, Dec. 7, 1910; C. M. Foraker, U.S. Marshal, New Mexico, Dec. 31, 1910, Albuquerque, to Attorney General, Washington, D.C., U.S. Department of Justice, Diplomatic Branch (NNFD), NARS 90755-397 812.00/624. A. V. Lomelí to Secretario de Relaciones Exteriores, El Paso, Aug. 4, 1909, AMGR, vol. 43, AGN, L.E. 947 XXX, ARE. "Comunicado," *El Heraldo*, Aug. 13, 1910.

Chapter 8. The Mexican Revolution

1. "Blancos, Blancos," *Regeneración*, Nov. 19, 1910. "Impundidad para los Linchadores," *Regeneración*, Dec. 24, 1910. Translations from Spanish are mine unless otherwise noted.

2. "Ambassador Cautions against Violence; Police Are Active," *Los Angeles Times*, Nov. 12, 1910. *Graham Guardian*, Nov. 18, 1910. "Americans Protests against Insult," *Copper Era*, Nov. 18, 1910. Lister and Lister, *Chihuahua*, 212.

3. Ricardo Flores Magón, "La Barbarie en los Estados Unidos," *Regeneración*, Aug. 5, 1911.

4. Carrigan, "Lynching of Persons of Mexican Origins," 413–415. "La Víctima de los 'Civilizados,' " *Regeneración*, Aug. 26, 1911. Ricardo Flores Magón, "A Salvar a un Inocente," *Regeneración*, Sept. 9, 1911. Ricardo Flores Magón, "Quemaron Vivo a un Hombre," *Regeneración*, Dec. 9, 1911.

5. Romo, *Ringside Seat to Revolution*, 223–227. " 'Viva Villa' Shouted in Riots at Juárez," *Los Angeles Times*, Jan. 29, 1917. The women were indignant about the deaths of several Mexican prisoners in March, who, after being bathed in a similar solution, caught fire and burned to death. Stories circulated about Euro-American soldiers pho-

tographing them while bathing. In shouting "¡Viva Villa!" they were expressing the symbol of the ultimate opposition to the United States and the Carranza forces that helped put down the rebellion. Pershing's expeditionary forces were still in Chihuahua. "Mexicans Given Baths," *Los Angeles Times*, Jan. 31, 1917. The practice was continued until a "compromise" was reached, whereby Mexicans were given a chemical bath in Juárez, where they received a certificate.

6. Simmons, "Attitudes toward United States," 34–36.

7. W. Estrada, "Los Angeles' Old Plaza," 110–111. "Plea Urges Plaza Peace," *Los Angeles Times*, May 26, 1935. Escobar, *Race, Police*, 42–49.

8. Kent and Huntz, "Spanish-Language Newspapers in United States," 449–451. For a comparison with Puerto Ricans, see Inglesias, *Memoirs of Bernardo Vega*, 84–85.

9. Luther Ellsworth, American Consul, San Antonio, to Secretary of State, Mar. 4, 1911, in Hanrahan, *Documents on Mexican Revolution*, 203–208. Luther T. Ellsworth, Eagle Pass, Texas, Dec. 23, 1910, to Secretary of State, in Hanrahan, *Documents on Mexican Revolution*, 100. Ellsworth to Secretary of State, Feb. 18, 1911, in Hanrahan, *Documents on Mexican Revolution*, 165. Hall and Coerver, *Revolution on Border*, 16–27. "Sonora Mines Again Active" *Copper Era*, Jan. 13, 1910. Pace, "Mexican Refugees in Arizona," 5, 8. The mining camps were a source of arms for many refugees.

10. Aboites Aguilar, *Breve historia de Chihuahua*, 121.

11. Meyer, *Pascual Orozco*, 9, 19. Wasserman, *Capitalists, Caciques, and Revolution*, 144.

12. Almada, *Revolución en Chihuahua*, 1:257–260. E. Turner, *Ricardo Flores Magón*, 217, 219, 222. Raat, *Revoltosos*, 283. Ellsworth, San Antonio, to Secretary of State, Mar. 2, 1911, 198–202 U.S. Department of Justice, RG 60 1413, no. 2, Justice 90755, Reel 1, Film 1413. E. Turner, *Revolution in Baja California*, 20–21. *Regeneración* blared out: "Madero Es un Traidor para la Causa de la Libertad" (Madero Is a Traitor to the Cause of Liberty). Beezley, *Insurgent Governor*, 34. The 1910 revolutionaries found recruits among those who took part in the 1906 and 1908 invasions and among workers in the mining camps.

13. E. Turner, *Revolution in Baja California*, 1–3, 6, 13, 23–24, 44–48, 50–51, 55–61. The *Los Angeles Times* carried extensive coverage. Cockcroft, *Precursors of Mexican Revolution*, 44–48, 50–51, 55–61. Blaisdell, "Chandler and Mexican Border Intrigue," 385. Blaisdell, "Was It Revolution?" 148–149.

14. Almada, *Revolución en Chihuahua*, 2:15, 21–22. Almada, *Revolución en Chihuahua*, 1:244–246, 278, 285–287, 291. Meyer, *Pascual Orozco*, 27, 38–40, 47, 49, 53–66, 94, 114. Aguilar Camín and Mayer, *In Shadow of Mexican Revolution*, 29–30. R. Estrada, "Border Revolution," 96, 102. Giese, "Sonoran Triumvirate," 459–460. Although Terrazas, along with other cattle barons, reportedly gave money to Orozco, many *magonistas* supported Terrazas because they shared his hatred for Madero. The Guerrero group also had a long history of taking money from Terrazas to lead revolts against Díaz, dating back to the 1880s and 1890s.

15. M. Anderson, *Villa's Revolution by Headlines*, 6–10. First converting Villa into a media star, the media then vilified him.

16. Hall and Coerver, *Revolution on Border*, 55.

17. Guzmán, *Memoirs of Pancho Villa*, 324–325, 371–372. Katz, *Life and Times of Villa*, 373. "Gen. Huerta Resigns," *Los Angeles Times*, July 16, 1914. M. Anderson, *Villa's Revolution by Headlines*, 49–52, 127. Chronology of events from April to November 1914 is based on *Los Angeles Times* and *New York Times* articles during this time period.

18. Katz, *Life and Times of Villa*, 551–553. Coerver and Hall, *Texas and Mexican Revolution*, 96–97. "Wave of Indignation Engulfs Lawmakers," *Los Angeles Times*, Jan. 13, 1916. "Tropas Americans Tienen Orden de Capturar a Pancho Villa," *El Tucsonense*, Mar. 11, 1916.

19. Yockelson, "Mexican Punitive Expedition," pt. 2.

20. "210,000 Men for Border Patrol," *Graham Guardian*, July 14, 1916. Eisenhower, *Intervention!* 103, 105, 231. Hall and Coerver, *Revolution on Border*, 57–77. Marvin, "Quick and Dead on Border," 295–296.

21. "¡Paciencia, Mexicanos!," *El Tucsonense*, May 6, 1916. "La Persecución de F. Villa," *El Tucsonense*, Apr. 8, 1916. "Tropas Americans Tienen Orden de Capturar a Pancho Villa," *El Tucsonense*, Mar. 11, 1916. "A Los Mexicanos de Tucson," *El Tucsonense*, June 24, 1916. Radding Murieta and Gracida Romo, *Sonora*, 135–140. The Liga Protectora was reported to have some 10,000 members in 1915.

22. Yockelson, "Mexican Punitive Expedition," pt. 2. Secretary of American Commission, "American and Mexican Joint Commission Report."

23. Bloch, "Facts about Mexican Immigration," 58. Hernández Alvarez, "Demographic Profile of Mexican Immigration," 477.

24. Rivera, in *Revolución en Sonora*, 126–127, 169, says that de la Huerta was a member of the PLM. Aguilar Camín, *Frontera nomada*, 105–106. J. Gutiérrez, *Relatos de mi pueblo*, 35–37. Campodónico's father was Italian and his mother from Sonora. Karp, *Cultura popular*, 58.

25. Rivera, *Revolución en Sonora*, 171. Aguilar Camín, *Frontera nomada*, 118–119, 133–134. Villa, *Historia de Sonora*, 411, 414, 421. Giese, "Sonoran Triumvirate," 199–200. M. J. Gonzales, "Copper Companies . . . and Mexican Revolution," 505. Radding Murieta and Gracida Romo, *Sonora*, 138. Chronology of events is based on accounts in the *Los Angeles Times*, which weekly carried several articles on the divisions within Sonora. See previous drafts in RFAC, Urband Archives, CSUN. According to Moore, "Adolfo de la Huerta," 4, de la Huerta was a quarter Yaqui. Moore states that de la Huerta left the PLM in 1907 (p. 6) and that he was a supporter of General Bernardo Reyes in 1907–08 and an early supporter of Maytorena (p. 73).

26. M. J. Gonzales, "Copper Companies . . . and Mexican Revolution," 510. George Young, to H. B. Paull, Duluth, Minnesota, Dec. 14, 1911, 4C Records, MS 1032, Box 1, Folder 6, AHS. In the main text, I shorten "Cananea Consolidated Copper Company" to "Cananea Consolidated," rather than to the more common, but less accessible "CCCC" or "4C." "Mexico Regains Stability," *Mining and Scientific Press* 104, no. 1 (Jan. 6, 1912): 5. Ulloa, *Revolución intervenida*, 81. Giese, "Sonoran Triumvirate," 75, 86. There were few soldiers on the border in 1910. This changed as U.S.

mobilizations and surveillance of the *revoltosos* increased. See J. Herbert Cole, Special Agent, El Paso, to Bureau of Investigation, Washington D.C., Jan. 5, 1911; Ellsworth to Secretary of State, Feb. 18, 1911; Luther Ellsworth, American Consul, San Antonio, to Secretary of State, Mar. 4, 1911, in Hanrahan, *Documents on Mexican Revolution*, 120–13, 165, 203–208, resp.

27. M. J. Gonzales, "Copper Companies . . . and Mexican Revolution," 507, 509, 510. "Federals Retake El Tigre Mines," *New York Times*, Sept. 17, 1912. Giese, "Sonoran Triumvirate," 116, 125–126. "Chihuahua," *Mining and Scientific Press* 104, no. 20 (May 18, 1912): 710.

28. George Young to D. Cirilo Ramirez, Hermosillo, Dec. 12 and 13, 1912, 4C Records, MS 1032, Box 1 folder 6. AHS.

29. Wasserman, "Enrique C. Creel," 659. Intimate advisers of Díaz, the *científicos* most prominently included José Yves Limantour. Creel, also a *científico*, returned to Mexico in the early 1920s and was an important financial adviser to Obregón. Geise, "Sonoran Triumvirate," 104.

30. Rivera, *Revolución en Sonora*, 119–120, 343. "New Republic Predicted in North Mexico," *Copper Era*, Apr. 4, 1913. "Unfortunate Cananea Incident," *Copper Era*, May 2, 1913. For multiple articles taken from the *Los Angeles Times*, Feb. 28 through Mar. 10, 1913, see RFAC, Urban Archives, CSUN. *Engineering and Mining Journal* 95, no. 19 (May 10, 1913): 976.

31. "Filibusters from Los Angeles Depart for the Mexican Border," *Los Angeles Times*, Mar. 12, 1913. Moore, "Adolfo de la Huerta," 101–106.

32. Aguilar Camín, *Frontera nomada*, 324–329. M. J. Gonzales, "Copper Companies . . . and Mexican Revolution," 512. Ulloa, *Revolución intervenida*, 91. Douglas Hardware and Phelps Dodge profiteered in the sale of arms and munitions. Byrkit, *Forging Copper Collar*, 54–55. In Oct. 1913, two Phelps Dodge officials were indicted for illegally trafficking in arms. William Brophy, general manager of the Phelps Dodge Mercantile Company, and F. E. Cole, manager of the company's hardware division, reportedly sold 90,000 rounds of ammunition to Carranza's agent, who paid in U.S. paper currency and gold. Two Mexicans took the blame. Brophy and Cole evaded testifying. Geise, "Sonoran Triumvirate," 185. The Douglas Hardware Store sold 400,000 rounds of ammunition in six months.

33. Emilio Kosterlitzky (1853–1928) was a Russian-born soldier of fortune, who eventually became a spy for the United States. Díaz appointed him commander of a mounted rural constabulary called the Gendarmería Fiscal, which operated in northeastern Sonora. Loosely referred to as "Rurales," Kosterlitsky's local troopers were confused with Díaz's national rural security units. Although no Cossack, Kosterlitzky was referred to as one by admirers and detractors alike.

34. There were daily reports in the *Los Angeles Times* and *New York Times* on the civil war. Only a few are cited. "Bullets Rain in Towns on Arizona Side," *Los Angeles Times*, Mar. 14, 1913. "Maytorena Anti-Alien Edict May Force Action by United States," *Los Angeles Times*, Sept. 1, 1913. Rivera, *Revolución en Sonora*, 343. Ulloa, *Revolución intervenida*, 79, 80. Sonora was extremely important to U.S. interests be-

cause of the large amount of U.S. capital there. Treasurer to J. S. Douglas, June 27, 1913, 4C Records, MS 1032, Box 1, Folder 6, AHS, informed Douglas that someone was listening in to his telephone conversations.

35. George Young to J. S. Douglas, General Manager, 4C, Douglas, Aug. 21, 1913, 4C Records, MS 1032, Box 1, Folder 6, AHS.

36. "Sonora Peons Face Famine," *Los Angeles Times*, Apr. 1, 1914. "Cananea Camps Much Agitated," *Los Angeles Times*, Mar. 15, 1914. "Mexican Miners Go on Strike at La Cananea," *Copper Era*, Apr. 17, 1914. M. J. Gonzales, "Copper Companies . . . and Mexican Revolution," 517. "Sonora," *Engineering and Mining Journal* 91, no. 17 (Apr. 25, 1914): 884, reported that a number of miners who said they were sympathizers of Huerta were deported. Because, however, they also said they had stayed out on strike until their leaders were brought back, they were most likely not *huertistas* but more militant miners, in favor of the Revolution.

37. "Cananea Mines Starting Anew," *Los Angeles Times*, May 10, 1914. "The Rioting at Cananea," *Los Angeles Times*, May 3, 1914. "Americans Will Reopen Sonora Mining Plants," *Los Angeles Times*, May 1, 1914. M. J. Gonzales, "Copper Companies . . . and Mexican Revolution," 515.

38. "Reporte oficial del Prefecto Político de Arizpe," as reproduced in Sariego Rodríguez, *Enclaves y minerales*, 143–148; Platt quotation on p. 145. See *Los Angeles Times* articles, Mar. 15, 1914 to July 3, 1914. "Mexican Miners Go on Strike at La Cananea," *Copper Era*, Apr. 17 and July 10, 1914. "Cananea Is Closed from End to End," *Copper Era*, July 17, 1914. Geise, "Sonoran Triumvirate," 209.

39. "Villa Saves Maytorena," *New York Times*, June 14, 1914. "Gov. Maytorena Besieged," *New York Times*, June 15, 1914. "Villa Plotting in Sonora," *New York Times*, June 24, 1914. Hall and Coerver, *Revolution on Border*, 31–33. Chronology of *villistas* fighting in Sonora is based on *Los Angeles Times* articles, Aug. 16 to Sept. 11, 1914.

40. General Superintendent (George Kingdon) to F. D. Hamilton, Cananea, Nov. 10, 1914; General Superintendent to F. D. Hamilton, Cananea, Nov. 17, 1914. General Superintendent, Douglas, Arizona, to F. W. Whitaker, Canada, Nov. 28, 1914. General Superintendent to L. D. Ricketts, Butte, Montana, Dec. 8, 1914. General Superintendent to L. D. Ricketts, President, New York City, Dec. 11, 1914. General Superintendent to L. D. Ricketts, President, Dec. 26, 1914. General Superintendent to L. D. Ricketts, President, Dec. 28, 1914, 4C Records, MS 1032, Box 2, Folder 22, AHS.

41. Chronology of the rupture between Villa and the constitutionalists and of the fight in and around Naco is based on *Los Angeles Times* articles, October 1914 to January 1915. "Cattle Baron Takes Bull by the Horns," *Los Angeles Times*, Nov. 8, 1914.

42. "Maytorena Kicked Out," *Los Angeles Times*, Jan. 4, 1915. "Hundred Dead in Mexican Flood," *Los Angeles Times*, Jan. 16, 1915. Hall and Coerver, *Revolution on Border*, 120. M. J. Gonzales, "Copper Companies . . . and Mexican Revolution," 519. D. J. Haff to Juan N. Amador, El Paso, Apr. 23, 1915, 4C Records, MS 1032, Box 2, Folder 33, AHS. In March, the copper companies were upset because Carranza raised tax rates on minerals. They claimed it was unconstitutional and that they employed 25,000 workers in northeastern Sonora.

43. Maytorena quotation from "Gen. Obregon for President," *Los Angeles Times*, Oct. 28, 1915. "American Machine Guns Trained into Mexico," *Los Angeles Times*, Oct. 31, 1915. Many of the headlines were provocative. Katz, *Life and Times of Villa*, 515, 524–525.

44. George Young, Warren, Arizona, to D. J. Haff, Kansas City, Nov. 16, 1915, 4C Records, MS 1032, Box 2, Folder 33, AHS. George Young, Warren, Arizona, to D. J. Haff, Kansas City, Night Letter, Nov. 16, 1915. 4C Records, MS 1032, Box 2, Folder 33, AHS.

45. *Engineering and Mining Journal* 100, no. 25 (Dec. 18, 1915): 1028. During October, 134 cars (4,689 tons) of ore valued at $1.2 million, consisting of $722,000 worth of copper, $293,000 worth of silver, and $186,000 worth of gold passed through Agua Prieta. "Villa Soldiers Executed," *New York Times*, Dec. 13, 1915. "Villa Forces Agree to Peace," *New York Times*, Dec. 21, 1915.

46. "Will Confiscate Sonora Property," *Los Angeles Times*, Jan. 30, 1916. "Stealing Mines of Americans," *Los Angeles Times*, Jan. 25, 1916. Villa, *Historia de Sonora*, 438.

47. "Bad Money on the Border," *Los Angeles Times*, Mar. 29, 1915. Giese, "Sonoran Triumvirate," 340, 391, 408, 420–422. "Sonora Chief Recalcitrant," *Los Angeles Times*, Sept. 6, 1916. M. J. Gonzales, "Copper Companies . . . and Mexican Revolution," 518–519.

48. Cleland, *History of Phelps Dodge*, 162. Hall and Coerver, *Revolution on Border*, 33–36, 119. "Peace Restores Mine Activities," *Los Angeles Times*, Jan. 9, 1916. "Counterfeiters Annoy Carranza," *Los Angeles Times*, Jan. 1, 1914. "Sonora Chief Recalcitrant," *Los Angeles Times*, Sept. 6, 1916. "Bad Money on the Border," *Los Angeles Times*, Mar. 29, 1915. "Widney Released on Cash Bond," *Los Angeles Times*, Jan. 8, 1915. "Mexicans Dissatisfied with Carranza Currency," *Los Angeles Times*, Feb. 9, 1916. "Induces Calles to Hold Office," *Los Angeles Times*, Feb. 11, 1916. Consul Danciger, Kansas City, to Weeks, Mexico City, Telegram, May 18, 1916, 4C Records, MS 1032, Box 2, Folder 34, AHS. Calles had discovered that foreigners owned property close to the border and that there was wholesale smuggling of cattle there. His decision to switch to hard currency was influenced by the unions, which demanded payment in gold. Weeks, Mexico City, to Consul Danciger, Kansas City, Cablegram, May 21, 1916, 4C Records, MS 1032, Box 2, Folder 34, AHS. C. S., Assistant Secretary, to George Young, Los Angeles, Aug. 8, 1916, 4C Records, MS 1032, Box 1, Folder 7, AHS.

49. Moore, "Adolfo de la Huerta," 129–132, 137–138. M. J. Gonzales, "Copper Companies . . . and Mexican Revolution," 503, 525–526. Moore, "Ejercito de gobierno," 231.

50. George Young, Secretary, Warren, Arizona, to D. J. Haff, Kansas City, July 11, 1916, 4C Records, MS32, Box 2, Folder 34, AHS. The quoted was also in "May Operations be Resumed? The Effect of the Mexican Revolution on American Mining Interest," Memorandum Submitted on Behalf of Forty-five Companies to the American Commission, Part 1, Sept. 1916, p. 12, 4C Records, MS 1032, Box 5, Folder 90, AHS. Part 2 of the report, p. 6., lists the mines in Sonora as the Moctezuma, the Sahuaripa, the Creston (east of Torres), La Dura (on the Río Yaqui) and the Arizpe.

51. "Six Catholic Priests Deported from Mexico," *Los Angeles Times*, Mar. 23, 1916. During June and July, there were frequent rumors that the United States would invaded Sonora. Sonoran women, who were no strangers to firearms, formed resistance groups. "Mexican Women Ready to Fight," *Los Angeles Times*, June 15, 1916.

52. John J. Pershing, Major General, Fort Sam Houston, Report no. 214, Apr. 28, 1917, Records of the Department of State Relating to Internal Affairs of Mexico, 1910–1929, NARS, 274, 60.

53. "Resultado de las Elecciones en Sonora," *El Tucsonense*, May 16, 1917. There was considerable support for Obregon's broter, who actually won in Nogales and Cananea. Calles, however, handily won the election overall. "La Compañia Politica y la Revolución en Sonora," *El Tucsonense*, Feb. 28, 1917.

54. Giese, "Sonoran Triumvirate," 424, 425–427, 427–433. William D. King, Douglas, to George Young, Secretary, Cananea, May 14, 1917, 4C Records, MS 1032, Box 2, Folder 34, AHS. In fairness to Calles, he did not roll over in the El Tigre Mine dispute. He told company officials that Cananea workers should be paid on the same scale as Ray, Clifton, and other Arizona camps. He was told that this not possible — the efficiency was not the same (something that Walter Douglas told Morenci Mexicans when they demanded parity with white miners). Calles said he knew that the Sonora mines were profitable; he insisted that workers' demands for decent housing were just and that the companies should care for the sick or disabled workers.

55. "Sonora Reform by Gen. Calles," *Los Angeles Times*, July 12, 1917. "Calles of Sonora to See Carranza," *Los Angeles Times*, July 17, 1917. "Calles to See Copper Magnates," *Los Angeles Times*, Aug. 5, 1917. Hall and Coerver, *Revolution on Border*, 39. Calles became angry with the copper companies for their brutal crackdown on strikers in Arizona in July 1917. Many of the Bisbee deportees returned to Sonora. According to Hall and Coerver, this strengthened Calles's resolve to reconstruct the Sonora economy and Mexico provide jobs for Mexicans.

56. J. Parker, Brigadier General, Fort Sam Houston, Report no. 223, June 30, 1917, Records of the Department of State Relating to Internal Affairs of Mexico, 1910–1929, NARS, 274, 61.

57. J. Parker, Brigadier General, Fort Sam Houston, Report no. 222, June 23, 1917, Records of the Department of State Relating to Internal Affairs of Mexico, 1910–1929, National Archives and Records Service, 274, 61. "Cananea Suspende Operaciones," *El Tucsonense*, June 23, 1917.

58. E. M. Lawton, Consul, Nogales, Mexico, to Secretary of State, "Leave of Absence Given to Governor Calles in Order to Assume Command of Military Zone," Aug. 14, 1917, Records of the Department of State Relating to Internal Affairs of Mexico, 1910–1929, NARS, 274, 61.

59. J. Parker, Brigadier General, Report no. 230, Aug. 18, 1917, Records of the Department of State Relating to Internal Affairs of Mexico, 1910–1929, NARS, 274, 61.

60. J. Parker, Brigadier General, Report no. 229, Aug. 11, 1917, Records of the Department of State Relating to Internal Affairs of Mexico, 1910–1929, NARS, 274, 61.

61. E. M. Lawton, Consul, to Secretary of State, "Periodical Report on Political and

General Conditions in Sonora," Nogales, Mexico, Sept. 12, 1917. Records of the Department of State Relating to Internal Affairs of Mexico, 1910–1929, NARS, 274, 61.

62. Quotation from Malvern-Hill-Barum, Colonel, General Staff, Fort Sam Houston, Report no. 240, "Internal Affairs of Mexico," Oct. 27, 1917. John W. Ruckman, Major General, Fort Sam Houston, Reports no. 237 and no. 239, Oct. 6 and 20, 1917, Records of the Department of State Relating to Internal Affairs of Mexico, 1910–1929, NARS, 274, 61.

63. American Vice Consul, Piedras Negras, Coahuila, to Secretary of State, "Conditions in the Torreón District and Vicinity, Aug. 1917." Malvern-Hill-Barum, Colonel, General Staff, Fort Sam Houston, Report no. 240, "Internal Affairs of Mexico," Oct. 27, 1917, Records of the Department of State Relating to Internal Affairs of Mexico, 1910–1929, NARS, 274, 61.

64. "Las Minas," *El Tucsonense*, Feb. 6, 1918. "De Cananea, Sonora," *El Tucsonense*, Apr. 5, 1919.

65. "Lamentos en Sonora," *El Tucsonense*, Nov. 14, 1917. American Vice Consul, Piedras Negras, Coahuila, to Secretary of State, "Conditions in the Torreón District and Vicinity," Aug. 1917, Records of the Department of State Relating to Internal Affairs of Mexico, 1910–1929, NARS, 274, 61. Hall and Coerver, *Revolution on Border*, 5, 40. Giese, "Sonoran Triumvirate," 414.

66. "Los Trabajos de Unificación," *El Tucsonense*, Jan. 11, 1919. "Los Seis Puntos de Alvaro Obregon," *El Tucsonense*, June 18, 1919. "La Capital de Sonora Cambia a Nogales," *El Tucsonense*, July 1, 1919. "Los Trabajadores Salen del Mineral de Cananea," *El Tucsonense*, Oct. 2, 1919. "El Gobierno Mexicano Vigila la Frontera," *El Tucsonense*, Dec. 11, 1919.

67. M. J. Gonzales, "Copper Companies . . . and Mexican Revolution," 531.

68. Almada, *Diccionario . . . sonorenses*, 230, 337–338. I. Muñoz, *Verdad y mito de la Revolución*, 55–57. Thanks to Ignacio Almada Bay for his advice on additional sources. E. Turner, *Ricardo Flores Magón*, 361. De Lara had represented the miners of Jerome before he went to Morenci to help in that strike. He went to Sonora, crossed the border to sell copies of his book. General Arnulfo Gómez, according to Ethel Turner, followed the orders of Calles and executed de Lara on Feb. 2, 1918. Aguilar Camín, *Frontera nomada*, 439. De Lara was rumored to have been close to Villa and to have purchased arms for him. A. M. Villareal to C. Aguilar, Secretario de Relaciones Exteriores, May 19, 1918, L.E. 803, ARE. "Say de Lara Put to Death by Enemies," *Los Angeles Times*, Feb. 17, 1918. Villarreal to Gompers, Jan. 12, 1924, in Snow, "Samuel Gompers," 191. "Se Confirma un Fusilamento," *El Tucsonense*, Feb. 19, 1918. "Sr. Lázaro Gutiérrez de Lara Luchador Socialista Fusilado en Saric," *El Tucsonense*, Jan. 26, 1918.

69. Kluger, *Clifton-Morenci Strike*, 23.

70. Calderón, *Guerra del Yaqui*, 15.

71. Albert R. Morawitz, Vice Consul, Nogales, Mexico, to David J. Hill, Aug. 4, 1899; Fred Becksmith, Arispe, Sonora, to F. W. Roberts, U.S. Consul, Nogales, Apr. 1, 1895, Despatches from United States Consuls in Nogales, 1889–1906, Micro Copy 283, Roll 2, NARA, 1964.

72. The *New York Times* and *Los Angeles Times* reported that Yaquis were on the "warpath." They wrote about the landing of Marines to protect U.S. property. "Admiral Howard Ordered to Land If Yaquis Again Threaten American Colonists," *New York Times*, June 17, 1915. "Marine Forces Sail for Mexico," *New York Times*, June 18, 1915. "Sonora Governor Says His Troops Would Oppose Americans," *New York Times*, June 20, 1915. "Admiral Howard Denies Reports That He Has Landed Marines," *New York Times*, June 29, 1915.

73. Chronology of events is based on following articles: "Charge Yaquis with Torturing;" *Los Angeles Times*, Apr. 10, 1913; "Pimas Join the Yaquis" and "Yaqui Danger Overshadowed," *Los Angeles Times*, Sept. 4, 1913; "Would Make Beef Cheap by Annexing Sonora," *Los Angeles Times*, Sept. 24, 1913; "Raid American Property," *New York Times*, July 10, 1916. Hall and Coerver, *Revolution on Border*, 33, 40–41, 109, 115. Calderón, *Guerra del Yaqui*, 20–21. Rivera, *Revolución en Sonora*, 24. Evans, "Yaquis vs. Yanquis." Dabdoub, *Historia del valle del yaqui*, 3, 386. For a good synthesis of early Sonoran history, see Aguilar Camín, *Frontera nomada*, 46–55, 48.

74. Quoted in Evans, "Yaquis vs. Yanquis." Banister, "Río Yaqui Delta," 397. Richardson Construction, "Compañia . . . in Yaqui Valley," 11. Aguilar Camín, *Frontera nomada*, 56–59.

75. Hewitt de Alcantara, *Modernización de agricultura mexicana*, 131. Dabdoub, *Historia del valle del yaqui*, 293. Balbas, *Recuerdos del yaqui*, 37. "Settlers Flock to Mexico Yaqui Valley Lands," *Los Angeles Times*, Nov. 8, 1908.

76. Giese, "Sonoran Triumvirate," 486, 489. Rivera, *Revolución en Sonora*, 511–523. General B. J. Viljoen, "Tribe at War for a Century," *Los Angeles Times*, Feb. 13, 1916.

77. Conferencia entre el Sr. Adolfo de la Huerta y el Gerente Gral. De la Compañia de la 4C, Cananea, Sonora, Mar. 18, 1919, 4C Records, MS 1032, Oversized Box, AHS. George Young to J. W. Allen, Treasurer, Greene Cananea Copper Company, New York, May 23, 1919, 4C Records, MS 1032, Box 1, Folder 8, AHS.

78. See *Los Angeles Times*, Mar. 31 to July 12, 1920. Brush, "De La Huerta Rebellion," 39–41, 73–74. Snow, "Samuel Gompers," 184–195. Giese, "Sonoran Triumvirate," 438–439, 445, 567. Trujillo, *De la Huerta*, 4–5, 39–41, 159–160, 190–194. Raat, *Revoltosos*, 274. Treviño, "Prensa y Patria," 457. Lerner, "Exiliados de la Revolución mexicana." Lerner Sigal, "Exiliados mexicanos en Estados Unidos," 21–25. "Mexicans in Celebration," *Los Angeles Times*, Sept. 16, 1926. Many of the exile leaders participated in this gigantic celebration. "Many Exiles May Go Home," *Los Angeles Times*, July 2, 1935.

Chapter 9. To the Other Side of La Linea

1. B.W.J. Lauck, "Labor Conditions in Arizona Smelters," *Mining and Scientific Press* 104, no. 5 (Feb. 3, 1912): 212.

2. U.S. Census, "1910 World Immigration." The attitudes and biases of census compilers can be often deduced from their notes and esp. from their alterations of notes. The 1910 census listed Norberto Subia as "Norberto Supia."

3. D. Martin, "Douglas Dynasty." Mailsey, "Douglas, Arizona," 3–10. Hall and Coerver, *Revolution on Border*, 135. Pendleton, "Labor in Arizona Irrigated Agriculture," 57–58. The *Graham Guardian* ran frequent articles on agricultural production. See RFAC, Urban Archives, CSUN. Crawford, "Goodhue, Douglas, and Tyrone," 25. Trained at Columbia University's School of Mines, Walter Douglas took over from his father in 1916. By 1900, Phelps Dodge dominated the copper production in the Southwest; by 1909, Arizona led the world in copper production. McWilliams, *Factories in Field*.

4. José Galván Amaro interviews, June 2 and 6, 1977, pp. 5, 8, 14, 22–23, 28–29.

5. W. S. Schengler, Brigadier General, Fort Huachuca, to Adjutant General of Army, Washington, D.C., Mar. 5, 1911, in Hanrahan, *Documents on Mexican Revolution*, 212–218.

6. Liga Protectora de Refugiados Políticos, El Paso, Dec. 19, 1912, ARE. "Revolutionary Information," El Paso, Texas, Jan. 3, 1913. L.E. 741, p. 3, ARE.

7. "Americans Are Leaving Mexico" and "Mexico Needs Spanking," *Graham Guardian*, Apr. 26, 1912.

8. W. S. Schengler, Brigadier General, Fort Huachuca, to Adjutant General of Army, Washington, D.C., Mar. 5, 1911, in Hanrahan, *Documents on Mexican Revolution*, 212–218. Unsigned letter to Madero, Hermosillo, Sonora. Oct. 5, 1911, Archivo de José María Maytorena, Patronato de la Historia de Sonora, AMGR, vol. 44, AGN.

9. Miguel Aguilar to Secretario de Relaciones Exteriores, Feb. 19, 1911, L.E. 639, ARE. V. Salado Alvárez, Mar. 14, 1911, Distrito Federal, L.E. 640, ARE.

10. *Copper Era*, Sept. 1, 1911, pt. 1, ARE, 4-8-11. S. M. del Toro to Secretario de Relaciones Exteriores, Apr. 21, 1912, ARE, 4-8-11. Siriani to Relaciones Exteriores, May 31, 1912, pt. 1, ARE, 4-8-22. S. M. del Toro, Clifton, to Secretario de Relaciones Exteriores, June 10, 1912, ARE, 39-9-48.

11. *Miners' Magazine*, Aug. 17, 1911, 1. *Miners' Magazine*, Apr. 17, 1913, 1. Abraham Salcido to Abraham González, Nogales, July 2, 1911. Corespondencia Particular del ex-Gobernador A. G. Gómez Palacio, Archivo del Supremo Tribunal de Justicia de Chihuahua, AMGR, vol. 44, AGN. I searched for but could not find further traces of Salcido.

12. *Miners' Magazine*, July 9, 1914, 7. *Miners' Magazine*, Aug. 13, 1914, 15. *Miners' Magazine*, Mar. 19, 1914, 2.

13. For an excellent, clear article on the revolutionary factions, see "What Is the I.W.W.?" *Miners' Magazine*, May 2, 1912, 12. Hildebrand and Mangum, *Capital and Labor*, 126–127, 128–129. Mellinger, " 'Men Have Become Organizers,' " 325.

14. Ben Goggia, "Situation at Jerome, Arizona, April 18, 1911," *Miners' Magazine*, Apr. 27, 1911, 9. Letter to Charles W. Clark, General Manager of United Verde Copper Mine, Jerome, Arizona, May 26, 1911, *Miners' Magazine*, June 22, 1911, 6. *Miners' Magazine*, Aug. 13, 1914, 15. *Miners' Magazine*, Dec. 28, 1911, 11.

15. Mellinger, *Race and Labor*, 124.

16. The charge that they lacked class consciousness was a sore point among Mexican activists. *Regeneración* was replete with articles expressing the theme of class consciousness. *Regeneración*, Feb. 11, 1911. *Regeneración*, June 29, 1912.

17. Luther T. Ellsworth, "Informe al Secretario de Estado, Fechado el 12 de Octubre de 1910 en Ciudad Porfirio Díaz, México," in Hanrahan, *Documents on Mexican Revolution*. Also quoted in Lomas, "Transborder Discourse," 52.

18. Mellinger, *Race and Labor*, 131–132, 163. *Regeneración*, Oct. 22, 1912. "La Huelga General," *Regeneración*, July 19, 1913. The only "Fernando Velarde" listed in the 1910 census as living in Phoenix was Fernando Velarde, born in California, whose parents were originally from New Mexico. He was married and had five children. A blacksmith by trade, he had his own shop. Phoenix, Maricopa County, Arizona, Series T624, Roll 40, Page 65B, Enumeration District 58, Part 2, Line 20. World War I Draft Registration Cards, 1917–1918. Fernando Velarde, born Apr. 4, 1873, white, living in Los Angeles. Velarde probably had family in Los Angeles. His wife, Louise, was born in California; their children, in Arizona. In 1920, Fernando and his family lived in Redondo Beach near Los Angeles, where he lived in a largely white neighborhood. See 1920 census, Redondo, Los Angeles, Series T625, Roll 118, Page 5A, Enumeration District 536, Image 11.

19. "Police Have Hot Times," *Los Angeles Times*, Apr. 15, 1912. "Police Kill Rioter in Battle with Mob," *Los Angeles Times*, Aug. 12, 1912. "Mexicans Threaten Life of Patrolman," *Los Angeles Times*, Aug. 13, 1912. "Clubs, Guns on Foaming Riot," *Los Angeles Times*, Jan. 6, 1913. "Arms Overawe Red Agitators," *Los Angeles Times*, Apr. 27, 1914. "Strikers Join Zapatistas in the Mexican Revolt," *Los Angeles Times*, Jan. 20, 1912. "Congressmen Hear Strikers' Children," *Los Angeles Times*, Mar. 5, 1912. The union listed José María Ibarra as president and Epifanio Regalado as secretary.

20. Mellinger, *Race and Labor*, 135–138. "Order I.W.W. from El Paso," *Los Angeles Times*, Apr. 24, 1913. California Fernando Palomarez, or Palomares according to his Social Security record, was born on Aug. 13, 1882, in Mexico, and he died on Dec. 10, 1951, in Los Angeles. His mother's maiden name was "Palomarez." According to the 1920 census, Series T625, Roll 119, Page 20A, Enumeration District 547, Image 42, "Rosendo Dorame" was living in Rowland Heights, a suburb of Los Angeles. Listed as born in Arizona in 1877 and a farmworker. "Order I.W.W. from El Paso," *Los Angeles Times*, Apr. 24, 1913. *Miners' Magazine*, May 22, 1913, 15. *Miners' Magazine*, Aug. 13, 1914, 15. "To the El Paso Smelting Workers," *Miners' Magazine*, May 8, 1913, 8–9. Hall and Coerver, *Revolution on Border*, 121–122. Charles H. Tanner, "The Situation at El Paso, Texas, July 11, 1913," *Miners' Magazine*, July 17, 1913, 9–10. Tanner's narrative was filled with racist remarks; he referred to blacks as "niggers." *Miners' Magazine*, June 5, 1913, 10. "Situation at El Paso," *Miners' Magazine*, May 26, 1913.

21. Narrative is based on articles in *Los Angeles Times*. "Louis Duncan Mayer, Letter June 28, 1914, *Miners' Magazine*, July 16, 1914, 5, 8. Mellinger, *Race and Labor*, 129–130. WFM, *Official Proceedings of 21st Annual Convention*, July 20–Aug. 3, 1914, 32, 83, 84.

22. Narrative is based on articles in *Los Angeles Times*. "Louis Duncan Mayer, Letter June 28, 1914, *Miners' Magazine*, July 16, 1914, 5, 8. Mellinger, *Race and Labor*, 129–130. Western Federation of Miners, *Official Proceedings of 21st Annual Convention*, July 20–Aug. 3, 1914, 32, 83, 84.

23. Pascasio Hériz to Granjon, Hayden, July 14, 1914, AAM; also in RFAC, Urban Archives, CSUN.

24. Paschasius Hériz to unnamed priest, June 2, 1913, AAM.

25. Hugginie, " 'Strikitos,' " 109, 157, 172. Sain, "History of Miami Area," 134.

26. Hugginie, " 'Strikitos,' " 157.

27. Kluger, *Clifton-Morenci Strike*, 26. "Eighty Per Cent Law Changes," *Copper Era*, July 31, 1914. "The Flag and Eighty Per Cent," *Copper Era*, Sept. 4, 1914. "Eighty Per Cent Case Before Court," *Copper Era*, Oct. 22, 1915. "80 Per Cent Law Invalid Says Court," *Copper Era*, Nov. 5, 1915.

28. "Race War in Arizona; Death List Is Sixteen," *Los Angeles Times*, Aug. 20, 1914.

29. "Guerra de Razas en Arizona" *Regeneración*, Aug. 22, 1914.

30. Mellinger, *Race and Labor*, 140.

31. Through its many articles, the *Los Angeles Times* whipped up war hysteria. See earlier drafts in RFAC, Urban Archives, CSUN. "Maytorena Refuses to Accept Gen. Scott's Terms," *Los Angeles Times*, Jan. 2, 1915. "Villa Hopes to Stop Firing across the Border," *Los Angeles Times*, Jan. 4, 1915. "Gen. Scott to Deal with Villa Directly for Peace along the Border with Mexico," *Los Angeles Times*, Jan. 5, 1915. "Gen. Scott Leaves for Naco to Induce Maytorena to Agree to Maintain Peace on the Border with Mexico," *Los Angeles Times*, Jan. 11, 1915.

32. William Palm, "Pioneer Days Are Recalled; American in Sonora Defy Murderous Yaquis," *Los Angeles Times*, May 21, 1915. "Wilson's Farewell to 'Watchful Waiting,' " *Los Angeles Times*, May 29, 1915. "Yaquis Burn Sonora Town," *Los Angeles Times*, June 13, 1915. "Yaqui Bands Raid Ranches," *Los Angeles Times*, June 18, 1915.

33. Mellinger, *Race and Labor*, 157. "Border Raiders Carranza's Men," *Los Angeles Times*, Jan. 24, 1920. Starr County Sheriff Octavio Gutiérrez testified before a Senate committee that Carranza and other Mexican officials were aware of the Plan de San Diego. He said that the rebels used German weapons.

34. Coerver and Hall, *Texas and Mexican Revolution*, 87.

35. *Regeneración*, Oct. 2, 1915. *Regeneración*, Oct. 15, 1910.

36. Marvin, "Quick and Dead on Border," 295.

37. W. Webb, *Texas Rangers*, xv.

38. W. Webb, *Texas Rangers*, 478.

39. Barnes, "Plan of San Diego." Hager, "Plan of San Diego," 330–336. Gómez-Quiñones, "Plan de San Diego," 125–126. Cumberland, "Border Raids in Lower Rio Grande," 290–294. B. Johnson, "Plan de San Diego Uprising," 285.

40. Mellinger, *Race and Labor*, 138–140.

41. Mellinger, *Race and Labor*, 147–149.

42. Thomas A. French, "History of the Arizona State Federation of Labor," *Miners' Magazine*, July 1920. WFM, *Official Proceedings of 20th Annual Convention*, July 15–26, 1912, 10, 220, 406, 410. McBride, "Henry S. McCluskey," 20.

43. Mellinger, *Race and Labor*, 150–153.

44. Bruere, "Following Trail of I.W.W.," pt. 2, *New York Evening Post*, Nov. 17, 1917. "Miners' Union Is after Globe Saloons," *Copper Era*, Mar. 3, 1910. Rivera, *Revolución en Sonora*, 436–452. Kluger, *Clifton-Morenci Strike*, 24–25.

45. Mellinger, *Race and Labor*, 160–162.

46. Parrish, "Labor, Progressives, and Copper," 6. Cogut and Conger, *History of Arizona's Clifton-Morenci*, 164. Leslie D. McLean, Superintendent, "History of the Morenci Company," Morenci Clipping File, AHS. Byrit, *Forging Copper Collar*, 55–62. "Morenci Southern R.R. Suspends Mail Train," *Copper Era*, Oct. 23, 1914.

47. Cogut and Conger, *History of Arizona's Clifton-Morenci*, 15, 115. "Arizona Metal Production in 1912," *Miners' Magazine*, Jan. 16, 1913, 9. Vinson, "Vanished Clifton-Morenci," 191.

48. "Strike Fine Ore Showing," *Los Angeles Times*, Nov. 9, 1913. "To Finish Smelter Soon," *Los Angeles Times*, June 29, 1913. "London-Arizona Consolidated," *Los Angeles Times*, Sept. 9, 1913.

49. "En Defensa de los Mexicanos," *Regeneración*, Sept. 20, 1913. The oldest son of Tomás de Urrea and Gabriela Cantúa (listed as "Gabriela Urrea" in the 1900 census) was named Jesús. Jesús M. Urea, Home in 1900: Precincts 3, 11, 19, and 15, Graham County, Arizona Territory; Age: 17; Estimated Birth Year: 1883; Birthplace: Mexico; Race: White; Relationship to Head-of-House: Son; Occupation: Wood Hauler; Immigration Year: 1891. World War I Draft Registration Cards, 1917–1918, list "Jesús Maria Urrea" and his closest relative as his mother, "Mrs. Gabriela de Lara." (Gabriela Cantúa/Urrea may have married). His birthdate is Oct. 2, 1883. He worked for the Arizona Copper Company during the 1930 census, while he was still living in Clifton with his wife, Antonia, 24. In 1930, he was a warehouseman for a department store. See 1930 census, Clifton, Greenlee County, Arizona, Roll 56, Page 13B, Enumeration District 1, Image 387.0.

50. "Nine Men Killed," *Graham Guardian*, Aug. 22, 1913.

51. "Mexicans Observe Independence Day" *Copper Era*, Sept. 19, 1913.

52. "Murder and Suicide Again Hold Stage in Morenci," *Copper Era*, Apr. 10, 1914. "Three Suicides in Clifton during Week Cast Gloom over Community," *Copper Era*, Mar. 20, 1914. "Mexican Is Killed by Plunging House," *Copper Era*, Feb. 20, 1914. "Quarrel over Taxes," *Los Angeles Times*, Nov. 20, 1913.

53. *Miners' Magazine*, Apr. 14, 1904, 6. *Miners' Magazine*, Jan. 2, 1908, 4. John M, O'Neil, "My Answer to the Bishop of Scranton," *Miners' Magazine*, Jan. 2, 1908, 5. *Miners' Magazine*, July 1, 1909, 8. *Miners' Magazine*, May 4, 1911, 5. "Pledges Catholics to Union Labor, *Miners' Magazine*, Feb. 24, 1910. *Miners' Magazine*, Oct. 12, 1911, 8. "Cardinal Gibbons against the People," *Miners' Magazine*, May 4, 1911, 5. *Miners' Magazine*, Feb. 22, 1912, 7. *Miners' Magazine*, Dec. 28, 1911, 4. "Bishop Carroll Again Hysterical, *Miners' Magazine*, Sept. 17, 1912, 7–8. On the other side, Ricardo Flores Magón wrote: "American people awake. Lulled to sleep by the church of the gold coins of your masters, you have not opened your eyes or contemplated the tragedy that is taking place in the south. Awake people, awake! Cease adoring the wealth of your executioners!" *Regeneración*, Feb. 25, 1911.

54. Special thanks to Merce Gras Casanovas, archivera de Arxiu de los Carmelites Descalcos de Catolunya (ACDC), Barcelona, and to Armando Miguelez, Universidad de Alicante, Spain, for access to his personal archives. Doctor Miguelez and a colleague rescued several hundred letters to and from the Carmelite Fathers, which were roaming around in Tucson, Arizona.

55. Esequiel to Pedro, Sept. 27, 1902, AAM. Many of the Church reforms before the 1857 War of Reform were a return to an orthodoxy foreign to the Mexican clergy. Pedro de San Elías, Vistador, ca. 1903, to General de los Carmelitas, P. Esequiel; Esequiel, Rome, to Padre Pedro, Padre Vistador, Dec. 5, 1903. Esequiel to Pedro, Oct. 27, 1904. Esequiel to Pedro, Jan. 17, 1905, AAM. "Datos Historicos sobre las Fundaciones de la Provincia de San José de Cataluna en Norteamerica," ACDC. Alejo de la Virgen del Carmen, *Breve resumén historico*, 151–153; Esequiel to Pedro, Aug. 31, 1903; Reynaldo de San Francisco to the General of the Carmelitas Descalzos, Rome, Sept. 7, 1903; Esequiel to Pedro, July 2, 1903, AAM. Apuntes para una Historia, Tucson, Arizona, Estados Unidos, N.S., ACDC. Reverend Lucas de San José Vilario, Provincial de la Semi Provincia de Cataluna, sent Reverend Pedro de San Elías to seek appointment in United States.

56. Levario, "History of Discalced Carmelite Friars," 17–21. Letter to N.R.P. José Castalla, Provincial de los Carmelitas Descalzos, Barcelona, from Casa Generalizia Carmelitani Scalzi, Rome, Oct. 5, 1983, ACDC. "Documentos, Hechos y Fechas," Bishop Henry Granjon, Padre Provincial de Los Carmelitas Descalzos de Cataluna, Barcelona, Pinal County, Feb. 6, 1912, [signed] Enrique Granjon, Bishop's House, Tucson, concedes that Father Pedro de San Elias and his faculty — order — were assigned to Winkelman, Hayden, Kelvin, Sonoratown, Christmas, and Mammoth. Pamphlet, "Beautiful Flower of Carmel" (Sonora, Arizona), Jan. 13, 1913, AAM. Pedro, Sonora, Arizona, to unnamed correspondent, Tarragona, Spain, Jan. 13, 1913, AAM. Letters cited from AAM are also available in RFAC, Urban Archives, CSUN.

57. Granjon to Father Pedro, Tucson, Aug. 2, 1913; Granjon to Alexis Colle, May 27, 1913, AAM. Names Alejo pastor of Morenci, which was without a parish priest. Granjon to F. Alexis, June 10, 1913; Alejo to Lucas, June 18, 1913; Pedro to Lucas, July 1, 1913; Alejo to Lucas, July 1, 1914; Granjon to Pedro, July 6, 1933, AAM.

58. Alejo de la Virgen del Carmen, *Breve resumén historico*, 1–5. "Great Crime Wave Sweeps over Morenci," *Copper Era*, July 18, 1913. "Try Again to Blow up Morenci Church," *Copper Era*, Sept. 19, 1913. Lucas Vicario de Carmelitas to Padre Pedro, Jan. 27, 1914, AAM.

59. Parchasius Hériz to Father Amado, Hayden, Feb. 16, 1913, AAM.

60. Pascasio Hériz to Granjon, Hayden, July 14, 1914, AAM. Paschasius Hériz to unnamed priests, June 2, 1913, AAM.

61. Henry Granjon to Father Paschasius, May 14, 1913; Granjon to Paschasius, Nov. 6, 1913, AAM, The bishop wrote to Pascasio, telling him he could have midnight Mass, but to be careful.

62. Granjon to Pedro, July 6 and 10, 1913; Pedro to Lucas, July 11, 1913; Granjon to Pedro, July 12, 1913, AAM.

63. Pedro to Lucas, from Clifton, Aug. 6, 1913; Lucas to Alejo de la Virgen del Carmen, Aug. 8, 1913; Granjon to Pedro, Aug. 12, 1913; Granjon to Pedro, Sept. 2, 1913, AAM.

64. Pedro to Lucas Aug. 27, 1913, AAM.

65. Granjon to Pedro, Nov. 25, 1913; Granjon to Father Alexis, Feb. 22, 1914, AAM. "Vandalism in Clifton," *Los Angeles Times*, Sept. 24, 1913.

66. Granjon to Alejo, July 15, 1913; Granjon to Pedro, Aug. 2, 1913. Pedro to Lucas, Aug. 4, 1913; Alejo to Lucas, Aug. 23, 1913. Simon to Lucas, Durango, July 9, 1913; Justino to Lucas, Aug. 5, 1913, Mazatlán; Simon to Lucas Aug. 6, 1913. Salvador, Mazatlán, to Lucas, June 5, 1913; Salvador to Lucas, Aug. 31, 1914, AAM.

67. Pedro to Lucas, Sept. 24, 1914; José María, Clifton, to Lucas, Oct. 19, 1913. Pedro, Morenci, to Lucas, Oct. 19, 1913, AAM. Father Pedro and Father Pascasius were twin brothers. Pascasio, Hayden, to [Lucas?], Nov. 5, 1913; Alejo to Lucas, Nov. 13, 1913; Lucas to Pedro, Nov. 10, 1913, AAM.

68. Lucas to Alejo July 17, 1914, AAM.

69. There was a lot of gossiping. Lucas to Alejo, Sonora, July 24, 1914. Pedro to Pascasio, Aug. 8, 1914. Pedro to Lucas, Aug. 9, 1914; Pedro to Lucas, Aug. 18, 1914, AAM. Alejo left the names of three people. Pedro to Lucas, Nov. 5, 1915. Granjon to Pedro, Aug. 20, 1914; Pedro to Lucas, Aug. 21, 1914. Granjon to Pedro, July 30, 1914; Pedro to Lucas, Aug. 31, 1914. Pedro to Lucas, Sept. 18, 1914. Pedro to Alejo, Metcalf, Oct. 11, 1914, AAM. Numerous letters were exchanged between the Arizona Carmelites and the Catholic Church Extension Society of Chicago. Although their parishes were poor, the friars spent most of the money on imported art from Grandes Talleres de Escultura y Pintura Religiosa Tomás Márques.

70. *Epitaph*, Oct. 31, 1915. Pascasio to Lucas, Morenci, Sept. 17, 1915. José María to [Lucas?], Sept. 19, 1915. José María to Pascasio, Sept. 20, 1915; Pascasio to Lucas, Sept. 21, 1915. Lucas to Alejo, Sept. 24, 1915; Pascasio to Lucas, Oct. 4, 1915, AAM. My colleague Jorge García recalls that his father and relatives told him the expulsion of Pascasio split the workers and there may well have been some defections. However, the correspondence clearly shows that Pascasio was anti-union and, in all probability, worked against the strike. This is a complex question—even church attendance was often along class lines.

71. Alejo to Lucas, Nov. 4, 1915; Lucas to Alejo, Nov. 8, 1915. Pascasio Hériz [Sonora, Arizona] to [Lucas?] Nov. 12, 1915, AAM.

72. Pascasio Hériz to Alejo Coll, Nov. 13, 1915. Pascasio to Lucas, Nov. 18, 1915; Alejo to Lucas, Nov. 18, 1915; Paschasius Hériz, Florence, Arizona, to Alejo, Nov. 18, 1915. Lucas to Alejo, Nov. 20, 1915. Pascasio to Alejo, Nov. 23, 1915; Pascasio to Alejo, Morenci, Nov. 29, 1915, AAM.

73. Alejo to Pedro, Jan. 3, 1916, AAM.

74. Pascasio, Florence, Arizona, to Alejo, May 5, 1916. Pascasio to Alejo, Dec. 28, 1915, AAM.

75. Paschasius Hériz to Alejo, June 21, 1916. In this note, Hériz sends his regards to Frank Wild and Angela Vargas. According to the 1910 census, Series T624, Roll 39, Part

3, Page 96A, there was an "Angela M. Vargas" in Morenci, born in 1871. Vargas was probably a widow. She was thirty-nine and had three sons and two daughters; the oldest was sixteen and the youngest four. The children had all been born in Arizona. Vargas is listed as having come to the United States in 1898, which meant that she had been here previously because her son Guadalupe was sixteen. He worked in the smelter. All of her neighbors were male heads of household. Most were born in Mexico but three were from Texas, New Mexico, and Arizona. Vargas is listed in the 1900 census, Precincts 3, 11, 19, and 15, Graham County, Arizona Territory, Series T623, Roll 45, Page 15A, Enumeration District 19. In 1900, she was married to Francisco Vargas, born 1849, who was a miner, and they had six children. Francisco's oldest son, Francisco, lived with them, born in Mexico. Pascasio to Alejo, Oct. 5, 1916; Pascasio, Washington, D.C., to Alejo, Oct. 6, 1916, AAM.

76. Granjon to Alejo, Mar. 29, 1917, AAM.

77. Lucas, Washington, D.C., to Alejo, Sept. 13, 1917, AAM. José María was also in Washington at this time. "Notas de Morenci," ACDC. "Afectuosa Despedida," *El Tucsonense*, Nov. 5, 1921. Fathers Eufrasio, Salvador, and Alejo leave Arizona. "El M.R.P. Lucas en Durango," *El Tucsonense*, Mar. 7, 1922.

78. Lucas, Rome, to Gercke, Jan. 24, 1928. Father Guillermo to Pedro, Jan. 24, 1928. Lucas, Rome, to Pedro, Jan. 24, 1928. Lucas, Rome, to Pedro, Feb. 11, 1928, AAM.

79. Pedro to Lucas, Feb. 13, 1928; Pedro to Father Romauldo, Feb. 19, 1928. Father Pedro, Provincial in Arizona, to Father Guillermo de San Alberto, Vicar General, Dec. 3, 1929, AAM.

80. Father Lucas de San José, C.D., Rome, Mar. 8, 1928 to M.R.P. Pedro de San Elías, Vice Provincial de C.C.D.D., Tucson. Lucas to Pedro, Mar. 8, 1928, AAM. Corbella, "¿Un Milagro?" 43–44.

Chapter 10. The Great Copper Wars

1. "Say Arizona Bill Violates Treaties," *New York Times*, Dec. 5, 1914. Hugginie, " 'Strikitos,' " 63–67.

2. "Struggle in Arizona," *Miners' Magazine*, Feb. 3, 1915. Cogut and Conger, *History of Arizona's Clifton-Morenci*, 116–117. Patton, *History of Clifton*, 33, 36. Mellinger, *Race and Labor*, 154–155.

3. Mellinger, *Race and Labor*, 154. Frank Roberts, Nogales, to Edwin F. Hill, Assistant Secretary of State, July 5, 1995, Despatches from United States Consuls in Nogales, 1889–1906, Micro Copy 283, Roll 2, NARA, 1964. Kluger, *Clifton-Morenci Strike*, 27. *Copper Era*, Aug. 27, 1915. Mellinger, " 'Men Have Become Organizers,' " 342. The Ray strike was the springboard to Morenci.

4. "Organizers Receive Cold Reception from Mexicans," *Copper Era*, Aug. 27, 1915. "Federation Again Attempts to Control Clifton District," *Copper Era*, Aug. 20, 1915. "Clifton Citizens and Red Cross," *Copper Era*, July 23, 1915. See Refugio G. Murillo in 1910 census, Metcalf, Graham County, Arizona Territory, Series T624, Roll 39, Page 148B, Enumeration District 45, Part 3, Line 37.

5. See Canuto Vargas [Sr.] in 1900 census, Precincts 3, 11, 19, and 15, Graham County, Arizona Territory, Series T623, Roll 45, Page 20A, Enumeration District 19; see also Pascual Vargas in 1910 census, Series T624, Roll 39, Part 3, Page 79A. Vargas's estimated birth year was 1891; he lived in Morenci and is listed as a "lodger." He was born in Mexico; his mother is listed as a "Spaniard." Canuto Vargas Jr. was the dominant figure and later wrote "A Short History of the Organized Labor Movement in the Clifton-Morenci-Metcalf District, Arizona," *Pan-American Labor Press/Obrero Pan-American*, San Antonio, Oct. 16, 1918.

6. Charles H. Mage, "Strike in Clifton District of Arizona," *Miners' Magazine*, Oct. 7, 1915. "Arizona Miners' Strike," *Miners' Magazine* (newspaper format), Oct. 7, 1915. Mellinger, *Race and Labor*, 158–159. Goff, *George W. P. Hunt*, 64.

7. *Miners' Magazine* (newspaper format), Oct. 7, 1915. Mellinger, *Race and Labor*, 154, 162–164, 165. McBride, "Development of Labor Unions in Arizona," 76. "Miners on Strike," *Graham Guardian*, Sept. 17, 1915. Rico had tried to join the AFL Typographers' Union in San Antonio in 1914, but was rejected because he was not a white man.

8. "Copper Miners on Rampage," *Los Angeles Times*, Sept. 28, 1915. In 1900, Pedro Michelena lived in Solomonville; his estimated birth year was 1858. Born in Mexico, he immigrated in 1863. See 1900 census, Series T623, Roll 45, Page 10B, Enumeration District 20. In 1910, he still lived in Solomonville. See 1910 census, Series T624, Roll 39, Part 3, Page 249A. Michelena was first listed in 1870 as living in Tucson. See 1870 census, Tucson, Arizona Territory, Series M593, Roll 46, Page 64, Image 122. In 1880, he was listed as a farmer, living in the Lower Gila Valley, Apache, Arizona. See 1880 census, Series T9, Roll 36, Family History Film 1254036, Page 4C, Enumeration District 35, Image 0012.

9. A. Johnson, "Governor G.W.P. Hunt," 56–58. Kluger, *Clifton-Morenci Strike*, 36. Hunt claimed to be related to George Washington.

10. Kluger, *Clifton-Morenci Strike*, 37, 38. E. S. Edmundson to Theodore Hollingsworth, June 20, 1916, JMC, Box 5, pp. 2–4, ASU. "Arizona Miners' Strike," *Miners' Magazine* (newspaper format), Oct. 7, 1915. A. Johnson, "Governor G.W.P. Hunt," 57. "Mexican Orator Concludes the Meeting and Darkness Had Fallen before the Crowd," *Copper Era*, Oct. 1, 1915.

11. Barr, "Integrated Results of Sixty Years' Operation" 172. Kluger, *Clifton-Morenci Strike*, 26–27. "Miners on Strike," *Graham Guardian*, Sept. 17, 1915. "Mexican Orator Concludes the Meeting and Darkness Had Fallen before the Crowd," *Copper Era*, Oct. 1, 1915.

12. E. S. Edmundson, to Theodore Hollingsworth, June 20, 1916, JMC, Box 5, pp. 2–4, ASU.

13. Celidonia Trujillo: 1910 census, Clifton, Graham County, Arizona Territory, Series T624, Roll 39, Page 56A, Enumeration District 42, Part 3, Line 3. "Western Federation Tactics in Clifton-Morenci," *Prescott Journal-Miner*, Oct. 19, 1915.

14. "Farmers to Gain Millions as a Result of War," *Copper Era*, Oct. 2, 1914. "Carmichael, Bennie and McLean Want Us to Starve; We Will Fight before We Starve; Abajo con los Gerentes," *Copper Era*, Oct. 8, 1915. Kluger, *Clifton-Morenci Strike*, 51.

15. Cogut and Conger, *History of Arizona's Clifton-Morenci*, 127. Patton, *History of Clifton*, 38. Kluger, *Clifton-Morenci Strike*, 38–40. "Managers Fear to Go to Phoenix," *Copper Era*, Oct. 8, 1915.

16. *Graham Guardian*, Oct. 1, 1915. *Miners' Magazine* (newspaper format), Oct. 7, 1915. McBride, "Development of Labor Unions in Arizona," 77–79. Kluger, *Clifton-Morenci Strike*, 40. "Farmers to Gain Millions As a result of War," *Copper Era*, Oct. 2, 1914. "Governor with Agitators," *Los Angeles Times*, Oct. 10, 1915. "Arizona Miners' Strike," *Miners' Magazine* (newspaper format), Oct. 7, 1915. A. Johnson, "Governor G.W.P. Hunt," 58–59. 66. "Probe Has Begun," *Graham Guardian*, Nov. 26, 1915. "Federal Probe Clifton Strike," *Graham Guardian*, Oct. 29, 1915. McBride, "Henry S. McCluskey," 37.

17. *Epitaph*, Oct. 31, 1915. Pascasio to Lucas, Morenci, Sept. 17, 1915; José María to [Lucas?], Sept. 19, 1915; José María to Pascasio, Sept. 20, 1915; Pascasio to Lucas, Sept. 21, 1915; Lucas to Alejo, Sept. 24, 1915; Pascasio to Lucas, Oct. 4, 1915; Alejo to Lucas, Nov. 4, 1915, AAM.

18. Kluger, *Clifton-Morenci Strike*, 40. "A. & N.M. Engine Crew Assaulted by Strikers" *Copper Era*, Oct. 8, 1915. "Deportation of Store Employee Resented," *Copper Era* Oct. 10, 1915. Gregorio Ramírez: 1910 census, Series T624, Roll 39, Part 3, Page 36A. "Labor Commission Coming," *Copper Era* Oct. 8, 1915. *Graham Guardian*, Oct. 20, 1915.

19. "Western Federation Tactics in Clifton-Morenci," *Prescott Journal-Miner*, Oct. 19, 1915.

20. "Western Federation Tactics in Clifton-Morenci Strike District Shown Up in Affidavits by Men Who Suffered Attacks," *Prescott Journal-Miner*, Oct. 21, 1915. Issues of the *Prescott Journal-Miner* can be found at Bisbee Deportation: Newspaper, http://digital.library.arizona.edu/bisbee/main/prescojm.php.

21. See Carlos Casalay in 1900 Census, Graham County, Arizona Territory, Series T623, Roll 45, Page 5B, Enumeration District 19. "Mines Are without Remedy, States Judge," *Copper Era* Oct. 8, 1915. "Gov. Hunt Encourages Riots by His Attitude," *Los Angeles Times*, Oct. 11, 1915. *Graham Guardian*, Oct. 20, 1915.

22. "Clifton Strike Is Endorsed by Federation," *Copper Era*, Oct. 8, 1915; "Further Developments of Clifton Strike" *Epitaph*, Oct. 10, 1915; "News of Developments in Strike District," *Epitaph*, Oct. 13, 1915; "Arizona Is Paying $1,000 per Day to Keep Armed Guard," *Arizona Gazette*, Oct. 26, 1915; "Continuation of Costly Strike Put Squarely Up to Governor Hunt," *Arizona Gazette*, Oct. 25, 1915. "Hunt's Recall Popular Move," *Los Angeles Times*, Oct. 28, 1915. "Governor Hunt, the Friend of Criminals, *Los Angeles Times*, Nov. 11, 1915. "Welfare of Criminals," *Epitaph*, Oct. 31, 1915. "Miners Disgusted with Federation; Dissension Grows," *Arizona Gazette*, Oct. 27, 1915.

23. "Arizona Is Paying $1,000 per Day to Keep Armed Guard," *Arizona Gazette*, Oct. 26, 1915. "Continuation of Costly Strike Put Squarely Up to Governor Hunt," *Arizona Gazette*, Oct. 25, 1915, M 97, ASU. "Hunt's Recall Popular Move," *Los Angeles Times*, Oct. 28, 1915. "Governor Hunt, the Friend of Criminals," *Los Angeles*

Times, Nov. 11, 1915. "Welfare of Criminals," *Epitaph*, Oct. 31, 1915. "Miners Disgusted with Federation; Dissension Grows," *Arizona Gazette*, Oct. 27, 1915.

24. "Conference Arranged with Managers and Employees" *Copper Era*, Oct. 15, 1915. "Mine Managers Explain Their Side" *Copper Era*, Oct. 22, 1915.

25. "Strike District Quiet during Week" *Copper Era*, Oct. 29, 1915. "Spanish American Orders Preceded Unions," *Copper Era*, Oct. 29, 1915. *Dunbar's Weekly* 2, no. 42 (Oct. 30, 1915): 4, editorial comment.

26. Kluger, *Clifton-Morenci Strike*, 37, 46–48. Cogut and Conger, *History of Arizona's Clifton-Morenci*, 91–92. W. Jackson, *Enterprising Scot*, 183.

27. "No Strikebreaker in Refugee Camp," *Copper Era* Dec. 3, 1915. "Harris Pronounces Report of Interview Inaccurate," *Copper Era*, Dec. 3, 1915. "Mass Meeting of Businessmen — Town Hall," *Copper Era*, Nov. 19, 1915. Casimiro Martínez, born about 1891, lived in Morenci, Graham County, Arizona. See 1910 census, Series T624, Roll 39, Part 3, Page 116A. "No Strikebreaker in Refugee Camp," *Copper Era*, Dec. 3, 1915.

28. Kluger, *Clifton-Morenci Strike*, 65–72. "1915 Production of Copper Breaks Record," *Copper Era*, Jan. 14, 1916. "Clifton Strike Ends," *Arizona Republican*, Jan. 25, 1916. Patton, *History of Clifton*, 42. *Copper Era* Jan. 25, 1916. "Long Strike in District Is Ended by Vote of Former Employees," *Copper Era*, Jan. 28, 1916. "Smelter Stacks Give Evidence Strike Is Over," *Copper Era*, Feb. 4, 1916.

29. Mellinger, *Race and Labor*, 158–159.

30. Hugginie, " 'Strikitos,' " 151. "D.C. Co. Employees Threaten Strike," *Copper Era*, Mar. 31, 1916.

31. Parrish, *Mexican Workers*, 13–14. Mellinger, in "How IWW Lost Western Heartland," 319–320, says that the IWW, whose centers of operation were Phoenix and Bisbee, was totally unprepared upon entering Arizona.

32. Parrish, *Mexican Workers*, 12. "By Order of the President's Mediation Commission, Oct. 31, 1917"; "Basis of Settlement: Clifton-Morenci-Metcalf Strike," JMC, Box 5, pp. 2–3, ASU. "Walkout Is Settled at Morenci," *Copper Era*, Feb. 11, 1916. "Los Trabajadores Mineros en Clifton," *El Tucsonense*, Feb. 26, 1916. "Union League Is Organized in Clifton," *Copper Era*, Mar. 17, 1916. "Managers in Session with Employee," *Copper Era*, Feb. 18, 1916. "By Order of the President's Mediation Commission, Oct. 31, 1917"; "Basis of Settlement: Clifton-Morenci-Metcalf Strike," JMC, Box 5, pp. 2–3, ASU.

33. Parrish, *Mexican Workers, Progressives, and Copper*, 11. "Labor Unions Recruit Many Members" *Copper Era*, May 26, 1916. "Employees Must Abide by Their Agreement" *Copper Era*, June 16, 1916, "Official Request to Governor for Troops" *Copper Era*, June 23, 1916. "Morenci Union to President," *Copper Era*, Aug. 4, 1916.

34. "I.W.W. Is Gaining Foothold in Morenci," *Copper Era*, Sept. 1, 1916. Azuara's name was spelled "Azora" and "Azore." "Editor of 'El Rebelde' Shy," Oct. 2, 1917. "I.W.W. Chiefs to Spend Twenty Years in Prison," *Los Angeles Times*, Aug. 31. 1918. "Writes Period to Red Career," *Los Angeles Times*, Oct. 23, 1919. Aurelio Vincenti Azuara, was born on Oct. 1, 1884. He registered for the draft while in Leavenworth

Penitentiary. His father was living in Manzanera, Spain. See 1920 census, Series T625, Roll 537, Page 6A, Enumeration District 97, Image 0693. which lists him as "Vincente Azuara."

35. "Donnelly Placed under Peace Bond," *Copper Era*, Sept. 8, 1916.

36. "Mexican Miners Might Cause Trouble Any Time," *Los Angeles Times*, Nov. 26, 1916.

37. "Miners Discuss 'Closed Shop,' " *Copper Era*, Nov. 3, 1916. Parrish, *Mexican Workers, Progressives, and Copper*, 15. "Labor Quiet in Arizona Mines," *Los Angeles Times*, Nov. 26, 1916. Patton, *History of Clifton*, 43–44. Mellinger, in " 'Men Have Become Organizers,' " says that the 1915 strike resolved the issue of whether Mexicans could be organized (p. 325), and that the WFM conducted major campaigns in Utah and Nevada between 1911 and 1914, but neglected Arizona (p. 337).

38. Parrish, *Mexican Workers, Progressives, and Copper*, 6–7, 8–10.

39. Parrish, "Labor, Progressives, and Copper,' " 6–15, 16–21. Parrish, *Mexican Workers, Progressives, and Copper*, 18.

40. Walter Douglas, "Makes Answer," *Copper Era*, Feb. 20, 1920. *United States v. Haywood et al.* was part of the deposition of John W. Hughes for *Simmons v. El Paso & Southwestern RR Co.*, SC, AZ 114, Box 1, Folder 1, Exhibit 48, UA.

41. Parrish, *Mexican Workers, Progressives, and Copper*, 20–23.

42. Parrish, "Labor, Progressives, and Copper," 41–50. Overstreet, "On Strike!" 197–218, http://digital.library.arizona.edu/bisbee/docs2/jahover.php. "True Copy of the Notes of Hon. Thomas E. Campbell," written between 1934 and 1939, MS 132, Campbell Family Papers, Folder 6, pp. 27, 34, AHS.

43. "The Arizona Strike," *New Republic*, Mar. 18, 1916, 185–186. The *New Republic* responded that Douglas was not even in the district; it pointed out that millionaire Frantz gave substantial support to the strikers, and it was his conduct and of Governor Hunt that prevented a Ludlow (pp. 186–187). "From Governor Hunt," *New Republic*, Apr. 15, 1916, 293: "Mr. Douglas's implied charge that the strikers were in any degree responsible for the burning of an abandoned mill, which was covered by insurance, is not supported by the report of the commanding officer of the guardsmen, who wrote that the cause of this fire was defective electric wiring in contact with the roof of the structure."

44. Byrkit, "Bisbee Deportation," 86. Byrkit, *Forging Copper Collar*, 17, 114–115, 119. The Burns International Detective Service and the chief of the Bureau of Investigation of the Department of Justice campaigned for the copper companies and against the IWW. The managers went all out to discredit labor. This network set the stage for Bisbee. Espionage and strikebreakers were essential, as proven during Ludlow in 1915. Ludlow Balwin-Felts Agency had several hundred gunmen, whom it could muster into the militia or deputize. The Broff Brothers Agency had a file of 10,000 mechanics.

45. From 1915 to 1918, Douglas reversed the politics of the state. Byrkit, *Forging Copper Collar*, 72, 81, 109–115.

46. Byrkit, *Forging Copper Collar*, 226.

47. Wallace, "Colonel McClintoch and 1917 Copper Strike," 24–26.

48. Robert W. Breure, "Following the Trail of the I.W.W.," pt. 4, *New York Evening Post*, Dec. 1, 1917, M 94, ASU. Also see McBride, "Development of Labor Unions in Arizona," 104–107. Wallace, "Colonel McClintoch and 1917 Copper Strike," 24–26.

49. Patton, *History of Clifton*, 43–44.

50. "Federal Mediator Arrives in Clifton," *Copper Era*, July 27, 1917.

51. See JMC, Box 5, pp. 6–7, ASU.

52. Robert W. Breure, "Following the Trail of the I.W.W.," pt. 5, *New York Evening Post*, Dec. 8, 1917, ASU. See also HSMC, Box 2, File 2 ("Jerome File"), ASU. McBride, "Henry S. McCluskey," 63.

53. Byrkit, *Forging Copper Collar*, 170. Parrish, *Mexican Workers, Progressives, and Copper*, 17. "Old Union Will Vote on Strike," *Arizona Republican*, July 7, 1917.

54. Robert W. Breure, "Following the Trail of the I.W.W.," pt. 3, *New York Evening Post*, Nov. 24, 1917, M 94, ASU.

55. Superior Court Judge G. Walter Shute, as quoted in Parrish, *Mexican Workers, Progressives, and Copper*, 22.

56. Hamilton, *Exploring Dangerous Trades*, 208–222; Hamilton quotation on p. 210. Also see Katherine Benton-Cohen, "Docile Children and Dangerous Revolutionaries," 30–50. This is an important article; however, the actions of the Bisbee mob went beyond a display of "manliness."

57. "A Record Output for Arizona Mines," *Copper Era*, Jan. 16, 1917. Casillas, "Mexicans, Labor, and Strife," 117.

58. Byrkit, *Forging Copper Collar*, 118–119. Casillas, "Mexicans, Labor, and Strife," 117. Byrkit, "Bisbee Deportation," 86.

59. IWW, *Songs of Workers*, 5–6. "Protective League Is Organized in Bisbee," *Copper Era*, Sept. 15, 1916. "I.W.W. Claims of Gains at Bisbee Unsubstantiated," *Arizona Republican*, July 2, 1917. "Indications Are That Bisbee Strike Has Failed," *Arizona Republican*, July 2, 1917. "Bisbee Situation Is Improving," *Arizona Republican*, July 2, 1917. Most evidence points to the fact that there was no danger. "Organization or Anarchy," *New Republic*, July 21, 1917, 321.

60. Grace McCool, "Russian Trick Pulled in Cochise County by Anti-Labor Mining Co. in 1917," *Gateway Times*, Sept. 8, 1960. Parrish, *Felix Frankfurter*, 90.

61. "Truth about Bisbee." Parrish, *Felix Frankfurter*, 90.

62. Benton-Cohen, "Docile Children and Dangerous Revolutionaries," 35.

63. Byrkit, "Walter Douglas," 23–24. After the deportations, Wheeler enlisted in the Army Air Force and had to be brought back from France to stand trial. As expected, the vigilantes were acquitted. Afterward, Wheeler worked trick shots in carnival and performed in Wild West shows in Europe. Grace McCool, "Russian Trick Pulled in Cochise County by Anti-Labor Mining Co. in 1917," *Gateway Times*, Sept. 8, 1960.

64. Byrkit, "Life and Labor in Arizona," 7. Byrkit, *Forging Copper Collar*, 10–11. Cox, "History of Bisbee," 14. Casillas, "Mexican Labor," 117–118. Harrison, "Development of Arizona Labor," 20–25.

65. Byrkit, "Walter Douglas," 23–24. Byrkit, *Forging Copper Collar*, 190.

66. Byrkit, "Life and Labor in Arizona," 23.

67. Byrkit, "Life and Labor in Arizona," 15.

68. Benton-Cohen, "Docile Children and Dangerous Revolutionaries, 30.

69. Benton-Cohen, "Docile Children and Dangerous Revolutionaries," 30. Byrkit, *Forging Copper Collar*, 213. "Credentials of Attorney Are Ignored by Bisbee and Deportation Follows," *Arizona Republican*, July 30, 1917. "Moore Arrives in Douglas and Tells of Deportation from Bisbee by Citizen's League," *Arizona Republican*, July 30, 1917.

70. "Organization or Anarchy," *New Republic*, July 21, 1917, 320.

71. "Bisbee's Deported Mexicans Reach Agua Prieta Afoot," *Arizona Republican*, Oct. 5, 1917. "Put Up Bars to Keep Out Deported Men," *Arizona Republican*, July 13, 1917.

72. "Los Trabajos de Bisbee, Ariz.," *El Tucsonense*, June 30, 1917. Claims 65 percent of the workers were fooled by agitators. "La Huelga de Globe, Miami, Clifton y Morenci," *El Tucsonense*, July 4, 1917. "La Situación en Globe, Ariz.," *El Tucsonense*, July 7, 1917. *Tucson Citizen*, July 13, 1917. "Los 'I.W.W.' Son Expulsados de Bisbee," *El Tucsonense*, July 14, 1917 "Los Disturbios Huegistas," *El Tucsonense*, July 21, 1917. "Los 'I.W.W.' Saliendo de Bisbee en Carros de Ganado par Columbus," *El Tucsonense*, July 28, 1917. "Inauguración del Estandarte de la Liga Protectora," *El Tucsonense*, July 28, 1917. Byrkit, "Bisbee Deportation," 87. Byrkit, *Forging Copper Collar*, 153–154. Byrkit, "Life and Labor in Arizona," 8. Chester Johnson, "Arizona I.W.W. Troubles Detailed by Man on Ground," *San Diego Union*, July 20, 1917.

73. Joseph D. Cannon, "No Wobblies Wanted—Loyal Americans Only to Get Work in Globe-Miami Mines—A White Man's Camp," *Miners' Magazine* (newspaper format), Oct. 1917.

74. Law of Necessity as Applied in State of Arizona," HSMC, Box 7, Folder 7, III, pp. 2–3, 20, 22, ASU. *Copper Era*, Jan. 23, 1920.

75. Byrkit, *Forging Copper Collar*, 276–280. Linquist, "Jerome Deportation," 241–245. Dos Passos, *"Mr. Wilson's War"*, 54.

76. Thomas A. French, Secretary Treasurer, Arizona State Federation of Labor, Phoenix, Sept. 21, 1917, JMC, Box 1, ASU. Mellinger, *Race and Labor*, 189–190. "Union Submit Proposition to Citizens," *Copper Era*, Sept. 8, 1917. "Strike Situation Unchanged at Present," *Copper Era*, Sept. 14, 1917. "Mine Managers Offer to Resume Operations *Copper Era*, Sept. 21, 1917. "Clifton District Mines Are to Close If Men Do Not Go to Work," *Arizona Republican*, Sept. 26, 1917.

77. "The Honor Roll Is Increased by Forty-Four," *Copper Era*, Sept. 24, 1917. The draftees included Arthur Ruiz and Juan Hernández from Clifton, Gustavo B. Escobedo from Morenci, and Geronimo Sierra from Metcalf. Private Juan G. Medina of Company B of the 158th Infantry at Camp Kearney, California, would later write home that he knew of three sergeants who were Mexican and that "some of the companies have schools for their Mexican boys." "Mex. Boy Writes Local Board Good Letter," *Copper Era*, Nov. 30, 1917.

78. "Sheriff Has Clifton Situation in Hand," *Arizona Republican*, Oct. 2, 1917.

79. "Clifton Miners Now Vote Against Return," *Arizona Republican*, Oct. 1, 1917. "Clifton Mines to Be Idle While Commission Probes," *Arizona Republican*, Oct. 5, 1917. E. Gutiérrez, Clifton, to Guillermo M. Segura, Consul at El Paso, Oct. 2, 1917, ARE, 17-7-120. "Informes sobre Huelgas en Arizona," ARE, 17-7-120. Memos to San Francisco and El Paso Consuls, Clifton, Arizona, Oct. 4, 1917; Ramón P. de Negri, Consul San Francisco, Enrique Gutiérrez, Clifton, to M. Seguín, Consul El Paso, Oct. 5, 1917; E. Gutiérrez, Clifton, Arizona, Oct. 5, 1917, ARE, 17-7-120. Memo Murray, Oct. 8, 1917, JMC, Box 5, ASU.

80. T. S. Curtis, Secretary, to Commissioners, Clifton, Oct. 22, 1917, JMC, Box 5, ASU.

81. Daguerre, Clifton, C. A. Vargas, Morenci, L. E. Soto, Metcalf, Telegram to Woodrow Wilson, Oct. 15, 1917, JMC, Box 5, ASU. The telegram, addressed to the "President of the United States," stated that three unions of Mexican miners in Clifton, Morenci, and Metcalf, with a membership of 4,000, 90 percent of whom were Mexican citizens, unanimously passed a resolution on Oct. 4, 1917, after consulting with their resident Mexican consul to request the Mexican president to repatriate them. The memo speaks to grievances and instances of oppression. The workers were not intimidated by the mine owners threats to seal up the mines. They reminded the president that there were 14,000 Mexican mine workers in Arizona.

82. Some white youths with means avoided the draft. "Deserters from Greenlee Draft," *Copper Era*, June 14, 1918. McCluskey, "Absentee Capitalists."

83. *Proceedings of President's Mediation Commission Session at Clifton*, 84–85, 104, 111, 112.

84. *Proceedings of President's Mediation Commission Session at Clifton*, 271–275, 284, 297, 301, 305.

85. *Proceedings of President's Mediation Commission Session at Clifton*, 521–530.

86. *Proceedings of President's Mediation Commission Session at Clifton*, 479–502. "La Liga Termina Su Trabajo," *El Tucsonense*, Sept. 18, 1918. Names Emilio Valdez, J. Y. Aisna, Jesús Estrada, and Francisco Benites of Clifton; Amado Cota Robles of Tucson. The Legislative Committee was headed by Ainsa, who was born in California and raised in Hermosillo. He was a notary in Morenci, and a member of the better element. "La Cuestión Algodonera en Arizona," *El Tucsonense*, Nov. 20, 1918.

87. H. S. McCluskey, "Arizona Conditions Are Still Unsettled," *Miners' Magazine* (newspaper format), Dec. 1917. "Strike at Clifton, Morenci, and Metcalf, Arizona, Settled," *Miners' Magazine*, Nov. 1917. "Arizona Conditions Are Still Unsettled," *Miners' Magazine* (newspaper format), Dec. 1917. "La Liga Termina Su Trabajo," *El Tucsonense*, Sept. 18, 1918. "El Trabajador Mexicano en E.U.," *El Tucsonense*, Mar. 13, 1918. "La Cuestión Algodonera en Arizona," *El Tucsonense*, Nov. 20, 1918.

88. Parrish, *Felix Frankfurter*, 93, 94. Parrish, *Mexican Workers, Progressives, and Copper*, 29–30.

89. Parrish, *Mexican Workers, Progressives, and Copper*, 34, 35.

90. Parrish, *Mexican Workers, Progressives, and Copper*, 33.

91. R. G. Riggs, Globe, to Gompers, Mar. 8, 1918; Thomas J. Groaf, President,

Arizona State Federation of Labor, Mar. 19, 1918, to Samuel Gompers, "Copper Situation" File A-B71, RG 61, Record of the War Industries Board, Entry 8-81, Labor Division, General Correspondence. Croaff to McCluskey, American Council of Defense, Mar. 20, 1918, HSMC, Box 2, Folder 3, ASU.

92. Francisca Subia, Death Certificate, Arizona State Board of Health, Mar. 16, 1919; Cause of Death: Influenza; Contributing Cause: Pregnancy.

93. Moyer to McCluskey, Denver, Feb. 20, 1919, HSMC, Box 3, Folder 2, ASU. P. M. Vargas to McCluskey in San Francisco, Sept. 10, 1917, HSMC, Box 2, Folder 7, ASU. "Walter Douglas Reviews Copper Situation," *Arizona Mining Journal*, Feb. 1919, 14.

94. Charles H. Moyer to H. S. McCluskey, Denver, Nov. 20, 1919. HSMC, Box 2, Folder 5a, ASU. For years, Moyer and indeed most labor union leaders had labeled Mexican Americans "un-American" and, by implication, unpatriotic. Yet hundreds of Mexican Americans in Arizona alone honorably served in the U.S. military during World War I. One such vet was José Ortega, who had been born in New Mexico and who had fought in France. Upon his death in 1920, Ortega was eulogized by the Liga Protectora Latina and the local American Legion. He was 27. "First War Veteran Dies at Clifton A.C. Hospital," *Copper Era*, Apr. 9 1920.

95. "Mr. Hunt Declara Suyo Puesto de Gobernador," *El Tucsonense*, Sept. 2, 1916. "La Gran Figura de Mr. Olney," *El Tucsonense*, Sept. 6, 1916. *El Tucsonense*, Sept. 9, 1916. *El Tucsonense*, Aug. 16, 1916. "Mr. Hunt Arrebata Derechos Inalineables al Pueblo Mexicano de Arizona," *El Tucsonense*, Aug. 30, 1916. *Proceedings of President's Mediation Commission Session at Clifton*, 123, 126, 129. "El Consul de Tucson Acusado," *El Tucsonense*, July 25, 1917. "Los 'I.W.W.' Son Expulsados de Bisbee," *El Tucsonense*, July 14, 1917. *El Tucsonense*, Feb. 2, 1918. "Las Minas," *El Tucsonense*, Feb. 6, 1918 "Ecos De Sonora," *El Tucsonense*, June 30, 1917. "Los Trabajos de Bisbee, Ariz.," *El Tucsonense*, June 30, 1917. "La Huelga de Globe, Miami, Clifton y Morenci," *El Tucsonense*, July 4, 1917. "Bisbee Deportees Wandering in New Mexico; Marooned in Desert; Hermanas," *Tucson Citizen*, July 13, 1917. "Los 'I.W.W.' Son Expulsados de Bisbee," *El Tucsonense*, July 14, 1917. "Los Disturbios Huegistas," *El Tucsonense*, July 21, 1917. "Plutarco Elías Calles Esta Loco," *El Tucsonense*, Dec. 20, 1919. "El Trabajador Mexicano en E.U.," *El Tucsonense*, Mar. 13, 1918.

96. "El Progeso del Comercio en Tucson," *El Tucsonense*, Dec. 28, 1918. "Tercera Convención de la Liga Protectora Latina," *El Tucsonense*, Sept. 14, 1918. "Gano Campbell," *El Tucsonense*, Nov. 6, 1918. "Al Público," *El Tucsonense*, Mar. 17, 1915: "We shall labor for the betterment of our race, which is at the head of Latin America." Teodoro Olea, Jan. 13, 1916, Phoenix, to Jesús Acuña, Ministro de Relaciones Exteriores, ARE, 6-12-18. *El Tucsonense*, July 10, 1915. McBride, "Liga Protectora Latina," 83–84. "Eighty Per Cent Law," *Copper Era*, Jan. 8, 1915. Federal District Judge J. M. Lally held the law unconstitutional. Vélez-Ibáñez, *Border Visions*, 69. Sheridan, *Tucsonenses*, 165–175. "Demanda de Los Operarios de la Redonda de Tucson con Relación a Sueldos," *El Tucsonense*, Aug. 5, 1919. "Los Ferrocarrileros Locales Tomaron Parte de la General Que Se Avecina," *El Tucsonense*, Aug. 2, 1919, "Los Operarios de la

Redonda Pediran, Justificadamente Aumento de Salario," *El Tucsonense*, July 31, 1919. Briegel, "Alianza Hispano Americana," 10–11. "Mexican Lodge Official," *Copper Era*, July 17, 1914. *El Tucsonense*, Jan. 25, 1919. McBride, "Liga Protectora Latina," 85–87. Pichardo, "Role of Community in Social Protest," 81. *El Tucsonense*, Aug. 24, 1918.

97. Amado Cota Robles, "La Igualidad de las Razas," *El Tucsonense*, Nov. 30, 1918. Amado Cota Robles, "La Liga Protectora Latina," *El Tucsonense*, Feb. 12, 1919. Amado Cota Robles, "La Igualdad de las Razas," *El Tucsonense*, Dec. 16, 1919. *El Tucsonense*, Mar. 15, 1919, has a biography of Amado Cota Robles, education director of the Liga Proctectora Latina. See Cota Robles Family Web page, http://www.cota-robles.com/generations (accessed Dec. 7, 2004). "Informe del Delegado C. C. Goodwin de la A.H.A.," *El Tucsonense*, Feb. 6, 1918. The Liga's 1918 annual convention was held at the Los Angeles Convention Center. Manuel Garza of Clifton was present. Quotation from Sheridan, *Tucsonenses*, 179. McBride, "Liga Protectora Latina," 83. "Declaraciones Patriotas del Candidato Tom Campbell," *El Tucsonense*, May 4, 1918. *El Tucsonense* endorsed Campbell and was rabid in its condemnation of the IWW. *El Tucsonense*, July 10, Aug. 16, Sept. 9, Oct. 18, 25, and 28, Nov. 8, 1916.

98. "Ramon Soto, President of Vigilance Commission of Legislature, Respetuosa y Oportuna Protesta Dirigida a la Camara del Senado," *El Tucsonense*, Mar. 5, 1919. *El Tucsonense*, Jan. 27, 1917. La Liga Protectora Latina protests against proposed law no. 23. McBride, "Liga Protectora Latina," 85, 86, 87. *El Tucsonense*, Mar. 15, 1919. *El Tucsonense*, June 17, 1919. A chapter of the Sociedad Mexicana Americana was approved for Morenci. Letter from A. I. Villarreal, *Pan-American Labor Press/Obrero Pan-American*, Sept. 18, 1918, PAFL, RG 63, JMC, Bancroft Library, UCB. "Las Fiestas Patrias," *El Tucsonense*, Sept. 19, 1917. A chapter of the Sociedad Mexicana Americana, sponsored by Amado Cota Robles, was established in Hayden, Arizona. "Formación de un Club de Hispano-Americanos," *El Tucsonense*, Sept. 2, 1916.

99. Letter from A. I. Villarreal, *Pan-American Labor Press/Obrero Pan-American*, Sept. 18, 1918, PAFL, RG 63, JMC, Bancroft Library, UCB.

100. Letter from A. I. Villarreal, *Pan-American Labor Press/Obrero Pan-American*, Sept. 18, 1918, PAFL, RG 63, JMC, Bancroft Library, UCB. Even though Mc-Cluskey was among the most politically advanced of the organizers, he could not get past his ethnic prejudice. McCluskey, "Absentee Capitalists." "Pan-American Federation of Labor Organized by International Labor Conference in Laredo, Texas," *Pan-American Labor Press/Obrero Pan-American*, Dec. 4, 1918, PAFL, RG 63, JMC, Bancroft Library, UCB. *Proceedings of President's Mediation Commission Session at Clifton*, 2, 3, 11, 13. There was a certain irony to McCluskey's nativism. Testifying before the president's commission, he said that the 1915 strike had produced a better class of workers, who were interested in the customs of country. A greater percentage of Mexicans had registered to vote. The *Arizona Labor Journal* carried a special section in Spanish. In Clifton, 90 percent of the schoolchildren were Mexican; the town had its own hall where the union taught English, and the Mexican workers contributed to campaigns. Morenci had a $10,000 strike fund.

101. CROM (Confederación Regional Obrera Mexicana) was a national federation of unions, founded in Mexico in May 1916.

102. Snow, "Samuel Gompers," 81–83, 89, 90, 100–102, 162.

Chapter 11. The Cotton Corridor

1. "Arizona Prepares to Battle Influenza," *Los Angeles Times*, Oct. 19, 1918. "Arizona Reports 700 Cases of Influenza," *Los Angeles Times*, Oct. 25, 1918. Crosby, *America's Forgotten Pandemic*, 207. Barry, *Great Influenza*, 13, 605. "Cases in Camps," *New York Times*, Oct. 10, 1918. Francisca Subia, Original Certificate of Death, Bureau of Vital Statistics, Arizona Board of Health, State Index no. 160, County Register no. 71, Local Registrar no. 47. Date of Death: Mar. 16, 1919; Age: 40; Pregnant; Cause of Death: Influenza.

2. Parrish, *Mexican Workers, Progressives, and Copper*, 35.

3. Statistics from Miguel A. Limón, Consul Clifton, to Don Salvador Diego Fernández, Official Mayor Interino Encargado de Despacho de Relaciones Exteriores, "Resenas Politicas," Aug. 21, 1919, ARE, 17-14-162. Andrés G. García, El Visitador General Encargado to Ernesto Garcia Perez, Relaciones Exteriores, Mar. 17, 1919, El Paso, Vol. 1919, Roll 1, ARE, 3-17-68. Limón to A. G. Garcia Mar. 20, 1919; Miguel A. Limón, Clifton, May 3, 1919, to Don Salvador Diego Fernández, Consulado de Mexico en Clifton, Arizona; Solicita Repatriación de Trabajadors Mexicanos Que Fueron a Ese Lugar, Vol. 1919, Roll 1, 8/82, ARE, 44-1-65, pp. 8–4. Limón resigned on May 10, 1920. Lucas Villareal to Daniel Garza Perez, Secretario de la Sección de Personal, Relaciones Exteriores, May 18, 1919; Miguel A. Limón, Clifton, May 28, 1919, to Don Salvador Diego Fernández, Oficial Encagado de Despacho, Vol. 1919, Roll 1, 8/82, ARE, 44-1-65. *Reglamento del "Gran Círculo Cooperativo,"* ARE, 17-14-162, pp. 3, 7. Nuestro Consulado en California, Arizona Envia la General Comprendia de Eñero a Agosto, Aug. 21, 1917, ARE, 17-14-162.

4. "Pedro Gómez," in Björkquist, "Mexican Americans in Morenci." Harner, "Copper Mining and Regional Identity," 1–2, 30.

5. Björkquist, "Mexican Americans in Morenci."

6. "Mexico Willing to Pay Fares to All Wishing Return," *Copper Era*, May 13, 1921. Over 1,700 were older than 6; many more were younger. "Mexicans Are Given Transportation to El Paso," *Copper Era*, Apr. 15, 1921. "Output of Metals in Arizona during Past Year of 1920," *Copper Era*, Jan. 7, 1921. "Phelps Dodge Will Close Operations at Morenci," *Copper Era*, Mar. 25, 1921. "Red Metal Situation Is Explained by Mr. Douglas," *Copper Era*, Apr. 8, 1921. "Moctezuma Mine Closes Apr. 15," *Copper Era*, Apr. 8, 1921.

7. Newspaper accounts trace the consolidation of copper production and transportation by Phelps Dodge. "General Mgr. States Shut Down Will Be Complete," *Copper Era*, May 27, 1921." "Phelps Dodge Negotiating for A.C. Co. Holdings," *Copper Era*, July 15, 1921. "Entire Holdings of A.C. Co. Ltd. Are Now Owned by Phelps Dodge Corp.," *Copper Era*, Oct. 7, 1921. "Copper Industry Must Have High Taxes Reduced," *Copper Era*, Mar. 3, 1922. "Recurrence of I.W.W.ism Noted in State," *Copper Era*,

Sept. 29, 1922. "Capacity of Morenci Mill to Be Doubled — More Miners Wanted," *Copper Era*, Oct. 20, 1922. Watt, "History of Morenci," 78–80. David Velásquez interview. Arrieta, "Mexican Community of Clifton-Morenci," 129.

8. "What Irrigation Projects Mean to Arizona," *Copper Era*, Jan. 30, 1914. "Seven to Eight Million Acres of Arizona Land is Irrigable," *Copper Era*, Jan. 2, 1914.

9. In this as in other sections, the basic chronology is based on day-to-day coverage in the *Los Angeles Times* and the *New York Times*. Joe Soto interview. Sowards, "Reclamation, Ranching, and Reservation," 301, 333. Friedricks, "Phoenix," 443–445. Luckingham, *Minorities in Phoenix*, 8, 17. Brown, "Early Inhabitants and Canals," 14. P. Taylor, "Mexicans North of Rio Grande," 135–136.

10. "Southern Pacific Buys Land near Phoenix," *Los Angeles Times*, Sept. 24, 1907. "First Cotton Picking Heavier than Expected," *Los Angeles Times*, Oct. 27, 1908. "Reclaiming Dry Lands," *Los Angeles Times*, Aug. 7, 1910. "Angelenos Are Heavy Buyers of Lots in Parker Townsite," May 17, 1910. "Phoenix Has Boom, Epoch," *Los Angeles Times*, Oct. 8, 1909. "Los Angeles Pledges a Hundred Thousand," *Los Angeles Times*, Sept. 18, 1912. "Settlers Push Verde Project," *Los Angeles Times*, Sept. 12, 1913. "Cotton Harvest in Full Swing," *Los Angeles Times*, Oct. 11, 1914.

11. "Twenty-Million-Dollar Tire Factory Coming to Los Angeles Soon," *Los Angeles Times*, June 29, 1919. "Flood of Mexican Aliens a Problem," *Los Angeles Times*, Nov. 3, 1919. McWilliams, *Ill Fares Land*, 79. "Using Mexicans to Pick Cotton," *Los Angeles Times*, Oct. 12, 1919. Peterson, "Twentieth-Century Search for Cibola," 117, 119–121. "Flood of Mexican Aliens a Problem," *Los Angeles Times*, Nov. 3, 1919.

12. Reisler, *By Sweat of Brow*, 38–39. "Asks Relief for Cotton Pickers," *Los Angeles Times*, Feb. 25, 1921. "Urges That State Aid Stranded Mexicans," *Copper Era*, Feb. 25, 1921.

13. Peterson, "Twentieth-Century Search for Cibola," 117, 119–121.

14. Peterson, "Twentieth-Century Search for Cibola," 101, 103. "Asks Relief for Cotton Pickers," *Los Angeles Times*, Feb. 25, 1921. "Urges That State Aid Stranded Mexicans," *Copper Era*, Feb. 25, 1921. Reisler, *By Sweat of Brow*, 38–39.

15. P. Taylor, "Mexican Labor in United States," 7–8, 12, 17.

16. Delmatier, McIntosh, and Waters, *Rumble of California Politics*, 212–216. "Industrial Relations and Labor Conditions," *Labor Monthly Review*, Mar. 1929, 59. P. Taylor, "Mexican Labor in United States," 2–3. McWilliams, *Factories in Fields*, 185, 188. "Relief in Labor Shortage," *Los Angeles Times*, Feb. 3, 1926. "Valley Labor Issue Settled," *Los Angeles Times*, Apr. 12, 1926. "California's Farm Labor Situation One Calling for Careful Study," *Los Angeles Times*, May 2, 1926. "Peril Cited in Box Bill," *Los Angeles Times*, Feb. 28, 1928. Cramp, Shields, and Thomson, *Mexican Population in Imperial Valley*, 2.

17. P. Castillo, "Making of Mexican Barrio," 20. Romo, *East Los Angeles*, 102.

18. Abel, "Mexicans and Tuberculosis Control," 823–849. Scott, "Mexican-American in Los Angeles," 77, 79–80. Kienle, "Housing Conditions among Mexican Population," 6. "No Plague Cases for Four Days," *Los Angeles Times*, Nov. 11, 1924. Romo, "Mexicanos in Los Angeles," 157.

19. Scott, "Mexican-American in Los Angeles," 67–71. Gustavson, "Ecological Analysis of Hollenbeck," 43. "Los Angeles Is Mecca of Mexican Refugees," *Los Angeles Times*, May 17, 1920.

20. "Los Angeles Is Mecca of Mexican Refugees," *Los Angeles Time*, May 17, 1920. "Mexican Señoritas Now Adorn Local Society," *Los Angeles Times*, Oct. 22, 1922. "Sonora Town, Backwater in Swirling Life of City," *Los Angeles Times*, Sept. 9, 1923. "Cinco de Mayo Gala Day" *Los Angeles Times*, May 6, 1923. "Mexicans Bow to Queen," *Los Angeles Times*, Sept. 17, 1924. Agnes Pallen, "Mexicans in Los Angeles," *Los Angeles Times*, May 3, 1925.

21. Sánchez, *Becoming Mexican American*, 75, 115. Medeiros, "*La Opinion*," 65–87. Ortegón, "Religious Status of Mexican Population," 8, 15, 17, 24, 26.

22. Ortegón, "Religious Status of Mexican Population," 8, 15, 17, 24, 26. Sánchez, *Becoming Mexican American*, 75.

23. I. Bernstein, *History of American Worker*, 47–50. For a general treatment of East Los Angeles, see Compeán, "Where Only Weeds Grow."

24. "Man Beaten in Jail, Is Charged," *Los Angeles Times*, May 19, 1921 "Mexicans in Gangs Fight with Police," *Los Angeles Times*, Oct. 12, 1925.

25. *California v. Pompa*, 192 Cal. 412 (1923). "Verdict of Murder Is Returned," *Los Angeles Times*, Mar. 14, 1923. "Slayer to Give Life for Crime," *Los Angeles Times*, Jan. 3, 1924. Cardoso, "Mexican Emigration to United States," 122–123. "Pompa to Hang, Governor Says," *Los Angeles Times*, May 24, 1924. Gamio, *Mexican Immigrant*, 103–107.

26. "At the Athletic Club," *Los Angeles Times*, July 27, 1896. "Herrera Knocks Out the Cleveland "Kid" *Los Angeles Times*, June 14, 1903. "One-Time Hero Jailed for Vag[rancy]," *Los Angeles Times*, Dec. 19, 1926. The *Los Angeles Times* chronicled Herrera's career in twenty-one articles. Gregory S. Rodriguez, "Boxing and the Formation of Ethnic Mexican Identities in 20th-Century Southern California," and "Aurelio Herrera, Southern California's First 'Mexican' Boxing Legend," *La Prensa*, Nov. 12, 1999.

27. "Manley Defeated by Colima," *Los Angeles Times*, Mar. 19, 1924. *Los Angeles Times*, Apr. 17, 1924. "Bell Calls Colima to Altar Soon," *Los Angeles Times*, Feb. 4, 1926. "Willis Hands Colima Kayo," *Los Angeles Times*, June 30, 1926. "Bert Colima Knocks out Judge in Tenth Round of Star Bout at Hollywood," *Los Angeles Times*, Aug. 13, 1927. "Colima in Win over Auerback," *Los Angeles Times*, Oct. 15, 1927. "Colima Wins Mexican Title," *Los Angeles Times*, Oct. 8, 1928. From July 1920 to October 1936, the *Los Angeles Times* alone published 318 articles on Colima. Even in the late 1940s, my father, hardly a boxing fan, would rave about Bert Colima, who he claimed paid for Jack Doyle's Olympic auditorium. Monroy, *Mexican Los Angeles*, 56.

28. García, *Race, Labor, and Citrus*, 109. "Teachers Plan to Aid Mexicans," *Los Angeles Times*, Nov. 23, 1925. Sánchez, *Becoming Mexican American*, 95, 99, 103–106, 122. Verner C. Beck, "Making Americans," *Los Angeles Times*, Oct. 27, 1929.

29. Medina, *Cotton-Picking Time*, 51–54. "Arizona Mines Labor Checked," *Los Angeles Times*, Mar. 28, 1932. "Copper District Sky Dark," *Los Angeles Times*, July 4, 1932.

30. P. Taylor, "Mexican Labor in United States," 29, 32.

31. Jamieson, *Unionism in American Agriculture*, 18, 76–78.

32. P. Taylor, "Mexican Labor in United States," 29, 32, 45, 64, 75. Wollenberg, "Huelga, 1928 Style," 48. Lowenstein, "Strike Tactics in California Agriculture," 25. "Melon Pickers Launch Strike Critical Situation," *Los Angeles Times*, May 9, 1928. "Strike in Melon Area Is Failure," *Los Angeles Times*, May 12, 1928. This was not the first time Mexican workers organized in agriculture in the Salt River and Imperial Valleys. Mexican consuls and La Liga Protectora were also involved in work actions in the period 1919–21.

33. Harvey, "Into Imperial Valley in 1930," 7–12. Jamieson, *Unionism in American Agriculture*, 80–81. Greenfield, *Migratory Farm Labor Problems*, 344.

34. "Lettuce Strike Blows Up," *Los Angeles Times*, Feb. 21, 1930. "Legion Men Warned of Red Danger," *Los Angeles Times*, Mar. 15, 1930. "Jury Demands Restitution," *Los Angeles Times*, May 18, 1929. "Second Gillett Trial Today," *Los Angeles Times*, Oct. 29, 1929. "Gillett under Arrest Again," *Los Angeles Times*, Feb. 20, 1930. Jamieson, *Unionism in American Agriculture*, 83. "Strike Agitators Named," *Los Angeles Times*, May 1, 1930. "El Centro Convicts Nine Reds," *Los Angeles Times*, June 14, 1930.

35. Reisler, *By Sweat of Brow*, 234. Daniel, *Bitter Harvest*, 110–113, 127. "Five Vacaville Officers among Injured," *Los Angeles Times*, Nov. 26, 1932. "Town Battles Striking Mob " *Los Angeles Times*, Dec. 5, 1932. "Labor Defense Group Wires Rolph Protests," *Los Angeles Times*, Dec. 6, 1932. "Vacaville 'Mob Rule' Protested," *Los Angeles Times*, Dec. 7, 1932. "Strikers Painted Red by Mob in California," *New York Times*, Dec. 6, 1932. Pat Chambers interview, Oct. 4, 1973.

36. Pat Chambers interview, Apr. 14, 1978. Jamieson, *Unionism in American Agriculture*, 83–89. Mitchell, *Lie of Land*, 124–129. Halcomb, "Efforts to Organize Migrant Workers," 8. "Walnut Strike Hits Wide Area," *Los Angeles Times*, Sept. 30, 1933. Pichardo, "Community in Social Protest," 152.

37. "City Leads World in Industrial Growth," *Los Angeles Times*, July 27, 1930. James Davis, "City Leads World in Industrial Growth," *Los Angeles Times*, July 27. 1930. "Industrial Growth Told," *Los Angeles Times*, Feb. 1, 1931. James L. Davis, "City's Great Industrial Growth Revealed," *Los Angeles Times*, Sept. 6, 1931. Clem S. Glass, "Eastern Trend Promises Hope," *Los Angeles Times*, Apr. 3, 1932. " 'Industrial and Labor Conditions,' Annual report of the Secretary of Labor, 1930," *Monthly Labor Review*, Jan. 1931: 83–89. "Southern California Breaks All Records," *Los Angeles Times*, Jan. 2, 1931. R. D. Sangster, "The Rise of Industry in Southern California," *Los Angeles Times*, Jan. 2, 1931.

38. Sánchez, *Becoming Mexican American*, 211. Ruiz, *Cannery Women*, 5. "Schooling Aid Unit Planned," *Los Angeles Times*, June 20, 1942. Ted Le Berthon, "Why It's Hard for Mexicans to Become Americans," *Los Angeles Times*, Aug. 28, 1932. "Americanization Honored," *Los Angeles Times*, May 22, 1931.

39. Stein, *California and Dust Bowl Migration*, 17, 36. S. Sjupp, "In the Mexican Quarter," *Los Angeles Times*, Oct. 25, 1931. "Use of Marijuana Spreading in West,"

New York Times, Sept. 16, 1934. Woll, "Latin Images in American Films," 20, 31. "Mexicans' Ire Often Roused by Hollywood," *Los Angeles Times*, Nov. 26, 1933. "Mexico Urges Film Embargo," *Los Angeles Times*, Jan. 21, 1934. Abel, "From Exclusion to Expulsion," 823–825, 838.

40. R. López, "Repatriados," 3, 63, in GCP, SC, UCLA. López's seminar paper is a treasure trove of information about the repatriation of Mexicans. Clements to Arnoll, Aug. 17, 1931, GCP, SC, UCLA. A. G. Arnoll was the Secretary Manager of the Los Angeles Chamber of Commerce. Hoffman, "Stimulus to Repatriation," 110. "California Has Fifty Thousand Less Mexicans," *Los Angeles Times*, Oct. 4, 1931.

41. "*Excelsior* Fiercely Attacks Bliss Bill," *Los Angeles Times*, Apr. 5, 1931. "Useless Bills Gum Up Hopper," *Los Angeles Times*, Mar. 16, 1929. "Bliss Offers Bill Changes," *Los Angeles Times*, Apr. 16, 1931. "Bliss Bill Irks Church Group," *Los Angeles Times*, Apr. 17, 1931. "New Protests on Bliss Bill," *Los Angeles Times*, Apr. 5, 1933. "Teacher Raps Race Division," *Los Angeles Times*, Apr. 6, 1931.

42. López, "El Monte Berry Strike," 58. Hoffman, *Unwanted Mexican Americans*, 52, 55. Hoffman, "Stimulus to Repatriation," 113, 116, 118. McWilliams, *North from Mexico*, 193. McLean, "Good-bye, Vincente," 195. "Great Migration Back to Mexico Under Way," *Los Angeles Times*, Apr. 12, 1931. "Trains to Take Mexicans Home," *Los Angeles Times*, Jan. 12, 1932. "Two Hundred Thousand Mexicans Are Taking American Customs into 'The Big Land' of Their Nativity," *Los Angeles Times*, Apr. 24, 1932. Joseph M. Park, "The Repatriados," *Los Angeles Times*, Apr. 24, 1932. "The Mexicans Who Went Home," *Los Angeles Times*, Mar. 20, 1933. "The Mexican Migration," *Los Angeles Times*, Apr. 18, 1931.

43. Pichardo, "Community in Social Protest," 178.

44. Sánchez, *Becoming Mexican American*, 217–221. Joseph M. Park, "The Repatriados," *Los Angeles Times*, Apr. 24, 1932. Jack Starr-Hunt, "The Mexicans Who Went Home," *Los Angeles Times*, Mar. 20, 1933. Balderama and Rodríguez, *Decade of Betrayal*, 194.

45. Bogardus, *Mexican in United States*, 42. Sánchez, *Becoming Mexican American*, 200–202. Ruiz, *Cannery Women*, 9, 14.

46. Pesotta, *Bread upon Waters*, 27–28.

47. Pesotta, *Bread upon Waters*, 28, 32, 45, 50, 51.

48. Fearis, "California Farm Worker," 89. "Farm Strikers to Start Drive," *Los Angeles Times*, June 25, 1933. Azuma, "Racial Struggle, Immigrant Nationalism." Ginzberg, "State Agrarianism versus Democratic," 341–372. Pichardo, "Community in Social Protest," 145. At this point, Mexican officials seem to be paranoid about communist activity in Mexico. "Mexico Orders Moscow Legation to Come Home," *Los Angeles Times*, Jan. 24, 1930. "Mexico Uprising Subdued," *Los Angeles Times*, Apr. 7, 1930. "Plot Aimed at Daniels," *Los Angeles Times*, Apr. 16, 1933.

49. "Seven in Berry Strike Jailed," *Los Angeles Times*, June 11, 1933. "Officers Watch Picketing Army," *Los Angeles Times*, June 30, 1933. "Action to End Strike Begun," *Los Angeles Times*, July 1, 1933.

50. "Seven in Berry Strike Jailed," *Los Angeles Times*, June 11, 1933. "Officers

Watch Picketing Army," *Los Angeles Times*, June 30, 1933. "Action to End Strike Begun," *Los Angeles Times*, July 1, 1933. Chretien, "Dual Unionism." Lenin, *Left-Wing Communism*, 117–118.

51. González, *Mexican Consuls and Labor Organizing*, 82–115, 101–103. Daniel, *Bitter Harvest*, 146–149. "The Los Angeles County Strike of 1933," 10–12. Jamieson, *Unionism in American Agriculture*, 90–92. Pat Chambers interview, Apr. 13, 1978. Spaulding, "Mexican Strike at El Monte," 571–572. López, "El Monte Berry Strike," 105.

52. Steinbeck's *In Dubious Battle* was based on interviews of organizers Pat Chambers and Caroline Decker, among others. Loftis, *Witnesses to Struggle*, 2, 45–65. Jamieson, *Unionism in American Agriculture*, 15, 19–21, 36, 93; quotation on p. 15. Pat Chambers interview, Apr. 19, 1978.

53. "Farm Workers' Pay Increased," *Los Angeles Times*, Aug. 2, 1933. "Recovery Act Hits First Snag near Fresno," *Los Angeles Times*, Aug. 2, 1933. "Tulare County Backs Recovery Act Plan," *Los Angeles Times*, Aug. 2, 1933.

54. Halcomb, "Efforts to Organize Migrant Workers," 12. "Ranch Produces Enormous Crops," *Los Angeles Times*, Aug. 10, 1931. "Tagus Ranch Strike Called," *Los Angeles Times*, Aug. 12, 1933. "Tulare Fruit Strike Fizzles," *Los Angeles Times*, Aug. 14, 1933.

55. Darcy, "Excerpts," 262–263. "Tulare County Backs Recovery Act Plan," *Los Angeles Times*, Aug. 2, 1933 "Tulare Fruit Strike Fizzles," *Los Angeles Times*, Aug. 14, 1933. "Strike Plot Laid to Reds," *Los Angeles Times*, Aug. 17, 1933. "Fruit Workers Talk of Strike," *Los Angeles Times*, Aug. 25, 1933. For one of the best studies on the CWA&IU, see Halcomb, "Efforts to Organize Migrant Workers," 9–37.

56. *Fresno Bee*, Aug. 15, 1933.

57. The *Los Angeles Times* had a flow of articles on Creel and the NRA Code. Halcomb, "Efforts to Organize Migrant Workers," 24–25. "Creel Continues As West Chief," *Visalia Times Delta*, Oct. 4, 1933. "Fruit Peace Hopes Rise," *Los Angeles Times*, Aug. 17, 1933.

58. *Chico Record*, Aug. 24, 1933. "Kern County Sheriff Deputized 300 Growers, 600 Ranchers Issued Gun Permits," *Visalia Times Delta*, Sept. 22, 1933.

59. McWilliams, *Factories in Fields*, 213–219. *Bakersfield Californian*, Sept. 14, 1933. "Grape Pickers Threaten Strike for More Wages," *Los Angeles Times*, Sept. 6, 1933. Walter Garrison was infamous in the San Joaquin Valley. See 1920 census, Series T625, Roll 143, Page 19B, Enumeration District 146, Image 0310; and 1930 census, Elkhorn, San Joaquin County, California, Roll 210, Page 8B, Enumeration District 17, Image 935.0. Garrison was born in 1876 in California; his father was from Missouri and mother from Pennsylvania. Listed as a farmer, the "Colonel" did not register for the draft during World War I, nor could I find any evidence that he had ever served in the military. He lived in Elkhorn, and his neighbors were mostly Japanese. "Fruit Workers Talk of Strike," *Los Angeles Times*, Aug. 25, 1933. "Peach Pickers Delegate Arrested for Trespass" *Los Angeles Times*, Aug. 25, 1933. "Fruit Ranch Picket Line Broken Up," *Los Angeles Times*, Sept. 1, 1933.

60. Jamieson, *Unionism in American Agriculture*, 97–98; the Municipal Court Justice quotation is on page 9. "Vineyards Row Leads to Killing," *Los Angeles Times*, Oct. 6, 1933.

61. "Plan Farmers Organizing Units," *Bakersfield Californian*, Sept. 9, 1933. McFarland and Earlimart growers formed chapters of precursors to the Associated Farmers. "Labor Agitator under Arrest," *Visalia Times Delta*, Sept. 9, 1933. A representative of the C&AWIU was arrested for criminal syndicalism. There was a drive to round up all union agitators in the San Joaquin Valley.

62. Pat Chambers interview, Apr. 13, 1978.

63. Daniel, *Bitter Harvest*, 180. Jamieson, *Unionism in American Agriculture*, 95–96.

64. *Bakersfield Californian*, Sept. 14, 1933. "Plan Farmers Organizing Units" *Bakersfield Californian*, Sept. 9, 1933. "Strike Leaders Move Activity," *Los Angeles Times*, Sept. 13, 1933. *Bakersfield Californian*, Sept. 12, 1933. Guerin-Gonzales, *Mexican Workers and American Dreams*, 119–122. A report to J. H. Fallin of the Farm Labor Division of the Employment Service in Los Angeles predicted that strikers in the El Monte strike would agitate in the San Joaquin Valley, as they had in the berry fields. Fallin informed Frank Palomares, who withdrew his offer to place unemployed strikers in the cotton fields. Clements to Mr. Arnoll, July 12, 1933, "Mexican Labor," GCP, SC, UCLA.

Chapter 12. The San Joaquin Valley Cotton Strike of 1933

1. See McNally, "E. P. Thompson." See also Winn, *Weavers of Revolution*, unnumbered dedication page.

2. Most pickers came over a winding road the workers called the Grapevine from Los Angeles. Others including the Oklahomans came over the Tehachapi Mountains into the Lower San Joaquin Valley. Mitchell, *Lie of Land*, 13, discusses the Joads' astonishment at seeing the San Joaquin Valley in the "morning glow." See Steinbeck, *Grapes of Wrath*, 309–310.

3. Large, "Cotton in San Joaquin Valley," 367.

4. Burton L. Smith, "Cotton Has Come to Stay in the Valley of the San Joaquin," *Los Angeles Times*, Dec. 27, 1925. "Quality of Cotton Starts Demand for Tipton Land," *Los Angeles Times*, Feb. 22, 1925.

5. "Cotton Price Pegged at ten Cts. Lb.," *Bakersfield Californian*, Sept. 23, 1933. Fearis, "California Farm Worker," 97–98. Rasmussen, *Department of Agriculture*, 23–24. On June 19, 1933, FDR initiated a cotton plow-up program of 10 million acres, one-fourth of crop. Cotton producers received rental payments for plowing up — and keeping out of production — 25 to 50 percent of their cotton acreage.

6. "Facts about 100-Degree Temperatures at Bakersfield."

7. Middlebrook, "Localization of Cotton Culture," 6, 9–12. Goldschmidt, *As You Sow*, 13, 32–34, 38–40, 44.

8. "Autos Increase Ranch Troubles," *Los Angeles Times*, Sept. 25, 1924. Jamieson, *Unionism in American Agriculture*, 72–73.

9. D. A. Weber, *Dark Sweat, White Gold*, 86–90. For similar activity in Mexico, see Carr, "Mexican Communist Party," 371, 373. Carr discusses the role of salaried peasants in organizing in this area in the 1930 and the role of the Communist Party. He points out that syndicalism and agrarianism were distinct views of agricultural reform in Mexico. It should not be assumed that Mexican rural workers came to the United States without a worldview; the Revolution had politicized much of Mexican society.

10. Jamieson, *Unionism in American Agriculture*, 87. Mitchell, *Lie of Land*, 134.

11. Mitchell, *Lie of Land*, 90–91, 115, Halcomb, "Efforts to Organize Migrant Workers," 4. Chaffee, *Cannery and Agricultural Workers*, 2–3. D. A. Weber, *Dark Sweat, White Gold*, 39–40, 42, 46, 80, 128. Reisler, *By Sweat of Brow*, 81. According to the 1930 census, Fresno, California, Roll 116, Page 11A, Frank J. Palomares lived in Fresno. The 1920 census, Monterey, California, Series T625, Roll 122, Page 13A, lists him as working for Spreckels Sugar in Monterey. Palomares was born (about 1871) in California, as were both of his parents and his wife Virginia's parents.

12. George West, "Communists Tried under I.W.W. Law," *New York Times*, Jan. 20, 1935. McWilliams, *Factories in Fields*, 212.

13. *Visalia Times Delta*, Sept. 16, 1933. "Growers Launch Organization to Assist Farmers," *Bakersfield Californian*, Sept. 19, 1933. *Visalia Times Delta*, Sept. 28, 1933. Darcy, "Excerpts," pp. 334–336. Sam Darcy interview.

14. Fearis, "California Farm Worker," 87–88. Rasmussen, *Department of Agriculture*, 23–24. "Valley Cut Requested," *Los Angeles Times*, June 23, 1933.

15. Halcomb, "Efforts to Organize Migrant Workers," 10–12, 69. P. Taylor and Kerr, "Documentary History of Strike," 19947, 19949.

16. Daniel, *Bitter Harvest*, 182.

17. J. E. Morgan: 1930 census, Corcoran, Kings County, California, Roll 122, Page, Enumeration District, Image: Caroline Decker interview, Aug. 8, 1973. Pat Chambers interview, Aug. 24, 1973.

18. Alejandro Torralva Rodríguez interview. Rodríguez assured me there was plenty of food at the Corcoran camp—a view that was contradicted by Lilly Cuellar, other strikers, and news accounts. He died Feb. 11, 1980, in Kings County. California Death Index, 1940–1997. He was not listed in the Social Security Death Index, which suggests that was Rodríguez always in farm labor.

19. Lilly Cuellar interview.

20. Matteo (Mateo) Castro: 1930 census, Corcoran, Kings County, California, Roll 122, Page 4A, Enumeration District 5, Image: 715.0. Although others refer to Mateo as a foreman or contractor, the census lists him as "farm laborer."

21. Arax and Wartzman, *King of California*, 138–139, 140.

22. Arax and Wartzman, *King of California*, 138–150; Rudy Castro quotations on pp. 138 and 150; nurse quotation on p. 146.

23. Paul S. Taylor Field Notes, Dec. 20–24, 1933. Daniel, *Bitter Harvest*, 187. P.

Taylor and Kerr, "Documentary History of Strike," 19981–19982. Lino Sanchez: 1920 census, Corcoran, Kings County, California, Series T625, Roll 101, Page 15A, Enumeration District, Image.

24. "Arvin Agitators Fail in Efforts to Halt Picking," *Bakersfield Californian*, Oct. 2, 1933.

25. John Cass Walser: 1930 census, Bakersfield, Kern County, California, Roll 121, Page 7B. The 1880 census, Calienta, Kern County, California, Series T9, Roll 66, Page, lists Walser as living in Calienta. *Visalia Times Delta*, Oct. 3, 1933. "Growers Form Group to Buck Cotton Strike," *Hanford Morning Journal*, Oct. 6, 1933. "Growers Evict Cotton Strikers in Kings Area," *Fresno Bee*, Oct. 5, 1933. "11 Arrested, Kern Cotton Strike," *Bakersfield Californian*, Oct. 3, 1933. *Agricultural Worker* (Cannery and Agricultural Workers Industrial Union) 1, no. 2 (Feb. 20, 1934): 1–2. R. Torres, "San Joaquin Valley Cotton Strike," 23.

26. *Visalia Times Delta*, Oct. 7, 1933. R. Torres, "San Joaquin Valley Cotton Strike," 32–34. Robert Hill: 1930 census, Visalia, Tulare County, California, Roll 226, Page 10A. Walter C. Haight, Social Security no.: 552-54-5703; Birth Date: Oct. 26, 1874; Birthplace: Illinois; Death Date: Nov. 2, 1962; Death Place: Tulare, California. Death Index, 1940–1997, Record.

27. Delos O. Howard: 1930 census, Alila, Tulare County, California, Roll 225, Page 3B, Enumeration District 1, Image 589.0. Hiram C. May: 1930 census, Alila, Tulare County, California, Roll 225, Page, Enumeration District, Image.

28. *Visalia Times Delta*, Oct. 7, 1933. R. Torres, "San Joaquin Valley Cotton Strike," 32–34. Robert Hill: 1930 census, Visalia, Tulare County, California, Roll 226, Page 10A. Walter C. Haight, Social Security no.: 552-54-5703; Birth Date: Oct. 26, 1874; Birthplace: Illinois; Death Date: Nov. 2, 1962; Death Place: Tulare, California. Social Security Records and California Death Index, 1940–1997.

29. Strikers statement in "Brief History of the San Joaquin Valley Cotton Strike," PSTC, Bancroft Library, UCB.

30. "Tulare Described as Powder Barrel," *Bakersfield Californian*, Oct. 9, 1933. "Growers Plan to Drive Out Agitators," *Visalia Times Delta*, Oct. 9, 1933. "Kern County Legion Post Inducts Officers,"*Los Angeles Times*, Oct. 9, 1933.

31. *San Francisco Examiner*, Oct. 10, 1933, as quoted in Chaffee, *Cannery and Agricultural Workers*, 17–18. "Rabbi's Message," *San Francisco Chronicle*, Oct. 7, 1933. "New Strike Declared," *Los Angeles Times*, Oct. 10, 1933.

32. "Growers Plan to Drive Out Agitators," *Visalia Times Delta*, Oct. 9, 1933. Chaffee, *Cannery and Agricultural Workers*, 27, 31. Darcy, "Excerpts," 334.

33. "Kern County American Legion Post Inducts Officers" *Los Angeles Times*, Oct. 9, 1933. "4,000 Growers to Protect Labor," *Bakersfield Californian*, Oct. 9, 1933. The Sam Darcy interview and Darcy, "Excerpts," give the impression that Darcy masterminded the Tagus Ranch and San Joaquin Valley strikes. The Porter Chafee interviews of May 25 and June 7, 1977, 43, 72–73, give most of the credit to Caroline Decker and Pat Chambers, suggesting some tension between Darcy and other members of the party who were not as ideological. Sam White, *Kern County Labor Journal*, Bakersfield, Nov.

17, 1933, in PSTC, Bancroft Library, UCB. Halcomb, "Efforts to Organize Migrant Workers," 42, 45. Fearis, "California Farm Worker," 105.

34. *Visalia Times Delta*, Oct. 10, 1933. Darcy, "Excerpts," 335–336. By Oct. 9, there were more than 10,000 pickers on strike, with some 8,000 still in the field. Darcy, "Excerpts," 338. R. Taylor, *Chavez and Farm Workers*, 52.

35. R. Torres, "San Joaquin Valley Cotton Strike," 46. Joe Ambris: 1930 census, Los Angeles, Roll 163, Page 25A, Enumeration District 711, Image 520.0. Joe's sons Albert and Raymond were born in Texas; his son Tony, in Kansas. From this and other census profiles, the indication is that many of the strikers had made California their residence.

36. Halcomb, "Efforts to Organize Migrant Workers," 61–62. P. Taylor and Kerr, "Documentary History of Strike," 19963; Chaffee, *Cannery and Agricultural Workers*, 49.

37. Ira Knox: 1930 census, Alpaugh, Tulare County, California, Roll 225, Page 2A.

38. R. Taylor, *Chavez and Farm Workers*, 51. *Visalia Times Delta*, Oct. 11, 1933. "Red Leader Incited Men by Speeches," *San Francisco Chronicle*, Oct. 11, 1933. "Ranchers Charge Meet," *Hanford Morning Journal*, Oct. 11, 1933. R. Torres, "San Joaquin Valley Cotton Strike," 51. Clifford Fox, "Score Wounded in Labor War of Three Counties," *San Francisco Chronicle*, Oct. 11, 1933. Fox columns were the opposite of *Los Angeles Times* columnist Chapin Hall, who had a lynch mob boss mentality.

39. Letter to the Editor from Mabel M. Richardson, San Marino, *Los Angeles Times*, Oct. 12, 1933. *San Francisco Chronicle*, Oct. 11, 1933. Darcy, "Excerpts," 339–342. Sam Darcy interview. "Four Dead and Scores Hurt in Cotton Strike," *Los Angeles Times*, Oct. 11, 1933. "4 Slain in State Strike," *San Francisco Chronicle*, Oct. 11, 1933.

40. O. W. Bryan interview. Bryan was a local hardware store owner and community leader.

41. Ronald Taylor interview. R. Taylor, *Chavez and Farm Workers*, 53–55.

42. Ira B. Cross to Raymond V. Cato, Feb. 20, 1934, PSTC, Bancroft Library, UCB.

43. Hugh S. Jewett: 1930 census, Bakersfield, Kern County, California, Roll 121, Page 11B. Lloyd W. Frick: 1930 census, Township 15, Kern County, California, Roll 122, Page 35B. Frick spelled his name "Fricke" on the 1930 census, which listed him as a "land developer."

44. "Eight Men Jailed Here for Arvin Battle Probe," *Bakersfield Californian*, Oct. 11, 1933. "Gun and Club Battles near Arvin and Pixley Described," *Bakersfield Californian*, Oct. 11, 1933. "Conflict at Arvin Ranch Is Described," *Bakersfield Californian*, Oct. 11, 1933. "Report Three Slain, Several Beaten in Arvin Strike Riot," *Bakersfield Californian*, Oct. 10, 1933. Leo Raridan, "Sheriff's Aid Asked When Peril Looms," San Francisco Chronicle, Oct. 12, 1933.

45. *Pixley Enterprise*, Nov. 10, 1933. Clifford Fox, "Score Wounded in Labor War of Three Counties," *San Francisco Chronicle*, Oct. 11, 1933. Loftis, *Witnesses to Struggle*, 25.

46. Pedro Subia's son, Pedro (Pete) M. Subia, was born on Mar. 31, 1913. Pete said

his father migrated from Camargo, Chihuahua, in 1891. It is probable that Pedro Subia had returned to Mexico for a visit. Pete's mother was Frances Markus, born in New Mexico, although some documents list her birthplace as Mexico. Pete had been the general manager of Schwartz, Inc., a clothing story, where he worked for twenty-five years. He was reluctant to talk about the cotton strike and discouraged me from talking to his sister in Burbank, who, he said, was suffering from hypertension. Pedro M. Subia interview. Pete died of a stroke at the Valley Medical Center in Fresno on August 21, 1990. As a result of his father's killing, he had a history of hypertension. Certification of Death, State of California, State File no. 90-119477. His surviving spouse was Grace Muñoz. He was buried at the Belmont Memorial Park Cemetery in Fresno.

47. Pedro Subia, no. 4717, Coroners's Court of the County of Kern, State of California, N. C. Houze, Coroner of the County of Kern, Oct. 14, 1933. "Picker Tells His Story of Arvin Battle," *Bakersfield Californian*, Oct. 11, 1933. "Strikers Deny Using Guns in Wasco Area," *Bakersfield Californian*, Oct. 11, 1933.

48. Undersheriff Tom Carter interview. See also Thomas J. Carter: 1930 census, Bakersfield, Kern County, California, Roll 121, Page 12B.

49. "Rolph Acts on Strike," *Los Angeles Times*, Oct. 12, 1933.

50. Darcy, "Excerpts," 341. Sam Darcy interview, Feb. 2, 1992. "Mexico Consul Sees No Ill in Kings County," *San Francisco Chronicle*, Oct. 12, 1933. *La Follette Hearings*, pt. 72, p. 26515. Chacón, "Labor Unrest and Industrialized Agriculture," 336–353. Hugh S. Allen: 1930 census, Bakersfield, Kern County, California, Roll 121, Page 5B. See also 1900 census, Township 12, Kern County, California, Series T623, Roll 87, Page 3B.

51. Leo Raridan, "Sheriff's Aid Asked When Peril Looms," *San Francisco Chronicle*, Oct. 12, 1933.

52. District Attorney Clarence Wilson, as quoted in Fearis, "California Farm Worker," 92. Halcomb, "Efforts to Organize Migrant Workers," 59–60, 66. Chambers, 31 and Decker, 21. "Suspected Agitator in Valley Strike Arrested," *Los Angeles Times*, Oct. 13, 1933. "Arvin Riot Trial Prosecution Closes," *Los Angeles Times*, Jan. 19, 1934.

53. Clarence H. Wilson interview.

54. Clifford Fox, "Score Fall in Pitched Ranch Strike Battles," *San Francisco Chronicle*, Oct. 11, 1933. P. Taylor and Kerr, "Documentary History of Strike," 19974.

55. "Mexican Consul Says Labor War at Delano Over," *Los Angeles Times*, Apr. 14, 1932. *Visalia Times Delta*, Oct. 12, 1933. "Mexican Consul to Seek Strike Death Prosecutions," *Pixley Enterprise*, Oct. 13, 1933." "Mexican Consul to Seek Death Prosecutions," *Los Angeles Times*, Oct. 12, 1933. "Mexico to Probe Riot Death," *Bakersfield Californian*, Oct. 13, 1933. González, *Mexican Consuls and Labor Organizing*, 122, 145–146. Enrique Bravo: 1930 census, Los Angeles, Roll 147, Page, Enumeration District, Image.

56. "Mexico Consul Sees No Ill in Kings County," *San Francisco Chronicle*, Oct. 12, 1933. Fearis, "California Farm Worker," 106.

57. Halcomb, "Efforts to Organize Migrant Workers," 65. *Tulare Advance Register*, Oct. 16, 1933. Clifford Fox, "Mexican Boycott Threatened by Consul," *San Francisco*

Chronicle, Oct. 13, 1933. Clifford Fox, "400 Rifles Arm Ragged Regiment for Strike Burial," *San Francisco Chronicle*, Oct. 14, 1933. González, *Mexican Consuls and Labor Organizing*, 133–137. Leoncio Acosta: 1930 census, Fresno, California, Roll 116, Page 84B, Enumeration District 14, Image 169.0.

58. D. A. Weber, *Dark Sweat, White Gold*, 102. Clifford Fox, "4,300 Women, Children Hungry in Tent Cities," *San Francisco Chronicle*, Oct. 13, 1933.

59. Clifford Fox, "400 Rifles Arm Ragged Regiment for Strike Burial," *San Francisco Chronicle*, Oct. 14, 1933. Johns, "Field Workers in California," 67. Fearis, "California Farm Worker," 106. "Strikers Gather in Visalia to Demand Prosecutions," *Los Angeles Times*, Oct. 12, 1933.

60. George Aydelotte interview. "Counties Push N.R.A. Campaign," *Los Angeles Times*, Aug. 17, 1933. "Rolph Acts on Strike," *Los Angeles Times*, Oct. 12, 1933. Clarence S. Morrill, chief of the state criminal intelligence bureau, named Pat Chambers as a communist. "Legion to Investigate Communism in Kern," *Bakersfield Californian*, Oct. 13, 1933. The American Legion Committee of the Frank S. Reynolds Post worked with Morrill and Cato to keep watch on strikers.

61. W. L. Walker interview. W. L. Walker, as quoted in Fearis, "California Farm Worker," 109. Pat Chambers: Social Security no.: 545-20-3453, issued in California (before 1951); Last Residence: San Pedro 90731, Los Angeles; Birth Date: Sept. 13, 1901; Death Date: May 8, 1990.

62. "Offers to Name Arbitrator," *Los Angeles Times*, Oct. 12, 1933. "Rolph Acts on Strike," *Los Angeles Times*, Oct. 12, 1933. "Ultimatum Delivered to Both Groups," *San Francisco Chronicle*, Oct. 12, 1933.

63. *Visalia Times Delta*, Oct. 11, 1933.

64. P. Taylor and Kerr, "Documentary History of Strike," 19959.

Chapter 13. Bitter Warfare

1. Winter, *Not to Yield*, 194–196. Chapter title was inspired by Benson and Loftis, "Steinbeck and Farm Labor Unionization," 197.

2. "Score Fall in Pitched Ranch Strike Battles," *San Francisco Chronicle*, Oct. 11, 1933. "Infant Starves in Strike Camp," *San Francisco Chronicle*, Oct. 11, 1933. Darcy, "Excerpts," 341, 343. Sam Darcy interview.

3. Clifford Fox, "Laborer Shot When Parade Is Dispersed," *Los Angeles Times*, Oct. 12, 1933; see photo by Jack French of cotton pickers at the Visalia Courthouse on p. 5. Clifford Fox, "400 Rifles Arm Ragged Regiment for Strike Burial," *San Francisco Chronicle*, Oct. 14, 1933. *Visalia Times Delta*, Oct. 14, 1933.

4. "Growers Plan to Starve Out Strikers." *San Francisco Chronicle*, Oct. 12, 1933. Editorial, "Farmers and Workers Both Need Protection," *San Francisco Chronicle*, Oct. 13, 1933. "Cotton Strike Hearing Asked," *Los Angeles Times*, Oct. 14, 1933. Other newspapers besides the *Chronicle* made the point that the planters were intentionally starving out the strikers. See, for example, Frederick F. Forbes, "California Clash Called 'Civil War,'" *New York Times*, Oct. 22, 1933.

5. Clifford Fox, "4,300 Women, Children Hungry in Tent Cities," *San Francisco*

Chronicle, Oct. 13, 1933, "Cotton Strike Hearing Asked," *Los Angeles Times*, Oct. 14, 1933. The number of infant deaths was uncounted because many of the mothers did not have papers and would be afraid to register the deaths. The infants were buried at the edge of the highway.

6. R. Torres, "San Joaquin Valley Cotton Strike," 68.

7. Darcy, "Excerpts," 345.

8. R. Torres, "San Joaquin Valley Cotton Strike," 81–82. Clifford Fox, "Sheriff Hits Creel Visit to Strikers," *San Francisco Chronicle*, Oct. 20, 1933. Darcy, "Excerpts," 345. Sam Darcy interview. Daniel, *Bitter Harvest*, 215. D. A. Weber, *Dark Sweat, White Gold*, 106. "San Joaquin Valley News," *Los Angeles Times*, Oct. 21, 1933.

9. Daniel, *Bitter Harvest*, 215. D. A. Weber, *Dark Sweat, White Gold*, 106. "San Joaquin Valley News," *Los Angeles Times*, Oct. 21, 1933.

10. "Growers Plan to Starve Out Strikers" *San Francisco Chronicle*, Oct. 12, 1933.

11. "Federal Action in Strike Asked," *Los Angeles Times*, Oct. 13, 1933. D. A. Weber, *Dark Sweat, White Gold*, 126–127. C. Chambers, *California Farm Organizations*, 83, 92. Goldschmidt, *As You Sow*, 46. J. Webb, *Migratory-Casual Worker*, 1, 5.

12. D. A. Weber, "Raiz Fuerte." *San Francisco Examiner*, Oct. 13, 1933, as quoted in Chaffee, *Cannery and Agricultural Workers Union*, 36–38.

13. D. A. Weber, *Dark Sweat, White Gold*, 103–107. "Farm Act Commended by Leader," *Los Angeles Times*, Oct. 12, 1933. "Cotton Strike Truce Ignored," *Los Angeles Times*, Oct. 17, 1933. *Bakersfield Californian*, Oct. 12, 1933.

14. *Tulare Advance Register*, Oct. 16, 1933. Halcomb, "Efforts to Organize Migrant Workers," 69.

15. Chaffee, *Cannery and Agricultural Workers*, 35, 49. "Relief Roll Census Made," *Los Angeles Times*, Dec. 11, 1933.

16. "Mexican Labor Blamed in Row," *San Francisco Chronicle*, Oct. 14, 1933.

17. Joe Gladney interview. Joseph F. Gladney, 51, born in 1878, was a farmer. See 1930 census, Tipton, Tulare County, California, Roll 226, Page, Enumeration District 61, Image 740.0. Joe Gladney's son, Joseph W., 17, lived with his father, mother, two older brothers, one younger brother and three sisters in Tipton, Tulare County, California. Joseph W. and his fifteen-year-old brother were born in Texas; his parents, in Oklahoma. Two of his sisters, ages eleven and nine, were born in Arizona; his youngest sister was born in California. His twenty-one-year-old brother was born in Oklahoma; his nineteen-year-old brother, in California. Chaffee, *Cannery and Agricultural Workers*, 12.

18. Enid Hubbard, "Mapped for Slain Picker, *San Francisco Chronicle*, Oct. 16, 1933.

19. Tipton dairy farmer interview. Charges were dropped against A. D. Stark and Monroe Stark, who were found not to be at Pixley during the shootings. Anthony Solo interview.

20. J. Boyd interview.

21. "Jail Trio in Kern," *Bakersfield Californian*, Oct. 12, 1933. "Strikers Gather in Visalia to Demand Protection" *Los Angeles Times*, Oct. 12, 1933. "Cotton Strikers

Make Plea to Gov. Rolph," *Los Angeles Times*, Oct. 13, 1933. "Strikers Gather in Visalia," *Los Angeles Times*, Oct. 13, 1933. "Governor Acts to End Strike," *Los Angeles Times*, Oct. 13, 1933. Leo Raridan, "Strike Murder Laid to Seven in Bakersfield," *San Francisco Chronicle*, Oct. 14, 1933.

22. *Bakersfield Californian*, Oct. 14, 1933.

23. *Bakersfield Californian*, Oct. 14, 1933. "Open Verdict Given in Killing of Striker" *Los Angeles Times*, Oct. 15, 1933. "Cotton Strike Comes to End," *Los Angeles Times*, Oct. 15, 1933. "Arbitration near in Cotton Pickers' Strike," *Los Angeles Times*, Oct. 15, 1933. "Seven to Face Rioting Charges" *Bakersfield Californian*, Oct. 27, 1933. Conspiracy charges were dropped against Viola Andrews, Alonzo Andrews, Herschel Real, Jesse McHenry, H. E. Clark, and William Johnson.

24. Telephone conversation with Ralph Kreiser, July 18, 1973; Ralph Kreiser interview. Ralph Kreiser, Social Security no.: 548-01-0053; Birth Date: Feb. 22, 1908; Death Date: Nov. 1975; Last Residence: Bakersfield 93308, Kern County, California. Kreiser was from Kansas. He said it was natural that many should want to talk to him about the strike because he was the oldest and only living reporter on the scene.

25. McWilliams, *Factories in Fields*, 222. Clifford Fox, "400 Rifles Arm Ragged Regiment for Strike Burial," *San Francisco Chronicle*, Oct. 14, 1933.

26. "Strikers Honor Slain 'Comrade,' " *Bakersfield Californian*, Oct. 16, 1933. Enid Hubbard, "Subia Rites Strip Camps of Families," *San Francisco Chronicle*, Oct. 17, 1933. "Cotton Pickers Parade 2,000 Strong in Bakersfield," *Los Angeles Times*, Oct. 17, 1933.

27. Clifford Fox, "Cotton Strike," *San Francisco Chronicle*, Oct. 22, 1933.

28. Clifford Fox, "Cotton Strikers Vote War to Finish: Women Called into Picket Lines Today," *San Francisco Chronicle*, Oct. 16, 1933. Clifford Fox, "Strike Bull Pen Seen in Cotton Area," *San Francisco Chronicle*, Oct. 18, 1933.

29. Clifford Fox, "Strike Zone Invaded by Armed Band," *San Francisco Chronicle*, Oct. 17, 1933. *San Francisco Chronicle*, Oct. 18, 1933. Bravo's taunt to the workers might have carried more weight had this upper-middle-class Mexican himself spent a single day in the fields.

30. Halcomb, "Efforts to Organize Migrant Workers," 74. P. Taylor and Kerr, "Documentary History of Strike," 19984. Editorial in *Hanford Morning Journal*, reprinted in *Tulare Advance Register*, Oct. 18, 1933. "Cotton Strike Hearing Asked," *Los Angeles Times*, Oct. 14, 1933. "Cotton Strike Area Quiet," *Los Angeles Times*, Oct. 18, 1933.

31. "100 Highway Police Sent into Corcoran Area to Halt Riots," *Bakersfield Californian*, Oct. 24, 1933. "Strike Situation in Corcoran Dangerous," *Bakersfield Californian* Oct. 24, 1933.

32. Clifford Fox, "Kern Asks U.S. to Halt Strikes; Pupils in Field," *San Francisco Chronicle*, Oct. 23, 1933. Chacón, "San Joaquin Valley Cotton Strike," 58–61.

33. "Cotton Strike Comes to End," *Los Angeles Times*, Oct. 15, 1933. "Kings County Sheriff Increases Deputies," *Los Angeles Times*, Oct. 21, 1933. "Cotton Picking Proceeds," *Bakersfield Californian*, Oct. 21, 1933. "Sheriff Hits Creel Visit to Strik-

ers," *San Francisco Chronicle*, Oct. 20, 1933. Chacón, "San Joaquin Valley Cotton Strike," 39.

34. Loftis, *Witnesses to Struggle*, 30–33.

35. Darcy, "Excerpts," 345. See also Sam Darcy interview. "Hearing Held on Cotton Strike."

36. "Hearing Held on Cotton Strike."

37. Johns, "Field Workers in California," 68. Goldschmidt, *As You Sow*, 156.

38. Louis D. Ellett, was from Texas, as were his parents and wife. Ellett was chairman of the Kings County Growers' Committee and agent for the Pacific Coast Seed Products Company. See 1930 census, Corcoran, Kings County, California, Roll 122, Page 11A, Enumeration District 4, Image 693.0. P. Taylor and Kerr, "Documentary History of Strike," 19982. "From the Proceedings of State Sheriffs Assn, 1934," 20, 23. PSTC, Bancroft Library, UCB. Darcy, "Excerpts," 347. "San Joaquin Valley News; Cotton Strike Views Related," *Los Angeles Times*, Oct. 21, 1933.

39. "Report on Cotton Strikers," 2, 3.

40. "Pickers' Wage Raise Advised," *Los Angeles Times*, Oct. 24, 1933. *San Francisco Chronicle*, Oct. 24, 1933. Halcomb, "Efforts to Organize Migrant Workers," 68, 72.

41. San Joaquin Valley planter, as quoted in Fearis, "California Farm Worker," 38. Clark Kerr interview, in P. Taylor and Kerr, "Documentary History of Strike," 20009.

42. *Visalia Delta Times*, Oct. 25, 1933. Halcomb, "Efforts to Organize Migrant Workers," 73. Edson Abel to Cross, Nov. 8 and Dec. 8, 1933; Ira Cross to Edson Abel, Jan. 6, 1934, PSTC, Bancroft Library, UCB. "Cotton Loans Held at Stake," *Los Angeles Times*, Oct. 22, 1933. Loftis, *Witnesses to Struggle*, 31.

43. Chapin Hall, "Cotton Growers Accept Proposal to End Strike," *Los Angeles Times*, Oct. 26, 1933. Chapin Hall, "Why Has Los Angeles So Many on Relief Roll?" *Los Angeles Times*, Dec. 1, 1933.

44. "Cotton Men Consider 75-cent Picking Rate but Demand U.S. Aid," *Bakersfield Californian*, Oct. 24, 1933. "Cotton Men Accept 75-Cent Rate," and "Higher Wage for Pickers Is Approved," *Bakersfield Californian*, Oct. 25, 1933. Chaffee, *Cannery and Agricultural Workers*, 37–40. Chapin Hall, "Cotton Growers Accept Proposal to End Strike," *Los Angeles Times*, Oct. 26, 1933. *Pixley Enterprise*, Oct. 27, 1933. "Cotton Strike Comes to End," *Los Angeles Times*, Oct. 28, 1933.

45. "Money Talking against Project," *Bakersfield Californian*, Nov. 28, 1933. "Grapes Coming Back after Volstead Spree," *San Francisco Chronicle*, Nov. 22, 1933.

46. "Kern Growers Get More Than Million Dollars from Co-operative," *Bakersfield Californian*, Jan. 6, 1934. "Cotton Men's Income Twice That of 1932," *Bakersfield Californian*, Jan. 13, 1934. "Farm Administration Satisfied with Cotton, Wheat Reduction Plan," *San Francisco Chronicle*, Jan. 13, 1934. Paul C. Smith, "Melon Cut by Giannini Organization," *San Francisco Chronicle*, Jan. 6, 1934.

47. *Tulare Advance Register*, Dec. 12, 1933. "The Source of Trouble," *Bakersfield Californian*, Nov. 28, 1933. "Chambers' Fate Rests with Jury," *Los Angeles Times*, Dec. 6, 1933. *Tulare Advance Register*, Dec. 6, 1933. "Chambers May Call Notables," *Los*

Angeles Times, Dec. 7, 1933. *Pixley Enterprise*, Dec. 8, 1933. *Tulare Advance Register*, Dec. 9, 1933. "Strike Leader Bond Returned to Owners," *Los Angeles Times*, Dec. 16, 1933. *Pixley Enterprise*, Dec. 15, 1933.

48. "Cotton Pickers' Strike, San Joaquin Valley," Dec. 20–24, 1933. Paul S. Taylor Field Notes, PSTC, Bancroft Library, UCB. "Non-Union Workers Ordered to Cotton Fields," *Los Angeles Times*, Oct. 28, 1933. P. Taylor and Kerr, "Documentary History of Strike," 19968. MacDonald, "California's Agricultural Labor," 19903–19905.

49. Clifford Fox, "Ku Klux Crosses Flame in Warning to Valley Strikers," *San Francisco Chronicle*, Oct. 27, 1933. William V. Buckner was born in 1859 in Kansas; his parents were from Tennessee and Missouri and, as a longtime resident of the area, he had raised five children there. He had been sheriff since at least the turn of the century.

50. W. V. Buckner interview. "3,500 Strikers at Corcoran Flatly Refuse to Vacate Camp," *Bakersfield Californian*, Oct. 26, 1933. See 1930 census, Hanford, Kings County, California, Roll 122, Page 3A, Enumeration District 21, Image 871.0; 1920 census, Hanford, Kings County, California, Series T625, Roll 101, Page 9B, Enumeration District 134, Image 444; and 1900 census, Hanford, Kings County, California, Series T623, Roll 87, Page 2A, Enumeration District 37. Image 444.

51. "3,500 Strikers at Corcoran Flatly Refuse to Vacate Camp," *Bakersfield Californian*, Oct. 26, 1933. MacDonald, "California's Agricultural Labor," 19903–19905. Joseph Warner Guiberson: 1930 census, Corcoran, Kings County, California, Roll 122, Page 1B, Enumeration District: 5; Image: 710.0. Darcy, "Excerpts," 347. Sam Darcy identified Guiberson and Edson Abel, a high-powered lawyer, as ringleaders among the planters. Abel was born in Colton, California, on Apr. 8, 1890, and died in Aug. 1982 in Santa Rosa, Sonoma County, California. Social Security Death Index. Abel registered for the World War I draft in Kern County. WWI Civilian Draft Registrations. Chacón, "San Joaquin Valley Cotton Strike," 58–61. See also MacDonald, "California's Agricultural Labor," 19903–19905.

52. Clifford Fox, "Ku Klux Crosses Flame in Warning to Valley Strikers," *San Francisco Chronicle*, Oct. 27, 1933. P. Taylor and Kerr, "Documentary History of Strike," 19972. Chacón, "San Joaquin Valley Cotton Strike," 44–46. It was widely reported that the strikers would be put in bull pens. When authorities threatened to deport them, they became defiant. Requests to deport the strikers were made by Tulare County District Attorney Walter C. Haight, Chairman of the Tulare Board of Supervisors Alfred J. Elliot, and Foreman of the Grand Jury James R. Fauver.

53. *Bakersfield Californian*, Oct. 27, 1933. "Frank C. MacDonald to Governor James Rolph, Jr., on San Joaquin Valley Cotton Strike," *La Follette Hearings*, pt. 54 (Sept.–Oct. 1933), pp. 19899–19901. González, *Mexican Consuls and Labor Organizing*, 140. Chapin Hall, "Reds Still in Saddle," *Los Angeles Times*, Oct. 27, 1933. *Bakersfield Californian*, Oct. 27, 1933. Clarence H. Wilson interview. "Cato Report to Rolph Denies Strike Headway," *Los Angeles Times*, Nov. 7, 1933.

54. "Porterville Strives to Keep Campers Away," *Los Angeles Times*, Oct. 27, 1933.

55. "Six Held to Answer in Rioting," *Los Angeles Times*, Nov. 3, 1933.

56. Darcy, "Excerpts," 348.

57. Undersheriff Tom Carter interview.

58. Winter, *Not to Yield*, 194–196. Loftis, *Witnesses to Struggle*, 13–29.

59. "Pickets Found Guilty, Maximum for Rioting two years," *Pixley Enterprise*, Nov. 24, 1933. *Tulare Advanced Register*, Nov. 25, 1933.

60. Clifford Fox, "Ku Klux Crosses Flame in Warning to Valley Strikers," *San Francisco Chronicle*, Oct. 27, 1933. Halcomb, "Efforts to Organize Migrant Workers," 75–76. *San Francisco Chronicle*, Oct. 29, 1933.

61. "Grand Jury Starts Strikers Death Inquiry," *Los Angeles Times*, Oct. 14, 1933. Chacón, "San Joaquin Valley Cotton Strike," 53. Jasper N. Stark: 1930 census, Tipton, Tulare County, California, Roll 226, Page 58, Enumeration District 60, Image 720.0. Listed as "farmer" in the 1930 census, Stark, like Culpepper and McAvee, lived in Tipton, with his wife and four children. Stark and his wife were born in Texas; his oldest daughter was born in Oklahoma, and the other children were born in California. Robert Culpepper: 1930 census, Tulare, Tulare County, California, Roll 226, Page 12A, Enumeration District 62, Image 337.0 Culpepper, listed in the 1930 census as a "farm laborer," was from in Texas, as were his wife and son.

62. "Four Convicted on Riot Counts," *Bakersfield Californian*, Jan. 23, 1934. "Strike-Murder Trial Started," *Los Angeles Times*, Jan. 10, 1934. "Story of Fight near Arvin Told in Court by Growers of Kern," *Bakersfield Californian*, Jan. 10, 1934. "Negro Girls Are Chief Witnesses at Rioting Trial," *Bakersfield Californian*, Jan. 12, 1934. "Ned Barlow Tells of Seeing Peter Subia Killed; Says Many Guns Fired," *Bakersfield Californian*, Jan. 12, 1934. "Arvin Riot Trial Testimony Repetitive," *Los Angeles Times*, Jan. 12, 1934. "Rioters Armed, Witness Avers," *Los Angeles Times*, Jan. 13, 1934. "Riot Hearing Is Continued by Judge until January 18," *Bakersfield Californian*, Jan. 13, 1933. "Lawyers Mildly Rebuffed at Kern Riot Count Trial," *Bakersfield Californian*, Jan. 18, 1934. "Riot Defendant Claims Farmer Killed P. Subia," *Bakersfield Californian*, Jan. 19, 1934. "Arvin Trial Hearing Continued," *Los Angeles Times*, Jan. 20, 1934. Born in South Dakota of Russian parents, Marvin Hayes is listed as "rancher" in the 1930 census, Township 15, Kern County, California, Roll 122. Page 20A, Enumeration district 65, Image 537.0 Census records suggest Hayes had been a migrant. His two sons had been born in Texas; his daughters in Oklahoma. Hayes died in 1987 in Visalia. Social Security Records and California Death Index, 1940–1997.

63. *Pixley Enterprise*, Nov. 3, 1933. *Pixley Enterprise*, Jan. 12, 1934. *Tulare Advance Register*, Jan. 12, 1934. Newpapers list Kruger as "Krueger." "Four Linked to Pixley Gun Play in Visalia Trial," *Los Angeles Times*, Jan. 13, 1934, says "Krueger" got his badge from Kern County. Edward G. Kruger, whose father and mother were from Russia and Germany, resp., was born in North Dakota; he lived with his wife and infant son in Kern County. See 1930 census, Township 9, Kern County, California, Series T625, Roll 100, Page 13B, Enumeration District 117, Image 1145, which lists him as "E. G. Kruger."

64. Henry Santens: 1930 census, Alila, Tulare County, California, Roll 225, Page 24A. Santens was born in Pennsylvania; his parents were French and spoke Flemish. He owned his farm. Leland Thompson was not listed in the 1930 census. "Strikers Give

Riot Evidence," *Los Angeles Times*, Jan. 20, 1934. "Allen Denies Riot Shooting," *Los Angeles Times*, Jan. 25, 1934. "News of San Joaquin Valley; Strikers Give Riot Evidence State," *Los Angeles Times*, Jan. 20, 1934. "Suspect Denies Pixley Killing," *Los Angeles Times*, Jan. 31, 1934.

65. *Tulare Advance Register*, Jan. 16, 1934. "Fatal Strike Riot Depicted," *Los Angeles Times*, Jan. 17, 1934. *Tulare Advance Register*, Jan. 17, 1934. "Witness Names Pixley Sniper," *Los Angeles Times*, Jan. 18, 1934.

66. Pixley Trial near End," *Los Angeles Times*, Feb. 1, 1934. *Tulare Advance Register*, Feb. 2, 1934. *Pixley Enterprise*, Feb. 2, 1932. *Tulare Advance Register*, Feb. 3, 1934. "Eight Acquitted in Tulare Cotton Strike Killings," *Los Angeles Times*, Feb. 2, 1934. "Vigilante Committees Need to Stop Rackets," *Porterville Recorder*, reprinted in *Tulare Advance Register*. Feb. 3, 1934. Editorial, *Tulare Advance Register*, Feb. 6, 1934.

67. Chapin Hall, "Church and Schools Used by Red Propagandists," *Los Angeles Times*, Dec. 19, 1933. "Clergy Urge Rolph to Act," *San Francisco Chronicle*, Oct. 12, 1933. "Red Programs in Schools Scored by Legion Chief," *Los Angeles Times*, Dec. 1, 1933. H. B. Walker interview. Clifford Fox, "Strike Zone Invaded by Armed Band," *San Francisco Chronicle*, Oct. 17, 1933. "Berkeley Students Act as Cotton Strike Leaders," *Los Angeles Times*, Oct. 28, 1933. "The Real Source," *Bakersfield Californian*, Oct. 30, 1933.

68. "Cagney Red Aid Listed," *Los Angeles Times*, Aug. 18, 1934. "Four Film Stars' Names Drawn into Red Inquiry," *Los Angeles Times*, Aug. 19, 1934. "Film Stars and Reds," *Los Angeles Times*, Aug. 21, 1934. "Actor Named in Red Trial," *Los Angeles Times*, Jan. 23, 1935. "Suit Calls Film Stars Communists," *Los Angeles Times*, Dec. 10, 1937. According to Buhle and Wagner, *Radical Hollywood*, 81–82, screenwriter John Bright, later married to Josefina Fierro, a Chicana activist, got Cagney to support the 1933 strike. The Hearst press crucified them. Cagney was also photographed with Caroline Decker. Martin Dies hounded Cagney and made innuendoes about him. "Radicals Slate Talks at Visalia," *Los Angeles Times*, Mar. 8, 1935. "Cagney Denies Story," *New York Times*, Aug. 18, 1934. "Film Actor Named in Coast Red Plot," *New York Times*, Aug. 18, 1934. "3 More Film Stars Face 'Red' Inquiry," *New York Times*, Aug. 19, 1934.

69. Pat Chambers, Social Security no.: 545-20-3453; Birth Date: Sept. 13, 1901; Death Date: May 8, 1990; Death Place: San Pedro, California, Social Security Death Index. See Pat Chambers interviews, Aug. 24, 1973, and Apr. 14, 1978. Caroline Decker, Social Security no.: 548-04-6861: Birth Date: Apr. 26, 1912; Death Date: May 1992, Social Security Death Records. Decker later married attorney Richard Gladstein; her last residence was in San Rafael, California. See also interviews by others of Chambers and Decker in Ewart, "Interviews" and in Paul S. Taylor Field Notes, PSTC, Bancroft Library, UCB. R. Taylor, *Chavez and Farm Workers*, 48, 50–57, is based on Taylor's Nov. 27, 1933, interview of Chambers. *San Francisco Chronicle*, Oct. 19, 1933.

70. Red Threats to Judge and Jury Stir Trial," *Los Angeles Times*, Mar. 1, 1935. Halcomb, "Efforts to Organize Migrant Workers," 7. "Bomb Ruse Tips Voiced," *Los Angeles Times*, Mar. 5, 1935. Caroline Decker interview, Aug. 8, 1973. By July 1933,

Decker was organizing farmworkers. She entered the San Joaquin Valley Cotton Strike with Chambers. By most accounts, Decker was a Southerner. In interviews, however, she makes it clear that she was from Pennsylvania and that her father worked around the coal mines. She was attracted to politics through her brother, who belonged to liberal college groups, and from whom she got her radical sense. According to California Death Records and the Social Security Death Index, Decker died as "Caroline Gladstein" — married to a prominent San Rafael, California, attorney. Her parents were probably Russian Jews. Her father's surname was Dwofsky and her mother's, Rackson. Her death certificate lists her birth date as Apr. 26, 1912, and her birthplace as Georgia. The only Dwofsky listed by the census in Georgia was Bernard Dwofsky, born on Jan. 6, 1878, from Macon, Bibb County, Georgia, where he registered for the World War Draft, 1917–1918. Decker was always private, and by misleading others about her family, she may only have been trying to protect them. Being from the South, she most probably experienced anti-Semiticism.

71. Winter, *Not to Yield*, 190. See Decker and other interviews, in Ewart, "Interviews." D. W. Magee, Los Angeles, "Communist Infiltration in Vultee Aircraft," Dec. 10, 1940, on Activities, Nov. 13–28, 1940, RG 165, USMID, 10104-1387-53. An undercover informant reported that Pat Chambers, true name "Henry Patterson," was an organizer for the United Construction Workers Organization Committee and was observed on the picket line at Vultee. On Nov. 28, 1933, Chambers told the undercover informant that Lou Michener had gone to San Diego after the Vultee settlement. Supposedly a close associate of Sam Darcy, Chambers was convicted of criminal syndicalism in a second trial in 1934 and sent to San Quentin.

72. *Visalia Times Delta*, Oct. 10, 1933. Daniel, *Bitter Harvest*, 185. William D. Hamett: 1930 census, Township 2, Fresno County, California, Roll 115, Page 7A. Hamett lived in Fresno with his wife and four sons, twenty-two, twenty, seventeen and eleven, at the time of the strike. Although Hamett was born in Texas, his sons were all born in Oklahoma and had lived there for some time.

73. "Active Communists in California Compiled by Advisory Associates," Jan. 30, 1934, RG 165, USMID, 10110-2666-72. D. A. Weber, *Dark Sweat, White Gold*, 91–95. "California War on Reds Opened on Many Fronts," *Los Angeles Times*, July 21, 1934: "Enrique Rodriguez, who was seized at the Maritime Workers' Industrial Union (Communist) here. When prosecutors produced a long police record and proof that Rodriguez was an alien, he was turned over to immigration authorities for deportation to Mexico."

74. Arax and Wartzman, *King of California*, 20.

75. Arax and Wartzman, *King of California*, 130–131; J. G. Boswell quotation on p. 152.

76. Arax and Wartzman, *King of California*, 153–154. Clarence Salyer, Social Security no.: 562-48-6296, issued 1953 in California; Birth Date: Feb. 4, 1895; Death Date: Jan. 1974; Last Residence: Hanford 93230, Kings County, California, Social Security Death Index; 1930 census, Corcoran, Kings County, California, Roll 122, Page 2B, Enumeration District 5, Image 712.0; 1920 census, Series T625, Roll 101, Page 9B, Enumeration District 120, Image 0068. Salyer came by way of Arkansas to California,

where he purchased an 80-acre farm. Among his holdings were the Salyer Grain and Milling Company. "Ex-Farmhand Operates 35,000-Acre Holdings," *Los Angeles Times*, Jan. 23, 1955.

77. *La Follette Hearings*, pt. 49 (Dec. 16, 1939), pp. 17911–17945. Wofford B. Camp interview, 20–22, 207, 213, 221.

78. Ormond W. Bryan, Social Security no.: 573-44-3342, issued 1951 in California; Birth Date: June 9, 1902; Death Date: Nov. 23, 1993; Last Residence: Earlimart 93219, Tulare County, California, Social Security Death Index; 1920 census, Pomona, Ward 3, Los Angeles County, California, Series T625, Roll 118, Page 17E, Enumeration District 593, Image 923. Listed as "Ormond H. Bryan" on census and as "Ormond W. Bryan" on death certificate. Johns, "Field Workers in California," 62–63. Daniel, *Bitter Harvest*, 195–196. O. W. Bryan, Earlimart, to Dr. Rudy Acuña, Aug. 26, 1973: "I have several friends locally that were involved and as I told you before, I would elect not to review the tragic days and the hard feelings that developed during this ill fated struggle. I elect to let the past remain burie[d] and forget the incident." See RFAFN, June 27, 1973, RFAC, Urban Archives, CSUN.

79. "State Has Farm Peace," *Los Angeles Times*, Sept. 29, 1935. "Pair Sentenced for Exhibition of Red Films," *Los Angeles Times*, June 7, 1934. A postscript: Lillian Dinkin and Lester Balog showed film clips of the strike in a pool hall. They were arrested, tried, and convicted for showing a film without a license in Tulare. Lester had filmed the cotton strike as a young man. When we met years later, the subject never came up, even though I was working on it. Lester's union, United Auto Workers Local 645 in Van Nuys, California, had one of the few copies of *Salt of the Earth*, which had been banned. The union would not lend it out but would let Lester show it whenever he liked, which he did, to young Chicanos, dozens of times.

Chapter 14. La Mula No Nació Arisca

1. Galarza, "Mula No Nació Arisca," 199–200.

2. Frederick F. Forbes, "California Clash Called 'Civil War,'" *New York Times*, Oct. 22, 1933.

3. "Ex-Farmhand Operates 35,000-Acre Holdings," *Los Angeles Times*, Jan. 23, 1955. "Southland Views and News; South Coast," *Los Angeles Times*, Mar. 24, 1960.

4. Wofford B. Camp interview, 20–22, 207, 213, 221. "King Cotton Shifts West," *Los Angeles Times*, Apr. 15, 1934. As the principal economist and representative for the western region of the cotton section of the Agricultural Adjustment Administration, Camp protected the interests of California and Arizona cotton growers. Kreiser called Camp the leader of the growers during 1933. Ralph Kreiser interview, July 25, 1973.

5. Robert B. Powers interviews, 1969. Robert B. Powers interview, Sept. 20, 1973. Robert B. Powers: 1920 census, Camp Furlong, Luna, New Mexico, Series T624, Roll 1076, Page 40A, Enumeration District 72, Image 534. See also 1930 census, Bakersfield, Kern County, California, Roll 121, Page 2A, Enumeration District 16, Image 881.0. Estimated birth year: 1900; Birthplace: New Mexico; Race: White. In 1920, Powers lived at Camp Furlong, Luna, New Mexico. He later became police chief in

Bakersfield. He was appointed by Governor Earl Warren to be coordinator of state law enforcement; he also worked for the progressive attorney general of California, Robert W. Kenny.

6. Ralph Kreiser interview, July 25, 1973.

7. Ralph Kreiser interview, July 25, 1973. Robert B. Powers interview, Sept. 20, 1973.

8. In searching the Camargo Registro Civil de Nacimientos, Rolls I and II, from October 1864 through 1886, ARCCC, I could not find the elusive Pedro Subia or even Pedro Zubia. It was at this point that Marty Grejada, founder of La Familia, found the baptismal certificate for Pedro Zubia at the Church of Santa Rosalía de Camargo, Chihuahua, for which I thank him very much. Although the "Pedro Zubia" recorded on the certificate shows every sign of being our cotton striker Pedro Subia, because Subia's relatives refused to confirm it I cannot be certain it was.

9. Pedro Subia: 1900 census, Precincts 3, 11, 19, and 15, Graham County, Arizona Territory, Series T623, Roll 45, Page 5B, Enumeration District 19, Birth Date: 1873; Birthplace: Mexico; Race: White; Immigration year: 1894. Pedro registered twice, once under "Suvia" and once under "Subia." That year, Pedro Subia also registered under the name of "Pedro Suvia," same wife and child. See 1900 census, Precincts 1, 5, 6, 7, 10, 12, and 13, Graham County, Arizona Territory, Series T623, Roll 45, Page 18A, Enumeration District 21. Pedro Jr. said his father arrived in Arizona in 1891.

10. George Subia, Bakersfield, to Rodolfo Acuña, Jan. 27, 1977, RFAC, Urban Archives, CSUN. Pedro Subia Jr. was living in Mendota, California, where he was a prominent citizen.

11. Pedro M. Subia (Pedro Subia Jr.) interview, Jan. 10, 1981.

12. See 1930 census, Township 15, Kern County, California, Enumeration District 66, Series T626, Roll 122, Page 7A, Image 0591.

13. There are various persons named Subia in eastern Arizona. Valentine Subia Herrera, for example, was born in Sheldon (about three miles from Clifton), Arizona, on May 21, 1920. His mother, Paz Subia Herrera, and his father, Serapio Herrera, were from Chihuahua. The family traveled to Arizona from Juárez, stopping in Silver City and moving along the Gila River to the Clifton area. "Valentine Subia Herrera," in Björkquist, "Mexican Americans in Morenci."

14. Presumed to be San Pablo de Meoqui, an agricultural area north of Santa Rosalía de Camargo.

15. Pedro Subia (other Pedro Subia) interview, June 30, 1980. The other Pedro Subia died in April 1986 in Safford, Arizona; the Social Security Death Index says that he was born on June 29, 1887.

16. Robert B. Powers to Rodolfo F. Acuña, Aug. 18, 1973, RFAC, Urban Archives, CSUN. Articles of Incorporation of Associated Farms of California, [signed by] S. Parker Frisselle, Kearney Park, Fresno, and Lloyd W. Frische Kern County.

17. Williams, *California*, 162. C. Chambers, *California Farm Organizations*, 33, 53, 69. Jamieson, *Unionism in American Agriculture*, 40–41. Lowenstein, "Strike Tactics in California Agriculture," 95, 120. Kirkendall, *Social Scientists and Farm Politics*,

118–119. *La Follette Hearings*, pt. 49, pp. 17911–17945. *La Follette Hearings*, pt. 67, Exhibit 11327-A, p. 24459. Articles of Incorporation of Associated farmers of California.

18. George P. Clements, M.D., to Guernsey Fraze, Executive Secretary, Associated Farmers of California, Jan. 23, 1935, GCP, SC, UCLA.

19. C. Chambers, *California Farm Organizations*, 38–40.

20. P. Bancroft, "Farmer and Communists."

21. Lubin, "Can Radicals Capture Farms of California?" *La Follette Hearings*, pt. 68, pp. 24967–24971.

22. Halcomb, "Efforts to Organize the Migrant Workers," 109–110. "Cotton Picker Woes Studies," *Los Angeles Times*, Jan. 16, 1940. Jamieson, *Unionism in American Agriculture*, 113–114. For an insightful discussion, see Benson and Loftis, "Steinbeck and Farm Labor Unionization," 194–223.

23. George P. West, "Communists Tried under I.W.W.," *New York Times*, Jan. 20, 1935.

24. "Rioting Told in Red Trial," *Los Angeles Times*, Feb. 9, 1935. Floyd J. Healey, "Lynch Talk Enters Case," *Los Angeles Times*, Feb. 22, 1935. "Aide of Reds Helps State," *Los Angeles Times*, Feb. 6, 1935. "Work with Reds Told," *Los Angeles Times*, Feb. 12, 1935. "Exhibits at Reds' Trial Give Revolt Plot Plans," *Los Angeles Times*, Feb. 23, 1935. Chapin Hall, "High Drama Marks Trial," *Los Angeles Times*, Feb. 26, 1935. Chapin Hall, "Soviets Get Rebuffs in Reds' Trial," *Los Angeles Times*, Feb. 27, 1935. Chapin Hall, "Red Threats to Judge and Jury Stir Trial," *Los Angeles Times*, Mar. 1, 1935. "Eight Reds Convicted in Sacramento," *Los Angeles Times*, Apr. 2, 1935. "California Serves Notice," *Los Angeles Times*, Apr. 3, 1935. "Eight Reds Sentenced," *Los Angeles Times*, Apr. 11, 1935.

25. Chapin Hall, "Red Threats to Judge and Jury Stir Trial," *Los Angeles Times*, Mar. 1, 1935."Eight Reds Convicted in Sacramento," *Los Angeles Times*, Apr. 2, 1935. "California Serves Notice," *Los Angeles Times*, Apr. 3, 1935. "Eight Reds Sentenced," *Los Angeles Times*, Apr. 11, 1935. *California v. Chambers et al.* 22 Cal. App. 2d 687 (1937).

26. "Syndicalism Convicts Win; Guilty Verdict of Eight Reversed by Appellate Court," *Los Angeles Times*, Sept. 29, 1937.

27. "Syndicalism Convicts Win; Guilty Verdict of Eight Reversed by Appellate Court," *Los Angeles Times*, Sept. 29, 1937. Jamieson, *Unionism in American Agriculture*, 113–115. "Communist Primary Petition Submitted," *Los Angeles Times*, May 18, 1934. Fearis, in "California Farm Worker," 85–86, says that the C&AWIU was pragmatic: borrowing from the IWW, it was the only union to work with Mexicans before World War I.

28. Perry, Kramer, and Schneider, *Operating during Strikes*. In *Copper Crucible*, Jonathan Rosenblum clearly demonstrates the role conservative academics played in breaking the United Steelworkers. The union-busting strategies advanced by these academics have become standard practice in labor relations.

29. Kingsolver, *Holding Line*, 3, 5, 10, 15.

30. Rosenblum, *Copper Crucible*, 150.

31. Henry Weinstein, "Unions, Firm in a Pivotal Struggle," *Los Angeles Times*, Aug. 30, 1983; see esp. photos, which are good. Harry Bernstein, "Labor, Unions Using Strikes Less," *Los Angeles Times*, Feb. 27, 1985. William Serrin, "Concessions in Labor Pacts Seen as Reflection of Growing Employer Power," *New York Times*, Mar. 10, 1985. Nicholas D. Kristof, "Profit Follows Cost Cutting; Phelps Dodge's Turnaround," *New York Times*, Mar. 19, 1986. PBS, *Los Mineros*.

Sources Cited

Archives and Collections

Acuña, Rodolfo F., Collection (RFAC). Urban Archives, California State University at Northridge.

Almada, Francisco, Collection. Ciudad Chihuahua.

Archivo de Armando Miguelez (AAM). Universidad de Alicante, Spain

Archivo del Ayuntamiento de Ciudad Guerrero (AACG). Coleción de Comunicación de Inferiores, Archivo de Manuel González Ramírez, Archivo General de la Nación.

Archivo General de la Nación (AGN). Mexico City.

Archivo de José María Maytorena, Archivo de Manuel González Ramírez, Archivo General de la Nación. Mexico City.

Archivo de Manuel González Ramírez, Archivo General de la Nación (AMGR, AGN). Mexico City.

Archivo de Manuel González Ramírez, Gobernación, Archivo General de la Nación (AMGR Gobernación, AGN). Mexico City.

Archivos de Registro Civil de Ciudad Camargo (ARCCC).

Archivos de Relaciones Exteriores (ARE). Mexico City.

Arhelger, Edward, Papers. Arizona Historical Society, A.695.

Arizona Historical Society (AHS). Tucson.

Arizona State Library, Archives and Public Records, Archives Division (ASA). Phoenix.

Arizona State University Libraries, Special Collections Department (SC, ASU).

Arxiu de los Carmelites Descalcos de Catolunya (ACDC). Balears Avineuda, Diagonal 42408037. Barcelona.

Bancroft, Philip, Papers, 1908–1959. Bancroft Library, University of California at Berkeley.

Bassett, J. H., folder. Arizona State Library, Archives and Public Records, Archives Division.

Compañia Constructora Richardson Papers, 1904–1927. Arizona State University Libraries, Special Collections Department.

Clements, George, Papers (GSP). University of California at Los Angeles Library, Special Collections.

Darcy, Samuel, Collection. New York University.

Davis, Nicholas Schenck, Collection (NSDC). Arizona Historical Society.

Fall, Albert, Collection. Huntington Library.

Freudenthal, Sam J., Biographical Files (SJFBF). Arizona State University Libraries, Special Collections Department Arizona State University Libraries, Special Collections Department.

Graham County Historical Society. Safford, Arizona.

McCluskey, Henry S., Collection (HSMC). Arizona State University Libraries, Special Collections Department.

Murray, John, Collection (JMC). Arizona State University Libraries, Special Collections Department.

Murray, John, Collection. Bancroft Library, University of California at Berkeley.

Pan-American Federation of Labor (PAFL). Record Group 63, Records of the Committee on Public Information. Selected Items to the American Federation of Labor-GSA, National Archives and Records Administration, 1959. Washington, D.C.

Rochlin, Harriett, Collection of Western Jewish History (F&HRC). Special Collections, University of California at Los Angeles.

Rochlin, Fred and Harriett, Collection. University of Arizona Library, Special Collections, SJA 002.

Ryder, Ridgeway, Collection (RRC). Arizona State University Libraries, Special Collections Department.

Taylor, Paul S., Collection (PSTC). Bancroft Library, University of California at Berkeley.

U.S. National Archives and Records Administration (NARA). Washington, D.C.

University of California at Los Angeles Library, Special Collections (SC, UCLA).

University of Arizona Library, Special Collections (SC, UA).

Waterman, Fred L., Collection (FLMC). Arizona State Library, Archives and Public Records, Archives Division.

Interviews

Armendáriz, Arturo. Interview by Rodolfo F. Acuña, July 10, 1982. Camargo, Chihuahua. RFAC, Urban Archives, CSUN.

Aydelotte, George, NRA director. Interview by Paul S. Taylor, Dec. 22, 1933. PSTC, Bancroft Library, UCB.

Bachelder, John L. "Reminiscences of John L. Bachelder." As told to Mrs. George Kitt, 1921. AHS.

Boyd, J., Tipton independent farmer. Interview by Paul S. Taylor, Dec. 23, 1933. PSTC, Bancroft Library, UCB.

Buckner, W. V. Interview by Paul S. Taylor, Dec. 22, 1933.

Bryan, O. W. Interview by Rodolfo F. Acuña, June 22, 1973. RFAC, Urban Archives, CSUN.

Camp, Wofford B. Interview by Willa Klug Blum, 1971. In "Cotton, Irrigation, and the AAA." Regional Oral History Office, Bancroft Library, UCB.

Carter, Undersheriff Tom. Interview by Paul S. Taylor, Nov. 17, 1933. Bakersfield. PSTC, Bancroft Library, UCB.

Chaffee, Porter. "Porter Chaffee: Labor Organizer." Interviews by Randall Jarrell, May 25 and June 7, 1977. Regional Oral History Office, Bancroft Library, UCB.

Chambers, Pat. Interviews by Rodolfo F. Acuña, Aug. 24 and Oct. 4, 1973, Apr. 13, 14, and 19, 1978. California State University at Northridge. RFAC, Urban Archives, CSUN.

Cuellar, Lilly, 57, from Brawley, California. Interview by Rodolfo F. Acuña, July 11, 1973. RFAC, Urban Archives, CSUN.

Darcy, Sam. Interview by Nelson Pichardo, Feb. 2,[?] 1992. Audio file from archives of Oral History Program, New York State University, Albany.

Decker, Caroline. Interview by Paul S. Taylor, Nov. 27, 1933. PSTC, Bancroft Library, UCB.

Decker, Caroline. Interview by Rodolfo F. Acuña, Aug. 8, 1973. RFAC, Urban Archives, CSUN.

Ewart, George, ed. "Interviews on the Organization of the Cannery and Agricultural Workers' Industrial Union in California in the 1930s by Jack Warnick and Others." Sound recording. Non-music interviews, Bancroft Library, UCB.

Frías Prieto, Professor Apolinar. Interviews by Rodolfo F. Acuña, July 10 and 15, 1982. Calle Ignacio Camargo, no. 1114, Ciudad Chihuahua. RFAC, Urban Archives, CSUN.

Galván Amaro, José, Mexican American field hand. Interviews by Meri Knaster, June 2 and 6, 1977. Watsonville, California. Regional History Project. Bancroft Library, UCB.

Gladney, Joe. Interview by Rodolfo F. Acuña, July 10, 1973. RFAC, Urban Archives, CSUN.

Kreiser, Ralph. Interview by Rodolfo F. Acuña, July 18, 1973. By telephone. RFAC, Urban Archives, CSUN.

Kreiser, Ralph. Interview by Rodolfo F. Acuña, July 25, 1973. RFAC, Urban Archives, CSUN.

Powers, Robert B. Interviews by Amelia R. Fry in 1969. Earl Warren Oral History Project, Law Enforcement, Race Relations: 1930–1960. With an Introduction by Robert W. Kenny.

Powers, Robert. Interview by Rodolfo F. Acuña, Sept. 20, 1973. Los Angeles. RFAC, Urban Archives, CSUN.

Rodríguez, Alejandro Torralva. Interview by Rodolfo F. Acuña, July 12, 1973. RFAFN, Urban Archives, CSUN.

Solo, Anthony. Interview by Rodolfo F. Acuña, July 10, 1973. RFAC, Urban Archives, CSUN.

Soto, Joe. Interview by Scott Solliday, Jan. 25, 1994. Narrated by Joe Soto. Tempe Oral History, Barrios Oral History Project. Interview no. OH-139.

Subia, Pedro (other Pedro Subia). Interview by Rodolfo F. Acuña, June 30, 1980. La Logia, San Jose, Arizona.

Subia, Pedro M. (Pedro Subia Jr.). Interview by Rodolfo F. Acuña, Jan. 10, 1981. Mendota, California. RFAC, Urban Archives, CSUN.

Taylor, Paul S. Interview by Rodolfo F. Acuña, Aug. 2, 1973. Taylor office, University of California at Berkeley. RFAC, Urban Archives, CSUN.

Taylor, Ronald, correspondent, *Fresno Bee*. Interview by Rodolfo Acuña, July 11, 1973. Visalia, California. RFAC, Urban Archives, CSUN.

Tipton dairy farmer, 73. Interview by Rodolfo Acuña, July 10, 1973. Tipton, California. RFAC, Urban Archives, CSUN.

Velásquez, David, 65. Interview by Rodolfo F. Acuña, June 20, 1982. Clifton, Arizona. RFAC, Urban Archives, CSUN.

Walker, H. B., Socialist City Councilman. Interview by Paul S. Taylor, Oct. 24, 1933. Tulare, California. PSTP, Bancroft Library, UCB.

Walker, W. L. Interview by Paul S. Taylor, Nov. 18, 1933. PSTP, Bancroft Library, UCB.

Wilson, Clarence H., District Attorney, Kings County. Interview by Paul S. Taylor, Dec. 22, 1933, Hanford, California. PSTP, Bancroft Library, UCB.

Newspapers and Magazines

Arizona Bulletin (Jan. 12, 1900).
Arizona Champion (Sept. 28, 1889).
Arizona Citizen (1890–91) AHS.
Arizona Daily Star (2000).
Arizona Enterprise (1891) AHS.
Arizona Gazette (1880) AHS; (1915) ASU.
Arizona Labor Journal (1917).
Arizona Miner (1867).
Arizona Mining Journal (Feb. 1919).
Arizona Republican (1890, 1905, 1916–17, 1925).
Arizona Star (Apr. 25, 1873) ASU.
Bakersfield Californian (1933–34).
El Centenario (Cananea, Sonora; May 12, 1906).
Chico Record (Aug. 24, 1933).
Clifton Clarion (1885).
Copper Era (Clifton; 1899–1900, 1905–06, 1910–11, 1913–18, 1920–22).
Dunbar's Weekly (Phoenix; Oct. 30, 1915).
El Eco de Sonora (Apr. 17, 1871).
Engineering and Mining Journal (1882, 1913–15).
Epitaph (Tombstone; 1915).
La Estrella de Occidente (Sonora; 1859, 1868, 1874).
Excelsior (Mexico City; 1931).
Fresno Bee (1933).
El Fronterizo (Tucson; 1878, 1880–82, 1891, 1896).
Gateway Times (El Paso; Sept. 8, 1960).
Graham Guardian (1910, 1912–13, 1915–16).
Hanford Morning Journal (1933).
El Heraldo (Morenci; Aug. 13, 1910).

Jerome Mining News (Nov. 20, 1899).

Labor Monthly Review (*Los Angeles Times*; Mar. 1929).

Los Angeles Mining Review (Mar. 21, 1901) AHS.

Los Angeles Times (1882–83, 1891, 1995–97. 1899–1900, 1902–03, 1906–11, 1912–21, 1926, 1935).

Mining and Scientific Press (1912).

Miners' Magazine (Western Federation of Miners; 1900–1917, 1920).

Morenci Leader (1905–1907).

New York Evening Post (1917).

New York Times (1858, 1892–93, 1895, 1904, 1906, 1912–16, 1918, 1932–35. 1985).

El Norte (Ciudad Chihuahua; 1893).

Pan-American Labor Press/Obrero Pan-American (1918) JMC, ASU.

El Paso Evening Tribune (1893).

El Paso Herald (1899, 1903).

El Paso Times (1893).

Periodico Oficial del Gobierno del Estado (Chihuahua; 1878, 1882, 1884–85, 1892). Francisco Almada Collection, Ciudad Chihuahua.

Prescott Journal-Miner (1915).

Prescott Weekly Courier (Aug. 8, 1884).

La Prensa (San Diego; Nov. 12, 1999).

Regeneración (1910–1915).

San Francisco Bulletin (May 27, 1857).

San Francisco Chronicle (1933–34).

San Francisco Examiner (1933).

San Diego Union (July 20, 1917).

Southwest Sentinel (Silver City; June 14, 1884) F&HRC, SC, UCLA.

La Sonora (Tucson; 1879–80).

El Tucsonense (1915–19, 1921–22).

Tucson Citizen (1904, 1917) SC, UA.

Tulare Advance Register (1933–34).

Visalia Times Delta (1933).

La Voz de Sonora (1856–57, 1885).

Weekly Arizona Republican (Jan. 19, 1905).

Other Sources

Abel, Emily K. "From Exclusion to Expulsion: Mexicans and Tuberculosis Control in Los Angeles, 1914–1940." *Bulletin of the History of Medicine* 77, no. 4 (2003): 823–849.

Aboites Aguilar, Luis. *Breve historia de Chihuahua*. Mexico City: Fondo de Cultura Economica, 1994.

———. "José Fuentes Mares y la histografía del norte de México: Una aproximación desde Chihuahua (1950–1957)." *Historia Mexicana* 49, no. 3 (Jan.–Mar. 2000): 477–507.

——. *Norte precario: Poblamiento y colonización en México (1760–1940)*. Mexico City: Colegio de México, 1995.

——, ed. *Agua y tierra en la región del conchos San Pedro, Chihuahua. 1720–1938*. Mexico City: Centro de Investigacion y Estudios Superiores en Antopologia Social, 1986.

Aboites Aguilar, Luis, and Alba Dolores Morales Cosme. *Breve compilación sobre tierras y aguas de Santa Cruz de Tapacolmes, Chihuahua (1713–1927)*. Mexico City: Centro de Investigaciones y Estudies Superiores, 1998.

Acosta, Roberto. *Apuntes historicos sonorenses: La conquista temporal y espiritual del Yaqui y del Mayo*. Mexico City: Apuntes Historicos Sonorenses, Imprenta Aldina, 1949.

Acuña, Rodolfo F. "Ignacio Pesqueira: Sonoran Caudillo." *Arizona and the West* 12, no. 2 (Summer 1970):

——. *Sonoran Strongman: Ignacio Pesqueira and His Times*. Tucson: University of Arizona Press, 1972.

Aguilar Camín, Hector. *La frontera nomada: Sonora y la Revolucion Mexicana*. Mexico City: Siglo Veintiuno, 1977.

Aguilar Camín, Hector, and Lorenzo Mayer. *In the Shadow of the Mexican Revolution: Contemporary Mexican History, 1910–1918*. Austin: University of Texas Press, 1993.

Aguirre Beltrán, Gonzalo. *La población negra de México*. Mexico City: Colección Firme, 1972.

Albro, Ward S. *Always a Rebel: Ricardo Magón and the Mexican Revolution* Fort Worth: Texas Christian University Press, 1992.

Alejo de la Virgen del Carmen, O.C.D. *Breve resumén historico de la restauración de la provincia carmelitana San José de Cataluna*. N.p.: Palma de Mallorca, 1939. In ACDC.

Algier, Keith Wayne. "Feudalism on New Spain's Northern Frontier: Valle De San Bartolomé, a Case Study." Ph.D. diss., University of New Mexico, 1966.

Allen, James B. *The Company Town in the American West*. Norman: University of Oklahoma Press, 1966.

Almada, Francisco R. *Diccionario de historia, geografia y biografia chihuahenses*. 2nd ed. Ciudad Juárez: Universidad de Chihuahua, 1968.

——. *Diccionario de historia, geografia, y biografia sonorenses*. Ciudad Chihuahua: n.p., n.d.

——. "La imprenta y el periodismo en Chihuahua." *Boletin de la Sociedad Chihuahuense de Estudios Historicos* 1, no. 3 (Jan. 15, 1939).

——. *La rebelión de Tomochi*. Ciudad Chihuahua: n.p., 1936.

——. *Resumén de historia del estado de Chihuahua*. Mexico City: Libros Mexicanos, 1955.

——. *La revolución en el Estado de Chihuahua*. Vol. 1. Mexico City: Biblioteca del Instituto Nacional de Estudio Historicos de la Revolución Mexicana, 1964.

Alonso, Ana María. *Thread of Blood: Colonialism, Revolution, and Gender on Mexico's*

Northern Frontier. Tucson: University of Arizona Press, 1995.

Altamirano, Graziella, and Guadalupe Villa. *Chihuahua: Textos de su historia, 1824–1921.* Vol. 1: *La Villa of Juárez.* Ciudad Chihuahua: Ediciones del Gobierno del Estado de Chihuahua; Instituto de Investigaciones Universidad Autonoma de Chihuahua, 1988.

———. *Chihuahua: Una historia compartida, 1824–1921.* Ciudad Juárez: Universidad Autonoma de Ciudad Juárez, 1988.

Anderson, Mark Cronlund. *Pancho Villa's Revolution by Headlines.* Norman: University of Oklahoma Press, 2000.

Anderson, Rodney D. *Outcasts in Their Own Land. Mexican Industrial Workers, 1906–1911.* De Kalb: Northern Illinois University Press, 1976.

Araiza, Luis. *Ricardo Flores Magón en la historia.* Mexico City: Ediciones Casa del Obrero Mundial, 1976.

Arax, Mark, and Rick Wartzman. *The King of California: J. G. Boswell and the Making of a Secret American Empire.* New York: Public Affairs, 2003.

Arrieta, Olivia "The Alianza Hispano Americana in Arizona and New Mexico: The Development and Maintenance of a Multifunctional Ethnic Organization." In Renato Rosaldo Lecture Series Monograph, vol. 7 (1991): 55–71. Mexican American Studies and Research Center, University of Arizona, Tucson.

———. "The Mexican Community of the Clifton-Morenci Mining District: Organizational Life in the Context of Change." In Mary Romero and Vandelaria Canadelaria, eds., *Community Empowerment and Chicano Scholarship.* Selected Proceedings of the National Association for Chicano Studies, 1992.

Azuma, Eiichiro. "Racial Struggle, Immigrant Nationalism, and Ethnic Identity: Japanese and Filipinos in the California Delta." *Pacific Historical Review* 67, no. 2 (May 1998): 163–199.

Bakewell, Peter J. *Silver Mining and Society in Colonial Mexico: Zacatecas, 1546–1700.* New York: Cambridge University Press, 1971.

———. *Silver Mining and Society in Colonial Mexico, Zacatecas 1546–1700.* New York: Cambridge Press, 2002.

Balbas, Manuel. *Recuerdos del yaqui: Principales episodios durante la campaña de 1899 a 1901.* Mexico City: Sociedad y Libreria Franco Americana, 1927.

Balderama, Francisco E., and Raymond Rodríguez. *Decade of Betrayal: Mexican Repatriation in the 1930s.* Albuquerque: University of New Mexico Press, 1995.

Ball, Larry Durwood. "The Office of the United States Marshal in Arizona and New Mexico's Territories, 1851–1912." Ph.D. diss., University of Colorado at Boulder, 1970.

Bancroft, Hubert Howe. *History of Arizona and New Mexico, 1530–1888.* San Francisco: History, 1889.

———. *History of the North Mexican States and Texas.* Vol. 1: *1553–1800.* San Francisco: A. L. Bancroft, 1884.

———. *History of the North Mexican States and Texas.* Vol. 2: *1801–1889.* San Francisco: History, 1889.

Bancroft, Philip. "The Farmer and the Communists." Address before the Commonwealth Club of San Francisco, Apr. 26, 1935. In Bancroft's Speeches and Writings, 1935–1955, Carton 1, Folder 10, Philip Bancroft Papers, 1908–1959, Bancroft Library, UCB.

Banister, Jeff. "The Rio Yaqui Delta: Early Twentieth-Century Photos from the Richardson Construction Company." *Journal of the Southwest* 40, no. 3 (Autumn 1998): 397–401.

Barnes, Robert L. "Mexican Affairs: Plan of San Diego." Feb. 14, 1912–Dec. 13, 1913. Bureau of Investigation. AFC, Box 72 (Special Agents), Folder 12, Huntington Library.

Barr, F. Remington. "Integrated Results of Sixty Years' Operation," Phelps Dodge Corporation, Morenci Branch, and "A Chronicle of Early Operations of the Principal Original Companies," Arizona Copper Company and the Detroit Copper Mining Company of Arizona, Nov. 1940. Revised RRC, ASU.

Barry, John M. *The Great Influenza: The Epic Story of the Deadliest Plague in History.* New York: Viking Adult, 2004.

Barta, Armando. *Regeneración, 1900–1918: La corriente más radical de la revolución de 1910 a tráves de su periódicos de cambate.* Mexico City: Hadise, 1972.

Bartlett, John Russell. *Personal Narrative of Explorations and Incidents in Texas, New Mexico, California, Sonora and Chihuahua: 1850–1853.* Vol. 1. New York: Appleton, 1856. In e-book form at http://www.discoverseaz.com/History/Bartlett.html.

Bauer, Arnold. "Modernizing Landlords and Constructive Peasants: In the Mexican Countryside." *Mexican Studies/Estudios Mexicanos* 14, no. 1 (Winter 1998): 191–212.

Bayman, James M., Manuel R. Palacios-Fest, and Lisa W. Huckell. "Botanical Signatures of Water Storage Duration in a Hohokam Reservoir." *American Antiquity* 62, no. 1 (Jan. 1997): 103–111.

Beezley, Willam H. *Insurgent Governor: Abraham González and the Mexican Revolution in Chihuahua.* Lincoln: University of Nebraska Press, 1973.

Benedict, H. Bradley. "Hacienda Management in Late Colonial Northern Mexico: A Case Study of Juan Bustamante and the Hacienda of Dolores, 1790–1820." *Proceedings of the American Philosophical Society*, 123, no. 6 (Dec. 28, 1979): 391–409.

Benson, Jackson J., and Anne Loftis. "John Steinbeck and Farm Labor Unionization: The Background of 'In Dubious Battle.'" *American Literature* 52, no. 2 (May 1980): 194–223.

Benton-Cohen, Katherine. "Docile Children and Dangerous Revolutionaries: The Racial Hierarchy of Manliness and the Bisbee Deportation of 1917." *Frontiers: A Journal of Women Studies* 24, nos. 2–3 (2003): 30–50. http://muse.jhu.edu/journals/frontiers/v024/24.2benton-cohen.html#authbio (accessed Mar. 1, 2004).

Bernstein, Irving. *History of the American Worker 1920–1933: The Lean Years.* Boston: Houghton-Mifflin, 1960.

Bernstein, Marvin D. "Colonel William C. Greene and the Cananea Copper Bubble." *Bulletin of the Business Historical Society* 26, no. 4 (Dec. 1952): 179–198.

Bideaux, Richard A., and Terry C. Wallace. "Arizona Copper." *Rocks and Minerals* 72, no. 1 (Jan. 1997): 10–27. http//www.rocksandminerals.org.

Björkquist, Elena Díaz. "In the Shadow of the Smokestack: An Oral History of Mexican Americans in Morenci, Arizona." Audiotape. Available online at http://www.geoci ties.com/our_morenci/interviewees.html.

Blaisdell, Lowell L. "Harry Chandler and Mexican Border Intrigue, 1914–1917." *Pacific Historical Review* 35, no. 4 (Nov. 1966): 385–393.

———. "Was It Revolution or Filibustering? The Mystery of the Flores Magón Revolt in Baja California." *Pacific Historical Review* 23, no. 2 (May 1954): 147–164.

Bloch, Louis. "Facts about Mexican Immigration before and since the Quota Restriction Laws." *Journal of the American Statistical Association* 24, no. 165 (Mar. 1929): 50–60.

Bogardus, Emory. *The Mexican in the United States.* Los Angeles: University of Southern California Press, 1934.

Borah, Woodrow, and Sherburne F. Cook. *Aboriginal Population of Central Mexico on the Eve the Spanish Conquest.* Berkeley: University of California Press, 1963.

Bowden, Charles. *Killing the Hidden Waters.* Austin: University of Texas Press, 1977.

Brand, Donald D. "The Historical Geography of Northwestern Chihuahua." Ph.D diss., University of California at Berkeley, 1933.

Briegel, Kaye Lynne. "Alianza Hispano-Americana, 1894–1965: A Mexican American Fraternal Insurance Society." Ph.D. diss., University of Southern California, 1974.

Brooks, Francis J. "Revising the Conquest of Mexico: Smallpox, Sources, and Populations." *Journal of Interdisciplinary History* 24, no. 1 (Summer 1993): 1–29.

Brophy, Blake. *Foundlings on the Frontier: Racial and religious conflict in Arizona Territory, 1904–1905.* Tucson: University of Arizona Press, 1972.

Brown, David. "Early Inhabitants and Their Canals Pave Way for Newcomers." *Arizona History* 65, no. 1 (Jan. 2003):

Bruere, Robert W. "Following the Trail of the I.W.W." *New York Evening Post*, Nov. 17, 24, and Dec. 1, 8, 1917. Reprinted, 1918. HSMC, Box 2, Folder 3, SC, ASU.

Brush, David Allen "The de La Huerta Rebellion in Mexico, 1923–1924." Ph.D. diss., Syracuse University, 1975.

Buhle, Paul, and Dave Wagner. *Radical Hollywood: The Untold Story behind Anerica's Favorite Movies.* New York: New Press, 2002.

Bunker, Steven B. " 'Consumers of Good Taste': Marketing Modernity in Northern Mexico, 1890–1910." *Mexican Studies/Estudios Mexicanos* 13, no. 2 (Summer 1997): 227–269.

Byrkit, James. "The Bisbee Deportation." In James C. Foster, ed., *American Labor in the Southwest: The First One Hundred Years*, 86–102. Tucson: University of Arizona Press, 1982.

———. *Forging the Copper Collar: Arizona's Labor Management War of 1901–192.* Tucson: University of Arizona Press, 1982.

——. "Life and Labor in Arizona, 1901–1921: With Particular Reference to the Deportations of 1917." Ph.D. diss., Claremont College, 1972.

——. "Walter Douglas and Labor Struggles in the Early 20th Century." *Southwest Economy and Society* 1, no. 1 (Spring 1976): 14–26.

Calderón, Esteban B. *Juicio sobre la guerra del yaqui y génesis de la huelga de Cananea.* Mexico City: Centro de Estudios Históricos del Movimiento Obrero Mexicano, 1975.

California v. Chambers et al. 22 Cal. App. 2d 687 (1937). Crim. no. 1533. Court of Appeals of California, Third Appellate District; 72 P.2d 746; 1937 Cal. App. LEXIS 196. Decided Sept. 28, 1937.

California v. Pompa, 192 Cal. 412 (1923). 1923 Cal. LEXIS 367, Nov. 26, 1923.

Calvo Berber, Laureano. *Nociones de historia de Sonora.* Mexico City: Librería De Manuel Porrúa, 1958.

Canty, J. Michael, and Michael N. Greeley, eds. *History of Mining in Arizona.* Tucson: Mining Club of the Southwest Foundation, 1987.

Cardoso, Lawrence Anthony. "Mexican Emigration to the United States, 1900–1930: An Analysis of Socio-Economic Causes." Ph.D. diss., University of Connecticut, 1974.

——. *Mexican Emigration to the United States, 1897–1931.* Tucson: University of Arizona Press, 1980.

Carmack, Robert M., Janine Gasco, and Gary H. Gossen. *The Legacy of Mesoamerica: History and Culture of a Native American Civilization.* Upper Saddle River, N.J.: Prentice Hall, 1996.

Carman, Michael Dennis. *United States Customs and the Madero Revolution.* El Paso: University of Texas at El Paso Press, 1976

Carmichael, Norman, and John Kiddie. "Development of Mine Transportation in Clifton-Morenci District." *Transactions of the American Institute of Mining and Metallurgical Engineers,* Mar. 1924.

Carr, Barry. "The Mexican Communist Party and Agrarian Mobilization in the Laguna, 1920–1940: A Worker-Peasant Alliance?" *Hispanic American Historical Review* 67, no. 3 (Aug. 1987): 371–404.

Carrigan, William D. "The Lynching of Persons of Mexican Origin or Descent in the United States, 1848 to 1928." *Journal of Social History* 37, no. 2 (2003): 411–438.

Casillas, Michael E. "Mexican Labor Militancy in the U.S., 1896–1915." *Southwest Economy and Society* 4, no. 1 (Fall 1975): 35, 45.

——. "Mexicans, Labor, and Strife in Arizona, 1896–1917." Master's thesis, University of New Mexico, 1979.

——. "The Partido Liberal Mexicano and the Union Movement in Territorial Arizona, 1906–1909." Arizona State University.

Castañeda González, Rocío. *Irrigación y reforma agraria: Las comunidades de riego del Valle de Santa Rosalía, Chihuahua, 1920–1950.* Mexico City: Comisión Nacional del Agua: Centro de Investigaciones y Estudios Superiores en Antropología Social, 1995.

Castillo, Pedro. "The Making of a Mexican Barrio: Los Angeles, 1890–1920." Ph.D. diss., University of California at Santa Barbara, 1979.

Caulfield, Norman. "Mexican Labor and the State in the 20th Century: Conflict and Accommodation." Ph.D. diss., University of Houston, 1990.

Caywood, Louis "The Spanish Missions of Northwestern New Spain. Jesuit Period, 1607–1767." *Kiva* (Arizona Archaeological and Historical Society) 5, no. 2 (Nov. 1939): 5–8.

Chacón, Ramon D. "The 1933 San Joaquin Valley Cotton Strike: Strikebreaking Activities in California Agriculture." In Mario Barrera, Alberto Camarillo, and Francisco Hernández, eds., *Work, Family, Sex Roles, Language: Selected Papers.* Berkeley, Calif.: Tonatiuh-Quinto Sol, 1980.

———. "Labor Unrest and Industrialized Agriculture in California: The Case of the 1933 San Joaquin Valley Cotton Strike." *Social Science Quarterly* 65, no. 2 (June 1984): 336–353.

Chaffee, Porter M. *A History of the Cannery and Agricultural Workers Industrial Workers Union.* Oakland, Calif.: Federal Writers Project, 1930–39. Available in Bancroft Library, UCB.

Chambers, Clark. *California Farm Organizations.* Berkeley: University of California Press, 1952.

Chance, John K. "On the Mexican Mestizo." *Latin American Research Review* 14, no. 3 (1979): 153–168.

Chávez Calderón, Plácido. *La defensa de Tomochic.* Mexico City: Editorial Jus, 1964.

Chilcott, John H. "Yaqui World View and the School: Conflict and Accommodation." *Journal of American Indian Education* 24, no. 1 (Jan. 1985), http://jaie.asu.edu/v24/V24S1Yaq.html.

Chretien, Todd. "Dual Unionism or 'Boring from Within': The Communist Party and the San Francisco General Strike." *Ex Post Facto* 4 (1997). Available online from journal.

Cleland, Robert Glass. *A History of Phelps Dodge, 1834–1950.* New York: Knopf, 1952.

"Clifton, New Mexico: Its Copper Mines and Furnaces." *Engineering and Mining Journal*, Sept. 2, 1882, 121–122.

Cockcroft, James D. *Intellectual Precursors of the Mexican Revolution, 1900–1913.* Institute of Latin American Studies. Austin: University of Texas Press, 1968.

Coerver, Don M., and Linda B. Hall. *Texas and the Mexican Revolution: A Study in State and National Border Policy, 1910–1920.* San Antonio: Trinity University Press, 1984.

Cogut, Ted, and Bill Conger. *History of Arizona's Clifton-Morenci Mining District: A Personal Approach.* Vol. 1: *The Underground Years.* Thatcher, Ariz.: Mining History, 1999.

Colmenares, Germán. *Haciendas de los jesuitas en el Nuevo Granada, Siglo XVIII.* Bogotá: Universidad Nacional de Colombia, 1969.

Colquhoun, James. *The Early History of the Clifton-Morenci District.* Pamphlet. London: William Clowes and Sons, n.d. Sam Freudenthal, Biographical Files, ASU.

——. *The Early History of the Clifton-Morenci District*. London: William Clowes and Sons, 1924. Reprinted in Carlos E. Cortés, ed., *The Mexican Experience in Arizona*. New York: Arno Press, 1976.

Compeán, Guadalupe. "Where Only the Weeds Grow: An Ecological Study of Mexican Housing in Boyle Heights, 1910–1940." School of Architecture and Urban Planning, University of California at Los Angeles, Dec. 1984

Cook, Noble David. *Born to Die: Disease and New World Conquest*. New York: Cambridge University Press, 1998.

Corbella, C. D. Carmelo "¿Un Milagro en Los Aires?" *Boletin de Revista Carmelitana*, 43–44.

Corle, Edwin. *The Gila: River of the Southwest*. Lincoln: University of Nebraska Press, 1967.

Corral, Ramón. *Obras historicas, reseña historica del estado de Sonora, 1856–1877: Biografía de José María Leyva Cajeme*. Las razas indigenas de Sonora. Hermosillo: Biblioteca Sonorenses de Geografía e Historia, 1959.

Cox, Annie M. "History of Bisbee, 1877–1937." Master's thesis, University of Arizona, 1938.

Cott, Kenneth. "Mexican Diplomacy and the Chinese Issue, 1876–1910." *Hispanic American Historical Review* 67, no. 1 (Feb. 1987): 63–85.

Cramaussel, Chantal. *La provincia de Santa Bárbara en Nueva Vizcaya, 1563–1631*. Ciudad Juárez: Universidad Autónoma de Ciudad Juárez, 1990.

Cramp, Kathryn, Louise F. Shields, and Charles A. Thomson. *Study of the Mexican Population in the Imperial Valley, California*. New York: Committee on Farm and Cannery Migrants, Council of Women for Home Missions, Mar. 31–Apr. 9, 1926.

Crawford, Margaret. "Bertram Goodhue, Walter Douglas, and Tyrone, New Mexico." *Journal of Architectural Education* 42, no. 4 (Summer 1989): 25–33.

Crosby, Alfred W. *The Columbian Exchange: Biological and Cultural Consequences of 1492*. Westport, Conn.: Greenwood Press, 1972.

——. *America's Forgotten Pandemic: The Influenza of 1918*. 2nd ed. New York: Cambridge University Press, 2003.

Cruz, Shamil. "African Americans in the Caribbean and Latin America." *IPOAA* (Indigenous People of Africa and Latin America) *Magazine*, Spring 2000 http://ipoaa .com/blacks _ latin _ america _ etc.htm.

Cue Cánovas, Austín. *Historia social y económica de México (1521–1854)*. Mexico City: Trillas, 1972.

Cumberland, Charles C. "Border Raids in the Lower Rio Grande Valley — 1915." *Southwestern Historical Quarterly* 57 (Jan. 1954): 285–311.

Dabdoub, Claudio. *Historia del Valle de Yaqui*. Mexico City: Libreria de Manuel Porrúa, 1964.

Daniel, Cletus E. *Bitter Harvest: A History of California Farmworkers, 1870–1941*. Berkeley, University of California Press, 1981

Darcy, Sam [Adams]. "Excerpts from the Writings of Sam Darcy, Written in the 1930s: Agricultural Strikes, California." Compiled by Pat Darcy. Samuel Darcy Collection, NYU.

Deeds, Susan M. *Defiance and Deference in Mexico's Colonial North: Indians under Spanish Rule in Nueva Vizcaya*. Austin: University of Texas Press, 2003.

———. "Land Tenure Patterns in Northern New Spain." *Americas* 41, no. 4 (Apr. 1985): 446–461.

———. "Mission Villages and Agrarian Patterns in a Nueva Vizcayan Heartland, 1600–1750." *Journal of the Southwest* 33, no. 3 (Fall 1991): 345–365.

———. "Rural Work in Nueva Vizcaya: Forms of Labor Coercion on the Periphery." *Hispanic American Historical Review* 69, no. 3 (Aug. 1, 1989): 429–443.

De La Vara, Martín González. "The Return to Mexico: The Relocation of New Mexican Families to Chihuahua and the Confirmation of a Frontier Region, 1848–1854." In Erlinda Gonzales-Berry and David R. Maciel, eds., *The Contested Homeland: A Chicano History of New Mexico*, 43–57. Albuquerque: University of New Mexico Press, 2000.

Delmatier, Royce D., Clarence F. McIntosh, and Earl G. Waters, eds. *The Rumble of California Politics, 1848–1970*. New York: Wiley, 1970.

del Río, Ignacio. "Auge y decadencia de los placeres y el real de la Cieneguilla, Sonora (1771–1783)." *Estudios de Historia Novohispana* 8 (May 1985): 83–96.

Dennis, Philip A. "The Anti-Chinese Campaigns in Sonora, Mexico." *Ethnohistory* 26, no. 1 (Winter 1979): 65–80.

Deutsch, Sarah. *No Separate Refuge: Culture, Class, and Gender on an Anglo-Hispanic Frontier in the American Southwest, 1880–1940*. New York: Oxford University Press, 1987.

Domecq, Brianda. "Teresa de Urrea." In *Temas sonorenses: A través de los simposios de historia*. Hermosillo: Gobierno del Estado de Sonora, 1984:

Dos Passos, John. *"Mr. Wilson's War": From the Assassination of McKinley to the Defeat of the the League of Nations*. Garden City, N.Y.: Doubleday, 1962.

Duarte, Carmen. "Mama Santos's Story: An Arizona Life." *Arizona Daily Star*, Feb. 13, 2000 through Mar. 18, 2000. Series, http://www.azstarnet.com/azlife/Day18.html (accessed July 2, 2003).

Dunbier, Roger. *The Sonoran Desert: Its Geography, Economy, and People*. Tucson: University of Arizona Press, 1968.

Eisenhower, John S. D. *Intervention! The United States and the Mexican Revolution: 1913-1917*. Baltimore: Johns Hopkins University Press 1995.

Emersley, J. D. "The Clifton Copper Mines, Arizona." *Engineering and Mining Journal*, Feb. 21, 1880, 133.

Emmons, David M. *The Butte Irish: Class and Ethnicity in an American Mining Town, 1875–1925*. Urbana: University of Illinois, 1989.

Endfield, Georgina H., and Sarah L. O'Hara. "Degradation, Drought, and Dissent: An Environmental History of Colonial Michoacán, West Central Mexico." *Annals of the Association of American Geographers* 89, no. 3 (Sept. 1999): 402–419.

Engerman, Stanley L., and Kenneth L. Sokoloff. "Factor Endowments, Inequality, and Paths of Development among New World Economies." *Economia* 3, no. 1 (2002):

Ensor, Bradley E. "Social Formations, Modo de Vida, and Conflict in Archaeology (Critical Essay)." *American Antiquity* 65, no. 1 (Jan. 2000): 15–42.

Escobar, Edward J. *Race, Police, and the Making of a Political Identity: Mexican Americans and the Los Angeles Police Department.* Berkeley: University of California Press, 1999.

Estrada, Richard Medina. "Border Revolution: The Mexican Revolution in the Ciudad Juárez–El Paso Area, 1906–1915." M.A. thesis, University of Texas at El Paso, 1975.

Estrada, William D. "Los Angeles' Old Plaza and Olvera Street: Imagined and Contested Space." *Western Folklore* 58, no. 2 (Winter 1999): 107–129.

Evans, Sterling. "Yaquis vs. Yanquis: An Environmental and Historical Comparison of Coping with Aridity in Southern Sonora." *Journal of the Southwest* 40, no. 3 (Autumn 1998): 363–396.

Fabela, Isidro ed. *Documentos históricos de la Revolución mexicana: Precusores de la Revolución mexicana, 1906–1910.* Vol. 11. Mexico City: Editorial Jus, 1966.

"Facts about 100-Degree Temperatures at Bakersfield." http://www.wrh.noaa.gov/han ford/climo/bfl100degreefacts.htm (accessed June 14, 2003).

Fearis, Donald Friend. "The California Farm Worker, 1930–1942." Ph.D. diss., University of California at Davis, 1971.

Fenn, Al. *Clifton Editor: Morenci, Duncan, and Other Famous Places.* Phoenix: Image, 1977.

Finley, James P. "The Yaqui Fight in Bear Valley." *Huachuca Illustrated* 2 (1996).

Flynn, Dennis Owen, and Arturo Giráldez. "Cycles of Silver: Global Economic Unity through the Mid-Eighteenth Century." *Journal of World History* 13, no. 2 (2002): 391–427.

Foley, E. S. "Estado Chihuahua, Its Places and People," *West Texas Geological Society* (164): 130–139.

Fong, Lawrence Michael. "Sojourners and Settlers: The Chinese Experience." *Journal of Arizona History* 21 (Autumn 1980): 1–30.

Forbes, Jack D. *Apache, Navaho and Spaniard.* Norman: University of Oklahoma Press, 1960.

Foster, James C., ed. *American Labor in the Southwest.* Tucson: University of Arizona Press, 1982.

Freeman, Joshua B. "Catholics, Community, and the Republicans: Irish Workers and the Organization of the Transport Workers Union." In Michael H. Frisch and Daniel J. Walkowitz, eds., *Working-class America: Essays on Labor, Community, and American Society.* Urbana: University of Illinois Press, 1983.

Freudenthal, Sam J. "Narrative of Sam J. Freudenthal." SJFBF, ASU.

Frías, Heriberto. *Tomochic: Novela histórica mexicana.* Mexico City: Editorial Nacional, 1973.

Friedricks, William B. "Phoenix: The History of a Southwestern Metropolis." *Business History Review* 65, no, 2 (Summer 1991): 443–445.

Fuentes Mares, José. *México se refugió en el desierto: Luis Terrazas: Historia y destino.* Mexico City: Editorial Jus, 1954.

Furlong, Thomas. *Fifty Years: A Detective.* Saint Louis: C. E. Barnett, 1912.

Gaillard, D. D. "The Papago of Arizona and Sonora." *American Anthropologist* 7, no. 3 (July 1894): 293–296.

Galarza, Ernesto. "La Mula No Nació Arisca." In John Burma, ed., *Mexican Americans in the United States: A Reader*, 199–206. Cambridge, Mass.: Schenkman, 1970.

Gamble, George B. "Clifton and Old Graham County." 1932. AHS.

Gamio, Manuel. *The Mexican Immigrant: His Life Story*. Chicago: University of Chicago Press, 1931.

García, Matt. *A World of Its Own: Race, Labor, and Citrus in the Making of Greater Los Angeles, 1900–1970*. Chapel Hill: University of North Carolina Press, 2001.

García-Acevedo, María Rosa "The Forgotten Diaspora: Mexican Immigration to New Mexico." In Erlinda Gonzales-Berry and David R. Maciel, eds., *The Contested Homeland: A Chicano History of New Mexico* Albuquerque: University of New Mexico Press, 2000.

García Ayluardo, Clara. "A World of Images: Cult, Ritual, and Society in Colonial Mexico City." In William H. Beezley, Cheryl English Martin, and William E. French, eds., *Rituals of Rule, Rituals of Resistance: Public Celebrations and Popular Culture in Mexico*. Washington, D.C.: Scholarly Resources, 1994.

Garza, Ramiro de. "Don Ignacio Pesqueira? Es Un Hero?" Revista Directorio Sonora. Manuel Humberto Ramirez, ed. Navojoa, Sonora, 1957, 19–22.

Gerhard, Peter. *The North Frontier of New Spain*, Revised Edition. Norman: University of Oklahoma Press, 1993.

Getty, Harry T. "Interethnic Relationships in the Community of Tucson." Ph.D. diss., University of Chicago, 1950.

Giese, Anna Mae. "The Sonoran Triumvirate: Preview in Sonora, 1910–1920." Ph.D. diss., University of Florida, 1975.

Ginzberg, Eitan. "State Agrarianism versus Democratic Agrarianism: Adalberto Tejeda's Experiment in Veracruz, 1928–32." *Journal of Latin American Studies* 30, no. 2 (May 1998): 341–372.

Glasscock, C. B. *The War of the Copper Kings*. New York: Gosset & Dunap, 1966.

Gleicher, Sheri Goldstein. "The Spiegelbergs of New Mexico: A Family Story of the Southwestern Frontier." *Southwest Jewish History* 1, no. 2 (Winter 1992).

Goff, John S. *George W. P. Hunt and His Arizona*. Pasadena: Socio Technical Publications, 1973.

Goldschmidt, Walter Rochs. *As You Sow*. New York: Harcourt, Brace, 1947.

Goldsmith, Raquel Rubio. "Hispanics in Arizona and Their Experiences with the Humanities." in F. Arturo Francisco Rosales and David William Foster, eds., *Hispanics and the Humanities in the Southwest: A Directory of Resources*. Tempe: Center for Latin American Studies, Arizona State University, 1983.

———. "Seasons, Seeds, and Souls: Mexican Women Gardening in the American Southwest, 1900–1940." In Heather Fowler-Salamini and and Mary K. Vaughan, eds., *Women of the Mexican Countryside: Creating Spaces, Shaping Transitions, 1850–1990*, 141–153. Tucson: University of Arizona Press, 1994.

Goldstein, Marcy Gail. "Americanization and Mexicanization: The Mexican Elite and

Anglo-Americans in the Gadsden Purchase Lands, 1853–1880." Ph.D. diss., Case Western Reserve University, 1977.

Gómez-Quiñones, Juan. "Plan de San Diego Reviewed." *Aztlán* (Spring 1970): 124–132.

Gonzales, Manuel G. *The Hispanic Elite of the Southwest*. El Paso: University of Texas at El Paso, 1989.

———. "Mariano G. Samaniego." *Arizona Journal of Arizona History* 31, no. 2 (Summer 1990): 141–160.

Gonzales, Michael J. "United States Copper Companies, the State, and Labour Conflict in Mexico, 1900–1910." *Journal of Latin American Studies* 26, no. 3 (Oct. 1994): 651–680.

———. "U.S. Copper Companies, the Mine Workers' Movement, and the Mexican Revolution, 1910–1920." *Hispanic American Historical Review* 76, no. 3 (Aug. 1996): 503–534.

Gonzales-Berry, Erlinda, and David R. Maciel, eds. *The Contested Homeland: A Chicano History of New Mexico*. Albuquerque: University of New Mexico Press, 2000.

Gonzales Ramírez, Manuel. *Manifestos politicos, 1892–1912*. Vol. 4. Mexico City: Fondo de Cultura Economica, 1957.

González, Gilbert G. *Mexican Consuls and Labor Organizing: Imperial Politics in the American Southwest*. Austin: University of Texas Press, 1999.

González Navarro, Moisés. "El mestizaje mexicano en el periodo nacional." *Revista Mexicana de Sociología* 30, no. 1 (Jan.–Mar. 1968): 35–52.

Gordon, Linda. *The Great Arizona Orphan Abduction*. Cambridge, Mass.: Harvard University Press, 1999.

Graeme, R. W. "Bisbee, Arizona's Dowager Queen of Mining Camps: A Look at Her First 50 Years." In J. Michael Canty and Michael N. Greeley, eds., *History of Mining in Arizona*, 51–76. Tucson: Mining Club of the Southwest Foundation, 1987.

Grant, Ulysses S. *Personal Memoirs*, 22–24. New York, 1885. Quoted at http://www.sewanee.edu/faculty/Willis/Civil _ War/documents/Grant.html (accessed Nov. 7, 2005).

Greenfield, Margaret. *Migratory Farm Labor Problems: Summary of Findings and Recommendations Made by Principal Investigative Committees, with Special Reference to California, 1915 to 1950*. Berkeley: University of California, Bureau of Administration, 1950.

Griffen, William B. *Apaches at War and Peace: The Janos Presidio, 1750-1858* Norman: University of Oklahoma Press, 1988.

———. *Indian Assimilation in the Franciscan area of Nueva Vizcaya*. Tucson: University of Arizona Press, 1979.

Guerin-Gonzales, Camille. *Mexican Workers and American Dreams: Immigration, Repatriation, and California Farm Labor, 1900–1939*. New Brunswick, N.J.: Rutgers University Press, 1994.

Gustavson, Cloyd V. "An Ecological Analysis of the Hollenbeck Area of Los Angeles." Master's thesis, University of Southern California, 1940.

Gutiérrez, Juan Ramón. *Relatos de mí pueblo: La microhistoria de Hermosillo.* Hermosillo: Servircios de Tipografía Guerrero, 1983.

Gutiérrez, Marcela Tostado. *El álbum de la mujer de las mexicanas.* Vol. 2: *Época colonial.* Mexico City: Instituto Nacional de Antropología e Historia, 1991.

Gutiérrez, Ramón A. *When Jesus Came, the Corn Mothers Went Away.* Stanford, Calif.: Stanford University Press, 1991.

Gutmann, Myron P., Robert McCaa, Rodolfo Gutierrez-Montes, and Brian Gratton. "The Demographic Impact of the Mexican Revolution in the United States." Texas Population Research Center Paper no. 99-00-01, Jan., 2000, http://www.prc.utexas.edu/working_papers/wp_pdf/99-001.pdf#search='u.s.%201910%20census%20mexican' (accessed Jan. 1, 2006).

Guzmán, Martin Luis. *Memoirs of Pancho Villa.* Translated by Virgina H. Taylor. Austin: University of Texas Press, 1965.

Hadley, Phillip L. *Minería y sociedad en el centro mineral de Santa Eulalia, Chihuahua (1709–1759).* Mexico City: Fondo de Cultural Económica, 1979.

Hager, William M. "The Plan of San Diego: Unrest on the Texas Border in 1915." *Arizona and the West* 5, no. 4 (Winter 1963).

Halcomb, Ellen L. "Efforts to Organize the Migrant Workers by the Cannery and Agricultural Workers." Master's thesis, Chico State College, 1963.

Hale, Charles A. "José María Luis Mora and the Structure of Mexican Liberalism." *Hispanic American Historical Review* 45, no. 2 (May 1965): 196–227.

Hall, Linda B., and Don M. Coerver. *Revolution on the Border: The United States and Mexico, 1910–1920.* Albuquerque: University of New Mexico Press, 1988.

Hamilton, Alice, M.D. *Exploring the Dangerous Trades: The Autobiography of Alice Hamilton, M.D.* Boston: Little, Brown, 1943.

Hanrahan, Gene Z., ed. *Documents on the Mexican Revolution.* Vol. 1. Salisbury, N.C.: Documentary, 1976.

Hansen, Lawrence Douglas Taylor. "La fiebre del oro en Sonora durante la decada de 1850 y sus repercusiones diplomáticas con Estados Unidos." *Revista de El Colegio de Sonora* 7, no. 12 (1996): 109, 112.

Harner, John P. "Copper Mining and Regional Identity in Sonora, Mexico." Ph.D diss., Arizona State University, 1996.

Harrison, Charles Buxton. "The Development of the Arizona Labor Movement." Master's thesis, Arizona State University, 1954.

Hart, John M. *Empire and Revolution: The Americans in Mexico since the Civil War.* Berkeley: University of California Press, 2002.

Harvey, B. H. "How We First Went into the Imperial Valley in 1930." Manuscript. Bancroft Library, UCB.

Havstad, K. M. "Improving Sustainability of Arid Rangelands." *New Mexico Journal of Science* 39 (Nov. 1999): 174–197.

"Hearing Held on the Cotton Strike in San Joaquin Valley by Fact-Finding Committee Appointed by James Rolph, Governor of the State of California." Oct. 19, 1933, Civic Auditorium, Visalia. PSTC, Folder 38, C-R 3I, Bancroft Library, UCB.

Hearings on S. Res. 106. 66th Cong., 2d sess. (1920). Report of Chairman, Committee on Foreign Relations, U.S. Senate. S. Doc. 285.

Henderson, Peter V. N. "Mexican Rebels in the Borderlands, 1910–1912." *Red River Valley Historical Review,* Summer 1975, 207–219.

Hernández Alvarez, José. "A Demographic Profile of the Mexican Immigration to the United States, 1910–1950." *Journal of Inter-American Studies* 8, no. 3 (July 1966): 471–496.

Hernández Padilla, Salvador. *El Magonismo: Historia de una pasión libertaria 1900– 1922.* Mexico City: Ediciones Era, 1984.

Heyman, Josiah. *Life and Labor on the Border: Working People of Northeastern Sonora, Mexico, 1886–1986.* Tucson: University of Arizona Press, 1991.

———. "Oral History of the Mexican American Community of Douglas, Arizona, 1901–1942." *Journal of the Southwest* 35, no. 2 (Summer 1993):

Híjar, Alberto. "Notas sobre cultura obrera mexicana." In Victor Novelo et al., *Monografías Obreras.* Vol. 1. Mexico City: Cuadernos de la Casa Chata, Sept. 1987.

Hildebrand, George H., and Garth L. Mangum. *Capital and Labor in American Copper, 1845–1990: Linkages between Product and Labor Markets.* Cambridge, Mass.: Harvard University Press, 1992.

"Historical Annual National Guard of the State of Arizona, 1938–1939." N.p.: Army-Navy Publishing, n.d. Brochure retells the story of June 1903 Morenci flood, as recalled in "Morenci Flood Claimed Score, Save Hundreds." *Phoenix Gazette,* June 9, 1953.

Hoffman, Abraham. "Stimulus to Repatriation: The 1931 Federal Deportation Drive and the Los Angeles Mexican Community." In Norris Hundley, ed., *The Chicano.* Santa Barbara, Calif.: Clio, 1975.

———. *Unwanted Mexican Americans in the Great Depression.* Tucson: University of Arizona Press, 1974.

Holbert, Jerry Edward. "Rural/Urban Conflict over Water Control in the Rio Grande Valley of Texas." Ph.D. diss., Texas A&M University, 1984.

Holden, Robert H. "Priorities of the State in the Survey of the Public Land in Mexico, 1876–1911." *Hispanic American Historical Review* 70, no. 4 (Nov. 1990): 579–608.

Holden, William Curry. *Teresita.* Owings Mills, Md.: Stemmer House, 1978.

Hopkins, Ernest J. *Financing the Frontier: A Fifty-Year History of the Valley National Bank.* Phoenix: Valley National Bank, 1950.

Huberman, Leo. *The Labor Spy Racket.* New York: Modern Age Books, 1937.

Hu-DeHart, Evelyn. *Missionaries, Mines and Indians: Spanish Contact with the Yaqui Nation of Northwestern New Spain, 1533–1820.* Tucson: University of Arizona Press, 1981.

———. *Yaqui Resistance and Survival: The Struggle for Land and Autonomy, 1821– 1910.* Madison: University of Wisconsin Press, 1984.

Huginnie, Andrea Yvette. " 'Strikitos': Race, Class, and Work in the Arizona Copper Industry, 1870–1920." Ph.D. diss., Yale University, 1991.

Hyde, Charles K. *Copper for America: The United States Copper Industry from Colonial Times to the 1990s.* Tucson: University of Arizona Press, 1998.

Industrial Workers of the World (IWW). *Songs of the Workers: To Fan the Flames of Discontent,* 34th ed. Chicago: Industrial Workers of the World, 1973.

Inglesias, César Andreu, ed. *Memoirs of Bernardo Vega: A Contribution to the History of the Puerto Rican Community in New York.* New York: Monthly Review Press, 1984.

Jackson, Robert H. "Demographic Change in Northwestern New Spain." *Americas* 41, no. 4 (Apr. 1985): 462–479.

————. *Indian Population decline: The Missions of Northwest New Spain, 1687–1840.* Albuquerque: University of New Mexico Press, 1995.

————, ed. *New Views of Borderland History.* Albuquerque: University of New Mexico Press, 1998.

————. "Northwestern New Spain: The Pimería Alta and the Californias." In Jackson, ed., *New Views of Borderland History.* Albuquerque: University of New Mexico Press, 1998.

Jackson, W. Turrentine. *The Enterprising Scot: Investors in the American West after 1873.* Edinburgh: Edinburgh University Press, 1968.

Jamieson, Stuart. *Labor Unionism in American Agriculture.* New York: Arno Press, 1976.

Jeffrey, John Mason. *The Story of the Arizona Territorial Prison.* La Jolla, Calif.: Prospect Ave Press, 1969.

Jenkins, Myra Ellen. "Ricardo Flores Magón and the Mexican Liberal Party." Ph.D. diss., University of New Mexico, 1953.

Johns, Bryan Theodore. "Field Workers in California." Master's thesis, University of California at Berkeley, 1948.

Johnson, Alan Vernon. "Governor G.W.P. Hunt and Organized Labor." Master's thesis, University of Arizona, 1964.

Johnson, Benjamin. "The Plan de San Diego Uprising and the Making of the Modern Texas-Mexican Borderlands." In Samuel Truett and Elliott Young, eds., *Continental Crossroads: Remapping U.S.-Mexico Borderlands History.* Durham, N.C.: Duke University Press, 2004.

Johnson, Susan L. "Sharing Bed and Board: Cohabitation and Cultural Difference in Central Arizona Mining Towns." *Frontiers: A Journal of Women Studies* 7, no. 3 (Women on the Western Frontier; 1984): 36–42.

Karp, Lian. *Cultura popular/cultura urbana.* Mexico City: El Colegio de Sonora, 1987.

Katz, Friedrich. *The Life and Times of Pancho Villa.* Stanford, Calif.: Stanford University Press, 1998.

Kellogg, Susan. "Hegemony Out of Conquest: The First Two Centuries of Spanish Rule in Central Mexico." *Radical History Review* 53 (Spring 1992): 27–46.

Kent, Robert B., and Maura E. Huntz. "Spanish-Language Newspapers in the United States." *Geographical Review* 86, no. 3 (Latin American Geography; July 1996): 446–456.

Kerig, Dorothy Pierson. "A United States Consul on the Border During the Mexican Revolution: The Case of Luther T. Ellsworth." Master's thesis, San Diego State College, 1974.

Kienle, John Emmanuel. "Housing Conditions among the Mexican Population of Los Angeles." Master's thesis, University of Southern California, 1912.

Kingsolver, Barbara. *Holding the Line: Women in the Great Arizona Mine Strike of 1983.* Ithaca, N.Y.: Cornell University Press, 1996.

Kirkendall, Richard S. *Social Scientists and Farm Politics in the Age of Roosevelt.* Columbus: University of Missouri Press, 1966.

Kluger, James R. *The Clifton-Morenci Strike: Labor Difficulty in Arizona, 1915–1916.* Tucson, University of Arizona Press, 1970.

Knowlton, Robert J. "Expropriation of Church Property in Nineteenth-Century Mexico and Colombia: A Comparison." *Americas* 25, no. 4 (Apr. 1969): 387–401.

Kroeber, A. L. *Uto-Aztecan Languages of Mexico.* Ibero-Americana, 8. Berkeley: University of California Press, 1934.

Lamb, Blaine Peterson. "Jewish Pioneers in Arizona, 1850–1920." Ph.D. diss., Arizona State University, 1982.

Lambert, Adolfo D. "Zona Minera de Naica." Feb. 22, 1890. Archivo de Arturo Armendariz.

Langham, Thomas C. *Border Trials: Ricardo Flores Magón and the Mexican Liberals.* El Paso: Texas Western Press 1981.

"La opinión de Chihuahua ante el Congreso: Instrucción dirigidas por la diputación provincial de Chihuahua a sus diputados en el Congreso General Constituyente Mexicano." Mexico City: Imprenta a Cargo de Martin Rivera, 1823. In Graziella Altamirano and Guadalupe Villa, eds., *Chihuahua: Textos de su historia, 1824–1921,* 1–11. Ciudad Juárez: Universidad de Juárez, 1988.

Large, David C. "Cotton in the San Joaquin Valley: A Study of Government in Agriculture." *Geographical Review* 47, no. 3 (July 1957): 365–380.

Lempriere, Charles. *Notes in Mexico in 1861 and 1862: Politically and Socially Considered.* London: Green, Longman, Roberts and Green, 1850.

Lenin, V. I. *Left-Wing Communism: An Infantile Disorder.* In *Collected Works,* 31:17–118. Moscow: Progress, 1964. *http://www.marxists.org/archive/lenin/works/1920/lwc/* (accessed Jan. 31, 2005).

Lerner Sigal, F. Victoria. "Los exiliados mexicanos en Estados Unidos, 1910–1940," http://136.142.158.105/Lasa2003/LernerSigalVictoria.pdf (accessed Nov. 15, 2003).

———. "Exiliados de la Revolución mexicana: El caso de los villistas (1915–1921)." *Mexican Studies/Estudios Mexicanos* 17, no. 1 (Winter 2001): 109–141.

Levario, Gilbert. "A History of the Discalced Carmelite Friars in Southern Arizona." *Carmelite Digest* 2, no. 4 (Autumn 1987): 17–21.

Linquist, John H. "The Jerome Deportation." *Arizona and the West* 11, no. 3 (Autumn 1969): 233–246.

Lister, Florence C., and Robert H. Lister. *Chihuahua: Storehouse of Storms.* Albuquerque: University of New Mexico Press, 1966.

Liverman, Diana M. "Drought Impacts in Mexico: Climate, Agriculture, Technology, and Land Tenure in Sonora and Puebla." *Annals of the Association of American Geographers* 80, no. 1 (Mar. 1990): 49–72.

Lloyd, Jane Dale. *El proceso de modernización capitalista en el noroeste de Chihuahua (1880–1910).* Mexico City: Universidad Iberoamericana, 1987.

Lloyd, Jane Dale, and Elena Azoala. *La formación y actividades politicas del Partido Libreral Mexicano en 1905–1906.* Mexico City: Cuadernos de la Casa Chata, 1974.

Loftis, Anne. *Witnesses to the Struggle: Imaging the 1930s California Labor Movement.* Reno: University of Nevada Press, 1998.

Lomas, Clara. "Transborder Discourse: The Articulation of Gender in the Borderlands in the Early Twentieth Century: 2. Contextualizing." *Frontiers — A Journal of Women's Studies* 24, nos. 2–3 (June–Sept. 2003): 51–75.

López, Ronald W. "The El Monte Berry Strike of 1933." *Aztlán* 1, no. 1 (Spring 1970): 101–114.

———. "Los Repatriados." Seminar paper, History Department, University of California at Los Angeles, 1968. Available in GCP, SC, UCLA.

Love, Frank. *Mining Camps and Ghost Towns.* Los Angeles: Westernlore Press, 1974.

Lowenstein, Norman. "Strikes and Strike Tactics in California Agriculture: A History." Master's thesis, University of California at Berkeley, 1940.

Lubin, Simon L. "Can the Radicals Capture the Farms of California?" Speech before the Commonwealth Club of San Francisco, Mar. 23, 1934.

Luckingham, Bradford. *Minorities in Phoenix: A Profile of Mexican American, Chinese American, and African American Communities, 1860–1992.* Tucson: University of Arizona Press, 1994.

MacDonald, Frank. "A Brief History of California's Agricultural Labor." In *La Follette Hearings: Violations of Free Speech and Rights of Labor.* Hearings before a Subcommittee of the Committee on Education and Labor. United States Senate. 76th Cong., 3d sess. Pursuant to S. Res. 266 (74th Congress), pp. 19903–19905. Exhibits entered in Los Angeles, California, Jan. 13, 1940. Washington, D.C.: Government Printing Office, 1940.

Macklin, Barbara June, and N. Ross Crumrine. "Three North Mexican Folk Saint Movements." *Comparative Studies in Society and History* 15, no. 1 (Jan. 1973): 89–105.

Madrid, Enrique R. La. "El Corrido de Tomochic: Honor, Grace, Gender, and Power in the First Ballad of the Mexican Revolution." *Journal of the Southwest* 41, no. 4 (Winter 1999): 441–460.

Magon et al. v. United States, 212 U.S. 589 (1909). 29 S. Ct. 691; 53 L. Ed. 663; 1909 U.S. LEXIS 2126 Jan. 4, 1909. Appeal from the Circuit Court of the United States for the Southern District of California. Dismissed.

Mailsey, F. R. "Douglas, Arizona: Chamber of Commerce and Mines." Douglas, Arizona, 1913. ASA.

Manson, Clara. "Indian Uprisings in Sonora, Mexico." Master's thesis, University of Southern California, Los Angeles, 1936.

Marez, Curtis "Signifying Spain, Becoming Comanche, Making Mexicans: Indian Captivity and the History of Chicana/o Popular Performance." *American Quarterly* 53, no. 2 (2001): 267–307.

Martin, Cheryl English. *Governance and Society in Colonial Mexico: Chihuahua in the Eighteenth Century.* Stanford, Calif.: Stanford University Press, 1996.

Martin, Douglas D. "The Douglas Dynasty." File A29, SC, UA.

Martínez-Echazabal, Lourdes. "Mestizaje and the Discourse of National/Cultural Identity in Latin America, 1845–1959." *Latin American Perspectives* 25, no. 3 (May 1998): 21–42.

Martínez Nuñez, Eugenio. *Historia de la Revolución Mexicana: Los mártires de San Juan de Ulúa.* Mexico City: [Talleres Gráficos de la Nación], 1968.

——. *La vida heroica de Práxedis G. Guerrero.* Mexico City: Bibloteca del Instituto Nacional de Estudios Historicos de la Revolución Mexicana, 1960.

Martínez, Oscar J. *Border Boom Town: Ciudad Juárez since 1848.* Austin: University of Texas Press, 1978.

Marvin, George. "The Quick and the Dead on the Border." *World's Work*, Jan. 1917, 295–296.

Mayer, Vincent Villanueva, Jr. "The Black Slave on New Spain's Northern Frontier: San José de Parral 1632–1676." Ph.D. diss., University of Utah, 1975.

McBride, James D. "The Development of Labor Unions in Arizona Mining, 1884–1818." Master's thesis, Arizona State University, 1974.

——. "Henry S. McCluskey: Workingman's Advocate." Ph.D. diss., Arizona State University, 1982.

——. "The Liga Protectora Latina: A Mexican-American Benevolent Society in Arizona." *Journal of the West*, Oct. 1975, 83–84.

McCaa, Robert. "The Peopling of Mexico from Origins to Revolution." Preliminary draft, Dec. 8, 1997 (notes omitted from Web version). Michael R. Haines and Richard H. Steckel, eds., *A Population History of North America.* Cambridge: Cambridge University Press. http://www.hist.umn.edu/rmccaa/mxpoprev/cambri dg3.htm (accessed July 19, 2003).

McClintock, James H. *Arizona: The Youngest State.* Vol. 2. Chicago: Clarke, 1916.

McCluskey, H. S. "Absentee Capitalists: Menace Popular Government in Arizona." Reprint of Articles Appearing in *Miami Daily Silver Belt* from Aug. 17 to Oct. 4, 1921. Box 7, Folder 1, HSMC, ASU.

McLean, Robert N. "Good-bye, Vincente." *Survey* (May 1931): 195.

McNally, David. "E. P. Thompson: Mass Struggle and Historical Materialism." *International Socialism Journal* 61 (Winter 1993). *http://pubs.socialistreviewindex.org.uk/ isj61/mcnally.htm* (accessed Sept. 23, 2004).

McWilliams, Carey. *California: The Great Exception.* Westport, Conn.: Greenwood Press 1971.

——. *Factories in the Fields: The Story of Migratory Labor in California.* Santa Barbara, Calif.: Peregrine, 1971.

———. *Ill Fares the Land: Migrants and Miratory Labor in the United States*. Boston: Little, Brown, 1942.

———. *North from Mexico: The Spanish-Speaking People of the United States*. Westport: Greenwood Press, 1968.

Medeiros, Francine. "*La Opinion*, a Mexican Exile Newspaper: A Content Analysis of Its First Years, 1926–1929." *Aztlan* 11, no. 1 (Spring 1980): 65–87.

Medina, Frank. *Once upon a Cotton-Picking Time*. New York: Vantage Press, 1975.

Medina Hoyos, Francisco. *Cananea: Cuna de la Revolución mexicana*. Mexico City, 1956.

Meinig, D. W. *Southwest: Three Peoples in Geographical Change 1600–1970*. New York: Oxford University Press, 1971.

Meier, Matt S., and Feliciano Rivera. *Dictionary of Mexican American History* Westport, Conn.: Greenwood Press, 1981.

Mellinger, Phillip J. "How the IWW Lost Its Western Heartland: Western Labor History Revisited." *Western Historical Quarterly* 27, no. 3 (Autumn 1996): 303–324.

———. " 'The Men Have Become Organizers': Labor Conflict and Unionization in the Mexican Mining Communities of Arizona, 1900–1915." *Western Historical Quarterly* 23, no. 3 (Aug. 1992): 323–347.

———. *Race and Labor in Western Copper: The Fight for Equality, 1896–1918*. Tucson: University of Arizona Press, 1995.

Menchaca, Martha. *Recovering History, Constructing Race: Indian, Black, and White Roots of Mexican Americans*. Austin: University of Texas Press, 2001.

Méndoza Magallanes, Víctor. *Pueblo Viejo*. [Chihuahua, Mexico]: Gobierno del Estado de Chihuahua, 1986.

Meredith, John D. "The Yaqui Rebellion of 1740: A Jesuit Account and Its Implications." *Ethnohistory* 22, no. 3 (Summer 1975): 222–261.

Meyer, Michael C. *Mexican Rebel: Pascual Orozco and the Mexican Revolution, 1910–1915*. Lincoln: University of Nebraska Press, 1967.

———. *Water in the Hispanic Southwest: A Social and Legal History, 1550–1850*. Tucson: University of Arizona Press, 1996.

Middlebrook, Pearl Hepsie. "Localization of Cotton Culture in the Kern County County Area, California." Master's thesis, University of Chicago, 1929.

Miller, Robert Ryal. "Plácido Vega: A Mexican Secret Agent in the United States, 1864–1866." *Americas* 19, no. 2 (Oct. 1962): 137–148.

Mitchell, Don. *The Lie of the Land: Migrant Workers and the California Landscape*. Minneapolis: University of Minnesota Press, 1996.

Morgan, Richard E. *Domestic Intelligence Monitoring Dissent in America*. Austin: University of Texas Press, 1980.

Monroy, Douglas. *Rebirth: Mexican Los Angeles from the Great Migration to the Great Depression*. Berkeley: University of California Press, 1999.

Montoya, Camila. "Empowered or Subordinated? The Role of Mexican American Women in the Popular Religious Traditions of the Borderlands and in the Us Catholic and Protestant Churches." *History* 486 (March 2000). *http://www.msu.edu/eldersjo/camila.htm* (accessed Aug. 26, 2004).

Moore, Walter. "Adolfo de la Huerta: His Political Role in Sonora, 1906–1920." Ph.D. diss., University of California at San Diego, 1982.

———. "Un ejercito de gobierno: Adolfo de la Huerta, Plutarco Elías Calles y las reformas de 1916–1917." In *Memoria: XI Simposio de Historia y Antropología de Sonora*, 226–245. Hermosillo: Universidad de Sonora, 1987.

Morehouse, Barbara J., Rebecca H. Carter, and Terry W. Spouse. "The Implications of Sustained Drought for Transboundary Water Management in Nogales, Arizona, and Nogales, Sonora." *Natural Resources Journal* 40, no. 4 (Fall 2000): 783–811.

Morgan, Richard E. *Domestic Intelligence Monitoring Dissent in America.* Austin: University of Texas Press, 1980.

Mosk, Sanford A. "Economic Problems in Sonora in the Late Eighteenth Century." *Pacific Historical Review* 8, no. 3 (Sept. 1939): 341–345.

Mulligan, Raymond A. "New York Foundlings at Clifton-Morenci: Social Justice in Arizona Territory, 1904–1905." In Manuel P. Servin, ed., *The Mexican Americans: An Awakening Minority*, 2nd ed. Beverly Hills, Calif.: Glencoe Press, 1970.

Muñoz, Ignacio. *Verdad y mito de la Revolución mexicana (relatada por un protagonista).* Vol. 2. Mexico City: Ediciones Populares, 196

Myrick, David F. *Railroads of Arizona, Clifton, Morenci and Metcalf: Rails and Copper Mines.* Vol. 3. Glendale, Calif.: Trans-Anglo Books, 1984.

Nabhan, Gary Paul. "Cultural Dispersal of Plants on the Islands of the Sea of Cortes: Integrating Indigenous Human Dispersal Agents into Island Biogeography." *Journal of the Southwest* 42, no. 3 (Autumn 2000): 545–558.

Nugent, Daniel. *Spent Cartridges of Revolution: An Anthropological History of Namiquipa, Chihuahua.* Chicago: University of Chicago Press, 1993.

NY Foundling Hosp. v. Gatti, 203 U.S. 429 (1906). 27 S. Ct. 53; 51 L. Ed. 254; 1906 U.S. LEXIS 1606. Argued Apr. 26, 1906. Decided Dec. 3, 1906.

O'Connor, Mary. "Two Kinds of Religious Movements among the Mayo Indians of Sonora, Mexico." *Journal for the Scientific Study of Religion* 18, no. 3 (Sept. 1979): 260–268.

Officer, James E. "Barriers to Mexican Integration in Tucson." *Kiva* 17 (Nov.–Dec. 1951): 7–16.

———. *Hispanic Arizona, 1536–1856.* Tucson: University of Arizona Press, 1987.

O'Horo, Kevin. *American Foreign Investments and Foreign Policy, 1865–1898.* New Brunswick, N.J.: Rutgers University, 1976.

Orozco, Victor, ed. *Las guerras indias en la historia de Chihuahua: Antología.* Ciudad Juárez: Universidad de Ciudad Juárez, Instituto Chihuahuahuense de la Cultura, 1987.

Ortegón, Samuel M. "The Religious Status of the Mexican Population of Los Angeles." Master's thesis, University of Southern California, 1932.

Osorio, Rubén. *Tomochic en llamas.* Mexico City: Consejo Nacional para la Cultura y las Artes, 1995.

Otero, Gerardo. "The New Agrarian Movement: Self-Managed, Democratic Production." *Latin American Perspectives* 16, no. 4 (Views and Debates: Autumn, 1989): 28–59.

Owens, Stephen L. "The Growth and Development of Safford, Arizona." Master's thesis, Arizona State University, 1953.

Pace, Anne. "Mexican Refugees in Arizona, 1910–1911." *Arizona and the West* 16, no. 1 (Spring 1974): 5–18.

Park, Joseph Franklin. "The 1903 'Mexican Affair' at Clifton." *Journal of Arizona History* 18 (Summer 1977): 119–148.

———. "The History of Mexican Labor in Arizona during the Territorial Period." Master's thesis, University of Arizona, 1961.

Perrigo, Lynn I. *Our Spanish Southwest*. Dallas: Banks Upshaw, 1960.

Parrish, Michael E. *Felix Frankfurter and His Times, The Reform Years*. New York: Free Press, 1982.

———. "Labor, Progressives, and Copper: The Failure of Industrial Democracy in Arizona during World War 2." History Department, University of California at San Diego.

———. *Mexican Workers, Progressives and Copper: The Failure of Industrial Democracy in Arizona During the Wilson Years*. Southwest Border Series. San Diego: Chicano Research Publications, 1979.

Patch, Robert W. "Imperial Politics and Local Economy in Colonial Central America: 1670–1770." *Past and Present Society* 143 (May 1994): 77–107.

Patton, James Monroe. *History of Clifton*. Clifton, Ariz.: Greenlee County Chamber of Commerce, 1977.

Pendleton, Edwin C. "History of Labor in Arizona Irrigated Agriculture." Ph.D diss., University of California at Berkeley, 1950.

Pérez de Ribas, Andrés. *History of the Triumphs of Our Holy Faith amongst the Most Barbarous and Fierce Peoples of the New World*. Translated by Daniel T. Reff, Maureen Ahern, and Richard K. Danford. Tucson: University of Arizona Press, 1999.

Perry, Charles R., Andrew M. Kramer, and Thomas J. Schneider. *Operating during Strikes: Company Experience, NLRB Policies, and Governmental Regulations*. Philadelphia: University of Pennsylvania, Wharton School, Industrial Research Unit, 1982.

Pesotta, Rosa. *Bread upon the Water*. New York: Dodd, Mead, 1944.

Pesqueira, Fernando. "Documentos para la historia de Sonora." 2nd series, vol. 3 [4?], Feb. 26, 1868. Secretaría de Gobernación, Archivos Viejos, Legajo 1833–1854, AGN. Typewritten copy in Biblioteca y Museo de Sonora, Hermosillo.

Peterson, Herbert B. "Twentieth-Century Search for Cibola: Post World War I Mexican Labor Exploitation in Arizona." In Manuel Servín, ed., *An Awakening Minority: The Mexican American,* 2nd ed. Beverly Hills, Calif.: Glencoe Press, 1974.

Phillips, David A., Jr. "Prehistory of Chihuahua and Sonora, Mexico." *Journal of World Prehistory* 3, no. 4 (Dec. 1989): 373–402.

Pichardo, Nelson Alexander. "The Role of Community in Social Protest: Chicano Working Class Protest, 1845–1933." Ph.D. diss., University of Michigan, 1990.

Población total nacional y estatal, serie censal y proyecciones. Monografías Socioeconómicas. Centro de Estudios Sociales y de Opinión Pública, Demografía Sonora, México, 1900–2010, http://www.conapo.gob.mx/m _ en _ cifras/proyecta 50/26.xls (accesed Jan. 1, 2006).

Polzer, Charles W., S.J. "The Evolution of the Jesuit Mission System in Northwest New Spain, 1600–1767." Ph.D. diss., University of Arizona, 1972.

Ponce de León, José María. *Datos geográficos y estadísticos del Estado de Chihuahua.* Ciudad Chihuahua: Imprenta del Gobierno a cargo de Gilberto A. de la Garza, 1907.

Powell, T. G. "Mexican Intellectuals and the Indian Question, 1876–1911." *Hispanic American Historical Review* 48, no. 1 (Feb. 1968): 19–36.

Pradeau, Alberto Francisco. *Sonora y sus casas de moneda: Alamos y Hermosillo.* Mexico City: Edición Privada, 1959.

Prewitt, Steven W. " 'We Didn't Ask to Come to this Party': Self-Determination Collides with the Federal Government in the Public Schools of Del Rio, Texas, 1890–1971." Ph.D. diss., University of Houston, 2000.

Proceedings of the President's Mediation Commission Session at Clifton, Arizona, Oct. 25–30, 1917. Reported by N. L. Rudcrow, Phoenix, Arizona. JMC, Bancroft Library, UCB.

Public Broadcasting System (PBS). *Los Mineros.* Hector Galan Productions, 1990. Video (58 min.).

Raat, W. Dirk. *Revoltosos: Mexico's Rebels in the United States, 1903–1923.* College Station: Texas A&M University Press, 1981.

Radding, Cynthia. "Cultural Dialogues: Recent Trends in Mesoamerican Ethnohistory." *Latin American Research Review* 33, no. 1 (Winter 1998): 193–211.

———. "From the Counting House to the Field and Loom: Ecologies, Cultures, and Economies in the Missions of Sonora (Mexico) and Chiquitanía (Bolivia)." *Hispanic American Historical Review* 81, no. 1 (2001): 45–87.

———. "Insurgencia y autonomia: Historia de los pueblos yaquis, 1821–1910." *Hispanic American Historical Review* 79, no. 1 (Feb. 1999): 157–158.

———. *Wandering Peoples: Colonialism, Ethnic Spaces, and Ecological Frontiers in Northwestern Mexico, 1700–1850.* Durham, N.C.: Duke University Press, 1997.

Radding Murieta, Cynthia, and Juan José Gracida Romo. *Sonora: Una Historia Compartida.* Hermosillo: Gobierno del Estado de Sonora, 1989.

Rasmussen, Wayne David. *The Department of Agriculture.* New York, Praeger 1972.

Redfield, Robert. "The Indian in Mexico." *Annals of the American Academy of Political and Social Science* 208 (Mexico Today; Mar. 1940): 132.

Reid, John C. *Reid's Tramp; or, A Journal of Incidents of Ten Months of Travel Through Texas, New Mexico, Arizona, Sonora, and California.* Selma, Alabama: John Hardy, 1858.

Reisler, Mark. *By the Sweat of Their Brow: Mexican Immigrant Labor in the United States, 1900–1940.* Westport, Conn.: Greenwood Press, 1976.

Rénique, Gerardo. "Frontier Capitalism and Revolution in Northwest Mexico, Sonora, 1830–1910." Ph.D. diss., Columbia University, 1990.

Report of Cases Argued and Determined in the Supreme Court of the Territory of Arizona from 1904 to 1906 Inclusive. Vol. 9. San Francisco: Bancroft-Whitney, 1908.

"Report on Cotton Strikers, Kings County." PSTC, Bancroft Library, UCB.

"Reporte oficial del Perfecto Político de Arizpe, Sonora, Sr. Federico Platt, al Gobernador, relato al paro general que tuvo lugar en la CCCCo, S.A. en julio de 1914." As reproduced in Juan Luis Sariego Rodríguez, *Enclaves y minerales en el norte de México: Historia social de los mineros de Cananea y Nueva Rosita, 1900–1970,* 143–148. Mexico City: Centro de Investigaciones y Estudios Superiores en Antropología Social, 1988.

Richardson Construction. "What the Compañía Constructora Richardson Is Doing in the Yaqui Valley, Sonora, Mexico." Brochure. N.p., 1917. Compañía Constructora Richardson Papers, SC, UA.

Richmond, Douglas. "The Legacy of African Slavery in Colonial Mexico, 1519–1810." *Journal of Popular Culture* 35, no. 2 (Fall 2001): 1–16.

Ridgway, William R. "Sanchez Name Spices Graham County History." *Journal of Graham County History* 5, no. 1 (1969). Graham County Historical Society, Safford, Arizona.

Ringgold, Jennie Parks. *Frontier Days in the Southwest: Pioneer Days in Old Arizona.* San Antonio, Tex.: Naylor, 1952.

Rivera, Antonio G. *La Revolución en Sonora, México.* Mexico City, 1969.

Roca, Paul M. *Spanish Jesuit Churches in Mexico's Tarahumara.* Tucson: University of Arizona Press, 1979.

Rocha Chávez, Rubén. *Tres siglos de historia y biografía de una ciudad: Parral.* Ciudad Chihuahua: La Prensa, 1976.

Rodríguez, Richard, and Gloria L. Rodríguez "Teresa Urrea: Her Life, as It Affected the Mexican-U.S. Frontier." *El Grito* (Summer 1972) 48–68.

Rogers, Allen H. "Character and Habits of the Mexican Miner." *Engineering and Mining Journal* 85, no. 14 (Apr. 4, 1908): 700–701.

Romo, Ricardo. *East Los Angeles: History of a Barrio.* Austin: University of Texas Press, 1983.

———. *Ringside Seat to a Revolution: An Underground Cultural History of El Paso and Juarez: 1893–1923.* El Paso, Tex.: Cinco Puntos Press, 2005.

———. "Work and Restlessness: Occupational and Spatial Mobility among Mexicanos in Los Angeles, 1918–1928. *Pacific Historical Review* 46, no. 2 (May 1977): 157–180.

Ronstadt, Federico José María. "The Memoirs of Federico José María Ronstadt." Transcription of the original text from the manuscript in the Ronstadt Family Archives. SC, UA.

Rosales, F. Arturo Francisco, and David William Foster, eds. *Hispanics and the Humanities in the Southwest: A Directory of Resources.* Tempe: Center for Latin American Studies, Arizona State University, 1983.

Rosales Villa, Manuel. *Mis puntes: Santa Rosalía de Camargo, Chihuahua.* Ciudad

Camargo: Imprenta "Pedroza" de Camargo, Apartación Cultural Manuel Rosales Villa, 1993.

Rosenblum, Johnathan D. *Copper Crucible: How The Arizona Miners' Strike of 1983 Recast Labor-Management Relations in America.* Ithaca, N.Y.: Cornell University Press, 1995.

Ross, Margaret Wheeler. *The Tale Is Told: History of the Arizona Federation of Women's Clubs and Its Forerunners.* N.p.: Arizona Federation of Women's Clubs, 1944.

Ruiz, Ramón Eduardo. *The People of Sonora and Yankee Capitalists.* Tucson: University of Arizona Press, 1988.

Ruiz, Vicki L. *Cannery Women, Cannery Lives: Mexican Women, Unionization, and the California Food Processing Industry, 1930–1950.* Albuquerque: University of New Mexico Press, 1987.

Ruiz y Sándoval, Alberto. *El algodón en México.* Mexico City: Ofina de la Secretaria de Fomento, 1884.

Rynning, Thomas H. *Gun Notches: The Life of a Cowboy-Soldier.* New York: Frederick A. Stokes, 1931.

Sain, Wilma Gray. "A History of the Miami Area, Arizona." Master's thesis, University of Arizona, 1944.

Sale, Kirkpatrick. "What Columbus Discovered." *Nation* 251, no. 13 (Oct. 22, 1990): 444–446.

Salutan Luengo, Fr. Josemaria. *A History of the Manila-Acapulco Slave Trade (1565–1815).* Tubigon, Bohol, Philippines: Mater Dei Publications, 1996.

Sánchez, George J. *Becoming Mexican American: Ethnicity, Culture and Identity in Chicano Los Angeles, 1900–1944.* New York: Oxford University Press, 1993.

Sandels, Robert L. "Silvestre Terrazas, the Press, and the Origins of the Mexican Revolution in Chihuahua." Ph.D. diss., University of Oregon, 1967.

Sargent, Charles S. "Copper Star of the Arizona Urban Firmament." In Carlos A. Schwantes, ed., *Bisbee: Urban Outpost on the Frontier*, 30–31. Tucson: University of Arizona Press, 1992.

Sariego Rodríguez, Juan Luis. *Enclaves y minerales en el norte de México: Historia social de los mineros de Cananea y Nueva Rosita, 1900–1970.* Mexico City: Centro de Investigaciones y Estudios Superiores en Antropología Social, 1988.

Schell, William, Jr. "American Investment in Tropical Mexico: Rubber Plantations, Fraud, and Dollar Diplomacy, 1897–1913." *Business History Review*, June 22, 1990, 217–254.

———. "Money as Commodity: Mexico's Conversion to the Gold Standard, 1905." *Mexican Studies/Estudios Mexicanos* 12, no. 1 (Winter 1996): 67–89.

Schlesinger, Andrew Bancroft. "Las Gorras Blancas, 1889–1891." *Journal of Mexican American History* (Spring 1971): 87–143.

Schmal, John P. "Indigenous Chihuahua: A Story of War and Assimilation." An educational project of the Houston Institute for Culture, http://www.houstonculture.org/mexico/chihuahua.html.

———. "Indigenous Identity in the Mexican Census," http://www.indigenouspeople.net/CENSUSSTORY.htm.

Schoonover, Thomas. "Mexican Cotton and the American Civil War." *Americas* 30, no. 4 (Apr. 1974): 429–447.

Schwantes, Carlos A., ed. *Bisbee: Urban Outpost on the Frontier*. Tucson: University of Arizona Press, 1992.

Scott, Robin Fitzgerald. "The Mexican-American in the Los Angeles Area, 1920–1950: From Acquiescence to Activity." Ph.D. diss., University of Southern California, 1971.

Secretary of the American Commission. To the Secretary of State. "American and Mexican Joint Commission Report on the Proceedings of the Commission with Accompanying Papers," Sept. 22, 1916. Records of the Department of State Relating to Internal Affairs of Mexico, 1910–1929, NARS, 274, 60.

Servín, Manuel P. *An Awakened Minority: The Mexican-Americans*. Beverly Hills, Calif.: Glencoe Press 1974.

Sheridan, Thomas E. *Arizona: A History*. Tucson: University of Arizona, 1995.

———. "The Limits of Power: The Political Ecology of the Spanish Empire in the Greater Southwest." *Antiquity* 66 (1992): 153–171.

———. *Los Tucsonenses: The Mexican Community in Tucson 1854–1941*. Tucson: University of Arizona Press, 1986.

———, ed. *Empire of Sand: The Seri Indians and the Struggle for Spanish Sonora, 1645–1803*. Tucson: University of Arizona Press, 1999.

Simmons, Merle E. "Attitudes toward the United States Revealed in Mexican *Corridos*." *Hispania* 36, no. 1 (Feb. 1953): 34–42.

Sinclair, John L. "The Town That Vanished into Thin Air." *New Mexico Magazine*, Mar. 1985, http://www.zianet.com/snm/santarit.htm. Reprinted in *New Mexico Magazine*, July 1997.

Smith, Michael M. "The Mexican Secret Service in the United States, 1910–1920." *Americas* 59, no. 1 (July 2002): 66–76.

Snow, Sinclair. "Samuel Gompers and the Pan-American Federation of Labor." Ph.D. diss., University of Virginia, 1960.

Sobarzo, Alejandro. *Deber y consciencia: Nicolás Trist, el negociador norteamericano en la Guerra del 47*. Mexico City: Fondo de Cultura Económica, 1996.

Sobarzo, Horacio. *Vocabulario sonorense*. Mexico City: Editorial Porrúa, 1966.

Socolow, Susan Migden. "Introduction to the Rural Past." In Louisa Schell Hoberman and Susan Migden Socolow, eds., *The Countryside in Colonial Latin America*, 3–18. Albuquerque: University of New Mexico Press, 1996.

Solomon, Isador Elkan. "Solomonville: A Jewish Town on the Frontier in Arizona Territory: The Memoirs of Isador Elkan Solomon." *Southwest Jewish History* 2, no. 3 (Spring 1994), http://www.v23issolomonville.htm.

Sonnichsen, C. L. *Colonel Greene and the Copper Skyrocket: The Spectacular Rise and Fall of William (Colonel) Greene, Copper King, Cattle Baron, and Promoter Extraordinaire*. Tucson: University of Arizona Press, 1974.

"Sonoran Pioneers in the Arizona Territory." Mexico/Arizona Biographical Survey, http://www.mexicoarizona.com/h2 _ mpa.htm (accessed July 20, 2003).

Soulie, Maurice. *The Wolf Cub: The Great Adventure of Count Gaston de Raousset-Boulbon in California and Sonora, 1850–1854*. Translated by Farrel Symons. Indianapolis: Bobbs-Merrill, 1921.

Sowards, Adam M. "Reclamation, Ranching, and Reservation: Environmental, Cultural, and Governmental Rivalries in Transitional Arizona." *Journal of the Southwest*, 40, no. 3 (Autumn 1998): 333–361.

Spaulding, Charles B. "The Mexican Strike at El Monte, California." *Sociology and Social Research*, July–Aug. 1934, 571–572.

Spicer, Edward H. *Cycles of Conquest: The Impact of Spain, Mexico and the United States on the Indians of the Southwest, 1533–1960*. Tucson: University of Arizona, 1962.

——. *The Yaquis: A Cultural History*. Tucson: University of Arizona Press, 1980.

——, ed. *Perspectives in American Indian Culture Change*. Chicago: University of Chicago Press, 1961.

Spude, Robert L. "The Walker-Weaver Digging and the Mexican Placero, 1863–1864." *Journal of the West*, Oct. 1975, 64–74.

Stein, Walter J. *California and the Dust Bowl Migration*. Westport, Conn: Greenwood Press, 1973.

Steinbeck, John. *In Dubious Battle*. New York: Penguin Books, 1992.

——. *The Grapes of Wrath*. New York: Penguin, 2002.

Stern, Peter, and Robert Jackson. "*Vagabundaje* and Settlement Patterns in Colonial Northern Sonora." *Americas* 44, no. 4 (Apr. 1988): 461–481.

Stevens, Robert C. "Mexico's Forgotten Frontier: A History of Sonora, 1821–1846." Ph.D. diss., University of California at Berkeley, 1963.

Sued-Badillo, Jalil. "Christopher Columbus and the Enslavement of the Amerindians in the Caribbean." Review of *Columbus and the New World Order, 1492–1992*. *Monthly Review* 44, no. 3 (July 1992): 71–102.

Swann, Michael M. "Population and Settlement in Late-Colonial Nueva Vizcaya: The Causes, Patterns, and Consequences of Demographic Change in a Frontier Region." Ph.D. diss., Syracuse University, 1980.

Taylor, Paul S. "Mexican Labor in the United States: Imperial Valley." In *Mexican Labor in the United States*. New York: Arno Press, 1970.

——. *Mexican Labor in the United States*. New York: Arno Press, 1970.

——. "Mexicans North of the Rio Grande." *Survey* 46, no. 3 (May 1, 1931): 137–140.

Taylor, Paul S., and Clark Kerr. "Documentary History of the Strike of the Cotton Pickers in California: San Joaquin Valley Cotton Strike, 1933." In *La Follette Hearings: Violations of Free Speech and Rights of Labor*. Hearings before a Subcommittee of the Committee on Education and Labor. United States Senate. 76th Cong., 3d sess. Pursuant to S. Res. 266 (74th Congress). Pt. 54: *Agricultural Labor in California*, pp. 19945–20036. Exhibits entered in Los Angeles, California, Jan. 13, 1940. Washington, D.C.: Government Printing Office, 1940.

Taylor, Ronald. *Chavez and the Farm Workers*. Boston: Beacon Press, 1975.

Taylor, William, and Elliot West. "Patron Leadership at the Crossroads: Southern Colorado in the Late Nineteenth Century." In Norris Hundley Jr., ed., *The Chicano*. Santa Barbara, Calif.: Clio, 1975.

Terrazas y Quezada, D. Joaquín. *Memorias del Sr. Coronel D. Joaquin Terrazas*. Ciudad Juárez: El Agricultor Mexicoro, 1905.

Tinker Salas, Miguel. *In the Shadow of the Eagles: Sonora and the Transformation of the Border during the Porfiriato*. Berkeley: University of California Press, 1997.

Torres, Jose Ignacio. "The Globe Strike (Lockout) of 1896." Arizona State University Library.

Torres, Robert. "The 1933 San Joaquin Valley (California) Cotton Strike." Master's thesis, California State University at Fresno, 1994.

Treutlein, Theodore E. "The Economic Regime of the Jesuit Missions in Eighteenth Century Sonora." *Pacific Historical Review* 8, no. 3 (Sept. 1939): 289–300.

Treviño, Roberto R. "Prensa y Patria: The Spanish-Language Press and the Biculturation of the Tejano Middle Class, 1920–1940." *Western Historical Quarterly* 4 (Nov. 1991): 451–472.

Troncoso, Francisco P. *Las guerras con las tribus yaqui y mayo del estado de Sonora* Mexico City: Tipografía del Departmento del Estado Mayor, 1905.

Trueba Urbina, Alberto. *Evolución de la Huelga*. Mexico City: Ediciones Botas, 1950.

Truett, Samuel, and Elliott Young, eds. *Continental Crossroads: Remapping U.S.-Mexico Borderlands History*. Durham, N.C.: Duke University Press,, 2004.

Trujillo, Rafael. *Patriot in Profile: De la Huerta and the Bucareli Treaties*. Hawthorne, Calif.: Omni, 1981.

"The Truth about Bisbee: An Account, Compiled from Legal Evidence and Other Authenticated Documents, of the I.W.W. Deportation on July 12, 1917, from Bisbee, Arizona, and its Aftermath." In *Arizona v. Wooten*. SC, 21-22. UA.

Tuck, Frank J. "Fifty Years of Mining in the State of Arizona, 1912 — 1962." M91, AHS.

Turner, Ethel Duffy. *Revolution in Baja California: Ricardo Flores Magon's High Noon*. Edited and annotated by Rey Devis. Detroit: Blaine Ethridge Books, 1981.

——. *Ricardo Flores Magón y el Partido Mexicano*. Morelia: Editorial "Esandi" del Gobierno del Estado Morelia, Michoacán, 1960.

Turner, John Kenneth. *Barbarous Mexico*. Austin: University of Texas Press, 1984

Uhl, David, and Moses Meglorin. "Chihuahuita in the 1930s: Tough Times in the Barrio." Borderland: An El Paso Community College History Project, http://www .epcc.edu/ftp/Homes/monicaw/borderlands/12 __ chihuahuita.htm (accessed Jan. 13, 2004).

Ulloa, Berta. *Revolución intervenida: Relaciones diplomáticas entre México y Eastados Unidos (1910–1914)*. Mexico City: Colegio de México, 1971.

United States v. Haywood et al. This exhibit was part of the deposition of John W. Hughes for *Simmons v. El Paso & Southwestern RR Co.* SC, UA.

U.S. House of Representatives. *Alleged Persecution of Mexican Citizens by the Government of Mexico*, 61st Cong., 2d sess. Report of Special Committee set up under H. J. Res. 201. Hearings held June 9, 10, 11, 13, and 14. 1910. Washington, D.C.: Government Printing Office, 1910.

Valadés, José C. *El porfirismo: Historia de un régimen.* Vol. 2: *El Crecimiento.* Mexico City: Editorial Patria, 1948.

———. *Porfirio Díaz contra el gran poder de Dios: Las rebeliones de Tomohic y Temosachic.* Mexico City: Ediciones Leega/Jucar Valades, 1985.

Valerio-Jiménez, Omar S. "Neglected Citizens and Willing Traders: The Villas del Norte (Tamaulipas) in Mexico's Northern Borderlands, 1749–1846." *Mexican Studies/Estudios Mexicanos* 18, no. 2 (Summer 2002): 251–296.

Vanderwood, Paul J. *The Power of God against Guns of Government: Religious Upheaval in Mexico at the Turn of the Nineteenth Century.* Stanford, Calif.: Stanford University Press, 1998.

———. "Using the Present to Study the Past: Religious Movements in Mexico and Uganda a Century Apart." *Mexican Studies/Estudios Mexicanos* 10, no. 1 (Winter 1994): 99–134.

Vaughan, Tom. "Everyday Life in a Copper Camp." In Carlos A. Schwantes, ed., *Bisbee: Urban Outpost on the Frontier,* 57–83. Tucson: University of Arizona Press, 1992.

Velasco, José Francisco. *Sonora: Its Extent, Population, Natural Production, Indian Tribes, Mines, Mineral Lands, Etc.* Translated by William F. Nye. San Francisco: H. H. Bancroft, 1861. Reprint, Hermosillo: Gobierno del Estado de Sonora, 1985.

Vélez-Ibáñez, Carlos G. *Border Visions: Mexican Cultures of the Southwest United States.* Tucson: University of Arizona Press, 1996.

Vigil, Ralph H. "Spanish Bluecoats: The Catalonian Volunteers in Northwestern New Spain, 1767–1810." *Latin American Research Review* 29, no. 1 (Winter 1994): 155–171.

Villa, Eduardo W. *Galeria de sonorenses ilustres.* Hermosillo: Impulsora de Artes Graficos, 1948.

———. *Historia del Estado de Sonora,* 2nd ed. Hermosillo: Editorial Sonora, 1951.

Villa-Flores, Javier. " 'To Lose One's Soul': Blasphemy and Slavery in New Spain, 1596–1669." *Hispanic American Historical Review* 82, no. 3 (2002): 435–468.

Vincent, Theodore G. *The Legacy of Guerrero: Mexico's First Black Indian President.* Gainesville: University Press of Florida, 2001.

Vinson, Mark C. "Vanished Clifton-Morenci: An Architect's Perspective." *The Journal of Arizona History* 33, no. 2 (Summer 1992): 183–206.

Voss, Stuart F. *On the Periphery of Nineteenth-Century Mexico: Sonora and Sinaloa, 1810–1877.* Tucson: University of Arizona Press, 1982.

———. "Societal Competition in Northwest New Spain." *Americas* 38, no. 2 (Oct. 1981): 185–203.

Wagoner, Jay J. *Arizona Territory 1863–1912: A Political History.* Tucson: The University of Arizona Press, 1970.

Wallace, Andrew. "Colonel McClintoch and the 1917 Copper Strike." *Arizonian,* Spring 1962, 24–26.

Wasserman, Mark. *Capitalists, Caciques, and Revolution: The Native Elite and Foreign Enterprise in Chihuahua, Mexico, 1854–1911.* Chapel Hill: University of North Carolina Press, 1984.

———. "Enrique C. Creel: Business and Politics in Mexico, 1880–1930." *Business History Review* 59, no. 4 (Business in Latin America: Winter 1985): 645–662.

———. "Foreign Investment in Mexico, 1876–1910: A Case Study of the Role of Regional Elites." *Americas* 36, no. 1 (July 1979): 3–21.

———. "The Social Origins of the 1910 Revolution in Chihuahua." *Latin American Research Review* 15, no. 1 (1980): 15–38.

Watt, Roberta. "History of Morenci, Arizona." Master's thesis, University of Arizona, 1956.

Webb, John W. *The Migratory-Casual Worker*. Monograph 7. Works Progress Administration. Division of Social Research. Washington, D.C.: Government Printing Office, 1937.

Webb, Walter Prescott. *The Texas Rangers*. 2nd ed. Austin: University of Texas Press, 1965.

Weber, David J. *The Mexican Frontier, 1821–1846: The American Southwest under Mexico*. Albuquerque: University of New Mexico Press, 1982.

———. *The Spanish Frontier in North America*. New Haven: Yale University Press, 1992.

———, ed. *Foreigners in Their Native Land*. Albuquerque: University of New Mexico Press, 1973.

Weber, Devra Anne. *Dark Sweat, White Gold: California Farm Workers, Cotton, and the New Deal*. Berkeley: University of California Press, 1994.

———. "Raiz Fuerte: Oral History and Mexicana Farmworkers." http://www.stolaf.edu/people/kutulas/Weber–RaizFuerte.htm (accessed Oct. 5, 2004).

Weckmann, Luis. *The Medieval Heritage of Mexico*. Translated by Frances M. López-Morillas. New York: Fordham University Press, 1992.

Weigand, Phil C., and Acelia García de Weigand. "Huichol Society before the Arrival of the Spanish." *Journal of the Southwest* 42, no. 1 (Spring 2000): 13–36.

Weigle, Marta. *Hispanic Villages of Northern New Mexico*. Santa Fe: Lighting Tree, 1975.

Western Federation of Miners (WFM). *Official Proceedings of the . . . Annual Convention of the Western Federation of Miners of America*. 1894–1917. Microfilms in RFAC, Urban Archives, CSUN.

———. *Strike for Liberty!: Songs, Poetry, and Comments by Workers of the Western Federation of Miners, 1900–1907*. Albuquerque, N.M.: Southwest Economy and Society, 1979. Reprinted in *Southwest Economy and Society* 5, nos. 1–2 (Fall 1979–Winter 1979/1980).

Willeford, Glenn P. "Mexican Settlers in the Big Bend Region of Texas, 1880–1945." Oral presentation for La Semana de Humanismo, La Universidad Autónoma de Chihuahua, Facultad de Filosofia y Letras, presented on Nov. 6, 2001, at La Quinta Gameros.

Winn, Peter. *Weavers of Revolution: The Yarur Workers and Chile's Road to Socialism*. New York: Oxford University Press, 1986. http://ojinaga.com/MexstlrsBB.html (accessed July 21, 2003).

Winter, Ella. *And Not to Yield: An Autobiography*. New York: Harcourt Brace and World, 1963.

Wolf, Eric. *Sons of the Shaking Earth: The People of Mexico and Guatemala — Their Land, History, and Culture*. Chicago: Phoenix Books, 1959.

Woll, Allan F. "Latin Images in American Films, 1929–1939." *Journal of Mexican American History* (1974): 28–40.

Wollenberg, Charles "Huelga, 1928 Style: The Imperial Valley Cantaloupe Worker's Strike." *Pacific Historical Review* (Feb. 1969): 45–58.

Wyllys, Rufus Kay. *The French in Sonora (1850–1854): The Story of French Adventurers from California into Sonora*. Berkeley: University of California Press, 1932.

Yetman, David. *Sonora: An Intimate Geography*. Albuquerque: University of New Mexico Press, 1996.

Yockelson, Mitchell. "The United States Armed Forces and the Mexican Punitive Expedition." Pt. 2. *Quarterly of the National Archives and Records Administration* 29, no. 4 (Winter 1997): 334–343. http://www.nara.gov/publications/prologue/mpep2.html.

"Yuma Territorial Prison Cemetery, Yuma, Yuma County, Arizona." Compiled and contributed by Steve Paul Johnson, http://www.interment.net/data/us/az/yuma/prison/prison.htm.

Zamora, Emilio. *The World of the Mexican Worker in Texas*. College Station: Texas A&M University Press, 1993.

Zavala, Lorenzo de. *Journey to the United States of America*. Translated by Wallace Woolsey. Edited by John-Michael Rivera. Houston: Arte Publico Press, 2005.

Index

About the Author

Rodolfo F. Acuña received his PhD in Latin American Studies from the University of Southern California in 1968. The following year Acuña was named the founding chair of the Chicano Studies Department at now California State University at Northridge, the largest Chicana/o Studies department in the nation, with thirty tenured professors. The author of eighteen books — three of which have received the Gustavus Myers Award as an Outstanding Book on Race Relations in North America — Acuña has written more than 300 articles and book reviews. In recognition of his role as an activist-scholar, the National Association for Chicana and Chicano Studies awarded him its Distinguished Scholar Award; *Black Issues in Higher Education* named him one of the 100 Most Influential Educators of the 20th Century; the Southern California Library for Social Studies and Research honored him with the Emil Freed Award for Community Service; and the Liberty Hill Foundation granted him the Founders Award for Community Service. Among his best-known books are *Occupied America: A History of Chicanos* (currently in its sixth edition); *Anything But Mexican: Chicanos in Contemporary Los Angeles; Sometimes There Is No Other Side: Chicanos and the Myth of Equality; Community under Siege; Sonoran Strongman: Ignacio Pesqueira and His Times;* and *U.S. Latino Issues.* Acuña has also written three children's books and has a three-volume work that he is co-editing with his wife, Guadalupe Compeán, in production.